WORLD TRADE ORGANIZATION

Dispute Settlement Reports

2011
Volume VII

Pages 3751-4286

CAMBRIDGE
UNIVERSITY PRESS

Shaftesbury Road, Cambridge CB2 8EA, United Kingdom

One Liberty Plaza, 20th Floor, New York, NY 10006, USA

477 Williamstown Road, Port Melbourne, VIC 3207, Australia

314–321, 3rd Floor, Plot 3, Splendor Forum, Jasola District Centre, New Delhi – 110025, India

103 Penang Road, #05–06/07, Visioncrest Commercial, Singapore 238467

Cambridge University Press is part of Cambridge University Press & Assessment, a department of the University of Cambridge.

We share the University's mission to contribute to society through the pursuit of education, learning and research at the highest international levels of excellence.

www.cambridge.org
Information on this title: www.cambridge.org/9781107033733

First published 2013

A catalogue record for this publication is available from the British Library

ISBN 978-1-107-03373-3 Hardback

THE WTO DISPUTE SETTLEMENT REPORTS

The *Dispute Settlement Reports* of the World Trade Organization (the "WTO") include panel and Appellate Body reports, as well as arbitration awards, in disputes concerning the rights and obligations of WTO Members under the provisions of the *Marrakesh Agreement Establishing the World Trade Organization*. The *Dispute Settlement Reports* are available in English. Volumes comprising one or more complete cases contain a cumulative list of published disputes. The cumulative list for cases that cover more than one volume is to be found in the first volume for that case.

This volume may be cited as DSR 2011:VII

TABLE OF CONTENTS

UNITED STATES – ANTI-DUMPING ADMINISTRATIVE REVIEWS AND OTHER MEASURES RELATED TO IMPORTS OF CERTAIN ORANGE JUICE FROM BRAZIL

Report of the Panel
WT/DS382/R

Adopted by the Dispute Settlement Body on 17 June 2011

BCI DELETED, AS INDICATED [[XX]]

TABLE OF CONTENTS

LIST OF ANNEXES

ANNEX A

EXECUTIVE SUMMARY OF THE FIRST WRITTEN SUBMISSIONS OF THE PARTIES

ANNEX B

THIRD PARTIES' WRITTEN SUBMISSIONS OR EXECUTIVE SUMMARIES THEREOF

ANNEX C

ORAL STATEMENTS OR EXECUTIVE SUMMARIES THEREOF OF THE PARTIES AT THE FIRST SUBSTANTIVE MEETING OF THE PANEL

ANNEX D

ORAL STATEMENTS OF THIRD PARTIES OR EXECUTIVE SUMMARIES THEREOF

ANNEX E

EXECUTIVE SUMMARIES OF THE SECOND WRITTEN SUBMISSIONS OF THE PARTIES

ANNEX F

EXECUTIVE SUMMARIES OF THE PARTIES STATEMENTS
AT THE SECOND SUBSTANTIVE MEETING OF THE PANEL

ANNEX G

REQUESTS FOR CONSULTATIONS AND THE
ESTABLISHMENT OF A PANEL

TABLE OF CASES CITED IN THIS REPORT

WTO DISPUTE SETTLEMENT REPORTS

Short Title	Full Case Title and Citation
Argentina – Poultry Anti-Dumping Duties	Panel Report, *Argentina – Definitive Anti-Dumping Duties on Poultry from Brazil*, WT/DS241/R, adopted 19 May 2003, DSR 2003:V, 1727
Brazil – Aircraft	Panel Report, *Brazil – Export Financing Programme for Aircraft*, WT/DS46/R, adopted 20 August 1999, as modified by Appellate Body Report WT/DS46/AB/R, DSR 1999:III, 1221
Canada – Aircraft	Appellate Body Report, *Canada – Measures Affecting the Export of Civilian Aircraft*, WT/DS70/AB/R, adopted 20 August 1999, DSR 1999:III, 1377
Canada – Aircraft	Panel Report, *Canada – Measures Affecting the Export of Civilian Aircraft*, WT/DS70/R, adopted 20 August 1999, as upheld by Appellate Body Report WT/DS70/AB/R, DSR 1999:IV, 1443
Chile – Price Band System	Appellate Body Report, *Chile – Price Band System and Safeguard Measures Relating to Certain Agricultural Products*, WT/DS207/AB/R, adopted 23 October 2002, DSR 2002:VIII, 3045 (Corr.1, DSR 2006:XII, 5473)
Dominican Republic – Import and Sale of Cigarettes	Panel Report, *Dominican Republic – Measures Affecting the Importation and Internal Sale of Cigarettes*, WT/DS302/R, adopted 19 May 2005, as modified by Appellate Body Report WT/DS302/AB/R, DSR 2005:XV, 7425
EC – Bed Linen	Appellate Body Report, *European Communities – Anti-Dumping Duties on Imports of Cotton-Type Bed Linen from India*, WT/DS141/AB/R, adopted 12 March 2001, DSR 2001:V, 2049
EC – Bed Linen	Panel Report, *European Communities – Anti-Dumping Duties on Imports of Cotton-Type Bed Linen from India*, WT/DS141/R, adopted 12 March 2001, as modified by Appellate Body Report WT/DS141/AB/R, DSR 2001:VI, 2077

Short Title	Full Case Title and Citation
EC – Bed Linen (Article 21.5 – India)	Appellate Body Report, *European Communities – Anti-Dumping Duties on Imports of Cotton-Type Bed Linen from India – Recourse to Article 21.5 of the DSU by India*, WT/DS141/AB/RW, adopted 24 April 2003, DSR 2003:III, 965
EC – Chicken Cuts	Appellate Body Report, *European Communities – Customs Classification of Frozen Boneless Chicken Cuts*, WT/DS269/AB/R, WT/DS286/AB/R, adopted 27 September 2005, and Corr.1, DSR 2005:XIX, 9157
EC – Computer Equipment	Appellate Body Report, *European Communities – Customs Classification of Certain Computer Equipment*, WT/DS62/AB/R, WT/DS67/AB/R, WT/DS68/AB/R, adopted 22 June 1998, DSR 1998:V, 1851
EC – Salmon (Norway)	Panel Report, *European Communities – Anti-Dumping Measure on Farmed Salmon from Norway*, WT/DS337/R, adopted 15 January 2008, and Corr.1, DSR 2008:I, 3
EC – Tube or Pipe Fittings	Appellate Body Report, *European Communities – Anti-Dumping Duties on Malleable Cast Iron Tube or Pipe Fittings from Brazil*, WT/DS219/AB/R, adopted 18 August 2003, DSR 2003:VI, 2613
EC – Tube or Pipe Fittings	Panel Report, *European Communities – Anti-Dumping Duties on Malleable Cast Iron Tube or Pipe Fittings from Brazil*, WT/DS219/R, adopted 18 August 2003, as modified by Appellate Body Report WT/DS219/AB/R, DSR 2003:VII, 2701
Egypt – Steel Rebar	Panel Report, *Egypt – Definitive Anti-Dumping Measures on Steel Rebar from Turkey*, WT/DS211/R, adopted 1 October 2002, DSR 2002:VII, 2667
Guatemala – Cement I	Appellate Body Report, *Guatemala – Anti-Dumping Investigation Regarding Portland Cement from Mexico*, WT/DS60/AB/R, adopted 25 November 1998, DSR 1998:IX, 3767
Japan – Alcoholic Beverages II	Appellate Body Report, *Japan – Taxes on Alcoholic Beverages*, WT/DS8/AB/R, WT/DS10/AB/R, WT/DS11/AB/R, adopted 1 November 1996, DSR 1996:I, 97

Short Title	Full Case Title and Citation
Mexico – Corn Syrup (Article 21.5 – US)	Appellate Body Report, *Mexico – Anti-Dumping Investigation of High Fructose Corn Syrup (HFCS) from the United States – Recourse to Article 21.5 of the DSU by the United States*, WT/DS132/AB/RW, adopted 21 November 2001, DSR 2001:XIII, 6675
US – Anti-Dumping Measures on Oil Country Tubular Goods	Appellate Body Report, *United States – Anti-Dumping Measures on Oil Country Tubular Goods (OCTG) from Mexico*, WT/DS282/AB/R, adopted 28 November 2005, DSR 2005:XX, 10127
US – Anti-Dumping Measures on Oil Country Tubular Goods	Panel Report, *United States – Anti-Dumping Measures on Oil Country Tubular Goods (OCTG) from Mexico*, WT/DS282/R, adopted 28 November 2005, as modified by Appellate Body Report WT/DS282/AB/R, DSR 2005:XXI, 10225
US – Anti-Dumping Measures on PET Bags	Panel Report, *United States – Anti-Dumping Measures on Polyethylene Retail Carrier Bags from Thailand*, WT/DS383/R, adopted 18 February 2010
US – Certain EC Products	Appellate Body Report, *United States – Import Measures on Certain Products from the European Communities*, WT/DS165/AB/R, adopted 10 January 2001, DSR 2001:I, 373
US – Continued Zeroing	Appellate Body Report, *United States – Continued Existence and Application of Zeroing Methodology*, WT/DS350/AB/R, adopted 19 February 2009
US – Continued Zeroing	Panel Report, *United States – Continued Existence and Application of Zeroing Methodology*, WT/DS350/R, adopted 19 February 2009, as modified as Appellate Body Report WT/DS350/AB/R
US – Corrosion-Resistant Steel Sunset Review	Appellate Body Report, *United States – Sunset Review of Anti-Dumping Duties on Corrosion-Resistant Carbon Steel Flat Products from Japan*, WT/DS244/AB/R, adopted 9 January 2004, DSR 2004:I, 3
US – Gasoline	Appellate Body Report, *United States – Standards for Reformulated and Conventional Gasoline*, WT/DS2/AB/R, adopted 20 May 1996, DSR 1996:I, 3

Short Title	Full Case Title and Citation
US – Gasoline	Panel Report, *United States – Standards for Reformulated and Conventional Gasoline*, WT/DS2/R, adopted 20 May 1996, as modified by Appellate Body Report WT/DS2/AB/R, DSR 1996:I, 29
US – Hot-Rolled Steel	Appellate Body Report, *United States – Anti-Dumping Measures on Certain Hot-Rolled Steel Products from Japan*, WT/DS184/AB/R, adopted 23 August 2001, DSR 2001:X, 4697
US – 1916 Act	Appellate Body Report, *United States – Anti-Dumping Act of 1916*, WT/DS136/AB/R, WT/DS162/AB/R, adopted 26 September 2000, DSR 2000:X, 4793
US – Oil Country Tubular Goods Sunset Reviews	Appellate Body Report, *United States – Sunset Reviews of Anti-Dumping Measures on Oil Country Tubular Goods from Argentina*, WT/DS268/AB/R, adopted 17 December 2004, DSR 2004:VII, 3257
US – Shrimp (Ecuador)	Panel Report, *United States – Anti-Dumping Measure on Shrimp from Ecuador*, WT/DS335/R, adopted on 20 February 2007, DSR 2007:II, 425
US – Shrimp (Thailand) / US – Customs Bond Directive	Appellate Body Report, *United States – Measures Relating to Shrimp from Thailand / United States – Customs Bond Directive for Merchandise Subject to Anti-Dumping/Countervailing Duties*, WT/DS343/AB/R / WT/DS345/AB/R, adopted 1 August 2008, DSR 2008:VII, 2385 / DSR 2008:VIII, 2773
US – Shrimp (Thailand)	Panel Report, *United States – Measures Relating to Shrimp from Thailand*, WT/DS343/R, adopted 1 August 2008, as modified by Appellate Body Report WT/DS343/AB/R / WT/DS345/AB/R, DSR 2008:VII, 2539
US – Softwood Lumber V (Article 21.5 – Canada)	Appellate Body Report, *United States – Final Dumping Determination on Softwood Lumber from Canada – Recourse to Article 21.5 of the DSU by Canada*, WT/DS264/AB/RW, adopted 1 September 2006, DSR 2006:XII, 5087
US – Stainless Steel (Mexico)	Appellate Body Report, *United States – Final Anti-Dumping Measures on Stainless Steel from Mexico*, WT/DS344/AB/R, adopted 20 May 2008, DSR 2008:II, 513

Short Title	Full Case Title and Citation
US – Stainless Steel (Mexico)	Panel Report, *United States – Final Anti-Dumping Measures on Stainless Steel from Mexico*, WT/DS344/R, adopted 20 May 2008, as modified by Appellate Body Report WT/DS344/AB/R, DSR 2008:II, 599
US – Upland Cotton	Appellate Body Report, *United States – Subsidies on Upland Cotton*, WT/DS267/AB/R, adopted 21 March 2005, DSR 2005:I, 3
US – Zeroing (EC)	Appellate Body Report, *United States – Laws, Regulations and Methodology for Calculating Dumping Margins ("Zeroing")*, WT/DS294/AB/R, adopted 9 May 2006, and Corr.1, DSR 2006:II, 417
US – Zeroing (EC)	Panel Report, *United States – Laws, Regulations and Methodology for Calculating Dumping Margins ("Zeroing")*, WT/DS294/R, adopted 9 May 2006, as modified by Appellate Body Report WT/DS294/AB/R, DSR 2006:II, 521
US – Zeroing (EC) (Article 21.5 – EC)	Appellate Body Report, *United States – Laws, Regulations and Methodology for Calculating Dumping Margins ("Zeroing") – Recourse to Article 21.5 of the DSU by the European Communities*, WT/DS294/AB/RW and Corr.1, adopted 11 June 2009
US – Zeroing (EC) (Article 21.5 – EC)	Panel Report, *United States – Laws, Regulations and Methodology for Calculating Dumping Margins ("Zeroing") – Recourse to Article 21.5 of the DSU by the European Communities*, WT/DS294/RW, adopted 11 June 2009, as modified by Appellate Body Report WT/DS294/AB/RW
US – Zeroing (Japan)	Appellate Body Report, *United States – Measures Relating to Zeroing and Sunset Reviews*, WT/DS322/AB/R, adopted 23 January 2007, DSR 2007:I, 3
US – Zeroing (Japan)	Panel Report, *United States – Measures Relating to Zeroing and Sunset Reviews*, WT/DS322/R, adopted 23 January 2007, as modified by Appellate Body Report WT/DS322/AB/R, DSR 2007:I, 97
US – Zeroing (Japan) (Article 21.5 – Japan)	Appellate Body Report, *United States – Measures Relating to Zeroing and Sunset Reviews – Recourse to Article 21.5 of the DSU by Japan*, WT/DS322/AB/RW, adopted 31 August 2009

Short Title	Full Case Title and Citation
US – Zeroing (Japan) (Article 21.5 – Japan)	Panel Report, *United States – Measures Relating to Zeroing and Sunset Reviews – Recourse to Article 21.5 of the DSU by Japan*, WT/DS322/RW, adopted 31 August 2009, as upheld by Appellate Body Report WT/DS322/AB/RW

GATT PANEL REPORTS

European Economic Community – Imposition of Anti-Dumping Duties on Imports of Cotton Yarn from Brazil ("EEC – Cotton Yarn"), ADP/137, adopted 30 October 1995, BISD 42S/17

I. INTRODUCTION

1.1 On 27 November 2008, the Government of Brazil ("Brazil") requested consultations with the Government of the United States of America (the "United States") under Articles 4 of the Understanding on Rules and Procedures Governing the Settlement of Disputes (the "DSU"), Article XXII:1 of the General Agreement on Tariffs and Trade of 1994 (the "GATT 1994") and Articles 17.2 and 17.3 of the Agreement on Implementation of Article VI of the General Agreement on Tariffs and Trade of 1994 (the "AD Agreement"), with regard to certain laws, regulations, administrative procedures, practices and methodologies for calculating dumping margins in administrative reviews, involving the alleged use of so-called "zeroing", and their application in anti-dumping duty administrative reviews regarding imports of certain orange juice from Brazil (case No A-351-840).[1] On 22 May 2009, Brazil requested further consultations with the United States with regard to the alleged use of "zeroing" in the anti-dumping duty investigation and in the second administrative review related to case No A-351-840 as well as to the continued use of the United States "zeroing procedures" in successive anti-dumping proceedings regarding imports of certain orange juice from Brazil.[2] The consultations were held on 16 January and 18 June 2009, respectively. The consultations failed to resolve the dispute.

1.2 On 20 August 2009, Brazil requested, pursuant to Articles 4.7 and 6 of the DSU, Article XXIII of the GATT 1994, and Article 17.4 of the AD Agreement, that the Dispute Settlement Body ("DSB") establish a Panel with regard to the following measures:

(a) The anti-dumping duty investigation on certain orange juice from Brazil (the "Original Investigation").

[1] WT/DS382/1.
[2] WT/DS382/1/Add.1.

(b) The 2005-2007 anti-dumping duty administrative review on certain orange juice from Brazil (the "First Administrative Review").

(c) The 2007-2008 anti-dumping duty administrative review on certain orange juice from Brazil (the "Second Administrative Review").

(d) The continued use of the US "zeroing procedures" in successive anti-dumping proceedings, in relation to the anti-dumping duty order issued in respect of imports of certain orange juice from Brazil.[3]

1.3 At its meeting on 25 September 2009, the DSB established a panel pursuant to the request of Brazil in document WT/DS382/4, in accordance with Article 6 of the DSU.

1.4 The Panel's terms of reference are the following:

> "To examine, in the light of the relevant provisions of the covered agreements cited by the parties to the dispute, the matter referred to the DSB by Brazil in document WT/DS382/4 and to make such findings as will assist the DSB in making the recommendations or in giving the rulings provided for in those agreements."

1.5 On 29 April 2010, Brazil requested the Director-General to determine the composition of the Panel, pursuant to paragraph 7 of Article 8 of the DSU. This paragraph provides:

> "If there is no agreement on the panelists within 20 days after the date of the establishment of a panel, at the request of either party, the Director-General, in consultation with the Chairman of the DSB and the Chairman of the relevant Council or Committee, shall determine the composition of the panel by appointing the panelists whom the Director-General considers most appropriate in accordance with any relevant special or additional rules or procedures of the covered agreement or covered agreements which are at issue in the dispute, after consulting with the parties to the dispute. The Chairman of the DSB shall inform the Members of the composition of the panel thus formed no later than 10 days after the date the Chairman receives such a request."

1.6 On 10 May 2010, the Director-General accordingly composed the Panel as follows:

Chairman: Mr. Miguel Rodriguez Mendoza

Members: Mr. Pierre S. Pettigrew

Mr. Reuben Pessah

---

3 WT/DS382/4.

1.7 Argentina; the European Union; Japan; Korea; Mexico; the Separate Customs Territory of Taiwan, Penghu, Kinmen and Matsu ("Chinese Taipei"); and Thailand reserved their rights to participate in the Panel proceedings as third parties.

1.8 The Panel met with the parties on 15-16 July and 12 October 2010. It met with the third parties on 16 July 2010. The Panel issued its interim report to the parties on 20 December 2010. The Panel issued its final report to the parties on 21 February 2011.

II. FACTUAL ASPECTS

2.1 Brazil's complaint is focused on the alleged use by the United States Department of Commerce ("USDOC") of a particular methodology, known as "zeroing", when calculating the margin of dumping of investigated exporters in the anti-dumping proceedings conducted against certain orange juice products from Brazil (case No. A-351.840). In particular, Brazil challenges the alleged use of "simple zeroing" for the purpose of calculating the margins of dumping, cash deposit rates and relevant importer-specific assessment rates for two respondents, Sucocítrico Cutrale S.A. ("Cutrale") and Fischer S.A. Comércio, Indústria e Agricultura ("Fischer") in the First and Second Administrative Reviews.[4] In addition, Brazil challenges the USDOC's alleged "continued use of zeroing" as "ongoing conduct" in successive anti-dumping proceedings, including in the original investigation resulting in the imposition of the anti-dumping duty order on certain orange juice products from Brazil[5], and each of the first three administrative reviews related to that order.[6]

2.2 Brazil alleges two types of "zeroing" in this dispute, which it describes as constituting different aspects of the same methodology: "model zeroing" and "simple zeroing". According to Brazil, "model zeroing" involves a number of steps: First, the product under consideration is sub-divided into a series of "averaging groups" or "models", and an annual weighted-average normal value and export price is calculated for the transactions falling within each group or model. A comparison is then made between the annual weighted-average price of all export transactions and the annual weighted-average price of all domestic market transactions in the same group or model. Next, the multiple comparison results are aggregated and divided by the total value of all comparable export transactions for all groups or models to arrive at a weighted-average margin of dumping. In summing the comparison results by group or model, positive differences (i.e., where the weighted average price of export transactions is less than the

---

4 Final Results of the First Administrative Review, 11 August 2008, 73 Fed. Reg. 46584. Exhibit BRA-21 ("First Administrative Review"); and Final Results of the Second Administrative Review, 11 August 2009, 74 Fed. Reg. 40167. Exhibit BRA-22 ("Second Administrative Review").

5 Anti-Dumping Duty Order: Certain Orange Juice from Brazil, 9 March 2006, 71 Fed. Reg. 12183 ("Anti-Dumping Duty Order"). Exhibit BRA-3.

6 First Administrative Review; Second Administrative Review; and Final Results of the Third Administrative Review, 18 August 2010, 75 Fed. Reg. 50999. Exhibit BRA-49.

weighted-average normal value of the model or group) are added to determine the total amount of dumping, but all comparison results showing negative results are disregarded or given a value of zero in the aggregation exercise. This practice of disregarding or counting as zero the negative results of weighted-average normal value to weighted-average export price comparisons ("W-W") is what Brazil describes as "model zeroing". Brazil notes that the USDOC ceased to apply "model zeroing" in February 2007[7], after the results of the original investigation into exports of orange juice products from Brazil were issued.

2.3 Brazil describes "simple zeroing" as very similar to "model zeroing", with the key difference stemming from the fact that the latter takes place when using the W-W comparison methodology, whereas the former arises when comparing the weighted-average normal value by model or group to the price of individual export transactions ("W-T"). As with W-W comparisons, results of W-T comparisons are aggregated and divided by the total value of all comparable export transactions to arrive at a weighted average margin of dumping. Again, in making this calculation, only the positive comparison results are aggregated, with all negative results (i.e., where the export price is higher than weighted average normal value) disregarded or given a value of zero. This practice of disregarding or counting as zero the negative comparison results when using the W-T comparison methodology is what Brazil describes as "simple zeroing".

III. PARTIES' REQUESTS FOR FINDINGS AND RECOMMENDATIONS

A. Brazil

3.1 Brazil requests that the Panel find:

(i) the United States' two administrative reviews concerning imports of certain orange juice from Brazil inconsistent with Articles 2.4 and 9.3 of the AD Agreement and Article VI:2 of the GATT 1994 due to the above-mentioned alleged use of "zeroing"; and

(ii) the continued use by the United States of "zeroing" in successive anti-dumping proceedings, in relation to the anti-dumping duty order issued in respect of imports of certain orange juice from Brazil, including the original investigation and subsequent administrative reviews, by which duties are applied and maintained over a period of time, inconsistent with Articles 2.4, 2.4.2 and 9.3 of the AD Agreement and Article VI:2 of the GATT 1994.

---

7 In particular, Brazil explains that on "December 27, 2006, the USDOC published a notice in the Federal Register announcing that it would no longer make W-to-W comparisons in investigations without providing offsets for non-dumped comparisons (71 Fed. Reg. 77722). The effective date of entry into force of this modification was February 22, 2007 (72 Fed. Reg. 3783)". Brazil, First Written Submission ("FWS"), footnote 31, citing Exhibits BRA-10 and BRA-11.

3.2 Pursuant to Article 19.1 of the DSU, Brazil requests that the Panel recommend that the United States bring its measures, found to be inconsistent with the AD Agreement and the GATT 1994, into conformity with its obligations under the covered agreements.

B. The United States

3.3 The United States asks the Panel to reject the entirety of Brazil's claims concerning the First and Second Administrative Reviews as well as Brazil's claim regarding the alleged "continued use" of "zeroing". The United States also asks the Panel to make two preliminary rulings concerning Brazil's claims with respect to the Second Administrative Review and the alleged "continued use" of "zeroing" in the orange juice anti-dumping proceedings.[8]

IV. ARGUMENTS OF THE PARTIES

4.1 The arguments of the parties are set out in their written submissions, oral statements to the Panel and their answers to questions. Executive summaries of the parties' written submissions, and where provided oral statements[9], are attached to this Report as annexes (see List of Annexes, pages iv and v).[10]

V. ARGUMENTS OF THE THIRD PARTIES

5.1 Argentina; the European Union; Japan; Korea; Mexico; Chinese Taipei; and Thailand reserved their rights to participate in the Panel proceedings as third parties. Thailand and Chinese Taipei did not submit third party written submissions; and Argentina, Mexico, Chinese Taipei and Thailand did not submit third party oral statements. The arguments of Argentina and Mexico are set out in their written submissions and answers to questions, and the arguments of the European Union, Japan and Korea are set out in their written submissions, oral statements and their answers to questions. Third parties' written submissions and oral statements, or executive summaries thereof, are attached to this Report as annexes (see List of Annexes, pages iv and v).

VI. INTERIM REVIEW

6.1 On 20 December 2010, we submitted our Interim Report to the parties. On 12 January 2011, Brazil and the United States submitted written requests for

---

[8] United States, First Written Submission ("FWS"), paras. 37-52.

[9] The parties' closing oral statements from the first substantive meeting with the Panel are attached in full.

[10] In accordance with the Working Procedures, executive summaries of the parties' answers to the Panel's questions were not provided. The arguments made in the parties' answers are therefore not reflected in the annexes to this Report.

review of precise aspects of the Interim Report. On 7 February 2011, Brazil and the United States submitted written comments on each other's requests for interim review. Neither party requested an additional meeting with the Panel.

6.2 Due to changes as a result of the interim review, the numbering of paragraphs and footnotes in the Final Report has changed from the Interim Report. The text below refers to the paragraph and footnote numbers in the Interim Report. Where we have made changes, a reference to the corresponding paragraph or footnote number in the Final Report is included in parentheses for ease of reference. In addition to the modifications mentioned below, we have corrected a number of typographical and other non-substantive errors throughout the report.

A. Review Requested by Brazil

6.3 Brazil requests review of paragraphs 7.25, 7.51-7.54, 7.65, 7.69, 7.72, 7.73, 7.77-7.81, 7.86, 7.115, 7.119, 7.125-7.127, 7.135, 7.136, 7.174, 7.180-7.182, 7.185 and 8.1, and footnotes 119-121, 124, 125, 135, 229, 271, 275-278. In addition, Brazil asks for the insertion a new paragraph after paragraph 7.86.

6.4 In the absence of any objections from the United States, we have decided to accept the changes requested to paragraphs 7.25, 7.53 (paragraph 7.59 in the Final Report), 7.54 (7.60), 7.65 (7.71), 7.69 (7.75), 7.72 (7.78), 7.73 (7.79), 7.78 (7.84), 7.79 (7.85), 7.80 (7.86), 7.81 (7.87), 7.86 (7.92), 7.115 (7.122), 7.119 (7.126), 7.125 (7.132), 7.127 (7.134), 7.135 (7.142), 7.136 (7.143), 7.174 (7.181), 7.180 (7.187), 7.181 (7.188), 7.182 (7.189), 7.185 (7.192), 8.1 and footnotes 119-121 (127-129), 124 (132), 125 (133), 219 (229), 229 (241), 271 (284), 277 (290) and 278 (291), albeit not always on the exact terms proposed by Brazil. For the reasons explained below, we have also agreed to inserting a new paragraph after paragraph 7.86 (7.92), and to modify the language used in paragraphs 7.126, 7.127 and 8.1. However, we have declined Brazil's requests to amend paragraphs 7.51, 7.52 and 7.77.

Paragraphs 7.51 and 7.52

6.5 Brazil considers that paragraphs 7.51 and 7.52 of the Interim Report failed to accurately convey its arguments concerning the impact of "zeroing" in response to what it characterizes as the United States submission that, in certain of the instances challenged by Brazil, the USDOC's recourse to "zeroing" had no impact, and therefore did not violate Article 9.3 of the AD Agreement and Article VI:2 of the GATT 1994. Brazil recalls that it had argued that the United States' use of "zeroing" under the orange juice anti-dumping duty order had three impacts: First, it resulted in the exclusion of a large number of negative comparison results from the determination of the margin; second, it resulted in the determination of positive margins of dumping higher than would have been the case without the use of "zeroing"; and third, it resulted in the determination of cash deposit rates ("CDRs") and importer-specific assessment rates ("ISARs") that were above *de minimis* levels. Brazil argues that paragraphs 7.51 and 7.52

failed to convey the first two arguments and did not convey accurately the gist of Brazil's third argument. Thus, Brazil requests that these paragraphs be modified to ensure that they set out a more complete and accurate description of Brazil's arguments. The United States did not comment on Brazil's request.

6.6 We note that the section of the Interim Report Brazil refers to sets out Brazil's arguments in support of its claim that "simple zeroing" in the First and Second Administrative Reviews was inconsistent with Article 9.3 of the AD Agreement and Article VI:1 of the GATT 1994. Brazil presented essentially two lines of argument in support of this claim: First, that the use of "simple zerong" irrespective of its impact on the amount of anti-dumping duty collected is inconsistent with these provisions; and second, that even if "simple zeroing" were required to impact the amount of anti-dumping duty collected in order to violate these provisions (which is what is argued by the United States), the facts of the First and Second Administrative Reviews confirm that there was such an impact for both respondents. Paragraphs 7.51 and 7.52 sought to describe this latter argument, that is, what Brazil considered to be the impact of "simple zeroing" on the amount of anti-dumping duty collected that caused the United States to be in breach of its obligations under Article 9.3 of the AD Agreement and Article VI:2 of the GATT 1994.

6.7 While it is true that Brazil identified the three impacts of "simple zeroing" described above, it did not claim that all three impacts resulted in a violation of Article 9.3 of the AD Agreement and Article VI:2 of the GATT 1994, which is the focus of paragraphs 7.51 and 7.52. Therefore, we see no need to include Brazil's additional arguments in the relevant paragraphs, and consequently decline Brazil's request.

Paragraph 7.77

6.8 Brazil notes that the description of United States Administrative Reviews found in paragraph 7.77 of the Interim Report characterized a cash deposit as "an estimate of an importer's final amount of anti-dumping duty". Brazil recalls, however, that the parties disagree on the legal characterization of cash deposits as a matter of WTO law, and that the Panel has not ruled on the matter. Thus, Brazil suggests that the Panel reformulate its characterization by noting that a CDR is determined by reference to each exporter's margin of dumping, and that the description of a cash deposit as an estimate of future liability, reflects the position of the United States. The United States disagrees with Brazil's proposed revision, arguing that the Interim Report text reflects more clearly and accurately the way in which the United States sets cash deposits.

6.9 Brazil's requested modification suggests that it is of the view that by describing a cash deposit as "an estimate of an importer's final amount of anti-dumping duty liability", the Panel has effectively prejudged one of the matters in dispute, namely, the question whether cash deposits amount to anti-dumping duties or whether they are securities. However, in our view, the mere description of cash deposits as "an estimate of an importer's final amount of anti-dumping duty liability" does not express any view or conclusion on whether that "estimate" amounts to a duty or a security. Indeed, the very sentence Brazil focuses upon in paragraph 7.77 makes clear that it is the United States that considers cash deposits to represent a "security", not the Panel. Thus, we consider the proposed modification to be unnecessary and therefore decline Brazil's request.

Paragraph 7.86

6.10 Brazil considers that paragraph 7.86 does not fully reflect the contextual arguments it made regarding the correct interpretation of the concept of "dumping". In order to do so, Brazil proposes specific text for an additional paragraph it suggests could be inserted after paragraph 7.86. The United States does not agree with Brazil's proposed insertion as written, stating that it does not make clear that the suggested language reflects only Brazil's view of the interpretation of "dumping". The United States therefore asks the Panel to revise Brazil's proposed text to make clear that the proposed statements are Brazil's assertions. We have decided to accept Brazil's requested modification to paragraph 7.86 (7.92), but slightly edited it to address the United States' concern.

Paragraphs 7.126, 7.127 and 8.1

6.11 Brazil finds certain views expressed by the Panel in paragraphs 7.126, 7.127 and 8.1 of the Interim Report on the impact of "zeroing" disputes on the WTO dispute settlement system unacceptable. According to Brazil, these views: "call into question the wisdom" of Brazil and other Members in bringing "zeroing" disputes; extend beyond the Panel's mandate; and do not serve to advance the interests of the dispute settlement system. Thus, Brazil requests the Panel to delete certain portions of these paragraphs and suggests revisions to this effect.

6.12 The United States considers that there is no basis to accept Brazil's request. The United States recalls that Article 11.7 of the DSU provides that "the report of the panel shall set out ... the basic rationale behind any findings and recommendations that it makes", and notes that the passages at issue explain why the Panel concludes as a legal matter that "dumping" cannot have a transaction-specific meaning. The United States argues that Brazil's disagreement with some elements of the Panel's reasoning provides no basis for its deletion. To the contrary, according to the United States, the language challenged by Brazil is part of the Panel's discussion of the systemic issues related to the Panel's conclusions, and therefore should not be deleted.

6.13 We note that the passages of text that Brazil objects to were not intended, as Brazil puts it, to "question the wisdom" of Members in bringing "zeroing" disputes. We fully recognize that Members are entitled to bring challenges where they believe that their rights under the WTO Agreement have been nullified or impaired. The relevant passages were simply intended to draw attention to the continuing difficulties of interpretation arising in respect of this issue, which we believe reflect the lack of clarity in how the AD Agreement defines "dumping". The views expressed in the Interim Report that Brazil takes issue with were intended to highlight this interpretative problem, its effects and potential consequences. In the light of the parties' comments, we have decided to revise the relevant passages of paragraphs 7.126 (7.133), 7.127 (7.134) and 8.1 in order to avoid any misunderstanding.

B. Review Requested by the United States

6.14 The United States requests review of paragraphs 2.1, 7.3, 7.12-7.14, 7.22, 7.25, 7.26, 7.28, 7.38, 7.58, 7.63, 7.66, 7.74, 7.80, 7.86, 7.87, 7.102, 7.106, 7.184, 7.185 and footnotes 126 and 147.

6.15 In the absence of any objections from Brazil, we have decided to accept the United States' requests to make changes to paragraphs 2.1, 7.3, 7.12-7.14, 7.22, 7.25, 7.58 (7.64), 7.63 (7.69), 7.66 (7.72), 7.74 (7.80), 7.86 (7.92), 7.87 (7.94), 7.102 (7.109), and footnote 147 (155), albeit not always on the exact terms proposed by the United States. In addition, for the reasons expressed below, we have decided to accept the modifications the United States requests to paragraphs 7.26, 7.28, 7.81 (7.87) and 7.106 (7.113) and, in part, the change requested to paragraph 7.80 (7.86). However, we have declined the United States request concerning paragraphs 7.184 (7.191) and 7.185 (7.192), but have decided to modify the language used in these paragraphs in order to avoid confusion and to clarify our conclusions.

Paragraphs 7.26 and 7.28

6.16 The United States argues that the Panel's findings in the Interim Report concerning its request for a preliminary ruling in respect of Brazil's challenge to the "continued zeroing" measure addressed only two of the three arguments it made in support of its request. In particular, the United States notes that the Panel's ruling did not take into account its argument that "continued zeroing" should not fall within the Panel's terms of reference because of Article 17.4 of the AD Agreement. The United States asks the Panel to reflect this argument in the Final Report and, in addition, calls upon the Panel to evaluate its merits as a separate jurisdictional basis for finding the alleged "continued zeroing" measure outside of its terms of reference.

6.17 Brazil suggests two edits to the changes sought by the United States to paragraphs 7.26 and 7.28 in order to reflect the fact that the particular argument the United States now asks the Panel to refer to was made for the first time in its Opening Statement at the Panel's First Substantive Meeting. In addition, in the light of the United States' request, Brazil asks the Panel to insert one additional paragraph into the Final Report in order to capture an argument it advanced in response to the United States. Brazil objects to the United States' request to have the Panel evaluate the merits of the argument it made concerning Article 17.4 of the AD Agreement, recalling that Panels are not specifically required to address all of the arguments advanced by parties. In any case, Brazil considers that the United States' argument should be rejected on its substance.

6.18 We have decided to decline Brazil's suggested modifications to paragraphs 7.26 and 7.28, but have accepted its request to refer to the additional argument it made in response to the United States' request for a preliminary ruling. Paragraph 7.30 has been modified accordingly. We have also accepted the United States' request to describe the argument it advanced in respect of Article 17.4 of the AD Agreement in paragraphs 7.26 and 7.28, and have evaluated its merits in our findings at paragraphs 7.43-7.49 of the Final Report.

Paragraph 7.80

6.19 The United States submits that paragraph 7.80 inaccurately describes its position with regard to the margin of dumping for Fischer in the Second Administrative Review. The United States does not agree that the bracketed number referred to in this paragraph is a weighted-average margin ("WAM") for Fischer, and explains that the USDOC publishes exporters' WAMs in the Federal Register. The United States argues that the computer programme output from which the bracketed number is drawn is not the same as the official final WAM published in the Federal Register. The United States asks the Panel to modify the language in the penultimate sentence and delete the entirety of the last sentence of paragraph 7.80 in order to clarify this distinction. Brazil objects to the United States' request to delete the last sentence, arguing that it cannot be justified.

6.20 We note that the last sentence of paragraph 7.80 was not intended to be understood to suggest that the United States believes that Fischer's *official* WAM, published in the Federal Register, was the same as the output from the computer programme run by the USDOC. Rather, the last sentence was intended to convey the fact that the United States does not contest that the WAM published in the Federal Register for Fischer was 0%, precisely because a WAM of [[XX]] was determined for Fischer through the computer programme. Thus, we do not consider the changes the United States has requested to this paragraph to be necessary. Nevertheless, we have redrafted the last sentence of paragraph 7.80 (7.86) in order to avoid any misunderstanding.

Paragraph 7.81

6.21 The United States suggests that footnote 126, which appears in paragraph 7.81, be revised to reflect the fact that all transactions, including transactions where export price was not below normal value, were taken into account in the denominator of the calculation of Fischer's ISAR in the Second Administrative Review. To this end, the United States proposes that certain specific textual changes be made to the footnote. Brazil objects to the United States' proposed modification, arguing that it is premised on a definition of "dumping" that is disputed between the parties and rejected by the Panel. Brazil advances its own textual modifications to footnote 126, which it considers would address the United States' concern while avoiding any confusion about the correct interpretation of the notion of "dumping".

6.22 Footnote 126 explains and refers to evidence of the United States' use of "simple zeroing" in the calculation of Fischer's ISAR in the Second Administrative Review. The description of how the United States determined this ISAR is consistent with how the "simple zeroing" methodology is described elsewhere in the Report (e.g. paragraph 7.79). In our view, it does not prejudge our views on the correct interpretation of the definition of "dumping". Thus, we fail to see the problem that Brazil raises with the language proposed by the United States and therefore accept the United States requested modifications to this footnote.

Paragraph 7.106

6.23 The United States considers that paragraph 7.106 contains an incomplete summary of its position regarding what it asserts is Brazil's use of "zeroing" under its prospective normal value system. In particular, whereas the Interim Report indicated that the United States had pointed to only "one particular instance" of Brazil's alleged recourse to "zeroing" when collecting duties on the basis of a prospective normal value, the United States recalls that it had in fact identified the collection of duties by Brazil in this manner with respect to products from "at least seven countries". The United States asks that this submission be fully reflected in the Final Report. Brazil objects to the United States' request, stating that the United States' allegations are factually wrong. According to Brazil, and contrary to the United States' assertions, the Brazilian investigating authority did not treat the amount of duties imposed in relation to a single entry as a margin of dumping in the instances identified by the United States. Rather, Brazil argues that the relevant exhibits show that the amount of duties was capped at the level of a margin of dumping previously established.

6.24 We note that the relevant passage at issue in paragraph 7.106 does not represent a factual finding on our part, but merely a description of an assertion made by the United States concerning how Brazil has allegedly collected anti-dumping duties in a number of cases. To this extent, we have decided to grant the United States' request and have consequently modified the language of this paragraph in order to fully reflect the United States' factual assertions. Although Brazil did not immediately respond to the United States' assertions when they were made during the Second Substantive Meeting of the Panel with the parties, we have decided to reflect the position it has now communicated with respect to the United States' allegations in the Final Report. We have modified footnote 177 (187) for this purpose.

Paragraph 7.184 and 7.185

6.25 The United States considers that the inferences drawn in paragraphs 7.184 and 7.185 from the Issues and Decision Memoranda Brazil submitted to substantiate its claim in respect of "continued zeroing" are inherently speculative. According to the United States, it is "incorrect" to read these Decision Memoranda as stating what approach the USDOC would take in a future proceeding because they pertain to the particular determinations at issue. In this regard, the United States also notes that in *US – Continued Zeroing*, the Appellate Body did not take a position as to what the USDOC would do in the future, relying only on what had been done to date. Thus, the United States requests the deletion of the relevant statements from paragraphs 7.184 and 7.185.

6.26 Brazil objects to the United States' request on two grounds. First, Brazil considers that the United States is, in essence, stating that the Panel's factual findings concerning the Issues and Decision Memoranda are "incorrect" on the ground that it disagrees with the Panel's assessment. Brazil recalls, however, that it is a Panel's task to examine and weigh evidence as the trier of facts in WTO dispute settlement. Thus, the fact that the United States disagrees with the Panel's assessment does not render it "incorrect". Secondly, Brazil considers that the Panel correctly concluded that the Issues and Decision Memoranda support Brazil's claims concerning "continued zeroing", submitting that in the absence of any change to the United States' "zeroing" policy, the Memoranda show that the use of "zeroing" is part of the USDOC's calculation methodology.

6.27 We note that the statements in paragraphs 7.184 and 7.185 that are the focus of the United States' request do not conclude that the USDOC will continue to use the "zerong procedures" in future administrative reviews under the orange juice anti-dumping duty order. Rather, the statements indicate only that the Issues and Decision Memoranda "strongly suggest" or "leave little doubt" that this would be the case. Moreover, we do not agree with the United States view that the Appellate Body in *US – Continued Zeroing* did not take a position on whether the USDOC would continue to use the "zeroing procedures" in the administrative reviews at issue in that dispute. On the contrary, the Appellate Body expressly concluded in that dispute that the evidence before it provided a sufficient basis to find that "the zeroing methodology *would likely continue* to be applied in successive proceedings".[11] Thus, we see no reason to delete the relevant statements made in paragraphs 7.184 and 7.185, and therefore decline the United States' request. Nevertheless, we have decided to amend the language in these paragraphs in order to clarify that the Panel's evaluation of the contents of the Issues and Decision Memoranda reflects an assessment of the intention held by the USDOC at the time those documents were published. A modification to this end has been made in the Final Report at paragraphs 7.191 and 7.192.

VII. FINDINGS

A. United States' Requests for Preliminary Rulings

1. Second Administrative Review

(a) Arguments of the United States

7.1 The United States asserts that Brazil's request for the establishment of a panel ("panel request"), which it submits defines this Panel's terms of reference, identified the "2007-2008 anti-dumping duty administrative review on certain orange juice from Brazil (the 'Second Administrative Review')" as one of the measures at issue. However, the United States points out that the final results in Second Administrative Review were issued on 11 August 2009, well after the

[11] Appellate Body Report, *US – Continued Zeroing*, para. 191 (emphasis added).

date of Brazil's request for consultations, dated 27 May 2009. Thus, according to the United States, the measure that Brazil challenges in its panel request did not exist at the time of its consultations request, and therefore could not have been subject to consultations.[12]

7.2 The United States recognizes that the preliminary results of the Second Administrative Review had been issued by the time of Brazil's request for consultations. However, the United States explains that preliminary results are not final, and their publication simply affords interested parties an opportunity to provide comments, which the United States Department of Commerce ("USDOC") considers before making a final determination. The United States submits that prior to the issuance of the final results of the Second Administrative Review, it was entirely possible that no definitive duties would have been levied at all. The United States asserts that this is exactly what happened for one of the two respondents (Fischer) in the Second Administrative Review.[13]

7.3 The United States recalls that a panel's terms of reference are determined by the complaining party's panel request, and that pursuant to Article 4.7 of the DSU, a complaining party may request establishment of a panel only if "consultations fail to settle a dispute".[14] The United States argues that Articles 17.3 through 17.5 of the AD Agreement contain requirements that parallel those of the DSU, and the AD Agreement clarifies further the relationship between consultations and panel requests under that Agreement. The United States notes that Article 17.4 provides that a Member may only refer "the matter" to the DSB following a failure of consultations to achieve a mutually agreed solution, and final action by the administering authorities to levy definitive antidumping duties or accept price undertakings. The United States submits further that, in *Guatemala – Cement*, the Appellate Body found that the term "matter" has the same meaning in Article 17.3, relating to the request for consultations, and in Articles 17.4 and 17.5, relating to the referral of a matter to the DSB and the request for the establishment of a panel. Thus, the United States submits that a Member may only file a panel request with respect to a measure upon which the consultations process has run its course; and the United States considers that no such consultations were held in respect of the "2007-2008 anti-dumping duty administrative review on certain orange juice from Brazil (the 'Second Administrative Review')". In this light, the United States asks the Panel to make a preliminary ruling that Brazil's claims against this measure are outside of its terms of reference.

(b) Arguments of Brazil

7.4 Brazil notes that although Article 6.2 of the DSU requires that consultations be held between parties in dispute, it does not require that the measures identified in the panel request be identical to the measures identified in the consultations request. Brazil recalls that the Appellate Body has on several occa-

---

12 United States, FWS, paras. 37, 46 and 48.

13 US, FWS, para. 47.

14 US, FWS, para. 39.

sions explained that "Articles 4 and 6 of the DSU [do not] ... require a precise and exact identity between the specific measures that were the subject of consultations and the specific measures identified in the request for the establishment of a panel".[15] Rather, Brazil argues that panels and the Appellate Body have consistently held that a panel's terms of reference may include a measure properly identified in the panel request, even if that measure was not included in the consultations request, provided that doing so does not change the "essence" of the dispute.[16]

7.5 Brazil submits that its consultations and panel requests both identified the Second Administrative Review, which was ongoing when the consultations request was filed.[17] According to Brazil, the consultations request also included a reference to "any on-going or future antidumping administrative reviews ... related to the imports of certain orange juice from Brazil (case no. A-351-840)", as well as the "continued use of zeroing procedures" by the United States in successive anti-dumping proceedings under the orange juice anti-dumping duty order. Thus, Brazil argues that the relevant measures were identified with sufficient clarity for the United States to comprehend that the Second Administrative Review was part of the dispute.

7.6 Brazil also submits that the Second Administrative Review has very close substantive connections to, and the same essence as, the First Administrative Review. Brazil explains that the Second Administrative Review followed the First Administrative Review adopted under the same anti-dumping duty order. The Second Administrative Review also involved the same type of determinations as the First Administrative Review, made by the same United States administering authority, concerning the same products, the same exporters, and the

---

15 Brazil, Comments on US Preliminary Rulings Request ("Brazil, Preliminary Rulings"), para. 7, referring to Appellate Body Report, *Brazil – Export Financing Programme for Aircraft* ("*Brazil – Aircraft*"), WT/DS46/AB/R, adopted 20 August 1999, DSR 1999:III, 1161, para. 132. *See also, e.g.*, Panel Report, *United States – Continued Existence and Application of Zeroing Methodology* ("*US – Continued Zeroing*"), WT/DS350/R, adopted 19 February 2009, as modified by Appellate Body Report WT/DS350/AB/R, para. 7.23; Appellate Body Report, *United States – Continued Existence and Application of Zeroing Methodology* ("*US – Continued Zeroing*"), WT/DS350/AB/R, adopted 19 February 2009, para. 222; and Appellate Body Report, *United States – Subsidies on Upland Cotton* ("*US – Upland Cotton*"), WT/DS267/AB/R, adopted 21 March 2005, DSR 2005:I, 3, para. 285.

16 Brazil, Preliminary Rulings, paras. 9-22, referring *inter alia* to Panel Report, *Canada – Measures Affecting the Export of Civilian Aircraft* ("*Canada – Aircraft*"), WT/DS70/R, adopted 20 August 1999, as upheld by Appellate Body Report WT/DS70/AB/R, DSR 1999:IV, 1443, para. 9.14; Appellate Body Report, *Brazil – Aircraft*, para. 132; Appellate Body Report, *Chile – Price Band System and Safeguard Measures Relating to Certain Agricultural Products* ("*Chile – Price Band System*"), WT/DS207/AB/R, adopted 23 October 2002, DSR 2002:VIII, 3045 (Corr.1, DSR 2006:XII, 5473), para. 139; Panel Report, *Dominican Republic – Measures Affecting the Importation and Internal Sale of Cigarettes* ("*Dominican Republic – Import and Sale of Cigarettes*"), WT/DS302/R, adopted 19 May 2005, as modified by Appellate Body Report WT/DS302/AB/R, DSR 2005:XV, 7425, para. 7.21; Appellate Body Report, European *Communities – Customs Classification of Frozen Boneless Chicken Cuts* ("*EC – Chicken Cuts*"), WT/DS269/AB/R, WT/DS286/AB/R, adopted 27 September 2005, and Corr.1, DSR 2005:XIX, 9157, para. 157; Appellate Body Report, *US – Continued Zeroing*, in particular paras. 222 and 228.

17 Brazil, Preliminary Rulings, paras. 3-4 and 23.

same exporting country. Brazil also highlights that the First and Second Administrative Reviews provide succeeding bases for the continued imposition of anti-dumping duties under the orange juice anti-dumping duty order. Brazil submits that these connections are confirmed by the fact that, under the USDOC's Regulations, all administrative (and other) reviews occurring under a single order are mere "segments" of a single "proceeding" that continues until revocation.[18]

7.7 Finally, Brazil argues that, if the Second Administrative Review were excluded from the panel's terms of reference, it would be difficult, if not impossible, to pursue WTO dispute settlement with respect to United States' administrative reviews. Because the United States conducts administrative reviews on an annual basis, Brazil argues that if a complainant were required to file a new consultations request for every administrative review, WTO dispute settlement would become a "moving target", and the recommendations and rulings of the DSB could not address the latest measure. According to Brazil, this would needlessly prevent the prompt settlement of disputes.[19]

7.8 Thus, Brazil asks the Panel to reject the United States' request for the exclusion of the Second Administrative Review from its terms of reference, and instead find that it properly falls within the scope of this dispute.

(c) Arguments of the Third Parties

(i) European Union

7.9 The European Union considers that Brazil's consultations and panel requests adequately identified the Second Administrative Review as one of the challenged measures.[20] Moreover, the European Union argues that since the Second Administrative Review is part of the "continued zeroing" measure, which the European Union considers is within the panel's terms of reference, the fact that the final results were published only after consultations were held is irrelevant.[21] Thus, the European Union urges the Panel to reject the United States' request for preliminary ruling.

(ii) Japan

7.10 Japan recalls that the Appellate Body has found that Articles 4 and 6 of the DSU "set forth a process by which a complaining party must request consultations, and consultations must be held, before a matter may be referred to the DSB for the establishment of a panel".[22] Moreover, Japan also notes that the Appellate Body has held that "consultations provide the parties an opportunity to

---

18 Brazil, Preliminary Rulings, para. 25, referring to 19 C.F.R. § 351.102. Exhibit BRA-44.

19 Brazil, Preliminary Rulings, para. 27.

20 EU, Third Party Written Submission ("TPWS"), para. 5.

21 EU, TPWS, para. 8.

22 Appellate Body Report, *Brazil – Aircraft*, para. 131.

define and delimit the scope of the dispute between them"[23]; and that Articles 4 and 6 do not "require a *precise and exact identity* between the specific measures that were the subject of consultations and the specific measures identified in the request for the establishment of a panel".[24] Rather, "[a]s long as the complaining party does not expand the scope of the dispute", the Appellate Body has said it would "hesitate to impose too rigid a standard for the 'precise and exact identity' between the scope of consultations and the request for the establishment of a panel, as this would substitute the request for consultations for the panel request".[25]

7.11 Japan notes that the Second Administrative Review was subject to consultations and is included in the Panel's terms of reference. Japan recognizes that the final results of the Second Administrative Review had not been issued at the time of Brazil's request for consultations. However, it asserts that the Review had been initiated and a final result was expected to be issued within a certain period. Japan observes that Brazil's panel request mentioned the date and contents of the final result of the Second Administrative Review. Thus, Japan argues that, in the light of the description in the request for consultations, Brazil's consultations provided the parties with an opportunity to define and delimit the scope of the dispute between them. After reviewing Brazil's consultations request and panel request, Japan concludes that it is sure that Brazil's panel request has not broadened the scope of the dispute. Thus, Japan submits that the Panel should dismiss the United States' request.[26]

(iii) Korea

7.12 Korea submits that there is no basis to support the United States' request for a preliminary ruling because a combined reading of Articles 17.3 and 17.4 of the AD Agreement indicate that consultations may be requested before "final action" is taken by the administering authorities, while the establishment of a panel may not be requested until after that "final action" has occurred. In particular, Korea notes that Article 17.3 of the AD Agreement, which authorizes WTO Members to request consultations, does not contain any language that might be read to suggest that a Member must wait to request consultations until a final determination has been issued. By contrast, the first sentence of Article 17.4, which authorizes WTO Members to refer matters to the DSB for establishment of a panel, does specifically require complaining Members to wait until (1) consultations under Article 17.3 "have failed to achieve a mutually agreed solution", *and* (2) "final action has been taken by the administering authorities of the importing Member to levy anti-dumping duties ....". Korea argues that if the administrative authorities have not yet taken "final action", the matter may not be

---

23 Appellate Body Report, *Mexico – Anti-Dumping Investigation of High Fructose Corn Syrup (HFCS) from the United States – Recourse to Article 21.5 of the DSU by the United States* ("*Mexico – Corn Syrup (Article 21.5 – US)*"), WT/DS132/AB/RW, adopted 21 November 2001, DSR 2001:XIII, 6675, para. 54.

24 Appellate Body, *Brazil – Aircraft*, para. 132 (Emphasis original).

25 Appellate Body Report, *US – Upland Cotton*, para. 293.

26 Japan, Third Party Written Submission ("TPWS"), paras. 13-17.

referred to the DSB for establishment of a panel (except to the extent permitted by the second sentence of Article 17.4, concerning panel review of "provisional measures").

7.13 According to Korea, the clear implication of this combined reading of the two provisions is that consultations may be requested before "final action has been taken by the administering authorities". Korea submits that if this were not the case, there would be no need to include a requirement of "final action" in the first sentence of Article 17.4. If consultations could be requested only after "final action" by the administering authorities, Korea argues that the provisions of the first sentence of Article 17.4 requiring that consultations be held (and "have failed") would embody a requirement of "final action" as well. Under such an interpretation, Korea considers that the language requiring "final action" in the first sentence of Article 17.4 would be redundant.

7.14 Thus, Korea argues that, consistent with the principle of effective treaty interpretation, Article 17.3 of the AD Agreement must be read to allow for the possibility of holding consultations on measures before "final action" has been taken. Accordingly, Korea asks the Panel to reject the United States' request for a preliminary ruling.[27]

(iv) Mexico

7.15 Mexico considers that the United States' arguments for seeking the exclusion from the Panel's terms of reference of Brazil claims against the Second Administrative Review are factually incorrect and misstate the role of consultations in defining the Panel's terms of reference. Mexico asserts that, as a factual matter, Brazil did specifically seek consultations, and in fact did consult with the United States, in respect of the Second Administrative Review. Moreover, Mexico argues that Brazil was not required to request consultations precisely with respect to the Second Administrative Review in order to properly include it in its panel request, recalling that neither Articles 4 and 6 of the DSU "require a *precise and exact identity* between the specific measures that were the subject of consultations and the specific measures identified in the request for the establishment of a panel".[28] Thus, according to Mexico, as long as Brazil made clear that it was challenging the application of zeroing in recent and ongoing administrative reviews, sufficient notice was provided to the United States, and the Second Administrative Review could properly be challenged in the panel request as a measure subject to the Panel's terms of reference. In this regard, Mexico recalls that the panel was confronted with, and dismissed, a similar request for a preliminary ruling in *US – Continued Zeroing*. Mexico invites the Panel to do the same in the present dispute.[29]

---

[27] Korea, Third Party Written Submission ("TPWS"), paras. 8-10.

[28] Mexico, Third Party Written Submission ("TPWS"), para. 15, quoting from Appellate Body Report, *Brazil – Aircraft*, para. 132 (emphasis original).

[29] Mexico, TPWS, paras. 11-20.

(d) Evaluation by the Panel

7.16 In general, a panel's terms of reference are found in the panel request[30], where pursuant to Article 6.2 of the DSU, a complaining Member must "indicate whether consultations were held, identify the specific measures at issue and provide a brief summary of the legal basis of the complaint sufficient to present the problem clearly". The United States' request for a preliminary ruling concerning Brazil's complaint against the Second Administrative Review does not take issue with whether the measure being challenged, or the claims being made, are properly described in the Panel's terms of reference. Rather, the United States asks that we rule that Brazil's claims are outside of the terms of reference of this dispute because it alleges that the *final results* of the "2007-2008 anti-dumping duty administrative review on certain orange juice from Brazil (the 'Second Administrative Review')" did not exist at the time of Brazil's consultations request, and therefore they could not have been the subject of consultations.

7.17 It is well established that in order to bring a matter before a WTO dispute settlement panel, a Member must first make a request for consultations and consultations must take place in respect of that matter. In *Brazil – Aircraft*, the Appellate Body observed that:

> "Articles 4 and 6 of the DSU ... set forth a process by which a complaining party must request consultations, and consultations must be held, before a matter may be referred to the DSB for the establishment of a panel".[31]

Article 4.4 of the DSU prescribes that a consultations request must "be submitted in writing and shall give the reasons for the request, including identification of the measures at issue and an indication of the legal basis for the complaint". Moreover, for the purpose of dispute settlement, the scope of consultations are defined by what is expressed in the consultations request (and not by any record of what was actually discussed).[32] A Member cannot, therefore, challenge a measure in panel proceedings unless it has been identified in its request for consultations. However, it is not necessary for there to be "a precise and exact identity between the specific measures that were the subject of consultations and the specific measures identified in the request for the establishment of a panel" in order for the latter to properly fall within a panel's terms of reference.[33] In this regard, the Appellate Body in *US – Upland Cotton* explained that:

> "As long as the complaining party does not expand the scope of the dispute, we hesitate to impose too rigid a standard for the 'precise and exact identity' between the scope of consultations and the

---

30 Article 7.1 DSU.

31 Appellate Body Report, *Brazil – Aircraft*, para. 131. A parallel process is envisaged under Articles 17.3 to 17.5 of the AD Agreement. See Appellate Body Report, *Guatemala – Cement I*, paras. 57-80.

32 Appellate Body Report, *US – Upland Cotton*, paras. 286-287.

33 Appellate Body Report, *Brazil – Aircraft*, para. 132.

request for the establishment of a panel, as this would substitute the request for consultations for the panel request. According to Article 7 of the DSU, it is the request for the establishment of a panel that governs its terms of reference, unless the parties agree otherwise."[34]

7.18 Thus, in evaluating the merits of the United States' request for a preliminary ruling, we see the main question to be resolved to be whether Brazil's reference to the *final results* of Second Administrative Review in its panel request has expanded the scope of the dispute beyond the contours of what the United States could have reasonably understood from Brazil's request for consultations. We start by reviewing Brazil's request for consultations.

7.19 Brazil's request for consultations is constituted by two documents: an original request for consultations and an addendum. Brazil's original request is dated 27 November 2008 (circulated on 1 December 2008). This request identified the First Administrative Review under the orange juice anti-dumping duty order and "any on-going or future antidumping administrative reviews, and the final results thereof, related to the imports of certain orange juice from Brazil (case no. A-351-840)" as the USDOC "determinations" raising concern.[35] As regards the First Administrative Review, the original consultations request reveals that Brazil took issue with the USDOC's alleged application of "zeroing".

7.20 The addendum to Brazil's original request for consultations is dated 22 May 2009 (circulated on 27 May 2009). This document states that Brazil and the United States held consultations on 16 January 2009 covering the First and Second Administrative Reviews "pursuant to the original request for consultations, which included among others: the First Administrative Review ... and, any ongoing or future antidumping administrative reviews" under the orange juice anti-dumping duty order.[36] In other words, although not expressly mentioned in Brazil's original request for consultations, the Second Administrative Review appears to have been discussed during the 16 January 2009 consultations between the two parties. In this regard, we note that the Second Administrative Review was in progress at the time of the January 2009 consultations, with preliminary results being issued on 6 April 2009.[37] Reflecting this state of affairs, the addendum to Brazil's original consultations request explicitly identified the Second Administrative Review as one of the measures Brazil wished to consult about with the United States.[38]

7.21 Brazil's request for establishment of a panel is dated 20 August 2009 (circulated 21 August 2009). This document recalls that by virtue of the addendum

---

34 Appellate Body Report, *US – Upland Cotton*, para. 293 (footnotes omitted).

35 Request for Consultations by Brazil, 1 December 2008, WT/DS382/1, p. 1

36 Request for Consultations by Brazil (Addendum), 27 May 2009, WT/DS382/1/Add.1, p. 1

37 Second Administrative Review, Final Results, Exhibit BRA-22.

38 Request for Consultations by Brazil (Addendum), 27 May 2009, WT/DS382/1/Add.1, p. 2 ("The Antidumping Duty Administrative Review from 1 March 2007 to 29 February 2008 (the 'Second Administrative Review'), related to the imports of certain orange juice from Brazil (case n° A-351-840)").

to its original request for consultations, Brazil had requested further consultations with the United States concerning "the use of 'zeroing' in the anti-dumping duty investigation and in the second administrative review related to case No A-351-840 ...".[39] The same document explains that a second round of consultations was held on 18 June 2009. It also identifies the *final results* of the Second Administrative Review, which had been issued on 11 August 2009[40], as one of the measures at issue in the following terms:

> "(c) The 2007-2008 anti-dumping duty administrative review on certain orange juice from Brazil (the 'Second Administrative Review')
>
> This anti-dumping proceeding concerns the administrative review of anti-dumping duties on certain orange juice from Brazil (case No A-351-840) for the period 1 March 2007 through 29 February 2008. The final results of this Second Administrative Review were published in 74 Fed. Reg. 40167 on 11 August 2009. ..."[41]

7.22 In our view, Brazil's reference to the final results of the Second Administrative Review in its panel request does not expand the scope of the complaint presented in its request for consultations. Not only do Brazil's original consultations request and addendum respectively identify a concern with "any on-going or future antidumping administrative reviews, and the final results thereof, related to the imports of certain orange juice from Brazil (case no. A-351-840)" and the "Second Administrative Review", but it appears that the USDOC's conduct during the Second Administrative Review was discussed in both consultations that were actually held. While it is true that the *final results* of the Second Administrative Review were not yet issued at the time of those consultations, we do not consider this to mean that Brazil's focus on these results in its panel request expanded the scope of its complaint beyond what the United States could have reasonably understood the dispute to be about. On the contrary, we see the explicit reference to the final results of the Second Administrative Review as merely confirming the content of the complaint Brazil appears to have always been making.

7.23 In support of its objection to Brazil's inclusion of the final results of the Second Administrative Review in the panel request, the United States refers to *US – Certain EC Products* dispute. In that controversy, the European Communities sought to challenge two measures taken by the United States in retaliation to the EC's alleged failure to implement the recommendations and rulings of the DSB in the *EC – Bananas* dispute. The first measure, taken by the US Customs Service, imposed increased bonding requirements on imports of certain EC products, which subject to the decision of the arbitrator in the *EC – Bananas* dispute,

---

[39] Request for the Establishment of a Panel by Brazil, 21 August 2009, p. 1.

[40] Second Administrative Review, Final Results, Exhibit BRA-22.

[41] Request for the Establishment of a Panel by Brazil, 21 August 2009, p. 1.

could potentially result in the payment of additional duties of 100%. This measure was effective as of 3 March 1999, and was identified in both the consultations and panel requests. The second measure was adopted by the USTR and imposed 100% duties on some, but not all, of the designated products that were previously subject to the increased bonding requirements, in the light of the arbitrator's ruling in *EC – Bananas*. This second measure was adopted on 19 April 1999 and was identified only in the panel request. Thus, at the time of the consultations request, dated 4 March 1999, the second measure did not exist.

7.24 The panel and Appellate Body found that the 19 April 1999 measure was outside of the panel's terms of reference, not only because it did not exist at the time of consultations (and therefore could not have been subject to consultations), but also because they found it to be "legally distinct" from the 3 March 1999 measure. Among the factors considered by the Appellate Body to indicate that the two measures were "legally distinct" included the fact that the substance of the two measures was not entirely the same; that different legal bases and different United States government agencies were responsible for each measure; and the fact that the first measure was not in any way a prerequisite for the second measure.[42]

7.25 In our view, the circumstances surrounding the United States' request for a preliminary ruling in the present dispute are clearly different to the particular facts of *US – Certain EC Products*. For instance, as we have already noted, although the *final results* of the Second Administrative Review were not mentioned in Brazil's original consultations request and addendum, the *Second Administrative Review and its preliminary results* were in fact identified. The *final results* of the same Second Administrative Review are part of the same proceeding undertaken by the same United States' agency in relation to the same product. The final results of the Second Administrative Review represent the US-DOC's final determination of the issues at stake in the Second Administrative Review under the orange juice anti-dumping duty order; issues which included those Brazil had identified in its original consultations request and addendum. It is also important to note that Brazil's claims in respect of the final results of the Second Administrative Review are identical to those raised in its original consultations request and addendum concerning the Second Administrative Review and its preliminary results. Thus, we cannot see how Brazil's focus on the *final results* of the Second Administrative Review in its panel request expands the scope of its complaint beyond what the United States could have reasonably understood through Brazil's consultations request. Indeed, as we have already observed, the explicit reference to the final results of the Second Administrative Review merely confirms the content of the complaint Brazil appears to have always been making. We therefore reject the United States request for a prelimi-

---

42 Appellate Body Report, *United States – Import Measures on Certain Products from the European Communities* ("*US – Certain EC Products*"), WT/DS165/AB/R, adopted 10 January 2001, DSR 2001:I, 373, paras. 74-77.

nary ruling and find that the final results of the Second Administrative Review fall within our terms of reference.

2. *"Continued Zeroing"*

(a) Arguments of the United States

7.26 The United States requests the Panel to make a preliminary ruling that Brazil's claims against the "continued use" of "zeroing" do not fall within its terms of reference because: (i) Brazil's panel request lacks specificity as regards the alleged measure; (ii) Brazil's challenge purports to include future measures that were not in existence at the time of the establishment of this Panel; and (iii) the alleged measure did not involve a final action to levy definitive anti-dumping duties or accept price undertakings as required by Article 17.4 of the AD Agreement.

7.27 The United States argues that Brazil's focus on "continued zeroing" is nothing more than a challenge to "an indeterminate number of potential measures". The United States recalls that in order to satisfy the requirements of Article 6.2, a panel request must identify the "specific" measures at issue. According to the United States, in challenging "continued zeroing" Brazil is speculating as to what may happen in the future, and such speculation is not an identification of a "specific" measure.[43]

7.28 Referring to previous terms of reference rulings by the panels in the *US – Upland Cotton* and *Indonesia – Autos* disputes, the United States also submits that future measures that are not yet in existence at the time of panel establishment are not within a panel's term of reference under the DSU. The United States asserts that the alleged "continued zeroing" measure is focused on "indeterminate future measures that did not exist at the time of Brazil's panel request (and may never exist)". The United States submits that such measures cannot be "impairing any benefits accruing to Brazil", within the meaning of Article 3.3 of the DSU, and therefore they cannot be within the Panel's terms of reference.[44] Furthermore, the United States argues that including "continued zeroing" within the Panel's terms of reference would be contrary to Article 17.4 of the AD Agreement because it would ignore the fact that, for any given importation, the imposition of anti-dumping duties is grounded in a specific final action, and no such final action has been taken in the case of "continued zeroing".

(b) Arguments of Brazil

7.29 Brazil recalls that the Appellate Body has observed that the specificity requirement in Article 6.2 of the DSU means that "the measures at issue must be identified *with sufficient precision so that what is referred to adjudication by a*

[43] US, FWS, para. 51.
[44] US, FWS, para. 52.

panel may be discerned from the panel request".[45] Brazil notes that in *US – Continued Zeroing*, the Appellate Body found that the European Communities had satisfied this standard when it identified a "specific measure" that the Appellate Body described as "the use of the zeroing methodology in successive proceedings, in each of the 18 [anti-dumping] cases, by which the anti-dumping duties are maintained".[46] Brazil submits that the measure it has described in its panel request uses very similar language, noting that the only material difference between Brazil's description and the measure at issue in *US – Continued Zeroing* is that in Brazil's case, the measure addresses continued conduct under a different anti-dumping duty order from the orders implicated by the European Communities.[47] Indeed, given the Appellate Body's own formulation of the "continued use" measure in *US – Continued Zeroing*, Brazil argues that the formulation used in the panel request is more than sufficient for the Panel, the United States, and the third parties to "identify[] with sufficient precision ... what is referred to adjudication". In particular, according to Brazil, the panel request specifies that: (1) the measure involves the use of "zeroing" in successive anti-dumping proceedings; (2) the relevant proceedings in which "zeroing" is used are those conducted pursuant to a named anti-dumping duty order; (3) the particular types of anti-dumping proceedings in which "zeroing" is used include original investigations and administrative reviews; and (4) the determinations made in these proceedings using "zeroing" provide the basis for the application and maintenance of anti-dumping duties under the order over a period of time.[48]

7.30 Brazil rejects the United States allegations to the effect that the measure at issue is of a type that cannot be challenged in WTO dispute settlement and that it does not exist, recalling that faced with similar arguments in *US – Continued Zeroing*, the Appellate Body explained that "... the identification of the specific measures at issue, pursuant to Article 6.2, is different from a demonstration of the existence of such measures"; and that "an examination regarding the specificity of a panel request does not entail substantive consideration as to what types of measures are susceptible to challenge in WTO dispute settlement".[49] In addition, Brazil considers that the United States' characterization of its complaint as a challenge to potential future measures misses the point. According to Brazil, the United States' position fails to appreciate the difference between a "continued use" measure and challenges to individual determinations. Brazil argues that the "continued use" measure involves ongoing conduct in the form of use of the "zeroing" methodology under a particular anti-dumping order. In its view, this is not a "potential future measure[]",[50] but an actual measure that exists today.[51]

---

[45] Brazil, Preliminary Rulings, para. 33, quoting Appellate Body Report, *US – Continued Zeroing*, para. 168.
[46] Brazil, Preliminary Rulings, para. 34, quoting Appellate Body Report, *US – Continued Zeroing*, para. 166.
[47] Brazil, Preliminary Rulings, para. 39.
[48] Brazil, Preliminary Rulings, paras. 40-41.
[49] Brazil, Preliminary Rulings, paras. 43-45, quoting from Appellate Body Report, para. 169.
[50] US, FWS, para. 52.
[51] Brazil, Preliminary Rulings, para. 54.

7.31 Thus, Brazil asks the Panel to reject the United States' request for the exclusion of the "continued use" measure from its terms of reference, and find instead that it falls within the scope of this dispute.[52]

(c) Arguments of the Third Parties

(i) European Union

7.32 The European Union recalls that the Appellate Body in *US – Continued Zeroing* was faced with essentially the same issue that is before the Panel in the present dispute, namely, whether the European Union's complaint against the United States' alleged "continued zeroing" as "ongoing conduct" was within the panel's terms of reference. The European Union recalls that in *US – Continued Zeroing*, the Appellate Body ruled that "the identification of the specific measures at issue, pursuant to Article 6.2, is different from a demonstration of the existence of such measures", rejecting "the proposition that an examination of the specificity requirement under Article 6.2 of the DSU must involve a substantive inquiry as to the existence and precise content of the measure".[53] As regards the proper identification of the alleged measure in its panel request, the European Union notes that the Appellate Body saw "no reason to exclude ongoing conduct that consists of the use of the zeroing methodology from challenge in WTO dispute settlement".[54] The European Union asks the Panel to come to the same result in respect of Brazil's challenge to the United States' "continued zeroing" in the orange juice anti-dumping proceedings.[55]

(ii) Japan

7.33 Japan finds no substantial difference between the "continued zeroing" measure Brazil challenges in this dispute and the "continued zeroing" measures at issue in *US – Continued Zeroing*. In response to the United States argument that the alleged measure includes an indeterminate number of potential future measures and is not properly within the Panel's terms of reference, Japan argues that the United States overlooks Brazil's description of the alleged measure that "[i]n particular, the use of zeroing continues in the 'most recent administrative review' … by which duties are 'currently' applied and maintained".[56] In this light, Japan urges the panel to reject the United States' request for a preliminary ruling and find that the "continued use" of the zeroing methodology in successive anti-dumping proceedings, in relation to the anti-dumping duty order issued in respect of imports of certain orange juice from Brazil, constitutes a "measure" that falls within the Panel's terms of reference under Article 6.2 of the DSU.

---

52 Brazil, Preliminary Rulings, paras. 29-56.

53 EU, TPWS, para. 6, quoting from Appellate Body Report, *US – Continued Zeroing*, para. 169.

54 EU, TPWS, para. 7, quoting from Appellate Body Report, *US – Continued Zeroing*, para. 181.

55 EU, TPWS, para. 8.

56 Request for the Establishment of a Panel by Brazil, WT/DS382/4, p. 3.

(iii) Korea

7.34 Korea recalls that the specificity requirement under Article 6.2 of the DSU is designed to ensure that a panel request "present[s] the problem clearly" and that "the identification of a measure within the meaning of Article 6.2 need be framed only with sufficient particularity so as to indicate the nature of the measure and the gist of what is at issue".[57] According to Korea, it is clear from item (d) of Brazil's panel request that its complaint relates to "a string of connected and sequential determinations" in which the United States uses the zeroing methodology by which duties are maintained over a period of time under the anti-dumping duty order. Thus, Korea argues that Brazil has satisfied the standard under Article 6.2 of the DSU. Moreover, Korea agrees with Brazil that the "continued zeroing" measure it is challenging in this dispute is virtually the same "ongoing conduct" that was at issue in *US – Continued Zeroing*. However, Korea notes that it would be inappropriate to address the existence of the measure for the purpose of responding to the United States' request for a preliminary ruling, recalling that the Appellate Body in *US – Continued Zeroing* stated that "the identification of the specific measures at issue, pursuant to Article 6.2, is different from a demonstration of the existence of such measures".[58]

(iv) Mexico

7.35 Mexico argues that the United States' request for a preliminary ruling confuses the specificity requirement under Article 6.2 of the DSU with the susceptibility of ongoing conduct to WTO dispute settlement. Mexico recalls that the Appellate Body has observed that "the identification of the specific measures at issue, pursuant to Article 6.2, is different from a demonstration of the existence of such measures"; and that "the specificity requirement under Article 6.2 is intended to ensure the sufficiency of a panel request in presenting the problem clearly".[59] According to Mexico, the problem at issue in this dispute – the United States' continued application of zeroing in successive anti-dumping proceedings – is clear and easy to discern. Accordingly, Mexico contends that Brazil's panel request satisfies the specificity requirement of Article 6.2 of the DSU.

7.36 In addition, Mexico argues that the United States' reliance on *US – Upland Cotton* in support of its view that future measures not yet in existence at the time of panel establishment are not within a panel's term of reference is misplaced. According to Mexico, the facts in *US – Upland Cotton* can be distinguished from the facts at issue in the present dispute. In particular, Mexico notes that in *US –Upland Cotton*, the panel found that payments under the Agricultural Assistance Act of 2003 (the "Act") were not within its terms of reference because the Act was not enacted until *after* the panel request. As a result, consulta-

---

[57] Korea, TPWS, para. 12, quoting Appellate Body Report, *US – Continued Zeroing*, paras. 168 and 169.

[58] Korea, TPWS, paras. 14-16.

[59] Mexico, TPWS, para. 23, quoting from Appellate Body Report, *US – Continued Zeroing*, paras. 168 and 169.

tions were not sought or held on the payments under the Act. In making its finding, Mexico recalls that the panel specifically "noted[d] that the cottonseed payments for each year were ad hoc appropriations, each with a separate legal basis, which did not follow a single model". Moreover, Mexico recalls that the panel found that the relevant section "did not amend or modify any existing or previous programme". Mexico also notes that the panel concluded that the evidence before it disclosed "the existence of separate and legally distinct cottonseed payment programmes for crops in different years rather than a single cottonseed payment programme".[60]

7.37 Mexico observes that, in contrast, in the present dispute Brazil challenges the continued application of zeroing in periodic reviews conducted as stages of a continuous proceeding involving the imposition, assessment, and collection of duties under the same anti-dumping duty order. With respect to the proceeding on certain orange juice from Brazil, Mexico argues that the USDOC has applied zeroing at every stage of the proceeding and has given no indication that it will change its approach in the future. Mexico submits that it is this recurring and ongoing conduct under the single anti-dumping duty order that Brazil challenges. After recalling that the Appellate Body in *US – Continued Zeroing* found a series of similar "ongoing conduct" measures to be susceptible to WTO dispute settlement proceedings, Mexico asks the Panel to deny the United States' request for a preliminary ruling to exclude Brazil's claims from its terms of reference.[61]

(d) Evaluation by the Panel

7.38 The United States' request for a preliminary ruling in respect of Brazil's "continued zeroing" claim is based on three lines of argument. First, the United States submits that in seeking to describe the alleged "continued zeroing" measure, Brazil's panel request provides only a "general reference to an indeterminate number of potential measures" based on "speculation" as to what may happen in the future. According to the United States, such "speculation" cannot satisfy the Article 6.2 requirement that a panel request "identify the *specific* measures at issue".[62] Secondly, the United States argues that by challenging "continued zeroing", Brazil appears to challenge "an indeterminate number of potential future measures", which were not in existence at the time of panel establishment and may never exist, and therefore cannot fall within the Panel's terms of reference.[63] Thirdly, the United States argues that the inclusion of "continued zeroing" in the Panel's terms of reference is inconsistent with Article 17.4 of the AD Agreement, because no "final action" within the meaning of that provision has been taken in the case of "continued zeroing".

---

[60] Mexico, TPWS, para 25, quoting from Panel Report, *US – Upland Cotton*, paras. 7.162, 7.165 and 167.

[61] Mexico, TPWS, paras. 26-28.

[62] US, FWS, paras. 49-51 (United States' emphasis).

[63] US, FWS, para. 52.

7.39 Before turning to examine Brazil's panel request, we note that the first two of the arguments described above served as the basis for a similar request for a preliminary ruling made by the United States in *US – Continued Zeroing*. Although the panel in that dispute agreed with the United States[64], the Appellate Body reversed the panel's findings. In particular, the Appellate Body held that the United States could reasonably have been expected to understand, from reading the panel request as a whole, that the European Communities was challenging the use of "zeroing" in successive proceedings, as "ongoing conduct", in each of 18 separate anti-dumping cases. The Appellate Body saw confirmation of this in the fact that the European Communities was seeking a prospective remedy.[65] The Appellate Body also rejected the panel's view that "in order to successfully raise claims against a measure, the complaining Member must in the first place demonstrate the existence and the precise content of such measure, consistently with the requirements of Article 6.2 of the DSU".[66] In this regard, the Appellate Body made the following observation:

> "... the identification of the specific measures at issue, pursuant to Article 6.2, is different from a demonstration of the existence of such measures. For the latter, a complainant would be expected to present relevant arguments and evidence during the panel proceedings showing the existence of the measures, for example, in the case of challenges brought against unwritten norms.{} Moreover, although a measure cannot be identified without some indication of its contents, the identification of a measure within the meaning of Article 6.2 need be framed only with sufficient particularity so as to indicate the nature of the measure and the gist of what is at issue. Thus, an examination regarding the specificity of a panel request does not entail substantive consideration as to what types of measures are susceptible to challenge in WTO dispute settlement. Such consideration may have to be explored by a panel and the parties during the panel proceedings, but is not prerequisite for the establishment of a panel. To impose such prerequisite would be inconsistent with the function of a panel request in commencing panel proceedings and setting the jurisdictional boundaries of such proceedings. Therefore, we reject the proposition that an examination of the specificity requirement under Article 6.2 of the DSU must involve a substantive inquiry as to the existence and precise content of the measure."[67]

7.40 In the present dispute, Brazil's panel request describes the alleged measure at issue in the following terms:

> "Measures and claims

---

64 Panel Report, *US – Continued Zeroing*, para. 7.61.
65 Appellate Body Report, *US – Continued Zeroing*, para. 171.
66 Panel Report, *US – Continued Zeroing*, para. 7.50.
67 Appellate Body Report, para. 169.

The measures at issue are the following:

...

(d) The continued use of the U.S. 'zeroing procedures' in successive anti-dumping proceedings, in relation to the anti-dumping duty order issued in respect of imports of certain orange juice from Brazil

This measure concerns the continued use by the United States of "zeroing procedures" in successive anti-dumping proceedings, in relation to the anti-dumping duty order issued in respect of imports of certain orange juice from Brazil (case No A-351-840), including the original investigation and any subsequent administrative reviews, by which duties are applied and maintained over a period of time. In particular, the use of zeroing continues in the most recent administrative review, identified under item (c) above, by which duties are currently applied and maintained."

7.41 The language in Brazil's panel request explicitly identifies the measure at issue as "the continued use by the United States of 'zeroing procedures' in successive anti-dumping proceedings" under the orange juice anti-dumping duty order, "including the original investigation and any subsequent administrative reviews, by which duties are applied and maintained over a period of time". We note that this language reveals that Brazil's concern is focused on the "continued use" of "zeroing procedures" in "*successive*" proceedings "*including* the original investigation *and any* subsequent reviews". In other words, Brazil objects to the United States' alleged "continued use" of "zeroing procedures" over time, starting from the original investigation that resulted in the imposition of the orange juice anti-dumping duty order to any subsequent proceeding under the same order. In our view, it is reasonably clear from this description, when read in the light of the panel request as a whole[68], that the alleged measure Brazil challenges is the United States' "continued use" of "zeroing procedures" as "ongoing conduct".

7.42 We see no need, for the purpose of responding to the United States request for a preliminary ruling, to pronounce on whether such "ongoing conduct" is susceptible to challenge in WTO dispute settlement. As the Appellate Body observed in the above-quoted passage from *US – Continued Zeroing*, "an examination regarding the specificity of a panel request does not entail substantive consideration as to what types of measures are susceptible to challenge in WTO

[68] For instance, we note that in addition to making claims against the "continued use" of "zeroing procedures" in "successive anti-dumping proceedings", Brazil's panel request challenges the original investigation and First and Second Administrative Reviews *individually*, as three *separate* measures.

dispute settlement".[69] Likewise, we do not see that it is our task, when considering the United States' preliminary ruling request, to decide whether the "ongoing conduct" measure Brazil objects to actually exists, even assuming that it can be challenged in WTO dispute settlement. Again, as the Appellate Body explained in *US – Continued Zeroing*, "the identification of the specific measures at issue, pursuant to Article 6.2, is different from a demonstration of the existence of such measures".[70]

7.43 The third argument the United States advances to support its request for a preliminary ruling is related to Article 17.4 of the AD Agreement. This provision reads:

> "If the Member that requested consultations considers that the consultations pursuant to paragraph 3 have failed to achieve a mutually agreed solution, and if final action has been taken by the administering authorities of the importing Member to levy definitive anti-dumping duties or to accept price undertakings, it may refer the matter to the Dispute Settlement Body ("DSB"). When a provisional measure has a significant impact and the Member that requested consultations considers that the measure was taken contrary to the provisions of paragraph 1 of Article 7, that Member may also refer such matter to the DSB."

7.44 The United States notes that Article 17.4 provides that a member may only refer a matter to the DSB following a failure of consultations to achieve a mutually agreed solution, and "final action" has been taken by the administering authorities to levy definitive anti-dumping duties or accept price undertakings. According to the United States, "continued zeroing" does not amount to "final action" within the meaning of Article 17.4 of the AD Agreement and, therefore, it cannot fall within our terms of reference. Although the Appellate Body in *US – Continued Zeroing* did not directly address this argument, it did appear to take this provision (as well as Article 17.3 of the AD Agreement) into account in the process of overturning the panel's findings on the merit of the European Communties' "continued zeroing" claims. In particular, in examining the question whether "continued zeroing" is a measure susceptible to WTO dispute settlement, and after recalling its observation from a previous case where it stated that "in principle, any act or omission attributable to a WTO Member can be a measure of that Member for purposes of dispute settlement proceedings"[71], the Appellate Body noted that:

> "Articles 17.3 and 17.4 of the *Anti-Dumping Agreement* are also relevant to the question of the types of measures that can be submitted to dispute settlement under the *Anti-Dumping Agreement*. Closely resembling Article 3.3 of the DSU, Article 17.3 provides

[69] Appellate Body Report, *US – Continued Zeroing*, para. 169.

[70] *Ibid.*.

[71] Appellate Body Report, *US – Corrosion-Resistant Steel Sunset Review*, para. 81.

that, '[i]f any Member considers that any benefit accruing to it, directly or indirectly, under [the *Anti-Dumping Agreement*] is being nullified or impaired ... by another Member or Members, it may, with a view to reaching a mutually satisfactory resolution of the matter, request in writing consultations with the Member or Members in question.'{} Article 17.4 of the *Anti-Dumping Agreement* further specifies that a Member may refer a matter to the DSB if it considers that the consultations have failed to achieve a mutually agreed solution 'and if final action has been taken by the administering authorities of the importing Member to', *inter alia*, 'levy definitive anti-dumping duties'.[72]"

7.45 In the very next paragraph, the Appellate Body agreed with the panel that "measures examined by WTO panels and the Appellate Body include 'not only measures consisting of acts that apply to particular situations, but also those consisting of acts setting forth rules or norms that have general and prospective application'." The Appellate Body then went on to observe that "[i]n order to be susceptible to challenge, a measure need not fit squarely within [the "as such" or "as applied"] categories, that is, either as a rule or norm of general and prospective application, or as an individual instance of the application of a rule or norm". Finally, the Appellate Body described the "continued zeroing" measure challenged by the European Communities using terms that are very similar to those used by Brazil in the present dispute, and concluded that it saw "no reason to exclude ongoing conduct that consists of the use of the zeroing methodology from challenge in WTO dispute settlement"[73].

7.46 In our view, the clear implication to draw from the Appellate Body's reasoning and findings in *US – Continued Zeroing* is that Article 17.4 of the AD Agreement does not limit Brazil's right in the present dispute to challenge "continued zeroing" under the AD Agreement. This conclusion finds support in the Appellate Body's observations in *US – 1916 Act*, where in allowing the European Communities and Japan to challenge certain United States' anti-dumping legislation, the Appellate Body explained *inter alia* that:

"Important considerations underlie the restriction contained in Article 17.4. In the context of dispute settlement proceedings regarding an anti-dumping investigation, there is tension between, on the one hand, a complaining Member's right to seek redress when illegal action affects its economic operators and, on the other hand, the risk that a responding Member may be harassed or its resources squandered if dispute settlement proceedings could be initiated against it in respect of each step, however small, taken in the course of an anti-dumping investigation, even before any concrete measure had been adopted.{} In our view, by limiting the availabil-

---

72 Appellate Body Report, *US – Continued Zeroing*, para. 177.

73 Appellate Body Report, *US – Continued Zeroing*, paras. 180-181.

ity of dispute settlement proceedings related to an anti-dumping investigation to cases in which a Member's request for establishment of a panel identifies a definitive anti-dumping duty, a price undertaking or a provisional measure{}, Article 17.4 strikes a balance between these competing considerations.

Therefore, Article 17.4 sets out certain conditions that must exist before a Member can challenge action taken by a national investigating authority in the context of an anti-dumping investigation. However, Article 17.4 does not address or affect a Member's right to bring a claim of inconsistency with the *Anti-Dumping Agreement* against anti-dumping legislation as such.

Moreover, as we have seen above, the GATT and WTO case law firmly establishes that dispute settlement proceedings may be brought based on the alleged inconsistency of a Member's legislation as such with that Member's obligations. We find nothing, and the United States has identified nothing, inherent in the nature of anti-dumping legislation that would rationally distinguish such legislation from other types of legislation for purposes of dispute settlement, or that would remove anti-dumping legislation from the ambit of the generally-accepted practice that a panel may examine legislation as such.[74]"

7.47 Thus, in the *US – 1916 Act* dispute, the Appellate Body found that the European Communities and Japan were entitled to bring a complaint against legislation they considered to be inconsistent with the AD Agreement before a panel, even though that legislation did not amount to a "final action" or a provisional measure within the meaning of Article 17.4 of the AD Agreement. In doing so, the Appellate Body described the relevance of Article 17.4 as being limited to complaints related to the conduct of investigating authorities in an anti-dumping investigation. However, in the present dispute, Brazil's challenge to the United States' alleged "continued use" of "zeroing" does not pertain to the conduct of the USDOC in one particular anti-dumping investigation. Rather, as we more fully explain below[75], Brazil's complaint is focused on the USDOC's alleged "use of zeroing" in multiple proceedings, under the orange juice anti-dumping duty order, as a single "*ongoing conduct*" measure. In our view, an "ongoing conduct" measure is broader than the type of conduct envisaged under Article 17.4 of the AD Agreement, and as such, falls outside of its scope of operation.

---

[74] Appellate Body Report, *United States – Anti-Dumping Act of 1916* ("*US – 1916 Act*"), WT/DS136/AB/R, WT/DS162/AB/R, adopted 26 September 2000, DSR 2000:X, 4793, at paras. 73-75 (footnote omitted).

[75] See below, paras. 7.171-7.176.

7.48 In any case, we note that the evidence Brazil has advanced in support of the existence of the alleged "continued zeroing" measure includes instances where the United States authorities have, in fact, levied definitive anti-dumping duties.[76] Thus, Brazil does not challenge the alleged "continued zeroing" measure in the absence of any connection between this alleged measure and "final action". On the contrary, the evidence of United States' "final action" lies at the heart of Brazil's complaint.

7.49 In conclusion, we find that Brazil's panel request is sufficiently precise to satisfy the standards of Article 6.2 of the DSU in that it reasonably identifies "the nature of the measure and the gist of what is at issue". Furthermore, we also find that the inclusion of Brazil's claim against the alleged "continued zeroing" measure in our terms of reference is not inconsistent with the requirements of Article 17.4 of the AD Agreement. We therefore dismiss the United States' request for a preliminary ruling.

B. Brazil's Claims Concerning the Alleged Use of "Simple Zeroing" in Administrative Reviews

1. Arguments of Brazil

7.50 Brazil claims that by allegedly calculating the margins of dumping, relied upon for the purpose of establishing the cash-deposit rates ("CDRs"), and the importer-specific assessment rates ("ISARs") for Cutrale and Fischer in the First and Second Administrative Reviews through the use of "simple zeroing", the USDOC acted inconsistently with its obligations under Articles 2.4 and 9.3 of the AD Agreement and Article VI:2 of the GATT 1994.[77]

(a) Article 9.3 of the AD Agreement and Article VI:2 of the GATT 1994

7.51 Brazil argues that Article 9.3 of the AD Agreement and Article VI:2 of the GATT 1994 establish an obligation on Members not to impose an anti-dumping duty on any dumped product in an amount that is greater than the "margin of dumping" determined in respect of that product. Relying upon the findings of the Appellate Body in a series of disputes involving the USDOC's application of "simple zeroing" in administrative reviews[78], Brazil submits that a

[76] The evidence Brazil has advanced to establish the existence of the alleged "continued zeroing" measure is set out and evaluated below, at paras. 7.177-7.192.

[77] Brazil, FWS, paras. 97 and 118; Brazil, Second Written Submission ("SWS"), para. 47; Brazil, Answers to Panel Questions 2 and 3.

[78] In particular, Brazil refers to the following Appellate Body Reports: Appellate Body Report, *United States – Laws, Regulations and Methodology for Calculating Dumping Margins ("Zeroing")* ("*US – Zeroing (EC)*"), WT/DS294/AB/R, adopted 9 May 2006, and Corr.1, DSR 2006:II, 417; Appellate Body Report, *United States – Measures Relating to Zeroing and Sunset Reviews* ("*US – Zeroing (Japan)*"), WT/DS322/AB/R, adopted 23 January 2007, DSR 2007:I, 3; Appellate Body Report, *United States – Measures Relating to Zeroing and Sunset Reviews – Recourse to Article 21.5 of the DSU by Japan* ("*US – Zeroing (Japan) (Article 21.5 – Japan)*"), WT/DS322/AB/RW, adopted 31 August 2009; Appellate Body Report, *United States – Final Anti-Dumping Measures on Stainless*

"margin of dumping" can only be calculated with respect to the product under consideration "as a whole", encompassing all export transactions of the product under consideration; and that it cannot be found to exist only for a type, model or category of that product. Brazil recalls that the Appellate Body has repeatedly found that Article 2.1 of the AD Agreement and Article VI:1 of the GATT 1994 define "dumping" as a concept related to the product "as a whole". In addition, Brazil notes that the Appellate Body has previously indicated that "dumping" and "margin of dumping" relate to the pricing practices of individual exporters or foreign producers; and that this interpretation is supported by several other provisions of the AD Agreement, including Articles 2.2, 2.3, 5.8, 6.10, 8.1, 9.4 and 9.5. Furthermore, Brazil recalls that the Appellate Body has found that the AD Agreement and the GATT 1994 are not concerned with dumping *per se*, but with dumping that causes or threatens to cause material injury to the domestic industry, a condition that by the terms of Article 3.1 of the AD Agreement cannot be found to exist in relation to individual transactions, but only for the product as a whole.[79]

7.52 Brazil argues that the fact that Article 9.4(ii) of the AD Agreement recognizes that variable anti-dumping duties may be collected on a transaction-specific basis does not mean that Article 2 of the AD Agreement authorizes a determination of dumping on the same basis. Brazil emphasizes that Article 9 of the AD Agreement governs the imposition and collection of duties, noting that these rules are "distinct and separate" from the rules governing the determination of dumping under Article 2. Thus, while Article 9 permits collection of variable anti-dumping duties on a transaction-specific basis, Brazil argues that "dumping" must be determined for the "product as a whole" in accordance with Article 2.[80]

7.53 In addition, Brazil submits that the possibility that a general prohibition on "zeroing" may result in "mathematical equivalence" between the result obtained when calculating a margin of dumping, for the purpose of Article 2.4.2, through the use of the W-W and W-T methodologies, does not undermine its legal argument, because "mathematical equivalence" may arise only "under a specific set of assumptions" that do not always apply. Furthermore, Brazil argues that the interpretation of the exceptional comparison methodology in Article 2.4.2 (i.e., "W-T") – and whether it permits "zeroing" – cannot govern the interpretation of the general rule regarding the definition of "dumping". In any case, Brazil recalls that the Appellate Body has noted that some Members have argued that the second sentence of Article 2.4.2 does not permit "zeroing".[81]

7.54 Brazil observes that the Appellate Body has repeatedly confirmed that the interpretation of the concepts of "dumping" and "margin of dumping" that it is advancing in the present dispute is the only "permissible" interpretation under

Steel from Mexico ("*US – Stainless Steel (Mexico)*"), WT/DS344/AB/R, adopted 20 May 2008; and *US – Continued Zeroing*.

[79] Brazil, FWS, paras. 6, 49-76; Brazil, First Confidential Opening Oral Statement ("FCOOS"), paras. 12-37.

[80] Brazil, FCOOS, paras. 47-51; Brazil, SWS, para. 5.

[81] Brazil, FCOOS, paras. 52-58; Brazil, SWS, para. 5.

the terms of Article 17.6(ii) of the AD Agreement, noting that the application of customary rules of treaty interpretation cannot result in a rival transaction-specific definition of these concepts.[82]

7.55 Thus, on the basis of essentially the same line of reasoning expounded by the Appellate Body in previous disputes involving "simple zeroing", Brazil argues that if a Member determines a margin of dumping for a particular exporter in an administrative review that exceeds the overall margin of dumping for that exporter's "product as a whole" because of the systematic exclusion of certain export transactions, that determination must be inconsistent with Article 9.3 of the AD Agreement and Article VI:2 of the GATT 1994. Brazil urges the Panel to come to the same conclusion, emphasizing the importance of resolving the same legal questions in the same way in subsequent disputes for the "security and predictability" and "consistency and stability" of the WTO dispute settlement system.[83]

7.56 Brazil argues that the facts show that the USDOC calculated the margins of dumping for Cutrale and Fischer in the First and Second Administrative Reviews through the use of "simple zeroing", and that in the absence of "simple zeroing", both respondents would have had no margins of dumping at all.[84] According to Brazil, the mere *use* of "simple zeroing" by the USDOC to calculate these margins, irrespective of any impact they may have had on the amount of anti-dumping duties actually collected, is inconsistent with Article 9.3 of the AD Agreement and Article VI:2 of the GATT 1994. In particular, Brazil argues that pursuant to these provisions, a Member must establish a margin of dumping for the "product as a whole" in accordance with Article 2 of the AD Agreement. Referring to a statement made by the panel in *US – Zeroing (Japan)(Article 21.5 – Japan)*, Brazil submits that a failure to comply with this requirement vitiates a determination made under Article 9.3 of the AD Agreement and Article VI:2 of the GATT 1994, irrespective of the amount of duties that is ultimately collected.[85]

7.57 In any case, Brazil notes that the margins of dumping determined for Cutrale and Fischer did have an impact on the amount of anti-dumping duties collected. Brazil notes that the margins of dumping were in fact relied upon by the USDOC to set the CDR for Cutrale in the Second Administrative Review and Fischer in the First Administrative Review.[86] According to Brazil, CDRs amount to anti-dumping duties and are subject to the disciplines of Article 9.3, as is well established in WTO case-law.[87] Therefore, if the impact of the use of "zeroing" is relevant to establish a violation of Article 9.3 of the AD Agreement and Arti-

---

[82] Brazil, FCOOS, paras. 2-4, 8-11.

[83] Brazil, FCOOS, para. 2; Brazil, SWS, para. 4.

[84] Brazil, FWS, para. 5; Brazil, FCOOS, paras. 66-75; Brazil, SWS, paras. 19, 35; Brazil, Answer to Panel Question 2.

[85] Brazil, Answer to Panel Question 2; Brazil, SWS, paras. 11-13, citing Panel Report, *US – Zeroing (Japan)(Article 21.5 – Japan)*, para. 7.162.

[86] Brazil, FWS, paras. 77-96; Brazil, Answer to Panel Question 2.

[87] Brazil, FCOOS, para. 35; Brazil, Answer to Panel Question 3.

cle VI:2 of the GATT 1994, the USDOC's reliance upon margins of dumping calculated using "simple zeroing" for the purpose of the CDRs collected on imports of the respondents' products in the periods subsequent to the relevant administrative reviews must be inconsistent with those provisions.[88]

7.58 Brazil also notes that the facts show that the ISARs determined for Cutrale in the First and Second Administrative Reviews, and for Fischer in the First Administrative Review, were calculated through the use of "simple zeroing".[89] Thus, again, if the *impact* of the use of "zeroing" is relevant to establish a violation of Article 9.3 of the AD Agreement and Article VI:2 of the GATT 1994, the USDOC's use of "simple zeroing" when establishing the relevant ISARs must be inconsistent with those provisions.[90]

7.59 Brazil rejects the United States' view that CDRs do not amount to anti-dumping duties falling within the scope of Article 9.3 of the AD Agreement. In its view, CDRs have the essential characteristics of anti-dumping duties imposed under Article 9 of the AD Agreement, and not reasonable securities within the meaning of the Ad Note to Article VI:2 and VI:3 of the GATT 1994. Relying on various observations of the Appellate Body in the *US – Shrimp/Bond* dispute[91], Brazil concludes that a reasonable security is "a response to a determination of a risk of non-payment of future anti-dumping duties that is commensurate with that risk"[92] and that a CDR neither reflects nor is commensurate with the likely magnitude of the risk of non-payment by an importer. Indeed, Brazil submits that the characteristics of a CDR match those of an anti-dumping duty because: it is imposed on all imports from exporters found to be engaged in injurious dumping; it is imposed as a specific response to a dumping determination made in connection with a particular exporter; and it is fixed at the level of the individual margin of dumping determined by the USDOC for the exporter in question, and cannot exceed that margin. As such, Brazil argues a CDR is an anti-dumping duty.

7.60 That CDRs are anti-dumping duties subject to Article 9 of the AD Agreement is, Brazil argues, confirmed by the case-law concerning United States' administrative reviews. First, Brazil recalls that in *US – Shrimp/Bond*, the Appellate Body, despite holding that it did not have to rule on the issue, disagreed with the "reasoning" that led the panel in that case to find CDRs to be securities within the meaning of the Ad Note, and not anti-dumping duties subject to Article 9 of the AD Agreement. Moreover, Brazil submits that the Appellate Body in the same dispute emphasized that even under United States' law, the role of cash deposits differs from a security, and that they are fixed at the level of an ex-

---

88 Brazil, Answer to Panel Question 2.

89 Brazil, FWS, paras. 77-96; Brazil, Answer to Panel Question 2.

90 Brazil, FCOOS, para. 72; Brazil, SWS, paras. 20-21; Brazil, Answer to Panel Question 2.

91 In particular, Appellate Body Report, *United States – Measures Relating to Shrimp from Thailand / United States – Customs Bond Directive for Merchandise Subject to Anti-Dumping/Countervailing Duties* ("*US – Shrimp (Thailand) / US – Customs Bond Directive*"), WT/DS343/AB/R, WT/DS345/AB/R, adopted 1 August 2008, paras. 221, 256, 258-263.

92 Brazil, Answer to Panel Question 3.

porter's margin of dumping. Second, Brazil argues that the Appellate Body has found several times that CDRs calculated through "zeroing" are inconsistent with Article 9.3 of the AD Agreement and Article VI:2 of the GATT 1994.[93]

7.61 Thus, Brazil argues that the applicability of Article 9.3 of the AD Agreement and Article VI:2 of the GATT 1994 to CDRs is well established and that security and predictability in the multilateral trading system dictate that the conclusion reached in disputes involving several other Members should also apply to Brazil's claims.[94]

(b) Article 2.4 of the AD Agreement

7.62 Brazil argues that the use of "simple zeroing" to calculate an exporter's margin of dumping in any stage of an anti-dumping proceeding infringes the requirement that a "fair comparison shall be made between export price and normal value" under Article 2.4 of the AD Agreement. According to Brazil, the obligation under Article 2.4 to make a "fair comparison" applies independently of the amount of anti-dumping duties that are collected by an importing Member. Brazil recalls that the Appellate Body has on numerous occasions observed that there is "an inherent bias in a zeroing methodology" and that as a "way of calculating" margins, the "zeroing" methodology "cannot be described as impartial, even-handed, or unbiased".[95] Moreover, Brazil notes that one panel and the Appellate Body have previously found that the maintenance and application of "zeroing" in the context of administrative reviews is inconsistent with Article 2.4 of the AD Agreement.[96] Brazil asks the Panel to come to the same conclusion, and in the light of the evidence it asserts shows the USDOC used "simple zeroing" to

---

[93] Brazil, Answer to Panel Question 3, referring to Appellate Body Report, *United States – Final Anti-Dumping Measures on Stainless Steel from Mexico* ("*US – Stainless Steel (Mexico)*"), WT/DS344/AB/R, adopted 20 May 2008, paras. 133-134 and 156(a), Appellate Body Report, *US – Continued Zeroing*, paras. 315-316 and 395(d), Appellate Body Report, *United States – Laws, Regulations and Methodology for Calculating Dumping Margins ("Zeroing") – Recourse to Article 21.5 of the DSU by the European Communities* ("*US – Zeroing (EC) (Article 21.5 – EC)*"), WT/DS294/AB/RW and Corr.1, adopted 11 June 2009, para. 304, and Appellate Body Report, *United States – Measures Relating to Zeroing and Sunset Reviews – Recourse to Article 21.5 of the DSU by Japan* ("*US – Zeroing (Japan) (Article 21.5 – Japan)*"), WT/DS322/AB/RW, adopted 31 August 2009, para. 156.

[94] Brazil, Answer to Panel Question 3.

[95] Brazil, FCOOS, para. 68 and Brazil, SWS, paras. 16-17, quoting Appellate Body Report, *United States – Sunset Review of Anti-Dumping Duties on Corrosion-Resistant Carbon Steel Flat Products from Japan* ("*US – Corrosion-Resistant Steel Sunset Review*"), WT/DS244/AB/R, adopted 9 January 2004, DSR 2004:I, 3, para. 135, and Appellate Body Report, *US – Zeroing (Japan)*, para. 146, quoting Appellate Body Report, *United States – Final Dumping Determination on Softwood Lumber from Canada – Recourse to Article 21.5 of the DSU by Canada* ("*US – Softwood Lumber V (Article 21.5 – Canada)*"), WT/DS264/AB/RW, adopted 1 September 2006, DSR 2006:XII, 5087, para. 142.

[96] Brazil, SWS, para. 17, referring to Panel Report, *United States – Measures Relating to Zeroing and Sunset Reviews – Recourse to Article 21.5 of the DSU by Japan* ("*US – Zeroing (Japan) (Article 21.5 – Japan)*"), WT/DS322/RW, adopted 31 August 2009, as upheld by Appellate Body Report WT/DS3227AB/RW, paras. 7.168 and 8.1(b); Appellate Body Report, *US – Zeroing (Japan)(Article 21.5 – Japan)*, para. 195, 197 and 213(c); and Appellate Body Report, *US – Zeroing (Japan)*, paras. 169, 176, 190(d) and 190(e).

calculate the margins of dumping of Cutrale and Fischer in the First and Second Administrative Reviews, find that the United States acted inconsistently with Article 2.4 of the AD Agreement.[97]

2. *Arguments of the United States*

7.63 The United States rejects Brazil's claims, arguing that they are grounded on an interpretation of Articles 2.4 and 9.3 of the AD Agreement and Article VI:2 of the GATT 1994 that finds no textual basis in the language of these provisions. Moreover, even accepting Brazil's legal arguments, the United States submits that Brazil's claims are at least in part factually flawed.

(a) Article 9.3 of the AD Agreement and Article VI:2 of the GATT 1994

7.64 The United States submits that, in *US – Softwood Lumber V*, the Appellate Body concluded that "zeroing" is prohibited in the context of weighted-average to weighted-average comparisons in investigations by interpreting the terms "margins of dumping" and "all comparable export transactions" as they are used in Article 2.4.2 in an integrated manner. The United States argues that a general prohibition on "zeroing" cannot be reconciled with this interpretation.. In this regard, the United States recalls that the language of Article 2.4.2 of the AD Agreement explicitly requires that "all comparable export transactions" be taken into account when establishing the margin of dumping through W-W comparisons. The United States notes that this language cannot be found elsewhere in the AD Agreement. Were there a general prohibition on "zeroing" applying in all proceedings and all comparison methodologies, the United States submits that the "all comparable export transactions" language in Article 2.4.2 would be redundant. Thus, according to the United States, the fact that no such language is found elsewhere in the AD Agreement suggests that there is no general prohibition on "zeroing" beyond W-W comparisons in original investigations.[98]

7.65 The United States argues that there is no textual basis in Articles 2.1 and 9.3 of the AD Agreement or Article VI:2 of the GATT 1994 to conclude that the definition of the terms "dumping" and "margin of dumping" must be exclusively understood to mean that dumping and margins of dumping can only exist for the product "as a whole" through the aggregation of comparison results of all transactions. The United States submits that the "product is always 'introduced into the commerce of another country' through individual transactions, and thus 'dumping', as defined in Article 2.1 of the AD Agreement, is most certainly transaction-specific". The United States observes that this "definition describes

---

[97] Brazil, FCOOS, para. 67; Brazil, SWS, para. 47.

[98] US, FWS, paras. 53-59; US, First Confidential Opening Oral Statement ("FCOOS"), paras. 23-25.

the real-world commercial conduct by which a product is imported into a country, i.e., transaction by transaction".[99]

7.66 The United States draws support for its interpretation of the concept of "dumping" from the 1960 Report of the Group of Experts, which it asserts indicated that the "ideal method" for applying anti-dumping duties "was to make a determination of both dumping and material injury in respect of each single importation of the product concerned". The United States considers that the view expressed by the Group of Experts reflects the rules as they stood under Article VI of the GATT 1947, which was incorporated into the GATT 1994 without any change or revision. The United States finds this transposition significant arguing that the "normal inference one draws from the absence of a change in language is that the drafters intended no change in meaning". Furthermore, the United States submits that if the negotiators intended to make "such a fundamental change" to the meaning of "margin of dumping", they would have done so clearly, and "it would not have come as a surprise to the major users of anti-dumping remedies, such as the EU and the United States, after the fact through dispute settlement".[100]

7.67 The United States rejects the view that the definition of dumping in Article 2.1 of the AD Agreement can only be read to mean that dumping can exist exclusively with respect to the "product as a whole". The United States notes that the expression "product as a whole" does not appear anywhere in the AD Agreement, and that the Appellate Body has not cited any actual text that would support a finding that a margin of dumping must occur at the level of multiple transactions, nor any text that would preclude the calculation of dumping from occurring at a transaction-specific level. Moreover, for the United States, the notion of "product as a whole" denies that the ordinary meaning of the word "product" used in Article 2.1 admits of a meaning that is transaction-specific.[101] According to the United States, the words "product" and "products" in Article 2.1 of the AD Agreement and Article VI of the GATT 1994 cannot be interpreted in such an exclusive manner so as to deprive them of one of their ordinary meanings. The United States comes to a similar conclusion with respect to the term "margin of dumping".[102]

7.68 The United States submits that a general prohibition on the use of "zeroing" outside of the limited circumstances of W-W comparison methodology in original investigations under Article 2.4.2 would render the third methodology (W-T) redundant because of "mathematical equivalence". The United States rejects the Appellate Body's explanation of how "mathematical equivalence" might be avoided, arguing that by suggesting that the comparison take place in respect of a *subset* of export transactions, the Appellate Body proposes a methodology

---

[99] US, FWS, paras. 61-68; US, FCOOS, para. 29; US, Second Written Submission ("SWS"), paras. 23-27.

[100] US, FWS, paras. 69-72, citing Second Report of the Group of Experts, L/1141, adopted on 27 May 1960, BISD 9S/194, para. 7.

[101] US, FWS, paras. 73-81.

[102] US, FWS, paras. 82-84; US, FCOOS, paras. 26-28.

that would itself be inconsistent with its view that the margin of dumping can only be established for the "product as a whole". In this regard, the United States recalls that a treaty "interpreter is not free to adopt a reading that would result in reducing whole clauses or paragraphs of a treaty to redundancy or inutility".[103]

7.69 The United States recalls that prospective normal value systems, which are explicitly provided for in Article 9.4(ii) of the AD Agreement, assess anti-dumping duties through a comparison of the import price of a given transaction with the prospective normal value, without considering the prices paid for other import transactions. According to the United States, if the liability for the payment of anti-dumping duties can be determined on a transaction-specific basis in prospective normal value systems, there is no reason why the same cannot be the case in retrospective duty assessment systems. Moreover, the United States submits that requiring, as the Appellate Body has ruled, that any margin of dumping determined for the purpose of Article 9.3 assessment be calculated on the basis of aggregating all comparison results of all transactions would turn prospective normal value systems of duty assessment into retrospective systems. The United States also notes that Articles 9.3, 9.3.1, and 9.3.2 are silent as to the period of review for any such assessment proceeding, and submits that the negotiators of the Antidumping Agreement would not have provided explicitly for a prospective normal value system and at the same time require that such systems conduct retrospective assessment proceedings that aggregate all the transactions occurring over some unspecified period of time.[104]

7.70 Thus, the United States urges the Panel to make its own objective assessment of the matter, as it is required to do under Article 11 of the DSU, and refrain from adopting the interpretations of the AD Agreement advanced by Brazil and developed by the Appellate Body in previous disputes involving "simple zeroing". Instead, the United States asks the Panel to find, consistent with the objective assessment made by previous panels, that the United States' approach rests on a permissible interpretation of the AD Agreement within the meaning of Article 17.6(ii) of the AD Agreement. In this regard, the United States argues, *inter alia*, that the very inclusion of the special standard of review contained in Article 17.6(ii) confirms that the text of the AD Agreement may be susceptible to more than one interpretation. To find that it is not possible to arrive at conflicting interpretations of the text would, according to the United States, mean depriving the second sentence of Article 17.6(ii) of meaning.[105]

7.71 In any event, the United States emphasizes that the obligation in Article 9.3 of the AD Agreement is about ensuring that the "*amount of the anti-dumping duty* shall not exceed the margin of dumping as established under Article 2". According to the United States, this means that even if "simple zeroing" were

---

[103] US, FWS, paras. 93-98, citing Appellate Body Report, *United States – Standards for Reformulated and Conventional Gasoline* ("*US – Gasoline*"), WT/DS2/AB/R, adopted 20 May 1996, DSR 1996:I, 3, para. 23; US, FCOOS, para. 34; US, SWS, paras. 74-79.

[104] US, FWS, paras. 109-115; US, FCOOS, para. 31; US, Answer to Panel Question 12; US, SWS, paras. 58-69; US, SCOOS, paras. 21-23.

[105] US, FWS, paras. 5, 23-33; US, FCOOS, paras. 3-7; US, Answer to Panel Questions 8 and 9.

used in an administrative review, it cannot result in any violation of the obligation contained in this provision if no anti-dumping duties were in fact collected.[106] The United States notes that this is precisely the situation with respect to Fischer in the Second Administrative Review, whose ISAR was [[XX]]. Thus, the United States argues that Brazil has failed to substantiate its claims with respect of Fischer in the Second Administrative Review.

7.72 Similarly, the United States observes that although Cutrale was assessed as having dumped at a rate of 0.45% in the First Administrative Review, no CDR was applied because under United States law, a rate of less than 0.5% is *de minimis*. Thus, the United States argues that regardless of whether "simple zeroing" was applied to determine the CDR for Cutrale in the First Administrative Review, a *de minimis* margin of dumping cannot exceed any "ceiling" provided for in the covered agreements. To this extent, the United States submits that the treatment of Cutrale in the First Administrative Review was not inconsistent with Article 9.3 and Article VI of the GATT 1994, even by Brazil's own interpretation of the obligations contained in those provisions.[107]

7.73 The United States also argues that Brazil errs in characterising CDRs as anti-dumping duties that are subject to the disciplines of Article 9.3 of the AD Agreement and Article VI:2 of the GATT 1994. In its view, CDRs are a security for the payment of anti-dumping duties and are governed by the AD Note to paragraphs 2 and 3 of the GATT 1994.[108] The United States recalls that the Ad Note allows a Member to "require a reasonable security (bond or cash deposit) for the payment of anti-dumping or countervailing duty pending final determination of the facts in any case of suspected dumping or subsidization". According to the United States, the "determination of the facts" identified in the Ad Note refers to the "determination of final liability for payment of anti-dumping duties" described in Article 9.3.1 of the AD Agreement. Moreover, the United States explains that a CDR is only an estimate of future anti-dumping duties, based on past dumping, that serves as a security pending determination of final liability to pay anti-dumping duties. The United States disagrees with Brazil's characterization of the Appellate Body findings in *US – Stainless Steel (Mexico)* and *US – Continued Zeroing*, submitting that they did not reflect a conclusion that CDRs are anti-dumping duties, but rather a conclusion that the application of "zeroing" in administrative reviews was inconsistent with Article 9.3 of the AD Agreement because it "results in the levy of an amount of anti-dumping duty that exceeds an exporter's margin of dumping".[109] Similarly, the United States argues that the other Reports mentioned by Brazil do not stand for the proposition that CDRs amount to anti-dumping duties.[110]

---

[106] US, SWS, para. 80.

[107] US, FWS, para. 121; US, FCOOS, para. 35.

[108] US, FWS, footnote 8; US, Answer to Panel Question 5.

[109] US, Answer to Panel Question 5, referring to Appellate Body Report, *US – Stainless Steel (Mexico)*, para.133 and Appellate Body Report, *US – Continued Zeroing*, para. 315.

[110] US, Answer to Panel Question 5.

(b) Article 2.4 of the AD Agreement

7.74 The United States submits that Brazil's interpretation of the obligation in Article 2.4 to conduct a "fair comparison" has no textual basis in the language of this provision and is misconceived. In its view, the text of Article 2.4 makes clear that it only addresses the adjustments that must be made to export price and normal value in order to account for "differences which affect price comparability" and render a "fair comparison". Thus, the United States argues that Article 2.4 does not create an obligation with respect to how the results of such comparisons are treated. According to the United States, its interpretation of Article 2.4 is supported by previous panel and Appellate Body Reports as well as the negotiating history of the AD Agreement. Moreover, given the highly subjective nature of the term "fair", the United States argues that its meaning in the context of Article 2.4 must have a principled basis, and not the open-ended and subjective meaning advanced by Brazil. Thus, the United States urges the Panel to reject Brazil's expansive interpretation of Article 2.4, which, in its view, would lead to a flood of anti-dumping disputes that are virtually impossible to resolve in any credible manner.[111]

3. *Arguments of the Third Parties*

(a) Argentina

7.75 Argentina does not address the merits of Brazil's specific claims, but rather the consistency of "zeroing", in general, under the AD Agreement. Recalling the Appellate Body's findings in *EC – Bed Linen*, Argentina argues that zeroing is inconsistent with Article 2.4.2, regardless of the methodology used.[112] In addition, according to Argentina, the "zeroing" methodology, by not producing a result that takes into account all the variables to be taken into consideration when determining a margin of dumping, ultimately results in the levying of anti-dumping duties in excess of the margin of dumping, and is consequently inconsistent with Articles 9.3 of the AD Agreement and VI:2 of the GATT 1994. However, Argentina emphasizes that the imposition and collection of duties cannot be confused with the calculation of the margin of dumping, which the implementing authority is required to make prior to the imposition phase.[113]

(b) European Union

7.76 The European Union submits that the United States' view that the prohibition on zeroing found in Article 2.4.2 of the AD Agreement is limited to W-W comparisons in the context of original investigations should be rejected in its entirety. According to the European Union, when the language of this provision is correctly interpreted, following the rules of interpretation of the Vienna Con-

---

[111] US, SWS, paras. 4-22; US, Second Confidential Opening Oral Statement ("SCOOS"), paras. 26-28.

[112] Argentina, Third Party Written Submission ("TPWS"), paras. 8-18.

[113] Argentina, TPWS, paras. 21-22.

vention, there can be no result other than a finding that Article 2.4.2 prohibits "zeroing" in all forms except targeted dumping[114], and in all types of anti-dumping proceedings.[115]

7.77 Drawing on essentially the same line of reasoning developed in previous Appellate Body reports, the European Union argues that the "margin of dumping" referred to in Article 9.3 of the AD Agreement must be interpreted and understood in the context of the definition of "dumping" contained in Article 2.1 of the AD Agreement and Article VI:1 of the GATT 1994 – i.e., that dumping can only be found in relation to the "product as a whole", as defined by the investigating authority. According to the European Union, "dumping" cannot be found to exist for only a type, model or category of a product, including a "category" in one or more low priced export transactions. Thus, the European Union submits that whatever method is used to calculate the margin of dumping, that margin must be and can only be established for the "product as a whole", subject to targeted dumping provisions.[116]

7.78 The European Union asserts that it is uncontested that the USDOC's use of "zeroing" in administrative reviews "systematically and inevitably inflates the dumping margin and the amount of duty, compared with a computation without zeroing". Thus, it submits that the use of "zeroing" in the administrative reviews at issue constitute a "direct violation of Article 9.3".[117] The European Union argues that the possibility for Members to use prospective normal value systems of duty collection offers no support to the United States' interpretation of the obligations in Article 9.3. In particular, the European Union is of the view that such prospective systems of duty assessment will always remain subject to Article 9.3.2, which calls for duty refunds to be made on request. In other words, the margin of dumping that should be used to assess the final duty liability must be determined on the basis of all export transactions, even those with a value above the prospective normal value.[118] Similarly, the European Union rejects the United States' reliance on "mathematical equivalence", arguing that there are ways of using the targeted dumping methodology without "zeroing"; and that in any case, permitting "zeroing" in circumstances where the third methodology applies might be acceptable, given that it is an exception to the rule.[119]

(c) Japan

7.79 Japan submits that the legal principles governing the WTO-inconsistency of the "zeroing" procedures at issue in this dispute have been thoroughly canvassed by the Appellate Body in past WTO disputes, and are now well established. Japan recalls that the Appellate Body has, on numerous occasions, determined that Article 2.1 of the AD Agreement and Article VI:1 of the GATT

[114] EU, TPWS, paras. 23-24, 163, 165 and 175.
[115] EU, TPWS, paras. 22-159.
[116] EU, TPWS, paras. 160-163.
[117] EU, TPWS, para. 169.
[118] EU, TPWS, paras. 171-174.
[119] EU, TPWS, paras. 175-176.

1994, when properly interpreted according to the Vienna Convention, define "dumping" on an exporter-specific basis for the "product as a whole". Japan notes that this definition applies throughout the AD Agreement, and is therefore relevant to all anti-dumping proceedings involving the determination of a margin of dumping, including duty assessment under Article 9.3 of the AD Agreement. Japan argues that the consequences of the USDOC's use of "zeroing" in the administrative reviews at issue in the present dispute are the same as those addressed in previous controversies. Japan asserts that by excluding all negative comparison results, the USDOC makes a "dumping" determination that disregards an entire category of the export transactions making up the "product" – namely, those transactions that generate the negative comparison results. Thus, Japan submits that the USDOC does not determine "dumping" for the "product" as defined by the investigating authority, but for a sub-part of that product. In conclusion, Japan argues that by applying "zeroing" in the measures at issue, the USDOC failed to comply with the definition of "dumping". Japan therefore urges the Panel to find that the United States acted inconsistently with Article 9.3 of the AD Agreement and Article VI:2 of the GATT 1994.[120]

(d) Korea

7.80 Korea recalls that in repeatedly ruling that the USDOC's practice of "zeroing" in administrative reviews is inconsistent with Article 9.3 of the AD Agreement and GATT Article VI:2, the Appellate Body has explicitly rejected the United States' arguments that "dumping" and "margin of dumping" can be found to exist at the level of individual transactions. Korea notes that the Appellate Body has found contextual support for this view in other provisions of the AD Agreement, such as Articles 5.8, 6.10 and 9.5 as well as the concept of injurious dumping. Korea submits that, like the Appellate Body, it too is unable to find "a textual or contextual basis in the GATT 1994 or the *Anti-Dumping Agreement* for treating transactions that occur above normal value as 'dumped', for purposes of determining the existence and magnitude of dumping in the original investigation, and as 'non-dumped', for purposes of assessing the final liability for payment of anti-dumping duties in a period review".[121]

7.81 Thus, Korea urges the Panel to follow the Appellate Body's reasoning in previous cases, and find that Brazil has established that the United States has acted inconsistently with its obligations under the AD Agreement and the GATT 1994.[122]

(e) Mexico

7.82 Mexico asserts that Brazil's claims against the United States' "zeroing" methodology are substantially the same as those brought against the United

---

[120] Japan, TPWS, paras. 4-12, 24-53, 57-69 and 72.

[121] Korea, TPWS, paras. 21-23, referring to and quoting Appellate Body Report, *US – Continued Zeroing (EC)*, paras. 285 and 287.

[122] Korea, TPWS, paras. 23-24.

States in previous disputes. Mexico notes that the WTO-inconsistency of this methodology has now been firmly established with the Appellate Body rulings in *US – Zeroing (EC)*, *US – Zeroing (Japan)*, *US – Stainless Steel* and *US – Continued Zeroing*. According to Mexico, in responding to Brazil's claims, the United States has raised no new substantive arguments in defence of "zeroing" that have not already been fully addressed in these cases. Mexico urges the Panel follow the Appellate Body on this matter and find that Brazil has fully made out its claims. Mexico considers that the Panel should do this not only because the prior rulings are correct, but also because there are strong systemic reasons to adhere to the Appellate Body's consistent body of case-law. In this regard, Mexico recalls the point made by the Appellate Body in *US – Oil Country Tubular Goods Sunset Reviews*, where it stated that "following the Appellate Body's conclusions in earlier disputes is not only appropriate, but is what would be expected from panels, especially where the issues are the same".[123] Thus, as the United States is, in Mexico's view, unable to identify any new substantive arguments not already rejected in previous WTO disputes, and as the substance of all of Brazil's legal claims have been considered and affirmed in a long line of consistent prior Appellate Body reports, Mexico asks the Panel to adopt the reasoning from those prior rulings and find "(yet again)" that the United States' "zeroing" methodology is inconsistent with the AD Agreement and the GATT 1994.[124]

4. *Evaluation by the Panel*

(a) Relevant Facts

(i) Administrative Reviews under United States' Law

7.83 The United States operates a retrospective system of duty assessment whereby liability for the payment of anti-dumping duties attaches at the time of entry, yet the final amount of such liability is not actually determined at that moment. Instead, at the time of entry, the United States collects what it characterizes as a "security" in the form of a cash deposit, which represents an estimate of an importer's final amount of anti-dumping duty liability. Once a year (during the anniversary month of the anti-dumping duty orders) interested parties may request an administrative review to determine the final amount of duties that is actually owed on each entry made during the period of review.[125] Thus, an administrative review serves two purposes. First, it establishes an overall dumping

---

[123] Appellate Body Report, *United States – Sunset Reviews of Anti-Dumping Measures on Oil Country Tubular Goods from Argentina* ("*US – Oil Country Tubular Goods Sunset Reviews*"), WT/DS268/AB/R, adopted 17 December 2004, DSR 2004:VII, 3257, para. 188.

[124] Mexico, TPWS, paras. 1-10.

[125] The period of review covered by United States duty assessment proceedings is normally twelve months. However, in the case of the first assessment proceeding following the original investigation imposing the anti-dumping duty order, the period of time may extend to a period of up to 18 months in order to cover all entries that may have been subject to provisional measures.

margin for each exporter, which becomes the new cash deposit rate ("CDR") for entries made after the publication of the review determination, and continues to apply until the completion of the next administrative review. Second, it establishes the final amount of anti-dumping duty that must be paid by each respective importer on imports that occurred during the relevant period of review – the importer-specific assessment rate ("ISAR"). If the ISAR results in an amount of duties that is less than the total amount of cash deposits that were paid by the importer on importation, the difference is refunded, with interest. Conversely, if the ISAR results in an amount of duties that is greater than the total amount of the cash deposits, the importer is requested to pay the difference, plus interest. If the ISAR results in an amount of duties that is equal to the cash deposits, the importer is notified of assessment at that rate. If no review is requested, the duty is assessed at the estimated rate, and the cash deposits made on the entries during the previous year are retained to pay the final duties.

(ii) Measures at Issue

7.84 The measures at issue under this part of Brazil's complaint relate to the anti-dumping duty order issued by the United States on 9 March 2006 covering exports of certain orange juice from Brazil.[126] In particular, Brazil challenges the final results for two respondents, Cutrale and Fischer, in the First and Second Administrative Reviews, which were respectively published in the United States Federal Register on 11 August 2008 and 11 August 2009. The weighted average dumping margins ("WAM"), the cash-deposit rates ("CDR") and the importer-specific assessment rates ("ISAR") determined for Cutrale and Fischer in the two administrative reviews are shown in the following table:

	WAM[127]	*CDR*[127]	*ISAR*[128]
First Administrative Review			
Cutrale	**0.45%**	**0%**	[[XX]]
Fischer	**4.81%**	**4.81%**	[[XX and XX]]
Second Administrative Review			
Cutrale	**2.17%**	**2.17%**	[[XX]]
Fischer	0%	0%	[[XX]]

[126] Anti-Dumping Duty Order: Certain Orange Juice from Brazil, 9 March 2006, 71 Fed. Reg. 12183 ("Anti-Dumping Duty Order"). Exhibit BRA-3.

[127] As published in the Final Results of the First Administrative Review, Exhibit BRA-21, and the Final Results of the Second Administrative Review, Exhibit BRA-22.

[128] Figures drawn from Exhibits BRA-34 (BCI) and BRA-37 (Cutrale's computer programme outputs), penultimate page; and BRA-35 (BCI) and BRA-39 (Fischer's computer programme outputs), penultimate page.

7.85 In each of the challenged administrative reviews, the USDOC used a computer programme to process the export price and normal value data of each exporter in order to calculate individual WAMs. In essence, this calculation followed three steps: First, the price of each individual export transaction was compared to a weighted-average normal value for a contemporaneous month; second, the results of these comparisons were aggregated; and third, the aggregated comparison results were divided by the total value of all export transactions, and the resulting fraction expressed in percentage terms. When undertaking the second step (aggregation), the programme included language that instructed the computer to disregard or count as zero any comparison results that were negative (i.e., where weighted-average normal value was lower than the relevant individual export price). In other words, the computer programme called for negative comparison results to be disregarded or given a zero value in the process of their aggregation for the purpose of establishing the numerator of the fraction representing the margin of dumping. It is this treatment of negative weighted-average normal value and individual export price comparison results that Brazil describes as "simple zeroing".

7.86 In addition to the support found in certain passages of the Issues and Decision Memoranda from the First and Second Administrative Reviews[129], the computer programme log and output evidence advanced by Brazil demonstrates that the "simple zeroing" instruction was in fact executed in the WAM calculations performed for each of the two respondents.[130] Moreover, we note that the

[129] We note that the United States asserts that the Issues and Decision Memorandum from the First Administrative Review submitted by Brazil does not demonstrate that the USDOC applied "simple zeroing" in that administrative review. In particular, the United States does not accept that it demonstrates that "Fischer's or Cutrale's sales presented [USDOC] with instances of non-dumped sales such that any denial of an offset for a non-dumped sale actually occurred" (US Answer to Panel Question 10). However, in our view, various statements made in this Issues and Decision Memorandum strongly suggest that the "simple zeroing" instruction was in fact used. For instance, "In the preliminary results, we followed our standard methodology of not using non-dumped comparisons to offset or reduce the dumping found on other comparisons (commonly known as 'zeroing'). ... We have not changed our calculation of the weighted-average margin of dumping margin as suggested by the respondents in these final results". Exhibit BRA-28, pp. 3 and 5. Similar language can be found in the Issues and Decision Memorandum from the Second Administrative Review, Exhibit BRA-43, pp. 3 and 6.

[130] Regarding Cutrale in the First Administrative Review, see Exhibits BRA-29 (BCI) (Computer programme log); BRA-28 (Issues and Decision Memorandum), pp. 3-6; BRA-34 (BCI) (Computer programme output); and BRA-31 (BCI) (Ferrier Affidavit). Regarding Fischer in the First Administrative Review, see Exhibits BRA-45 (BCI) (Computer programme log); BRA-28 (Issues and Decision Memorandum), pp. 3-6; BRA-35 (BCI) (Computer programme output); and BRA-31 (BCI) (Ferrier Affidavit). Regarding Cutrale in the Second Administrative Review, see Exhibits BRA-36 (BCI) (Computer programme log); BRA-43 (Issues and Decision Memorandum), pp. 3-6; BRA-37 (BCI) (Computer programme output); and BRA-31 (BCI) (Ferrier Affidavit). Regarding Fischer in the Second Administrative Review, see Exhibits BRA-38 (BCI) (Computer programme log); BRA-43 (Issues and Decision Memorandum), pp. 3-6; BRA-39 (BCI) (Computer programme output); and BRA-31 (BCI) (Ferrier Affidavit). Although the United States initially challenged the authenticity of one piece of evidence Brazil relied upon for the purpose of demonstrating that the WAM of Fischer in the First Administrative Review was calculated through the use of "simple zeroing" (Exhibit BRA-30 (BCI) (Computer programme log)), Brazil subsequently introduced a replacement exhibit, the authenticity of which the United States has not challenged. See, US, FWS, para. 122; US, FCOOS,

WAMs for Fischer in the First Administrative Review (4.81%) and Cutrale in the Second Administrative Review (2.17%) were relied upon to set equivalent CDRs. In the First Administrative Review, the WAM for Cutrale of 0.45% was deemed to be *de minimis* under United States law, and therefore a 0% CDR was applied.[131] Although the WAM (and consequently the CDR) published in the Final Results of the Second Administrative Review for Fischer were 0%[132], the computer programme evidence submitted by Brazil shows that the calculation run by the USDOC resulted in a WAM of [[XX]].[133] Thus, it appears that a WAM of 0%, and an equivalent CDR, were imposed on Fischer in the Second Administrative Review because of the WAM of [[XX]] determined through the application of the USDOC's computer programme. We note that the United States does not argue that a WAM and CDR of 0% were imposed on Fischer for any other reason.

7.87 To determine the ISARs applicable to entries of the respective exporter's products, the computer programme applied by the USDOC followed the same methodology described in paragraph 7.85 but, for a given importer, it included only those transactions imported by that importer in the calculation. In other words, the computer programme sorted and aggregated transactions where the export price was below normal value on an importer-specific basis, thereby applying "simple zeroing".[134] Accordingly, ISARs of [[XX]] and [[XX]] were calculated for Cutrale in, respectively, the First and Second Administrative Reviews; and for Fischer, ISARs of [[XX]] and [[XX]] were determined in the First Administrative Review.[135] Although a [[XX]] ISAR was applied to Fischer's imports in the Second Administrative Review, the evidence demonstrates that the computer programme used by the USDOC to calculate Fischer's ISAR applied "simple zeroing".[136]

---

para. 36. Exhibit BRA-45 (BCI). See also the summary of information on the use of "zeroing", submitted as Exhibit BRA-48.

131 Exhibit BRA-21.

132 Exhibit BRA-22.

133 Exhibit BRA-39 (BCI), last page, right-hand column, "Wt avg percent margin".

134 Regarding Cutrale in the First Administrative Review, see Exhibits BRA-29 (BCI) (Computer programme log); and BRA-31 (BCI) (Ferrier Affidavit). Regarding Fischer in the First Administrative Review, see Exhibits BRA-45 (BCI) (Computer programme log); and BRA-31 (BCI) (Ferrier Affidavit). Regarding Cutrale in the Second Administrative Review, see Exhibits BRA-36 (BCI) (Computer programme log); and BRA-31 (BCI) (Ferrier Affidavit). Regarding Fischer in the Second Administrative Review, see Exhibits BRA-38 (BCI) (Computer programme log); and BRA-31 (BCI) (Ferrier Affidavit). See also the summary of infromation on the use of "zeroing", submitted as Exhibit BRA-48.

135 See above, footnote 127.

136 In particular, the computer programme evidence reveals that the numerator in the calculation of Fischer's ISAR in the Second Administrative Review included only the total amount by which export price of individual transactions was below normal value. These accounted for [[XX]] out of a total of [[XX]] transactions. See Exhibits BRA-38 (BCI), p.76; and BRA-31 (BCI) (Ferrier Affidavit), paras. 53-56. We note that the ISAR determined on this basis ([[XX]]) was considered to be [[XX]]. Exhibit BRA-39 (BCI), p. 105. See also the summary of information on the use of "zeroing", submitted as Exhibit BRA-48.

(b) Introduction

7.88 As the parties recognize[137], Brazil's complaint against the United States' alleged use of "simple zeroing" in the relevant administrative reviews is, first and foremost, premised on the view that "dumping" is defined, as a general matter, in the AD Agreement and the GATT 1994 in relation to the "product as a whole". Thus, the fundamental question that lies at the heart of Brazil's claims is the following: how does the AD Agreement define the notion of "dumping"? Is Brazil correct in submitting that "dumping" is a concept that relates to an exporter's overall pricing behaviour that Members are only entitled to measure with respect to the "product as a whole"? Or does the AD Agreement, as the United States argues, permit both this and a transaction-specific conception of "dumping"?

(c) The definition of "dumping"

7.89 We start our assessment of the parties' arguments by reviewing Article VI:1 of the GATT 1994 and Article 2.1 of the AD Agreement, which respectively read:

> *Article VI:1 of the GATT 1994*
>
> "The contracting parties recognize that dumping, by which products of one country are introduced into the commerce of another country at less than the normal value of the products, is to be condemned if it causes or threatens material injury to an established industry in the territory of a contracting party or materially retards the establishment of a domestic industry. For the purposes of this Article, a product is to be considered as being introduced into the commerce of an importing country at less than its normal value, if the price of the product exported from one country to another
>
> (*a*) is less than the comparable price, in the ordinary course of trade, for the like product when destined for consumption in the exporting country, or,
>
> (*b*) in the absence of such domestic price, is less than either
>
> (i) the highest comparable price for the like product for export to any third country in the ordinary course of trade, or
>
> (ii) the cost of production of the product in the country of origin plus a reasonable addition for selling cost and profit.

[137] Brazil, FCOOS, para. 6; US, FWS, paras. 60-61.

> Due allowance shall be made in each case for differences in conditions and terms of sale, for differences in taxation, and for other differences affecting price comparability.*"
>
> *Article 2.1 of the AD Agreement*
>
> "For the purpose of this Agreement, a product is to be considered as being dumped, i.e. introduced into the commerce of another country at less than its normal value, if the export price of the product exported from one country to another is less than the comparable price, in the ordinary course of trade, for the like product when destined for consumption in the exporting country."

7.90 Both Article VI:1 of the GATT 1994 and Article 2.1 of the AD Agreement describe "dumping" in the same terms, namely, as occurring whenever a product is "introduced into the commerce of another country at less than its normal value" or, more specifically, when the export "price of the product exported from one country to another is less than the comparable price, in the ordinary course of trade, for the like product when destined for consumption in the exporting country". There is no disagreement between the parties that this description, as it appears in Article 2.1, defines "dumping" for the purpose of the entire AD Agreement. Moreover, although both parties consider the ordinary meaning of the text of these provisions to support their own interpretations of the notion of "dumping", they do not argue that the text *alone* resolves the question whether "dumping" may be measured on the basis of individual transactions or whether it must necessarily always be determined through aggregation of all transactions relating to the "product as a whole".[138] Previous panels and the Appellate Body have generally come to the same conclusion, and have looked beyond the language of Article 2.1 in order to decipher the meaning of "dumping". When it comes to the issue of "zeroing", the inconclusive nature of the definition of "dumping" contained in Article 2.1 was perhaps most clearly articulated in *US – Continued Zeroing*, where the Appellate Body declared that:

> "Mere scrutiny of the particular terms – such as product and export price – in Article 2.1 does not resolve the issue of whether the concept of dumping is concerned with individual transactions or whether it is necessarily an aggregative concept attributable to an exporter".[139]

Similarly, the Concurring Opinion in the same Appellate Body report observed:

> "... Nothing could be more important than the definition of the concept of 'dumping'. It is foundational and applies throughout the

[138] See, for instance, Brazil, FWS, paras. 49-60; and US, FWS, paras. 63-68.

[139] Appellate Body Report, *US – Continued Zeroing*, para. 282. See further, e.g., Panel Report, *US – Zeroing (Japan)*, paras. 7.103-7.112; Panel Report, *US – Stainless Steel (Mexico)*, para. 7.119.

> Agreement, as the clear wording of Article 2.1 makes plain. It cannot have variable or contradictory meanings, for that would infect the entire Agreement. Yet the definition is cast at a high level of generality. The definition makes no attribution of agency; it does not say who introduces a product into the commerce of another country. Article 2.1 might so easily have included the words 'by an exporter', but it does not. So too, the definition might have referred to the product as a whole, and not simply a product. The definition is inchoate, and thus it must be interpreted."[140]

7.91 In our view, the language of Article 2.1 of the AD Agreement and Article VI:1 of the GATT 1994 is drafted in such general terms that render both provisions potentially capable of capturing either of the two conceptions of "dumping" advanced by the parties. We are mindful, however, that this conclusion is only the starting point of our analysis, as pursuant to the customary rules of interpretation of public international law reflected in the Vienna Convention, we must test and explore our understanding of the relevant text in the light of its context and the object and purpose of the AD Agreement.

(i) Articles 3, 5.8, 6.10, 8.1, 9.1, 9.3 and 9.5 of the AD Agreement

7.92 Drawing from various findings of the Appellate Body in prior disputes[141], Brazil argues that Articles 3, 5.8, 6.10, 8.1, 9.1, 9.3 and 9.5 of the AD Agreement all support the position that "dumping" must be understood in terms of the pricing behaviour of individual exporters or foreign producers determined through the calculation of a single margin of dumping with respect to the "product as a whole".[142] In particular, Brazil highlights, *inter alia*, that pursuant to Article 5.8, there shall be "immediate termination" of an anti-dumping investigation against an exporter where the margin of dumping determined for that exporter is *de minimis*, recalling that the Appellate Body has said that the term "margin of dumping" in this provision "refers to a single margin established for each exporter by aggregation of its export transactions".[143] Similarly, Brazil points to: (i) Article 6.10, which it emphasizes requires that investigating authorities "shall, as a rule, determine an *individual* margin of dumping for each

---

140 Appellate Body Report, *US – Continued Zeroing*, para. 300.

141 Including, Appellate Body Report, *European Communities – Anti-Dumping Duties on Imports of Cotton-Type Bed Linen from India – Recourse to Article 21.5 of the DSU by India* ("*EC – Bed Linen (Article 21.5 – India)*"), WT/DS141/AB/RW, adopted 24 April 2003, DSR 2003:III, 965, para. 115; Appellate Body Report, *US – Softwood Lumber V*, footnote 158; Appellate Body Report, *United States – Final Dumping Determination on Softwood Lumber from Canada – Recourse to Article 21.5 of the DSU by Canada* ("*US – Softwood Lumber V (Article 21.5 – Canada)*"), WT/DS264/AB/RW, adopted 1 September 2006, DSR 2006:XII, 5087, para. 108; Appellate Body Report, *US – Zeroing (Japan)*, para. 126; Appellate Body Report, *US – Stainless Steel (Mexico)*, paras. 86-87, 99, 108; and Appellate Body Report, *US – Continued Zeroing*, paras. 268, 283.

142 Brazil, FWS, paras. 54-56; Brazil, FCOOS, paras. 20-28.

143 Brazil, FWS, para. 55; Brazil, FCOOS, para. 20, referring to Appellate Body Report, *US – Continued Zeroing*, para. 283.

known exporter or producer concerned of *the product* under investigation"[144]: (ii) Articles 6.10.2 and 9.5, which according to Brazil, contain similar language[145]; (iii) Article 8.1, which Brazil submits provides that price undertakings must not be greater than necessary "to eliminate *the* margin of dumping"[146]; and (iv) Articles 9.1 and 9.3, which Brazil notes stipulate that duties imposed and collected must be no greater than "*the* margin of dumping".[147] Brazil also asserts that the injurious effects of "dumped imports" are assessed under Article 3, not on a transaction-by-transaction basis, but rather by examining the effects of all imports of the exporter engaged in dumping. Brazil argues that a uniform interpretation of the term "dumping" ensures that transactions treated as "dumped" for purposes of a dumping determination are also treated as "dumped" for the purpose of injury, and *vice versa.*[148]

7.93 Brazil adds that there is both a consistency and logic to the text of the AD Agreement. According to Brazil, Article 6.10 expressly requires that a single margin of dumping be determined for each exporter of the product. In Brazil's view, the singularity of that determination has a series of important legal consequences that affect the product as a whole: under Article 5.8, the decision to terminate an investigation is based on a single dumping determination made for all transactions relating to the "product"; under Article 3, on the basis of a product-wide dumping determination, all entries of the "product" are treated as dumped for the purposes of an injury determination; under Articles 8 and 9, the extent of permissible remedial action to counter injurious "dumping" is fixed by reference to a single margin of dumping, and that remedy applies to all future imports of the "product".[149]

7.94 The United States considers that Brazil's contextual arguments in support of its legal case are misplaced. Although agreeing with Brazil that the margin of dumping referred to in Article 5.8 of the AD Agreement may refer to an aggregation of multiple transactions, the United States considers that its relevance is limited to original investigations conducted under Article 5 of the AD Agreement, where an investigating authority must determine whether dumping exists above a 2 per cent *de minimis* threshold, and whether such dumping causes injury to the domestic industry. The United States argues that, in contrast, duty assessment under Article 9.3 of the AD Agreement is about the collection of duty, not the determination of the existence of dumping and injury. Thus, according to the United States, the differences between an Article 5 original investigation and duty assessment under Article 9.3 undermine Brazil's reliance on Article 5.8.[150]

---

144 Brazil, FWS, para. 56; Brazil, FCOOS, para. 21 (emphasis original).
145 Brazil, FCOOS, para. 21.
146 Brazil, FCOOS, para. 25 (emphasis original).
147 *Ibid.*
148 Brazil, FWS, para. 58; Brazil, FCOOS, para. 23.
149 Brazil, FCOOS, para. 26.
150 US, SWS, paras. 30-37.

7.95 The United States submits that the term "individual" appearing in Article 6.10 does not, as Brazil argues, refer to a "single" margin of dumping calculated on the basis of the "product as a whole". Rather, the United States argues that this term must be read as meaning that any calculated margin must *correspond* to the individual exporter. The United States finds support for this view in the Spanish text, which it notes provides that the investigating authority determine a margin of dumping "que corresponda a cada exportador", i.e., "that corresponds to each exporter". The United States explains that a margin may correspond to an exporter while being based on one transaction – as long as that transaction is the exporter's. According to the United States, Article 6.10 has nothing to do with how many transactions form the basis for any such margin, a fact it argues has been recognized by previous panels.[151]

7.96 The United States also argues that Brazil's interpretation of Articles 6.10, 8.1, 9.1, 9.3 and 9.5, overstates the importance of the term "margin of dumping" in the singular.[152] According to the United States, Brazil has itself admitted that "the use of the singular is not decisive".[153] Thus, drawing on previous panel and Appellate Body findings, the United States submits that a term that is used in the AD Agreement in the singular form may have "both singular and plural meanings".[154] In addition, the United States counters Brazil's reliance on how injury is determined under Article 3 by recalling that no injury determination is required in Article 9.3 assessment proceedings. The United States explains that Article 9 focuses on the amount of duty to be assessed on particular entries, an exercise that is separate and apart from the calculation of an overall dumping margin and determination of injury or threat of material injury during the original anti-dumping investigation.[155]

7.97 We agree with the parties that Article 5.8 makes it necessary to determine a "single" overall margin of dumping for an investigated producer or exporter in order to ensure compliance with the *de minimis* dumping rule it prescribes. However, it is equally apparent to us that Article 5.8 says nothing about *how* any such single margin of dumping must be calculated – i.e., whether it should involve an aggregation of the results of *all* normal value and export price comparisons or only those where normal value exceeds export price. We note that the question that must be answered when examining the WTO-consistency of "zeroing" is not simply whether there must be aggregation of multiple normal value and export price comparison results, but also whether any such aggregation must *always*

---

[151] US, SWS, paras. 38-42, referring to *inter alia* Panel Report, *US – Zeroing (Japan)*, para. 7.111; Panel Report, *US – Stainless Steel (Mexico)*, para. 7.127; and Panel Report, *US - Continued Zeroing*, para. 7.163.

[152] US, SWS, para. 43.

[153] US, SWS, para. 43, citing Brazil, FCOOS, para. 13.

[154] US, SWS, para. 43, referring to Panel Report, *United States – Anti Dumping Measures on Oil Country Tubular Goods (OCTG) from Mexico*, WT/DS282/R, adopted 28 November 2005, as modified by Appellate Body Report WT/DS282/AB/R, para. 7.149; and Appellate Body Report, *United States –Anti Dumping Measures on Oil Country Tubular Goods (OCTG)* from Mexico, WT/DS282/AB/R, adopted 28 November 2005, para. 147.

[155] US, FWS, paras. 87-92.

necessarily take account of *all* those comparison results.[156] In our view, the fact that Article 5.8 envisages the calculation of a "single" overall margin of dumping clarifies little about *how* that margin of dumping is supposed to be calculated.[157]

7.98 Similarly, the fact that all imports are treated as "dumped" for the purpose of determining injury in an original investigation under Article 3 might also be understood to provide support for the view that "dumping" concerns the "product as a whole".[158] In this regard, Brazil recalls that the Appellate Body has highlighted "the contradiction that arises when the same type of transactions are treated as 'dumped' for purposes of injury determination in the original investigation and as 'non-dumped' in periodic reviews for duty assessment".[159] Brazil argues that such contradictions have no place in a "harmonious and coherent" interpretation of the AD Agreement.[160] However, as we see it, contradiction and incoherence arises only if the qualitative differences in the rules governing original investigations (where authorities must perform an injury analysis) and duty assessment proceedings (where the focus is purely on duty collection) are not considered sufficient to justify the possibility of two conceptions of the notion of "dumping" co-existing in the AD Agreement. Obviously, the Appellate Body believes the differences are not so great.[161]

7.99 We find the language that Brazil has pointed to in the remainder of the above-mentioned provisions relatively weak and consider that it provides no particularly useful guidance for the purpose of determining which of the two conceptions of "dumping" is favoured under the AD Agreement. Again, it is difficult to see what obligations which refer to "the" margin of dumping or "an individual" margin of dumping can tell us about the definition of "dumping" when they do not speak at all to *how* "the" margin of dumping or any "individual" margin of dumping must be calculated – should it be through an aggregation of the results of all normal value and export price comparisons or only those where normal value exceeds export price?[162]

(ii) "Dumping" is an exporter-specific, not importer-specific, concept

7.100 Brazil recalls that the Appellate Body has found that "dumping" is determined with respect to an individual exporter, and not on an importer-specific

156 See above, para. 7.90.

157 A similar view was expressed in the Concurring Opinion of one Appellate Body Member in Appellate Body Report, *US – Continued Zeroing*, paras. 309-310.

158 We note that there is no disagreement between the parties that a margin of dumping determined through the use of the first methodology described in Article 2.4.2 of the AD Agreement must be established on the basis of a comparison of weighted average normal value with a weighted average of prices of all comparable export transactions. See, e.g., Brazil, FWS, para. 114; US, FWS, para. 54.

159 Appellate Body Report, *US – Stainless Steel (Mexico)*, para. 108.

160 Brazil, FCOOS, para. 23.

161 See, e.g, Appellate Body Report, *US – Continued Zeroing*, paras. 284-285.

162 A similar view was expressed with respect to Articles 6.10 and 9.5 of the AD Agreement in the Concurring Opinion of one Appellate Body Member in Appellate Body Report, *US – Continued Zeroing*, paras. 309-310.

basis. Relying upon the position articulated by the Appellate Body in *US – Stainless Steel (Mexico)*, Brazil submits that the elements of the definition of "dumping" – namely, that "dumping" occurs when a product is "*introduced* into the commerce of *another country*" at an "*export price*" that is less than the "comparable price for the like product in the *exporting country*" – indicate that Article VI:1 of the GATT 1994 and Article 2.1 of the AD Agreement address the pricing practices of an exporter.[163] Brazil also refers to Articles 2.2, 2.3, 5.8, 6.10, 8.1, 9.4 and 9.5 of the AD Agreement, drawing support for its position from the language in these provisions which identifies or focuses upon the "*export price*", the "*exporter*", the "*volume of exports*", the "*exporting country*", "any *known exporter*", "*any exporter*", "*exporters or foreign producers*" and the "*selected exporters or producers*".[164] In addition, Brazil cites another series of Appellate Body statements where it is observed that:

> "[d]umping arises from the pricing practices of exporters as both normal value and export prices reflect their pricing strategies in home and foreign markets".[165]
>
> "Indeed, it is the exporter, not the importer that engages in practices that result in situations of dumping".[166]
>
> "The fact that 'dumping' and 'margin of dumping' are exporter-specific concepts under the *Anti-Dumping Agreement* is not altered by the fact that the export price may be the result of negotiation between the importer and the exporter. Nor is it altered by the fact that it is the importer that incurs the liability to pay anti-dumping duties".[167]

7.101 The United States submits that "dumping" may be both exporter-specific and transaction-specific at the same time. According to the United States, an exporter orientation does not, of itself, require that transactions be aggregated under Article 9.3 of the AD Agreement because a dumping margin determination on the basis of an exporter's actions with respect to an individual transaction is no less exporter-specific than one on the basis of multiple transactions by that exporter. Moreover, the United States argues that a transaction-specific meaning is equally exporter-specific and importer-specific since each transaction has both an exporter and an importer.[168]

---

[163] Brazil, FWS, para. 53, referring to Appellate Body Report, *US – Stainless Steel (Mexico)*, para. 86 (emphasis original).

[164] Brazil, FWS, paras. 54-56, referring to Appellate Body Report, *US – Stainless Steel (Mexico)*, paras. 86-87 (emphasis original).

[165] Brazil, FWS, para. 57, citing Appellate Body Report, *US – Stainless Steel (Mexico)*, para. 95 and Appellate Body Report, *US – Zeroing (Japan)*, para. 156.

[166] Brazil, FWS, para. 57, citing Appellate Body Report, *US – Zeroing (EC)*, para. 129.

[167] Brazil, FWS, para. 57, citing Appellate Body Report, *US – Stainless Steel (Mexico)*, para. 95.

[168] US, FWS, paras. 85-86.

7.102 We agree with Brazil and the Appellate Body that "dumping" is a concept that relates to an individual exporter's pricing behaviour. However, in our view, this tells us little about *how* to make a determination of "dumping", and in particular, whether the focus of such a determination should be an individual exporter's overall pricing behaviour in respect of the "product as a whole", or an exporter's pricing behaviour considered on a transaction-specific basis. As the United States has submitted, the question at issue in this dispute is not whether "dumping" is an exporter-specific or importer-specific concept, but rather to what extent individual transactions of a particular exporter must be aggregated when making a determination of "dumping".[169] Brazil's arguments concerning the exporter-specific nature of "dumping" elucidate very little in this regard.

(iii) Article VII:3 and the Ad Note to Article VI:1 of the GATT 1994, and Articles 2.2 and 2.3 of the AD Agreement

7.103 The United States submits that the term "product" used throughout the AD Agreement and the GATT 1994 carries with it a variable meaning, implying that it cannot be presumed that the same term has the exclusive meaning Brazil argues in the context of Article 2.1 of the AD Agreement and Article VI:1 of the GATT. For instance, the United States points to Article 2.6 of the AD Agreement, which defines the term "like product" in relation to "the product under consideration". According to the United States, this provision plainly uses the term "product" in the collective sense. The United States notes that, by contrast, Article VII:3 of the GATT 1994 – which refers to "[t]he value for customs purposes of any imported product" – plainly uses the term "product" in the individual sense of the object of a particular transaction (*i.e.*, a sale involving a specific quantity of merchandise that matches the criteria for the "product" at a particular price).[170]

7.104 In addition, the United States argues that the term "margin of dumping" found in the Ad Note to Article VI:1 of the GATT 1994 and Article 2.2 of the AD Agreement does not refer exclusively to the aggregated results of comparisons for the "product as a whole". As used in the Ad Note to Article VI:1, the United States submits that the term "margin of dumping" cannot relate to aggregated results of all comparisons for the "product as a whole" because an exporter or foreign producer may make export transactions using multiple importers. Similarly, according to the United States, were Brazil correct, the term "margin of dumping" as it appears in Article 2.2 of the AD Agreement, would require the use of constructed normal value for the "product as a whole", even if the condition precedent for using constructed normal value under Article 2.2 relates only to a portion of the comparisons. In this regard, the United States recalls that the panel in *US – Softwood Lumber V (Article 21.5 – Canada)* observed that this "would run counter to the principle that constructed normal value is an alterna-

169 US, FWS, para. 85.
170 US, FWS, para. 79.

tive to be used only in the limited circumstances provided for in Article 2.2. ... We are not convinced that the Appellate Body could have intended its *US – Softwood Lumber V* findings to be applied in this manner".[171]

7.105 Brazil argues that the United States' reliance on Article VII:3 of the GATT 1994 misunderstands the role of context in treaty interpretation. According to Brazil, the fact that the same word appears in two (or more) proximate treaty provisions does not mean that the word carries the same meaning in each provision. Thus, Brazil submits that a single word used in two provisions may have different meanings in each provision, depending on the context. In its particular context, the word "product" appearing in Article VII:3 has a meaning that is relevant to what is regulated under that provision – customs valuation, which is necessarily undertaken on a transaction-specific basis. This is an entirely different context to Article VI:1, which is about dumping. Therefore, Brazil is of the view that the United States is wrong to assume that the same word, "product", must be given the same meaning in Article VI:1 and Article VII:3 of the GATT 1994.[172]

7.106 Brazil also disputes the United States' interpretation of the Ad Note to Article VI:1, arguing that it does not provide a definition of either "dumping" or "margins of dumping", nor does it state implicitly or otherwise that "margins" may be transaction-specific. Brazil argues that like Article 2.3 of the AD Agreement, the Ad Note to Article VI:1 simply permits an authority to use an importer's resale price to an independent buyer as the starting-point for determining the export price in circumstances where the importer is related to the exporter. In its view, neither Article 2.3 nor the Ad Note to Article VI:1 alters the requirement that an individual margin of dumping be determined for each exporter on the basis of all relevant export transactions.[173]

7.107 Finally, Brazil rejects the United States' reliance on Article 2.2 of the AD Agreement, recalling that the Appellate Body has previously rejected the same argument.[174] In particular, Brazil notes that the Appellate Body has held that an authority may sub-divide the product in conducting intermediate comparisons on a model-specific basis, and on this basis assess whether the conditions in Article 2.2 for construction of normal value are met. Brazil emphasizes that the results of all intermediate comparisons must be aggregated to determine "dumping" on a product-wide basis to meet the definition in Article 2.1.

7.108 We agree with the United States that the transaction-specific meaning of the word "product" when used in Article VII:3 of the GATT 1994 tends to support the view that it cannot be *presumed* that the same word, when it appears in Article 2.1 of the AD Agreement and Article VI:1 of the GATT 1994, must necessarily refer to the "product as a whole", with all the consequences that follow

---

[171] US, FWS, para. 83, referring to Panel Report, *US – Softwood Lumber V (Article 21.5 – Canada)*, para. 5.62.

[172] Brazil, FCOOS, paras. 39-43.

[173] Brazil, FCOOS, paras. 44-45.

[174] Brazil, FCOOS, para. 46, referring to Appellate Body Report, *US – Softwood Lumber V (Article 21.5 – Canada)*, para. 104.

for the definition of "dumping". However, we note that Brazil's arguments are based on more than just the ordinary meaning of the word "product", but also the particular context in which it is found in both the AD Agreement and the GATT 1994. In other words, Brazil does not *presume* that the word "product" in abstract has the meaning it argues. Rather, Brazil submits that this meaning is confirmed from how the notion of "dumping" is described in other provisions it considers form part of the relevant context of Article 2.1 of the AD Agreement and Article VI:1 of the GATT 1994. Thus, in our view, the fact that the word "product" in Article VII:3 has a transaction-specific meaning does not detract from Brazil's complaint. It does, however, suggest that the drafters of the GATT understood that the meaning of the word "product" could have a transaction-specific meaning in the particular context of customs valuation, which in turn also suggests that it cannot be categorically excluded that the negotiators may have held the same view about the meaning of "product" when it appears in Article 2.1 of the AD Agreement and Article VI:1 of the GATT 1994. As we have said before, the ordinary meaning of the word "product" as it appears in Article 2.1 of the AD Agreement does not resolve which of the two definitions of "dumping" must prevail.

7.109 The United States argues that the Ad Note to Article VI:1 of the GATT 1994 expressly defines a particular form of dumping – "hidden dumping" – in relation to individual transactions and that the text of that provision contemplates that a "margin of dumping" may be calculated for a specific sale by an importer, implying that "dumping" cannot be exclusively defined with respect to the "product as a whole". It is not entirely clear to us that this is the correct reading of the Ad Note. In our view, the plain language of the Ad Note might equally be interpreted as merely identifying one particular situation ("Hidden dumping by associated houses") in which investigating authorities are entitled to construct export price on the basis of an importer's resale price. In any case, because the Ad Note is silent about *how* any comparison results involving normal value and one or more constructed export prices must be aggregated, it does not provide any useful guidance on the question whether "dumping" relates exclusively to the "product as a whole" or whether it can also be transaction-specific. The same can be said about Article 2.2 of the AD Agreement. As Brazil notes, it is possible to sub-divide a product when multiple averaging, and explore whether the conditions in Article 2.2 for constructed normal value are satisfied for each averaging group. However, again, because Article 2.2 (like Article 2.3) says nothing about how comparisons involving constructed normal value must be aggregated, this provision is, in our view, inconclusive about how to interpret the notion of "dumping".

(iv) Duty collection on the basis of a prospective normal value

7.110 The United States argues that the existence of prospective normal value systems of duty collection demonstrates that the notion of "dumping" cannot be exclusively understood to relate to the "product as a whole".[175] Drawing on descriptions found in previous panel reports[176], as well as information concerning how Canada administers its own prospective normal value system[177], the United States explains that under such systems, the amount of liability for payment of anti-dumping duties is determined at the time of importation on the basis of a comparison between the price of the individual export transaction and the prospective normal value. Thus, according to the United States, duties will be payable only when the price of an imported product is below the prospective normal value, with the prices of all other transactions playing no part in this determination. The United States recalls that the transaction-specific nature of prospective normal value systems has led previous panels to find that a transaction-specific conception of "dumping" must also be permissible under the AD Agreement. For instance, the United States points to the following observation of the panel in *US – Zeroing (Japan)*:

> "the fact that express provision is made in the AD Agreement for this sort of system confirms that the concept of dumping can apply on a transaction-specific basis to prices of individual export transactions below the normal value and that the AD Agreement does not require that in calculating margins of dumping the same significance be accorded to export prices above the normal value as to export prices below the normal value".[178]

7.111 Brazil responds to the United States' submissions by recalling that the Appellate Body has considered and rejected the same arguments in previous "zeroing" disputes.[179] In particular, Brazil notes that the Appellate Body has explained "that the duty collected at the time of importation under a prospective normal value system does not represent the margin of dumping", and that the rules in the AD Agreement regarding duty "imposition and collection" are "distinct and separate" from those governing a determination of "dumping".[180] Moreover, Brazil observes that the Appellate Body has also explained that the amount of duties collected in a prospective normal value system is subject to review under Article 9.3.2 of the AD Agreement to ensure that the total amount of duties does not exceed the margin of dumping for the "product as a whole".[181]

---

175 US, FWS, paras. 109-115; US, SWS, paras. 59-69.

176 For example, Panel Report, *US – Zeroing (Japan)*, para. 7.201; and *US – Softwood Lumber V (Article 21.5 – Canada)*, para. 5.53.

177 US, Answer to Panel Question 13; and US, SWS, paras. 63-65, referring to Report on the Special Import Measures Act, House of Commons Canada, December 1996, submitted by the United States as Exhibit US-2; and Canada's WTO Trade Policy Review, WT/TPR/S/112, para. 68 and Table III.5.

178 Panel Report, *US – Zeroing (Japan)*, para. 7.205. The United State refers to a similar statement made by the panel in Panel Report, *US – Zeroing (EC)*, para. 7.206.

179 Brazil, SCOOS, paras. 14-16.

180 Brazil, FCOOS, paras. 47-48, referring to Appellate Body Report, *US – Zeroing (Japan)*, para. 160; Appellate Body Report, *US – Continued Zeroing*, para. 294; and Brazil, SWS, para. 5.

181 Brazil, FCOOS, para. 49; and Brazil, Answer to Panel Question 12.

7.112 Previous panels have generally disagreed with the view that duty collection in a prospective normal value system is subject to refund proceedings involving the calculation of a margin of dumping for the "product as a whole" under Article 9.3.2 of the AD Agreement, on the ground that it would be inconsistent with the fundamental nature of how such systems are intended to function.[182] The United States submits that accepting the Appellate Body's position would effectively transform the prospective normal value system into a retrospective system of duty collection.[183] We recognize that the functioning of prospective normal value systems of duty collection, as described by the United States and previous panels, would be fundamentally altered if subjected to the possibility of duty refunds involving the calculation of a margin of dumping on the basis of the "product as a whole". An approach that would permit transaction-specific determinations of a margin of dumping for the purpose of collecting anti-dumping duties, yet *require* "product as a whole" determinations when deciding whether there was over-collection, in our view, seems to be incongruent and not in keeping with how prospective normal value systems have traditionally operated. In this regard, we note that the United States asserts that Canada, a WTO Member that applies a prospective normal value system, grants refund ("re-determination") requests that are "usually transaction-specific".[184] Moreover, although the Canadian system envisages that, under certain conditions, importers may request a refund with respect to multiple transactions ("blanket request procedure")[185], this possibility is limited to transactions concerning "shipments of goods to the same importer".[186]

7.113 Brazil and a number of third parties that typically collect anti-dumping duties on a prospective basis, but with varying levels of experience in their collection on the basis of a prospective normal value, have stated that they *would* provide refunds of excessive duties collected through application of a prospective normal value on the basis of a margin of dumping determined for the "product as a whole".[187] However, neither Brazil nor any of the relevant third parties have explained how any such refunds would be determined. Thus, we do not know, for instance, what would be the length of the period of review covered by any such "product as a whole" assessment or whether any refund would be based

[182] See for instance, Panel Report, *US – Zeroing (Japan)*, para. 7.204; Panel Report, *US – Stainless Steel (Mexico)*, para. 7.133.

[183] US, FWS, para. 115; US, SWS, para. 64.

[184] US, Answer to Panel Question 13, footnote 11 citing Exhibit US-6, Canada Border Services Agency; *Procedures for making a request for a Re-Determination or an Appeal under the Special Import Measures Act*: Memorandum D14-1-3 (1 October 2008) (the "SIMA Memorandum"), paras. 19, 34-44.

[185] The SIMA Memorandum stipulates that "A blanket request is a procedure through which an importer may request re-determinations on more than one transaction under specific conditions provided that both the public and the CBSA receive administrative benefits". A "blanket request" may be refused where *inter alia* it "may result in administrative difficulties or processing delays". Exhibit US-6, paras. 50 and 53(b).

[186] SIMA Memorandum, para. 53(d). Exhibit US-6.

[187] Brazil, Answer to Panel Question 13. See also EU, Answer to Panel Question 2 to the Third Parties; and Mexico, Answer to Panel Question 2 to the Third Parties.

on a calculation involving exports to all importers or only those requesting a refund. Indeed, neither Brazil nor any of the relevant third parties have identified any instance in which refunds for duties collected on the basis of a prospective normal value have actually been requested and/or granted. In this regard, we note that the United States has questioned whether Brazil's system in fact operates as Brazil asserts, pointing to instances involving the collection of duties on the basis of a prospective normal value on products from seven WTO Members, where the United States asserts Brazil's Official Gazette stated that the anti-dumping duty would be calculated on a transaction-specific basis.[188]

7.114 In considering the United States' arguments in respect of prospective normal value systems, we cannot, however, overlook the absence from the AD Agreement of any complete description of how prospective normal value systems are intended to operate. Apart from Article 9.4(ii) of the AD Agreement – a provision explaining how anti-dumping duties may be collected from exporters or producers not included in a limited examination performed under Article 6.10 – the AD Agreement is silent about how such systems must be implemented. In the absence of any more detailed provisions explaining how prospective normal value systems are generally supposed to function, it is difficult to come to any firm conclusion about which of the two views should prevail.

(v) Article 2.4.2 and "mathematical equivalence"

7.115 The United States submits that the prohibition on "model zeroing" found by the Appellate Body to exist in *US – Softwood Lumber V* under Article 2.4.2 of the AD Agreement was based on the textual references to "margins of dumping" and "all comparable export transactions" appearing in the first sentence of this provision, which the Appellate Body stated had to be read in an "integrated manner". According to the United States, it was these textual references, and not any independent obligation found elsewhere in the AD Agreement, that led the Appellate Body to conclude that "product" must mean "product as a whole" and that "margins of dumping" may not be based on individual averaging group comparisons. The United States notes that no similar language appears else-

---

[188] US, SCOOS, paras. 13-19 and Ministry of Development, Industry and Foreign Trade, Office of the Secretary of Foreign Trade, *Circular No. 12 of 7 March 2008*, (imports of polyvinylchloride from the United States and Mexico) Exhibit US-9, para. 3 ("The anti-dumping duty is calculated on the basis of the absolute difference between the reference price and the price at which the transaction by which the product is imported from the USA or Mexico is executed, as the case may be. The anti-dumping duty will be charged only in a case in which the price of the imported product is lower than the proposed reference price.") See also Exhibits US-10 to US-12, containing other determinations with substantially similar language. Brazil submits that the United States' assertions are factually wrong. In its view, the measures at issue laid down a cap on the amount of duties that could be levied on each import entry, providing that this amount could not exceed the relevant margins of dumping previously established by the Brazilian investigating authority. Thus, according to Brazil, its investigating authority did not treat the amount of duties imposed in relation to a single entry as a margin of dumping, and instead, capped the amount of duties at the level of a margin of dumping previously estalished. Brazil, Comments on US Requests for Interim Review, paras. 19-22.

where in the AD Agreement, in its view suggesting that the "product as a whole" notion of "dumping" cannot extend, as a general matter, beyond the particular context of W-W comparisons in original investigations. Indeed, the United States submits that if, as Brazil argues, there were a general prohibition on "zeroing" applying to all anti-dumping proceedings and all comparison methodologies, the meaning ascribed to "all comparable export transactions" by the Appellate Body in *US – Softwood Lumber V*, would be redundant.[189]

7.116 The United States also argues that any interpretation of the AD Agreement and the GATT 1994 that gives rise to a general prohibition of "zeroing" – i.e., that establishes that "dumping" can only be defined with respect to the "product as a whole" – would render the second sentence of Article 2.4.2 redundant. In particular, the United States submits that the exceptional comparison methodology provided for in this sentence (the W-T methodology) would yield precisely the same result as a W-W comparison if, in both cases, "dumping" was determined for the "product as a whole". According to the United States, such an outcome would contradict a key rule of treaty interpretation, namely, that an "interpretation must give meaning and effect to all the terms of a treaty".[190] The United States recalls that previous panels have found this argument persuasive[191], and urges the Panel in this dispute to do likewise.[192]

7.117 Brazil does not appear to have *directly* responded to the United States' arguments concerning the implications of a general prohibition on "zeroing" in the light of the Appellate Body's findings in *US – Softwood Lumber V* and Article 2.4.2 of the AD Agreement. However, it has repeatedly emphasized that the Appellate Body has consistently found that Article 2.1 of the AD Agreement and Article VI:1 of the GATT 1994, when considered in the context of various other provisions and in the light of the object and purpose of the AD Agreement, establish a definition of "dumping" applicable to the *entire* AD Agreement that is focused on the "product as a whole". As regards the United States' "mathematical equivalence" argument, Brazil recalls that the Appellate Body has found there to be "considerable uncertainty as to how precisely the third methodology should be applied", noting that different approaches to its application could generate results that would not be mathematically equivalent. In addition, Brazil argues that the exceptional authority conferred under the second sentence of Article 2.4.2 cannot dictate how the general (non-exceptional) rules for calculating margins of dumping are to be interpreted.[193]

7.118 The United States is correct in recalling that an "integrated" reading of the terms "margins of dumping" and "all comparable export transactions" was

[189] US, FWS, paras. 54-59; US, FCOOS, paras. 23-25.

[190] US, FWS, para. 94, referring to Appellate Body Report, *US – Reformulated Gasoline*, p. 23.

[191] The United States refers to: Panel Report, *US – Zeroing (EC)*, para. 7.266; Panel Report, *US – Softwood Lumber V (Article 21.5 – Canada)*, para. 5.52; Panel Report, *US – Zeroing (Japan)*, para. 7.127; and Panel Report, *US – Stainless Steel (Mexico)*, para. 7.134.

[192] US, FWS, paras. 93-98; US, FCOOS, para. 34; US, Answer to Panel Question 14.

[193] Brazil, FCOOS, paras. 52-58; Brazil, Answer to Panel Question 14; Brazil, SWS, para. 5; Brazil, SCOOS, paras. 32-36.

central to the Appellate Body's "model zeroing" findings in *US – Softwood Lumber V*. However, there was no disagreement between the parties in that dispute about how the term "all comparable export transactions" should be interpreted. That is, all participants agreed that "all comparable export transactions" had to be taken into account in establishing margins of dumping. The parties' dispute was with respect to how the results of multiple comparisons should be interpreted and aggregated. The Appellate Body described this disagreement as flowing from the respective views on the meaning of "dumping" and "margins of dumping".[194] To resolve this difference of opinion, the Appellate Body turned to the definition of "dumping" found in Article 2.1 of the AD Agreement and Article VI:1 of the GATT 1994. The Appellate Body then explained:

> "It is clear from the texts of these provisions that dumping is defined in relation to a product as a whole as defined by the investigating authority. Moreover, we note that the opening phrase of Article 2.1—'[f]or the purpose of this Agreement'—indicates that the definition of 'dumping' as contained in Article 2.1 applies to the entire Agreement, which includes, of course, Article 2.4.2. 'Dumping', within the meaning of the *Anti-Dumping Agreement*, can therefore be found to exist only for the product under investigation as a whole, and cannot be found to exist only for a type, model, or category of that product."[195]

Thus, it appears to us that the same notion of "dumping" that Brazil advances in the present controversy was also at the heart of the Appellate Body's finding concerning "model zeroing" in *US – Softwood Lumber V*.

7.119 In its answer to Panel Question 14, the United States explained in detail how it considered the third (W-T) methodology described in Article 2.4.2 operates, demonstrating how "mathematical equivalence" would result if "zeroing" was generally prohibited. Brazil, on the other hand, has pointed to various descriptions found in previous panel and Appellate Body reports of how other Members give effect to, or potentially give effect to, the W-T methodology set out in Article 2.4.2 without yielding "mathematical equivalence". It is apparent that Members have different views on how the W-T methodology in Article 2.4.2 should be implemented, and whether it will result in "mathematical equivalence". This is not surprising as when it comes to understanding the modalities for how it should be applied, the text of Article 2.4.2 provides little guidance for those seeking a detailed explanation of what may or may not be permissible. Were the approach advocated by the United States correct, a general prohibition on "zeroing" (i.e., a definition of "dumping" in relation to the "product as a whole") applicable to the entire AD Agreement would render the text describing the W-T methodology in Article 2.4.2 redundant. Obviously, such a result would be inconsistent with the principle of effective treaty interpretation. This would

---

194 Appellate Body Report, *US – Softwood Lumber V*, para. 90.
195 Appellate Body Report, *US – Softwood Lumber V*, para. 93.

imply that no such general prohibition could exist, unless, as Brazil, two of the third parties[196] and the Appellate Body contend, the W-T methodology can be characterized as an "exception" to the otherwise generally applicable definition of "dumping". However, it could be argued that this point of view also has its weaknesses. First, the word "exception" does not appear in Article 2.4.2. Arguably, the fact that the first sentence of Article 2.4.2 directs Members to "normally" establish margins of dumping through the use of the W-W and T-T methodologies does not render the W-T methodology described in the following sentence an "exceptional" methodology, but rather one whose application is not *expected* to be the "norm".[197] Second, the fact that the definition of dumping contained in Article 2.1 of the AD Agreement is intended to apply "[f]or the purpose of this Agreement" could be viewed as suggesting that it is not subject to any "exception". Thus, on the issue of "mathematical equivalence", we find neither of the positions advanced by the parties' to be conclusive.

(vi) Historical background

7.120 The United States considers that the Second Report of the Group of Expert Report on anti-dumping and countervailing duties, adopted in May 1960, supports the view that the notion of "dumping" may be defined on a transaction-specific basis. The United States explains that the Group of Experts considered that the "ideal method" for applying anti-dumping duties "was to make a determination of both dumping and material injury in respect of each single importation of the product concerned".[198] The United States recalls that previous panels have found this evidence persuasive, with the panel in *US – Zeroing (Japan)* observing that it "shows that historically the concept of dumping has been understood to be applicable at the level of individual export transactions"[199]; and the panel in *US – Softwood Lumber V (Article 21.5 – Canada)* concluding that it demonstrates that "the Group of Experts did not consider that there was anything in the definition of dumping set forth in Article VI of the GATT that would preclude the calculation of such transaction-specific margins".[200]

7.121 In addition, the United States notes that two GATT 1947 panels asked to determine whether "zeroing" was prohibited under the provision of the Tokyo Round Anti-Dumping Code concluded that it was not, further reinforcing the validity of the Group of Experts' understanding of Article VI of the GATT 1947.[201] In this light, the United States finds it significant that Article VI of the GATT 1947 was incorporated into the GATT 1994 without revisions, notwith-

---

[196] EU, TPWS, para. 175; and Japan, Answer to Panel Question 3 to the Third Parties.

[197] In our view, there may well be situations where a particular product or market is affected by "targeted" dumping to such an extent that an investigating authority will resort to the W-T methodology more often than the W-W or T-T methodologies. In such circumstances, the W-T methodology could effectively become the "norm" with respect to that particular product or market.

[198] US, FWS, para. 69, citing *Anti-Dumping and Countervailing Duties*, Second Report of the Group of Experts, L/114, adopted on 27 May 1960, BISD 9S/194, para. 7.

[199] Panel Report, *US – Zeroing (Japan)*, para. 7.107.

[200] Panel Report, *US – Softwood Lumber V (Article 21.5 – Canada)*, para. 5.64.

[201] US, FWS, para. 71, referring to *EC – Audiocassettes*, para. 360 and *EC – Cotton Yarn*, para. 502.

standing the fact that the Uruguay Round negotiators had actively discussed whether the use of "zeroing" should be restricted. According to the United States, if the Uruguay Round negotiators had intended to make such a fundamental change to the notion of "dumping" they would have been clearer about it, and it would not have come to a surprise to the major users of dumping remedies, such as the EU and the United States, after the fact through dispute settlement.[202] In this regard, the United States advances evidence which it considers demonstrates that apart from the United States and the EU, at least two other major users of the anti-dumping remedy continued to calculate margins of dumping through the use of "zeroing" after the entry into force of the Uruguay Round Agreements.[203]

7.122 Brazil considers the United States' references to the methodologies allegedly used by other WTO Members to be irrelevant for the purpose of assessing whether the United States' own conduct in the orange juice proceedings was WTO-consistent. In any case, Brazil notes that the European Union has abandoned "zeroing" in order to comply with its WTO obligations; that the panel's findings in *Argentina – Poultry Anti-Dumping Duties*, relied upon by the United States, related in fact to the investigating authority's decision to initiate an investigation, and not to the determination of the margin of dumping in the investigation itself; and that Argentina's position as a third party in the present dispute is that it considers "zeroing" to be inconsistent with the AD Agreement.[204]

7.123 Brazil has not responded to the United States' arguments concerning the Group of Experts Report and the prior GATT panels. However, they have been addressed previously by the Appellate Body in a number of disputes, where it has denied the relevance of the Report and the previous GATT panel reports for various reasons, including because: (i) the Group of Experts' Report itself characterized the "ideal" transaction-specific method of determining injurious dumping as "clearly impracticable"; (ii) today, Article VI of the GATT 1994 has to be

---

202 US, FWS, paras. 69-72.

203 US, Answer to Panel Question 17, referring to Argentina and South Africa, who together with the European Communities and the United States, accounted for the largest number of initiations of anti-dumping investigations in 1995. As regards Argentina, the United States points out that in the *Argentina – Poultry Anti-Dumping Duties* dispute, the panel concluded *inter alia* that "if zeroing is inconsistent with Article 2.4.2, then Argentina's practice of totally disregarding certain export transactions [i.e., transactions with a price that was higher than or equal to normal value] would also be inconsistent with Article 2.4.2 because it does not compare the weighted average normal value with the weighted average of prices of all comparable transactions". In addition, the United States notes that Argentina stated that its methodology was also used by other WTO Members. Panel Report, *Argentina – Definitive Anti-Dumping Duties on Poultry from Brazil* ("*Argentina – Poultry Anti-Dumping Duties*"), WT/DS241/R, adopted 19 May 2003, DSR 2003:V, 1727, para. 7.78 and Annex B-4 (Replies of Argentina to Questions of the Panel – First Meeting, reply to question 11(b), at B-94). In respect of South Africa, the United States points to the Board of Tariffs and Trade Report, in the *Investigation into the Alleged Dumping of Meat of Fowls of the Species Gallus Domesticus, Originating in or Imported from the United States of America*, where the following statement was made: "In determining the dumping margin, the Board applied the 'zeroing' methodology ... This methodology is applied by a number of jurisdictions including the European Union and the United States". Exhibit US-13.

204 Brazil, Comments on US Answer to Panel Question 17.

interpreted in the light of the relevant AD Agreement framework including provisions such as Articles 2.1, 2.4, 2.4.2 and 9.3; (iii) the AD Agreement entered into force "long after" the 1960 Group of Experts Report; and (iv) the panel reports at issue examined "zeroing" under the Tokyo Round Anti-Dumping Code, which as a plurilateral agreement was legally separate from the GATT 1947, has been terminated, and in any case, contained provisions much less detailed than those found in the current AD Agreement.[205]

7.124 We have sympathy for the view that a transaction-specific notion of "dumping" was traditionally recognized by the Contracting Parties to the GATT 1947 as being at least permissible under Article VI, particularly given that the major users of the anti-dumping remedy were all Signatories to the Tokyo Round Anti-Dumping Code and therefore members of the Committee on Anti-Dumping Practices, which on 30 October 1995 adopted the *EEC – Cotton Yarn* panel report.[206] Indeed, Brazil, which was the complainant in that case, did not argue against the use of "zeroing" *per se*. Rather, "Brazil argued that in this case the large variations in dumping margins found by the EC were due to severe distortions in the Brazilian financial environment. In the circumstances of a volatile financial environment, so-called 'zeroing' produced a distortion which should have been the subject of a due allowance".[207] It is true, however, that the panel in the *EEC – Cotton Yarn* dispute examined Brazil's claims under Article 2.6 of the Tokyo Round Code, a provision which was modified in the WTO AD Agreement. Moreover, there was no equivalent of Article 2.4.2 of the WTO AD Agreement in the Tokyo Round Anti-Dumping Code.

7.125 As regards the Group of Experts Report, we note that the Experts considered that the "ideal method of fulfilling [the principles of Article VI] was to make a determination of *both dumping and material injury* in respect of each single importation of the product concerned".[208] However, they found that this "was clearly impracticable, *particularly as regards injury*".[209] In other words, the Group of Experts appear to have tied their acceptance of transaction-specific dumping determinations to transaction-specific injury determinations, which is not exactly what the United States is arguing in the present dispute.

---

[205] See e.g., Appellate Body Report, *US – Stainless Steel (Mexico)*, paras. 131-132; Appellate Body Report, *US – Continued Zeroing*, paras. 299-303.

[206] Minutes of the Meeting of the Committee on Anti-Dumping Practices, 21 February 1996, ADP/M/50. As regards the *EC – Audiocassettes* dispute, we note that although having expressed dissatisfaction with the ruling concerning "zeroing", Japan (the complainant) "welcomed the Report and strongly recommended the Committee to adopt it at this first opportunity". It was the EC that opposed the adoption of this report. See, e.g., Minutes of the Meeting of the Committee on Anti-Dumping Practices, 26 September 1995, ADP/M/49; and Minutes of the Meeting of the Committee on Anti-Dumping Practices, 8 April 1997, ADP/M/54.

[207] GATT Panel Report, *European Economic Community – Imposition of Anti-Dumping Duties on Imports of Cotton Yarn from Brazil*, ADP/137, adopted 30 October 1995, BISD 42S/17, para. 486.

[208] Emphasis added.

[209] Emphasis added.

(vii) Permissible Interpretations under Article 17.6(ii) of the AD Agreement

7.126 Brazil has characterized the notion of "dumping" as a "foundational concept" that must be defined uniformly for all Members.[210] Although this language does not appear in the AD Agreement, it goes without saying that the notion of "dumping" is indeed fundamental and of critical importance to the operation of the AD Agreement. However, as our analysis of the parties' arguments and relevant jurisprudence reveals, the express terms of the AD Agreement provide no precise definition of this important concept. Indeed, that the text used in the definition of "dumping" set forth in Article 2.1 of the AD Agreement and Article VI:1 of the GATT 1994 is, alone, inconclusive has already been recognized by previous panels and the Appellate Body.[211] Furthermore, in our view, even when interpreted in its relevant context and in the light of the object and purpose of the AD Agreement, the definition of "dumping" contained in these provisions does not result in one clear definition that is free from valid criticism, or that does not generate its own set of practical and legal problems. In this regard, we cannot help but agree with the Concurring Opinion in *US – Continued Zeroing* that the arguments the parties have advanced in respect of the definition of "dumping" create, for different reasons, their own interpretative dilemmas.[212] We view this objective lack of clarity in the definition of a concept that is as fundamental to the functioning of the AD Agreement as "dumping" to strongly suggest that Members held, if not accepted, differing views about what "dumping" meant at the time of the closure of the Uruguay Round.

7.127 The Appellate Body has expressed the opinion that the proper application of the rules of treaty interpretation set out in the Vienna Convention cannot result in conflicting interpretations. In particular, the Appellate Body has explained that:

> "... the rules and principles of the *Vienna Convention* cannot contemplate interpretations with mutually contradictory results. Instead, the enterprise of interpretation is intended to ascertain the proper meaning of a provision; one that fits harmoniously with the terms, context, and object and purpose of the treaty.{} The purpose of such an exercise is therefore to narrow the range of interpretations, not to generate conflicting, competing interpretations. Interpretative tools cannot be applied selectively or in isolation from one another. It would be a subversion of the interpretative disciplines of the *Vienna Convention* if application of those disciplines yielded contradiction instead of coherence and harmony among, and effect to, all relevant treaty provisions."[213]

---

210 See, e.g., Brazil, FCOOS, para. 31.

211 See above discussion concerning Article 2.1 of the AD Agreement and Article VI:1 of the GATT 1994, at paras. 7.89-7.91.

212 Appellate Body Report, *US – Continued Zeroing*, para. 305.

213 Appellate Body Report, *US – Continued Zeroing*, para. 273 (footnote omitted).

7.128 Brazil agrees with the Appellate Body.[214] On the other hand, the United States argues that such a view would render Article 17.6(ii) meaningless. According to the United States, Article 17.6(ii) reflects the Uruguay Round negotiators' recognition that they had left a number of issues unresolved and that customary rules of interpretation would not always yield only one permissible interpretation of a given provision. Thus, the United States submits that to conclude that "it is not possible to find that there are conflicting interpretations of the text would mean depriving the second sentence of Article 17.6(ii) of meaning. If the permissible interpretations are all 'harmonious' then it is difficult to see how a measure could be in conformity with only one of the interpretations".[215]

7.129 It is well established that the purpose of treaty interpretation through the use of the Vienna Convention is the identification of the *common intention* of the parties.[216] It follows that where the common intention of the parties to a treaty explicitly provides for two conflicting interpretations of the same term or treaty provision, the Vienna Convention rules on treaty interpretation must necessarily recognize both positions. In other words, where the very words of a treaty expressly provide for the legality of two rival interpretations, the Vienna Convention will respect both interpretations. The same result must also hold where the examination of a term's ordinary meaning, in the light of its context and the object and purpose of the treaty to which it pertains, establishes a *common intention* of the parties to accept two conflicting interpretations. To the extent that both circumstances give effect to the *common intention* of the parties, they are not only consistent with the rules of interpretation contained in the Vienna Convention, but also entirely coherent and representative of the particular order negotiated by the parties. Thus, we see the critical question before us in the present dispute to be the following: does application of the customary rules of interpretation of public international law reflected in the Vienna Convention rules of treaty interpretation lead us to understand the common intention of the Members at the end of the Uruguay Round as allowing for one exclusive ("product as a whole") interpretation of the concept of "dumping"; or does it accept the possibility that "dumping" may also have an additional ("transaction-specific") meaning?

(viii) Conclusion concerning the definition of "dumping"

7.130 The present controversy is the fifth dispute where a panel has been tasked with examining the notion of "dumping" in the context of a complaint against the United States' alleged use of "zeroing" administrative reviews.[217] In all but one

214 See, e.g,. Brazil, FCOOS, paras. 6-11.

215 US, FCOOS, para. 7; US, FWS, paras. 25-28.

216 See, e.g, Appellate Body Report, *European Communities – Customs Classification of Certain Computer Equipment* ("*EC – Computer Equipment*"), WT/DS62/AB/R, WT/DS67/AB/R, WT/DS68/AB/R, adopted 22 June 1998, DSR 1998:V, 1851, para. 84; and Appellate Body Report, *EC – Chicken Cuts*, para. 239.

217 See Panel and Appellate Body Reports, *US – Zeroing (EC)*; *US – Zeroing (Japan)*; *US – Stainless Steel (Mexico)*; and *US – Continued Zeroing*.

of these disputes, panels have taken the view that the AD Agreement does not *exclusively* define "dumping" in relation to the "product as a whole". These panels have found that it is permissible to measure "dumping" in the context of duty assessment proceedings in the United States on a transaction-specific basis.[218] On the other hand, the Appellate Body has consistently found that the *only* permissible interpretation of the notion of "dumping" is that it relates to the "product as a whole". Not surprisingly, the parties' arguments in the present dispute have closely followed the two currents of thought that have evolved in previous cases, with Brazil advocating the position taken by the Appellate Body and the United States the views of most of the previous panels.

7.131 For the reasons we have tried to explain in the above analysis, we find it difficult to accept, on the basis of the arguments and jurisprudence we have reviewed, that the AD Agreement entertains only one exclusive definition of "dumping". However, there is no doubt in our minds that on the question of "zeroing", and more particularly, the definition of "dumping", the string of Appellate Body reports concerning mainly the United States' use of "zeroing" in anti-dumping proceedings read loud and clear.

7.132 Although adopted panel and Appellate Body reports do not bind WTO Members beyond parties to a particular dispute[219], the Appellate Body has expressed the view that ensuring "'security and predictability' in the dispute settlement system, as contemplated in Article 3.2 of the DSU, implies that, absent cogent reasons, an adjudicatory body will resolve the same legal question in the same way in a subsequent case".[220] Indeed, the Appellate Body has held that "following the Appellate Body's conclusions in earlier disputes is not only appropriate, but is what would be expected from panels, especially where the issues are the same".[221] The Appellate Body's role in the WTO dispute settlement system is defined in terms of hearing appeals from panel cases and "limited to issues of law covered in the panel report and legal interpretations developed by the panel".[222] Members are entitled to express their views on an Appellate Body report. However, unless the DSB decides not to adopt it, an Appellate Body report "shall be adopted by the DSB and unconditionally accepted by the parties to the dispute".[223] Institutionally, the fact that all Appellate Body reports overturning panel findings on the question of "zeroing" have been adopted by the DSB implies acceptance by all WTO Members of their contents, and bestows upon them systemic legitimacy.

---

[218] Although the panel in *US – Continued Zeroing* "generally found the reasoning of earlier panels ... persuasive", it concluded that "the multiple goals of the DSU" would be best served by following the Appellate Body's adopted findings. Panel Report, *US – Continued Zeroing*, paras. 7.162-7.183.

[219] See, e.g., Appellate Body Report, *Japan – Taxes on Alcoholic Beverages* ("*Japan – Alcoholic Beverages II*"), WT/DS8/AB/R, WT/DS10/AB/R, WT/DS11/AB/R, adopted 1 November 1996, DSR 1996:I, 97 at 106-108; and Appellate Body Report, *US – Stainless Steel (Mexico)*, para. 158.

[220] Appellate Body Report, *US – Stainless Steel (Mexico)*, para. 160.

[221] Appellate Body Report, *US – Oil Country Tubular Goods Sunset Reviews*, para. 188.

[222] Article 17.6, DSU.

[223] Article 17.14, DSU.

7.133 WTO Members created the WTO dispute settlement system as "a central element in providing security and predictability to the multilateral trading system"[224], emphasizing that "the prompt settlement" of disputes is "essential to the effective functioning of the WTO".[225] Moreover, the "aim of the dispute settlement mechanism is to secure a positive solution to a dispute".[226] We recall that this is the fifth dispute where the United States' use of "simple zeroing" in administrative reviews has been challenged. It is also the tenth dispute that has involved the definition of "dumping" in the context of "zeroing".[227] Furthermore, two additional panels have recently been established to examine complaints that include claims not unlike those presented by Brazil in the present dispute.[228] Inevitably, irrespective of the position taken by those (and any future) panels on the definition of "dumping", the Appellate Body will decide the matter by following its previous rulings. Following this pattern, the "zeroing" question has tested the limits of the WTO dispute settlement system for almost 10 years now. It has occupied the work of Members, panels and the Appellate Body like no other controversy. We have no doubt that this experience has not served to advance the system's efficiency; and we note that Members have not only sought to resolve the issue of "zeroing" through WTO dispute settlement, but they are also trying to address it through negotiations in the Negotiating Group on Rules in the context of the Doha Development Agenda.[229].

7.134 Given the objective lack of clarity in the current definition of "dumping" that is set forth in the AD Agreement (a conclusion which we believe is inescapable after almost a decade of unprecedented, and often conflicting, panel and Appellate Body opinions on the matter), we firmly believe that all Members have a strong systemic interest in seeing that a lasting resolution to the "zeroing" controversy is found sooner rather than later[230].

7.135 With all these considerations in mind, and despite sometimes diverse positions existing even amongst ourselves as to different aspects of this debate, we believe that, on balance, our function under Article 11 of the DSU, and the integrity and effectiveness of the WTO dispute settlement system, are best served in the present instance by following the Appellate Body. Thus, we find that the

---

[224] Article 3.2, DSU.

[225] Article 3.3, DSU.

[226] Article 3.7, DSU.

[227] See Panel and Appellate Body Reports in *EC – Bed Linen*; *EC – Pipe Fittings*; *US – Zeroing (EC)*; *US – Zeroing (Japan)*; *US – Stainless Steel*; *US – Continued Zeroing*; *US – Softwood Lumber V; US – Shrimp (Ecuador)*; *US – Shrimp (Thailand) / US – Customs Bond Directive*; and *US – Anti-Dumping Measures on PET Bags*.

[228] *United States – Use of Zeroing in Anti-Dumping Measures on Products from Korea*, panel constituted on 16 July 2010, WT/DS402/4; *United States – Anti-Dumping Measures on Shrimp from Viet Nam*, panel constituted on 16 July 2010, WT/DS404/6.

[229] See, e.g, Draft Consolidated Chair Texts of the AD and SCM Agreements, 30 November 2007, TN/RL/W/213; and New Draft Consolidated Chair Texts of the AD And SCM Agreements, 19 December 2008, TN/RL/W/236.

[230] We note that Article 3.9 of the DSU states that its provisions are "without prejudice to the right of Members to seek authoritative interpretation of provisions of a covered agreement through decision-making under the WTO Agreement".

only permissible interpretation of the definition of "dumping" contained in Article 2.1 of the AD Agreement, with relevance for the entire AD Agreement, is one that is based on an understanding that "dumping" can only be determined for the "product as a whole", and not individual transactions.

7.136 Having concluded that "dumping" cannot have a transaction-specific meaning, we now move on to examine the merits of Brazil's claims under Articles 2.4 and 9.3 of the AD Agreement and Article VI:2 of the GATT 1994. Because "zeroing" takes place in the process of calculating margins of dumping, we consider it appropriate to commence our evaluation by focusing on Brazil's claim under Article 2.4 of the AD Agreement, the one legal basis for Brazil's complaint that, as the title to Article 2 indicates, is explicitly about the "determination of dumping".

(d) Brazil's claims under Article 2.4 of the AD Agreement

7.137 Brazil claims that the USDOC's use of "simple zeroing" in the First and Second Administrative Reviews to determine the WAMs, relied upon for the purpose of establishing the CDRs, and the ISARs of Cutrale and Fischer was inconsistent with Article 2.4 of the AD Agreement, irrespective of its impact on the amount of duties actually collected by the United States.[231] The United States rejects Brazil's claims, arguing *inter alia* that the obligations set forth in Article 2.4 do not prescribe how the results of multiple comparisons between export price and normal value must be aggregated.

7.138 Brazil submits that the first sentence of Article 2.4 contains an obligation that applies whenever an investigating authority calculates a margin of dumping in any anti-dumping proceeding.[232] According to Brazil, Article 2.4 is not only about "price comparability" but also "the nature of the comparison between export price and normal value", and therefore the "fairness of that comparison".[233] Relying on previous findings of the Appellate Body, and one panel in an Article 21.5 implementation dispute[234], Brazil argues that the calculation of a margin of dumping through the use of "simple zeroing" results in an unfair comparison

---

[231] Brazil, FCOOS, paras. 67-72 and 74-79, referring to *inter alia*, the explanation provided in the Ferrier Affidavit, Exhibit US-31 (BCI), paras. 35-38 (First Administrative Review - ISARs) and 40-44 (First Administrative Reviews - CDRs) and 48-65 (Second Administrative Review – ISARs and CDRs); Brazil, Answer to Panel Question 2.

[232] Brazil, Answer to Panel Question 2.

[233] Brazil, SCOOS, para. 82, citing from Panel Report, *Egypt – Definitive Anti-Dumping Measures on Steel Rebar from Turkey* ("*Egypt – Steel Rebar*"), WT/DS211/R, adopted 1 October 2002, DSR 2002:VII, 2667, paras. 7.333-7.335, and referring to Panel Report, *Argentina – Definitive Anti-Dumping Duties on Poultry from Brazil* ("*Argentina – Poultry Anti-Dumping Duties*"), WT/DS241/R, adopted 19 May 2003, DSR 2003:V, 1727, para. 7.265; and Panel Report, *EC – Tube or Pipe Fittings*, para. 7.140.

[234] Appellate Body Report, *US – Softwood Lumber V (Article 21.5 – Canada)*, paras. 101, 138; Appellate Body Report, *US – Corrosion-Resistant Steel Sunset Review*, para. 135; Appellate Body Report, *US – Zeroing (Japan)*, paras. 146, 169 and 190(d).

between export price and normal value and therefore infringes Article 2.4.[235] On the other hand, the United States argues that the obligation to make a fair comparison under Article 2.4 is limited to adjustments needed to ensure price comparability. The United States finds support for this position not only in the statements made by panels and the Appellate Body in other disputes, but also the alleged negotiating history of the AD Agreement and Member practice. Moreover, the United States counters Brazil's reliance on the alleged panel and Appellate Body findings in previous "zeroing" disputes, arguing that there were either no such findings made in the relevant disputes, or that they related to claims that are factually and legally distinct from those Brazil is making in the present dispute.[236]

7.139 Article 2.4 of the AD Agreement reads:

> "*A fair comparison shall be made between the export price and the normal value.* This comparison shall be made at the same level of trade, normally at the ex-factory level, and in respect of sales made at as nearly as possible the same time. Due allowance shall be made in each case, on its merits, for differences which affect price comparability, including differences in conditions and terms of sale, taxation, levels of trade, quantities, physical characteristics, and any other differences which are also demonstrated to affect price comparability.{} In the cases referred to in paragraph 3, allowances for costs, including duties and taxes, incurred between importation and resale, and for profits accruing, should also be made. If in these cases price comparability has been affected, the authorities shall establish the normal value at a level of trade equivalent to the level of trade of the constructed export price, or shall make due allowance as warranted under this paragraph. The authorities shall indicate to the parties in question what information is necessary to ensure a fair comparison and shall not impose an unreasonable burden of proof on those parties."[237]

7.140 Brazil's claim raises two main questions. The first is whether the obligation in the first (underlined) sentence of Article 2.4 to ensure a "fair comparison" between export price and normal value applies outside of the context of what is described in the remainder of this provision, namely, beyond the selection of

---

[235] Brazil, FCOOS, para. 68; Brazil, Answer to Panel Question 2.

[236] US, SWS, paras. 4-22, quoting Panel Report, *Egypt – Rebar*, para 7.335; Panel Report, *Argentina – Poultry Anti-Dumping Duties*, para. 7.265; Panel Report, *US – Softwood Lumber V*, para. 7.356; Appellate Body Report, *United States – Anti-Dumping Measures on Certain Hot-Rolled Steel Products from Japan* ("*US – Hot-Rolled Steel*"), WT/DS184/AB/R, adopted 23 August 2001, DSR 2001:X, 4697, para. 179, to support its position that Article 2.4 governs only adjustments needed to ensure price comparability; and quoting Panel Report, *US – Zeroing (Japan)*, para. 7.155; *US – Softwood Lumber V (Article 21.5 – Canada)*, para. 5.74; and Panel Report, *US – Zeroing (EC)*, para. 7.260, in support of the view that the notion of "fairness" must be interpreted in a principled fashion, in the context of the activity at issue, and not in the abstract, as it alleges Brazil argues. US, SCOOS, paras. 26-28.

[237] Underline added, footnote omitted.

transactions and use of adjustments to account for differences between export price and normal value which affect their comparability. Assuming it does, and that it applies to calculations of the margin of dumping in the way Brazil argues, including during duty assessment proceedings, the second question we would have to resolve is whether the use of "simple zeroing" to calculate a margin of dumping is unfair.

7.141 In previous "zeroing" disputes where claims under Article 2.4 have been made in the context of United States' administrative reviews, panels and the Appellate Body appear to have accepted that the first (underlined) sentence in Article 2.4 is applicable beyond the particular context of adjustments or the selection of transactions for purposes of price comparability. For instance, in *US – Zeroing (Japan)*, the panel explained its views on the scope of Article 2.4, first sentence, in the following terms:

> "We consider that the requirement of a fair comparison set out in the first sentence of Article 2.4 is an independent legal obligation that is not defined exhaustively by the specific requirements set out in the remainder of Article 2.4 and is not limited in scope to the issue of adjustments to ensure price comparability. In this regard, we agree with the analysis of the panel in *US – Zeroing (EC)* regarding the scope of the "fair comparison" obligation. *First*, as stated by that panel, not to give independent meaning to the "fair comparison" requirement would render this provision inutile. *Second*, the structure of Article 2.4 suggests that the chapeau of Article 2.4 and its sub-paragraphs must be interpreted as a whole. *Third*, the "comparison" referred to in Articles 2.4.1 and 2.4.2 of the *AD Agreement* is the "comparison" in Article 2.4. *Fourth*, the "fair comparison" requirement explicitly applies also to the subject matter of Article 2.4.2 by virtue of the phrase "subject to the provisions governing fair comparison in paragraph 4" in Article 2.4.2. {}"[238]

7.142 We note that the plain language of the first sentence of Article 2.4 implies that it is concerned with the "comparison" made between export price and normal value for the purpose of determining a margin of dumping; with the "fairness" requirement applying precisely to discipline that "comparison". While this requirement can (and should) be understood to inform the rules concerning price comparability issues addressed in the remainder of Article 2.4, we agree with previous panels and the Appellate Body that this does not exhaust its relevance. First, it is significant that the "fair comparison" requirement is stated in a separate sentence at the beginning of the provision. In this light, to read it as simply repeating the requirements that follow would render the first sentence of Article

[238] Panel Report, *US – Zeroing (Japan)*, para. 7.157 (footnote omitted).

2.4 redundant.[239] Secondly, unlike Article 2.4.2, which is explicitly limited to the "investigation phase", the application of Article 2.4 is not constrained to any particular anti-dumping proceeding. It follows that the entirety of Article 2.4, including its first sentence, must apply to discipline the "comparison" between export price and normal value whenever undertaken during an anti-dumping proceeding, including during duty assessment.[240]

7.143 One panelist wishes to emphasize that, in his view, the correct interpretation of the "fair comparison" requirement set out in the first sentence of Article 2.4 is not as clear as previous panels and the Appellate Body appear to have suggested. In particular, this panelist considers that the scope of the "fair comparison" requirement must be informed by its immediate context, which includes the last sentence of Article 2.4. This sentence establishes an obligation on investigating authorities to "indicate to the parties what information is necessary to ensure a fair comparison". In the view of this panelist, the "fair comparison" referred to in this last sentence of Article 2.4 is the same that is described in the first sentence. Moreover, the "information ... necessary to ensure a fair comparison" is not information pertaining to *any aspect* of the comparison between export price and normal value. Rather, it is information needed to make appropriate adjustments or transaction selection for the purpose of accounting for differences affecting price comparability. When this view of the operation of Article 2.4 is coupled with the arguments advanced by the United States in support of its view that the "fair comparison" requirement should have limited application, this panelist finds there to be strong grounds to doubt the broad interpretation of the scope of the "fair comparison" requirement made by previous panels and the Appellate Body. Nevertheless, this panelist considers that, on balance, and in the light of the systemic considerations previously mentioned in this report, the view of the Appellate Body should be followed on this issue.

7.144 We recall that "simple zeroing" takes place when aggregating multiple results of comparisons between individual export prices and weighted-average normal values. In our view, the process of *aggregation* is an integral part of the "comparison" that is undertaken between export prices and weighted-average normal values. It therefore falls squarely within the "comparison" that is envisaged and regulated under the first sentence of Article 2.4. Thus, in order to comply with what is prescribed in that sentence, "simple zeroing" must be "fair".

7.145 In terms of whether Article 2.4 prohibits margins of dumping calculated on the basis of "simple zeroing", it is not surprising to find that, in essence, the jurisprudence mirrors the findings of past panels and the Appellate Body with respect to the definition of "dumping". Thus, in *US – Zeroing (Japan)*, the panel

---

[239] Panel Report, *US – Zeroing (EC)*, para. 7.253. On appeal, the Appellate Body agreed with the panel that "the legal rule set out in the first sentence of Article 2.4 is expressed in terms of a general and abstract standard. One implication of this is that this requirement is also applicable to proceedings governed by Article 9.3". Appellate Body Report, *US – Zeroing (EC)*, para. 146 (footnote omitted).

[240] By this conclusion, we do not mean to say that a "comparison" between export price and normal value is *required* in *all* anti-dumping proceedings.

rejected Japan's claim that the USDOC's use of "simple zeroing" in 11 administrative reviews was inconsistent with Article 2.4 of the AD Agreement because it considered that a general prohibition on zeroing in any context would: (i) render the W-T methodology described under Article 2.4.2 *inutile*; and (ii) undermine the effectiveness of Article 9, which in the panel's view, permitted duty collection on a transaction basis.[241] In *US – Stainless Steel (Mexico)*, the panel dismissed Mexico's claim that the United States had acted inconsistently with Article 2.4 of the AD Agreement by using "simple zeroing" in five administrative reviews because, in its view, it was permissible under Article 9.3 for the United States to have used "simple zeroing". In other words, what was permissible under one provision of the AD Agreement could not be found to be "unfair" and impermissible under another provision.

7.146 In *US – Zeroing (Japan)*, the Appellate Body reversed the panel's findings under Article 2.4 and found instead that the United States use of "simple zeroing" was, "as such" and "as applied", inconsistent with this provision.[242] The Appellate Body explained its reasoning in the following terms:

> "We turn next to examine whether zeroing in periodic reviews and new shipper reviews is, as such, inconsistent with the "fair comparison" requirement in Article 2.4 of the *Anti-Dumping Agreement.*
>
> If anti-dumping duties are assessed on the basis of a methodology involving comparisons between the export price and the normal value in a manner which results in anti-dumping duties being collected from importers in excess of the amount of the margin of dumping of the exporter or foreign producer, then this methodology cannot be viewed as involving a 'fair comparison' within the meaning of the first sentence of Article 2.4.{} *This is so because such an assessment would result in duty collection from importers in excess of the margin of dumping established in accordance with Article 2,* as we have explained previously.{}"[243]

7.147 Although clearly rejecting the view expressed by the panel concerning the inconsistency of "simple zeroing" with Article 2.4, we note that the underlined text in the Appellate Body's reasoning appears to signal that the basis of its findings lay in the *effect* "simple zeroing" had on the amount of duties collected. Similarly, the Appellate Body appeared to express the same view in *US – Zeroing (Article 21.5 – Japan)*, where it upheld the panel's findings that the United

[241] Panel Report, *US – Zeroing (Japan)*, para. 7.159.

[242] In *US – Stainless Steel (Mexico)*, the Appellate Body reversed the panel's findings, but it refrained from making any findings of its own on the merits of Mexico's claim under Article 2.4 on the basis that it considered it unnecessary for the purpose of resolving the dispute. Appellate Body Report, *US – Stainless Steel (Mexico)*, paras. 143-144.

[243] Appellate Body Report, *US – Zeroing (Japan)*, paras. 167-168 (footnotes omitted, underline added).

States had failed to comply with the recommendations and rulings from the original proceeding when it acted inconsistently with Article 2.4 of the AD Agreement by using "simple zeroing" in a series of subsequent administrative reviews. In coming to its conclusion, the Appellate Body explained that ""[i]n this case, compliance with the DSB's recommendations and rulings required the cessation of zeroing *in the application of anti-dumping duties* by the end of the reasonable period of time".[244]

7.148 However, in general, the Appellate Body has on multiple occasions also described its views on "zeroing" in terms that strongly suggest that it is unfair because of its effect on the magnitude of the margin of dumping, whenever determined. For instance, in *US – Corrosion-Resistant Steel Sunset Review*, the Appellate Body stated:

> "When investigating authorities use a zeroing methodology such as that examined in *EC – Bed Linen* to calculate a dumping margin, whether in an original investigation or otherwise, that methodology will tend to inflate the margins calculated. Apart from inflating the margins, such a methodology could, in some instances, turn a negative margin of dumping into a positive margin of dumping. As the Panel itself recognized in the present dispute, "zeroing ... may lead to an affirmative determination that dumping exists where no dumping would have been established in the absence of zeroing." {} Thus, the inherent bias in a zeroing methodology of this kind may distort not only the magnitude of a dumping margin, but also a finding of the very existence of dumping."[245]

7.149 We are somewhat attracted by the logic underlying the panel's observation in *US – Zeroing (Japan)* that a general prohibition on "zeroing" operating through Article 2.4 of the AD Agreement, would render the W-T methodology described in the second sentence of Article 2.4.2 redundant. However, we see a parallel between this line of reasoning and the conundrum posed by "mathematical equivalence". In the latter context, we noted in our previous discussion that no redundancy would exist if the United States' views about how the W-T methodology actually operates were incorrect. Yet we observed that there appears to be considerable uncertainty as to precisely how the W-T methodology should be given effect. We also concluded that another way to avoid redundancy would be if the W-T methodology, as described by the United States, could be characterized as an "exception" to the otherwise generally applicable definition of "dumping", which operates to otherwise prohibit "zeroing". We did not, however, find this explanation to be convincing.[246] In our view, the same interpretative dilemmas can be found in the particular problem posed by the approach taken by the panel in *US – Zeroing (Japan)* to Article 2.4.

---

[244] Appellate Body Report, *US – Zeroing (Japan)(Article 21.5 – Japan)*, para. 193 (underline added).

[245] Appellate Body Report, *US – Corrosion-Resistant Steel Sunset Review*, para. 135.

[246] See discussion above, para. 7.119.

7.150 The United States argues further that if a general prohibition on "zeroing" existed by virtue of the operation of Article 2.4, there would be no need to articulate the same requirement through the use of the "all comparable export transactions" and "margins of dumping" language in Article 2.4.2 of the AD Agreement.[247] However, we note that Article 2.4 operates as the *chapeau* to Article 2.4.2, and therefore logically, it must inform whatever is governed under that provision. Indeed, Article 2.4.2 explicitly provides that it must be read "subject to the provisions governing fair comparison in paragraph 4".

7.151 The United States also submits that Brazil's interpretation of the "fair comparison" requirement is overly broad, unprincipled and, as we understand the United States' argument, would result in the establishment of an obligation to ensure that "any and all anti-dumping calculations are 'impartial, even-handed, or unbiased'".[248] In this regard, the United States refers to the panel in *US – Softwood Lumber V (Article 21.5 – Canada)*, which it argues "cautioned against the overly liberal use of the 'fair comparison' language of Article 2.4" in the following terms:

> "[W]e believe that a claim based on a highly general and subjective test such as 'fair comparison' should be approached with caution by treaty interpreters. For this reason, any conception of 'fairness' should be solidly rooted in the context provided by the *AD Agreement*, and perhaps the *WTO Agreement* more generally. As such, there must be a discernable standard within the *AD Agreement*, and perhaps the *WTO Agreement*, by which to assess whether or not a comparison has been 'fair' or 'unfair'. Thus, the fact that comparison methodology A produces a higher margin of dumping than comparison methodology B would only make comparison methodology A unfair if comparison methodology B were the applicable standard.{} If, however, the *AD Agreement* were to permit either comparison methodology A or B, this would not be the case."[249]

7.152 We agree with the United States and the panel in *US – Softwood Lumber V (Article 21.5 – Canada)* that the meaning of the notion of "fairness" as it is articulated in Article 2.4 will depend upon the particular context in which it is intended to operate. In our view, the search for this context must, first and foremost, start with understanding precisely what it is that must be "fair". This, of course, is the "comparison" between export price and normal value. Thus, contrary to the United States' argument, accepting that the scope of the "fair comparison" requirement extends beyond the subject matter of Article 2.4, does not establish a rule governing "any and all anti-dumping calculations".[250] The very language of the first sentence of Article 2.4 explicitly limits its relevance to

---

247 US, SCOOS, para. 26.
248 US, SWS, paras. 16-22; US, SCOOS, para. 28.
249 Panel Report, *US – Softwood Lumber V*, para. 5.74.
250 US, SWS, para. 22.

situations involving the "comparison" between export price and normal value. For instance, the "fair comparison" requirement does not extend to govern how an investigating authority establishes normal value. It is clear that this is comprehensively disciplined under Article 2.2 of the AD Agreement. Neither does the "fair comparison" requirement regulate how to establish constructed export price, which is addressed in Article 2.3 of the AD Agreement. However, pursuant to the first sentence of Article 2.4, the "comparison" between any export price and normal value, both individually established in accordance with the specific rules set out in Article 2, must be "fair".

7.153 An investigating authority will compare export price with normal value for the purpose of determining the existence of dumping or the magnitude of a margin of dumping. This implies that the comparison between export price and normal value must be informed by the definition of "dumping" that is contained in Article 2.1 of the AD Agreement. Above we have found that, on balance, and taking into account important systemic concerns, it is impermissible to compare export price with normal value in such a way that does not result in a determination of "dumping" for the "product as a whole". In this light, a comparison methodology (such as "simple zeroing") that ignores transactions, which if properly taken into account, would result in a lower margin of dumping, must be considered "unfair" and therefore inconsistent with Article 2.4.

7.154 Thus, for all of the above reasons, we conclude that "simple zeroing" is inconsistent with the "fair comparison" requirement that is prescribed in Article 2.4 of the AD Agreement.

(i) "Simple zeroing" in the First Administrative Review

7.155 We recall that we have found that the WAMs and ISARs determined for both Cutrale and Fischer in the First Administrative Review were calculated through the use of "simple zeroing".[251] In the case of Fischer, the WAM determined by the USDOC was relied upon for the purpose of establishing Fischer's CDR. Likewise, because the WAM determined for Cutrale was considered to be *de minimis* under United State law, a CDR of 0% was applied to entries of Cutrale's products in the subsequent period.

7.156 The United States argues that even under the Appellate Body's own rationale, the determination of Cutrale's *de minimis* margin of dumping, which was converted into a CDR of 0% through the operation of United States law, cannot be considered to infringe Article 2.4 because a *de minimis* margin cannot be said to be "artificially inflated" or "inherently unfair".[252] We disagree. In our view, the obligation under Article 2.4 is focused on the "comparison" between export price and normal value, not its impact. In other words, it is the nature of the "comparison" itself, and not the results of that comparison, that is disciplined

[251] See above, paras. 7.84-7.87.

[252] US, SWS, para. 18, citing from Appellate Body Report, *US – Softwood Lumber V (Article 21.5 – Canada)*, paras. 143-144.

under Article 2.4. Thus, a "comparison" between export price and normal value that involves "simple zeroing" will be "unfair" for the purpose of Article 2.4, irrespective of whether the final margin of dumping actually applied is considered to be *de minimis*. Moreover, in the present instance, although Cutrale's WAM was *de minimis*, the fact remains that absent "simple zeroing" it would have been non-existent.[253]

7.157 Thus, we find that by using "simple zeroing" to calculate the WAMs (relied upon for the purpose of setting CDRs) and the ISARs for both Cutrale and Fischer in the First Administrative Review, the United States failed to perform a "fair comparison" between export price and normal value, and thereby acted inconsistently with Article 2.4 of the AD Agreement.

(ii) "Simple zeroing" in the Second Administrative Review

7.158 We recall that we have found that the WAM and ISAR determined for Cutrale in the Second Administrative Review were calculated through the use of "simple zeroing".[254] We also made the same finding with respect to Fischer. In particular, we noted that although the WAM and corresponding CDR for Fischer were both declared to be 0% in the published Final Results, the WAM calculation actually run by the USDOC by means of its computer programme that involved "simple zeroing" determined a WAM of [[XX]].[255] Likewise, we concluded that "simple zeroing" was used in the computer programme applied by the United States for the purpose of calculating Fischer's ISAR, even though the ISAR actually imposed on imports of Fischer's products was [[XX]].[256]

7.159 The United States argues that, even according to the Appellate Body's rationale relied upon by Brazil, the determination of a 0% margin of dumping for Fischer cannot be considered to infringe Article 2.4 because a 0% margin cannot be said to be "artificially inflated" or "inherently unfair".[257] Similarly, the United States argues that even accepting the Appellate Body's line of reasoning with respect to Article 2.4, in order for there to be an infringement of the "fair comparison" requirement in the context of administrative reviews, any use of "simple zeroing" must result in excessive collection of duties.[258]

---

[253] The computer programme log for Cutrale indicates that [[XX]] out of [[XX]] export transactions generated negative comparison results, and were therefore excluded from the USDOC's calculation. These transactions represented [[XX]] of Cutrale's transactions. Exhibits BRA-29 (BCI), p. 63; and BRA-31 (BCI) (Ferrier Affidavit), para. 38. Moreover, Cutrale's computer programme output reveals that the *de minimis* margin of 0.45% was determined by taking into account export transactions accounting for [[XX]] of the total volume of transactions, and [[XX]] of their total value. Exhibit BRA-34 (BCI), last page.

[254] See above, paras. 7.84-7.87.

[255] See above, para. 7.86.

[256] *Ibid.*

[257] US, SWS, para. 18, citing from Appellate Body Report, *US – Softwood Lumber V (Article 21.5 – Canada)*, paras. 143-144.

[258] US, SWS, para. 17, citing from Appellate Body Report, *US – Zeroing (Japan)*, para. 168.

7.160 We are unable to agree with the United States' submissions. As we have already explained[259], the obligation under Article 2.4 is focused on the "comparison" between export price and normal value, not its impact. In other words, it is the nature of the "comparison" itself, and not the results of that comparison, that is disciplined under Article 2.4. Thus, in our view, it follows that a "comparison" between export price and normal value that involves "simple zeroing" will be "unfair" for the purpose of Article 2.4, irrespective of whether the final WAM or final ISAR actually imposed is 0%. Article 2.4 regulates the "comparison" that is made by an investigating authority; and it is this "comparison" (not its outcome) that falls within the scope of Article 2.4 of the AD Agreement.

7.161 Thus, we find that by using "simple zeroing" to calculate the WAMs (relied upon for the purpose of setting CDRs) and the ISARs for both Cutrale and Fischer in the Second Administrative Review, the United States failed to perform a "fair comparison" between export price and normal value, and thereby acted inconsistently with Article 2.4 of the AD Agreement.

(e) Brazil's claims under Article 9.3 of the AD Agreement and Article VI:2 of the GATT 1994

7.162 Having found that the measures challenged by Brazil are inconsistent with Article 2.4 of the AD Agreement, we consider it is not necessary, for the purpose of satisfactorily resolving this dispute, to make additional findings with respect to Brazil's claims that the same measures are also inconsistent with Article 9.3 of the AD Agreement and Article VI:2 of the GATT 1994. On this basis, we decide to exercise judicial economy and decline to make any findings in respect of these claims.

C. Brazil's Claims Concerning "Continued Zeroing"

1. Arguments of Brazil

7.163 Brazil challenges the alleged "continued use by the United States of zeroing procedures in successive anti-dumping proceedings under the Orange Juice Order, including the original investigation and any subsequent administrative reviews by which duties are applied and maintained over a period of time".[260]

7.164 Brazil characterizes the USDOC's alleged "continued use" of "zeroing" as "ongoing conduct" of virtually the same kind found to be inconsistent with Article 9.3 of the AD Agreement and Article VI:2 of the GATT 1994 by the Appellate Body in *US – Continued Zeroing*. Relying entirely upon the Appellate Body's reasoning in that dispute, and various pieces of evidence allegedly demonstrating the USDOC's use of "zeroing procedures" in the original investigation and First, Second and Third Administrative Reviews, Brazil asks the Panel to find that the USDOC's "continued use" of "zeroing" in successive proceedings under of the orange juice anti-dumping duty order, by which duties are applied

[259] See above, para. 7.156.

[260] Brazil, FWS, para. 48.

to imports of orange juice from Brazil, amounts to "ongoing conduct" that is inconsistent with Articles 2.4, 2.4.2 and 9.3 of the AD Agreement and Article VI:2 of the GATT 1994.[261]

2. *Arguments of the United States*

7.165 The United States argues that "continued zeroing" as "ongoing conduct" does not exist as a "measure" susceptible to challenge in WTO dispute settlement proceedings. In particular, the United States asserts that the alleged measure is focused on "indeterminate future measures that did not exist at the time of Brazil's panel request (and may never exist)". According to the United States, "measures that do not and may never exist are not within a dispute settlement panel's terms of reference", and for this reason, they cannot be challenged in WTO dispute settlement. Thus, the United States asks the Panel to find that "continued zeroing" as "ongoing conduct" is not a measure that can be challenged in this dispute.[262]

7.166 In any case, the United States submits that Brazil has failed to establish that the USDOC actually "zeroed", as a matter of fact, in "successive proceedings". The United States asserts that the computer programme evidence submitted by Brazil in Exhibits BRA-32 (BCI) and BRA-33 (BCI) does not demonstrate that the USDOC used "zeroing" in the original investigation. According to the United States, the various lines of the computer programme that Brazil focuses upon show that the "necessary condition for activating the 'zeroing' operation" was not satisfied, meaning that no comparison of export price and normal value resulted in a negative value. In other words, the United States asserts that Brazil's evidence shows that all comparison results were positive (i.e., all comparison results showed dumping).[263] The United States also argues that the computer programme evidence submitted by Brazil in Exhibit BRA-33 (BCI) was generated by Brazil's consultant, not the USDOC, and only after the USDOC made the relevant final determinations.[264] Moreover, the United States emphasizes that no CDR was applied to imports of Cutrale's products following the First Administrative Review, and no CDRs or ISARs were applied to Fischer's products as a result of the Second Administrative Review. Thus, the United States submits that whatever "zeroing" may have taken place in the calculation of Cutrale's or Fischer's margins of dumping, it did not result in a breach of the United States' obligation under Article 9.3 of the AD Agreement to ensure that any anti-dumping duty applied is not in excess of the margin of dumping established under Article 2.[265]

---

[261] Brazil, FWS, paras. 98-117; Brazil, FCOOS, paras. 80-96; Brazil, SWS, paras. 27-46; Brazil, SCOOS, paras. 86-93.

[262] US, FWS, paras. 52, 124 and 130-131; US, SWS, paras. 83-84.

[263] US, FWS, para. 128; US, FCOOS, para. 38; US, SWS, para. 87; US, Answer to Panel Question 24.

[264] US, Answer to Panel Question 24.

[265] US, FWS, para. 127; US, FCOOS, para. 39.

7.167 The United States submits that, at most, the evidence advanced by Brazil shows that "zeroing" was applied in order to determine the margin of dumping of one company in one proceeding covering a one year period. The United States contrasts this with the facts the Appellate Body found in *US – Continued Zeroing* to demonstrate the existence of "continued zeroing" as "ongoing conduct", namely: the use of "zeroing" in the original investigation; the use of "zeroing" in four successive administrative reviews; and reliance in a sunset review upon rates determined using "zeroing". According to the United States, the facts Brazil relies upon do not constitute "a string of determinations, made sequentially ... over an extended period of time". Thus, the United States argues that there is no basis for the Panel to find that the "zeroing" methodology was used without interruption, that it was used in different proceedings, and that it was used over an extended period of time. The United States therefore asks the Panel to reject Brazil's claim that it has established the USDOC's "continued zeroing" as "ongoing conduct".[266]

7.168 Finally, the United States notes that Brazil challenges "continued zeroing" under Article 2.4.2 of the AD Agreement, in addition to Article 9.3 and Article VI:2 of the GATT 1994. The United States argues that Brazil's reliance on this legal basis is misplaced because Article 2.4.2 is explicitly limited to the "investigation phase", and has therefore no application to duty collection or other anti-dumping proceedings. In this regard, the United States asks the Panel to follow the finding of the panel in *US – Zeroing (EC)*, and decline to extend the obligations of Article 2.4.2 to "successive proceedings" beyond the original investigation.[267]

3. *Arguments of the Third Parties*

(a) Japan

7.169 Japan argues that there is no substantial difference between the "continued zeroing" measure that Brazil challenges in the present dispute and the "continued zeroing" measure challenged by the European Communities in *US – Continued Zeroing*. Japan recalls that previous panels and the Appellate Body have found that "zeroing" is inconsistent with Article 2.4.2 (when performed in original investigations) and Article 9.3 of the AD Agreement and Article VI:2 of the GATT 1994 (when performed for the purpose of duty assessment proceedings). Thus, Japan calls on the Panel to follow these findings and rule that the USDOC's "continued zeroing" in the orange juice anti-dumping proceedings is inconsistent with Article 9.3 of the AD Agreement and Article VI:2 of the GATT 1994.[268]

---

[266] US, FWS, paras. 132-133; US, SWS, para. 87; US, SCOOS, paras. 39-40.
[267] US, FWS, paras. 134-135.
[268] Japan, TPWS, paras. 18-22 and 72.

4. *Evaluation by the Panel*

(a) Introduction

7.170 Brazil's complaint against the USDOC's alleged "continued use" of "zeroing" in the orange juice anti-dumping proceedings raises essentially three main questions: (i) whether it is possible to challenge a Member's "ongoing conduct" as a "measure" in WTO dispute settlement; (ii) if it is possible to challenge such a "measure", whether Brazil has demonstrated that it exists as a matter of fact; and (iii) if it does exist, whether the "measure" is inconsistent with Articles 2.4, 2.4.2 and 9.3 of the AD Agreement and Article VI:2 of the GATT 1994. Below we address each of these questions in turn.

(b) Whether the "continued use" of "zeroing" as "ongoing conduct" is a "measure" susceptible to WTO dispute settlement

7.171 It is well established that "in principle, any act or omission attributable to a WTO Member can be a measure of that Member for purposes of dispute settlement".[269] Measures that have been examined by panels and the Appellate Body in the past include "not only measures consisting of acts that apply to particular situations, but also those consisting of acts setting forth rules or norms that have general and prospective application".[270] Moreover, in *US – Zeroing (EC)*, the Appellate Body found that the European Communities was entitled to challenge an *unwritten* zeroing "norm" because it found no basis in the DSU and the AD Agreement to "conclude that 'rules or norms' can be challenged, as such, *only* if they are expressed in written form".[271]

7.172 In *US – Continued Zeroing*, the Appellate Body concluded that the USDOC's "continued use" of "zeroing" to calculate the margins of dumping in 18 different anti-dumping proceedings could be challenged as a "measure" it described as "ongoing conduct". The Appellate Body's reasoning included the following observations:

> "Thus, the measures at issue consist of neither the zeroing methodology as a rule or norm of general and prospective application, nor discrete applications of the zeroing methodology in particular determinations; rather, they are the use of the zeroing methodology in successive proceedings, in each of the 18 cases, by which duties are maintained over a period of time. We see no reason to exclude ongoing conduct that consists of the use of the zeroing methodology from challenge in WTO dispute settlement. The successive determinations by which duties are maintained are con-

---

[269] Appellate Body Report, *US – Corrosion Resistant Steel Sunset Review*, para. 81.

[270] Panel Report, *US – Continued Zeroing*, para. 7.45, cited with approval in Appellate Body Report, *US – Continued Zeroing*, para. 177.

[271] Appellate Body Report, *US – Zeroing (EC)*, para. 193. The panel in the same case come to the same conclusion on the basis of similar reasoning.

> nected stages in each of the 18 cases involving imposition, assessment, and collection of duties under the same anti-dumping duty order.{} The use of the zeroing methodology in a string of these stages is the allegedly unchanged component of each of the 18 measures at issue.{} It is with respect to this ongoing conduct that the European Communities brought its challenge, seeking its cessation. At the oral hearing, the European Communities confirmed that it is not seeking the revocation of the 18 anti-dumping orders but, rather, the cessation of the use of the zeroing methodology by which the duties are calculated and maintained in these 18 cases.{} In our view, the European Communities, in seeking an effective resolution of its dispute with the United States, is entitled to frame the subject of its challenge in such a way as to bring the ongoing conduct, regarding the use of the zeroing methodology in these 18 cases, under the scrutiny of WTO dispute settlement."[272]

7.173 Conceptually, the alleged "measure" that Brazil challenges in this dispute appears to be very similar, if not identical, to the measure that was the subject of the European Communities' complaint in *US – Continued Zeroing*. Indeed, Brazil has repeatedly emphasized that it is challenging the same type of "measure" that was at issue in *US – Continued Zeroing*, namely, a "measure" in the form of "ongoing conduct". Moreover, Brazil has explained that by challenging the alleged "measure" it is seeking to obtain a prospective remedy, namely, the "cessation of the use of the zeroing methodology" in the orange juice anti-dumping proceedings.[273]

7.174 According to the United States, the alleged "ongoing conduct" "measure" that Brazil challenges cannot be subject to WTO dispute settlement because it is based on "an indefinite number of future individual measures that do not and may never exist".[274] Moreover, the United States submits that if "continued use" were a "measure", it would "presumably ... cease to exist if at any point 'zeroing' is not used in a particular individual determination". Yet, the United States notes that "Brazil's argument requires the Panel to assume that it will be used".[275] Thus, the United States argues that Brazil's focus on "continued zeroing" as "ongoing conduct" involves "speculating as to what may happen in the future"[276], and for this reason the United States considers that such conduct cannot amount to a "measure" that is susceptible to WTO dispute settlement.

7.175 As we understand it, implicit in the United States' argument is the view that there is a prospective element to the alleged "ongoing conduct" "measure" Brazil challenges which cannot be established with any degree of certainty because it is inherently speculative. We note, however, that although describing the

---

272 Appellate Body Report, *US – Continued Zeroing*, para. 181 (footnotes omitted).

273 Brazil, Answer to Panel Question 2.

274 US, FWS, paras. 51 and 131.

275 US, SWS, para. 84.

276 *Ibid.*

"ongoing conduct" measure in *US – Continued Zeroing* in terms that contemplate its prospective operation, the Appellate Body did not require absolute certainty as to the future conduct it envisaged. In particular, the Appellate Body found that:

> "The density of factual findings in these cases, regarding the continued use of the zeroing methodology in a string of successive proceedings pertaining to the same anti-dumping duty order, provides a sufficient basis for us to conclude that the zeroing methodology *would likely continue* to be applied in successive proceedings whereby the duties in these four cases are maintained."[277]

7.176 Thus, ongoing conduct may be simply described as conduct that is currently taking place and is *likely to continue* in the future. Given that any act or omission attributable to a Member may, in principle, be challenged by a Member in WTO dispute settlement proceedings, we see no reason why "ongoing conduct" cannot also be the subject of a complaint. The particular "ongoing conduct" that Brazil objects to is the USDOC's alleged "continued use" of "zeroing procedures" under the orange juice anti-dumping duty order. Conceptually, we see no practical difference between this form of "ongoing conduct" and the "ongoing conduct" challenged in the *US – Continued Zeroing* dispute. Like the Appellate Body in that controversy, we consider that Brazil is entitled to bring a complaint against such a "measure" to WTO dispute settlement. However, accepting that the "continued use" of "zeroing" may be challenged in WTO dispute settlement as a "measure" in the form of "ongoing conduct" does not amount to accepting that any such "measure" actually exists. It is to this second question that we now turn.

(c) Has Brazil established that the alleged "continued zeroing" as "ongoing conduct" measure exists?

7.177 In *US – Continued Zeroing*, the Appellate Body explained the basis for its conclusion concerning the existence of "continued zeroing" as "ongoing conduct" in the following terms:

> "Thus, in each of the above four cases, the Panel's findings indicate that *the zeroing methodology was repeatedly used in a string of determinations, made sequentially in periodic reviews and sunset reviews over an extended period of time*. The density of factual findings in these cases, regarding the *continued use of the zeroing methodology in a string of successive proceedings pertaining to the same anti-dumping duty order*, provides a sufficient basis for us to conclude that the zeroing methodology would likely continue

[277] Appellate Body Report, *US – Continued Zeroing*, para. 191 (emphasis added).

to be applied in successive proceedings whereby the duties in these four cases are maintained."[278]

7.178 Thus, the evidence the Appellate Body considered demonstrated the existence of the "continued zeroing" measure covered the use of "zeroing" in the original investigation; the use of "zeroing" in four successive administrative reviews; and reliance in a sunset review upon rates determined using "zeroing". On the other hand, the Appellate Body found that the "continued zeroing" measure could not be established on the basis of evidence showing the use or reliance upon "zeroing" in only: (i) one anti-dumping proceeding – i.e., either one original investigation, one administrative review or one sunset review; (ii) two (three) administrative reviews in the same proceeding, where there was a lack of evidence showing that the use of "zeroing" in a third (fourth) administrative review related to the same anti-dumping duty order; and (iii) two administrative reviews and one sunset review related to the same anti-dumping duty order, where there was no evidence regarding any other proceedings submitted during the panel process.[279]

7.179 Brazil argues that the evidence it has introduced shows that the USDOC used "zeroing" to calculate the margins of dumping in the original investigation and the First, Second and Third Administrative Reviews. Moreover, according to Brazil, the facts it has presented also demonstrate that the USDOC will continue to apply the same methodology in all future proceedings under the orange juice anti-dumping duty order. On the other hand, the United States submits that Brazil has failed to satisfy the standard applied by the Appellate Body in *US – Continued Zeroing*, noting that in a number of instances, the USDOC did not use "zeroing" at all, or that even when it did, it had no bearing on the WAMs, CDRs or ISARs actually imposed. According to the United States, the facts Brazil relies upon have more in common with the facts the Appellate Body considered did not establish the existence of a "continued zeroing" measure, than those the Appellate Body found to demonstrate its existence.

7.180 We have previously concluded that Brazil has shown that the USDOC determined the WAMs (relied upon for the purpose of setting the CDRs) and the ISARs of Cutrale and Fischer in the First and Second Administrative Reviews through the use of "simple zeroing".[280] Below we examine the extent to which the evidence Brazil has submitted establishes the same with respect to the original investigation and the Third Administrative Review.

---

278 *Ibid.*

279 Appellate Body Report, *US – Continued Zeroing*, para. 194.

280 See above, paras. 7.84-7.87, 7.155 and 7.158.

(i) Original Investigation

7.181 Brazil asserts that the computer programme the USDOC applied in the original investigation[281] to calculate the respondents' margins of dumping "provided for the exclusion ... of negative comparison results where the weighted-average export price of any model exceeded normal value".[282] To substantiate this assertion, Brazil submits a copy of the relevant programme logs together with an explanation which identifies the "language to zero negative margins" appearing in each log.[283]

7.182 The United States asserts that the computer programme evidence submitted by Brazil demonstrates that no "zeroing" actually took place in the original investigation. According to the United States, there were no negative comparison results to "zero" in that investigation because all of the respondents transactions were dumped. Thus, the United States does not argue that the "zeroing" instruction was not present in the computer programme used in the Original Investigation. Rather, the United States points out that the instruction was not executed during the course of the calculation because of the absence of non-dumped transactions.

7.183 Brazil does not contest the United States' assertion about the absence of transactions sold at an export price above normal value. Indeed, the explanation provided in Exhibit BRA-31 (BCI) appears to confirm this point. However, Brazil does not accept that the "zeroing" instruction did not function in the original investigation. According to Brazil, the "zeroing" line ("WHERE EMARGIN GT 0") always functions to ensure that the total amount of dumping is based exclusively on positive comparison results. For this line not to function, Brazil submits that it must be removed from the computer programme.[284] Moreover, Brazil argues that in the light of the nature of its claim, the fact that the "zeroing procedures" did not exclude any transactions sold at an export price above normal value is irrelevant. Brazil explains the nature of its claim in the following terms:

> "In Brazil's view, a challenge to the continued use of zeroing under a single anti-dumping order does not fit squarely into either the 'as applied' or the 'as such' category. Indeed, the claim shares elements of both 'as such' and 'as applied' claims.

---

[281] Final Results of the Original Investigation, 71 Fed. Reg. 2183 (13 January 2006), Exhibit BRA-18; and Amended Final Results of the Original Investigation, 71 Fed. Reg. 8841 (21 February 2006), Exhibit BRA-19.

[282] Brazil, FWS, para. 102.

[283] Exhibits BRA-32 (BCI) (Programme log for Cutrale); BRA-33 (BCI) (Programme log for Fischer); and BRA-31 (BCI) (Ferrier Affidavit). The United States argues that Exhibit BRA-33 (BCI) was "generated by Brazil's consultant, not by the USDOC, and only after the USDOC made the relevant final determinations" (US, Answer to Panel Question 24). However, Brazil has presented evidence which we are satisfied confirms that Exhibit BRA-33 (BCI) was provided to Fischer's Counsel by the USDOC (See Exhibit BRA-58, and Brazil, Comment on US Answer to Panel Question 24). See also the summary of infromation on the use of "zeroing", submitted as Exhibit BRA-48.

[284] Brazil, Comment on US Answer to Panel Question 24.

> With respect to similarities to an 'as such' claim, the claim contests the continued use of zeroing in a series of determinations under a specific anti-dumping order that applies prospectively to all subject imports; the claim is, therefore, not confined to 'specific instances in which the zeroing methodology was applied, such as a periodic review or sunset review determination'.{} The evidence, as a whole, shows that, under the Orange Juice Order, the United States systematically uses the zeroing as part of its methodology for determining dumping and margins of dumping. Also similar to an 'as such' claim, the aim of the 'continued use' claim is to obtain 'the cessation of *the use of the zeroing methodology* by which the duties are calculated and maintained'.{} Thus, the 'continued use' claim contests zeroing on a relatively generalized basis, aiming to terminate its use on that basis.
>
> However, the claim is nonetheless different from an 'as such' claim with respect to the degree of generality of the claim. An 'as such' claim against the zeroing procedures as a rule or norm of general and prospective application would address the maintenance of zeroing for use in administrative (or other) reviews, under *all* anti-dumping orders. In contrast, Brazil's 'continued use' claim addresses the use of the zeroing in determinations under *one single* anti-dumping order, namely the Orange Juice Order. The claim is, therefore, 'narrower' than an 'as such' claim.{}"[285]
>
> "With respect to the 'continued use' measure, the conduct comprising this measure is the *use of zeroing* in determinations made under the Orange Juice Order, including in administrative reviews. As with an 'as such' claim against zeroing under all anti-dumping orders, the consistency of this measure, under Article 9.3 and Article VI:2, in the context of the Orange Juice Order, does not turn on the *outcome* of any specific determination resulting from the use of zeroing."[286]

Thus, Brazil argues that its challenge relates to the "continued use" of the US-DOC's "zeroing" methodology, not its impact. For this reason, Brazil argues that the fact that the "zeroing" instruction did not function to "zero" any export transactions sold at a price above normal value in the original investigation does not detract from its complaint.

7.184 We agree with Brazil. In our view, the nature of its complaint against "continued zeroing" is akin to a claim that could be made against a measure "as such", in the sense that Brazil challenges the "continued use" of the "zeroing methodology" under the orange juice anti-dumping duty order, *independent of*

[285] Brazil, Answer to Panel Question 1 (footnotes omitted).

[286] Brazil, Answer to Panel Question 2.

its application. However, whereas a measure subject to a typical "as such" claim in WTO dispute settlement would be generally applicable to all anti-dumping proceedings conducted under all United States anti-dumping duty orders, the "measure" Brazil objects to exists only in the limited context of the orange juice proceedings.

7.185 By bringing a complaint against such a "measure", Brazil is seeking to redress what it considers to be the root of the problem it has with the United States' conduct of the orange juice proceedings, namely, the USDOC's "continued use" of the "zeroing methodology". Brazil's challenge seeks to achieve a prospective remedy; a solution that would prevent the United States from using the "zeroing methodology" in future proceedings under the orange juice anti-dumping duty order. In this light, the fact that the particular circumstances of the original investigation were such that the "zeroing" instruction did not function to remove any negative export price to normal value comparisons does not invalidate Brazil's claim, because it is the very existence of the "zeroing" instruction in the computer programmes used to calculate the relevant margins of dumping, *independent of its application*, that is the subject of Brazil's complaint.

7.186 Thus, we conclude that the evidence Brazil has submitted demonstrates that the USDOC used the "zeroing methodology" in the original investigation, even though this conduct had no impact on the relevant margins of dumping determined for the respondents because of the particular set of facts that arose in that investigation.

(ii) Third Administrative Review

7.187 Brazil asserts[287] that the USDOC used "simple zeroing" in the Final Results of the Third Administrative Review to determine the following WAMs, CDRs and ISARs:

	WAM[288]	*CDR*[288]	*ISAR*[289]
Third Administrative Review			
Cutrale	**8.13%**	**8.13%**	[[XX]]
Fischer	5.26%	5.26%	[[XX]]

7.188 To substantiate its assertion, Brazil submits the same type of evidence it used to demonstrate the use of "simple zeroing" in the First and Second Administrative Reviews, namely, the relevant computer programme logs and output for each respondent, the Issues and Decision Memorandum, and a second Ferrier

287 Brazil, SWS, paras. 36-41.

288 Final Results, Third Administrative Review, Exhibit BRA-49.

289 BRA-54 (BCI) (Programme output for Cutrale), penultimate page; BRA-55 (BCI) (Programme output for Fischer), penultimate page.

Affidavit.[290] We have carefully reviewed this evidence and find that it confirms Brazil's assertions.

7.189 The United States does not contest that the USDOC used "simple zeroing" when determining the above WAMs, CDRs and ISARs[291], but it argues that the Third Administrative Review is not within the Panel's terms of reference.[292] However, apart from referring to a discussion contained in its first written submission where it explains why the Second Administrative Review is outside of the Panel's terms of reference, the United States presents no separate argumentation concerning the Third Administrative Review.

7.190 In our view, the United States' position with respect to Brazil's reliance on the results of the Third Administrative Review is misplaced. Brazil does not *challenge* the results of the Third Administrative Review, but instead uses them as *evidence* of the "continued zeroing" measure. A panel's terms of reference need only contain a sufficiently clear explanation of the legal basis of a complainant's claims and a description of the challenged measures[293]; they are not required to also identify the evidence. We therefore see no basis for the United States' objection to Brazil's reliance on the results of the Third Administrative Review.

(iii) Conclusion regarding the existence of the "continued zeroing" measure

7.191 Overall, the evidence submitted by Brazil reveals that the USDOC applied a computer programme that included an instruction to "zero" in the original investigation and in the First, Second and Third Administrative Reviews, for the purpose of calculating the WAMs and the ISARs of the relevant respondents. The evidence also shows that this instruction was actually executed in the first three administrative reviews under the orange juice anti-dumping duty order. Moreover, the Issues and Decision Memoranda from the three administrative reviews strongly suggest that, at the time they were issued, the USDOC intended to continue to take the same approach to calculating margins of dumping in the future. In this regard, we find the following USDOC statement, which appears in exactly the same language in all three Issues and Decision Memoranda, to be particularly revealing:

> "Section 771(35)(A) of the Act defines 'dumping margin' as the 'amount by which the normal value exceeds the export price or

---

290 Exhibits BRA-50 (Issues and Decision Memorandum), pp. 2-6; BRA-51 (BCI) (Ferrier Affidavit re 3rd Administrative Review); BRA-52 (BCI) (Programme log for Cutrale); BRA-54 (BCI) (Programme output for Cutrale); BRA-56 (BCI) (Programme log for Fischer); BRA-55 (BCI) (Programme output for Fischer). See also the summary of information on the use of "zeroing", submitted as Exhibit BRA-48.

291 US, Answer to Panel Question 24.

292 US, FWS, para. 126; US, Answer to Panel Question 24.

293 See, e.g., Appellate Body Report, *Guatemala – Anti-Dumping Investigation Regarding Portland Cement from Mexico* ("*Guatemala – Cement I*"), WT/DS60/AB/R, adopted 25 November 1998, DSR 1998:IX, 3767, para. 72.

> constructed export price of the subject merchandise'. Outside the context of antidumping investigations involving average-to-average comparisons, *the Department interprets this statutory definition to mean that a dumping margin exists only when NV is greater than EP or CEP. As no dumping margins exist with respect to sales where NV is equal to or less than EP or CEP, the Department will not permit these non-dumped sales to offset the amount of dumping found with respect to other sales. The CAFC has held that this is a reasonable interpretation of the statute.*"[294]

7.192 We recall that in *US – Continued Zeroing*, the evidence the Appellate Body considered was sufficient to establish the existence of the "continued zeroing" measure challenged in that dispute demonstrated that the USDOC: used "zeroing" in the original investigation; used "zeroing" in four successive administrative reviews; and relied in a sunset review upon margins of dumping determined through the use of "zeroing". Although the pattern of use of "zeroing" in the present dispute is not exactly the same, there is nevertheless, in our view, sufficient evidence to establish the existence of the "continued use" measure that Brazil challenges. Apart from the evidence showing the use of "zeroing procedures" in each of the successive proceedings, of particular significance are the statements contained in the Issues and Decision Memoranda, which in our view, leave little doubt about how the USDOC intended to interpret the notion of "dumping" in future proceedings under the orange juice anti-dumping duty order at the time the Memoranda were issued. Thus, we conclude that Brazil has established the existence of the USDOC's "continued use" of "zeroing procedures" as a "measure" in the form of "ongoing conduct" under the orange juice anti-dumping duty order.

(d) Whether the "measure" is inconsistent with Articles 2.4, 2.4.2 and 9.3 of the AD Agreement and Article VI:2 of the GATT 1994

7.193 We recall that we have already found that the USDOC's use of "simple zeroing" is inconsistent with Article 2.4 of the AD Agreement. In our view, it necessarily follows that the "continued use" of the "zeroing procedures" must also be inconsistent with the same provision. Thus, we find that the United States' "continued use" of "zeroing" under the orange juice anti-dumping duty order is inconsistent with Article 2.4 of the AD Agreement.

7.194 Brazil claims that the USDOC's "continued use" of "zeroing" is also inconsistent with Articles 2.4.2 and 9.3 of the AD Agreement and Article VI:2 of the GATT 1994. The United States submits that Brazil's reliance on Article 2.4.2 is misplaced because, in its view, the prohibition on "zeroing" in this provision is explicitly limited to the "investigation phase", which by definition does not include duty assessment proceedings or any other proceedings. Having found that

---

[294] Exhibits BRA-28, p 5; BRA-43, pp 4-5; and BRA-50, p 4.

the "continued zeroing" measure challenged by Brazil is inconsistent with Article 2.4 of the AD Agreement, we consider it is not necessary, for the purpose of satisfactorily resolving this dispute, to make additional findings with respect to the same measure under Articles 2.4.2 and 9.3 of the AD Agreement and Article VI:2 of the GATT 1994. On this basis, we decide to exercise judicial economy and decline to make any findings in respect of Brazil's claims under Articles 2.4.2 and 9.3 of the AD Agreement and Article VI:2 of the GATT 1994.

VIII. CONCLUSIONS AND RECOMMENDATIONS

A. Conclusions

8.1 As previously observed, the question at the centre of Brazil's complaint in this dispute has been well litigated in WTO dispute settlement. This core question concerns how the AD Agreement (and Article VI of the GATT 1994) defines the notion of "dumping": is it a concept that relates to an exporter's overall pricing behaviour that can only be measured with respect to the "product as a whole"; or can it also be conceived of and measured on a transaction-specific basis? Although fundamental and of critical importance to the operation of the AD Agreement, our evaluation of the parties' arguments and relevant jurisprudence has led us to conclude that there exists no *single* answer to this question. The objective lack of clarity on this issue, to some extent also recognized by the Appellate Body[295], lends legitimacy to both parties' positions. However, the Appellate Body has consistently only found room for there to be one permissible interpretation of "dumping"; and for the important systemic reasons described above[296], we have decided to follow this interpretation and come to the final conclusions expressed in this report. Nevertheless, we wish to once again emphasize that all Members have a strong systemic interest in seeing that a lasting resolution to the "zeroing" controversy is found sooner rather than later. In this regard, we note that Members have not only sought to resolve the issue of "zeroing" through WTO dispute settlement, but they are also trying to address it through negotiations in the Negotiating Group on Rules in the context of the Doha Development Agenda[297].

8.2 In the light of the findings set out in the foregoing sections of this Report, we conclude that Brazil ***has established*** that:

(a) the United States acted inconsistently with Article 2.4 of the AD Agreement when it used "simple zeroing" to determine the

[295] See, in particular, the Concurring Opinion of one Appellate Body Member in Appellate Body Report, *US – Continued Zeroing*, paras. 304-313.

[296] See above, paras. 7.132-7.135.

[297] See, e.g, Draft Consolidated Chair Texts of the AD and SCM Agreements, 30 November 2007, TN/RL/W/213; and New Draft Consolidated Chair Texts of the AD And SCM Agreements, 19 December 2008, TN/RL/W/236. We also note that Article 3.9 of the DSU states that its provisions are "without prejudice to the right of Members to seek authoritative interpretation of provisions of a covered agreement through decision-making under the WTO Agreement".

weighted-average margins of dumping (used to set the cash-deposit rates) and the importer-specific assessment rates of Cutrale and Fischer in the First and Second Administrative Reviews under the orange juice anti-dumping duty order; and

(b) the United States' "continued use" of "zeroing" in proceedings under the orange juice anti-dumping duty order is inconsistent with Article 2.4 of the AD Agreement.

8.3 Finally, in the light of the findings we have set out in paragraphs 8.2, we make no findings, based on judicial economy, in respect of Brazil's claims:

(a) under Article 9.3 of the AD Agreement and Article VI:2 of the GATT 1994, concerning the United States' alleged use of "simple zeroing" in the First and Second Administrative Reviews under the orange juice anti-dumping duty order; and

(b) under Articles 2.4.2 and 9.3 of the AD Agreement and Article VI:2 of the GATT 1994, concerning the United States' "continued use" of "zeroing" in proceedings under the orange juice anti-dumping duty order.

B. Recommendation

8.4 Pursuant to Article 3.8 of the DSU, in cases where there is infringement of the obligations assumed under a covered agreement, the action is considered *prima facie* to constitute a case of nullification or impairment of benefits under that agreement. Accordingly, we conclude that to the extent the United States has acted inconsistently with Article 2.4 of the AD Agreement, it has nullified or impaired benefits accruing to Brazil.

8.5 We recommend that the Dispute Settlement Body request the United States to bring its measures into conformity with its obligations under the AD Agreement.

ANNEX A

EXECUTIVE SUMMARY OF THE FIRST WRITTEN SUBMISSIONS OF THE PARTIES

ANNEX A-1

EXECUTIVE SUMMARY OF THE FIRST WRITTEN SUBMISSION OF BRAZIL

I. THE SUBJECT OF THE DISPUTE

1. This is yet another dispute in a long line of WTO challenges concerning the United States' "zeroing procedures". Including the present one, there have now been eleven disputes brought against the United States regarding zeroing, by eight different WTO Members, and, in each one so far decided, zeroing has been found to be WTO-inconsistent.

2. The current dispute concerns the United States' application of its zeroing procedures in the original anti-dumping investigation and administrative reviews of the anti-dumping duty order on certain orange juice from Brazil ("Orange Juice Order").[1] In the original investigation, in calculating the margin of dumping, the United States Department of Commerce ("USDOC") included its "model zeroing" procedures, under which the amount by which any model's average export price exceeded the average normal value for that model was eliminated or, in effect, set at zero ("zeroed").

3. In two administrative reviews of anti-dumping duties conducted since the issuance of the Orange Juice Order, the USDOC applied its "simple zeroing" procedures, under which the amount by which an individual export price exceeded normal value was ignored or zeroed. Individual export transactions with prices below normal value were treated under US law as having "dumping margins" or, in WTO parlance, "positive comparison results" in the amount of the

[1] 71 Fed. Reg. 12183 (9 March 2006). Exhibit BRA-3.

difference. On the other hand, the zeroing of the transactions with export prices above normal value means that the "negative comparison results" on these export sales are disregarded.

4. This dispute also concerns the USDOC's deliberate and continued use of its zeroing procedures in successive anti-dumping proceedings under the Orange Juice Order, including the original investigation and any subsequent administrative reviews, by which duties are applied and maintained over a period of time. This "ongoing conduct" continues to this day, as the USDOC is now imposing duties on entries of merchandise covered by the Orange Juice Order pursuant to the results of the second administrative review, and as it is conducting its third administrative review under the Orange Juice Order, again using zeroing.

5. The Appellate Body has, on numerous occasions, found that both model zeroing in investigations and simple zeroing in administrative reviews are inconsistent with the obligations of the GATT 1994 and the *Anti-Dumping Agreement*.

6. In light of the Appellate Body's consistent findings regarding the WTO-inconsistency of zeroing, Brazil's claims in this dispute are simple and straightforward. Brazil asks this Panel to find that (i) the two administrative reviews completed to date in respect of imports subject to the Orange Juice Order are inconsistent with Article VI:2 of the GATT 1994 and Article 9.3 of the *Anti-Dumping Agreement* due to the application of the zeroing procedures. Brazil also asks this Panel to rule that (ii) the continued use of the US zeroing procedures in successive anti-dumping proceedings in relation to the Orange Juice Order, including the original investigation and any subsequent administrative reviews, by which duties are applied and maintained over a period of time, is inconsistent with Article VI:2 of the GATT 1994 and Articles 2.4.2 and 9.3 of the *Anti-Dumping Agreement.*

II. ZEROING IS PROHIBITED UNDER THE GATT 1994 AND THE *ANTI-DUMPING AGREEMENT*

A. The Concepts of Dumping and Margins of Dumping under the GATT 1994 and the Anti-Dumping Agreement

7. According to the Appellate Body, there are three key elements to the definition of the concepts of "dumping" and "margin of dumping".[2] First, these linked concepts are defined in terms of a "product"; second, dumping determinations for the "product" are made with respect to an exporter or foreign producer; and, third, the WTO agreements are not concerned with "dumping" *per se*, but with injurious dumping.

8. Addressing these elements in greater detail, first, Article VI:I of the GATT 1994 defines dumping as occurring when "*products*" of one country are sold at less than the normal value of the "*products*". This definition of "dump-

[2] Appellate Body Report, *US – Zeroing (Japan)*, paras. 108 – 116.

ing" is carried into the *Anti-Dumping Agreement* by Article 2.1, which states that "*a product*" is "dumped" if it is exported at less than the comparable price of the like "*product*". The definition of "dumping" in Article VI:1 of the GATT 1994 is an important element of the context of Article VI:2, which refers to the "margin of dumping", inasmuch as Article VI:2 clarifies that the "margin of dumping" is determined in respect of a dumped "product".

9. Second, the elements of the definition of "dumping" in Article VI:1 of the GATT 1994 and Article 2.1 of the *Anti-Dumping Agreement* indicate that these provisions address the pricing practice of an exporter or foreign producer. The definition provides that "dumping" occurs when a product is "*introduced* into the commerce of *another country*" at an "*export price*" that is less than the "comparable price for the like product in the *exporting country*". These and other provisions of the GATT 1994 and the *Anti-Dumping Agreement* make clear that a dumping determination focuses on the pricing behavior of individual exporters or foreign producers with a view to calculating a single margin for them with respect to the product as a whole.

10. Third, the *Anti-Dumping Agreement* and the GATT 1994 are not concerned with dumping *per se*, but with dumping that causes or threatens to cause material injury to the domestic industry. Further, it is evident from Article 3.1 that the volume of transactions matters: injury cannot be found to exist in relation to individual transactions, but only for the *product as whole*.

11. On the basis of these three intertwining strands of analysis, the Appellate Body concluded that the concepts of "dumping" and "margin of dumping" are defined in relation to a product under investigation as a whole, encompassing all of the export transactions of the product pertaining to an investigated exporter, and they cannot be found to exist only for a type, model or category of a product. Thus, although an investigating authority may undertake multiple comparisons using averaging groups or models, the results of these comparisons are not "margins of dumping", but rather intermediate comparison results that must be aggregated to establish, for each exporter, a margin of dumping for the product under investigation as a whole.

B. Zeroing Is Prohibited under Article 9.3 of the Anti-Dumping Agreement and Article VI:2 of the GATT 1994

12. The opening phrase of Article 2.1 of the *Anti-Dumping Agreement* – "[f]or the purpose of this Agreement" – makes clear that the term "dumping" has the same meaning in all provisions of the *Agreement* and for all types of anti-dumping proceedings, including administrative reviews under Article 9.3. This understanding is confirmed by the text of Article 9.3, which provides that the "amount of the anti-dumping duty shall not exceed the margin of dumping as established under Article 2".

13. Pursuant to these provisions, the Appellate Body has held that, "[i]n a review proceeding under Article 9.3.1, the authority is required to ensure that the total amount of anti-dumping duties ... does not exceed the total amount of

dumping found in all sales made by the exporter or foreign producer, calculated according to the margin of dumping established for that exporter".[3] In other words, "under Article VI:2 and Article 9.3, the margin of dumping established for an exporter in accordance with Article 2 operates as a *ceiling* for the total amount of anti-dumping duties that can be levied on the entries of the subject merchandise from that exporter".[4]

14. The United States contravenes this obligation, because it does not calculate a margin of dumping for each exporter based on all the export transactions made by the exporter, and as a result, it does not ensure that the total margin of dumping for each exporter functions as a ceiling on the amount of anti-dumping duties that are levied on entries of that exporter's subject merchandise. Rather, the USDOC includes only those intermediate comparison results for export transactions with prices below normal value. Any export transactions with prices greater than normal value are disregarded, or "zeroed" when calculating the aggregate amount of the price differences.

15. By disregarding or treating as zero those comparison results for export prices that are greater than normal value, the USDOC's use of zeroing necessarily results in dumping margins that are higher than they would be if all export transactions were taken into account. This is because those price comparisons that generate "negative" comparison results – where export prices are higher than normal value – are not considered in the aggregate of the comparison results. They therefore cannot reduce the "positive" comparison results generated by those export transactions below normal value. By systematically excluding transactions with prices above normal value, the USDOC's use of zeroing generates dumping margins that are greater than the margins properly determined for "the product under investigation as a whole". Hence, the USDOC's use of zeroing in administrative reviews violates Article VI:2 of GATT 1994 and Article 9.3 of the *Anti-Dumping Agreement*.

16. This conclusion is confirmed by a consistent series of Appellate Body decisions. The Appellate Body first addressed the USDOC's practice of zeroing in administrative reviews in *US – Zeroing (EC)*. In that instance, the Appellate Body found that, by disregarding, "at the aggregation stage", all comparisons where "the export price exceeded the contemporaneous average normal value", the USDOC's methodology "is inconsistent with Article 9.3 of the *Anti-Dumping Agreement* and Article VI:2 of the GATT 1994".[5]

17. In at least four further rulings since *US – Zeroing (EC),* the Appellate Body has affirmed its ruling that the use of zeroing in administrative reviews is inconsistent with the GATT 1994 and the *Anti-dumping Agreement*.[6] Among

---

[3] Appellate Body Report, *US – Zeroing (Japan)*, para. 156.

[4] Appellate Body Report, *US – Stainless Steel (Mexico)*, para. 102. Original emphasis. *See* also Appellate Body Report, *US – Zeroing (EC)*, para. 130.

[5] Appellate Body Report, *US – Zeroing (EC)*, para. 133.

[6] In addition to Appellate Body Report, *US – Zeroing (EC)*, para. 135: Appellate Body Reports, *US – Zeroing (Japan)*, para. 176; *US – Stainless Steel (Mexico)*, para. 139; *US – Continued Zeroing (EC)*, para. 316; and *US – Zeroing (Japan) (21.5)*, paras. 195 and 197.

these rulings, the Appellate Body, in *US – Stainless Steel (Mexico)*, stated the conclusion succinctly: "We see no basis in Article VI:2 of the GATT 1994 or in Articles 2 and 9.3 of the *Anti-Dumping Agreement* for disregarding the results of comparison where the export price exceeds the normal value when calculating the margin of dumping for an exporter".[7] In light of this long line of decisions by the Appellate Body, there is no doubt that USDOC's use of zeroing in administrative reviews is inconsistent with the GATT 1994 and the *Anti-dumping Agreement.*

III. THE UNITED STATES VIOLATED ITS OBLIGATIONS BY USING ZEROING IN TWO ADMINISTRATIVE REVIEWS

18. The USDOC has completed two administrative reviews of exports of certain orange juice from Brazil since the anti-dumping duty order on this product was fist issued. The first administrative review covered exports by Cutrale and Fischer, the principal exporters of this product, for the period between 24 August 2005 and 28 February 2007. The second administrative review covered exports by Cutrale and Fischer between 1 March 2007 and 29 February 2008.

19. In the first administrative review the USDOC applied zeroing to exports by both Cutrale and Fischer, despite written objections from both companies that this practice violated the *Anti-Dumping Agreement* and the GATT 1994. In its Issues and Decision Memorandum in that review, the USDOC stated explicitly that "the Department has continued to deny offsets to dumping based on export transactions that exceed NV in this review".[8] Thus, the USDOC admitted that it used zeroing to exclude negative comparison results, derived from export transactions with prices above normal value, in its calculation of the overall dumping margin for each exporter.

20. This conclusion is confirmed by the computer program logs containing the computer programming language used by the USDOC to calculate cash deposit and duty assessment rates for both Cutrale and Fischer[9], and by the computer outputs generated in carrying out this calculation.[10] These documents show that the USDOC's programs excluded all negative comparison results – where export transaction prices were at or above normal value – despite the fact that for both companies these negative comparison results constituted a majority of the transactions under review. The "cash deposit rates" and the "importer-specific assessment rates" applied to both Cutrale and Fischer therefore overstated the dumping margins for both companies by failing to include all export transactions in the calculations.

---

7 Appellate Body Report, *US – Stainless Steel (Mexico)*, para. 103.

8 Exhibit BRA-28.

9 Exhibits BRA-29 and BRA-30.

10 Exhibits BRA-34 and BRA-35. *See* also Exhibit BRA-31, an expert affidavit that explains the USDOC's procedures and, in particular, the specific portions of the USDOC's computer program logs and outputs showing the use of zeroing.

21. In the second administrative review the Department again applied its policy of zeroing over the protests of both Cutrale and Fischer. In its Issues and Decision Memorandum, the Department stated even more explicitly than it had in the previous review, that it had excluded from its calculations those sales with negative comparison results. The Department said that it applied the policy "by aggregating all individual dumping margins, *each of which is determined by the amount by which NV exceeds EP* or CEP, and dividing this amount by the value of all sales. At no stage of the process is the amount by which EP or CEP exceed the NV permitted to offset or cancel out the dumping margins found on other sales".[11]

22. Responding to Cutrale's and Fischer's claims that this methodology violated the *Anti-Dumping Agreement* and the GATT 1994, the USDOC stated flatly that "Congress did not intend for WTO reports to automatically trump the exercise of the Department's discretion in applying the statute". Therefore, the USDOC said that it "has continued to deny offsets to duping based on CEP transactions that exceed NV in this review".

23. Again, the computer logs and outputs generated during the second administrative review confirm the USDOC's statements that it applied zeroing to exclude price comparisons where export prices were at or above normal value.[12] They show that the USDOC ignored the comparison results for a significant number of export transactions for Cutrale, and for the vast majority of export transactions for Fischer. The exclusion of these export transactions resulted in higher cash deposit and importer-specific assessment rates than would have been calculated for Cutrale had all export transactions been included in the calculation. For Fischer, the positive comparisons were too small in number to generate a margin of dumping, and the cash deposit rate was zero.

24. Since the USDOC has admitted that it applied zeroing in both administrative reviews to exclude transaction comparisons where the export price was at or above normal value, and since the computer program logs submitted by Brazil in both administrative reviews confirm this result, as do the outputs also submitted by Brazil, there is no doubt that the USDOC applied zeroing in both administrative reviews. Equally, there is no doubt, as the Appellate Body has said repeatedly, that the USDOC's practice of zeroing in administrative reviews is inconsistent with Article 9.3 of the *Anti-Dumping Agreement* and Article VI:2 of the GATT 1994.

---

[11] Exhibit BRA-43.

[12] Exhibits BRA-36, BRA-38 (computer program logs), BRA-37 and BRA-39 (computer program outputs).

IV. THE USDOC'S CONTINUED USE OF ZEROING AND ITS APPLICATION OF DUTIES CALCULATED USING ZEROING IS INCONSISTENT WITH THE GATT 1994 AND THE *ANTI-DUMPING AGREEMENT*

25. The USDOC has, to date, used its zeroing procedures in the first three proceedings that have taken place on this product – (1) the original anti-dumping investigation; (2) the first administrative review; and (3) the second administrative review. Moreover, it has used zeroing in reaching its preliminary determination in the third administrative review.[13] Together, these successive determinations constitute an "ongoing conduct" inconsistent with the requirements of the *Anti-Dumping Agreement* and the GATT 1994.

26. In the original anti-dumping investigation, the USDOC calculated the "dumping margin" using a comparison of weighted-average prices of each model sold in the United States to the normal value of that model. At the time when the final determination was made in the original investigation, the USDOC systematically applied this "model" zeroing to its price comparisons. The computer program used in the original investigation, as shown by the computer program logs submitted as Exhibits BRA-32 and BRA-33, provided for the exclusion from the calculation of negative comparison results where the weighted-average export price exceeded normal value.

27. The original investigation has been followed by two completed administrative reviews to date. In both of these reviews, as discussed above, the USDOC applied "simple zeroing" to exclude any US transactions whose price comparisons showed export prices at or above normal value. A third administrative review is currently in progress, and to date it has resulted in a preliminary determination in which the USDOC again applied simple zeroing. Accordingly, use of zeroing is common to all the successive stages of the case at issue, with the USDOC adopting a "string of connected and sequential determinations"[14] in which it disregarded comparison results where the price of the exports exceeded normal value. This string of determinations has provided a continuing basis for the United States to apply and maintain anti-dumping duties on imports of certain orange juice from Brazil since 9 March 2006.

28. In *US – Continued Zeroing (EC)*, the Appellate Body found that the use of the zeroing methodology in an original investigation and "successive stages" of administrative reviews constitute an "ongoing conduct" that amount to a "measure" subject to challenge in WTO dispute settlement.[15] The ongoing conduct at issue in that dispute is virtually identical to the ongoing conduct at issue in this dispute. Both disputes concern the continued use of the zeroing methodology in successive phases of an anti-dumping proceeding under a particular

---

13 *See* Exhibit BRA-20, "Summary of Information on the Use of Zeroing".

14 Appellate Body Report, *US – Continued Zeroing (EC)*, para. 180.

15 Appellate Body Report, *US – Continued Zeroing (EC)*, para. 185.

anti-dumping order whereby the USDOC applies and maintains anti-dumping duties.

29. The USDOC's zeroing procedures, as used in the original investigation and in the administrative reviews in this case, have repeatedly been found to be inconsistent with Article VI:2 of the GATT 1994 and Articles 2.4.2 and 9.3 of the *Anti-Dumping Agreement*. Consequently, the continued use of zeroing in these consecutive anti-dumping determinations constitutes an ongoing conduct that violates these provisions of the GATT 1994 and the *Anti-Dumping Agreement*.

ANNEX A-2

EXECUTIVE SUMMARY OF THE FIRST WRITTEN SUBMISSION OF THE UNITED STATES

I. INTRODUCTION

1. In this dispute, Brazil asks this Panel to read an obligation into the *Agreement on Implementation of Article VI of the General Agreement on Tariffs and Trade 1994* ("AD Agreement") and Article VI of the *General Agreement on Tariffs and Trade 1994* ("GATT 1994"), notwithstanding the fact that there is no textual basis for the obligation that Brazil proposes. This Panel should make an objective assessment of the matter before it and refrain from adopting Brazil's interpretation.

2. Brazil also challenges two "measures" that are not within the Panel's terms of reference. The United States requests that the Panel grant the requests for preliminary rulings with respect to these "measures".

II. GENERAL PRINCIPLES

3. The burden of proving that an obligation has not been satisfied is on the complaining party. In a dispute involving the AD Agreement, a panel must also take into account the standard of review set forth in Article 17.6(ii) of the AD Agreement. Article 17.6(ii) confirms that there are provisions of the Agreement that "admit[] of more than one permissible interpretation". Where that is the case, and where the investigating authority has relied upon one such interpretation, a panel is to find that interpretation to be in conformity with the Agreement.

4. Article 11 of the Dispute Settlement Understanding ("DSU") requires a panel to make an objective assessment of the matter before it, including an objective assessment of the facts and the applicability of and conformity with the relevant covered agreements. The Appellate Body has explained that the matter includes both the facts of the case (and the specific measures at issue in particular) and the legal claims raised.

5. Articles 3.2 and 19.2 of the DSU contain the fundamental principle that the findings and recommendations of a panel or the Appellate Body, and the recommendations and rulings of the Dispute Settlement Body ("DSB"), cannot add to or diminish the rights and obligations provided in the covered agreements. While prior adopted panel and Appellate Body reports create legitimate expectations among WTO Members, the Panel is not bound to follow the reasoning set forth in any Appellate Body report. The rights and obligations of the Members flow, not from panel or Appellate Body reports, but from the text of the covered agreements.

III. REQUESTS FOR PRELIMINARY RULINGS

A. The Second Administrative Review

6. A Member may only file a panel request with respect to a measure upon which the consultations process has run its course. Article 4.7 of the DSU provides that a complaining party may request establishment of a panel only if "the consultations fail to settle a dispute". Article 4.4 of the DSU, in turn, provides that a request for consultations must state the reasons for the request, "including identification of the measure at issue and an indication of the legal basis for the complaint". These rules apply with equal force to disputes brought under the AD Agreement, which contains parallel requirements in Articles 17.3 through 17.5.

7. In this dispute, Brazil seeks the establishment of a panel with respect to "[t]he 2007-2008 anti-dumping duty administrative review on certain orange juice from Brazil (the 'Second Administrative Review')". However, the final results of the second administrative review were issued after Brazil's request for consultations. As such, at the time of Brazil's consultations request, the second administrative review did not constitute a "measure" within the meaning of Article 4.4 of the DSU. As it was not, and could not have been, subject to consultations, the second administrative review is not within the Panel's terms of reference.

B. The "Continued Use of the US 'Zeroing Procedures'"

8. Under Article 6.2 of the DSU, a panel request must identify the "*specific* measure at issue in the dispute", and a panel's terms of reference under Article 7.1 are limited to those specific measures. Brazil's identification of the "continued use of the US 'zeroing procedures' in successive anti-dumping proceedings, in relation to the anti-dumping duty order issued in respect of imports of certain orange juice from Brazil" as a "measure" in its panel request fails to meet this requirement. A general reference to an indeterminate number of potential measures does not satisfy the requirement that a panel request identify the "*specific* measure at issue". Brazil is merely speculating as to what may happen in the future, and such speculation is not identification of a specific measure. There is no basis to conclude, for example, that the results of any future antidumping proceeding with respect to orange juice from Brazil would reflect "zeroing".

9. By including this purported measure in its panel request, Brazil appears to be challenging an indeterminate number of potential measures. However, measures that are not yet in existence at the time of panel establishment are not within a panel's terms of reference under the DSU. It is impossible for Members to consult on a measure that does not exist, and a non-existent measure cannot meet the requirement of Article 4.2 of the DSU that the measure be "affecting" the operation of a covered agreement.

10. Article 3.3 of the DSU provides that

> [t]he prompt settlement of situations in which a Member considers that any benefits accruing to it directly or indirectly under the covered agreements are being impaired by measures taken by another Member is essential to the effective functioning of the WTO and the maintenance of a proper balance between the rights and obligations of Members.

Accordingly, in *US – Upland Cotton*, the panel found that a measure that had not yet been adopted could not form part of its terms of reference, noting that such a "measure" could not have been impairing any benefits because it was not in existence at the time of the panel request. Similarly, in this case, indeterminate future measures that did not exist at the time of Brazil's panel request, and may in fact never exist, could not be impairing any benefits accruing to Brazil.

IV. BRAZIL'S CLAIMS REGARDING ASSESSMENT PROCEEDINGS SHOULD BE REJECTED

11. Brazil challenges the first and second administrative reviews as inconsistent with Article VI:2 of the GATT 1994 and Article 9.3 of the AD Agreement. The U.S. Department of Commerce ("Commerce") reviewed two companies in each of these reviews: Fischer and Cutrale. Aside from the fact that the second administrative review is outside the Panel's terms of reference, Brazil's claims with respect to these reviews should be rejected for the reasons below.

12. The AD Agreement provides no general obligation to consider transactions for which the export price exceeds normal value as an offset to the amount of dumping found in relation to other transactions at less than normal value. In *US – Softwood Lumber Dumping (AB)*, the Appellate Body found that the exclusive textual basis for an obligation to account for such non-dumping in calculating margins of dumping appears in connection with the obligation in Article 2.4.2 that "the existence of margins of dumping during the investigation phase shall normally be established on the basis of a comparison of a *weighted average normal value with a weighted average of prices of all comparable export transactions* ... ". This particular text of Article 2.4.2 applies only within the limited context of determining whether dumping exists in the investigation phase when using the average-to-average comparison methodology in Article 2.4.2. There is no textual basis for the additional obligations that Brazil would have this Panel impose.

13. Subsequent to *US – Softwood Lumber Dumping (AB)*, several panels examined whether the obligation not to "zero" when making average-to-average comparisons in an investigation extended beyond that context. In making an objective assessment of the matter, these panels determined that the customary rules of interpretation of public international law do not support a reading of the AD Agreement that expands the zeroing prohibition beyond average-to-average comparisons in an investigation. This Panel should likewise find that, at a minimum, it is permissible to interpret the AD Agreement as not prohibiting zeroing

outside the context where the interpretation of "all comparable export transactions" articulated in the Appellate Body report in *US – Softwood Lumber Dumping* is applicable.

14. In *US – Softwood Lumber Dumping (AB),* the Appellate Body specifically recognized that the issue before it was whether so-called "zeroing" was prohibited under the average-to-average comparison methodology found in Article 2.4.2. Thus, the report found only that "zeroing is prohibited when establishing the existence of margins of dumping under the weighted-average-to-weighted-average methodology". The Appellate Body reached this conclusion by interpreting the terms "margins of dumping" and "all comparable export transactions" as they are used in Article 2.4.2 in an "integrated manner". The obligation to provide offsets, therefore, was tied to text of the provision addressing the use of the average-to-average comparison methodology in an investigation, and did not arise out of any independent obligation to offset prices. An assertion by Brazil that there is a general prohibition of "zeroing", or one specifically applicable to the more particular context of assessment proceedings, cannot be reconciled with the interpretation articulated in *US – Softwood Lumber Dumping (AB)*. If there is a general prohibition of zeroing that applies in all proceedings and under all comparison methodologies, the meaning ascribed to "all comparable export transactions" in that dispute would be redundant of the general prohibition of zeroing.

15. The need to avoid such redundancy was recognized in *US – Zeroing (Japan)(AB)* when the Appellate Body changed its interpretation of this phrase. In *US – Softwood Lumber Dumping (AB)*, "margins of dumping" and "all comparable export transactions" were interpreted in an integrated manner. The Appellate Body found that in aggregating the results of the model-specific comparisons, "all" comparable export transactions must be accounted for. Thus, the phrase necessarily referred to all transactions across all models of the product under investigation, *i.e.* the product "as a whole". However, in *US – Zeroing (Japan)(AB)*, the Appellate Body reinterpreted "all comparable export transactions" to relate solely to all transactions within a model, and not across models of the product under investigation. In doing so, the Appellate Body abandoned the only textual basis for its reasoning in *US – Softwood Lumber Dumping (AB).*

16. In addition, a general prohibition of zeroing that applies beyond the context of average-to-average comparisons in investigations would be inconsistent with the remaining text of Article 2.4.2, which provides for an exceptional methodology that may be used in certain circumstances. This methodology was drafted as an exception to the obligation to engage in symmetrical comparisons in an investigation. The mathematical implication of a general prohibition of zeroing, however, is that the exceptional clause would be reduced to inutility. That is because the exceptional methodology, provided for in Article 2.4.2, mathematically must yield the same result as an average-to-average comparison if, in both cases, non-dumped comparisons are required to offset dumped comparisons. In this respect, a general prohibition of zeroing would render the exception in Article 2.4.2 a nullity. Such an interpretation would be disfavoured

under a key tenet of customary rules of treaty interpretation, that an interpretation must give meaning and effect to all the terms of a treaty.

17. In *US – Zeroing (EC)*, *US – Softwood Lumber Dumping (Article 21.5)*, *US – Zeroing (Japan)*, and *US – Stainless Steel (Mexico)*, each of the panels recognized that the customary rules of interpretation of public international law precluded an interpretation that rendered the exceptional provision of Article 2.4.2 redundant. Brazil has not offered any explanation as to how this defect is avoided under its interpretation of the AD Agreement.

18. Despite the findings of the panels that the results of the exceptional methodology "will necessarily always yield a result identical to that of an average-to-average comparison," under a general prohibition of zeroing, the Appellate Body has found this concern to be "overstated". The Appellate Body has asserted that mathematical equivalence will occur only in "certain situations" and represents "a non-tested hypothesis". These objections, however, are not persuasive. First, the panels have specifically addressed all of the situations under which it was argued that mathematical equivalence would not obtain and found these situations did not represent methodologies consistent with the AD Agreement. The exceptional provision is rendered inutile if the only alternative methodologies that do not result in mathematical equivalence are, themselves, not consistent with the AD Agreement.

19. In *US – Zeroing (Japan)*, the Appellate Body dismissed the redundancy caused by mathematical equivalence by concluding that it may be permissible to apply the exceptional methodology to a subset of export transactions. The AD Agreement says nothing about selecting a subset of transactions when conducting an analysis under the second sentence of Article 2.4.2. The exception provides that, when certain conditions are met, Members are permitted to compare average normal values to transaction-specific export prices. If the Appellate Body is correct that dumping may only be determined for the product as a whole (which the United States does not concede), there is no textual basis for inferring that the comparison methodology in the second sentence of Article 2.4.2 is an exception to that provision (which, as Article 2.1 provides, applies throughout the AD Agreement). The second sentence of Article 2.4.2 simply provides an exception to the average-to-average or transaction-to-transaction comparison requirement of the first sentence of Article 2.4.2. Consequently, the use of a subset of export transactions as a means of avoiding mathematical equivalency would also appear to be inconsistent with the AD Agreement. The redundancy of the second sentence of Article 2.4.2 occurs as a consequence of any interpretation that results in a general prohibition of "zeroing".

20. Article 2.1 of the AD Agreement and Article VI:1 of the GATT 1994 are definitional provisions that do not impose independent obligations. Article 2.1 of the AD Agreement and Article VI of the GATT 1994 do not define "dumping" and "margins of dumping" so as to require that export transactions be examined at an aggregate level. The definition of "dumping" in these provisions references "product ... introduced into the commerce of another country at less than its nor-

mal value". This definition describes the real-world commercial conduct by which a product is imported into a country, *i.e.*, transaction by transaction.

21. In addition, the term "less than normal value" is defined as when the "price of the product exported ... is less than the comparable price ...". This definition describes the real-world commercial conduct of pricing such that one price is less than another price. The ordinary meaning of "price" as used in the definition of dumping is the "payment in purchase of something". In *US – Zeroing (Japan)*, the panel found that this definition "can easily be applied to individual transactions and does not require an examination of export transactions at an aggregate level".

22. There is nothing in the GATT 1994 or the AD Agreement that suggests that injurious dumping that occurs with respect to one transaction is mitigated by the occurrence of another transaction made at a non-dumped price. Indeed, the foreign producer or exporter itself exclusively enjoys the benefit of the extent to which the price of a non-dumped export transaction exceeds normal value.

23. In *US – Zeroing (Japan)*, the panel noted that "the record of past discussions in the framework of GATT shows that historically the concept of dumping has been understood to be applicable at the level of individual export transactions". Well before the recent debate about "zeroing", a Group of Experts convened to consider issues with respect to the application of Article VI of the GATT 1947. The Group of Experts considered that the "ideal method" for applying antidumping duties "was to make a determination of both dumping and material injury in respect of each single importation of the product concerned". The methodology of not offsetting dumping based on comparisons where the export price was greater than normal value was examined by two GATT panels and found to be consistent with the Antidumping Code. In view of these findings, the Uruguay Round negotiators actively discussed whether the use of "zeroing" should be restricted. The text of Article VI of the GATT 1947, however, did not change as a result of the Uruguay Round agreements. The normal inference one draws from the absence of a change in language is that the drafters intended no change in meaning.

24. Brazil's claim ultimately depends on the reasoning set forth in Appellate Body reports that rejected the notion that dumping may occur with respect to an individual transaction in the absence of the textual basis that was present in *EC – Bed Linen (AB)* and *US – Softwood Lumber Dumping (AB)*. This interpretation relies on the term "product" as being solely and exclusively synonymous with the concept of "product as a whole". It denies that the ordinary meaning of the word "product" or "products" used in Article 2.1 of the AD Agreement and Article VI of the GATT 1994 admits of a meaning that is transaction-specific. However, as the panel report in *US – Zeroing (Japan)* explained, "[T]here is nothing inherent in the word 'product[]' (as used in Article VI:1 of the GATT 1994 and Article 2.1 of AD Agreement) to suggest that this word should preclude the possibility of establishing margins of dumping on a transaction-specific basis ...".

25. Examination of the term "product" as used throughout the AD Agreement and the GATT 1994 demonstrates that the term "product" in these provisions does not exclusively refer to "product as a whole." Instead, "product" can have either a collective meaning or an individual meaning. Therefore, the words "product" and "products" as they appear in Article 2.1 of the AD Agreement and Article VI of the GATT 1994 cannot be understood to provide a textual basis for an interpretation requiring that margins of dumping established in relation to the "product" must necessarily be established on an aggregate basis for the "product as a whole".

26. Likewise, examination of the term "margins of dumping" itself provides no support for Brazil's interpretation of the term as solely, and exclusively, relating to the "product as a whole". As the panel in *US – Softwood Lumber Dumping (Article 21.5)* observed:

> [T]here is dumping when the export "price" is *less* than the normal value. Given this definition of dumping, and the express linkage between this definition and the phrase "price difference", it would be permissible for a Member to interpret the "price difference" referred to in Article VI:2 as the amount by which the export price is less than normal value, and to refer to that "price difference" as the "margin of dumping".

Thus, the panel saw "no reason why a Member may not ... establish the 'margin of dumping' on the basis of the total amount by which transaction-specific export prices are less than the transaction-specific normal values".

27. Additionally, the term "margin of dumping", as used elsewhere in the GATT 1994 and the AD Agreement, does not refer exclusively to the aggregated results of comparisons for the "product as a whole". As used in the Note Ad Article VI:1, which provides for importer-specific price comparison, the term "margin of dumping" cannot relate to aggregated results of all comparisons for the "product as a whole" because an exporter or foreign producer may make export transactions using multiple importers. As used in Article 2.2 of the AD Agreement, the term "margin of dumping" would require the use of constructed value for the "product as a whole", even if the condition precedent for using constructed value under Article 2.2 relates only to a portion of the comparisons. The panel in *US – Softwood Lumber Dumping (21.5)* observed that this "would run counter to the principle that constructed normal value is an alternative to be used only in the limited circumstances provided for in Article 2.2".

28. Brazil argues that "'dumping and 'margin of dumping' are exporter-related concepts". However, individual transactions are exporter-specific; dumping may be both exporter-specific and transaction-specific at the same time. And, as explained above, the term "margin of dumping", as defined in Article 2.1 of the AD Agreement and Article VI of the GATT 1994, may be applied to individual transactions. This understanding of the term "margin of dumping" is particularly appropriate in the context of antidumping duty assessment. In administering antidumping regimes, the individual transactions are both the means by which less

than fair value prices are established and the mechanism by which the object of the transaction (i.e., the "product") is "introduced into the commerce of the importing country". Likewise, antidumping duties are assessed on individual entries resulting from those individual transactions. Thus, the obligation in Article 9.3 to assess no more in antidumping duties than the margin of dumping is similarly applicable at the level of individual transactions.

29. In Brazil's view, a Member breaches Article 9.3 of the AD Agreement and Article VI:2 of the GATT 1994 by failing to provide offsets because Members are required to calculate margins of dumping on an exporter-specific basis for the product "*as a whole*" and, consequently, a Member is required to aggregate the results of "*all*" "*intermediate comparisons*", including those for which the export price exceeds the normal value. The terms upon which Brazil's interpretation rests are conspicuously absent from the text of both Articles 2.1 and 9.3 and Article VI:2. Brazil's interpretation is not mandated by the definition of dumping contained in Article 2.1, as described above.

30. The panel in *US – Zeroing (Japan)* correctly rejected the conclusion that the "margin of dumping under Article 9.3 must be determined on the basis of an aggregate examination of export prices during a review period in which export prices above the normal value carry the same weight as export prices below the normal value ...". The panel explained that the importer- and import-specific obligation to pay an antidumping duty "lend[s] further support to the view ... that there is no general requirement to determine dumping and margins of dumping for the product as a whole, which, ... entails a general prohibition of zeroing".

31. Although dumping involves differential pricing behavior of exporters or producers between its export market and its normal value, dumping nevertheless occurs at the level of individual transactions. Moreover, the remedy for dumping provided for in Article VI:2 of GATT 1994, *i.e.*, antidumping duties, are applied at the level of individual entries for which importers incur the liability. This way, the importer may be induced to raise resale prices to cover the amount of the antidumping duty, thereby preventing the dumping from having further injurious effect. If, instead, the amount of the duty must be reduced to account for the amount by which some other transaction was sold at above normal value, possibly involving an entirely different importer, then the antidumping duty will be insufficient to have the intended effect. The importer of the dumped product would remain in a position to profitably resell the product at a price that continues to be injuriously dumped. For this reason, if Brazil's interpretation of the margin of dumping is adopted as the sole permissible interpretation of Article 9.3, the remedy provided under the AD Agreement and the GATT 1994 will be prevented from addressing injurious dumping. If a Member is unable to calculate and assess the duties on a transaction-specific basis, importers of the merchandise for which the amount of dumping is greatest will actually have an advantage over their competitors who import at fair value prices because they will enjoy the benefit of offsets that result from their competitors' fairly priced imports.

32. Brazil's argument that "dumping" must cause or threaten injury does not preclude an interpretation that dumping can occur at the level of individual trans-

actions in assessment proceedings. No Article 3 injury determination is required in Article 9.3 assessment proceedings. Article 9, by its terms, focuses on the amount of duty to be assessed on particular entries, an exercise that is distinct from the determination of injury or threat of injury that would have already been addressed in the affirmative in the investigation phrase.

33. Brazil's interpretation of Article 9.3, requiring that antidumping duty liability be determined for the product "as a whole", is also inconsistent with the specific provision in Article 9 that recognizes the existence of prospective normal value systems of assessment. Because in a prospective normal value system, liability for antidumping duties is incurred only to the extent that prices of individual export transaction are below the normal value, the panel in *US – Zeroing (Japan)* concluded, "the fact that express provision is made in the AD Agreement for this sort of system confirms that the concept of dumping can apply on a transaction-specific basis to prices of individual export transactions below the normal value and that the AD Agreement does not require that in calculating margins of dumping the same significance be accorded to export prices above the normal value as to export prices below the normal value". And, as the panel in *US – Stainless Steel (Mexico)* found, if in a prospective normal value system individual export transactions at prices less than normal value can attract liability for payment of antidumping duties, without regard to whether or not prices of other export transactions exceed normal value, there is no reason why liability for payment of antidumping duties may not be similarly assessed on the basis of export prices less than normal value in a retrospective system.

34. The Appellate Body has disagreed, stating that the duty collected at the time of importation under a prospective normal value system does not represent the margin of dumping within the meaning of Article 9.3 and noting such duty is subject to review under Article 9.3.2. But, to the extent that (as the Appellate Body suggests) Article 9.3 requires consideration of the "product as a whole", an importer seeking a refund in a prospective normal value system would have to provide evidence that relates to the "product as a whole", not just its own entries. This would make it difficult, if not impossible, for an importer to obtain a refund. Further, accepting Brazil's interpretation that a Member must aggregate the results of "*all*" comparisons on an exporter-specific basis would require that retrospective reviews be conducted, even in a prospective normal value systems, in order to take into account "*all*" of the exporters' transactions. This result is contrary to the very concept of the prospective normal value system.

35. For all of these reasons, because the conclusion that there is no general prohibition of "zeroing" in assessment proceedings is, at a minimum, a permissible interpretation of the covered agreements, the Panel should reject Brazil's claims.

36. Even under Brazil's interpretation of the scope of a Member's obligations, Brazil has not met its burden of proof as a factual matter. In the first administrative review, Commerce determined a *de minimis* margin of dumping for Cutrale. In the second administrative review, Commerce determined a zero margin of dumping and assessed no antidumping duties for Fischer. A zero or *de minimis*

margin of dumping cannot exceed any "ceiling" Brazil argues is provided for in the covered agreements, and, where no duties are assessed, no duties are imposed in excess of the margin of dumping, even under Brazil's interpretation of the obligations of those agreements. Additionally, Brazil has failed to meet its burden of proof to show that "zeroing" was used in the first administrative review with respect to Fischer. Brazil provided a margin program log that was generated after the first administrative review had been completed, which must have been run by someone other than Commerce.

V. BRAZIL'S CLAIMS REGARDING "CONTINUED USE" SHOULD BE REJECTED

37. As noted above, the "continued use of 'zeroing'" is not a measure within the Panel's terms of reference under Article 6.2 of the DSU. Should the Panel conclude otherwise, however, Brazil's claims that such "continued use" violates Article VI:2 of the GATT and Articles 2.4.2 and 9.3 of the AD Agreement should be rejected for multiple reasons.

38. Brazil's claim with respect to this purported "measure" is premised on dumping margins calculated in the original investigation, final results of the first and second administrative review, and preliminary results of the third administrative review. Neither the second nor the third administrative review is within the Panel's terms of reference as they were not consulted upon, and, with respect to the third administrative review, the calculations Brazil references are merely preliminary results and do not constitute a "final action" that can be challenged.

39. Moreover, Brazil's evidence with respect to the investigation indicates that "zeroing" had no impact on the margin calculations in the investigation. In particular, this evidence shows that there were no negative comparison results, meaning that the necessary condition for activating the "zeroing" line of the program was not satisfied, and the "zeroing" operation was not applied. The margins calculated as a result could not and did not exceed the margins contemplated by the covered agreements, even under Brazil's interpretation. With respect to the reviews, as noted above, in the first administrative review, the margin of dumping for Cutrale was *de minimis*. With respect to the second administrative review, the margin of dumping and assessment rate for Fischer was zero. As such, like the investigation, they do not provide a basis for a claim that the United States has continuously acted inconsistently with its obligations by "inflating" the margins via "zeroing".

40. Brazil's assertion that the facts of this case are "virtually identical" to the facts of cases found to be WTO-inconsistent by the Appellate Body in the *US – Zeroing II (EC)* dispute is not accurate. In that dispute, the Appellate Body found that the record supported findings of inconsistency where "the zeroing methodology was repeatedly used in a string of determinations made sequentially in periodic reviews and sunset reviews over an extended period of time". Here, in contrast, there have been no sunset reviews, and Brazil's own evidence

fails to establish that "zeroing" was applied to, or had any impact on, any margin in the investigation or first administrative review, one of the two margins in the second administrative review, or one of the two margins in the preliminary results of the third administrative review. This does not constitute "a string of determinations, made sequentially ... over an extended period of time" and does not provide a basis for concluding that "zeroing" would likely continue to be applied in successive proceedings.

41. Brazil's argument that the alleged "continued use of zeroing" is even a measure that can be challenged, as well as a violation of the covered agreements, is premised on its assertion that such "continued use" constitutes "ongoing conduct". Even were this a cognizable claim, as detailed above, the facts belie a conclusion that any such "ongoing conduct" exists or is likely to continue in the order that is at issue in this dispute.

42. In addition, with respect to Brazil's claim that the "continued use" violates Article 2.4.2 of the AD Agreement, the express terms of Article 2.4.2 limit its application to the "investigation phase" of a proceeding. To require the application of Article 2.4.2 to assessment proceedings, or the amorphous "continued use" of "zeroing" in successive proceedings, would read out of the AD Agreement the express limitation to investigations. Such a result would be inconsistent with the principle of effectiveness, under which all the terms of an agreement should generally be given meaning wherever possible.

VI. CONCLUSION

43. The United States requests that the Panel grant the requests for preliminary rulings and reject Brazil's claims.

ANNEX A-3

EXECUTIVE SUMMARY OF BRAZIL'S RESPONSE TO THE UNITED STATES' REQUESTS FOR PRELIMINARY RULINGS

I. INTRODUCTION

1. The United States has requested a preliminary ruling that the following two measures are not within the Panel's terms of reference: (i) the 2007-2008 anti-dumping duty administrative review on certain orange juice from Brazil (the "Second Administrative Review")[1]; and (ii) the continued use of the US zeroing procedures in successive anti-dumping proceedings in relation to the anti-dumping duty order issued in respect of imports of certain orange juice from Brazil.[2]

2. Nearly identical objections were raised by the United States, and rejected, in *US – Continued Zeroing*.[3]

II. THE SECOND ADMINISTRATIVE REVIEW FALLS WITHIN THE PANEL'S TERMS OF REFERENCE

A. Factual Background

3. Brazil filed its first request for consultations in the present proceedings on 27 November 2008. The request mentioned, in particular, the 2005-2007 anti-dumping administrative review on certain orange juice from Brazil (the "First Administrative Review"), and "any on-going or future antidumping administrative reviews, and the final results thereof, related to the imports of certain orange juice from Brazil (case no. A-351-840)".[4] On 6 April 2009, the United States adopted preliminary results in the Second Administrative Review. On 22 May 2009, Brazil filed an addendum to its request for consultations. This additional request for consultations indicated, among others, that Brazil wished to consult with the United States on the Second Administrative Review.[5]

4. On 11 August 2009, the United States adopted the final results in the Second Administrative Review. On 20 August 2009, Brazil filed the request for

---

1 US First Written Submission ("FWS"), paras. 37 – 48.

2 US FWS, paras. 38 and 49 – 52.

3 Panel Report, *US – Continued Zeroing*, paras. 7.11 – 7.13, 7.16; and Appellate Body Report, *US – Continued Zeroing*, paras. 156 – 157 and 217; and paras. 172 (and the reasoning in paras. 159 – 171) and 236 (and the reasoning in paras. 220 – 235).

4 Request for Consultations by Brazil, 27 November 2008, WT/DS382/1, p. 1.

5 Request for Consultations by Brazil, Addendum, 22 May 2009, WT/DS382/1/Add.1, para. 5 (3).

establishment of this Panel, listing the Second Administrative Review among the measures at issue, and specifically referring to the final results in this review.[6]

B. The United States' Objections under Article 6.2 of the DSU

5. The United States argues that because final results in the Second Administrative Review had not yet been adopted at the time of consultations, these were not the subject of consultations and, therefore, cannot fall within the Panel's terms of reference under Article 6.2 of the DSU.[7]

C. The Requirements of Article 6.2 of the DSU

6. A panel's terms of reference are determined by the panel request[8], which must be consistent with Article 6.2 of the DSU. Although Article 6.2 requires that consultations be held, it does not require that the measures identified in the panel request be identical to the measures identified in the consultations request. In several disputes, the Appellate Body has held that Article 4 and 6 of the DSU "do not ... require a *precise and exact identity* between the specific measures that were the subject of consultations and the specific measures identified in the request for the establishment of a panel".[9]

7. Panels and the Appellate Body have consistently held that a panel's terms of reference may include a measure properly identified in the panel request, even if that measure was not included in the consultations request, provided that doing so did not change the "essence" of the dispute, or in other words, that it did not "expand the scope" of the dispute.[10]

8. For example, in *US – Continued Zeroing*, the United States took a similar position to its position in this dispute, objecting to the inclusion in the panel's terms of reference of 14 anti-dumping reviews that were included in the European Communities' panel request, but not in its consultations request.[11] These 14 additional reviews were issued under anti-dumping duty orders included in the consultations request. The panel and the Appellate Body recalled that there is no need for strict identity between the consultations and panel requests, and that

---

[6] Request for the Establishment of a Panel by Brazil, 20 August 2009, p. 2.

[7] US FWS, paras. 37 and 39 – 48. These same arguments were made by the United States in *US – Continued Zeroing*, and rejected by both the panel and the Appellate Body. Panel Report, *US – Continued Zeroing*, paras. 7.17 – 7.28; Appellate Body Report, *US – Continued Zeroing*, paras. 220 – 236.

[8] *See, e.g.*, Appellate Body Report, *US – Continued Zeroing*, para. 161 ("... a panel's terms of reference are established by the claims raised in panel requests...").

[9] Appellate Body Report, *Brazil – Aircraft*, para. 132. *See also, e.g.*, Panel Report, *US – Continued Zeroing*, para. 7.23; Appellate Body Report, *US – Continued Zeroing*, para. 222; and Appellate Body Report, *US – Upland Cotton*, para. 285, 293.

[10] Panel Report, *Canada – Aircraft*, para. 9.14; Panel Report, *Brazil – Aircraft*, para. 7.11; Appellate Body Report, *Brazil – Aircraft*, para. 132; Appellate Body Report, *Chile – Price Band System*, para. 139; Panel Report, *Dominican Republic – Import and Sale of Cigarettes*, para. 7.15, 7.21; Appellate Body Report, *EC – Chicken Cuts*, para. 157; Appellate Body Report, *US – Continued Zeroing*, in particular paras. 222 and 228; Appellate Body Report, *US – Upland Cotton*, para. 293.

[11] *See, e.g.*, Appellate Body Report, *US – Continued Zeroing*, para. 223.

measures not included in a consultations request may form part of the terms of reference if they do not change the essence of the dispute.[12] The Appellate Body upheld the panel's findings that the 14 reviews fell within the panel's terms of reference.[13] The panel said that:

> ... as long as the consultations request and the panel request concern the same matter, or dispute, claims raised in connection with measures identified in the complaining Member's panel request would fall within a panel's terms of reference even if those precise measures were not identified in the consultations request.[14]

9. Thus, Panels and the Appellate Body assess the scope of a panel's jurisdiction on the basis of the *substantive* connections between the measures that were, and the measures that allegedly were not, part of the terms of reference. The Appellate Body has stated that this approach – which properly promotes substance over form – is "supported" by "the object and purpose of the WTO dispute settlement system."[15]

10. Additional support for this approach can be found in the Appellate Body's consideration of the scope of a panel's jurisdiction under Article 21.5 of the DSU.[16]

11. In sum, the case-law shows that a series of closely linked measures adopted over time – starting with measures identified in a consultations request, continuing with measures adopted during consultations[17], the original proceedings[18], and into implementation[19] – may all relate to "fundamentally the same 'dispute'"[20] such that jurisdiction is conferred, provided the measures share the

---

12 Panel Report, *US – Continued Zeroing*, paras. 7.22 – 7.23; Appellate Body Report, *US – Continued Zeroing*, in particular paras. 222 and 228.

13 Appellate Body Report, *US – Continued Zeroing*, paras. 235 – 236 and Panel Report, *US – Continued Zeroing*, para. 7.28.

14 Panel Report, *US – Continued Zeroing*, para. 7.22. In *US – Continued Zeroing*, the panel and the Appellate Body also rejected the argument, reiterated by the United States in this dispute, that the Appellate Body's decision in *US – Certain EC Products* supports its position. Appellate Body Report, *US – Continued Zeroing*, para. 60, 230-231; Panel Report, *US – Continued Zeroing*, paras. 7.26 and 7.27; *also*, Appellate Body Report, *US – Certain EC Products*, paras. 76 – 77.

15 Appellate Body Report, *Chile – Price Band System*, para. 140, 144.

16 The Appellate Body has concluded that measures with "a *particularly close relationship*", or having "*sufficiently close links*", to measures that are indisputably within the compliance panel's jurisdiction are themselves subject to a compliance panel's jurisdiction. *See, e.g.*, Appellate Body Report, *US – Softwood Lumber IV (Article 21.5 – Canada)*, para. 77, 79; *see also* Panel Report, *US – Zeroing (Japan) (21.5 – Japan)*, para. 7.114; and Appellate Body Report, *US – Zeroing (Japan) (21.5 – Japan)*, paras. 124 – 130.

17 Appellate Body Report, *Brazil – Aircraft*.

18 Appellate Body Report, *Chile – Price Band System*; Panel Report, *Dominican Republic – Import and Sale of Cigarettes*; Panel Report, *Argentina – Footwear (EC)*, para. 8.45; and Appellate Body Report, *EC – Chicken Cuts*.

19 Appellate Body Report, *US – Softwood Lumber IV (Article 21.5 – Canada)*; Panel Report, *Australia – Salmon (Article 21.5 – Canada)*, para. 6.5; and Panel Report, *Australia – Automotive Leather II (Article 21.5 – US)*, para. 7.10.

20 Panel Report, *Brazil – Aircraft*, para. 7.11.

same "essence"[21] or close substantive connections[22], and together manifest a common "problem" that the complaining Member's claims are seeking to "fix".[23]

D. The Second Administrative Review Is within the Panel's Terms of Reference

12. At the outset, Brazil recalls that its consultations and panel requests both identify the Second Administrative Review, which was ongoing when the consultations request was filed[24], and was adopted before the panel request was filed.

13. The sole issue is whether it is decisive that the Second Administrative Review was adopted after the consultations request was filed. The case law just discussed shows that this factor is not decisive. Panels and the Appellate Body have consistently found that new measures, adopted after a consultations request was filed, may form part of a panel's terms of reference, if the new measures were part and parcel of the same dispute.

14. The Second Administrative Review is properly regarded as part of the same dispute as the other measures at issue. This measure has very close substantive connections to – and, indeed, the same essence as – the First Administrative Review. These are successive annual administrative reviews adopted under the same anti-dumping order regarding certain orange juice from Brazil. They involve the *same type of determinations*, made by the *same US administering authority*, concerning the *same products*, the *same exporters*, and the *same exporting country*, and they provide *succeeding bases* for the continued imposition of anti-dumping duties under that order. These connections are confirmed by the fact that, under the USDOC's Regulations, all administrative (and other) reviews occurring under a single order are mere "*segments*" of a single "*proceeding*" that continues until revocation.[25]

15. In addition to the close substantive similarities between the First and Second Administrative Reviews, the claims made regarding the two measures are also identical. Thus, the nature, or "essence", of the dispute regarding the two measures is exactly the same, and the Second Administrative Review properly falls within the panel's terms of reference.

16. Brazil also notes that, if the Second Administrative Review were excluded from the panel's terms of reference, it would be difficult, if not impossible, to pursue WTO dispute settlement regarding US administrative reviews. As Brazil has explained in its First Written Submission, the United States typically

---

[21] Appellate Body Report, *Brazil – Aircraft*, para. 132; Appellate Body Report, *Chile – Price Band System*, para. 139; Panel Report, *Dominican Republic – Import and Sale of Cigarettes*, para. 7.21; Appellate Body Report, *EC – Chicken Cuts*, para. 157.

[22] Appellate Body Report, *US – Softwood Lumber IV (Article 21.5 – Canada)*, para. 77.

[23] Appellate Body Report, *US – FSC (Article 21.5 – EC II)*, para. 95.

[24] Request for Consultations by Brazil, Addendum, 22 May 2009, WT/DS382/1/Add.1, para. 5(3); and Request for the Establishment of a Panel by Brazil, 20 August 2009, p. 2.

[25] 19 C.F.R. § 351.102. Exhibit BRA-44.

conducts annual administrative reviews under an anti-dumping order.[26] Thus, every year, one administrative review is succeeded by another. If a complainant were required to file a new consultations request for every administrative review, WTO dispute settlement would become a "moving target", and the recommendations and rulings of the Dispute Settlement Body ("DSB") could not address the latest measure. This would needlessly prevent the prompt settlement of disputes. As noted, panels and the Appellate Body have rightly rejected this interpretation.

III. THE CONTINUED USE OF ZEROING IN SUCCESSIVE PROCEEDINGS UNDER THE ORANGE JUICE ORDER FALLS WITHIN THE PANEL'S TERMS OF REFERENCE

A. Background

17. In addition to challenging individual reviews in which zeroing was used, Brazil has challenged "[t]he continued use of the US. "zeroing procedures" in successive anti-dumping proceedings, in relation to the anti-dumping duty order issued in respect of imports of certain orange juice from Brazil".[27] Brazil refers to this as the "Continued Use" measure.

B. The United States' Objections under Article 6.2 of the DSU

18. Like in *US – Continued Zeroing*, where its arguments were rejected, the United States objects that the continued use of zeroing in successive anti-dumping proceedings relating to the orange juice order does not fall within the panel's terms of reference.[28]

C. The Requirements of Article 6.2 of the DSU

19. Article 6.2 of the DSU requires, among others, that a panel request "identify the *specific* measures at issue".[29] If a measure is not specifically identified in the panel request, it does not fall within the panel's terms of reference. In the words of the Appellate Body,

> ... the specificity requirement means that the measures at issue must be identified with sufficient precision so that what is referred to adjudication by a panel may be discerned from the panel request.[30]

---

26 Brazil's FWS, paras. 19 – 21.

27 Request for the Establishment of a Panel by Brazil, 20 August 2009, p. 3, heading (d).

28 US FWS, paras. 50-52. This line of argument was rejected in *US – Continued Zeroing*. Appellate Body Report, *US – Continued Zeroing*, paras. 159 – 172.

29 Compliance with the requirements of Article 6.2, including the requirement to identify the specific measures at issue, must be examined based "on the face" of the panel request, "read 'as a whole'". Appellate Body Report, *US – Continued Zeroing*, para. 161, quoting Appellate Body Report, *US – Carbon Steel*, para. 127, and Appellate Body Report, *US – OCTG Sunset Reviews*, para. 169.

30 Appellate Body Report, *US – Continued Zeroing*, para. 168.

20. In *US – Continued Zeroing*, the Appellate Body held that, under Article 6.2 of the DSU, the European Communities had properly identified a "specific measure" that the Appellate Body described as follows: "the use of the zeroing methodology in successive proceedings, in each of the 18 [anti-dumping] cases, by which the anti-dumping duties are maintained".[31]

21. In reaching this conclusion, the Appellate Body dismissed US arguments to the effect that such a measure did not exist. It emphasized that, under Article 6.2, the issue is whether a measure has been properly identified, adding that:

> ... the *identification* of the specific measures at issue, pursuant to Article 6.2, is different from a *demonstration of the existence* of such measures.[32]

22. The Appellate Body also dismissed the US arguments that a measure involving ongoing conduct in a series of anti-dumping determinations was of a type that could not be challenged in WTO dispute settlement.[33] Furthermore, after finding that the panel request sufficiently identified a "continued use" measure, the Appellate Body also held that, in certain instances, this measure violated the *Anti-Dumping Agreement* and the GATT 1994. Thus, the continued use of zeroing is a measure of a type that may be subject to WTO dispute settlement.

D. Brazil' Continued Use Measure Falls within the Panel's Terms of Reference

23. Brazil begins by noting that the content of the measure identified in its panel request is defined in very similar terms to the measure that the Appellate Body stated had been challenged by the European Communities in *US – Continued Zeroing*. The two sets of measures were defined as follows:

> [T]he continued use by the United States of "zeroing procedures" in successive anti-dumping proceedings, in relation to the anti-dumping duty order issued in respect of imports of certain orange juice from Brazil (case No A-351-840), including the original investigation and any subsequent administrative reviews, by which duties are applied and maintained over a period of time.[34]

> [T]he use of the zeroing methodology in successive proceedings, in each of the 18 [anti-dumping] cases, by which the anti-dumping duties are maintained.[35]

---

[31] Appellate Body Report, *US – Continued Zeroing*, para. 166, 169.

[32] Appellate Body Report, *US – Continued Zeroing*, para. 169.

[33] Appellate Body Report, *US – Continued Zeroing*, para. 169. *Also*, Appellate Body Report, *US – Corrosion-Resistant Steel Sunset Review*, para. 101.

[34] Request for the Establishment of a Panel by Brazil, 20 August 2009, p. 3, heading (d).

[35] Appellate Body Report, *US – Continued Zeroing*, para. 166.

24. Thus, Brazil identified the Continued Use measure at issue in similar terms to the formulation that the Appellate Body used to describe a similar measure. These similarities are not accidental. Brazil intended to bring claims concerning the same ongoing conduct challenged by the European Communities in *US – Continued Zeroing*, that is, the continued use of zeroing in successive anti-dumping proceedings under a particular anti-dumping order. The only material difference is that Brazil's claims address continued conduct under a different anti-dumping order from the orders implicated in *US – Continued Zeroing*.

25. Given the Appellate Body's own formulation of the "continued use" measure in *US – Continued Zeroing*, the formulation of Brazil's panel request is more than sufficient for the Panel, the United States, and the third parties to "identify[] with sufficient precision … what is referred to adjudication".[36] The United States has not argued that the panel request lacks clarity; it merely repeats the arguments made in *US – Continued Zeroing* to the effect that the measure at issue is of a type that cannot be challenged in WTO dispute settlement, and that the measure does not exist. For the same reasons as were given by the Appellate Body in *US – Continued Zeroing*, these arguments of the United States should be rejected.[37]

26. Brazil also notes that, in *US – Continued Zeroing*, the Appellate Body rejected the US argument that the continued use of zeroing in successive anti-dumping proceedings under specific anti-dumping orders is no different to a challenge to past individual determinations, an argument that the United States now repeats.[38] The Appellate Body observed that a challenge to a continued use measure of the type at issue is "narrower than a challenge to the zeroing methodology" as such, and "broader than specific instances in which the zeroing methodology was applied".[39]

27. With respect to the continued use measure, the Appellate Body found that the complaint was directed at:

> … the zeroing methodology as used in the final order and programmed to continue to be used until such time as the United States eliminates zeroing from the particular anti-dumping duty under consideration.[40]

28. The Appellate Body explained that a complainant "is entitled to frame the subject of its challenge in such a way as to bring the ongoing conduct [] under the scrutiny of WTO dispute settlement".[41]

29. As in *US – Continued Zeroing*, the conduct at issue in this case is the *continued use of the zeroing methodology in making determinations under a*

---

36 Appellate Body Report, *US – Continued Zeroing*, para. 168.

37 Appellate Body Report, *US – Continued Zeroing*, paras. 169, 171.

38 US FWS, para. 50.

39 Appellate Body Report, *US – Continued Zeroing*, paras. 179 – 181.

40 Appellate Body Report, *US – Continued Zeroing*, para. 180.

41 Appellate Body Report, *US – Continued Zeroing*, para. 181, footnotes omitted.

particular anti-dumping order, and the remedy requires the United States to cease using this methodology to make determinations under the *particular order*. In this regard, Brazil is entitled, as the European Communities was in *US – Continued Zeroing*, to bring claims regarding this measure in order to resolve a disagreement regarding the use of zeroing under the orange juice order.

30. The United States also argues that Brazil is "challenging an indeterminate number of potential future measures", which, it says, is contrary to the DSU.[42] This argument was also dismissed by the Appellate Body in *US – Continued Zeroing*, which stated:

> The prospective nature of the remedy sought by the European Communities is congruent with the fact that the measures at issue are alleged to be ongoing, with prospective application and a life potentially stretching into the future.[43]

31. Accordingly, Brazil is not precluded from challenging the Continued Use measure simply because it may be applied when future anti-dumping determinations are made under the orange juice order. To the contrary, this is the very reason why Brazil has brought this dispute over the continued use of zeroing under the orange juice order – it wishes to resolve a dispute regarding conduct that will likely "stretch[] into the future".[44] WTO dispute settlement is designed precisely to allow Members to settle such disputes promptly, by permitting Members to challenge the root of the problem. By challenging the root of the problem, Brazil avoids the situation where the United States has adopted new individual determinations using zeroing before the Panel proceedings have been completed, which would turn the US measures into "a 'moving target'".[45]

E. Conclusion

32. Thus, Brazil requests that the Panel reject the United States' requests for the Second Administrative Review and the Continued Use measure to be excluded from its terms of reference, and to find that these measures form part of its terms of reference.

---

[42] US FWS, para. 52.

[43] Appellate Body Report, *US – Continued Zeroing*, para. 171.

[44] *Ibid.*

[45] Appellate Body Report, *Chile – Price Band System*, para. 144.

ANNEX B

THIRD PARTIES' WRITTEN SUBMISSIONS OR
EXECUTIVE SUMMARIES THEREOF

ANNEX B-1

THIRD PARTY WRITTEN SUBMISSION
OF ARGENTINA

TABLE OF CONTENTS

I. INTRODUCTION

1. Argentina thanks the Panel for this opportunity to present its arguments concerning the correct interpretation of the *Anti-Dumping Agreement* (hereinafter ADA), to ensure that the Agreement is not interpreted in such a way as to diminish or impair the rights of Members.

2. Argentina will not discuss zeroing as applied in the specific case brought by Brazil. Rather, it will focus on a more systemic aspect, i.e. the inconsistency of zeroing as such.

3. As it has emerged from other cases submitted to the DSB, the practice and methodology applied by the United States Department of Commerce (USDOC), commonly known as "zeroing", is inconsistent with the ADA, since Article 1 of the ADA stipulates that "[a]n anti-dumping measure shall be applied only under circumstances provided for in Article VI of GATT 1994 and pursuant to investigations initiated and conducted in accordance with the provisions of this Agreement".

4. On the contrary, the zeroing methodology for calculating the margin of dumping during the investigation phase, by eliminating certain relevant transactions from the calculation, can lead to two situations: (a) artificial inflation of a margin of dumping; or, in the worst-case scenario, (b) creation of a margin of dumping where there is none.

5. Argentina will now present its arguments concerning the interpretation of the main provisions of the ADA raised in this dispute that may be affected as a result of applying the zeroing methodology to calculate margins of dumping.

6. Firstly, bearing in mind that Brazil referred to the zeroing methodology in original investigations ("model zeroing"), and more specifically to the inconsistency of the methodology with Article 2.4.2 of the ADA[1], we shall examine the consistency of that methodology with the said provision of the ADA.

7. Finally, in the light of Brazil's analysis of the inconsistency of the use of the zeroing methodology in administrative reviews with Article VI.2 of the GATT 1994 and Article 9.3 of the ADA, we shall address that issue.

II. INCONSISTENCY WITH ARTICLE 2.4.2 OF THE *ANTI-DUMPING AGREEMENT*

8. Both Panels and the Appellate Body have in several instances found the practice of zeroing to be inconsistent with Article 2.4.2 of the ADA.[2]

9. Article 2.4.2 refers to the various methods available to investigating authorities for calculating the margin of dumping. This provision specifies that "[*s*]*ubject to the provisions governing fair comparison in paragraph 4, the existence of margins of dumping during the investigation phase shall normally be established on the basis of a comparison of a weighted average normal value with a weighted average of prices of* ***all*** *comparable export transactions or by a comparison of normal value and export prices on a transaction to transaction*

1 First Written Submission of Brazil, page 38, para. 114.

2 See the Reports of the Appellate Body in *EC - Bed Linen,* para. 66; *US - Softwood Lumber V*, para. 117; *US - Zeroing (EC)*, para. 222. See also the reports of the Panels in *US - Zeroing (Japan)*, paras. 7.86 and 7.179; *US - Stainless Steel (Mexico)*, para. 7.63; and *US - Continued Zeroing*, paras. 7.109-111.

basis [thus providing the possibility of a weighted average/transaction under exceptional circumstances method]".

10. The above provision explains how domestic authorities must proceed in establishing "the existence of margins of dumping", that is, it explains how they must proceed in establishing that there is dumping.

11. As can be inferred from this provision, comparison for the purposes of calculating the "margin of dumping" in an investigation, regardless of the method used, must be based on "all" comparable transactions and not on the selection of some models or transactions.

12. Moreover, a methodology that fails to include all transactions in the calculation of the margin of dumping is not "fair", thus contravening the principle established in Article 2.4 of the ADA and the first sentence of Article 2.4.2 of the ADA.

13. In this connection, in *EC - Bed Linen* (paragraph 55) the AB held that:

> ... the investigating authorities are required to compare the weighted average normal value with the weighted average of prices of *all* comparable export transactions. Here, we emphasize that Article 2.4.2 speaks of "all" comparable export transactions. As explained above, when "zeroing", the European Communities counted as zero the "dumping margins" for those models where the "dumping margin" was "negative". As the Panel correctly noted, for those models, the European Communities counted "the weighted average export price to be equal to the weighted average normal value [...] despite the fact that it was, in reality, higher than the weighted average normal value." By "zeroing" the "negative dumping margins", the European Communities, therefore, did *not* take fully into account the entirety of the prices of *some* export transactions, namely, those export transactions involving models of cotton-type bed linen where "negative dumping margins" were found. [...] Thus, the European Communities did *not* establish "the existence of margins of dumping" for cotton-type bed linen on the basis of a comparison of the weighted average normal value with the weighted average of prices of *all* comparable export transactions ...

14. Furthermore, Article 2.4.2 of the *Anti-Dumping Agreement* also states that "the existence of margins of dumping during the investigation phase shall normally be established on the basis of a comparison of a weighted average normal value with a weighted average of prices of all *comparable* export transactions".

15. As regards the term "comparable", in *EC - Bed Linen* (paragraph 56) the AB held that:

> [T]he word "comparable" in Article 2.4.2 does not affect, or diminish in any way, the obligation of investigating authorities to establish the existence of margins of dumping on the basis of "a comparison of the weighted average normal value with the weighted average of prices of *all* comparable export transactions. (emphasis added)

16. By "zeroing" the difference between normal value and export price of certain transactions, deliberately setting aside a proportion of the export price, the United States appears to rely on at least two presumptions, that is:

(a) A certain proportion of the price is irrelevant for calculating the margin of dumping, whereas another part is not; and

(b) it prejudges the existence of a margin of dumping before even having made the pertinent determination, since it decides a priori which margin to apply as a parameter, at least for some transactions.

17. As regards the first presumption, the AB (*EC - Bed Linen*, paragraph 55) noted the inconsistency of this reasoning, in finding that "a comparison between export price and normal value that does not take fully into account the entirety of the prices of all comparable transactions" does not fulfil the fair comparison requirement under Article 2.4 and Article 2.4.2.

18. It should be emphasized that the definition of the term "margin of dumping" is always the same, regardless of the method used for its calculation, in accordance with Article 2.4.2 of the ADA. In *EC - Bed Linen* (paragraph 53), the AB held that "[w]hatever the method used to calculate the margins of dumping, [...] these margins must be, and can only be, established for the product under investigation as a whole".

III. INCONSISTENCY WITH ARTICLE 9.3 OF THE *ANTI-DUMPING AGREEMENT* AND ARTICLE VI:2 OF THE GATT 1994

19. Article 9.3 of the ADA, read in conjunction with Article VI:2 of the GATT 1994, provides that anti-dumping duties levied in order to offset the effects of dumping may not exceed the margin of dumping in respect of such product.

20. Article 9.3 stipulates that "*[t]he amount of the anti-dumping duty shall be established in accordance with the provisions of Article 2*".

21. The zeroing methodology, by not producing a result that takes into account all the variables to be taken into consideration in a margin-of-dumping determination, ultimately implies the levying of anti-dumping duties in excess of the margin of dumping, and is consequently inconsistent with Articles 9.3 of the ADA and VI:2 of the GATT 1994.

22. Nonetheless, Argentina wishes to make clear that the imposition and collection of duties cannot be confused with the calculation of the margin of dumping, which the implementing authority is required to make prior to the imposition phase.

IV. CONCLUSION

23. In view of the foregoing, Argentina considers that the zeroing methodology for calculating margins of dumping during the investigation phase is inconsistent with Article 2.4.2 of the ADA.

24. Furthermore, the imposition of an anti-dumping duty in excess of the amount of the margin of dumping is inconsistent with Article VI:2 of the GATT 1994 and Article 9.3 of the ADA, except as provided for in paragraph 24.

25. Accordingly, Argentina respectfully requests the Panel to ask the United States to bring its measures into conformity with WTO law.

ANNEX B-2

EXECUTIVE SUMMARY OF THE THIRD PARTY WRITTEN SUBMISSION OF THE EUROPEAN UNION

I. PRELIMINARY ISSUES RAISED BY THE US

1. The EU considers that the Panel should reject the US request for preliminary rulings. First, the EU considers that Brazil adequately identified the measure at issue in its Consultations and Panel Requests. Second, as regards the existence of the measures at issue and the requirements under Article 6.2 of the DSU, in *US – Continued Zeroing*, the Appellate Body rejected a similar argument raised by the US. Since the ongoing conduct at issue includes the original determination and any subsequent administrative review with respect to the same anti-dumping order, Brazil has identified with sufficient precision the measures at issue in the present case in accordance with Article 6.2 of the DSU. Since the second administrative review is part of the same measure, the fact that the definitive results were published only after consultations were held is irrelevant. All these measures thus fall within the Panel's terms of reference.

II. BURDEN OF PROOF

2. The EU understands that the programme used to determine the specific dumping margins is provided to each company in a disk so that the results can be verified. In that sense, running the programme later on is a simple operation which does not alter the results contained in the programme log. To the extent that the US disagrees with the documents provided by Brazil, in the EU's view, it is for the US to provide the relevant evidence. In addition, the US argues that Brazil cannot meet its burden of proof merely by alleging that "zeroing" may or will occur in the future. According to the US, there may in fact be no "zeroing" at all where there are no negative comparison results. In this respect, the EU considers that, even where all transactions are below or above the line, zeroing is embedded in the measure at issue. The fact that the zeroing procedures do not alter the dumping margin calculations is something which may be relevant when determining the level of nullification or impairment caused at a later stage (e.g., in Article 22.6 DSU proceedings). However, it does not eliminate the WTO inconsistent methodology which is part of the measure and that, depending on future transactions, may lead to negative comparison results. In essence, what the US seems to argue is that legislation which is not applied cannot be challenged since it does not lead to any results. However, the relevant case law has clarified that legislation can be challenged "as such" even if it has never been enforced. Consequently, the US contention should be dismissed.

III. STANDARD OF REVIEW: THE ROLE OF THE PRECEDENT IN THIS DISPUTE

3. In *US – Stainless Steel from Mexico* the Appellate Body clarified the role of its previous reports and indicated how panels should act in cases where the same legal issues arise (paras 157-162). The EU fully agrees with these statements without reservation. WTO panels are obliged to correctly apply the law; in the context of this dispute this also means that the Panel should follow the rulings of the Appellate Body where the Appellate Body has previously interpreted the same legal questions. Otherwise, the security and predictability enshrined in Article 3.2 of the DSU would be put in serious danger.

IV. OVERVIEW OF THE CORE PROBLEM

4. The term "zeroing" – which does not appear in the ADA, may be considered something of a misnomer, because it describes only part of the problem: that is, the downward adjustment of the relatively high export transactions; or, in other words, the setting to zero of the negative amounts. The heart of the matter, however, is the selection of the relatively low priced export transactions per se, as a sub-category, as the only or preponderant basis for the dumping margin calculation. This has nothing to do with "offsets" or "credits".

5. This is not a new problem. It is discussed at length in Jacob Viner's Memorandum, and was specifically addressed in the Uruguay Round negotiations, during which the Members were fully informed of the issue and knew exactly what they were talking about. After more than three years of public negotiations, the problem was nicely summarised by the WTO secretariat: it was generally considered that the practice of comparing a weighted average normal value with individual export transactions was obviously unfair to exporters – particularly from developing countries – and required amendment of the Tokyo Round AD Code; the US explained that such a method was necessary to reveal targeted dumping – that is, successive attacks on different parts of an importing market; the consensus was that the Membership should try to find a solution to accommodate the legitimate concerns of both sides. That compromise was the text of Article 2.4.2 of the ADA, as it stands today.

6. Looking at the overall design and architecture of Article 2.4.2, and reading its provisions intelligently, in the light of the underlying economic realities that the legal rules are intended to address and respond to – that is, the real world, it is clear that there are only three sub-categories of clustered low priced export transactions that it is permissible to respond to: those clustered by purchaser, region or time. These categories broadly correspond to typical market definition parameters: they make economic sense.

7. Thus, it is not permissible, and it is not fair, to pick up low priced export transactions clustered by model. The US has acknowledged as much. This is clear from the term "all" in the first sentence of Article 2.4.2, and the definition

of dumping in Article 2.1 of the ADA and Article VI:1 of the GATT 1994 in terms of the product; read together with the absence in the targeted dumping provisions of any reference to a sub-category by model. Thus, the relevant provisions, and particularly the normal rule and the exception, are read harmoniously, so as to give meaning – both legal and economic – to all the treaty terms.

8. In exactly the same way, it is not possible to pick up low priced export transactions per se as a sub-category. There is no reference to any such sub-category in the provisions on targeted dumping. To accept such a proposition would be to render the targeted dumping provisions useless; and to negate the compromise, negotiated and agreed by all the WTO Members (in return for other concessions), to which we have just referred. The proof of this is that for some 15 years the US has simply ignored the targeted dumping requirements, content to continue doing exactly what it was doing before, based on its own unilateral interpretation of Article 2.4.2. The further proof of this is that, by its own assertion, the US sought the insertion of the phrase "the existence of margins of dumping during the investigation phase" (the "Phrase") precisely with the intention of side-stepping the compromise and the obligations that we have just outlined. This is a highly significant point that bears repetition: the entire US position is premised on the implied admission that the overall design and architecture of Article 2.4.2 is to be interpreted in the manner advocated by the EU in previous cases.

9. We turn, therefore, to the Phrase "the existence of margins of dumping during the investigation phase", added – behind closed doors – after some three and a half years of public negotiations. According to the US, this means that the obligations in Article 2.4.2 do not apply to the re-calculation of dumping margins in assessment proceedings. Rather, the US is completely free to choose the methodology to be used for calculating a contemporaneous dumping margin and finally collecting duties. Since the results of the first retrospective assessment proceeding are applied with effect from the date on which duties were first imposed, this would negate entirely the compromise enshrined in Article 2.4.2.

10. In the view of the EU, assuming Members negotiate in full knowledge of the 1969 Vienna Convention on the Law of the Treaties (the "Vienna Convention"), it may reasonably be assumed that they negotiate in good faith, just as they agree that the terms of the ADA are to be interpreted in good faith. In such negotiations, the EU would neither expect nor accept that what is clearly given, after lengthy debate, with one hand (that is, agreement not to use asymmetry absent targeted dumping) would be surreptitiously entirely taken away with the other hand. The US position reflects what might be termed the "last minute" "spanner in the works" theory of international negotiation – a tactic that, in the view of the EU, is hardly suited to a multilateral organisation with 153 Members, including many developing countries.

11. However, assuming for the sake of argument, that such negotiation tactics are permissible, the EU would like to draw the Panel's very close attention to what a Member forfeits when it adopts such an approach. First, most obviously, the Member chooses to leave no trace of its intended unilateral interpretation in

the preparatory work. Second, and in similar vein, the Member chooses not to offer any explanation to its negotiating partners – many of whom are developing countries - as to what the object and purpose of such a provision might be. This is particularly problematic when the subsequent unilateral interpretation flies in the face of the overall design and architecture of the ADA. Especially when there is no object and purpose capable of explaining why, on the basis of identical data, the mere act of collection should inflate the dumping margin many times over – a proposition that is "manifestly absurd or unreasonable" within the meaning of the Vienna Convention – both in legal terms and in economic terms. Third, and in similar vein, the Member chooses to forego any attempt to reconcile conflicting context with its intended unilateral interpretation. The Panel may thus note that of the various elements of the interpretive rule in the Vienna Convention, by the US' own choice, there is only one that stands between the US and failure: the supposed ordinary meaning of the Phrase.

12. We believe we have previously amply demonstrated – and we do so again below - that the ordinary meaning of the Phrase is not that advocated by the US. We believe that, for the US, the term "investigation" was key in its intended unilateral interpretation. In fact, we have an express admission of this in the US Statement of Administrative Action (SAA), which accompanied the adoption of the US Uruguay Round Agreements Act, and which contains the words ("not reviews"). Obviously, the drafter of the SAA well appreciated that these words are not contained in Article 2.4.2 of the ADA, and do not result from a proper interpretation of that provision, which is precisely why they were inserted in the SAA in an attempt at ex post rationalisation – an attempt doomed to fail, as subsequent WTO litigation has demonstrated.

13. The discussion could stop here. But there are a multitude of other interpretative points against the US. First, the grammatical structure of the Phrase, in which the term "during … phase" is grammatically linked to a period of time in which margins exist (an investigation period) as opposed to one in which they are established (as the US would have it). This both confirms the EU interpretation and precludes the US interpretation. Second, the defined term "margin of dumping" has the same meaning throughout the ADA, and must inform the meaning of the Phrase – there being no support in the text for the view that the definition should change at the moment of final collection. Third, the overall design and architecture of Article 2.4.2, as outlined above. It is particularly significant in this respect that the EU position reads the normal rule referring to the investigation period in counterpoint to the exceptional rule permitting a response to time based targeted dumping. Thus, once again, the EU advances a harmonious reading of all the treaty terms, which makes legal and economic sense of all of them. Fourth, the numerous references in Article 2 to "investigations", which are considered, even in US municipal law, to refer to all types of investigations, including assessment proceedings. Fifth, the rule in Article 9.3 that the amount assessed cannot exceed the dumping margin – with an express cross-reference to all of Article 2. Sixth, the absence of any object and purpose argument capable

of supporting the US position. Seventh, the preparatory work, as outlined above … And the list goes on.

14. Finally, the US turns to some other general arguments, equally without merit. First, the so-called "mathematical equivalence" argument, which is obviously vitiated by a simple intellectual error: something can perfectly well be fair as a response to targeted dumping, but unfair absent targeted dumping. Second, the argument derived from Article 9(4)(ii) and the so-called "variable duty" or prospective normal value. This provision concerns sampling, and insofar as it implies the possibility that one of the measures that could be imposed pursuant to Article 9.2 ADA could be a variable duty, it equally implies that any such duty is ultimately subject to final assessment or refund under Article 9.3, with dumping margins re-calculated in accordance with all of the provisions of Article 2. This is completely logical. It plugs the gap that would otherwise arise in the refund system under Article 9.3.2, in which final liability cannot, by definition, increase. The only option for Members operating such systems who are fearful of targeted dumping is a variable duty, with refund in the event that the feared targeted dumping does not materialise. The proposition that Article 9(4)(ii) in any way contradicts any of the interpretative points that we have already outlined is thus without merit. Third, the proposition that because, in the US, assessment proceedings are importer driven, this should change the analysis. This practical assertion is without merit. The ADA responds to international price discrimination by exporters; and it is a matter of elementary accounting to calculate final liabilities for importers, whilst respecting the ceiling fixed by the amount of dumping practiced by an exporter.

15. If all of the interpretative elements in the Vienna Convention support the position of the EU and Brazil, and disprove the position of the US, the US interpretation cannot be said to be "permissible" within the meaning of Article 17.6 of the ADA.

V. CONCLUSION

16. The EU submits that the US new attempt to revisit the issue of zeroing should be rejected and trusts that the Panel will comply with its functions under Article 11 of the DSU.

ANNEX B-3

EXECUTIVE SUMMARY OF THE THIRD PARTY WRITTEN SUBMISSION OF JAPAN

1. In this dispute, Brazil presents a series of claims against the United States' continued use of the so-called "zeroing" procedures in calculating margins of dumping in a large number of anti-dumping proceedings.

2. To determine the overall amount of "dumping", the USDOC aggregated the multiple comparison results. Under the zeroing procedures, the USDOC disregarded – or treated as "zero" value – the negative comparison results for export transactions which the USDOC itself deemed to be comparable. By excluding all negative comparison results, the USDOC makes a "dumping" determination that disregards an entire category of the export transactions making up the "product" – namely, those transactions that generate the negative comparison results. "Dumping" is, therefore, *not* determined for the "*product*" as defined by the investigating authority, but for a sub-part of it.

3. The Appellate Body repeatedly ruled that a partial determination of this type is inconsistent with the definition of "dumping" in Article 2.1 of the *Anti-Dumping Agreement*, and Article VI of the GATT 1994, because it is *not* made for the "*'product' as a whole*" but for a sub-part of the product.[1] The Appellate Body also ruled that this definition of "dumping" "*applies to the entire [Anti-Dumping] Agreement*", including all the provisions governing reviews.[2] The United States' zeroing procedures, and anti-dumping measures adopted using these procedures, have been found to be incompatible with Articles 2.4 and 2.4.2, 9.3, 9.5 and 11.3 of the *Anti-Dumping Agreement* in a series of previous disputes.[3]

4. In the current dispute, the United States' defense consists entirely of a repetition of arguments that have been made in previous disputes. The purpose of WTO dispute settlement is to allow the Dispute Settlement Body – acting through panels and, ultimately, the Appellate Body – to resolve disputes by clarifying the meaning of the text on a multilateral basis. Japan does not consider that these ends would be served if the Panel were to reject the Appellate Body's previous rulings on zeroing, which are based on the text of the covered agreements, and have been consistently rendered.

---

[1] Appellate Body Report, *EC – Bed Linen*, para. 53; Appellate Body Report, *US – Softwood Lumber V*, para. 99; Appellate Body Report, *US – Zeroing (EC)*, para. 126; Appellate Body Report, *US – Softwood Lumber V (Article 21.5 – Canada)*, paras. 87 and 89; Appellate Body Report, *US – Zeroing (Japan)*, para. 115.

[2] Appellate Body Report, *US – Zeroing (Japan)*, para. 109; Appellate Body Report, *US – Softwood Lumber V*, para. 93; *and* Appellate Body Report, *US – Corrosion-Resistant Steel Sunset Review*, paras. 109 and 126.

[3] Appellate Body Report, *US – Zeroing (Japan)*, para. 190; Appellate Body Report, *US – Zeroing (EC)*, para. 263; Appellate Body Report, *US – Softwood Lumber V*, para. 183.

I. THE UNITED STATES' REQUEST FOR PRELIMINARY RULINGS SHOULD BE REJECTED

5. The United States argues that the Second Administrative Review is not properly within the Panel's terms of reference, because the final results of it had not been issued at the time of Brazil's request for consultations. However, in the present case, the Second Administrative Review was subject to consultations and included in the Panel's terms of reference. Even though the final result of the review had not been issued at the time of the request for consultations, the review had been initiated and a final result had been expected to be issued in a certain period. Japan thinks that, from the description of the request for consultations, Brazil's consultations provided the parties an opportunity to define and delimit the scope of the dispute between them.

6. The United States argues that the "continued use of zeroing" is not a measure with in the Panel's terms of reference under Article 6.2 of the DSU. To see Brazil's panel request, Japan finds no substantial difference between the measure at issue in the present case and the measures at issue in *US – Continued Zeroing (EC)*.[4] Japan thinks that the panel should reject the United States' request for preliminary rulings and find that the continued use of the zeroing methodology in successive anti-dumping proceedings, in relation to the anti-dumping duty order issued in respect of imports of certain orange juice from Brazil, constitute a "measure" that falls within the Panel's terms of reference under Article 6.2.

II. THE ZEROING PROCEDURES USED BY THE USDOC IN THE MEASURES CHALLENGED BY BRAZIL ARE INCONSISTENT WITH THE OBLIGATIONS ESTABLISHED BY THE *ANTI-DUMPING AGREEMENT* AND THE GATT 1994

7. As the United States accepts, the analysis of the zeroing issue begins with the concepts of "dumping" and "margins of dumping", as defined in Article VI:1 of the GATT 1994 and Article 2.1 of the *Anti-Dumping Agreement*. Article 2.1 has particular importance among the "agreed disciplines" set out in Article 2 for determining "dumping" and "margins of dumping"[5], because it provides a definition of "dumping". This provision reiterates the definition of "dumping" in Article VI:1 of the GATT 1994. The text of both of these provisions refers to the dumping of "a *product*". In addition, they state that dumping of "*a product*" occurs when "*the* [export] *price of the product*" is less than "*the* comparable *price* ... for *the like product*" (Emphasis added). The text, therefore, defines "dumping" in terms of the difference between two prices, each one of which is an *ag-*

4 Appellate Body Report, *US – Continued Zeroing (EC)*, para. 181

5 Appellate Body Report, *US – Corrosion-Resistant Steel Sunset Review*, para. 127.

gregate price for "the product". The "dumping" determination is, therefore, made by reference to an overall price difference for the product.[6]

8. Whether or not the investigating authority decides initially to make multiple comparisons at the sub-product level, the wording of Article 2.1 and Article VI emphasizes that "dumping is defined in relation to a product".[7] Thus, the Appellate Body further found, "it is only on the basis of aggregating all these 'intermediate values' that an investigating authority can establish margins of dumping for the product under investigation as a whole".[8]

9. For each individually examined producer or exporter, the text of the *Anti-Dumping Agreement* expressly contemplates the determination of only a *single* margin of dumping *for a product*. As stated by Article 2.1, this language underscores that a single, overall dumping determination is made for a product as a whole on the basis of aggregate price comparisons, even if multiple intermediate comparisons are undertaken at a sub-product level. Finally, as noted above, Article 2.1 sets forth a definition of "dumping" that applies "[f]or the purpose of this Agreement". Therefore, a uniform definition of "dumping" relating to a product as a whole applies throughout the *Anti-Dumping Agreement*, and to different types of anti-dumping proceedings that are conducted pursuant to the *Agreement*.[9]

10. Then, Japan addresses more specific arguments raised by the United States to support its argument that "dumping" in Article 2.1 and Article VI:1 need not be defined in relation to a "product" as a whole. *First*, the United States argues that the meaning of the treaty terms "dumping" and "margins of dumping" must be based on "real-world commercial conduct" in the marketplace, where prices are often determined for individual transactions. The text of the *Anti-Dumping Agreement* requires that a comparison be made of *aggregate* prices for a "product" to arrive at a *single* margin of dumping for each foreign producer or exporter. The fact that prices may be determined in the marketplace for individual transactions is not the sole consideration that motivated WTO Members.

11. *Second*, the United States relies on certain historical arguments in support of its argument that zeroing is permissible. Although the United States believes that the negotiating history produced an outcome permitting zeroing, nothing in the text shows that the Members agreed to this view. *Third*, the United States argues that the term "product" does not refer exclusively to "product as a whole". The analysis of the zeroing issue begins with the concepts of "dumping" and "margins of dumping" in Article VI:1 of the GATT 1994 and Article 2.1 of the *Anti-Dumping Agreement*. For each individually examined producer or exporter, the text of the *Anti-Dumping Agreement* expressly contemplates the determination of *single* margin of dumping *for a product*.

6 Appellate Body Report, *US – Zeroing (Japan)*, para. 109.
7 Appellate Body Report, *US – Softwood Lumber V*, para. 93.
8 Appellate Body Report, *US – Zeroing (Japan)*, para. 122.
9 Appellate Body Report, *US – Zeroing (Japan)*, para. 109.

12. *Fourth*, the United States argues that *Ad* Article VI:1 "provides for importer-specific comparisons" and, as a result, "the term 'margin of dumping' cannot relate to aggregated results of all comparisons for the 'product as a whole'". The *Ad* Article does not purport to alter the requirement in Article 2.1 and Article VI:1 that dumping and margins of dumping are determined for a "product". Instead, consistent with these provisions, the term "margin of dumping" in the *Ad* Article can, and must, be read to refer to a margin for a "product". *Fifth*, the United States relies on Article 2.2 of the *Anti-Dumping Agreement*, arguing that a product-wide definition of dumping "would require the use of constructed [normal] value for the 'product as a whole'". Whether or not normal value is constructed for some or all models under Article 2.2, the results of intermediate comparisons must all be aggregated to determine "dumping" on a product-wide basis to meet the definition in Article 2.1.

13. The United States contends that a "general prohibition of zeroing" would be "inconsistent" with the second sentence of Article 2.4.2 of the *Anti-Dumping Agreement*, and specifically would "reduce to inutility" the comparison methodology authorized by that sentence. The United States made this argument, without success, in *US – Zeroing (EC), US – Softwood Lumber V (Article 21.5 – Canada), US – Zeroing (Japan), US – Stainless Steel (Mexico) and US – Continued Zeroing (EC).*

14. In *US – Softwood Lumber V (Article 21.5 – Canada)*, the Appellate Body rejected the United States' argument that the prohibition of zeroing would render the second sentence of Article 2.4.2 inutile. *First*, it noted that the United States has never applied the methodology authorized by the second sentence and that the argument as to "mathematical equivalence" between W-to-W and W-to-T comparisons "rests on an untested hypothesis".[10] *Second*, the Appellate Body noted that the methodology authorized in the second sentence of Article 2.4.2 is an "exception" to the methodologies authorized in the first sentence, and as such, the second sentence "alone cannot determine the interpretation of the two methodologies provided in the first sentence ...".[11] *Third*, the Appellate Body noted that "there is considerable uncertainty regarding how precisely the third methodology [i.e. the methodology in the second sentence] should be applied", because it has never been invoked and that the United States could not provide details regarding how this never-used methodology would work.

15. The United States indicated to the Appellate Body that its use of W-to-T comparison method would be limited to the export transactions making up the "pricing pattern", and that W-to-W comparisons would be conducted for the remaining export transactions. However, "the United States failed to explain how precisely the results of the two comparison methodologies would be combined". *Finally*, applying the proper test for inutility, the Appellate Body found that "[i]t has not been proven that in all cases, or at least in most of them, the two

[10] Appellate Body Report, *US – Softwood Lumber V (Article 21.5 – Canada)*, para. 97.
[11] *Ibid.*

methodologies would produce the same results".[12] The Appellate Body, therefore, found that the concerns regarding "mathematical equivalence" were unwarranted.[13]

16. The Appellate Body added that the second sentence of Article 2.4.2 does not provide contextual support for a finding that zeroing is permissible because, "[i]n order to unmask targeted dumping, an investigating authority may limit the application of the W-T comparison methodology [under the second sentence] to the prices of export transactions falling within the relevant pattern".[14] On this interpretation, absent zeroing, a comparison based on this sub-set of transactions would not produce the same outcome as a W-to-W comparison under the first sentence. There is, therefore, no need to permit zeroing under the second sentence of Article 2.4.2 in order to avoid the inutility of the sentence.

A. Zeroing as Used by the USDOC in Original Investigations Is Inconsistent with Article 2.4.2 of the Anti-Dumping Agreement

17. After noting that "model zeroing" had already been found to be inconsistent with Article 2.4.2 in *US – Zeroing (EC)* when used in W-to-W comparisons, the Appellate Body in *US – Zeroing (Japan)* went on to explain that (simple) zeroing in T-to-T comparisons is likewise inconsistent.[15]

B. Zeroing as Used by the USDOC in Periodic Reviews Is Inconsistent with Article 9.3 of the Anti-Dumping Agreement

18. The requirement set forth in the *chapeau* of Article 9.3 parallels the language of Article VI:2 of the GATT 1994. It also reflects the rule in Article 9.1 that the amount of duty can be no more than the margin of dumping. As a discipline on the "magnitude" of the duty imposed[16], the rule that the maximum amount of anti-dumping duty cannot exceed the "margin of dumping" reflects the "*overarching principle*" in Article VI of the GATT 1994 and Article 11.1 of the *Anti-Dumping Agreement* that duties may be imposed solely "*to the extent necessary* to counteract *dumping*" during the time period covered by the review.[17]

19. On the basis of this treaty text, the Appellate Body held that "the margin of dumping established for an exporter or foreign producer operates as a *ceiling* for the total amount of anti-dumping duties that can be levied on the entries of the subject product (from that exporter) covered by the duty assessment proceeding".[18] The express reference to Article 2 in the *chapeau* of Article 9.3 includes, among others, Article 2.1, which, as noted above, sets forth a definition of

[12] Appellate Body Report, *US – Softwood Lumber V (Article 21.5 – Canada)*, para. 99.
[13] Appellate Body Report, *US – Softwood Lumber V (Article 21.5 – Canada)*, para. 100.
[14] Appellate Body Report, *US – Zeroing (Japan)*, para. 135.
[15] Appellate Body Report, *US – Zeroing (Japan)*, para. 123.
[16] Appellate Body Report, *US – Carbon Steel*, para. 70.
[17] Appellate Body Report, *US – OCTG Sunset Reviews (Mexico)*, para. 115.
[18] Appellate Body Report, *US – Zeroing (EC)*, para. 130. Original emphasis. *See also* Appellate Body Report, *US – Zeroing (Japan)*, para. 155.

"dumping" that applies "[f]or the purpose of this Agreement". In *US – Zeroing (EC)*, relying on these textual cross-references, the Appellate Body made an explicit interpretive connection between a "product as a whole" requirement of Article 2.1 and dumping determinations in periodic reviews under Article 9.3.[19]

20. Accordingly, if, in a periodic review, the investigating authority chooses to undertake multiple comparisons at an intermediate stage, it is not permitted to take into account the results of only some of the multiple comparisons, while disregarding others. Thus, for purposes of these reviews, the investigating authority must aggregate all multiple comparisons to establish a margin of dumping for the "product" under investigation as a whole. It is required to compare the anti-dumping duties collected on all entries of the subject merchandise from a given exporter or foreign producer with that exporter's or foreign producer's margin of dumping for the product as a whole, to ensure that the total amount of the former does not exceed the latter.[20]

21. The Appellate Body also rejected the United States' argument that, in a periodic review, "dumping" and "margins of dumping" can be determined on an importer- or import-specific basis. In doing so, the Appellate Body relied in part on Article 6.10 as context, which precludes the calculation of a margin of dumping for each individual import transaction, and it also requires that margins be calculated for exporters and foreign producers, not importers.[21] The United States objects to the Appellate Body's interpretation that margins of dumping are determined for foreign producers or exporters. However, as the Appellate Body previously explained, the United States' misgivings are misplaced. Although *margins of dumping* are established for foreign producers or exporters for a product as a whole, Members can assess anti-dumping *duties* on "a transaction- or importer-specific basis", "provided that the total amount of anti-dumping duties that are levied does not exceed the exporters' or foreign producers' margins of dumping".[22]

22. The United States argues that Members using a prospective normal value system are entitled to assess duties on the basis of a transaction-specific margin of dumping. And, it says, the same entitlement to make transaction-specific assessments should be afforded to users of retrospective systems. However, Articles 9.1 and 9.2, and Article VI:2 allow duties to be collected in appropriate amounts not exceeding the margin of dumping, determined either during the investigation or a subsequent review. The manner in which a Member chooses to impose and collect duties under Article 9 – retrospectively or prospectively – does not alter the uniform definition of "dumping" in Article 2.1 and Article VI:1.

---

[19] Appellate Body Report, *US – Zeroing (EC)*, para. 127, quoting Appellate Body Report, *US – Softwood Lumber V*, para. 99.

[20] Appellate Body Report, *US – Zeroing (EC)*, para. 132.

[21] Appellate Body Report, *US – Zeroing (EC)*, para. 128. *See also* Appellate Body Report, *US – Zeroing (Japan)*, para. 112.

[22] Appellate Body Report, *US – Zeroing (EC)*, para. 131.

C. Other Issues on Brazil's Claims

23. The United States argues that with respect to two administrative reviews Brazil has failed to satisfy its burden of proving that zeroing was applied to, or had an impact on, the challenged margins of dumping. Japan would like to note that in *US – Continued Zeroing (EC)*, the Appellate Body stated, "[w]e therefore consider that the Panel disregarded the significance of the submitted evidence when it failed to *give consideration to that evidence in its totality*, including evidence that, in the Panel's view, did not by itself show that simple zeroing was applied in a particular periodic review".[23]

24. The United States appears to be based on the premise that Brazil would claim that continued use of zeroing is inconsistent solely with Article 2.4.2 of the *Anti-Dumping Agreement*. It is not true, and Japan notes that Brazil claims that the continued use by the United States of its zeroing procedures violates Article 2.4.2 in relation to the original investigations; and Article VI:2 of the GATT 1994 and Article 9.3 in relation to the imposition and collection of anti-dumping duties.

III. CONCLUSION

25. Japan submits the following:

(1) two administrative reviews concerning imports of certain orange juice from Brazil are inconsistent with Article 9.3 of the *Anti-Dumping Agreement* and Article VI:2 of the GATT 1994 due to the use of zeroing;

(2) the continued use by the United States of zeroing procedures in successive anti-dumping proceedings, in relation to the anti-dumping duty order issued in respect of imports of certain orange juice from Brazil, including the original investigation and subsequent administrative reviews, by which duties are applied and maintained over a period of time, is inconsistent with Articles 2.4.2 and 9.3 of the *Anti-Dumping Agreement*, and Article VI:2 of the GATT 1994.

---

[23] Appellate Body Report, *US – Continued Zeroing (EC)*, para. 337. Underlining Added.

ANNEX B-4

EXECUTIVE SUMMARY OF THE THIRD PARTY WRITTEN SUBMISSION OF KOREA

1. Korea addresses in its submission (1) certain issues presented in the request by the United States for a preliminary ruling; and (2) some additional substantive issues raised by the parties in their submissions.

I. THE UNITED STATES' REQUEST FOR PRELIMINARY RULINGS SHOULD BE REJECTED

2. In its first written submission, the United States requests preliminary rulings with regard to two issues. First, the United States argues that the USDOC's final determination in the second administrative review of the antidumping order on Certain Orange Juice from Brazil is not within the Panel's terms of reference because that determination was not the subject of consultations between the parties. Second, the United States asks the Panel to find that the "continued use of the US 'zeroing procedures' in successive anti-dumping proceedings" lacks the required specificity and is not within the Panel's terms of reference.

3. The United States has contended that the USDOC's determination in the second administrative review was not adequately described in Brazil's request for consultations. Korea notes, however, that Brazil's Addendum to its initial request for consultations dated 22 May 2009 specifically indicated that "[t]he consultations, held on 16 January 2009, covered the ... the Antidumping Duty Administrative Review from 1 March 2007 to 29 February 2008 (the "Second Administrative Review")".

4. As a separate matter, it should be noted that it is beyond dispute that Brazil's 20 August 2009 request for establishment of a panel in this dispute did specifically identify the second administrative review as one of "the measures at issue". In describing that measure, Brazils' panel request also specifically referred to the USDOC's 11 August 2009 final determination in that review.

5. The preliminary ruling request by the United States does not address the significance of this statement in Brazil's panel request. This silence suggests that the United States believes that the USDOC's second administrative review can only fall within the Panel's terms of reference if the *final determination* in that review was specifically referenced in the consultation request, as well as in the panel request itself. However, that interpretation is not consistent with the provisions of the relevant agreements.

6. Article 17.3 of the *Anti-Dumping Agreement*, which authorizes WTO Members to request consultations, does not contain any language that might be read to suggest that a Member must wait to request consultations until a final

determination has been issued. By contrast, the first sentence Article 17.4 of the *Anti-Dumping Agreement*, which authorizes WTO Members to refer matters to the DSB for establishment of a panel, does specifically require complaining Members to wait until (1) consultations under Article 17.3 "have failed to achieve a mutually agreed solution", *and* (2) "final action has been taken by the administering authorities of the importing Member to levy anti-dumping duties...". If the administrative authorities have not yet taken "final action," the matter may not be referred to the DSB for establishment of a panel (except to the extent permitted by the second sentence of Article 17.4, concerning panel review of "provisional measures").

7. The clear implication is that consultations may be requested before "final action has been taken by the administering authorities". After all, if consultations could not be requested before such "final action," there would be no need to include a requirement of "final action" in the first sentence Article 17.4. Instead, if consultations could be requested only after "final action" by the administering authorities, then the provisions of the first sentence of Article 17.4 requiring that consultations be held (and "have failed") would embody a requirement of "final action" as well. Under such an interpretation, the language requiring "final action" in the first sentence of Article 17.4 would be redundant.

8. In accordance with the principle that "a treaty interpreter must give meaning and effect to all terms used in a treaty provision and must avoid interpretations which render treaty terms redundant" in WTO jurisprudence, the provisions of Articles 17.3 and 17.4 of the *Anti-Dumping Agreement* must be understood to indicate that consultations may be requested before "final action" by the administering authorities, while the establishment of a panel may not be requested until after that "final action" has occurred. Consequently, there is no basis for the argument by the United States that Brazil's request for consultations with respect to the second administrative review before the USDOC issued its final determination in that review was somehow improper or invalid.

9. The United States also requests that the Panel make a preliminary ruling that Brazil's reference to the "continued use of the US 'zeroing procedures'" does not properly describe a "measure" that can fall within the Panel's terms of reference. In particular, the United States argues that the description of the measure in Brazil's panel request lacks specificity because the alleged measure did not exist at the time of the panel request.

10. Korea notes that a measure may be identified either by the name or number of promulgation, law, regulations, etc. or by a narrative description of the nature of the measure, so that the measure may be discerned by the panel examining the panel request. As the Appellate Body has explained, the specificity requirement under Article 6.2 of the DSU is designed to ensure that a panel request "present[s] the problem clearly". The Appellate Body has also found that "the identification of a measure within the meaning of Article 6.2 need be framed only with sufficient particularity so as to indicate the nature of the measure and the gist of what is at issue".

11. In item (d) of its panel request, under the heading "Measures and claims", Brazil has identified the anti-dumping duty order, case No A-350-840 and the original investigation and subsequent administrative reviews under such order. It appears to be sufficiently clear in this dispute that the measure referred to is "a string of connected and sequential determinations" in which the United States uses the zeroing methodology by which duties are maintained over a period of time under the anti-dumping duty order.

12. It should also be noted that the Appellate Body in *US – Continued Zeroing* concluded that a Member's "ongoing conduct" constitutes a measure and is challengeable by another Member. According to the Appellate Body, such a measure would not fall squarely within the "as such" or "as applied" distinction, but that fact would not preclude a Member from bringing a challenge in WTO dispute settlement. As Brazil notes in its first written submission, the ongoing conduct that was at issue in the *US – Continued Zeroing* is virtually identical to the ongoing conduct at issue in this dispute. The zeroing practice by the USDOC maintained and applied in successive phases of the anti-dumping proceeding under the anti-dumping duty order on certain orange juice from Brazil is an ongoing conduct that is inconsistent with the *Anti-Dumping Agreement*.

13. In addition, it should be recalled that the identification of a measure is distinct from the demonstration of the existence of a measure. According to the Appellate Body, the demonstration of the existence of a measure can, if necessary, be made at subsequent stages of the dispute. It would be inappropriate, therefore, to dismiss Brazil's claims in whole or in part without allowing it a full opportunity to present its case.

II. THE PRACTICE OF "ZEROING" IN ORIGINAL INVESTIGATIONS IS INCONSISTENT WITH ARTICLE 2.4.2 OF THE *ANTI-DUMPING AGREEMENT*

14. In its first written submission, the United States concedes that its zeroing practice utilized in original investigations is inconsistent with Article 2.4.2 of the *Anti-Dumping Agreement*. There no longer appears to be any dispute with respect to this issue.

15. In light of the decisions holding zeroing in investigations to be inconsistent with Article 2.4.2, the USDOC has stated that, effective 22 February 2007 it will no longer utilize the practice of zeroing in new and pending investigations. However, this change in practice was not applied to the anti-dumping investigation that is the subject of this dispute, because the final results and the amended final results of the original investigation of anti-dumping duties on certain orange juice from Brazil were published on 13 January 2006 and 21 February 2006 - more than a year before the effective date of the USDOC's 22 February 2007 change in practice.

16. Because the USDOC has only implemented its change in practice for original investigations that were either pending on or commenced after 22 Feb-

ruary 2007, the final results of the original investigation that is the subject of this dispute were calculated using the zeroing methodology that the United States has admitted is inconsistent with Article 2.4.2 of the *Anti-Dumping Agreement*. Therefore, the Panel should find the practice of zeroing in the original investigation of anti-dumping duties on certain orange juice from Brazil inconsistent with Article 2.4.2 of the *Anti-Dumping Agreement*.

III. THE PRACTICE OF "ZEROING" IN PERIODIC REVIEWS IS INCONSISTENT WITH ARTICLE 9.3 OF THE *ANTI-DUMPING AGREEMENT* AND ARTICLE VI:2 OF THE GATT 1994

17. The Appellate Body has repeatedly ruled that the USDOC's practice of zeroing in periodic administrative reviews is inconsistent with the *Anti-Dumping Agreement* - and it has held that panels considering this issue should follow the Appellate Body's reasoning on this issue. However, the United States contends that, notwithstanding the rulings by the Appellate Body, the practice of zeroing in periodic "administrative reviews" should be found to be consistent with the *Anti-Dumping Agreement*. Korea considers the United States' arguments unconvincing and submits that the Panel should once again find that the United States' practice of zeroing in administrative reviews is inconsistent with the *Anti-Dumping Agreement*.

18. In ruling that the USDOC's practice of zeroing in periodic "administrative reviews" is inconsistent with Article 9.3 of the *Anti-Dumping Agreement* and GATT Article VI:2, the Appellate Body has explicitly rejected the United States' arguments that "dumping" and "margin of dumping" can be found to exist at the level of individual transactions.

19. The Appellate Body, in analyzing the concept of "dumping" and "margin of dumping," has examined the context in other provisions of the *Anti-Dumping Agreement*, such as Articles 5.8, 6.10, 9.5, as well as the concept of injurious dumping, and concluded that the *Anti-Dumping Agreement* does not refer to "dumping" and "margin of dumping" as existing at the level of individual transactions. Korea believes that the Appellate Body's analyses are readily available to the Panel and does not see the need to repeat all of the Appellate Body's reasoning. Like the Appellate Body, Korea is unable to find "a textual or contextual basis in the GATT 1994 or the *Anti-Dumping Agreement* for treating transactions that occur above normal value as "dumped", for purposes of determining the existence and magnitude of dumping in the original investigation, and as "non-dumped", for purposes of assessing the final liability for payment of anti-dumping duties in a period review". It is time that the United States bring its practice in periodic administrative reviews into conformity with requirements of the *Anti-Dumping Agreement* - as it already has with original investigations.

ANNEX B-5

EXECUTIVE SUMMARY OF THE THIRD PARTY WRITTEN SUBMISSION OF MEXICO

I. INTRODUCTION

1. As a WTO member likewise seeking compliance by the United States with its WTO obligations in relation to the practice of "zeroing" in anti-dumping duty "administrative reviews" conducted by the U.S. Department of Commerce, Mexico has a systemic interest in the proper interpretation and application of the various provisions of the *Antidumping Agreement*, GATT 1994, and the DSU. Also, Mexico, as well as other WTO Members, has been facing the application of zeroing by the United States in antidumping duty "administrative reviews", and has been dealing with the fact that the United States has not eliminated this practice despite several recommendations from the DSB.

2. The substantive core of Brazil's challenge in this dispute is the WTO-consistency of the United States' application of zeroing in anti-dumping administrative reviews. However, given that the principal substantive issue in this proceeding has been decided the same way many times over, Mexico will limit its response to three issues of systemic importance to Mexico and other WTO Members.

3. First, Mexico will address the compelling need for this Panel to follow the consistent body of Appellate Body jurisprudence in this area. Second, Mexico will discuss the United States' request for a preliminary ruling with respect to the inclusion within the Panel's terms of reference of an antidumping administrative review that was not final as of the date Brazil first requested consultations. Finally, Mexico will address the United States' request for a preliminary ruling that Brazil's challenge to "ongoing conduct" is not subject to the scrutiny of WTO dispute settlement.

II. THE PANEL SHOULD FOLLOW THE CONSISTENT LINE OF APPELLATE BODY JURISPRUDENCE IN THIS AREA

4. The United States requests that this Panel reconsider and reject the long line of consistent Appellate Body rulings in this area and instead chart a course of its own. This Panel should reject that suggestion and should adhere to the well-established WTO jurisprudence – not only because the prior Appellate Body decisions were correctly decided, but because there are strong systemic reasons to adhere to this consistent body of law.

5. As recognized both by WTO panels and the Appellate Body, there are important systemic reasons for following the reasoning of the Appellate Body in

previous disputes when issues already decided are presented again to a new panel. As one panel succinctly summarized, "following the Appellate Body's conclusions in earlier disputes is not only appropriate, but is what would be expected from panels, especially where the issues are the same".[1]

6. As the United States is unable to identify any new substantive arguments not already rejected in previous proceedings, and as the substance of all of Brazil's legal claims have been considered and affirmed in a long line of consistent prior Appellate Body decisions, this Panel should adopt the reasoning from those prior decisions and hold (yet again) the United States' zeroing methodology in violation of the *Antidumping Agreement* and the GATT 1994.

III. THE SECOND ADMINISTRATIVE REVIEW IS WITHIN THE PANEL'S TERMS OF REFERENCE

7. The United States seeks a preliminary ruling that the Panel's terms of reference do not include the Second Administrative Review on the grounds that this measure was not subject to consultations because the final results of that review were not published until after Brazil first requested consultations. The United is factually incorrect and misstates the role of consultations request in defining the Panel's terms of reference under the DSU.

8. Previous panels and the Appellate Body have specifically highlighted that a WTO panel's terms of reference are governed by the complaining Member's panel request, as opposed to it its consultations request. There is no dispute that the final results of the Second Administrative Review were published prior to Brazil's panel request. It is equally clear that Brazil's panel request identified the Second Administrative Review, and specifically the final results published on 11 August 2009, as a "measure at issue".

9. Moreover, the United States is incorrect in its suggestion that the consultations request sets the matter in stone, thereby limiting what can properly be included in the panel request. As long as Brazil made clear that it was challenging the application of zeroing in recent and ongoing periodic administrative reviews, sufficient notice was provided to the United States, and the Second Administrative Review could properly be challenged in the panel request as a measure subject to the Panel's terms of reference.

10. But even if this was not the case, Brazil's challenge to the United States' application of zeroing in the Second Administrative Review would still properly fall within the Panel's terms of reference because, as a factual matter, Brazil did specifically seek consultations-and, in fact, consulted with the United States-about this particular measure.

11. Accordingly, there is no question that Brazil properly included in its panel request its challenge to the application of zeroing in the Second Adminis-

[1] Appellate Body Report, *United States – Sunset Reviews of Anti-Dumping Measures on Oil Country Tubular Goods from Argentina*, WT/DS268/AB/R, adopted 17 December 2004, para. 188.

trative Review. Therefore, the United States' request for a preliminary ruling in this respect should be denied.

IV. THE CONTINUED USE OF THE US ZEROING PROCEDURES ARE PROPERLY CHALLENGED AND SUBJECT TO PANEL REVIEW IN THIS DISPUTE

12. The United States is equally misguided in its request for a preliminary ruling *(i)* that Brazil's challenge to the continued use of US zeroing procedures fails to meet the requirement under Article 6.2 of the DSU that panel requests identify specific measures at issue, and *(ii)* that Brazil appears to be challenging an indeterminate number of potential future measures that are outside of the scope of the Panel's terms of reference because the measures are not yet in existence.

13. First, as the Appellate Body has pointed out, the specificity requirement is intended to ensure the sufficiency of a panel request in presenting the problem clearly. The problem here-the United States' continued application of zeroing in successive antidumping proceedings-is clear and easy to discern. Accordingly, the requirement under Article 6.2 has been met.

14. Second, in this dispute Brazil challenges the continued application of zeroing in periodic reviews conducted as stages of a continuous proceeding involving the imposition, assessment, and collection of duties under the same antidumping duty order. With respect to the proceeding on certain orange juice from Brazil, the United States Department of Commerce has applied zeroing at every stage and has given no indication that it will change its approach in future stages. It is this recurring conduct under the single antidumping duty order that Brazil challenges here.

15. It is the ongoing conduct of the United States in continuing to use zeroing in successive determinations by which anti-dumping duties are applied and maintained that Brazil is challenging as "ongoing conduct" here. Brazil is entitled to frame its challenge in way that subjects this ongoing conduct to the scrutiny of WTO dispute settlement. Accordingly, the United States' request for a preliminary ruling in this respect should be denied.

V. CONCLUSION

16. For the foregoing reasons, Mexico respectfully requests that the Panel deny the United States' requests for preliminary rulings. Mexico also submits that the Panel should follow the well-established precedent holding the United States' application of zeroing in violation of the *Antidumping Agreement* and the GATT 1994.

17. Mexico appreciates the opportunity to participate in these proceedings, and to present its views to the Panel.

ANNEX C

ORAL STATEMENTS OR EXECUTIVE SUMMARIES THEREOF OF THE PARTIES AT THE FIRST SUBSTANTIVE MEETING OF THE PANEL

ANNEX C-1

EXECUTIVE SUMMARY OF THE OPENING STATEMENT OF BRAZIL AT THE FIRST MEETING OF THE PANEL

I. INTRODUCTION

1. Brazil responds, in turn, to the legal and factual arguments in the US First Written Submission ("FWS"). At the outset, Brazil notes that in this dispute, the US consistently encourages the Panel to depart from established precedent in *Zeroing* disputes. Brazil regrets such arguments, noting that "WTO Members attach significance to reasoning provided in previous panel and Appellate Body reports".[1] Contrary to the US suggestions, Article 11 of the DSU does not imply that relevant previous rulings by the Appellate Body should not be followed. On the contrary, respecting previous and repeated rulings – which have been adopted by the WTO Membership in the DSB – is part and parcel of, and even facilitates, a panel's objective assessment under Article 11 of the DSU.[2]

---

1 Appellate Body Report, *US – Stainless Steel*, para. 160.

2 *See* Appellate Body Report, *US – Stainless Steel*, paras. 157 – 162.

II. THE *ANTI-DUMPING AGREEMENT* AND THE GATT 1994 DEFINE "DUMPING" IN RELATION TO THE "PRODUCT" AS A WHOLE

2. The US rightly notes that "this dispute is about the definitions of 'dumping' and 'margin of dumping'".[3] Brazil argues that these concepts are defined by reference to the product as a whole. Conversely, the US argues that these concepts are sufficiently "flexible" that they may be defined by individual Members in relation (1) to the "product" as a whole; (2) to each individual transaction relating to the "product"; or even (3) to both conceptions.

3. As a basis for its plea for unilateral discretion, the U.S. relies on Article 17.6(ii) of the *Anti-Dumping Agreement*, but misreads it. Article 17.6(ii) comprises two sentences. The first enjoins a panel to interpret the *Anti-Dumping Agreement* using the customary rules of treaty interpretation. The second provides that, when these rules yield multiple permissible interpretations, a measure is WTO-consistent if it rests on one permissible interpretation. As the Appellate Body said in *US – Continued Zeroing*, "Article 17.6(ii) contemplates a sequential analysis", with a panel first applying the customary rules of interpretation in a "conscientious" manner. "Only *after* engaging in this exercise will a panel be able to determine whether the second sentence of Article 17.6(ii) applies".[4]

4. The Appellate Body has applied the rules of treaty interpretation to the definitions of "dumping" and "margin of dumping" in the past, and found that they lead to a product-wide meaning, and that therefore there is no room for resorting to the second sentence of Article 17.6(ii).[5] It has added that the notion of multiple permissible interpretations cannot be stretched to include *rival* interpretations.[6]

5. Brazil has set forth its interpretation of these terms, explaining that they refer to the product as a whole, in its FWS.[7] Brazil recalls that Article 2.1 of the *Anti-Dumping Agreement*, by defining "dumping" "[f]or the purpose of this Agreement", makes plain that "dumping" has the same meaning "in all provisions of the Agreement and for all types of anti-dumping proceedings".[8] The requirement to give the concept of "dumping" a consistent meaning throughout the *Anti-Dumping Agreement* is crucial because: "Nothing could be more important than the definition of the concept of "dumping". It is foundational and applies throughout the Agreement, as the clear wording of Article 2.1 makes plain.

---

[3] US FWS, para. 60.

[4] Appellate Body Report, *US – Continued Zeroing*, para. 271. Original emphasis. *See also*, Appellate Body Report, *US – Hot-Rolled Steel*, para. 60.

[5] Appellate Body Report, *US – Zeroing (Japan)*, para. 189.

[6] Appellate Body Report, *US – Continued Zeroing*, para. 273 and Concurring Opinion, para. 312.

[7] *See* Brazil's FWS, paras. 49 – 61.

[8] Appellate Body Report, *US – Zeroing (Japan)*, para. 109.

It cannot have variable or contradictory meanings, for that would infect the entire Agreement."[9]

6. The US argues that Brazil is wrong to interpret "dumping" and "margin of dumping" uniformly throughout the *Anti-Dumping Agreement* and Article VI:1 and VI:2 as referring to the product as a whole, and finds support in the use of the singular words "product" and "price" in Article VI:1 of the GATT 1994 and Article 2.1 of the *Anti-Dumping Agreement.* However, the cited provisions use "price" in the singular also when referring to "normal value", which is not defined in relation to a single transaction. Normal value is the "comparable price, *in the ordinary course of trade, for the like product*". "The ordinary course of trade" cannot be ascertained on the basis of one transaction; and the adjective "normal" indicates that the price is the "regular", "usual", "standard" or "common" price for "the like product". Such a "price" cannot be ascertained on the basis of one transaction, but must be based on all relevant transactions contributing to the "normal" price. The French and Spanish language versions of Article 2.1 confirm this view.

7. Numerous contextual provisions of the *Anti-Dumping Agreement* confirm that "dumping" and "margin of dumping" are defined in relation to the product as a whole. For example, *first*, Article 5.8 of the *Anti-Dumping Agreement* requires the termination of an investigation into an exporter if "the margin of dumping" is *de minimis*. The US position would mean that an authority's termination decision would be made for each individual export transaction. This is absurd.[10] *Second*, Article 6.10 requires that an authority determine "an *individual* margin of dumping for *each known exporter or producer* concerned of *the product* under investigation".[11] Similar language appears in Articles 6.10.2 and 9.5. *Third,* under Article 3, an authority must assess the injurious effects of "dumped imports", a term that covers *all* imports from an exporter engaged in "dumping".[12] For purposes of Article 3, and consistent with Article 6.10, a single dumping determination, based on all export transactions, is made for an exporter, and that single determination influences the treatment of all imports from that party.[13] *Fourth*, under Articles 8 and 9 of the *Anti-Dumping Agreement* and the GATT 1994, the extent of permissible remedial action to counter injurious "dumping" is fixed by reference to a single margin of dumping, and that remedy applies to *all* future imports of the "product".[14]

---

9 Appellate Body Report, *US – Continued Zeroing*, Concurring Opinion, para. 307. *See* also, e.g., Appellate Body Report, *US – Stainless Steel*, para. 107, and Appellate Body Report, *US – Continued Zeroing*, para. 285.

10 *See* Appellate Body Report, *US – Continued Zeroing*, para. 283.

11 *See* Appellate Body Report, *US – Softwood Lumber V*, footnote 158, citing Appellate Body Report, *US – Hot-Rolled Steel*, para. 118.

12 Appellate Body Report, *EC – Bed Linen (21.5)*, para. 115. *See also* Panel Report, *Argentina – Poultry Anti-Dumping Duties*, para. 7.303.

13 *See, e.g.,* Appellate Body Report, *US – Stainless Steel*, para. 108.

14 *See* Articles 8.1, 9.1 and 9.3, and Appellate Body Report, *US – Softwood Lumber V (21.5)*, para. 108.

8. In sum, there is both consistency and logic to the text of the *Anti-Dumping Agreement*. By defining "dumping" in relation to the product as a whole, the *Anti-Dumping Agreement* ensures parallelism between the scope of a dumping determination and the scope of the legal consequences this determination entails. This parallelism is important because, under Article II:2(b) of the GATT 1994, anti-dumping duties frequently exceed the level of a Member's bound rates. To justify imposing anti-dumping duties on a product-wide basis, a dumping determination must be made on an equivalent product-wide basis.[15]

9. The U.S. also argues that "dumping" may have a transaction-specific meaning because the word "product" in Article VII:3 of the GATT 1994, on customs valuation, refers to individual transactions. The US confuses proximity (of Article VII:3 with Articles VI:1 and VI:2) with context. The purpose and consequences of a customs valuation decision and of anti-dumping proceedings are altogether different.[16]

10. The Note *Ad* Article VI:1, on which the US also relies, does not alter the requirement to determine dumping for the product as a whole, but simply provides for the situation where sales to an importer may not be relied upon directly because the exporter and the importer are related. The US argument that a product-wide definition of "dumping" and a prohibition on zeroing under Article 9.3 prevent anti-dumping duties from being effective is also flawed, because "it is the exporter, not the importer, that engages in" dumping.[17] Other US arguments have been comprehensively dealt with and rejected by the Appellate Body, and in some cases by panels, too.[18]

---

15 Brazil also rejects the argument, in footnotes 8 and 144 of the US FWS, that cash deposits are not subject to the disciplines in Article 9.3 of the *Anti-Dumping Agreement*. In several disputes, the DSB has ruled that cash deposits rates calculated with zeroing are inconsistent with this provision (Appellate Body Reports, *US – Stainless Steel*, paras. 133 – 134 and 156(a); *US – Continued Zeroing*, paras. 315 – 316 and 395(d); *US – Zeroing (EC) (21.5)*, para. 294; and Panel Report, *US – Zeroing (Japan) (21.5)*, paras. 7.166 – 7.168 and 8.1(b). *See* also Appellate Body Report, *US – Zeroing (Japan)*, para. 156). In compliance proceedings in *US – Zeroing (Japan)*, the US itself argued in vain that its implementation obligations under Article 9.3 applied *solely* to cash deposit rates, and not assessment rates (*see* Panel Report, *US – Zeroing (EC) (21.5)*, para. 8.155(b); Appellate Body Report, *US – Zeroing (EC) (21.5)*, para. 6; Panel Report, *US – Zeroing (Japan) (21.5)*, para. 3.3; and Appellate Body Report, *US – Zeroing (Japan) (21.5)*, para. 12). Thus, the applicability of Article 9.3 to cash deposit rates is well-established, and has been accepted by the US.

16 Under Article 1.1 of the *Customs Valuation Agreement*, the customs value is the price actually paid or payable in a specific import transaction. The authority does not value goods following an investigation into a large number of transactions relating to a "product" that the authority itself has defined. Nor does the act of customs valuation for an individual entry necessarily entail, for example, the imposition of duties in excess of bound rates on all entries of the product.

17 Appellate Body Report, *US – Zeroing (Japan)*, para. 156.

18 *See*, respectively: (i) on Article 2.2, Appellate Body Report, *US – Softwood Lumber V (21.5)*, paras. 82, 97 and 104; (ii) on prospective normal value systems and the US confusion between duty collection under prospective normal value systems and the determination of the margin of dumping, Appellate Body Report, *US – Zeroing (Japan)*, paras. 160, 162 – 163 and 166; and Appellate Body Report, *US – Continued Zeroing*, para. 294; Panel Report, *US – Stainless Steel*, para. 7.131; and Appellate Body Report, *US – Stainless Steel*, para. 120; (iii) and on "mathematical equivalence", Appellate Body Report, *US – Zeroing (Japan)*, paras. 133 – 135; Appellate Body Report, *US – Soft-*

III. ZEROING AS A MATTER OF FACT IN THE MEASURES AT ISSUE

A. USDOC Program Logs

11. For the First Review, Brazil inadvertently submitted as Exhibit BRA-30 a log generated by its expert, Mr. Ferrier, when rerunning the USDOC software earlier this year. In *US – Continued Zeroing*, the Appellate Body has questioned the significance of the fact that logs were replicated using the USDOC programs, rather than being directly generated by the USDOC.[19] In any event, in Exhibit BRA-45, Brazil now submits the log that Fischer received from the USDOC with its final results in the First Review. The US also contests the provenance of the log for Fischer's Third Administrative Review (Exhibit BRA-25), although without explanation.[20] Fischer received the log in Exhibit BRA-25 directly from the USDOC, as evidenced by USDOC's email that Brazil submits as Exhibit BRA-46.

B. Cutrale's First and Fischer's Second Administrative Reviews

12. The US argues that Brazil has not met its burden of proving that zeroing was applied to, or had an impact on, the margin of dumping for Cutrale in the First Review, because the USDOC determined a margin of dumping lower than the US *de minimis* threshold. The US makes similar arguments regarding Fischer in the Second Review, because the cash deposit and importer-specific assessment rates were zero. The US is wrong on a number of counts.

13. *First*, as a matter of law, the *use* of zeroing is, in itself, sufficient to establish a violation of the *Anti-Dumping Agreement* and the GATT 1994.[21]

14. In this dispute, the use of zeroing to calculate margins of dumping in administrative reviews violates Articles 2.4 and 9.3 of the *Anti-Dumping Agreement*, and Article VI:2 of the GATT 1994. Brazil has already presented arguments on Article 9.3 and Article VI:2[22], and now presents arguments based on Article 2.4.[23] The Appellate Body has held that, as a "*way of calculating*" margins, the zeroing methodology "cannot be described as impartial, even-handed, or unbiased", because it necessarily excludes any negative comparisons results.[24] The Appellate Body has, therefore, ruled that the "maintenance" of zeroing procedures in administrative reviews is inconsistent with Article 2.4 of the *Anti-*

wood Lumber V (21.5), paras. 97 – 100; Appellate Body Report, *US – Stainless Steel*, paras. 126 – 127; Appellate Body Report, *US – Continued Zeroing*, para. 297.

[19] Appellate Body Report, *US – Continued Zeroing*, para. 340.

[20] US FWS, footnote 145.

[21] *See, e.g.,* Panel Report, *US – Zeroing (Japan) (21.5)*, para. 7.162.

[22] Brazil's FWS, paras. 62 – 76 and 97.

[23] Brazil's panel request, p. 3, includes claims under Article 2.4.

[24] Appellate Body Report, *US – Zeroing (Japan)*, para. 146, quoting Appellate Body Report, *US – Softwood Lumber V (21.5)*, para. 142. *See also* Appellate Body Report, *US – Softwood Lumber V (21.5)*, para. 138; and Appellate Body Report, *US – Corrosion-Resistant Steel Sunset Review*, para. 135.

Dumping Agreement.[25] Consequently, by including zeroing in its methodology for determining margins of dumping in the administrative reviews at issue, the US failed to conduct a "fair comparison".

15. Brazil has established that the USDOC *used* zeroing for Cutrale's determination in the First Review, and for Fischer's determination in the Second Review[26], and the US does not contest this. As a result, the US violated Articles 2.4 and 9.3 of the *Anti-Dumping Agreement* and Article VI:2 of the GATT 1994 in its dumping determinations for Cutrale in the First Review, and for Fischer in the Second Review.

16. Moreover, even though it was not required to do so, Brazil has also shown that the use of zeroing had an *impact* on the USDOC's calculation.[27] The logs and outputs for Cutrale and Fischer show that the vast majority of export transactions – in number, volume and value – generated negative comparison results, but were excluded from the calculation of the margins of dumping.[28] These facts provide an illustration of the "inherent bias in a zeroing methodology".[29]

17. The resulting overall weighted average margin of dumping for Cutrale in the First Review was 0.45 per cent, and not zero.[30] Furthermore, also using zeroing, the USDOC determined an importer-specific assessment rate for Cutrale's goods that above the US *de minimis* threshold, with anti-dumping duties collected at that rate.[31] Thus, zeroing had an impact on the calculation, and also led to the collection of duties where none would have otherwise been collected. For Fischer in the Second Review, the tiny minority of sales with a positive comparison result generated a positive margin, albeit a small one, of 0.002 per cent[32], whereas without zeroing the margin would not have been positive.

C. Existence of the Continued Use Measure

18. The US argues that Brazil has not proven the existence of the Continued Use measure to the standard set out in *US – Continued Zeroing*. In that case, the Appellate Body sought to complete the analysis on the continued use measures, which the panel had ruled to be outside the terms of reference. The Appellate Body found that the existence of continued use of zeroing in a specific anti-dumping case was established when it was proven that the zeroing methodology had been used, without interruption, in different types of proceedings over an

[25] Appellate Body Report, *US – Zeroing (Japan)*, paras. 169 and 190(d).

[26] As explained in detail in Exhibit BRA-31.

[27] This is explained in detail at paras. 35 – 38 and 40 – 44 of the Ferrier Affidavit. Exhibit BRA-31.

[28] For Cutrale, Exhibit BRA-29, p. 63 and Exhibit BRA-34, last page. For Fischer, Exhibit BRA-38, p. 76 and Exhibit BRA-39, last page. *See also* Exhibit BRA-31, paras. 38 and 56.

[29] Appellate Body Report, *US – Corrosion-Resistant Steel Sunset Review*, para. 135.

[30] Exhibit BRA-34, p. 93, "wt avg percent margin". *See also* Exhibit BRA-20.

[31] Exhibit BRA-34, p. 92, "percent ad valorem assessment".

[32] Exhibit BRA-39, p. 106, right-most column "Wt avg percent margin".

extended period of time[33], or in other words, when there was a "density of factual findings"[34] showing that zeroing had been used in successive proceedings in the same case.

19. In this dispute, Brazil has shown that zeroing has been used by the USDOC at *every available opportunity* under the Order in proceedings extending over five years from the original investigation, initiated in February 2005, through the First and Second Reviews, to the preliminary determination in the Third Review in April 2010. Furthermore, in its Issues and Decision Memoranda under the Order, the US affirmed its continued use of zeroing in administrative reviews, stating expressly that its zeroing policy in reviews is unchanged despite WTO rulings.[35] These Memoranda show that the use of zeroing continues to be part of the USDOC's calculation methodology. In sum, there is the required "density" of facts.

20. The US also repeats its arguments on the impact of zeroing. However, the conduct at issue is the continued *use* of zeroing over time, and not the continued *impact* of zeroing. It is well-established that, irrespective of the impact of zeroing, it is contrary to WTO law to maintain zeroing procedures to calculate margins, whether for their continued use in proceedings under specific anti-dumping orders[36] or for their continued use in anti-dumping proceedings generally.[37] The Appellate Body reached this conclusion in reply to a similar US argument made in *US – Continued Zeroing*.[38]

21. The US arguments that the Second and Third Review are outside the panel's terms of reference are, in this context, irrelevant, because with regard to the Continued Use measure, these reviews serve as *evidence* of the continued use of zeroing.

---

33 Appellate Body Report, *US – Continued Zeroing*, para. 195. The Appellate Body also explained that the approach it was taking was "cautious", because the panel had failed to make findings on continued use, and the Appellate Body has no mandate to find facts.

34 Appellate Body Report, *US – Continued Zeroing*, para. 191.

35 Exhibit BRA-28, pp. 5 – 6; and Exhibit BRA-43, pp. 4 – 6.

36 Appellate Body Report, *US – Continued Zeroing*, paras. 199 and 395(a)(v).

37 Appellate Body Report, *US – Zeroing (Japan)*, paras. 166, 169 – 170, 190(c) and 190(d).

38 Appellate Body Report, *US – Continued Zeroing*, para. 192.

ANNEX C-2

EXECUTIVE SUMMARY OF THE OPENING STATEMENT OF THE UNITED STATES AT THE FIRST MEETING OF THE PANEL

1. The United States would like to focus on a few points concerning Brazil's arguments. First, we will discuss how Brazil is improperly trying to include measures that fall outside of the scope of the Panel's terms of reference. Second, we will refute Brazil's claims that the United States has acted inconsistently with obligations under the *Agreement on Implementation of Article VI of the General Agreement on Tariffs and Trade 1994* ("Antidumping Agreement") or the *General Agreement on Tariffs and Trade 1994* ("GATT 1994"). A plain reading of the text of those agreements makes clear that there is no obligation to provide offsets outside of the context of average-to-average comparisons in original investigations. Reading the text to impose such obligations would render certain provisions of the Antidumping Agreement meaningless. In addition, with respect to the challenged "continued use" of "zeroing", Brazil has failed to show any basis for concluding that such alleged "ongoing conduct" exists, or any basis for a dispute settlement panel to make findings based on speculation about what measure may or may not exist in the future.

2. We recognize that this is not the first time a dispute settlement panel has considered the issue of "zeroing," that is, the alleged obligation to provide offsets for non-dumped transactions. On the one hand, the Appellate Body has found in other disputes that "zeroing" in Article 9 assessment proceedings is inconsistent with provisions of the Antidumping Agreement and the GATT 1994. Reliance upon those findings is the basis of Brazil's claims. On the other hand – as panels have found in those disputes, and as discussed fully in the US first written submission – there is no textual basis for imposing the obligations that Brazil suggests. Consistent with the standard of review provided for in Article 17.6 of the Antidumping Agreement, and the responsibilities of panels provided for in the *Understanding on Rules and Procedures Governing the Settlement of Disputes* ("DSU"), we ask this Panel to remain faithful to the text of the negotiated agreements and refrain from making the findings that Brazil suggests.

Standard of Review

3. Article 11 of the DSU generally defines a panel's task in reviewing the consistency with the covered agreements of measures taken by a WTO Member. In a dispute involving the Antidumping Agreement, a panel must also take into account the standard of review set forth in Article 17.6(ii) with respect to various permissible interpretations of a provision of the Antidumping Agreement.

4. The question under Article 17.6(ii) is whether an investigating authority's action rests upon a permissible interpretation of the Antidumping Agreement.

Article 17.6(ii) confirms that there are provisions of the Agreement that "admit[] of more than one permissible interpretation". Where that is the case, and where the investigating authority's action rests upon one such interpretation, a panel is to find that interpretation consistent with the Agreement.

5. Under Article 11 of the DSU, this Panel is charged with making an objective assessment of the matter before it, including an objective assessment of the facts and the conformity of the challenged measures with the relevant covered agreements, applying the customary rules of interpretation. The Panel cannot make findings or recommendations that add to or diminish the rights and obligations provided in the covered agreements.

6. The United States is aware that the Appellate Body has rejected the view that the covered agreements do not impose an obligation to provide offsets in assessment reviews. However, the fact that for the Appellate Body there is an interpretation under which there would be an obligation to provide offsets is not a basis for concluding that no other interpretation is permissible. The very inclusion of Article 17.6(ii) confirms that the text of the Antidumping Agreement may be susceptible to more than one interpretation. To find that it is not possible to find that there are conflicting interpretations of the text would mean depriving the second sentence of Article 17.6(ii) of meaning. If the permissible interpretations are all "harmonious", then it is difficult to see how a measure could be in conformity with only one of the interpretations. And it is not surprising that the Antidumping Agreement could be subject to more than one permissible interpretation. For example, in many instances, the text was drafted to cover varying and complex antidumping systems around the world. A number of previous panels that considered the issue have found that the interpretation that there is no obligation to provide offsets beyond the context of the average-to-average comparison methodology in investigations rests on a permissible interpretation of the Antidumping Agreement. It is difficult to understand how, if these various panels found that this interpretation is permissible, then it is not permissible.

Scope of this Dispute

7. The United States has requested a preliminary ruling that two of the measures identified in Brazil's panel request are outside the Panel's terms of reference.

8. Brazil suggests that the scope of a dispute includes any measure, adopted at any time (from before consultations through implementation), as long as the measures share the same "essence" or "close substantive connections" and together "manifest a common 'problem' that the complaining Member's claims are seeking to 'fix'". Such a sweeping approach is not based in the text of the DSU.

9. The Appellate Body has explained that the identification in a panel request may be considered to include subsequent measures in more limited circumstances, namely where those measures do not change the essence of the measure properly identified in the panel request. However, this is not the case here. Each administrative review is separate and distinct from the reviews that

proceed or follow it. The second administrative review is not a measure with the same "essence" as the first administrative review. It is a distinct measure dealing with different entries during a different period of time with different results. The final results of one administrative review do not apply to entries of merchandise for any other review. The fact that the second administrative review is a distinct measure is confirmed by Article 17 of the Antidumping Agreement which requires that there have been "final action" to "levy antidumping duties". The "final action" under the second administrative review is distinct from the "final action" under the first administrative review.

10. In addition, with respect to Brazil's claims concerning the "continued use of the US 'zeroing procedures'", this is not a "measure" that even exists. Brazil purports to include in this "measure" an indefinite number of future proceedings, none of them in existence. Any findings with respect to any such hypothetical future measure would be based only on speculation. It is not possible to have consulted on a measure not in existence or to "identify" a "specific" non-existent measure, and any findings based only on speculation could not comport with an "objective assessment" of the matter.

11. Moreover, the "essence" of a non-existent measure is nothing but speculation. In that vein, it should be noted that, apart from the *US – Zeroing II* dispute, the cases cited by Brazil in support of its broad approach to a panel's jurisdiction address situations in which the challenged "future" measures were in fact in existence, such that there was a measure that the panel could evaluate. This is not the case here with respect to the "continued use of the US 'zeroing procedures'". Rather, Brazil requests the Panel to speculate as to whether any such measure will come into existence, what that measure will consist of, and find inconsistent an indefinite number of measures that do not exist. It is not known whether any of these hypothetical future measures will even reflect "use of the US 'zeroing procedures'". For example, there may be no negative value comparisons that could be "zeroed", such that neither the margin of dumping nor the duties assessed will reflect "zeroing". (Indeed, as discussed in our first written submission, the facts Brazil itself presents bear this out.) The Panel of course is unable to analyze any such future measure since there are no details or specifics to analyze.

12. Brazil's assertion that such an indeterminate measure could be within a panel's terms of reference is based on the reasoning of the Appellate Body in the *US – Zeroing II (EC)* dispute. As just explained, however, we fail to see how a reference to the "continued use of the US 'zeroing procedures' in successive antidumping proceedings" can in any way meet the requirement of Article 6.2 of the DSU to identify the specific measures at issue. Whether something is a "measure" goes to the very question of what a Member may challenge under the DSU, and therefore what may fall within a panel's terms of reference. If something is not a "measure", then it is not, and cannot be, a measure "specifically" identified within the meaning of Article 6.2. Brazil may wish to be free of needing to provide evidence as to the existence, content, and relationship of any future measure

to the WTO agreements, but that is not consistent with the WTO dispute settlement system.

13. Furthermore, Article 17.4 of the Antidumping Agreement provides that, if consultations have failed, and if "final action" has been taken by the administering authorities of the importing Member to levy definitive antidumping duties or to accept price undertakings, a Member may refer "the matter" to dispute settlement. At the time of Brazil's consultations request, neither the second administrative review nor the alleged "continued use of the US 'zeroing procedures'" involved a final action to levy definitive antidumping duties or accept price undertakings. (While provisional measures may also be challenged in certain circumstances, Brazil has made no allegations in this regard.) Including the second administrative review and "continued use" within the terms of reference would ignore the fact that, for any given importation, the imposition of antidumping duties is grounded in a specific final action.

14. The United States first requests a preliminary ruling that the "Second Administrative Review", which appeared in Brazil's panel request but was not the subject of consultations, is outside the Panel's terms of reference. Under Article 7.1 of the DSU, the measures within a panel's terms of reference are determined by the complaining party's request for the establishment of a panel. Article 6.2 in turn provides that a panel request must "identify the specific measures at issue" in a dispute. Under Article 4.7, however, a Member may not request the establishment of a panel with respect to any measure, but only with respect to a measure that was subject to consultations. Article 4.4 requires that the request for consultations state the reasons for the request, "including identification of the measures at issue and an indication of the legal basis for the complaint". As the United States explained in its first written submission, the Antidumping Agreement contains parallel requirements in Articles 17.3 through 17.5.

15. The covered agreements therefore establish a clear progression between the measures that are discussed in consultations conducted pursuant to Article 4.4 of the DSU and the measures identified in a request to establish a panel, which, in turn, form the basis of the panel's terms of reference. This is not a question of form over substance. Under the relevant provisions in the DSU and the Antidumping Agreement just discussed, a panel's terms of reference cannot include measures that were not the subject of a request for consultations.

16. Brazil seeks to include the second administrative review in this dispute. However, the final determination in the second administrative review was issued after Brazil's request for consultations, and even after those consultations were held. It was not, and could not have been, the subject of consultations and is therefore outside this Panel's terms of reference. Brazil's argument to the contrary is based on its assertion that the second administrative review "has the same essence as" the first administrative review. However, as explained earlier, the second administrative review is not essentially the same measure as the first administrative review, and is not within the scope of this dispute.

17. The United States also asks that the Panel find that Brazil's reference in its panel request to the "continued use of the US 'zeroing procedures' in successive anti-dumping proceedings" does not meet the specificity requirement of DSU Article 6.2. As noted above, by including this purported "measure" in its panel request, Brazil is merely speculating as to what might happen in the future, and speculation as to what might happen is not identification of a specific measure.

18. In addition, Article 3.3 of the DSU contemplates the "prompt settlement of situations where a Member considers that any benefits accruing to it directly or indirectly under the covered agreements *are being impaired*" by another Member's measures. While it appears that Brazil is challenging an indeterminate number of future measures by identifying "the continued use" in its panel request, a non-existent measure cannot be impairing any such benefits and cannot fall within the scope of a dispute.

19. Finally, we note that Brazil makes repeated references to what it suggests is the desired remedy in this dispute as justifying the expansion of the scope of this proceeding. First, there have been no recommendations and rulings yet in this dispute. Moreover, a Member's desired remedy (whatever that may be) does not dictate a panel's jurisdiction and does not provide a basis for departing from the requirements of the DSU. In determining its terms of reference, a panel does not start from what the complaining Member describes as the appropriate relief and work backwards. Rather, the Panel should be guided by the requirements of the DSU, including the requirement to identify the specific measures at issue.

The Claimed Obligation to Provide Offsets

20. We now turn to comments related to Brazil's argument that the Antidumping Agreement contains an obligation to provide offsets for instances of non-dumping in the context of assessment proceedings. Brazil argues that the Antidumping Agreement imposes on Members an obligation to provide an offset to dumping in all types of antidumping proceedings, including assessment proceedings. The key issue here is whether the text of the Antidumping Agreement actually contains such an obligation that applies in assessment proceedings. The starting point must be what the text of the Agreement actually says. It is fundamental that a treaty interpreter must not impute into an agreement words and obligations that are not contained in the text. But, in this dispute, Brazil asks this Panel to read an obligation into the Antidumping Agreement, notwithstanding the fact that there is no textual basis for the obligation that Brazil proposes.

21. In particular, Brazil seeks to infer an obligation to reduce antidumping duties to account for instances of non-dumping. This treats non-dumped imports as though they were a remedy for dumped imports. Brazil does so despite the fact that there is no textual basis for such an obligation and that there is a permissible interpretation of the Antidumping Agreement that does not require such offsets.

22. In the disputes that have addressed this issue, the only textual basis panels have identified for an obligation to provide offsets has been the "all comparable export transactions" language in the text of Article 2.4.2 of the Antidumping Agreement. This is entirely consistent with the approach articulated by the Appellate Body in *US – Softwood Lumber Dumping*. The phrase "all comparable export transactions" in Article 2.4.2 applies only to antidumping investigations and only when authorities use average-to-average comparisons pursuant to Article 2.4.2. Panels have consistently characterized as persuasive the argument that the obligation to provide offsets applies only as a consequence of the text-based obligation to include all comparable export transactions when making weighted-average to weighted-average comparisons in an investigation. With respect to the argument that there is an obligation to provide offsets outside this context, the panels addressing this question have consistently reasoned that there is no textual basis for such an obligation. The analysis offered by the prior panels is persuasive and correct.

23. Article 2.4.2 provides for three different types of comparisons: two symmetrical comparison types, average-to-average and transaction-to-transaction; and a third asymmetrical comparison type, average-to-transaction, which may be used under certain conditions. With respect to the average-to-average comparisons, the phrase "all comparable export transactions", as interpreted by the Appellate Body in *US – Softwood Lumber Dumping*, addresses whether the relevant comparison may be made at the level of averaging groups (or "models"). Under this reading, the word "all" in "all comparable export transactions" refers to all transactions across all models of the product under investigation. This is the textual basis for the conclusion that margins of dumping based on average-to-average comparisons must relate to the "product as a whole", rather than individual averaging group comparisons. This phrase, "all comparable export transactions", however, applies only to the use of average-to-average comparisons in an investigation. It does not apply to the use of transaction-to-transaction or average-to-transaction comparisons. Such comparisons will necessarily result in multiple comparisons where there are numerous transactions because each export transaction will result in its own separate comparison. The text of Article 2.4.2 does not address whether or how a Member should aggregate the results of such multiple comparisons into a single overall margin of dumping.

24. A general prohibition of zeroing that applies in all proceedings and with respect to all comparison types would negate and contradict the interpretation of the phrase "all comparable export transactions" that was the basis of the obligation to provide offsets in the context of average-to-average comparisons, and for the conclusion that the margin of dumping must be calculated for "the product as a whole".

25. Brazil argues that margins of dumping calculated in assessment proceedings must relate to the "product as a whole", and cannot be calculated for individual transactions. However, "product as a whole" is not a term found in the Antidumping Agreement, nor does it have any defined meaning. Furthermore, to the extent the concept of "product as a whole" has any relevance to the Anti-

dumping Agreement, it is only as a shorthand for the operation of the phrase "all comparable export transactions" in the context of average-to-average comparisons in investigations. Brazil's argument relies entirely on the concept of "product as a whole" being applied in a manner detached from that underlying textual basis.

26. Brazil offers no textual analysis to support its claim that offsets are required by Article 2.1 of the Antidumping Agreement and Article VI of the GATT 1994. This is because the text of these provisions defines and describes dumping as occurring in the course of individual commercial transactions. Prices are generally set in individual transactions, and products are "introduced into the commerce" of the importing country in individual transactions. In other words, dumping – as defined under these provisions – may occur in a single transaction. This is entirely consistent with the exporter-specific understanding of dumping because individual transactions are also exporter-specific. There is nothing in either the GATT 1994 or the Antidumping Agreement that suggests that dumping that occurs with respect to one transaction is mitigated by the occurrence of another transaction made at a non-dumped price. To the extent that some transactions introduce merchandise into the market of an importing country at a price above normal value, this benefits the seller, but does not undo the effects on the domestic industry of other (dumped) transactions made at less than normal value.

27. Nevertheless, Brazil asserts that dumping and margins of dumping "are defined in relation to a product under investigation as a whole, encompassing all of the export transactions of the product pertaining to an investigated exporter, and they cannot be found to exist only for a type, model, or category of that product". The Appellate Body reports relied upon by Brazil for this proposition are unpersuasive because they cannot alter the simple fact that the relevant text of these provisions, the relevant context for interpreting the meaning of these terms, and the well-established prior understanding of these concepts all confirm that dumping and margins of dumping do have a meaning in relation to individual transactions. Our written submission sets forth the textual, contextual, and other evidence that the concepts of dumping and margins of dumping, as defined in the Antidumping Agreement and GATT 1994, are applicable to individual transactions. That evidence establishes that the terms dumping and margins of dumping as used in Article 2.1 of the Antidumping Agreement and Article VI of the GATT 1994 do not support the existence of an obligation to provide offsets for instances of non-dumping in assessment proceedings.

28. Brazil has not demonstrated any inconsistency with Article 9.3 of the Antidumping Agreement or Article VI:2 of the GATT. Article 9.3 requires that the amount of the antidumping duty assessed shall not exceed the margin of dumping. The term "margin of dumping" may be applied to individual transactions. Individual transactions are both the means by which less than fair value prices are determined and by which the product is introduced into commerce. Antidumping duties are similarly assessed on individual entries resulting from those individual transactions. The obligation in Article 9.3 to assess no more in

antidumping duties than the margin of dumping, just like the term "margin of dumping" itself, may be applied at the level of individual transactions.

29. In this same vein, Brazil attempts to tie an obligation to provide offsets to a determination of injury, arguing that "injury cannot be found to exist in relation to an individual transaction, but only for the *product as a whole*". However, Brazil's argument actually reinforces the interpretation that any such obligation would be limited to the context of investigations because, in contrast to investigations, there is no obligation to address the existence of injury in Article 9.3 duty assessment proceedings.

30. In addition, Brazil's interpretation of Article 9.3, requiring that antidumping duty liability be determined for the product "as a whole", cannot be reconciled with the specific provision in Article 9 that recognizes the existence of prospective normal value systems of assessment. Under such systems, the amount of liability for payment of antidumping duties is determined at the time of importation on the basis of a comparison between the price of the individual export transaction and the prospective normal value. If the margin of dumping must relate exclusively to the "product as a whole", as Brazil argues, the administration of such an assessment system is an impossibility. This is because, among other reasons, future transactions that would need to be taken into account in such a margin of dumping would not yet have occurred. An obligation to account for other imports in assessing antidumping duties on a particular entry is contrary to the very concept of a prospective normal value system and, if accepted, would effectively render prospective normal value systems WTO-inconsistent unless they were converted to a retrospective system by adopting periodic retrospective assessment reviews.

31. Antidumping duties are applied at the level of individual entries for which importers incur the liability. An importer's cost of acquiring the entered merchandise is the sum of the dumped price and the antidumping duty. Accordingly, the importer has an incentive to raise resale prices to cover the full normal value of the merchandise, thereby providing an effective remedy for the dumping. The antidumping duty will be insufficient to have this effect if, instead, the amount of the duty must be reduced to account for the amount by which some other transaction was sold at above normal value, possibly involving an entirely different importer. The importer would remain in a position to profitably resell the exporter's dumped product at a price that continues to be less than normal value. If Brazil's reading of "margin of dumping" is accepted as the sole permissible interpretation of Article 9.3, the remedy provided under the Antidumping Agreement and the GATT 1994 will be prevented from fully addressing dumping.

31. In addition, as the panel in *US – Softwood Lumber Dumping (21.5)* observed, and as described in detail in our written submission, providing offsets creates perverse incentives and "absurd results" that undermine the remedial effect of antidumping duties.

32. Any interpretation that gives rise to a general prohibition of zeroing also renders the second sentence of Article 2.4.2 inutile. This is because the exceptional methodology provided for in Article 2.4.2 mathematically must yield the same result as an average-to-average comparison if, in both cases, non-dumped comparisons are required to offset dumped comparisons.

Brazil has not satisfied its Burden of Proving that "Zeroing" was applied to, or had an Impact on, the challenged Margins of Dumping

34. As detailed in our first submission, Brazil has also failed to make a *prima facie* case as to the facts for certain of its claims. Brazil has challenged the calculation of dumping margins determined for two respondents, Fischer and Cutrale, in two administrative reviews. However, aside from the fact that the second administrative review is outside the Panel's terms of reference, in each of the reviews, the margin was zero or *de minimis* for one of these two respondents. Consequently, Brazil cannot establish that the margin should have been any lower to be consistent with the covered agreements.

35. Also, with respect to the assessment for Fischer in the first administrative review, the exhibits Brazil submitted in support of its claim with its first written submission are not the actual computer program logs created by Commerce.

The "Continued Use of the US 'Zeroing Procedures'"

36. Brazil's claim with respect to the "continued use of the US 'zeroing procedures'" should also be rejected. Aside from the fact that this alleged "measure" is outside the Panel's terms of reference, as explained in our first written submission, even were there an obligation to provide offsets outside the context of average-to-average comparisons in investigations, there is no basis for concluding that such "continued use" constitutes "ongoing conduct" that violates Article VI:2 of the GATT 1994 or Articles 2.4.2 and 9.3 of the Antidumping Agreement.

37. First, Brazil's own evidence refutes its claim that "zeroing" had any impact on the dumping margins in the original investigation. As such, even applying Brazil's interpretations of the relevant provisions of the covered agreements, there is no basis for finding the margins in the original investigation were inconsistent with any provision of the covered agreements.

38. The evidence with respect to each of the first and second administrative reviews also undermines Brazil's claims regarding the alleged "continued use" of "zeroing." One of the two companies reviewed had a *de minimis* margin in the first administrative review, which Commerce essentially treats as zero. One of the two companies reviewed had a zero margin in the second administrative review.

39. Thus, each of the proceedings concluded to date in the orange juice case – the investigation, the first administrative review, and the second administrative review – include margins that were not impacted (or "inflated") by "zeroing". As explained in our submission, this does not reflect a sequential string of determi-

nations applying "zeroing", contrary to Brazil's assertion. It does not provide a basis for in turn projecting that the United States will act inconsistently in the future with respect to measures that may never come into existence.

40. As noted in our first written submission, our experience in the *US – Zeroing II (EC)* dispute demonstrates further that there is no basis to assume that "zeroing" will be used in any antidumping proceeding. In that dispute, the Dispute Settlement Body adopted recommendations and rulings with respect to the use of "zeroing" in four original investigations. Commerce then issued new determinations with respect to those four investigations. In doing so, however, Commerce discovered that in three of the four investigations there were no offsets to provide (that is, there was no "zeroing") because all of the comparisons demonstrated dumping, or the rates determined in the original determinations were based upon facts available rates that did not involve "zeroing". As such, the dumping margins did not change in Commerce's new determinations. Accordingly, among the many problems under Brazil's approach would be the fact that any recommendation with respect to a future measure would need to be conditioned on the use of zeroing, but there would be no mechanism to determine if that condition were fulfilled – that is, if zeroing were in fact used in any individual proceeding.

41. As noted in our first written submission, we have serious concerns about the approach taken by the Appellate Body in the *US – Zeroing II (EC)* dispute. However, because Brazil relies heavily upon the Appellate Body's reasoning in that dispute, it bears repeating that, as a factual matter, there is no basis for such an approach in this case. The facts of this case are not "virtually identical" to the cases in that dispute found to be WTO-inconsistent. They are instead more similar to the cases where the evidence was considered insufficient to support such a finding.

42. In summary, even were the alleged "continued use of the US 'zeroing procedures'" within the Panel's terms of reference, Brazil has failed to establish that any such "ongoing conduct" exists or is likely to continue into the future. Brazil has not and cannot demonstrate a basis for concluding that any measures that may come to be with respect to imports of orange juice will involve the application of "zeroing" and be inconsistent with the covered agreements.

ANNEX C-3

CLOSING STATEMENT OF BRAZIL AT THE FIRST MEETING OF THE PANEL

1. Mr. Chairman, Members of the Panel, Brazil thanks you for the opportunity to appear before you and answer your questions.

2. During the hearing yesterday, we heard opposing interpretations of the foundational terms "dumping" and "margin of dumping" in the *Anti-Dumping Agreement* and Article VI of the GATT 1994. According to Brazil, these concepts are defined by reference to the product as a whole. According to the United States, they are sufficiently "flexible" that they may be defined in relation to: the "product" as a whole; individual transaction; or, even a combination of these different conceptions.

3. Brazil takes the view that the meaning given to these terms must be based on the text, context, object and purpose of the *Anti-Dumping Agreement* and Articles VI:1 and VI:2 of the GATT 1994. The treaty interpreter must strive for an interpretation that "is harmonious and coherent and fits comfortably in the treaty as a whole".[1] Brazil also notes that the terms at issue have been interpreted numerous times in previous disputes concerning zeroing. The Appellate Body has now clarified the interpretation of these terms beyond any reasonable doubt. An important part of ensuring "security and predictability"[2] through the dispute settlement system is that panels must, in making an objective assessment under Article 11 of the DSU, follow the Appellate Body's rulings when the same legal questions are presented. Brazil, therefore, urges the Panel to adopt the interpretation of "dumping" and "margin of dumping" that the Appellate Body has given.

4. Yesterday, we also had a discussion on the relevance of the impact of zeroing to Brazil's claims. Brazil argues that the *use* of zeroing is prohibited, irrespective of its particular impact. In previous disputes, the use and maintenance of zeroing has been found to be WTO-inconsistent in original investigations and administrative reviews, irrespective of the impact of zeroing.[3]

5. The Panel has also enquired about the impact, "in the real world", of zeroing in the present case. Brazil therefore briefly summarizes the impact of zeroing under the Orange Juice Order.

6. *First*, the use of zeroing under this Order has resulted in the determination of positive margins in the administrative reviews completed so far under the

---

[1] Appellate Body Report, *US – Continued Zeroing*, para. 268.

[2] Article 3.2 of the DSU.

[3] *See, e.g.,* Panel Report, *US – Zeroing (Japan) (21.5)*, para. 7.162 and 8.1(b); Appellate Body Report, *US – Zeroing (Japan)*, paras. 190(b) and (c) ; Appellate Body Report, *US – Continued Zeroing*, para. 395(a)(v), second indent.

Orange Juice Order, where there would have been negative margins had zeroing not been used.

7. *Second*, the use of zeroing under the Orange Juice Order has resulted in the imposition of duties, where no duties would have otherwise been imposed. Cutrale and Fischer have so far incurred final anti-dumping duty liabilities of [[XX]] million US dollars, whereas they would have owed zero duties had the United States not used zeroing. Thus, "in the real world", zeroing has enabled the imposition of significant amounts of duties on Brazil's exports.

8. *Third*, under US law, the USDOC routinely terminates an anti-dumping order for any exporter that has zero margins in three consecutive administrative reviews.[4] Under the Orange Juice order, Cutrale and Fischer would both have had consecutive zero margins in the first two administrative reviews, with the final results of the third due in August 2010. Had the United States not used zeroing, the Brazilian exporters could now expect termination of the Order. Thus, "in the real world", zeroing perpetuates the duration of the order.

9. To answer the Panel's enquiry, the use of zeroing has a significant "real world" impact on the Brazilian exporters covered by the Order.

10. As regards Brazil's continued use claim, the United States goes not much further than to say that this "ongoing conduct" is based on "speculation". Brazil need only remind the Panel of the latest Issues and Decision Memorandum relative to the Orange Juice Order at issue, where the USDOC restates its position of maintaining the zeroing methodology.[5] That is indeed a new meaning to the word "speculation", especially in light of the facts in this dispute, where the "density" of facts is beyond doubt, not fragmented, and where zeroing is about to be re-used in the Third Administrative Review.

11. Finally, the continued used claim, already accepted by the Appellate Body[6], allows Members to avoid being victims of the "moving target" and "hit and run" scenarios typical of measures that are sequential over time.

12. Mr. Chairman, Members of the Panel, staff of the Secretariat, Brazil once again thanks you for this opportunity and for your hard work in this dispute.

---

4 19 C.F.R. § 351.222(b), available at http://frwebgate2.access.gpo.gov/cgi-bin/PDFgate.cgi?WAISdocID=68qIUf/103/2/0&WAISaction=retrieve.

5 Exhibit BRA-43, pp. 4 – 6, "Department's Position".

6 *See* Appellate Body Report, *US – Continued Zeroing*, para. 185.

ANNEX C-4

CLOSING STATEMENT OF THE UNITED STATES AT THE FIRST MEETING OF THE PANEL

Mr. Chairman, members of the Panel:

1. On behalf of the United States delegation, I would once again like to thank you and the members of the Secretariat for your work on this dispute. We appreciated the opportunity to provide you with preliminary thoughts on your questions and look forward to providing you with our written responses and our rebuttal submission.

2. As an initial matter, Brazil asserts its claims are not dependent upon whether zeroing had an effect on the calculations. We disagree. It is not sufficient to simply point to the presence of a zeroing line in a computer code. The zeroing line of programming language is itself conditional. It only operates when the requisite condition is satisfied. With respect to the investigation, Brazil has conceded that no comparison results were "zeroed". Thus, these dumping margins were calculated without using zeroing. While Brazil stated yesterday that it is only relying on the investigation as evidence as the "continued use" of zeroing, the investigation provides no such evidence. Because zeroing was not used in the calculation of these margins, Brazil's claim that there is any such "continued use" is not supported by the evidence.

3. With respect to the second administrative review determination, Brazil's position is equally incoherent. Brazil fails to explain how no antidumping duty for Fischer in the second administrative review determination is excessive under Article 9.3, or otherwise inconsistent with any other provision of the covered agreements. Likewise, Brazil did not explain how Commerce's determination to assess no duties on Fischer's entries during the period and to estimate that no antidumping duty would be due on Fischer's entries after the second administrative review determination could be inconsistent.

4. Turning to the issues of interpretation, Brazil argues that the term "margin of dumping" must always relate to the "product as a whole" regardless of the context in which the term is used. At the same time, Brazil also asserts, "The fact that the same word appears in two (or more) proximate treaty provisions does not mean that the word carries the same meaning in each provision ... a single word used in two provisions may have different meanings in each provision, depending upon the context". The United States agrees that context matters. As we have explained, the precise meaning of the term "margin of dumping" may be informed by the context in which the term is used. The terms "dumping" and "margin of dumping" are defined in relation to the term "product". The ordinary meaning of "product" may refer to a single transaction, or multiple transactions, or both. For example, in Article II of the GATT 1994, the term "product" is

used, including with respect to the imposition of an antidumping duty on a "product" "at the time of importation". Clearly, Article II is using "product" in the sense of an individual transaction and not in the sense of "product as a whole". No one has argued that tariffs on a product can exceed the bound rate for some transactions as long as they are below the bound rate in enough other transactions such that the average does not exceed the bound rate.

5. In particular, contrary to Brazil's assertion at paragraph 20 of its opening statement, the United States agrees that in the context of Article 5.8 the margin of dumping may refer to an aggregation of multiple transactions. Article 6.10 concerns the question of what information should be relied upon in calculating margins of dumping for exporters or producers. It ensures that each exporter or producer is assigned an antidumping duty based on its own pricing behavior, and not that of other exporters or producers, unless it is impracticable. In this context, this provision does not address whether the "margin of dumping" only has meaning in relation to the product as a whole (a term nowhere found in the text of the Antidumping Agreement) or individual transactions. With respect to Articles 6.10, 8.1, 9.1, 9.3, and 9.5, Brazil's interpretation relies solely on the use of the term "margin of dumping" in the singular as the basis for its interpretation. We, however, would agree with Brazil's observation in paragraph 13 of its opening statement that "the use of the singular is not decisive ...".

6. As detailed in our first written submission, Brazil's interpretation cannot be reconciled with the ordinary meaning of the terms with which dumping and margins of dumping are defined. Dumping is defined as occurring in the course of ordinary commercial transactions, where products are "introduced into the commerce" of the importing country transaction by transaction, not "as a whole". And, the prices of products are set in individual transactions, not "as a whole". Brazil's interpretation also cannot be reconciled with the Appellate Body's interpretation of the phrase "all comparable export transactions" in *US – Softwood Lumber Dumping*. Nor can it be reconciled with the exceptional provision in the second sentence of Article 2.4.2; or with the effective functioning of antidumping duties as a remedy for dumping.

7. In addition, Brazil's proposed obligation is contrary to the very concept of a prospective normal value system provided for in Article 9. As we explained yesterday, under such a system, the amount of liability for payment of antidumping duties is determined at the time of importation on the basis of a comparison between the price of the individual export transaction and the prospective normal value. The administration of such an assessment system cannot function as intended if the margin of dumping must relate exclusively to an aggregation of all transactions constituting the "product as a whole". As became apparent from Brazil's answers to the Panel's questions, Brazil's proffered understanding of how the prospective normal value systems should function is radically different from how Members operate these systems.

8. Under Brazil's interpretation, a prospective normal value assessment system necessarily requires retrospective reviews on the basis of the aggregation of transactions because the margin of dumping for the "product as a whole" can

never be known at the time of importation. Nothing in the text of Article 9, however, suggests that the refund proceeding described therein necessarily must relate to an aggregated examination of all transactions. Nor does Brazil attempt to explain why, if refund proceedings under Article 9.3 require aggregation of transactions for the "product as a whole", Article 9.3 fails to provide for any time frame over which the transactions would be aggregated.

9. In contrast, the United States has offered a harmonious and coherent interpretation that gives meaning to all provisions of the Antidumping Agreement and the GATT 1994. This interpretation has been endorsed by prior panels. Brazil would have you believe that none of these panels adopted an interpretation that is coherent, and that none of these panels had the interest of the dispute settlement system or the trading system at heart. But this interpretation, in contrast to Brazil's interpretation, is fully consistent with the text, context, and object and purpose of the covered agreements.

10. In its opening statement, Brazil categorically asserts that "the same legal questions must be resolved in the same way in subsequent disputes". On the contrary, the authority to adopt interpretations of the covered agreements rests exclusively with the Ministerial Conference and the General Council.[1] Therefore, while the dispute settlement system serves to resolve a particular dispute, and to clarify agreement provisions in the context of doing so, neither panels nor the Appellate Body can adopt authoritative interpretations that are binding with respect to another dispute.

11. Brazil would have this Panel merely follow Appellate Body reports without engaging in its own analysis. We disagree. To be clear, the United States is not asking the Panel blindly to follow the numerous panel reports that have found a general requirement to provide offsets does not exist in the Antidumping Agreement. Nor have we asked you to ignore Appellate Body reports finding zeroing to be WTO-inconsistent in certain circumstances.

12. What we have asked you to do, and are confident you will do, is to fulfill your function to make an objective assessment of the matter before you. As part of that, we have asked you to consider whether previous panel reports on this issue are persuasive; we believe they are. We have also asked you to consider whether previous Appellate Body reports on this issue are persuasive; we have explained they are not. Of course, the Panel must undertake its own consideration of these reports and determine their relevance to the issues here and their persuasiveness, as previous panels confronted with claims against "zeroing" have done.

13. Brazil would instead have the Panel abdicate its responsibility of making an objective assessment in the interest of "security and predictability". Security and predictability are provided by a dispute settlement system that does not add to or diminish the rights and obligations to which the Members agreed. This re-

[1] Article IX:2 of the *Marrakesh Agreement Establishing the World Trade Organization*. *See also*, United States' First Written Submission, n. 26.

quires the proper application of customary rules of interpretation of public international law to the provisions of the covered agreements. Any obligation to provide offsets must be found in the text of the covered agreements. There is no textual basis for a general prohibition of zeroing. The only textual basis for an obligation to provide offsets arises in the limited context of average-to-average comparisons in investigations.

14. Brazil's proposed obligation to reduce antidumping duty assessments for negative comparison results treats non-dumped imports as a remedy for dumping that replace the application of antidumping duties. However, the application of antidumping duties is the remedy provided for in the covered agreements. The prior panels addressing this issue have consistently recognized the deficiencies inherent in Brazil's proposed interpretation (and in the Appellate Body reports upon which Brazil relies). The panels have found that the relevant text, the relevant context, and the well-established prior understanding of the terms "dumping" and "margin of dumping" demonstrate that these concepts are not devoid of meaning except in relation to the product as a whole.

15. Mr. Chairman, Members of the Panel, we appreciate this opportunity to present these closing comments and look forward to continuing to work with you on these issues.

ANNEX D

ORAL STATEMENTS OF THIRD PARTIES OR EXECUTIVE SUMMARIES THEREOF

ANNEX D-1

THIRD PARTY ORAL STATEMENT OF THE EUROPEAN UNION

Mr. Chairman, distinguished Members of the Panel.

1. The European Union appreciates this opportunity to appear before you today. The European Union makes this third party oral statement because of its systemic interest in the *DSU*. This case also raises important substantive issues in relation to Article VI of the *GATT 1994* and the *Anti-Dumping Agreement*. However, none of the issues raised in this proceeding relating to anti-dumping are new. Brazil's claims appear to be supported by a consistent body of reasoning and findings, contained in all reports issued by panels and the Appellate Body, lastly in *US – Continued Zeroing*. Further, the United States has not raised anything new in its argumentation to defend its zeroing methodologies and practices.

2. The European Union's oral statement will therefore be brief. In its written submission the European Union set out at length the systemic reasons why in its view, this Panel should follow the findings and conclusions contained in previous panels and Appellate Body reports on zeroing. It is beyond dispute that the practice of zeroing in anti-dumping cases has been contested many times in WTO dispute settlement proceedings. The Appellate Body in particular has adjudicated on the issues raised in this case frequently, including in cases involving different variations of zeroing, both in original anti-dumping investigations and reviews, in different factual circumstances and between different parties.

3. The United States does not contest this, but argues that this Panel should not follow these Appellate Body reports. Further, the United States explicitly invites this Panel to re-apply findings and follow the reasoning contained in panel reports that have been rejected and overturned –in many cases more than once– by the Appellate Body, in reports which have subsequently been adopted

by the DSB. The European Union submits that the suggestion by the United States that, according to Article 11 of the *DSU* this Panel should be free to depart from adopted Appellate Body reports on issues of law and legal interpretations relating to the covered agreements, is misguided. It is rather the opposite. The Appellate Body itself has addressed this very question in several cases, notably in *US – Stainless Steel from Mexico*, and thus the US proposition should be rejected.

4. On the substance, the European Union has set out its views in its written submission, and has only a few comments in this oral statement, on two specific aspects of the US written submission.

5. First, zeroing has nothing to do with "offsets" or "credits". The key issue, however, and the fundamental problem raised by this methodology is the selection of the relatively low priced export transactions *per se*, as a sub-category, as the only or preponderant basis for the dumping margin calculation, regardless of whether or not they are clustered by purchaser, region or time. This was *not* the compromise achieved in the text of Article 2.4.2 of the *ADA*. It is clear that according to Article 2.4.2 of the *ADA* there are only three sub-categories of clustered low priced export transactions that it is permissible to respond to: those clustered by purchaser, region or time. Thus, it is not permissible, and it is not fair, to pick up low priced export transactions clustered by model or *per se*, as the US zeroing methodology does. This is also clear from the term "all" in the first sentence of Article 2.4.2, and the definition of dumping in Article 2.1 of the *ADA* and Article VI:1 of the *GATT 1994* in terms of the product as a whole; read together with the absence in the targeted dumping provisions of any reference to a sub-category by model or *per se*. Thus, the relevant provisions, and particularly the normal rule and the exception, are read harmoniously, so as to give meaning – both legal and economic – to all the treaty terms.

6. Second, the United States continues to rely on the legally erroneous proposition that the disciplines of Article 2.4.2 of the *ADA* are excluded from retrospective assessment proceedings. In this respect, we believe that the Panel does not need to enter into this issue. Confronted with the same argument by the United States, the Appellate Body has repeatedly found that Article VI of the *GATT 1994* and Articles 2.1 and 9.3 of the *ADA* require that the dumping margin must be established on the basis of the product under investigation *as a whole*. In any event, should the Panel enter into this discussion, we invite the Panel to take into account the analysis set out in our written submission.

7. The European Union stands ready to participate further in the discussion and answer any questions that this Panel may have in writing. Thank you for your attention.

ANNEX D-2

EXECUTIVE SUMMARY OF THE THIRD PARTY ORAL STATEMENT OF JAPAN

I. THE UNITED STATES' REQUEST FOR PRELIMINARY RULINGS SHOULD BE REJECTED

1. The United States argues that the Second Administrative Review is not properly within the Panel's terms of reference, because the final results of it had not been issued at the time of Brazil's request for consultations.[1] However, it is clear that, in reviewing Brazil's requests for consultations and panel establishment, the Second Administrative Review is included in the Panel's terms of reference.

2. Even though the final result of the Second Administrative Review had not been issued at the time of the request for consultations, the review had been initiated at the time and a final result had been expected to be issued in a certain period in light of the United States' anti-dumping system. In previous cases where a certain measure was subject to the dispute, certain amendments to that measure which took effective even after the consultation were also found as falling within the panel's terms of reference, for example, in *Chile – Price Band*, as not "*changing its essence*".[2]

3. In its panel request, Brazil mentioned the date and contents of the final result of the Second Administrative Review. From the description of the request for consultations and panel establishment, the Second Administrative Review shares the essential legal implication – the use of the zeroing methodology, as well as the same underlying antidumping duty order – with the Original Investigation and the First Administrative Review, and this shared point is exactly what Brazil is challenging in this dispute. Brazil does not raise any other issues than zeroing with regard to the review, therefore, the scope of the dispute has not been broadened. In this sense, the Second Administrative Review does not change the essence of the measure at issue. Brazil's requests for consultations and panel establishment thus provided an opportunity for the United States to define and delimit the scope of the dispute between them. With respect to US argument that the second administrative review "was not (and could not have been) subject to consultations"[3], the Appellate Body admitted "additional measures relate to the same duties identified in the consultations request"[4] being within the panel's terms of reference stating:[5]

---

1 United States' First Written Submission, paras. 39-48.

2 Appellate Body Report on *Chile – Price Band*, para. 139(emphasis in original).

3 US First Written Submission, para. 48.

4 Appellate Body Report, *US – Continued Zeroing (EC)*, para. 228.

5 Appellate Body Report, *US – Continued Zeroing (EC)*, para. 228. (footnote omitted)

> The proceedings listed in the consultations request and the panel request are therefore successive stages subsequent to the issuance of the same anti-dumping duty orders. More specifically, as regards the periodic reviews, the subsequent measures assessed actual duty liabilities and updated cash deposit rates that were imposed on the same products from the same countries as those listed in the consultations request. With respect to the sunset reviews, the subsequent measures related to the continued application of duties on the same products from the same countries as those listed in the consultations request. Moreover, in both its consultations request and panel request, the European Communities made clear that it was challenging the specific administrative review and sunset review proceedings because of the use of the zeroing methodology. Specifically, both the consultations request and the panel request allege that the USDOC "systematically" applies the zeroing methodology in all types of review proceedings, which, the European Communities contends, is a methodology found to be inconsistent with the covered agreements.

4. In light of the above, Japan considers that the Panel should reject the United States' request for preliminary rulings with regard to the Second Administrative Review.

5. With respect to US argument that the continued use of the US Zeroing procedures in successive anti-dumping proceedings is not within the Panel's terms of reference, Japan notes that the Appellate Body of *US-Continued Zeroing (EU)* states regarding an ongoing conduct:

> As discussed, we are of the view that it can be discerned from the panel request, read as a whole, that the measures at issue consist of an ongoing conduct, that is, the use of the zeroing methodology in successive proceedings in each of the 18 cases whereby anti-dumping duties are maintained. *The prospective nature of the remedy sought by the European Communities is congruent with the fact that the measures at issue are alleged to be ongoing, with prospective application and a life potentially stretching into the future.* Moreover, it is not uncommon for remedies sought in WTO dispute settlement to have prospective effect, such as a finding against laws or regulations, as such, or a subsidy programme with regularly recurring payments.[6] (emphasis added)

Appellate Body also states:

> *We see no reason to exclude ongoing conduct that consists of the use of the zeroing methodology from challenge in WTO dispute settlement.* The successive determinations by which duties are maintained are connected stages in each of the 18 cases involving

[6] Appellate Body Report, *US – Continued Zeroing (EC)*, para.171.

> imposition, assessment, and collection of duties under the same anti-dumping duty order.The use of the zeroing methodology in a string of these stages is the allegedly unchanged component of each of the 18 measures at issue. It is with respect to this ongoing conduct that the European Communities brought its challenge, seeking its cessation.[7] (emphasis added)

6. Therefore, given this conclusion of the Appellate Body, Japan considers that the Panel should reject the United States' request for preliminary rulings with regard to the continued use of the US Zeroing procedures in successive anti-dumping proceedings.

II. ZEROING AS USED BY THE USDOC IN PERIODIC REVIEWS IS INCONSISTENT WITH ARTICLE 9.3 OF THE *ANTI-DUMPING AGREEMENT*

7. The legal principles governing the WTO-inconsistency of the zeroing procedures have been thoroughly canvassed by the Appellate Body in past WTO disputes, and are well established by now. Japan notes again that, as the result of the interpretation of the *Anti-Dumping Agreement* under the customary rules of interpretation of public international law, the Appellate Body held;

... "dumping" and "margins of dumping" can be found to exist only in relation to [the] product as defined by [the] authority. They cannot be found to exist for only a type, model or category of that product. Nor, under any comparison methodology, can "dumping" and "margins of dumping" be found to exist at the *level* of an individual transaction.[8]

8. Then, with regard to Article 9.3 of the *Anti-Dumping Agreement*, the Appellate Body held that "the margin of dumping established for an exporter or foreign producer operates as a *ceiling* for the total amount of anti-dumping duties that can be levied on the entries of the subject product (from that exporter) covered by the duty assessment proceeding".[9] The express reference to Article 2 in the *chapeau* of Article 9.3 of the *Anti-Dumping Agreement* includes, among others, Article 2.1 of the *Anti-Dumping Agreement*, which, as noted above, sets forth a definition of "dumping" that applies "[f]or the purpose of this Agreement". In *US – Zeroing (EC)*, relying on these textual cross-references, the Appellate Body made an explicit interpretive connection between a "product as a whole" requirement of Article 2.1 and dumping determinations in periodic reviews under Article 9.3.[10]

---

[7] Appellate Body Report, *US – Continued Zeroing (EC)*, para. 181(footnote omitted).

[8] Appellate Body Report, *US – Zeroing (Japan)*, para. 115. (emphasis in original)

[9] Appellate Body Report, *US – Zeroing (EC)*, para. 130 (emphasis in original). *See also* Appellate Body Report, *US – Zeroing (Japan)*, para. 155.

[10] Appellate Body Report, *US – Zeroing (EC)*, para. 127, quoting Appellate Body Report, *US – Softwood Lumber V*, para. 99.

9. Accordingly, if, in a periodic review, the investigating authority chooses to undertake multiple comparisons at an intermediate stage, it is not permitted to take into account the results of only some of the multiple comparisons, while disregarding others. Thus, for purposes of these reviews, the investigating authority must aggregate all multiple comparisons to establish a margin of dumping for the "product" under investigation as a whole. It is required to compare the anti-dumping duties collected on all entries of the subject merchandise from a given exporter or foreign producer with that exporter's or foreign producer's margin of dumping for the product as a whole, to ensure that the total amount of the former does not exceed the latter.[11]

10. When applying zeroing as used by the USDOC in periodic reviews, the USDOC compares the prices of individual export transactions against monthly weighted average normal values, and disregards the amounts by which the export prices exceed the monthly weighted average normal values, when aggregating the results of the comparisons to calculate the going-forward cash deposit rate for the exporter and the duty assessment rate for the importer concerned. In this way, zeroing as used by the USDOC results in the levy of an amount of anti-dumping duty that exceeds an exporter's margin of dumping, which, under Article 9.3 of the *Anti-Dumping Agreement*, operates as the ceiling for the amount of anti-dumping duty that can be levied in respect of the sales made by an exporter.

11. The Appellate Body rejected the United States' argument that, in a periodic review, "dumping" and "margins of dumping" can be determined on an importer- or import-specific basis. In doing so, the Appellate Body relied in part on Article 6.10 of the *Anti-Dumping Agreement* as context, which precludes the calculation of a margin of dumping for each individual import transaction, and it also requires that margins be calculated for exporters and foreign producers, not importers.[12]

12. The United States objects to the Appellate Body's interpretation that margins of dumping are determined for foreign producers or exporters. However, as the Appellate Body previously explained, the United States' misgivings are misplaced. Although *margins of dumping* are established for foreign producers or exporters for a product as a whole, Members can assess anti-dumping *duties* on "a transaction- or importer-specific basis", "provided that the total amount of anti-dumping duties that are levied does not exceed the exporters' or foreign producers' margins of dumping".[13]

13. In light of the above, Japan submits that two administrative reviews concerning imports of certain orange juice from Brazil are inconsistent with Article 9.3 of the *Anti-Dumping Agreement* and Article VI:2 of the GATT 1994 due to the use of zeroing.

---

11 Appellate Body Report, *US – Zeroing (EC)*, para. 132.

12 Appellate Body Report, *US – Zeroing (EC)*, para. 128. *See also* Appellate Body Report, *US – Zeroing (Japan)*, para. 112.

13 Appellate Body Report, *US – Zeroing (EC)*, para. 131(footnote omitted).

14. Additionally, Japan notes the Appellate Body's findings in *US – Continued Zeroing (EC)* to address United States' argument concerning Article 17.6(ii) of the *Anti-dumping Agreement* as follows:

In our analysis, we have been mindful of the provisions of Article 17.6(ii) of the *Anti-Dumping Agreement*. The analysis offered above, applying the customary rules of interpretation of public international law, does not allow for conflicting interpretations. We have found, by the application of those rules, that zeroing is inconsistent with Article 9.3. A holding that zeroing is also consistent with Article 9.3 would be flatly contradictory. Such contradiction would be repugnant to the customary rules of treaty interpretation referred to in the first sentence of Article 17.6(ii). Consequently, it is not a permissible interpretation within the meaning of Article 17.6(ii), second sentence.[14]

15. Finally, Japan notes the Appellate Body's findings in *US – Stainless Steel (Mexico)* concerning whether the panels should follow previous adopted Appellate Body reports addressing the same issues as follows:[15]

The creation of the Appellate Body by WTO Members to review legal interpretations developed by panels shows that Members recognized the importance of consistency and stability in the interpretation of their rights and obligations under the covered agreements. This is essential to promote "security and predictability" in the dispute settlement system, and to ensure the "prompt settlement" of disputes. The Panel's failure to follow previously adopted Appellate Body reports addressing the same issues undermines the development of a coherent and predictable body of jurisprudence clarifying Members' rights and obligations under the covered agreements as contemplated under the DSU.

16. To provide the security and predictability to Members, Japan strongly expects the Panel to keep consistency with the Appellate Body's stabled findings regarding zeroing as used by the USDOC in periodic reviews.

III. THE CONTINUED USE OF ZEROING IN SUCCESSIVE ANTI-DUMPING PROCEEDINGS BY WHICH DUTIES ARE APPLIED AND MAINTAINED IS INCONSISTENT WITH THE *ANTI-DUMPING AGREEMENT* AND THE GATT 1994

17. The Appellate Body concluded with respect to the four "cases" for which it was able to complete the analysis in *US – Continued Zeroing (EC)*:

we conclude that the application and continued application of anti-dumping duties is inconsistent with Article 9.3 of the *Anti-Dumping Agreement* and Article VI:2 of the GATT 1994 to the extent that the duties are maintained at a level calculated through the use of the zeroing methodology in the periodic reviews in the following four cases...[16]

---

[14] Appellate Body Report, *US – Continued Zeroing (EC)*, para. 317.

[15] Appellate Body Report, *US – Stainless Steel (Mexico)*, para. 161.

[16] Appellate Body Report, *US – Continued Zeroing (EC)*, para. 199.

18. Again, Japan strongly expects the Panel to keep consistency with the Appellate Body's finding regarding the continued use of zeroing in the consecutive anti-dumping determinations, including the original investigation and subsequent administrative reviews.

ANNEX D-3

THIRD PARTY ORAL STATEMENT
OF KOREA

Mr. Chairman and Members of the Panel,

1. The Republic of Korea ("Korea") appreciates this opportunity to present its views to the Panel as a third party.

2. This dispute involves the practice, commonly referred to as "zeroing", by which the USDOC has treated transactions with negative dumping margins as having margins equal to zero in original investigations and administrative reviews. In Korea's view, this practice is plainly inconsistent with relevant provisions of the *Anti-Dumping Agreement* and Article VI of the GATT 1994. This view has been upheld by the Appellate Body in numerous previous disputes addressing the USDOC's zeroing practice.

3. Absent particular reasons for distinguishing the case at hand, the Panel is obliged to follow the rulings of the Appellate Body. There is no reason for the Panel in the current dispute to disregard the Appellate Body's decisions in the long line of cases involving the zeroing methodology. In this respect, Korea urges this Panel to follow the well-established WTO jurisprudence and requests that the Panel find the United States zeroing methodology inconsistent with the *Anti-Dumping Agreement* and the GATT 1994.

4. As in its Third Party Submission, Korea in this oral statement will present its views with regard to the preliminary ruling request by the United States and on the use of zeroing methodology in the USDOC's original investigations and periodic administrative reviews.

I. THE PANEL SHOULD DISMISS THE PRELIMINARY RULING REQUEST BY THE UNITED STATES

5. The United States has requested preliminary rulings with regard to two issues. The United States argues (1) that the final determination in the second administrative review of the antidumping order on Certain Orange Juice from Brazil is not within the Panel's terms of reference; and (2) that the "continued use of the US 'zeroing procedures' in successive anti-dumping proceedings" is not within the Panel's terms of reference due to lack of specificity.

A. The Panel Should Dismiss the United States' Claim that the Second Administrative Review is not Within the Panel's Terms of Reference

6. Contrary to the United States argument, the second administrative review is adequately described in Brazil's request for consultations. In the Addendum to Brazil's initial request for consultations, submitted 22 May 2009, Brazil specifically stated that "[t]he consultations, held on 16 January 2009, covered the ... the Antidumping Duty Administrative Review from 1 March 2007 to 29 February 2008 (the "Second Administrative Review")".[1]

7. It should first be noted that it is beyond dispute that Brazil's request for establishment of a panel specifically identified the second administrative review as one of "the measures at issue".[2] However, the preliminary ruling request by the United States does not address the significance of this statement in Brazil's panel request. This silence suggests that the United States believes that the US-DOC's second administrative review can only fall within the Panel's terms of reference if the *final determination* in that review was specifically referenced in the consultation request, as well as in the panel request itself. Yet, that interpretation is not consistent with the provisions of the relevant agreements.

8. Article 17.3 of the *Anti-Dumping Agreement* does not contain any language that might be read to suggest that a Member must wait to *request consultations* until a final determination has been issued. By contrast, the first sentence of Article 17.4 of the *Anti-Dumping Agreement*, which authorizes WTO Members to refer matters to the DSB for establishment of a panel, specifically requires complaining Members to wait until (1) consultations under Article 17.3 "have failed to achieve a mutually agreed solution", *and* (2) "final action has been taken by the administering authorities of the importing Member to levy anti-dumping duties...". If the administrative authorities have not yet taken "final action", the matter may not be referred to the DSB for establishment of a panel.

9. The clear implication is that *consultations* may be requested before "final action has been taken by the administering authorities". After all, if consultations could not be requested before such "final action", there would be no need to include a requirement of "final action" in the first sentence Article 17.4. Instead, if consultations could be requested only after "final action" by the administering authorities, then the provisions of the first sentence of Article 17.4 requiring that consultations be held (and "have failed") would embody a requirement of "final action" as well. Under such an interpretation, the language requiring "final action" in the first sentence of Article 17.4 would be redundant.

10. It is well established in WTO jurisprudence that "a treaty interpreter must give meaning and effect to all the terms used in a treaty provision and must avoid interpretations which render treaty terms redundant". In accordance with

---

[1] WT/DS382/1/Add.1, para. 3.

[2] WT/DS382/4.

that principle, the provisions of Articles 17.3 and 17.4 of the *Anti-Dumping Agreement* must be understood to indicate that consultations may be requested before "final action" by the administering authorities, while the establishment of a panel may not be requested until after that "final action" has occurred.

11. Korea is also unable to find the United States' reliance on the decision in *US – Certain EC Products* to be persuasive. In *US – Certain EC Products,* the EC's request for consultations made reference to a notice issued by the US Customs Service withholding liquidation (referred to as the "March 3rd Measure") but did not refer to the separate decision by the US Trade Representative (the "USTR") to impose 100 per cent duties on certain EC products (referred to as the "April 19th action"). The panel and Appellate Body held that the EC's failure to mention the April 19th action during the consultations meant that claims regarding that action were outside the panel's terms of reference.

12. The *US – Certain EC Products* decision can, therefore, be easily distinguished from the situation presented by Brazil's consultation request in this dispute. Unlike *US – Certain EC Products*, this is not a case in which the consultation request fails to mention the particular measure. Instead, as described above, the Addendum to Brazil's consultation request clearly refers to the second administrative review.

13. Moreover, the legal relationship between the March 3rd Measure and the April 19th action at issue in *US – Certain EC Products* is quite different from the legal relationship between the second administrative review described in the Addendum to Brazil's consultation request and the final determination mentioned in Brazil's panel request. In *US – Certain EC Products*, the Appellate Body focused on the fact that the March 3rd Measure and April 19th action involved two different government agencies acting separately pursuant to distinct statutory legal authority.[3] In particular, the United States Customs Service took its measure on March 3rd pursuant to Section 113.13 of the Code of Federal Regulations, Volume 19, while the USTR took its action on April 19th pursuant to Section 301 of the Trade Act of 1974.[4] In this case, the second administrative review was conducted by the same agency, the USDOC, that subsequently issued the final results of the review on 11 August 2009. In conducting the review and issuing the final results, the USDOC acted pursuant to the same statutory authority, Title VII of the Tariff Act of 1930, as amended, which establishes the framework for US antidumping proceedings.

14. The Appellate Body in *US – Certain EC Products* also noted that there was no "perceptible correlation" between the March 3rd Measure and the April 19th action. The situation in the present case is clearly different. It is difficult, if not impossible, to maintain that there is no perceptible correlation between the conduct of the second administrative review of the antidumping order on Certain Orange Juice from Brazil and final results of that review.

---

3 WT/DS165/AB/R, para. 75.

4 *Ibid.*

15. Consequently, there is no basis for the argument by the United States that Brazil's request for consultations with respect to the second administrative review before the USDOC issued its final determination in that review was somehow improper or invalid.

B. The Panel Should Find that the "Continued Use of the US 'Zeroing Procedures'" as Identified in Brazil's Panel Request Falls Within the Panel's Terms of Reference

16. Korea is also of the view that the "continued use of the US 'zeroing procedures'" is within the Panel's terms of reference. The United States argues that the description of the measure in Brazil's panel request lacks specificity because the alleged measure did not exist at the time of the panel request.

17. As the Appellate Body has explained, the specificity requirement under Article 6.2 of the DSU is designed to ensure that a panel request "present[s] the problem clearly". The Appellate Body has also found that "the identification of the specific measures at issue, pursuant to Article 6.2, is different from a demonstration of the existence of such measures".

18. Korea notes that item (d) of Brazil's panel request identifies the anti-dumping duty order, case No A-350-840 and the original investigation and subsequent administrative reviews under such order. It appears to be sufficiently clear also in this dispute that the measure referred to is "a string of connected and sequential determinations" in which the United States uses the zeroing methodology by which duties are maintained over a period of time under the anti-dumping duty order.

19. In this regard, the Appellate Body in *US – Continued Zeroing* concluded that a Member's "ongoing conduct" constitutes a measure and is challengeable by another Member.[5] As Brazil notes in its first written submission, the ongoing conduct that was at issue in *US – Continued Zeroing* is virtually identical to the ongoing conduct at issue in this dispute. The zeroing practice by the USDOC maintained and applied in successive phases of the anti-dumping proceeding under the anti-dumping duty order on certain orange juice from Brazil is an ongoing conduct that is inconsistent with the *Anti-Dumping Agreement*.[6]

II. THE PANEL SHOULD FIND THAT THE PRACTICE OF "ZEROING" IN ORIGINAL INVESTIGATIONS IS INCONSISTENT WITH ARTICLE 2.4.2 OF THE *ANTI-DUMPING AGREEMENT*

20. The USDOC's utilization of its zeroing methodology in original investigations has been found to be inconsistent, as such and as applied, with Article

---

[5] Appellate Body Report, *US – Continued Zeroing*, para. 180.
[6] Appellate Body Report, *US – Continued Zeroing*, para. 199.

2.4.2 of the *Anti-Dumping Agreement* in numerous past disputes.[7] There no longer appears to be any dispute with respect to this issue.

21. In fact, the USDOC has stated that, effective 22 February 2007, it will no longer utilize the practice of zeroing in new and pending investigations.[8] However, this change in practice was not applied to the anti-dumping investigation that is the subject of the present dispute, because the final results and the amended final results of the original investigation of anti-dumping duties on certain orange juice from Brazil were published more than a year before the effective date of the USDOC's 22 February 2007 change in practice.

22. Therefore, Korea considers it imperative that the Panel find the practice of zeroing in the original investigation of anti-dumping duties on certain orange juice from Brazil inconsistent with Article 2.4.2 of the *Anti-Dumping Agreement*.

III. AS THE APPELLATE BODY HAS CONSISTENTLY FOUND, THE PANEL SHOULD FIND THAT THE PRACTICE OF "ZEROING" IN PERIODIC REVIEWS IS INCONSISTENT WITH ARTICLE 9.3 OF THE *ANTI-DUMPING AGREEMENT* AND ARTICLE VI:2 OF THE GATT 1994

23. The Appellate Body has repeatedly ruled that the practice of zeroing in periodic administrative reviews is inconsistent with the *Anti-Dumping Agreement* — and it has held that panels considering this issue should follow the Appellate Body's reasoning on this issue.[9] Nevertheless, the United States contends that, notwithstanding the rulings by the Appellate Body, the practice of zeroing in periodic "administrative reviews" should be found to be consistent with the *Anti-Dumping Agreement*. Korea considers the United States' arguments unconvincing and submits that the Panel should once again find that the United States' practice of zeroing in administrative reviews is inconsistent with the *Anti-Dumping Agreement*.

24. In ruling that the USDOC's practice of zeroing in periodic "administrative reviews" is inconsistent with Article 9.3 of the *Anti-Dumping Agreement* and GATT Article VI:2, the Appellate Body has explicitly rejected the United States' arguments that "dumping" and "margin of dumping" can be found to exist at the level of individual transactions.[10] Like the Appellate Body, Korea is unable to

---

[7] *See* Panel Report, *US – Anti-Dumping Measures on PET Bags (Thailand)*; Panel Report, *US – Shrimp (Thailand)*; Appellate Body Report, *EC – Bed Linen (India)*; Appellate Body Report, *US – Zeroing (Japan)*; Appellate Body Report, *US – Continued Zeroing (EC)*.

[8] *See Antidumping Proceedings: Calculation of the Weighted-Average Dumping Margin During an Antidumping Investigation: Final Modification*, 71 Fed. Reg. 77722 (27 December 2006); and *Antidumping Proceedings: Calculation of the Weighted-Average Dumping Margins in Antidumping Investigations: Change in Effective Date of Final Modification*, 72 Fed. Reg. 3783 (26 January 2007).

[9] *See, e.g.*, Appellate Body Report, *United States – Mexican Stainless Steel*, para. 161 to 162.

[10] Appellate Body Report, *United States – Continued Zeroing (EC)*, para. 287.

find "a textual or contextual basis in the GATT 1994 or the *Anti-Dumping Agreement* for treating transactions that occur above normal value as "dumped", for purposes of determining the existence and magnitude of dumping in the original investigation, and as "non-dumped", for purposes of assessing the final liability for payment of anti-dumping duties in a periodic review".[11] Korea believes that the United States should bring its practice in periodic administrative reviews into conformity with requirements of the *Anti-Dumping Agreement* — as it already has with original investigations.

IV. CONCLUSION

25. Korea requests that the Panel find the United States' practice of zeroing as used in the original investigation and administrative reviews as well as its continued use in successive anti-dumping proceedings concerning imports from certain orange juice from Brazil to be inconsistent with the *Anti-Dumping Agreement.*

26. Korea appreciates this opportunity to participate in these proceedings and to present its views to the Panel.

---

[11] Appellate Body Report, *US – Continued Zeroing (EC)*, para. 285.

ANNEX E

EXECUTIVE SUMMARIES OF THE SECOND WRITTEN SUBMISSIONS OF THE PARTIES

ANNEX E-1

EXECUTIVE SUMMARY OF THE SECOND WRITTEN SUBMISSION OF BRAZIL

I. INTRODUCTION

1. The areas of disagreement between the two parties in this dispute have already been well canvassed in the respective submissions to this Panel. In its second written submission, therefore, Brazil, does not repeat the details of what has been said before. Instead, Brazil presents a summary of the key interpretive arguments, and select arguments on the three measures at issue: the First and Second Administrative Reviews and the continued use measure.

2. Before doing so, Brazil recalls that, following the First and Second Administrative Reviews, Cutrale and Fischer have so far incurred final anti-dumping duty liabilities of [[XX]] million US dollars under the Orange Juice Order. The payment of these duties is a direct consequence of the USDOC's use of zeroing, because, if zeroing had not been used, the United States would have collected no anti-dumping duties under the Order.

II. SUMMARY OF KEY INTERPRETIVE ARGUMENTS

3. The crucial legal arguments in this dispute relate to the definition of "dumping" and "margin of dumping". Brazil has explained that dumping and margin of dumping may only be defined in relation to the product as a whole. As required by Article 17.6(ii) of the *Anti-Dumping Agreement*, this reading is derived from the relevant text, context, and object and purpose, interpreted in accordance with the *Vienna Convention on the Law of Treaties*. In particular, Brazil's reading, like the Appellate Body's[1], is grounded in the text, context, object

---

[1] *See* Appellate Body Report, *US – Stainless Steel*, paras. 83 – 99.

and purpose of the following provisions: Articles II:1, VI:1 and VI:2 of the GATT 1994; and Articles 2.1, 2.2, 2.3, 3.1, 3.2, 5.2(ii), 5.8, 6.1.1, 6.7, 6.10, 6.10.2, 7.2, 7.4, 8.1, 9.1, 9.3, 9.5, 10.6 and 11.1 of the *Anti-Dumping Agreement*. The Appellate Body has repeatedly confirmed that this is the sole permissible interpretation of the terms "dumping" and "margin of dumping", overturning numerous panels that held otherwise.[2]

4. Conversely, the United States argues that "dumping" and "margin of dumping" may be defined in diverse ways, at an importing Member's discretion, to encompass both transaction-specific and product-wide definitions of "dumping". In its Opening Statement at the first Panel meeting, Brazil responded to each of the arguments presented by the United States in support of this interpretation. Because the United States has not elaborated further on its position since that meeting, in its Second Written Submission Brazil summarized the arguments presented earlier in this regard.[3]

5. The United States also argues that, assuming the use of zeroing gives rise to an inconsistency with WTO disciplines, to prove such an inconsistency Brazil must demonstrate that the use of zeroing had an impact on the outcome of the authority's determination. As Brazil discusses below, the United States is wrong on the law and the facts.

III. THE FIRST AND SECOND ADMINISTRATIVE REVIEWS VIOLATE ARTICLES 2.4 AND 9.3 OF THE *ANTI-DUMPING AGREEMENT*, AND ARTICLE VI:2 OF THE GATT 1994

6. Brazil has shown that, for the two Brazilian exporters at issue, Cutrale and Fischer, the USDOC used zeroing in the First Administrative Review under the Orange Juice Order to determine the "weighted average margins of dumping", the cash deposit rates ("CDR") and the importer-specific assessment rates ("ISAR").[4] The United States has not contested this fact. Instead, it argues that Brazil has not proven that the use of zeroing in this review had an *impact* on one of the two exporting companies, Cutrale.

7. With respect to the Second Administrative Review, Brazil has also shown that the USDOC used zeroing, for both Cutrale and Fischer, in determining the margins of dumping, CDRs and ISARs.[5] Again, the United States has not contested the use of zeroing for either Cutrale or Fischer. Instead, it contends that

---

[2] *See, e.g.*, Brazil's FWS, paras. 49 – 61; and Brazil's Opening Statement, paras. 6 – 37. *See* also Appellate Body Report, *US – Continued Zeroing*, concurring opinion, para. 312.

[3] Brazil's SWS, pp. 3 – 4.

[4] Brazil's FWS, paras. 77 – 85; and Brazil's Opening Statement, paras. 65 – 72. *See* also Exhibits BRA-31 (Ferrier Affidavit); BRA-28 (Issues and Decision Memorandum); BRA-29 and BRA-30 (computer program logs); and BRA-34 and BRA-35 (computer program outputs).

[5] Brazil's FWS, paras. 86 – 95; and Brazil's Opening Statement, paras. 73 – 79. *See* also Exhibits BRA-31 (Ferrier Affidavit); BRA-43 (Issues and Decision Memorandum); BRA-36 and BRA-38 (computer program logs); and BRA-37 and BRA-39 (computer program outputs).

zeroing did not have an impact on the determination for one of the companies, Fischer.

A. As a matter of Law, the Use of Zeroing violates Articles 2.4 and 9.3 of the Anti-Dumping Agreement and Article VI:2 of the GATT 1994, regardless of the Impact of Zeroing[6]

8. As set forth in the *chapeau* of Article 9.3 of the *Anti-Dumping Agreement*, a Member must establish a margin of dumping consistently with Article 2 of the *Anti-Dumping Agreement*. The obligation to comply with Article 2 in determining margins of dumping is not dependent on any other aspect of the anti-dumping proceeding or on the outcome of that proceeding in terms of duty collection. A failure to comply with Article 2 in determining the margin vitiates a determination made under Article 9.3, irrespective of the amount of duties that is ultimately collected.[7]

9. In *US – Zeroing (Japan)(21.5)*, the United States argued that Japan had not proven the impact of zeroing in the challenged administrative reviews, and that therefore Japan's challenge had to fail. The panel rejected the US argument. It noted that "the Appellate Body's findings in the original proceedings were not based on evidence that particular importers had sales with negative margins or that individual importer-specific assessment rates were affected by the application of zeroing procedures". Therefore, the Panel did not consider "that Japan must show that given importers had sales with negative margins" under the reviews at issue, "or the effect of zeroing on the importer-specific assessment rates determined in those Reviews".[8]

10. A showing of impact is also not necessary to prove a violation of Article 2.4 of the *Anti-Dumping Agreement*. Article 2.4 provides that, in the determination of dumping:

> A fair comparison shall be made between the export price and the normal value…

11. The focus of Article 2.4 is firmly on the *comparison* between export price and normal value, which must be "fair". In *Egypt – Rebar*, for example, the panel held that the "fair comparison" requirement concerns "the *nature of the comparison* of export price and normal value".[9] In reaching this interpretation, the panel observed that the first sentence of Article 2.4 explicitly focuses on the

---

6 *See* also Brazil's Opening Statement, paras. 66 – 68 and 74; and Brazil's Answers, paras. 8 – 11 and 18 – 21.

7 *See*, in particular, Panel Report, *US – Zeroing (Japan) (21.5)*, para. 7.162.

8 Panel Report, *US – Zeroing (Japan) (21.5)*, para. 7.162. The United States did not appeal this aspect of the panel's findings, and the Appellate Body upheld the panel's finding that the application of zeroing in these reviews was inconsistent with Article 9.3 of the *Anti-Dumping Agreement*, as well as Article 2.4 of the same agreement and Article VI:2 of the GATT 1994. Appellate Body Report, *US – Zeroing (Japan) (21.5)*, paras. 195 and 197.

9 Panel Report, *Egypt – Rebar*, paras. 7.333 – 7.335 (emphasis added). *See also* Panel Report, *Argentina – Poultry*, para. 7.265; and Panel Report, *EC – Pipe Fittings*, para. 7.140.

"the *fairness* of the *comparison*"; the second sentence elaborates on considerations pertaining to the "*comparison*"; the third, fourth and fifth sentence address issues relating to "price *comparability*"; and the final sentence concerns information necessary to make a "fair *comparison*".[10] The panel also considered that the surrounding context in Articles 2.4.1 and 2.4.2 confirmed that Article 2.4 imposes obligations on the nature of the "comparison" itself.[11]

12. Accordingly, in assessing a claim under Article 2.4, a panel must assess "the *nature of the comparison*" made between export price and normal value to determine whether it was "fair". Because the obligation in Article 2.4 to provide a fair comparison concerns "the nature of the comparison" that is made by an anti-dumping authority, it applies independently of the amount of anti-dumping duties that are collected by an importing Member.

13. In terms of ordinary meaning, "[t]he term 'fair" [in Article 2.4] is generally understood to connote impartiality, even-handedness, or lack of bias".[12] The Appellate Body has held that there "is an inherent bias in a zeroing methodology".[13] Focusing on "the nature of the comparison", the Appellate Body has also said that, as a "*way of calculating*" margins, the zeroing methodology "cannot be described as impartial, even-handed, or unbiased", because the comparison necessarily excludes any negative results.[14] A panel and the Appellate Body have, therefore, ruled that the maintenance and application of zeroing procedures in administrative reviews is inconsistent with Article 2.4 of the *Anti-Dumping Agreement*.[15]

14. In this dispute, by including zeroing in its methodology for determining margins of dumping in the administrative reviews at issue, the United States failed to conduct a "fair comparison". The United States has not contested Brazil's evidence that the USDOC did not "take fully into account the prices of all comparable export transactions"[16] for both companies in both the First and the Second Administrative Reviews. To recall, by using zeroing in the comparison, the USDOC excluded the vast majority of both companies' export transactions, in number, volume and value.[17] The *nature of the comparison* was, therefore, distorted and unfair, because it favored, very heavily, a positive dumping determination.

---

[10] Panel Report, *Egypt – Rebar*, para. 7.333 (original emphasis).

[11] Panel Report, *Egypt – Rebar*, para. 7.334.

[12] Appellate Body Report, *US – Softwood Lumber V (21.5)*, para. 138.

[13] Appellate Body Report, *US – Corrosion-Resistant Steel Sunset Review*, para. 135.

[14] Appellate Body Report, *US – Zeroing (Japan)*, para. 146, quoting Appellate Body Report, *US – Softwood Lumber V (21.5)*, para. 142.

[15] Panel Report, *US – Zeroing (Japan)(21.5)*, paras. 7.168 and 8.1(b); Appellate Body Report, *US – Zeroing (Japan)(21.5)*, paras. 195, 197 and 213(c); and Appellate Body Report, *US – Zeroing (Japan)*, paras. 169, 176, 190(d) and 190(e).

[16] Appellate Body Report, *EC – Bed Linen*, para. 55.

[17] *See* Exhibits BRA-34, BRA-35, BRA-37 and BRA-39, respective last page, "Percentage of value with AD margins" and "Percentage of quantity with AD margins".

B. *As a matter of Fact, the Use of Zeroing had an impact for both Companies in both the First and Second Administrative Reviews*

15. Even assuming, *arguendo*, that the United States were right in arguing that a showing of impact is necessary to establish a violation of Articles 2.4 and 9.3 of the *Anti-Dumping Agreement*, and Article VI:2 of the GATT 1994 (*quod non*), the United States' use of zeroing had an impact for both Cutrale and Fischer in the First and Second Administrative Reviews.

16. Brazil notes, first, that as regards Fischer in the First Administrative Review, and Cutrale in the Second Administrative Review, the United States has contested neither the use nor the impact of zeroing. Thus, the disagreement on the facts between Brazil and the United States concerns only Cutrale in the First, and Fischer in the Second Administrative Review.

17. Contrary to the US arguments, zeroing had an impact for Cutrale, too, in the First Administrative Review. *First*, through the use of zeroing, the United States established a positive margin of dumping for Cutrale.[18] Had the United States complied with its WTO obligations, this margin would have been zero. *Second*, through the use of zeroing, the United States established an ISAR for Cutrale which was positive and above the *de minimis* threshold in US law.[19] The United States, therefore, also collected anti-dumping duties on the relevant entries from Cutrale, on the basis of an ISAR determined using zeroing.

18. Finally, also contrary to the US argument, zeroing had an impact for Fischer in the Second Administrative Review. The dumping margin established for Fischer in this review, albeit very small, was a positive one, whereas it would have been zero had the United States not disregarded the overwhelming majority of export transactions.[20]

IV. THE UNITED STATES' CONTINUED USE OF ZEROING VIOLATES ARTICLES 2.4 AND 9.3 OF THE *ANTI-DUMPING AGREEMENT*, AND ARTICLE VI:2 OF THE GATT 1994

19. In addition to challenging zeroing "as applied" in the First and Second Administrative Reviews, Brazil claims that the continued use of zeroing in a string of determinations under the Orange Juice Order violates Articles 2.4, 2.4.2 and 9.3 of the *Anti-Dumping Agreement*, and Article VI:2 of the GATT 1994. Brazil's earlier arguments can be found in previous written and oral submissions.[21] Also, with regard to Article 2.4 of the *Anti-Dumping Agreement*, Brazil

---

[18] Exhibit BRA-21, p. 46585, "Percent margin". This plainly contradicts the US Opening Statement, para. 35.

[19] Exhibit BRA-34, penultimate page, "Percent ad valorem assessment".

[20] Exhibit BRA-39, right-most column, "Wt avg percent margin". This too contradicts the US Opening Statement, para. 35.

[21] *See* Brazil's FWS, paras. 98 – 117; Brazil's Opening Statement, paras. 80 – 96; and Brazil's Answers, paras. 3 – 6 and 9 – 20.

has developed interpretive arguments in this Submission and in its Opening Statement, and has explained why the use of zeroing violates that provision.[22] Those arguments are made also in respect of the United States' continued use of zeroing under the Orange Juice Order.

20. Here, Brazil focuses on U.S. arguments asserting that the evidence does not show the continued use of zeroing under the Orange Juice Order. The United States argues, in particular, that the series of determinations under the Orange Juice Order is not sufficiently long to establish the continued use of zeroing under this Order, and in support of this position, also repeats its arguments that Brazil must show the impact, not the use, of zeroing.

21. Brazil disagrees. In *US – Continued Zeroing*, the Appellate Body held that the continued use of zeroing is established if there is a sufficient "*density*" of evidence, that is *not* "*fragmented*" over time, showing that zeroing has been used in a string of successive proceedings under the same order.[23]

22. Under the Orange Juice Order, the USDOC has used zeroing at *every available opportunity* under the Orange Juice Order in proceedings extending over five years from the original investigation, initiated in February 2005, through the First and Second Administrative Reviews, to the preliminary determination in the Third Administrative Review in April 2010 and the final determination in this review in August 2010. Therefore, the evidence of the continued use of zeroing under the Orange Juice Order is perfectly consistent over an extended time, with no "fragmentation".

1. Zeroing was used in the original investigation

23. With respect to the *original investigation*, the United States contends that zeroing was not used, because there were no negative comparison results. It contends that the "lack of any negative comparison results means that "zeroing" had no impact on the dumping margin calculation".[24] In reply, Brazil has noted that the United States misunderstands the nature of the conduct, and hence measure, at issue, which is the continued *use*, and not impact, of zeroing[25]; in the Appellate Body's words, the measure at issue is "the *use* of the zeroing methodology as an ongoing conduct".[26]

24. The United States unsuccessfully raised a similar objection in *US – Continued Zeroing*. In that case, it argued that the continued use of zeroing under specific orders could not violate the *Anti-Dumping Agreement* because, in a given determination, there may be no negative comparison results. The Appellate Body disagreed. It said:

---

[22] *See* paras. 10 - 14 above; and Brazil's Opening Statement, paras. 67 – 72 and 74 – 79.

[23] Appellate Body Report, *US – Continued Zeroing*, paras. 191 and 194. *See* also, *ibid.*, paras. 193 and 195.

[24] US FWS, paras. 128 – 129.

[25] Brazil's Opening Statement, paras. 91 – 93.

[26] Appellate Body Report, *US – Continued Zeroing*, para. 193 (emphasis added). *See* also Brazil's Answers, paras. 3 – 6 and 9 – 11.

> ... even if zeroing may not manifest itself as a result of the particular factual circumstances of a case in which all export prices are below the normal value, this does not negate the fact that the repeated action by the USDOC in a string of determinations relating to these four cases confirms the use of the zeroing methodology as an ongoing conduct.[27]

Thus, irrespective of the impact of zeroing in a given determination, the continued use of zeroing is WTO-inconsistent.

2. Zeroing was used in the First and Second Administrative Reviews

25. With respect to the *First and Second Administrative Reviews*, the United States contends that zeroing did not have an impact for Cutrale in the First Administrative Review, and for Fischer in the Second Administrative Review. Again, for the reasons just elaborated, this argument misapprehends the nature of the measure at issue, which is the continued use of zeroing. The US arguments do not, therefore, show any "fragmentation" in the USDOC's decision to use zeroing as part of its margin calculation methodology. Indeed, in both reviews, the USDOC stated expressly in the respective Issues & Decisions Memoranda that it had decided to continue using zeroing despite objections from Brazil's exporters.[28]

26. Also, for the reasons already given[29], the United States is incorrect in asserting that zeroing had no impact on the dumping determinations made for Cutrale in the First Administrative Review, and for Fischer in the Second Administrative Review.

3. Zeroing was used in the Third Administrative Review

27. Since the Panel's first substantive meeting with the parties, the United States has seized yet another opportunity to use zeroing under the Order, in the Third Administrative Review, with predictable results. Although this determination is not itself challenged as a measure at issue in these proceedings, it serves as further evidence to show the continued use of zeroing under the Orange Juice Order.[30]

28. In April of 2009, the USDOC initiated the Third Administrative Review under the Orange Juice Order. On 13 April 2010, the USDOC published its preliminary results in this review, as set out in Brazil's First Written Submission.[31]

---

27 Appellate Body Report, *US – Continued Zeroing*, para. 193.

28 Exhibits BRA-28, pp. 5 – 6; and BRA-43, pp. 4 – 6.

29 *See* paras. 17 - 18 and 14 above.

30 *See* Brazil's Opening Statement, para. 95.

31 Brazil's FWS, para. 48, 98, 103, footnote 53 and Exhibits BRA-23, BRA-24 and BRA-25. *See* also Brazil's Opening Statement, paras. 88 and 95.

On 18 August 2010, the USDOC published its final results in this review.[32] In this review, the USDOC again used zeroing. As before, it dismissed the exporters' pleas that it stop using zeroing, and stated, again, that WTO dispute settlement reports do not trump the exercise of the USDOC's discretion under US law.[33]

29. The USDOC's computer logs and outputs, for both Cutrale and Fischer, confirm that the USDOC used zeroing in the Third Administrative Review to determine the margins of dumping, the CDRs, and the ISARs, excluding all negative comparison results, as explained in Mr. Ferrier's second affidavit.[34]

30. Furthermore, in the Issues and Decision Memorandum in the Third Administrative Review, the United States stated expressly that its zeroing policy in reviews remains unchanged despite WTO rulings.[35]

31. Thus, in the midst of these Panel proceedings, which are inquiring into the USDOC's continued use of zeroing under the Orange Juice Order, the United States has expressly confirmed that the use of zeroing continues to be part of the USDOC's calculation methodology for this Order. In these circumstances, the United States' arguments that the evidence before the Panel does not prove the continued use of zeroing ring hollow. Its actions outside these proceedings contradict its words in these proceedings.

32. Indeed, the United States' actions in using zeroing in the Third Administrative Review show precisely why Brazil challenges the continued use of zeroing. Brazil wishes to tackle the root of the problem under the Orange Juice Order, namely the United States' continued use of zeroing. It wishes to do so independent of the application of zeroing in individual determinations because, if Brazil's challenge were confined to such determinations, the challenged measures would be outdated before the Panel proceedings have even ended, with the dispute being prolonged by new measures that are not subject to the Panel's findings.

33. By challenging the continued use measure, Brazil seeks a ruling on a single measure involving the specific ongoing conduct that is the source of the dispute, namely, the continued use of zeroing under the Order. This measure is manifested by, and evidenced in, the string of individual determinations; yet its existence transcends those measures, and must be subject to a specific recommendation by the Dispute Settlement Body to ensure that the ongoing conduct ceases.

34. In sum, the United States has used zeroing with perfect consistency in every proceeding under the Orange Juice Order. Moreover, in rejecting exporters' requests for it to cease using zeroing, it has repeatedly affirmed its intent to persist in this conduct. The record before the Panel, therefore, shows that the continued use of zeroing as an ongoing conduct under the Orange Juice Order

---

[32] Exhibit BRA-49.

[33] Exhibit BRA-50, pp. 4 – 6. .

[34] Exhibit BRA-51. Brazil's SWS, pp. 13 – 15.

[35] Exhibit BRA-50, pp. 4 – 6.

exists. For reasons that Brazil has stated elsewhere[36], the continued use of zeroing is inconsistent with Articles 2.4, 2.4.2 and 9.3 of the *Anti-Dumping Agreement*, and Article VI:2 of the GATT 1994, and the Panel should find accordingly.

[36] *See* Brazil's FWS, paras. 98 – 117; Brazil's Opening Statement, paras. 80 – 96; and Brazil's Answers, paras. 7 – 20.

ANNEX E-2

EXECUTIVE SUMMARY OF THE SECOND WRITTEN SUBMISSION OF THE UNITED STATES

I. ARTICLE 2.4 DOES NOT IMPOSE OBLIGATIONS WITH RESPECT TO ZEROING

1. The obligation to make a "fair comparison" under Article 2.4 does not create an obligation to provide for offsets. Article 2.4 addresses only the required adjustments that must be made to export price and normal value in order to account for "differences which affect price comparability".

2. *First*, from the text of Article 2.4, it is clear that Article 2.4 establishes an obligation that a fair comparison be made between normal value and export price and provides detailed guidance as to how that fair comparison is to be made. The focus of Article 2.4 is on how the authorities are to select transactions for comparison and make the appropriate adjustments for differences that affect price comparability. As the panel in *Egypt – Steel Rebar* explained: "[A]rticle 2.4 in its entirety, including its burden of proof requirement, has to do with ensuring a fair comparison, through various adjustments as appropriate, of export price and normal value".

3. A number of other Appellate Body and panel reports that have considered the question of price comparability have interpreted Article 2.4 to address pre-comparison price adjustments that affect the comparability of prices between markets. For example, as the Appellate Body stated in *US – Hot-Rolled Steel*, "an examination of whether USDOC acted consistently with Article 2.4 of the *Anti-Dumping Agreement* must focus on ... whether there were 'differences', relevant under Article 2.4, which affected the comparability of export price and normal value". Thus, Brazil's proposed interpretation of Article 2.4 to encompass the *results* of comparisons between export price and normal value is erroneous. In short, there is no obligation in Article 2.4 to offset any negative differences between normal value and export price.

4. *Second*, the United States urges the Panel to reject Brazil's invitation to convert "fair comparison" into a broad-ranging mandate to determine whether any and all dumping calculations are "fair" or "unfair". As the panel report in *EC – Cotton Yarn*, which was adopted by the Tokyo Round Antidumping Committee, stated regarding the corresponding provision of the Tokyo Round Code: "The Panel was of the view that although the object and purpose of Article 2.6 is to effect a fair comparison, the wording of Article 2.6 '[i]n order to *effect* a fair comparison' made clear that if the requirements of that Article were met, any comparison thus undertaken was deemed to be 'fair'". The *EC – Cotton Yarn* panel rejected Brazil's argument that the term "fair comparison" in Article 2.6 of the Tokyo Round Antidumping Code provided a basis to strike down the EC's

zeroing practices. The panel interpreted Article 2.6 as relating solely to the "actual comparison of prices at the same level of trade and in respect of sales made as nearly as possible at the same time".

5. The term "fair comparison" originated in the 1967 Kennedy Round Antidumping Code. Article 2(f) specified that: "In order to effect a fair comparison between the export price and the domestic price in the exporting country ... the two prices shall be compared at the same level of trade, normally at the ex factory level, and in respect of sales made as nearly as possible at the same time. Due allowance shall be made in each case, on its merits, for the differences in conditions and terms of sale, for the differences in taxation, and for other differences affecting price comparability". This language was incorporated practically verbatim into Article 2.6 of the Tokyo Round Antidumping Code. The Uruguay Round AD Agreement adopted the original Kennedy and Tokyo Round language with minor modifications in Article 2.4.

6. *Third*, Brazil's claim of inconsistency with Article 2.4 does not rely on the text of Article 2.4. Instead it relies upon isolated statements from the Appellate Body reports in *US – Softwood Lumber (Article 21.5)*, *US – Corrosion-Resistant Steel Sunset Review*, and *US – Zeroing (Japan)*.

7. While the Appellate Body in *US – Zeroing (Japan)* found that the use of "zeroing" in assessment proceedings was inconsistent with Article 2.4, those findings flowed from its finding that the amount of the antidumping duty exceeded the margin of dumping under Article 9.3. Contrary to Brazil's argument, the Appellate Body stated that "[*i*]*f* antidumping *duties are assessed* on the basis of a methodology involving comparisons between the export price and the normal value *in a manner which results in anti-dumping duties being collected from importers in excess of the amount of the margin of dumping* of the exporter or foreign producer, then this methodology cannot be viewed as involving a 'fair comparison' within the meaning of the first sentence of Article 2.4". But in the second administrative review with respect to orange juice (aside from the fact that, as explained in our first written submission, it is outside of the Panel's terms of reference), for example, Commerce determined that the weighted-average dumping margin for Fischer was zero and assessed no antidumping duties on Fischer's entries of orange juice. Under these facts, even under the Appellate Body's rationale relied upon by Brazil, there can be no inconsistency with either Article 9.3 or 2.4 of the AD Agreement.

8. In *US – Softwood Lumber (Article 21.5)*, the Appellate Body stated that "the use of zeroing under the transaction-to-transaction comparison methodology artificially inflates the magnitude of dumping, resulting in higher margins of dumping and making a positive determination more likely". The Appellate Body limited this statement to margins in investigations that violated Article 2.4.2 of the AD Agreement, while accepting the panel's conclusion that higher margins are "fair" as long as they are otherwise WTO consistent. Article 2.4.2 does not apply in the context of the assessment proceedings. Additionally, where, as here, the United States determined either zero or *de minimis* dumping margins for Cutrale and Fisher in the first and second administrative reviews, respectively,

these margins cannot be characterized as "artificially inflate[d]" or "inherently unfair" even under the Appellate Body's rationale.

9. The Appellate Body's report in *US – Corrosion Resistant Steel Sunset Review*, concerned a sunset review, which is not at issue in this dispute. The Appellate Body declined to find an inconsistency with Article 2.4 of the AD Agreement, a salient fact that Brazil neglects to mention.

10. Moreover, any allegation of bias is based upon the assumption that a methodology "artificially" inflates the magnitude of dumping. It may be that a methodology always produces higher margins of dumping, and that exporters or foreign producers may consider that to be biased and "unfair". However, it is then equally true that prohibiting the methodology always produces lower margins of dumping, and the domestic industry – an industry that must have been found to be injured by dumping before the measure is imposed – may consider that to be biased and "unfair". Higher or lower margins are not inherently fair or unfair.

11. As the panel in *US – Zeroing (Japan)* noted, the "precise meaning of" the fair comparison requirement "must be understood in light of the nature of the activity at issue". The panel concluded that "the 'fair comparison' requirement cannot have been intended to allow a panel to review a measure in light of a necessarily somewhat subjective judgment of what fairness means in the abstract and in complete isolation from the substantive context". Other panels have reached the same conclusion. In *US – Softwood Lumber Dumping (Article 21.5)*, the panel cautioned against the overly liberal use of the "fair comparison" language of Article 2.4: "the fact that comparison methodology A produces a higher margin of dumping than comparison methodology B would only make comparison methodology A unfair if comparison methodology B were the applicable standard. If however, the *AD Agreement* were to permit either comparison methodology A or B, this would not be the case". In *US – Zeroing (EC)*, the panel similarly stated: "[C]aution ... is especially warranted where as in the case of the first sentence of Article 2.4, a legal rule is expressed in terms of a standard that by its very nature is more abstract and less determinate than most other rules in the *AD Agreement*".

12. Absent any principled basis for resolving such disputes, the Appellate Body and the panels would be required to apply a vague, subjective, and ill-defined legal standard to factual situations where "fairness" turns on the eye of the beholder. The Panel should reject an expansive interpretation of a "fair comparison" requirement that leads to a flood of antidumping disputes that are virtually impossible to resolve in any credible way.

II. THE TEXT OF ARTICLE VI:1 AND ARTICLE VI:2 OF THE GATT AND ARTICLE 2 OF THE AD AGREEMENT DO NOT PRECLUDE UNDERSTANDING OF THE TERMS "DUMPING" AND "MARGIN OF DUMPING" IN RELATION TO INDIVIDUAL TRANSACTIONS

13. The term "product as a whole" is not found anywhere in the AD Agreement and the GATT 1994, and Brazil's so-called "textual" argument is devoid of any textual analysis of the relevant provisions.

14. *First*, the precise meaning of the terms "dumping" and "margin of dumping" may be informed by the context in which the term is used. These terms appear in many different provisions of the covered agreements, and, in each case, must be interpreted in light of the text, context, and of the object and purpose, of the provision at issue. The terms "dumping" and "margin of dumping" are defined in relation to the term "product". The ordinary meaning of "product" may refer to a single transaction or multiple transactions. The fundamental problem with Brazil's interpretation is that it effectively denies the fact that the terms "dumping" and "margin of dumping" may apply in different contexts and the context matters.

15. Dumping is defined as occurring in the course of ordinary commercial transactions, where products are "introduced into the commerce" of the importing country transaction by transaction, not "as a whole". The drafters of the AD Agreement and the GATT 1994 wrote a *definition* of dumping and put into the *definition* the essential meaning of this fundamental, foundational concept. It defies logic to then redefine the terms "dumping" and "margin of dumping" by finding new additional components of its meaning hidden in other provisions of the AD Agreement that do not purport to define those terms.

16. Article 2.1 defines "dumping" in relation to the terms "export price" and "normal value". These fundamental concepts have flexible meaning because "normal value" and "export price" could relate to either an individual transaction or multiple transactions depending upon the context. Because the term "dumping" is defined in relation to the terms "normal value" and "export price," it would be illogical to conclude that the derivative term "dumping" may not have a similarly flexible definition.

17. *Second*, the United States agrees with Brazil that the AD Agreement establishes multilateral disciplines. However, contrary to what Brazil suggests, it does not follow that the terms "dumping" and "margin of dumping" must be construed only in terms of the "product as a whole". To the contrary, the fact that the Agreement expressly allows Members to maintain different systems for the assessment of antidumping duties and that Members assess duties differently demonstrates that the multilateral character of the Agreement does not mandate the definition Brazil seeks to impose.

18. Brazil also appears to suggest that there must always be the same result in determining "dumping" for the same set of export transactions, prices, products,

and exporters regardless of the context. Brazil's interpretation is contrary to the text of the AD Agreement, which expressly recognizes different assessment systems and different ways to make comparisons between the normal value and export price. If the AD Agreement provides for different comparison methodologies that could result in different amounts of dumping for the same set of transactions, there is no reason to assume that calculations must always result in a single invariable number in different contexts – such as assessment proceedings and investigations – particularly when a Member uses different comparison methodologies in these two contexts.

19. *Third*, Brazil conflates distinct proceedings – investigations and assessment proceedings – which are subject to different requirements and serve different functions. While investigations are conducted to determine the existence and degree of dumping pursuant to Article 5.1 and the existence of material injury, assessment proceedings are conducted to determine the final liability for payment of antidumping duties or whether a refund of excess antidumping duties is owed pursuant to Article 9.3. Prior panels found that this contextual difference is significant. In *US – Zeroing (EC)*, for example, the panel explained: "In our view, the fact that in an assessment proceeding in Article 9.3 the margin of dumping must be related to the liability incurred in respect of particular import transactions is an important element that distinguishes Article 9.3 proceedings from investigations within the meaning of Article 5".

III. BRAZIL'S CONTEXTUAL ARGUMENTS UNDER ARTICLES 3, 5.8, 6.10, 8.1, 9.1, 9.3 AND 9.5 ARE MISPLACED

20. *Article 5.8 of the AD Agreement*: Brazil argues that in the context of Article 5.8 the margin of dumping must refer to an aggregation of multiple transactions. The fundamental flaw of Brazil's contextual argument is that Brazil seeks to apply that understanding entirely removed from the context of Article 5. Article 9.3 assessment proceedings provide a very different context from Article 5 investigations. Article 2.4.2 sets forth the rules that govern the determination of the "existence" of margins of dumping for purposes of Article 5 investigations. The text of Article 2.4.2 expressly limits itself to an Article 5 investigation in two different ways. First, it expressly provides that it applies only in the "investigation phase." Second, it provides that its purpose is to establish the "existence" of dumping. There is only one investigation phase that requires a determination of the "existence" of dumping: the Article 5 investigation that follows the initiation of an anti-dumping investigation.

21. The Appellate Body and panels have found that the application of Article 2.4.2 is limited to Article 5 investigations. The Appellate Body in *EC – Bed Linen* found that there is no connection between Article 9.3 and Article 2.4.2. The panel in *Argentina – Poultry* found that "[i]f the drafters of the *AD Agreement* had intended to refer exclusively to Article 2.4.2 in the context of Article 9.3, the latter provision would have stated that 'the amount of the anti-dumping

duty shall not exceed the margin of dumping as established under Article 2.4.2'. This is not what Article 9.3 says".

22. *Article 6.10 of the AD Agreement*: Article 6.10 ensures that each exporter or producer is assigned an antidumping duty based on its own pricing behavior, and not that of other exporters or producers, unless it is impracticable. This provision does not address whether the "margin of dumping" only has meaning in relation to the "product as a whole" (a term nowhere found in the text of the AD Agreement) or individual transactions. This fact has been recognized by prior panels that examined this issue. In *US – Zeroing (Japan)*, for example, the panel explained that Article 6.10 does not mandate any particular methodologies for calculating the margin of dumping.

23. Further, if Article 6.10 is read in the manner suggested by Brazil, then prospective normal value systems cannot function in the manner that Members currently administering such systems are operating. The effect of the Appellate Body's and Brazil's reading of Article 6.10 would be to compel a Member using a prospective normal value system to calculate a margin based on all of the transactions for some particular period of time, rather than calculating a margin based on a particular transaction.

24. *Brazil Overstates the Significance of the Use of the Singular in the Term "Margin of Dumping"*: With respect to Articles 6.10, 8.1, 9.1, 9.3, and 9.5, Brazil's interpretation relies on the use of the term "margin of dumping" in the singular. However, by Brazil's own admission,"the use of the singular is not decisive ...". A term that is used in the AD Agreement in the singular form may have "both singular and plural meanings".

25. *Brazil Misinterprets Article VII:3 of the GATT 1994*: Brazil argues that the United States is wrong to assume that the same word, "product", must be given the same meaning in two proximate treaty provisions, namely Article VI:1 and Article VIII:3 of the GATT 1994. Brazil misstates the US argument. The United States argues that the term "product" may have either collective meaning or an individual meaning, depending upon the context. This term, used in a wide variety of contexts throughout the provisions of the GATT 1994 and the AD Agreement, incorporates a flexibility of meaning that derives from the fact that the term "product" ordinarily has a meaning that is either collective or transaction-specific.

26. Brazil attempts to draw contextual distinctions between Article VII:3 of the GATT 1994 and Article 9.3 of the AD Agreement. In describing the context of Article VII:3, for example, Brazil argues that "the customs authorities *assess* the value of particular goods that are listed in an import entry of an individual import transaction and, based on that valuation, impose duties on that specific entry". However, Article 9.3 of the AD Agreement also governs the *assessment* of the amount of the antidumping duty, and the antidumping duties are assessed on individual entries resulting from individual transactions. Therefore, the obligation set forth in Article 9.3 to assess no more in antidumping duties than the margin of dumping is similarly applicable at the level of individual transactions.

In *US – Stainless Steel (Mexico)*, the panel properly recognized the transaction-specific character of Article 9.3 assessment proceedings: "We note that the obligation to pay anti-dumping duties is not incurred on the basis of a comparison of an exporter's total sales, but on the basis of an individual sale between the exporter and its importer. It is therefore a transaction-specific liability".

27. *Brazil Misinterprets AD Article VI:1 of the GATT 1994*: Brazil asserts that Ad Article VI:1 does not provide a definition of "dumping" or "margin of dumping" and does not state that margins may be transaction specific. However, contrary to Brazil's assertions, Ad Article VI:1 defines a particular form of dumping – "hidden dumping" – in relation to individual transactions. The use of the term "price invoiced" is particularly significant, because an invoice is normally issued with respect to an individual transaction, and not with respect to *all* transactions covered by the period of review. Thus, the text of Ad Article VI:1 provides that the "margin of dumping" may be calculated on the basis of a specific sale by a particular importer rather than on the basis of the "product as a whole".

28. *Brazil Misinterprets Article 2.2 of the AD Agreement*: Brazil disagrees that the term "margin of dumping" as used in Article 2.2 of the AD Agreement would require the use of constructed value for the "product as a whole", even if the condition precedent for using constructed value under Article 2.2 relates only to a portion of the comparisons. Brazil argues that the Appellate Body stated that an authority may subdivide the "product as a whole" in conducting "intermediate comparisons" on a model-specific basis and, thus, may assess whether the conditions in Article 2.2 are met on a model-specific basis, and subsequently aggregate all intermediate comparisons to determining dumping for the product as a whole.

29. This interpretation is incorrect. Under Article 2.2, a Member may calculate normal value based on constructed value. Many Members do so on a model- or transaction-specific basis. That is, if the home market sales of a particular model were not in the ordinary course of trade, the importing Member might resort to using a constructed normal value as a basis for normal value for that particular model; however, normal value for other models might still be based on home market sales. If, however, the "margin of dumping" must refer, regardless of context, to the "product as a whole", then, when the conditions of Article 2.2 have been met, an investigating authority would be required to use constructed value for the "product as a whole", not just for specific models or transactions of the product. This would be inconsistent with the principle that constructed normal value is to be used only in limited circumstances. The panel in *US – Softwood Lumber Dumping (21.5)* observed that this "would run counter to the principle that constructed normal value is an alternative to be used only in the limited circumstances provided for in Article 2.2".

30. *Brazil's Interpretation Cannot Be Reconciled with the Effective Functioning of Antidumping Duties as a Remedy for Dumping*: Brazil gives no answer to the fact that, if offsets must be provided, importers of the merchandise for which the amount of dumping is greatest will actually have an advantage over their

competitors who import at fair value prices because they will enjoy the benefit of offsets that result from their competitors' fairly priced imports.

IV. BRAZIL'S PROPOSED OBLIGATION IS CONTRARY TO THE CONCEPT OF A PROSPECTIVE NORMAL VALUE SYSTEM PROVIDED FOR IN ARTICLE 9

31. Brazil's proposed obligation to provide offsets is contrary to the very concept of a prospective normal value system provided for in Article 9. The administration of such an assessment system cannot function as intended if the margin of dumping must relate exclusively to an aggregation of all transactions constituting the "product as a whole".

32. Brazil argues that the amount of duties in the prospective normal value system is subject to review under Article 9.3.2 to ensure that the total amount of duties does not exceed the margin of dumping for "the product as a whole". However, nothing in the text of Article 9 suggests that the refund proceeding described therein necessarily must relate to an aggregated examination of all transactions. The United States is not aware of a single prospective normal value system that conforms with Brazil's assertion that a refund mechanism must recalculate a margin of dumping based on an aggregation of all export transactions. The character of the prospective normal value system has led multiple panels that have examined this issue to conclude that final liability for antidumping duties may be determined with respect to individual transactions rather than the "product as a whole". It is implausible to think that the negotiators would agree to provisions in the AD Agreement providing explicitly for a prospective normal value system while simultaneously, and without making any textual provision whatsoever, requiring that such systems conduct retrospective assessment proceedings that aggregate all the transactions occurring over some unspecified period of time.

33. Another characteristic of the AD Agreement that supports the transaction-specific nature of the term "margin of dumping" in certain contexts, and not the aggregation of all transactions constituting "product as a whole", is the use of the term "importer" in Article 9.3.2. When an exporter or producer makes sales of the product subject to the antidumping duty, it is common for such sales to be made to multiple importers. If Importer A decides to request a refund of duty paid in excess of margin of dumping under Article 9.3.2, it would be concerned with its purchases and not the purchases of Importers B and C (or the "product as a whole"). Further, Importer A would not likely have access to the information relating to purchases by its competitors, Importers B and C. Therefore, Importer A would not be able to provide the necessary evidence to duly support a request for a refund if it was requesting a review for all Importers (i.e., for the "product as a whole").

V. BRAZIL'S ARGUMENTS REGARDING MATHEMATICAL EQUIVALENCY ARE WRONG

34. The United States demonstrated in its first written submission that a general prohibition against the use of zeroing would reduce the second sentence of Article 2.4.2 to inutility because the result of a comparison under the second sentence would yield the same result as a weighted average to weighted average comparison under the first sentence of that article. Brazil argues that the Appellate Body has noted that a comparison under the second sentence may yield different mathematical results from comparisons under other provisions if only a subset of data is analyzed, *i.e.*, using only those export transactions that make up the pricing pattern envisioned by Article 2.4.2. However, this argument is not supported by the text of Article 2.4.2.

35. The second sentence of Article 2.4.2 describes the situation in which an asymmetrical methodology may be used. It does not establish a set of circumstances under which a Member may select a subset of export transactions. If the drafters had intended for Members to limit its analysis to a subset of export transactions, then presumably Article 2.4.2 would have said so. Instead, the text provides for an asymmetrical comparison methodology, using the same universe of export transactions as the other two methodologies.

36. Brazil's interpretation of the second sentence of Article 2.4.2 essentially requires that the Panel read words into that sentence that do not appear there. Moreover, inferring those words in that provision would allow that provision to be applied in a manner that is similar to other provisions explicitly provided in the AD Agreement, but without any of the safeguards or limitations that the drafters found appropriate when explicitly permitting the kind of analysis contemplated by Brazil. Consequently, Brazil's interpretation would be inconsistent with both the specific text of the second sentence of Article 2.4.2 and with the broader context provided by the AD Agreement.

VI. THERE IS NO VIOLATION WHEN "ZEROING" HAS NO IMPACT

37. At the first substantive hearing, the United States explained that, even if Brazil were able to prove that a denial of offsets for non-dumped transactions was part of a particular dumping margin calculation, there could be no violation in the instances where there was no impact on the calculated dumping margin. Brazil argues that the "use" of zeroing is the violation, regardless of the impact. However, Brazil is wrong because when no duties are assessed, there can be no violation of any obligation not to assess duties in excess of the margin of dumping. Consequently, there can be no violation with respect to Fischer in the second administrative review (in which the dumping margin was zero).

38. It is worth noting in addition that, with respect to the perceived difference between the "use" and the "impact" of "zeroing", Brazil appears to suggest that

all that matters for purposes of finding an inconsistency with the covered agreements is that the "zeroing" line appear in the relevant calculation program. However, the "zeroing" line does not operate where there are no non-dumped sales. In those circumstances – as in the orange juice investigation – the calculations and comparisons made are exactly those that would have been made even if the "zeroing" line were not there.

VII. BRAZIL'S CLAIMS WITH RESPECT TO "CONTINUED USE" FAIL

39. The United States explained in its first written submission and in its oral statements at the first meeting with the Panel why Brazil's "continued use" claim is not a measure that may be subject to dispute settlement. Brazil's response to the US request for preliminary rulings, and its statements at the first meeting with the Panel, demonstrate this point further. They underline that Brazil seeks to obtain adverse findings against specific measures that do not exist, based on evidence of past conduct that does not demonstrate a violation of any obligation.

40. It is worth noting in light of Brazil's comparison of its "continued use" measure to an "as such" measure that a challenge to an "as such" measure requires certain evidentiary showings that Brazil has not offered here. Instead, the challenge to this alleged "measure" ignores the fact that any "use" of "zeroing" can only occur in individual "as applied" measures and tries to include an indefinite number of future individual measures that do not and may never exist. The Panel cannot analyze such measures, because there are no facts about them to analyze. In addition, presumably, if Brazil is challenging the "continued use" as a measure, such measure would cease to exist if at any point "zeroing" is not used in a particular individual determination – but Brazil's argument requires the Panel to assume that it will be used. Any recommendation with respect to a future measure would need to be conditioned on the use of zeroing, but there would be no mechanism to determine if zeroing were in fact used in any individual proceeding. In addition, under Article 4.2 of the Dispute Settlement Understanding ("DSU") a measure must be "affecting" the operation of a covered agreement, and a measure that does not exist cannot be "affecting" the operation of an agreement.

41. Brazil relies heavily upon the Appellate Body's findings in *US – Continued Zeroing (EC) (AB)* in support of its arguments that the "continued use" of "zeroing" is a measure that is subject to dispute settlement and WTO-inconsistent. Even aside from the fact that "continued use" is not properly within the Panel's terms of reference, the reasoning in that report does not support a similar finding in this case because this case is more similar to the cases in which the Appellate Body declined to find a "continued use" violation.

42. Contrary to Brazil's claim, the United States does not suggest that the Appellate Body created a specific standard for finding a "continued use" violation. But in light of Brazil's insistence that the findings in that dispute supported

its claim, we noted that the Appellate Body found an inconsistency only in circumstances that included the use of the zeroing methodology in the initial less than fair value investigation, the use of the zeroing methodology in four successive administrative reviews, and reliance in a sunset review upon rates determined using the zeroing methodology. We further explained that the Appellate Body declined to find a violation in 14 other cases that had facts more similar to this case. Brazil claims that the reason the Appellate Body declined to find a violation in most of the cases before it was that the evidence of zeroing was "fragmented" in those cases. However, continuity was only one aspect of the Appellate Body's analysis. In taking a cautious approach, the Appellate Body found a violation only where "the zeroing methodology was repeatedly used in a string of determinations made sequentially in periodic reviews and sunset reviews over an extended period of time". That is not the case here.

43. Brazil argues that, regardless of whether the zeroing methodology had any impact, its presence in the program is evidence of a violation. However, if the zeroing methodology has no impact, there can be no lesser dumping margin that could have been calculated and there could be no lesser duty assessed. It is not reasonable to find that a measure that is not itself WTO-inconsistent – for example, the original investigation in the orange juice case, in which Brazil's own evidence shows there were no non-dumped sales that could have been "zeroed" – can, nevertheless, be evidence of an ongoing and continuing violation. Even if Brazil's factual allegations were true and the zeroing line was present in each of the calculation programs at issue, Brazil has not shown the application of "zeroing" in "a string of determinations, made sequentially ... over an extended period of time". At most it would have shown that "zeroing" applied to one company in one proceeding that is within this Panel's terms of reference, covering a one year period, *i.e.*, Fischer in the first administrative review.

ANNEX F

EXECUTIVE SUMMARIES OF THE PARTIES STATEMENTS AT THE SECOND SUBSTANTIVE MEETING OF THE PANEL

ANNEX F-1

EXECUTIVE SUMMARY OF THE ORAL OPENING STATEMENT OF BRAZIL

I. INTRODUCTION

1. Zeroing has now been condemned in eight dispute settlement cases. Unfortunately, the United States continues to resist the rulings in these cases, and repeats yet again arguments that have already been rejected by the Appellate Body. Brazil is therefore compelled to address again a large number of interpretive points that should, by now, be accepted by all WTO Members.[1]

II. DEFINITIONS OF THE CONCEPTS OF DUMPING AND MARGIN OF DUMPING

A. Dumping is Defined in Relation to the Product as a Whole

2. Contrary to the United States' assertion, Brazil has explained in great detail[2] that the text of Article 2 of the *Anti-Dumping Agreement* and Articles VI:1 and VI:2 of the *General Agreement on Tariffs and Trade 1994* ("GATT 1994") shows that "dumping" and "margin of dumping" are defined in relation to the "product" as a whole, and not in relation to individual export transactions. Dumping, therefore, involves an "exporter's pricing behavior as reflected in all of its transactions over a period of time".[3] Such dumping may cause injury to the domestic industry – not on a transaction-specific basis, but through the exporter's pricing behavior over time. Brazil has shown that its interpretation of the terms

1 *See* Appellate Body Report, *US – Continued Zeroing*, para. 312.

2 *See* Brazil's First Opening Statement, paras. 12 – 37; Brazil's FWS, paras. 49 – 61.

3 Appellate Body Report, *US – Stainless Steel (Mexico)*, para. 98.

"dumping" and "margin of dumping" is confirmed by the context in Articles 2, 3, 5.8, 6.10, 8.1, 9.1, 9.3, and 9.5 of the *Anti-Dumping Agreement*.

3. Given the interconnectedness of all aspects of anti-dumping proceedings, with anti-dumping duties justified only "as long as and to the extent necessary to counteract dumping which is causing injury"[4], the Appellate Body's conclusion that the crucial notion of "dumping" should be defined uniformly throughout the *Agreement* – as Article 2.1 of the *Anti-Dumping Agreement* explicitly provides – is inescapable.

4. The United States disregards the very lucid, text-based, reasoning of the Appellate Body, and replaces it with an *à la carte* interpretation.[5]

B. The United States' Arguments Are Contrary to The Basic Principles Concerning the Determination of Dumping

5. The US argument that "dumping" and "margin of dumping" have different meanings in different proceedings, or even within the same type of proceedings, is unavailing.

6. The different proceedings at issue *all* concern a determination of the margin – or magnitude – of dumping, because anti-dumping duties involve a justified departure from Members' bound tariffs *only so long as and to the extent* necessary to counteract "dumping". The different procedural steps at which such magnitude is measured do not, therefore, justify a change in the definition of what is being measured, *i.e.*, dumping. At all stages, whether the *existence and extent* of the right to counter dumping is being determined in an original investigation; whether the *extent* of that right is being determined in an administrative review; or whether the *duration* of that right is being determined in a sunset review, a Member's right to take countermeasures is determined by reference to the same concept of "dumping". The *existence, extent, and duration,* of the right must be measured in the same way. The Appellate Body has made this point in no uncertain terms.[6]

7. The United States also argues that the existence of different systems for the assessment of duties justifies different interpretations of the concepts of "dumping" and "margin of dumping". At its core, the US argument is wrong because it confuses *duty collection* with the *determination of the margin of dumping*.[7] If the US argument were accepted, then a Member's administrative choices on how to *collect* duties would become the decisive consideration in how "dumping" is defined for each Member.

---

4 *Anti-Dumping Agreement*, Article 11.

5 *See, e.g.*, Appellate Body Report, *US – Zeroing (Japan)*, paras. 108 – 115; and Appellate Body Report, *US – Stainless Steel (Mexico)*, paras. 82 – 99.

6 Appellate Body Report, *US – Stainless Steel (Mexico)*, para. 96: "'dumping' and 'margin of dumping' have the same meaning throughout the *Anti-Dumping Agreement*".

7 Appellate Body Report, *US – Stainless Steel (Mexico)*, para. 120; Appellate Body Report, *US – Zeroing (Japan)*, paras. 162 – 163; Appellate Body Report, *US – Continued Zeroing*, paras. 293 – 294.

8. The United States adds that the multilateral character of the *Anti-Dumping Agreement* actually "*undermines*" the conclusion that "dumping" and "margin of dumping" have a single definition for purposes of the *Agreement*, because having multiple, open-ended meanings of terms is better suited to multilateral agreements, so as to "accommodate" the interpretation and practices of a large number of parties.[8]

9. The notion that the more parties there are to an agreement, the more the agreement's terms should be interpreted to accommodate all Members' practices, is absurd. This approach to treaty interpretation would unravel multilateral disciplines, replacing them with unilateralism based on the diverse practices of up to 153 Members.

10. The United States argues that the treaty interpreter should give meaning to "constructive ambiguity".[9] This confuses a negotiating tactic – *i.e.*, employing language that might seem to lend itself to a range of interpretations – with the task of treaty interpretation. Just because certain negotiators might resort to so-called "constructive ambiguity" as a negotiating tactic does not mean that the ordinary meaning of the ensuing agreement is incapable of being ascertained through the customary rules of treaty interpretation.

11. Indeed, this is the very purpose of treaty interpretation; namely, whatever the subjective views of this or that negotiator, the treaty interpreter must discern the common intent of the contracting parties as expressed through the words used.[10] Moreover, as Article 3.2 of the DSU sets forth, the purpose of dispute settlement is to resolve disputes regarding the existing covered agreements using the customary rules of treaty interpretation. The United States would deny this purpose.

12. As already explained, the text, context, and object and purpose of the *Agreement* define "dumping" uniformly "[f]or the purpose of [the] Agreement". The text of a treaty evidences the common intent and consent of the parties[11], leaving no grounds for arguing that the parties' subjective intent was different from that ascertained through an analysis of this text, in light of its context, and of the treaty's object and purpose.

C. The United States' Contextual Objections Lack Merit

13. In support of its *à la carte* view of the *Anti-Dumping Agreement*, the United States reiterates several contextual arguments that have already been dismissed by the Appellate Body. Brazil is therefore compelled to address these arguments again, together with some further objections that the United States raises with regard to provisions that Brazil relies upon as context.

---

[8] US SWS, Section III:B and para. 28.

[9] US Answers, para. 34.

[10] *See* Appellate Body Report, *EC – Computer Equipment*, para. 84; and Appellate Body Report, *EC – Chicken Cuts*, para. 239.

[11] *See, e.g.*, Isabelle van Damme, *Treaty Interpretation by the WTO Appellate Body*, Oxford University Press, 2009, p. 36.

14. *Ad Article VI:1 of the GATT 1994*: The United States argues that *Ad* Article VI:1 defines a particular form of dumping in relation to individual transactions, and therefore proves that dumping can be transaction-specific. However, *Ad* Article VI:1 does not set out a definition of "dumping". It is Article 2.1 of the *Anti-Dumping Agreement* that does so, "[f]or the purpose of [the] Agreement".

15. *Article VII:3 of the GATT 1994*: As already noted, the United States refuses to acknowledge that certain provisions on anti-dumping may provide context for the interpretation of the terms "dumping" and "margin of dumping". At the same time, it argues that the term "product" should have the same meaning in Article VII:3, on customs valuation, and in the WTO provisions on anti-dumping. Yet customs valuation is concerned with the establishment of the customs value of a single transaction, with the aim of levying duties on that single transaction. Anti-dumping, on the other hand, is concerned with establishing the margin of dumping for a product as defined by the investigating authority[12], as a basis for levying duties on all subsequent entries of that product during a particular period. Thus, the US attempts to assimilate the meaning of "product" from the customs valuation context to the anti-dumping context are without basis.

16. *Article 2.2 of the Anti-Dumping Agreement*: The United States also repeats its argument that Article 2.2 supports a transaction-specific interpretation of "dumping". The US argument is without merit. The Appellate Body has clarified that the conditions in Article 2.2 for the construction of normal value may be met on a model-specific basis, and model-specific intermediate comparisons may be made under Article 2.4.2, *provided* that the results of all intermediate comparisons are aggregated to determine "dumping" on a product-wide basis to meet the definition in Article 2.1. It does not exempt Members from the obligation to determine dumping for the product as a whole.[13]

17. *Mathematical equivalence under Article 2.4.2 of the Anti-Dumping Agreement*: The United States argues that the mathematical implication of a "general prohibition on zeroing" is that the second sentence of Article 2.4.2 "would be reduced to inutility", and therefore, there can be no general prohibition on zeroing.[14] But an exception such as that set out in the second sentence of Article 2.4.2, which is, moreover, inapplicable to the facts at issue in this dispute, cannot govern the interpretation of the general rule regarding the determination of dumping.[15] Further, the US argument is premised on the US interpretation of the third methodology set out in the second sentence, whereas "there is considerable uncertainty regarding how precisely the third methodology should be applied".[16]

---

[12] *See, e.g.*, Appellate Body Report, *US – Stainless Steel (Mexico)*, para. 115.

[13] Appellate Body Report, *US – Softwood Lumber V (21.5)*, paras. 82 and 97. *See* Brazil's First Opening Statement, para. 46; and Brazil's SWS, para. 5.

[14] US SWS, paras. 74 – 79.

[15] Brazil's First Opening Statement, paras. 52 – 58; Appellate Body Report, *US – Softwood Lumber V (21.5)*, para. 97; and Appellate Body Report, *US – Continued Zeroing*, para. 297.

[16] Appellate Body Report, *US – Softwood Lumber V (21.5)*, para. 98, *cited in* Brazil's Answers, para. 58.

18. *Article 5.8 of the Anti-Dumping Agreement*: While the United Sates insists that the meaning of "dumping" in Article 5.8 is unrelated to the meaning of "dumping" in other provisions of the *Anti-Dumping Agreement*, Brazil welcomes the United States' recognition that "in the context of an Article 5 investigation" the term "margin of dumping" "may refer to multiple transactions", by which it seems to mean "product as a whole".[17]

19. *Article 6.10 of the Anti-Dumping Agreement*: The United States' reliance on the Spanish language version of the text of Article 6.10 in support of its contention that Article 6.10 leaves open the possibility of establishing dumping in relation to individual transactions is based on a mistranslation of this language version ("a margin" in lieu of "the margin").[18] Brazil's interpretation gives meaning to the English, French and Spanish versions of Article 6.10.[19]

20. *The Use of the Singular:* According to the United States, Brazil overstates the significance of the term "margin of dumping" in the singular in Articles 6.10, 8.1, 9.1 and 9.3 of the *Anti-Dumping Agreement*. However, Brazil's interpretation is based on the text and context of the provisions relating to "dumping" and "margin of dumping", and on the object and purpose of the treaties in which these provisions are set out.[20] Brazil relies on the use of the singular as part of the textual choices made by negotiators. The US also refers to *US – OCTG from Mexico*. But in that case, the language at issue was the phrase "*any* anti-dumping duty", and the panel, upheld by Appellate Body, relied on the fact that "any" was different from "an", in that the former has both singular and plural meanings.[21]

21. *Prospective Normal Value ("PNV") Systems*: The United States repeats that "margin of dumping" must have a transaction-specific meaning because, in PNV systems, a margin of dumping is established for each import entry of the goods subject to measures. As explained by the Appellate Body, this argument is unfounded, because the United States is confusing the method for duty collection with the determination of the margin of dumping.[22] The United States argues that Brazil's interpretation transforms PNV systems into retrospective systems. This is not correct. Under PNV systems, duties on importation are still collected on the basis of a PNV. However, to ensure that the amount of duty collected is not excessive, the *Anti-Dumping Agreement* provides for a refund mechanism based on the product as a whole. The United States also argues that Brazil's view would discourage importers from requesting refund reviews under Article 9.3.2, because they could, as a result, "find out that [their] dumping liability increased".[23] This too is wrong. In a prospective duty assessment, based on the text, the outcome of a refund review is: (i) a refund; or (ii) no action.

---

[17] US SWS, para. 34.

[18] US SWS, para. 41.

[19] *See* Appellate Body Report, *US – Stainless Steel (Mexico)*, footnote 200.

[20] Brazil's FWS, paras. 49 – 69; and Brazil's First Opening Statement, paras. 6 – 34.

[21] Panel Report, *US – OCTG from Mexico*, para. 7.149; and Appellate Body Report, *US – OCTG from Mexico*, paras. 146 – 147.

[22] Brazil's First Opening Statement, paras. 47 – 49; and Brazil's SWS, para. 5.

[23] US SWS, para. 73.

Even if the authority establishes that "the actual margin of dumping" was higher than that established prospectively, it may not, as a result, retrospectively increase the anti-dumping duty liability, because the treaty refers to a "refund" procedure. Finally, the United States relies on the practice of one Member operating a PNV system, arguing that it gives preference to transaction-specific refunds. Yet, the practice of one – or even some – Members does not establish the proper interpretation of a treaty counting 153 parties.[24]

III. ARTICLE 2.4 OF THE *ANTI-DUMPING AGREEMENT* IMPOSES AN OBLIGATION TO CONDUCT A FAIR COMPARISON, AND IS NOT LIMITED TO ISSUES OF PRICE COMPARABILITY

22. The United States argues that "Article 2.4 addresses only the required adjustments that must be made to export price and normal value in order to account for 'differences which affect price comparability'".[25] This arguments overlooks the text of Article 2.4, as well as the case law setting out the proper interpretation of this provision.

23. Article 2.4 consists of a series of distinct sentences, the first of which states succinctly: "A fair comparison shall be made between the export price and the normal value". Thus, the panel in *Egypt – Steel Rebar*, for example, held that the "fair comparison" requirement in Article 2.4 generally concerns "the *nature of the comparison* of export price and normal value"[26], with the first sentence explicitly focused on the "the *fairness* of the *comparison*". Only the third, fourth and fifth sentences of Article 2.4 address issues relating to "price comparability".[27]

24. The Appellate Body confirmed this understanding in *US – Zeroing (EC)*. It saw "nothing incorrect" in the reasoning of the panel in that case. The Appellate Body "also agree[d] with the Panel that the legal rule set out in the first sentence of Article 2.4 is expressed in terms of a general and abstract standard", noting that "[o]ne implication of this is that this requirement is also applicable to proceedings governed by Article 9.3".[28] Contrary to the US arguments, the Appellate Body has repeatedly held that the use of zeroing in administrative reviews is inconsistent with the fair comparison requirement of Article 2.4.[29]

25. The negotiating history of the *Anti-Dumping Agreement* confirms that Article 2.4 imposes an independent obligation to conduct a fair comparison between export price and normal value. This conclusion is compelled by the fact

---

[24] *See, e.g.*, Appellate Body Report, *EC – Chicken Cuts*, paras. 258 ff.

[25] US SWS, para. 4 and Section II.A.

[26] Panel Report, *Egypt – Steel Rebar*, paras. 7.333 – 7.335 (emphasis added). *See also* Panel Report, *Argentina – Poultry*, para. 7.265; and Panel Report, *EC – Tube or Pipe Fittings*, para. 7.140.

[27] Panel Report, *Egypt – Steel Rebar*, para. 7.333 (original emphases).

[28] Appellate Body Report, *US – Zeroing (EC)*, para. 146.

[29] Appellate Body Report, *US – Softwood Lumber V (21.5)*, para. 138; Appellate Body Report, *US – Corrosion-Resistant Steel Sunset Review*, para. 135; and Appellate Body Report, *US – Zeroing (Japan)*, paras. 190(c) and 190(e).

that the drafters of the *Anti-Dumping Agreement* explicitly modified the text of this provision – as compared to that of the prior Anti-Dumping Codes[30] – to separate the "fair comparison" requirement in the first sentence of Article 2.4 into a stand-alone obligation.

IV. THE USE OF ZEROING IS INCONSISTENT WITH ARTICLES 2.4 AND 9.3 OF THE *ANTI-DUMPING AGREEMENT*, AND ARTICLE VI:2 OF THE GATT 1994, REGARDLESS OF ITS IMPACT

26. Brazil has demonstrated that the USDOC *used* zeroing in the First and Second Administrative Reviews, and that it *continues to use* zeroing under the Orange Juice Order.[31] The United States has not contested that it used or continues to use zeroing in these instances; rather, it has argued that the use of zeroing had *no impact* on *one* of the exporters in the First Administrative Review (*i.e.*, Cutrale) and on *one* of the exporters in the Second Administrative Review (*i.e.*, Fischer). In all other situations, it has no defence. But even in the two limited situations it identifies, the *use* of zeroing is inconsistent with Articles 2.4 and 9.3, and Article VI:2 of the GATT 1994, *regardless of its impact.*

A. Article 9.3 of the Anti-Dumping Agreement and Article VI:2 of the GATT 1994

27. Article 9.3, which parallels Article VI:2, sets forth two requirements: (i) that a margin of dumping be established in accordance with Article 2 of the *Anti-Dumping Agreement*; and (ii) that the amount of the anti-dumping duty not exceed the margin so established.

28. With respect to the first requirement, the obligation to comply with Article 2 in determining margins of dumping is *independent* of any other aspect of the anti-dumping proceeding or of the outcome of that proceeding in terms of duty collection. A failure to comply with Article 2 in determining the margin vitiates a determination made under Article 9.3, irrespective of the amount of duties that is ultimately collected.[32]

29. In *US – Zeroing (Japan) (21.5)*, the United States argued that Japan had not proven the impact of zeroing in the challenged administrative reviews, and that therefore Japan's challenge had to fail. The panel rejected the U.S. argument.[33] The United States did not appeal this aspect of the panel's findings, and the Appellate Body upheld the panel's finding that the application of zeroing in

[30] Article 2(f) of the Kennedy Round Anti-Dumping Code and Article 2.6 of the Tokyo Round Anti-Dumping Code.

[31] *See* Brazil's FWS, paras. 62 – 97, 98 – 104, and 114 – 117; and Brazil's First Opening Statement, paras. 66 – 69 and 74 – 75.

[32] *See*, in particular, Panel Report, *US – Zeroing (Japan) (21.5)*, para. 7.162. *See* also Mexico's Answers, paras. 21-23; the EU's Answers, para. 9; and Korea's Answers, para. 13.

[33] Panel Report, *US – Zeroing (Japan) (21.5)*, para. 7.162.

these reviews was inconsistent with Article 9.3 of the *Anti-Dumping Agreement*, as well as Article 2.4, and Article VI:2 of the GATT 1994.[34]

30. Further, in *US – Continued Zeroing*, the United States argued that the EU's "continued use" claim failed because there was no evidence of the impact of zeroing in any specific determinations. In particular, the United States argued that there was no evidence that there would be negative comparison results that would be zeroed in each and every determination. The Appellate Body rejected this argument, finding that the continued use of zeroing under a specific anti-dumping order is inconsistent with, among others, Article 9.3 of the *Anti-Dumping Agreement* irrespective of the outcome of the calculation.[35]

B. Article 2.4 of the Anti-Dumping Agreement

31. The United States' use of zeroing in the administrative reviews at issue is also inconsistent with Article 2.4 of the *Anti-Dumping Agreement*, irrespective of its impact. As discussed earlier, the "fair comparison" requirement in the first sentence of Article 2.4 concerns "the *nature of the comparison* of export price and normal value"[36], and is focused on "the *fairness* of the *comparison*".[37] Because the obligation concerns "the nature of the comparison" that is made by an anti-dumping authority, it applies independently of the amount of anti-dumping duties that are collected by an importing Member.

32. In terms of ordinary meaning, "[t]he term 'fair" [in Article 2.4] is generally understood to connote impartiality, even-handedness, or lack of bias".[38] The Appellate Body has held that there "is an inherent bias in a zeroing methodology".[39] It has also said that, as a "*way of calculating*" margins, the zeroing methodology "cannot be described as impartial, even-handed, or unbiased".[40] A panel and the Appellate Body have, therefore, ruled that *the maintenance and application* of zeroing procedures in administrative reviews is inconsistent with Article 2.4 of the *Anti-Dumping Agreement*.[41]

33. Thus, irrespective of impact, the use of zeroing in making determinations for all of the companies in all of the measures at issue violates Article 2.4 of the *Anti-Dumping Agreement* because it involves an unfair comparison.

---

[34] Appellate Body Report, *US – Zeroing (Japan) (21.5)*, paras. 195 and 197.

[35] Appellate Body Report, *US – Continued Zeroing*, para. 192.

[36] Panel Report, *Egypt – Steel Rebar*, paras. 7.333 – 7.335 (emphasis added). *See also* Panel Report, *Argentina – Poultry*, para. 7.265; and Panel Report, *EC – Tube or Pipe Fittings*, para. 7.140.

[37] Panel Report, *Egypt – Steel Rebar*, para. 7.333 (original emphasis).

[38] Appellate Body Report, *US – Softwood Lumber V (21.5)*, para. 138.

[39] Appellate Body Report, *US – Corrosion-Resistant Steel Sunset Review*, para. 135.

[40] Appellate Body Report, *US – Zeroing (Japan)*, para. 146, *quoting* Appellate Body Report, *US – Softwood Lumber V (21.5)*, para. 142.

[41] Panel Report, *US – Zeroing (Japan)(21.5)*, paras. 7.168 and 8.1(b); Appellate Body Report, *US – Zeroing (Japan)(21.5)*, paras. 195, 197 and 213(c); and Appellate Body Report, *US – Zeroing (Japan)*, paras. 169, 176, 190(d) and 190(e).

V. THE CONTINUED USE OF ZEROING IS INCONSISTENT WITH ARTICLES 2.4 AND 9.3 OF THE *ANTI-DUMPING AGREEMENT*, AND ARTICLE VI:2 OF THE GATT 1994

34. Brazil claims that the United States has violated Articles 2.4, 2.4.2 and 9.3 of the *Anti-Dumping Agreement*, and Article VI:2 of the GATT 1994, also through the continued use of zeroing under the Orange Juice Order.[42]

35. The United States maintains that Brazil's "continued use" claim is not a measure that may be subject to dispute settlement.[43] However, in *US – Continued Zeroing*, the Appellate Body found "no reason to exclude ongoing conduct that consists of the use of the zeroing methodology from challenge in WTO dispute settlement".[44] The US argument is also surprising because the United States is challenging a "continued use" measure in *EC – Large Civil Aircraft*, explicitly and extensively relying on the Appellate Body's reasoning in *US – Continued Zeroing*, which it is nonetheless encouraging this Panel to disregard.[45]

36. The United States also argues that Brazil has not made the evidentiary showings required for an "as such" challenge. However, as Brazil has explained[46], a challenge to the "continued use" of zeroing under the Orange Juice Order is narrower than a challenge to zeroing "as such" and, therefore, not subject to the identical evidentiary requirements.

37. Brazil has established that there is a sufficient "density of factual findings", that is not "fragmented" over time, showing that zeroing has been used in successive proceedings under the same order.[47] As Brazil has demonstrated, the USDOC used zeroing in the original investigation; in the First and Second Administrative Reviews; and in the Third Administrative Review. Indeed, with regard to the latter review, Brazil notes that while the United States stated before the Panel that it could not foretell whether it would continue to use zeroing under the Orange Juice Order, it then used zeroing shortly after the first meeting with the Panel, in the Third Administrative Review.[48] Thus, the United States has used zeroing with perfect consistency in *every* proceeding under the Orange Juice Order, including very recently.[49]

---

[42] *See* Brazil's FWS, paras. 98 – 117; Brazil's First Opening Statement, paras. 80 – 96; and Brazil's Answers, paras. 7 – 20.

[43] *See* U.S. SWS, paras. 83 – 87.

[44] Appellate Body Report, *US – Continued Zeroing*, para. 181.

[45] US Other Appellant's Submission, EC – Large Civil Aircraft, 23 August 2010, paras. 53-58, available at http://www.ustr.gov/trade-topics/enforcement/dispute-settlement-proceedings/wto-dispute-settlement/measures-affecting-t-0.

[46] *See* Brazil's Answers, paras. 3 – 6.

[47] *See* Brazil's SWS, paras. 29 – 30 and Appellate Body Report, *US – Continued Zeroing*, paras. 191 and 194.

[48] *See* Brazil's SWS, paras. 31 – 45.

[49] *See* Brazil's SWS, para. 42. It has also repeatedly affirmed its intent to persist in this conduct under the Orange Juice Order, despite WTO rulings. *See* IDM in the First Administrative Review, pp. 5 – 6; IDM in the Second Administrative Review, pp. 4 – 6; and IDM in the Third Administrative Review, pp. 4 – 6. Exhibits BRA-28, BRA-43 and BRA-50. On IDMs, *see* Appellate Body Report, *U.S. – Continued Zeroing*, footnote 767.

ANNEX F-2

EXECUTIVE SUMMARY OF THE ORAL OPENING STATEMENT OF THE UNITED STATES

1. In our statement today, we would like to focus on rebutting arguments made by Brazil in its second written submission and in response to the Panel's questions. We hope that our oral statement will clarify our views as Brazil's opening statement did not present them accurately. We first will highlight that interpreting the terms "dumping" and "margin of dumping" to have meaning in relation to individual transactions is a permissible and perfectly coherent interpretation of the *Agreement on Implementation of Article VI of the General Agreement on Tariffs and Trade 1994* ("Antidumping Agreement"). Brazil's proposed interpretation, in contrast, has no textual basis. In addition, Brazil's interpretation is inconsistent with the very concept of a prospective normal value system, both as provided for in the text and as such systems are actually used. Indeed, as we show in the exhibits submitted with this oral statement, and contrary to Brazil's representations, Brazil's own use of prospective normal value is inconsistent with Brazil's insistence that the Antidumping Agreement prohibits a transaction-specific definition of dumping.

2. We will then respond to four other lines of argument in this dispute: First, with respect to mathematical equivalence, as we demonstrated empirically in our response to the Panel's questions, Brazil's proposed interpretation of the Antidumping Agreement would render the second sentence of Article 2.4.2 meaningless. Second, with respect to "fair comparison" under Article 2.4, Brazil's interpretation invites a subjective examination that is not based on the text. Third, Brazil's arguments regarding cash deposits are similarly not based on the text of the Antidumping Agreement, which plainly allows Members to collect a cash deposit as security for payment of antidumping duties. Finally, with respect to its assertion that the "use" of "zeroing" is inconsistent with the covered agreements regardless of whether any duties were collected or whether there even were any negative comparison results to "zero", Brazil's interpretation is completely inconsistent with the text. Brazil has failed to demonstrate any basis for finding an inconsistent "continued use" measure, even were such a measure within the Panel's terms of reference.

I. A TRANSACTION-SPECIFIC INTERPRETATION OF "DUMPING" AND "MARGIN OF DUMPING" IS PERMISSIBLE

3. The text and context of the covered agreements, interpreted in accordance with the customary rules of interpretation of public international law, make clear that the terms "dumping" and "margin of dumping" may have meaning for indi-

vidual transactions. Brazil's interpretation, in contrast, is not consistent with either the text, or with how prospective normal value systems operate.

A. Standard of Review

4. As we have noted previously, in a dispute involving the Antidumping Agreement, the relevant standard of review includes that set forth in Article 17.6(ii) with respect to various permissible interpretations of a provision of the Agreement.

5. The question under Article 17.6(ii) is whether an investigating authority's action rests upon a permissible interpretation of the Antidumping Agreement. Article 17.6(ii) confirms that there are provisions of the Agreement that "admit[] of more than one permissible interpretation". Where that is the case, and where the investigating authority's action rests upon one such interpretation, a panel is to find the action consistent with the Agreement.

6. The United States has argued – and multiple previous panels have agreed – that an interpretation of the Antidumping Agreement that does not require offsets is permissible. This interpretation is permissible because the text and context of the Antidumping Agreement, interpreted in accordance with customary rules of interpretation of public international law, make clear that the terms "dumping" and "margin of dumping" may have meaning for individual transactions. The mere fact that this interpretation differs from another interpretation is not a basis for finding it impermissible.

7. An interpretation of the provisions of the Antidumping Agreement and the GATT 1994 that not only is consistent with the text, but also reflects how business is conducted, how trade in goods occurs, and the point at which duties are imposed – that is, in individual transactions – is hardly, as Brazil alleges, "incoherent". Multiple previous panels, applying the customary rules of interpretation of international law, have confirmed that this interpretation is permissible.

8. The interpretation by previous panels does not allow a Member to define dumping any which way it wants. As noted earlier, there is a definition of "dumping" in Article 2.1 of the Antidumping Agreement. The question is whether this definition, "the difference between normal value and export price", can apply at the level of individual transactions or must be applied to "the product as a whole", a term that does not even appear in the text. Brazil argues that the term "dumping margin" must relate, solely and exclusively, to the "product as a whole" regardless of the text and context of the provision in which the term is used. The United States argues – and previous panels have confirmed – that "dumping margin" may be understood as relating to the "product" that is the subject of an individual transaction, in accordance with the ordinary meaning of the word "product", and permits the text and context of the relevant provisions to inform the appropriate interpretation of the term as it is used.

B. There Is No Textual Basis for the Obligation That Brazil Proposes

9. To require, as Brazil asserts, that a Member calculate a "margin of dumping" only for the "product as a whole" does not reflect a "harmonious" interpretation of the Antidumping Agreement. There is no textual basis for such an obligation in either the Antidumping Agreement or the GATT 1994. Not surprisingly, then, in arguing that an investigating authority must calculate a margin of dumping for the "product as a whole" in assessment proceedings, Brazil does not rely on the text of the GATT 1994 or the Antidumping Agreement.

10. To accept Brazil's argument would mean that the major users of dumping remedies, which were not granting offsets at the time the WTO Agreements were negotiated, agreed to an obligation to provide offsets without including an express provision for such an obligation in the Antidumping Agreement and the GATT 1994. In fact, there were negotiating proposals to restrict "zeroing", but these proposals were not adopted. The major users of dumping remedies continued to use "zeroing" after the agreements came into effect. If the negotiators of the Uruguay Round agreements intended to make such a fundamental change in the meaning of "margin of dumping" as to require offsets, they would have been clear about it. As we noted in our first written submission, in settling disputes among Members, panels and the Appellate Body cannot add to or diminish the rights and obligations provided in the covered agreements.

11. A panel should not build an interpretation on terms that do not appear in the covered agreements, such as "product as a whole". Prior panels have found that there is no textual basis in the Antidumping Agreement for the obligation that Brazil proposes today. All these panels made an objective assessment of the matter before them and came to the same conclusion that no offsets are required in assessment proceedings. We respectfully request that this Panel reach the same conclusion in this proceeding.

C. Brazil's Arguments Are Inconsistent with Both the Concept of, and Its Own Application of, a Prospective Normal Value System

12. The United States has demonstrated that the obligation that Brazil seeks to impose on Members is contrary to the very concept of a prospective normal value system provided for in Article 9 of the Antidumping Agreement. Under such a system, the amount of liability for payment of antidumping duties is determined at the time of importation on the basis of a comparison between the price of the individual export transaction and the prospective normal value. For example, an importer who imports a product the export price of which is equal to or higher than the prospective normal value cannot incur liability for payments of antidumping duties. The converse is also true. A liability for a dumped sale would be determined by comparing the price of an individual export transaction with a prospective normal value and the prices of other transactions have no relevance to this determination. As the panel in *US – Zeroing (Japan)* found,

"there is no textual support in Article 9 for the proposition that export prices in other transactions are of any relevance".

13. The United States has provided evidence that demonstrates how prospective normal value systems operate and that the refund mechanism under a prospective normal value system normally addresses specific individual transactions. In contrast, there is no evidence to support the assertions that a refund mechanism must recalculate a margin of dumping based on an aggregation of all comparisons. Indeed, Brazil acknowledged that it has never granted a single refund when collecting antidumping duties on the basis of a prospective normal value.

14. Brazil nonetheless argues that an obligation to calculate the margin of dumping with respect to "product as a whole" is consistent with prospective normal value systems. In its answers to the Panel's Questions, Brazil asserts that when it has applied prospective normal value, "the collection of the duty was limited to a dumping margin determined in accordance with Article 2 of the *Anti-Dumping Agreement*". A review of the facts, however, raises questions about how this assessment comports with Brazil's proposed interpretation of the Antidumping Agreement.

15. Brazil has used prospective normal value to collect antidumping duties on products from at least seven countries: the United States, Mexico, Romania, Germany, France, Spain, and the United Kingdom. In each case, Brazil calculated the antidumping duty as the absolute difference between the normal value (or reference price) and the adjusted export price of a specific transaction. Brazil assessed the antidumping duty in instances where the price of the imported product (an entry) was lower than the established normal value. However, Brazil assessed no duty if the result of the comparison was less than or equal to zero. And, Brazil has never provided a refund or an offset based on non-dumped transactions.

16. The way that Brazil has collected duties on imports of polyvinylchloride from the United States and Mexico, for example, does not appear consistent with the arguments that Brazil made in this dispute. In that case, Brazil assessed duties on a transaction-specific basis without providing any offsets for non-dumped transactions. In addition, Brazil's Official Gazette specifically states that the antidumping duty is calculated on a transaction-specific basis:

> The anti-dumping duty is calculated on the basis of the absolute difference between the reference price and the *price at which the transaction by which the product is imported from the USA or Mexico is executed,* as the case may be. The anti-dumping duty will be charged only in a case in which the price of the imported product is lower than the proposed reference price.

17. There is no reason why liability for payment of antidumping duties in the retrospective system applied by the United States may not be similarly assessed on the basis of transaction-specific export prices. Accepting the interpretation

that a Member must aggregate the results of *"all"* comparisons on an exporter-specific basis would require that retrospective reviews be conducted even in a prospective normal value system. This result is contrary to the very concept of a prospective normal value system.

18. Despite its arguments that Members have an affirmative and fundamental obligation to determine the antidumping liability for the "product as a whole" regardless of the context, Brazil has never conducted a review under Article 9.3.2. Brazil suggests this is because no importer has ever asked for a review or a refund. As we explained previously, however, it is difficult to see why an importer would request such a review when the importer does not have information for the "product as a whole" and as such does not know if the importer's liability could actually increase. And, when importers do not request refunds, no offsets are provided.

19. It should be noted that Brazil's arguments in this respect are entirely inconsistent with its arguments regarding cash deposits. Under Brazil's argument, the supposed obligation to calculate a margin for the "product as a whole" in a prospective normal value system is apparently only triggered when someone requests a refund. In the meantime, duties are collected on a transaction-specific basis without providing offsets for non-dumped transactions. Of course, in a retrospective system such as that operated by the United States, cash deposits are expressly not a final assessment of duties. Cash deposits are only a security pending the final assessment of duties, which occurs later in a review initiated upon a request. Yet according to Brazil, cash deposits that similarly do not reflect offsets for non-dumped transactions are themselves WTO-inconsistent.

20. Before moving on, we would like to make one final but important point on the topic of prospective normal value systems: It is implausible to think that the negotiators of the Antidumping Agreement would provide explicitly for a prospective normal value system and at the same time, without making any textual provision whatsoever, require that such systems conduct retrospective assessment proceedings that aggregate all the transactions occurring over some unspecified period of time. Articles 9.3, 9.3.1, and 9.3.2 are silent as to the period of review for any such proceeding. These articles include no requirements with respect to whether an assessment proceeding must cover a time period of a certain length or even that assessment proceeding coverage be time-based at all.

21. In its responses to the Panel's questions, Brazil suggested that the period of review for refund proceedings is specified in footnote 4 to Article 2.2.1. Article 2.2.1 specifies certain conditions under which a Member may choose to disregard sales at prices below the per unit cost of production in the domestic market of the home country or a third country if "such sales are made within an extended period of time in substantial quantities and at prices which do not provide for the recovery of all costs". Footnote 4 specifies that "extended period of time" is "normally one year but shall in no case be less than six months". Contrary to Brazil's suggestion, footnote 4 specifies what constitutes an *"extended period of time"*. It does not specify the length of a "period of review" or "refund proceeding". Moreover, Article 2.2.1 and footnote 4 only apply in specific circum-

stances, when a Member decides to disregard certain below-cost sales. They do not apply in any other context.

22. If the drafters of the Antidumping Agreement had intended to adopt an obligation to provide an "offset" for non-dumped transactions, one would have expected the drafters also to agree on an obligation for assessment proceedings to cover some established time period over which transactions must be aggregated. Otherwise a Member's obligations might have differed in a significant, substantive fashion depending solely upon whether it elects to cover more or fewer entries, or more or less time, in conducting its assessment proceedings. Thus, Brazil's assertion that the Antidumping Agreement imposes, with no textual basis, an obligation to grant offsets for non-dumped transactions implies that the drafters neglected to provide for an essential element of the obligation, namely, the time period over which such an offset would be granted. Such an interpretation should not be adopted by the Panel.

II. BRAZIL'S INTERPRETATION RENDERS THE SECOND SENTENCE OF ARTICLE 2.4.2 OF THE ANTIDUMPING AGREEMENT A NULLITY

23. The United States would recall that it has demonstrated that Brazil's interpretation of the Antidumping Agreement does not fit with the text of Article 2.4.2 of the Antidumping Agreement. This is because the exceptional methodology provided for in the second sentence of Article 2.4.2 mathematically must yield the same result as an average-to-average comparison as provided for in the first sentence of Article 2.4.2 if, in both cases, non-dumped comparisons are required to offset dumped comparisons. Accordingly, Brazil's interpretation would be disfavored under a key tenet of customary rules of treaty interpretation, namely, as explained by the Appellate Body in *US – Gasoline*, that an "interpretation must give meaning and effect to all the terms of the treaty".

24. The United States demonstrated the mathematical equivalency empirically in its response to the Panel's questions. Brazil's only response to the mathematical equivalency argument is to cite certain Appellate Body reports. These reports are not persuasive because their reasoning is not based upon the text of the Antidumping Agreement and does not adequately resolve the problem of mathematical equivalency. Panels have specifically addressed all of the situations under which it was argued that there would not be mathematical equivalence and found these situations did not represent methodologies consistent with the Antidumping Agreement. The United States has demonstrated that if *all* export transactions are taken into account, and "zeroing" is prohibited, average-to-average and average-to-transaction comparisons produce the *same result*.

III. BRAZIL'S BROAD INTERPRETATION OF ARTICLE 2.4 OF THE ANTIDUMPING AGREEMENT SHOULD BE REJECTED

25. As the United States has explained, Brazil's arguments under Article 2.4 of the Antidumping Agreement – like its other interpretations of the Antidumping Agreement – require reading into the text of the Agreement words that are not there and were never agreed. There is no obligation in Article 2.4 to offset any negative differences between normal value and export price. The United States cannot be found to have violated an obligation that does not exist. Moreover, if Article 2.4 required offsets, there would be no need for such a requirement in Article 2.4.2 (which was the basis for the Appellate Body's finding in *US – Softwood Lumber Dumping*).

26. Brazil's proposed interpretation that Article 2.4 applies to the *results* of comparisons between export price and normal value is erroneous. As the Appellate Body stated in *US – Hot-Rolled Steel*, "an examination of whether USDOC acted consistently with Article 2.4 of the *Anti-Dumping Agreement* must focus on ... whether there were 'differences', relevant under Article 2.4, which affected the comparability of export price and normal value". Contrary to Brazil's assertions, because the "fair comparison" obligation in Article 2.4 refers to the required price adjustments, it does not create an obligation with respect to how the *results* of those comparisons are treated. Assessment of antidumping duties in the amount by which the normal value exceeded the export price on a transaction-specific basis does reflect a "fair comparison" made for each export transaction. The phrase "fair comparison" in Article 2.4 simply has nothing to do with the aggregation of comparison results, and Brazil has not explained how an offset to the dumping found on one export transaction as a result of a distinct export transaction having been sold at above normal value would be considered an adjustment or other comparison criterion that falls under Article 2.4.

27. Instead, Brazil would have the Panel use Article 2.4 to examine any and all antidumping calculations to determine whether they are "impartial, even-handed, or unbiased". However, such an open-ended approach would result in disputes that are nearly impossible to resolve in any principled, text-based way. The Panel should reject an expansive interpretation of a "fair comparison" requirement that requires a subjective evaluation of what is "fair" or "unfair".

IV. CASH DEPOSITS ARE A SECURITY, NOT DUTIES

28. The United States explained in its First Written Submission and in its responses to Panel questions that cash deposits are not duties covered by Article 9 of the Antidumping Agreement, but rather a security governed by separate provisions of the GATT 1994. The Ad Note to paragraphs 2 and 3 of GATT Article VI expressly provides that a Member may collect a "reasonable security (bond or cash deposit) for the payment of anti-dumping duty ... pending final determination of the facts". In the retrospective system used by the United States, cash deposits are held as a security pending determination of the anti-

dumping duty to ensure that funds are available to pay the duties. None of the cash deposit rates at issue in this dispute were applied as assessment rates.

29. In response to the US showing that cash deposits are a security, Brazil relies on the Appellate Body report in the *United States – Shrimp Bonding* dispute. That report, however, is inapposite to the issue in this dispute regarding cash deposits. In *Shrimp Bonding*, the Appellate Body analyzed the WTO-consistency, including the "reasonableness", of an extra bonding requirement that applied above cash deposits. The purpose of this extra requirement was to secure potential additional liability that might arise if the margin of dumping was determined to be greater than the cash deposit – that is, to address defaults on that portion of the duties that exceed the amount of cash deposited as a security. That is not an issue in this dispute, nor is it the standard for whether or not cash deposits are in fact a security.

V. BRAZIL'S ARGUMENTS REGARDING THE "USE" OF ZEROING HAVE NO BASIS IN THE TEXT

30. In the last meeting with the Panel, and in its second written submission, Brazil insists that the "use" of "zeroing" violates various provisions of the Anti-dumping Agreement and the GATT 1994, regardless of whether any duties were collected, and regardless of whether any transaction-specific comparisons were in fact "zeroed". To be clear, we have a defense to all of Brazil's claims as there is no basis in the text of the agreements for the obligations Brazil seeks to impose. However, in response to Brazil's claims on this point we would like to explain further how these assertions with respect to the "use" of "zeroing" are inconsistent with the text of the relevant provisions.

31. In this dispute, Brazil's allegations of WTO-inconsistency based on its "zeroing" theories extend to certain instances in which the United States in fact assessed no antidumping duties. As the United States has explained, where no antidumping duties have been assessed, there can be no breach of Article 9.3 of the Antidumping Agreement or Article VI:2 of the GATT.

32. In its second written submission, Brazil asserts that Article 9.3 and Article VI:2 – both of which expressly refer to the amount of the antidumping duty – can be violated "irrespective of the amount of duties that is ultimately collected". The United States fails to see how, as Brazil argues, it makes sense to find a violation of an obligation not to collect duties, when no duties are collected. Article VI:2 allows a Member to "levy on any dumped product an anti-dumping duty not greater in amount than the margin of dumping ...". Article 9.3 directs that "[t]he amount of the anti-dumping duty shall not exceed the margin of dumping as established under Article 2". Finding a violation of these provisions where no antidumping duties are levied and the antidumping duty is zero would render meaningless the provisions' references to "levy ... an anti-dumping duty" and "[t]he amount of the anti-dumping duty".

33. Brazil's meaning of the term "use" is different from what was at issue in prior panel and Appellate Body reports. Brazil claims that "use" refers to the line in the computer program. Prior reports refer to the final duties assessed. Consequently, those earlier reports do not support Brazil.

34. Brazil does not address the fact that these provisions specifically address the amount of the duty. Instead, Brazil's only support for its argument that there could be a violation even when no duties are assessed is (i) a cite to the Appellate Body report in *Continued Zeroing* and (ii) an argument that the *chapeau* of Article 9.3 refers to Article 2.

35. With regard to the *Continued Zeroing* report, it is not pertinent to the issue in this dispute. In particular, it does not address the argument in this case that there can be no violation of Article 9.3 or GATT Article VI:2 where a Member assesses no duties. That dispute involved the issue of whether alleged "continued use" was outside of the terms of reference because it purported to capture future measures. However, the argument in this case is not only about what might happen in the future. In this dispute, Brazil's own evidence demonstrates that zeroing had no effect in certain of the proceedings at issue.

36. Brazil's argument as to the *chapeau* is based solely upon the fact that the *chapeau* mentions Article 2. However, Brazil fails to cite the actual text of the *chapeau*, which states that "the amount of the anti-dumping duty shall not exceed the margin of dumping as established under Article 2". The text is clear that the obligation is based upon "the amount of duty" not *exceeding* the margin of dumping. Where the United States has applied an assessment rate of zero, "the amount of duty" is zero, which cannot exceed the margin of dumping.

37. The United States fails to see how there can be a violation of an alleged obligation to provide offsets for non-dumped transactions when there are no non-dumped transactions. As just noted, unlike in the *Continued Zeroing* dispute, in this dispute we are not just presented with a request to find an inconsistency with respect to measures that do not exist even though we do not know whether there will be any non-dumped transactions. We are also presented with a request to base a finding of future inconsistency on a proceeding in which the evidence shows there actually were no non-dumped transactions. Zeroing is not and cannot be "used" in such circumstances. It is mathematically impossible. In such circumstances, the comparisons made, and the amount of duties collected, are exactly the same as they would have been if there were no "zeroing" line in the computer program. Brazil's own evidence indicates the United States calculated the dumping margins in the orange juice investigation on the basis of *all* comparable transactions.

VI. ASIDE FROM THE FACT THAT IT IS OUTSIDE THE TERMS OF REFERENCE, BRAZIL'S CLAIMS WITH RESPECT TO THE "CONTINUED USE" MEASURE FAIL

38. Even if Brazil's "continued use" claim were properly before this Panel, it must fail because there is no evidence that zeroing affected any margin in the investigation, nor certain rates in the assessment proceedings at issue. Brazil has relied heavily upon the Appellate Body's report in *Continued Zeroing*, and the United States has explained why that reliance is misplaced. We have demonstrated that the Appellate Body's analysis in *Continued Zeroing* does not apply here. In that dispute, the Appellate Body found an inconsistency only in circumstances that included zeroing in the initial less than fair value investigation, zeroing in four successive administrative reviews, and reliance in a sunset review upon rates determined using the zeroing methodology.

39. In response to the US arguments, Brazil attempts to distinguish the circumstances in the current dispute from the cases in which the Appellate Body declined to find a violation in *Continued Zeroing* by arguing that the evidence of zeroing was "fragmented" in those cases. However, in this dispute, Brazil's own evidence shows that there was no zeroing in the investigation, zeroing had no effect on certain rates in the assessment proceedings, and there has been no sunset review. This is not a case where, to quote the Appellate Body report in *Continued Zeroing*, "the zeroing methodology was repeatedly used in a string of determinations made sequentially in periodic reviews and sunset reviews over an extended period of time". Moreover, as explained earlier, there is no textual basis for finding a violation where no duties are collected, or where there were no non-dumped transactions. Individual proceedings that are not inconsistent cannot be the basis of a finding of "ongoing" inconsistency stretching indefinitely into the future.

ANNEX G

REQUESTS FOR CONSULTATIONS AND THE ESTABLISHMENT OF A PANEL

ANNEX G-1

REQUEST FOR CONSULTATIONS BY BRAZIL

WORLD TRADE ORGANIZATION

WT/DS382/1
G/L/872
G/ADP/D75/1
1 December 2008

(08-5867)

Original: English

UNITED STATES – ANTI-DUMPING ADMINISTRATIVE REVIEWS AND OTHER MEASURES RELATED TO IMPORTS OF CERTAIN ORANGE JUICE FROM BRAZIL

Request for Consultations by Brazil

The following communication, dated 27 November 2008, from the delegation of Brazil to the delegation of the United States and to the Chairman of the Dispute Settlement Body, is circulated in accordance with Article 4.4 of the DSU.

Upon instructions from my authorities, I hereby request consultations with the Government of the United States pursuant to Article 4 of the *Understanding on Rules and Procedures Governing the Settlement of Disputes*

("DSU"), Article XXII:1 of the *General Agreement on Tariffs and Trade 1994* ("GATT 1994"), and Articles 17.2 and 17.3 of the *Agreement on Implementation of Article VI of GATT 1994* ("*Anti-Dumping Agreement*"), with regard to the matters listed hereunder:

The following determinations of the United States Department of Commerce (USDOC) concerning the imports of certain orange juice from Brazil, case nº A-351-840:

- the antidumping administrative review for the period from 24 August 2005 to 28 February 2007, and the final results thereof, in "*Certain Orange Juice from Brazil: Final results and Partial Rescission of Antidumping Duty Administrative Review*", published in 73 Fed. Reg. 46,584 (11 August 2008), as well as any assessment instructions and cash deposit requirements issued pursuant to them (the "Issues and Decision Memorandum", dated 5 August 2008, which discusses issues raised in this review, confirms that "zeroing" was applied by the USDOC in this review and specifically rejects the relevance of WTO Appellate Body precedents for administrative reviews conducted by the USDOC);
- any on-going or future antidumping administrative reviews, and the final results thereof, related to the imports of certain orange juice from Brazil (case nº A-351-840), as well as any assessment instructions and cash deposit requirements issued pursuant to them.

Any actions taken by United States Customs and Border Protection (USCBP) to collect definitive anti-dumping duties at duty assessment rates established in periodic reviews covered by the preceding paragraph, including through the issuance of USCBP liquidations instructions and notices.

The following US laws, regulations, administrative procedures, practices and methodologies:

- the Tariff Act of 1930, as amended, (the "Act"), in particular sections 736, 751, 771(35)(A) and (B), and 777A(c) and (d);
- the US Statement of Administrative Action that accompanied the Uruguay Round Agreements Act, H.R. Doc. No. 103-316, vol. I;
- the implementing regulations of USDOC, codified at Title 19 of the United States Code of Federal Regulations, 19 CFR Section 351, in particular sections 351.212(b), 351.414(c), and (e);
- the Import Administration Antidumping Manual (1997 edition), including the computer program(s) to which it refers;
- the general procedures and methodology employed by the United States to determine dumping margins in administrative reviews, whereby USDOC, in comparing weighted average normal value with transaction price of individual export transactions, treats as zero negative intermediate comparison results (i.e. situations in

which the individual export price is greater than the weighted average normal value). Such methodology is commonly referred to as "simple zeroing" and/or the US "zeroing procedures."

Brazil is concerned that the laws, regulations, administrative procedures, practices and methodologies described above are as such, and as applied in the determinations and actions listed above, inconsistent with the obligations of the United States under the *Marrakesh Agreement Establishing the World Trade Organization* ("WTO Agreement") and the Agreements annexed thereto. The provisions with which these measures appear to be inconsistent include, but are not limited to, the following:

- Articles II, VI:1 and VI:2 of the GATT 1994;
- Articles 1, 2.1, 2.4, 2.4.2, 9.1, 9.3, 11.2 and 18.4 of the *Anti-Dumping Agreement*;
- And Article XVI:4 of the WTO Agreement.

Brazil reserves the right to raise additional claims and legal matters during the course of the consultations. It looks forward to receiving the United States Government's response and to setting a mutually convenient date for consultations.

Please accept, Excellency, the assurances of my highest consideration.

ANNEX G-2

REQUEST FOR CONSULTATIONS BY BRAZIL – ADDENDUM

WORLD TRADE ORGANIZATION

WT/DS382/1/Add.1
G/L/872/Add.1
G/ADP/D75/1/Add.1
27 May 2009

(09-2552)

Original: English

UNITED STATES – ANTI-DUMPING ADMINISTRATIVE REVIEWS AND OTHER MEASURES RELATED TO IMPORTS OF CERTAIN ORANGE JUICE FROM BRAZIL

Request for Consultations by Brazil
Addendum

The following communication, dated 22 May 2009, from the delegation of Brazil to the delegation of the United States and to the Chairman of the Dispute Settlement Body, is circulated in accordance with Article 4.4 of the DSU.

---

1. This letter contains a request for consultations pursuant to Article 4 of the Understanding on Rules and Procedures Governing the Settlement of Disputes (the "DSU"), Article XXII:1 of the General Agreement on Tariffs and Trade 1994 (the "GATT 1994"), and Articles 17.2 and 17.3 of the Agreement on Implementation of Article VI of GATT 1994 (the "*Anti-Dumping Agreement*"). The present request complements, constitutes an addendum to, and must be read with, the original request for consultations presented on 27 November 2008 (Document WT/DS382/1, G/L/872, G/ADP/D75/1).

2. On 27 November 2008, the Government of Brazil requested consultations with the Government of the United States of America (the "United States") under Article 4 of the Understanding on Rules and Procedures Governing the Settlement of Disputes (the "DSU"); Article XXII:1 of the General Agreement on Tariffs and Trade 1994 (the "GATT 1994"); and Articles 17.2 and 17.3 of the Agreement on Implementation of Article VI of GATT 1994 (the "*Anti-Dumping*

Agreement"), with regard to the laws, regulations, administrative procedures, practices and methodologies for calculating dumping margins in administrative reviews, involving the use of "zeroing", and their application in antidumping duty administrative reviews regarding imports of certain orange juice from Brazil (case nº A-351-840).[1]

3. The consultations, held on 16 January 2009, covered the Antidumping Duty Administrative Review for the period from 24 August 2005 to 28 February 2007 (the "First Administrative Review") and the Antidumping Duty Administrative Review from 1 March 2007 to 29 February 2008 (the "Second Administrative Review"), pursuant to the original request for consultations, which included, among others: the First Administrative Review, the final results thereof, and any assessment instructions and cash deposit requirements issued pursuant thereto; and, any on-going or future antidumping administrative reviews related to the imports of certain orange juice from Brazil (case nº A-351-840), the final results thereof, and any assessment instructions and cash deposit requirements issued pursuant thereto.

4. In addition to the above matters, Brazil would like to consult with the United States with regard to the complementary matters listed hereunder:

(a) The Antidumping Duty Investigation on certain orange juice from Brazil (case nº A-351-840), for the period from 1 October 2003 to 30 September 2004, and the final results thereof, in "*Notice of Final Determination of Sales at Less Than Fair Value and Affirmative Final Determination of Critical Circumstances: Certain Orange Juice from Brazil*", published in 71 Fed. Reg. 2183 (13 January 2006); the corresponding antidumping order, entitled "*Antidumping Duty Order: Certain Orange Juice from Brazil*", published in 71 Fed. Reg. 12183 (9 March 2006); as well as any cash deposit requirements issued pursuant to them. In this measure, the United States Department of Commerce (the "USDOC") employed a methodology whereby it aggregated intermediate comparison results between weighted average normal value and weighted average export price for sub-groups of products within the product under investigation ("averaging groups"), treating as zero negative intermediate comparison results (*i.e.*, situations in which the weighted average export price was greater than the weighted average normal value of an "averaging group"). Such methodology is commonly referred to as "model zeroing" and/or US zeroing procedures; and

(b) The continued use of the US zeroing procedures ("model" or "simple" zeroing) in successive antidumping proceedings, in relation to the antidumping order issued in respect of imports of certain orange juice from Brazil (case nº A-351-840), including the original investigation and subsequent administrative reviews, by which du-

[1] WT/DS382/1, G/L/872, G/ADP/D75/1.

ties are imposed and maintained in place at a level in excess of the antidumping margin which would result from the correct application of the *Anti-Dumping Agreement* (whether duties or cash deposit rates or other form of measure).

5. Furthermore Brazil would like to further consult with the United States with regard to the following matter:

(c) The Antidumping Duty Administrative Review from 1 March 2007 to 29 February 2008 (the "Second Administrative Review"), related to the imports of certain orange juice from Brazil (case nº A-351-840).

6. Brazil is concerned that these measures are inconsistent with the obligations of the United States under the Marrakesh Agreement Establishing the World Trade Organization (the "WTO Agreement") and the Agreements annexed thereto. The provisions with which these measures appear to be inconsistent include, but are not limited to, the following:

- Articles II, VI:1 and VI:2 of the GATT 1994;
- Articles 1, 2.1, 2.4, 2.4.2, 9.1, 9.3, 11.2 and 18.4 of the *Anti-Dumping Agreement*;
- And Article XVI:4 of the WTO Agreement.

7. Brazil reserves the right to raise additional claims and legal matters during the course of the consultations. It looks forward to receiving the United States Government's response and to setting a mutually convenient date for consultations.

ANNEX G-3

REQUEST FOR THE ESTABLISHMENT OF
A PANEL BY BRAZIL

WORLD TRADE ORGANIZATION

WT/DS382/4
21 August 2009

(09-3998)

Original: English

UNITED STATES – ANTI-DUMPING ADMINISTRATIVE REVIEWS AND OTHER MEASURES RELATED TO IMPORTS OF CERTAIN ORANGE JUICE FROM BRAZIL

Request for the Establishment of a Panel by Brazil

The following communication, dated 20 August 2009, from the delegation of Brazil to the Chairman of the Dispute Settlement Body, is circulated pursuant to Article 6.2 of the DSU.

Upon instructions from my authorities, I hereby request the establishment of a panel pursuant to Articles 4.7 and 6 of the Understanding on Rules and Procedures Governing the Settlement of Disputes (the "DSU"), Article XXIII of the General Agreement on Tariffs and Trade of 1994 (the "GATT 1994") and Article 17.4 of the Agreement on Implementation of Article VI of the General Agreement on Tariffs and Trade of 1994 (the "*Anti-Dumping Agreement*"), with regard to the matters listed hereunder:

Consultations

On 27 November 2008, the Government of Brazil ("Brazil") requested consultations with the Government of the United States of America (the "United States") under Articles 4 of the DSU, Article XXII:1 of the GATT 1994 and Articles 17.2 and 17.3 of the *Anti-Dumping Agreement*, with regard to the laws, regulations, administrative procedures, practices and methodologies for calculating dumping margins in administrative reviews, involving the use of "zeroing", and their application in anti-dumping duty administrative reviews regarding imports of certain orange juice from Brazil (case No A-351-840). On 22 May 2009, Brazil requested further consultations with the United States with regard to the use of "zeroing" in the anti-dumping duty investigation and in the second administrative review related to case No A-351-840 as well as to the continued use of the US "zeroing procedures" in successive anti-dumping proceedings regarding imports of certain orange juice from Brazil. The consultations were held on 16 January 2009 and 18 June 2009, respectively. They allowed a better understanding of the parties' positions but failed to resolve the dispute.

Measures and claims

The measures at issue are the following:

(a) The anti-dumping duty investigation on certain orange juice from Brazil (the "Original Investigation")

This anti-dumping proceeding concerns the imposition of anti-dumping duties on certain orange juice for transport and/or further manufacturing produced in two different forms: (1) Frozen orange juice in a highly concentrated form, sometimes referred to as frozen concentrated orange juice for further manufacturing (FCOJM); and (2) pasteurized single-strength orange juice which has not been concentrated, referred to as Not-From-Concentrate (NFC) (case No A-351-840). The final results of this Original Investigation were published in 71 Fed. Reg. 2183 on 13 January 2006 and the amended final results were published in 71 Fed. Reg. 8841 on 21 February 2006. The anti-dumping duty order was published in 71 Fed. Reg 12183 on 9 March 2006. The period of investigation is 1 October 2003 through 30 September 2004, and the amended rate of the *ad valorem* anti-dumping duty was 12.46% for Fischer S.A.Comércio, Indústria, e Agricultura ("Fischer") and 19.19% for Sucocítrico Cutrale S.A. ("Cutrale").

In this Original Investigation, the United States Department of Commerce (the "USDOC") employed a methodology whereby it aggregated intermediate comparison results between weighted average normal value and weighted average export price for sub-groups of products within the product under investigation ("averaging groups"), treating as zero negative intermediate comparison results (i.e., situations in which the weighted average export price was greater than the weighted average normal value of an "averaging group"). Brazil refers to such methodology as "model zeroing" and/or US "zeroing procedures".

(b) The 2005-2007 anti-dumping duty administrative review on certain orange juice from Brazil (the "First Administrative Review")

This anti-dumping proceeding concerns the administrative review of anti-dumping duties on certain orange juice from Brazil (case No A-351-840) for the period of 24 August 2005 through 28 February 2007. The final results of this First Administrative Review were published in 73 Fed. Reg. 46584 on 11 August 2008. The rate of the *ad valorem* anti-dumping duty was 4.81% for Fischer and 0.45% for Cutrale.

In this First Administrative Review, in order to assess the importers' final liability for payment of anti-dumping duties and the going-forward cash deposit rates, the USDOC employed a methodology whereby it aggregated intermediate comparison results between weighted average normal value for each "averaging group" with the transaction price of individual export transactions, treating as zero negative intermediate comparison results (i.e., situations in which the individual export price was greater than the weighted average normal value of an "averaging group"). Brazil refers to such methodology as "simple zeroing" and/or U.S. "zeroing procedures".

(c) The 2007-2008 anti-dumping duty administrative review on certain orange juice from Brazil (the "Second Administrative Review")

This anti-dumping proceeding concerns the administrative review of anti-dumping duties on certain orange juice from Brazil (case No A-351-840) for the period of 1 March 2007 through 29 February 2008. The final results of this Second Administrative Review were published in 74 Fed. Reg. 40167 on 11 August 2009. The rate of the *ad valorem* anti-dumping duty was 0% for Fischer and 2.17% for Cutrale.

In this Second Administrative Review, the USDOC applied again "simple zeroing" and/or US "zeroing procedures".

The measures at issue also include any assessment instructions issued by the USDOC and cash deposit requirements imposed pursuant to the measures listed in items (a), (b) and (c) above, as well as any measures taken by the United States Customs and Border Protection (USCBP) to collect definitive anti-dumping duties at the duty assessment rates established in those measures, including through the issuance of USCBP liquidations instructions and notices.

(d) The continued use of the U.S. "zeroing procedures" in successive anti-dumping proceedings, in relation to the anti-dumping duty order issued in respect of imports of certain orange juice from Brazil

This measure concerns the continued use by the United States of "zeroing procedures" in successive anti-dumping proceedings, in relation to the anti-dumping duty order issued in respect of imports of certain orange juice from Brazil (case No A-351-840), including the original investigation and any subsequent administrative reviews, by which duties are applied and maintained over a period of time. In particular, the use of zeroing continues in the most recent administrative review, identified under item (c) above, by which duties are currently applied and maintained.

Claims

Brazil considers that the measures described above are inconsistent with the following provisions:

- Article 2.1 of the *Anti-Dumping Agreement* and Articles VI:1 and VI:2 of the GATT 1994 because the United States did not determine a margin of dumping for the product as a whole;
- Article 2.4.2 of the *Anti-Dumping Agreement* because the United States' use of "zeroing procedures" precluded a determination for the product as a whole in the Original Investigation;
- Article 2.4 of the *Anti-Dumping Agreement* because the comparison of normal value and export price using "zeroing procedures" is unfair;
- Article VI:2 of the GATT 1994 and Article 9.3 of the *Anti-Dumping Agreement* insofar as the imposition and collection of anti-dumping duties is made in excess of the margin of dumping properly determined pursuant to Article 2 of the *Anti-Dumping Agreement*;
- Article II:1(a) and II:1(b) of the GATT 1994 insofar as the United States subjects the importation of certain orange juice to duties in excess of the duties permitted by the United States' Schedule of Concessions; and
- Article XVI:4 of the Marrakesh Agreement establishing the World Trade Organization and Article 18.4 of the *Anti-Dumping Agreement* insofar as the United States has not taken all necessary steps, of a general or particular character, to ensure the conformity of its laws, regulations and administrative procedures with the provisions of GATT 1994 and the *Anti-Dumping Agreement*.

Request

Brazil hereby respectfully requests that a panel be established pursuant to Article XXIII of the GATT 1994, Articles 4.7 and 6 of the DSU and Article 17.4 of the *Anti-Dumping Agreement*, with standard terms of reference. Brazil asks that this request be placed on the agenda of the next meeting of the WTO Dispute Settlement Body that will take place on 31 August 2009.

EUROPEAN COMMUNITIES - DEFINITIVE ANTI-DUMPING MEASURES ON CERTAIN IRON OR STEEL FASTENERS FROM CHINA

Report of the Appellate Body

WT/DS397/AB/R

Adopted by the Dispute Settlement Body on 28 July 2011

European Communities[1] – Definitive Anti-Dumping Measures on Certain Iron or Steel Fasteners from China

European Union, *Appellant/Appellee*
China, *Appellee/Other Appellant*
Brazil, *Third Participant*
Canada, *Third Participant*
Chile, *Third Participant*
Colombia, *Third Participant*
India, *Third Participant*
Japan, *Third Participant*
Norway, *Third Participant*
Separate Customs Territory of Taiwan, Penghu, Kinmen and Matsu, *Third Participant*
Thailand, *Third Participant*
Turkey, *Third Participant*
United States, *Third Participant*

Present:
Oshima, Presiding Member
Hillman, Member
Unterhalter, Member

---

1 This dispute began before the entry into force of the *Treaty of Lisbon amending the Treaty on European Union and the Treaty establishing the European Community* (done at Lisbon, 13 December 2007) on 1 December 2009. On 29 November 2009, the World Trade Organization received a Verbal Note (WT/L/779) from the Council of the European Union and the Commission of the European Communities stating that, by virtue of the *Treaty of Lisbon*, as of 1 December 2009, the "European Union" replaces and succeeds the "European Community". On 13 July 2010, the World Trade Organization received a second Verbal Note (WT/Let/679) from the Council of the European Union confirming that, with effect from 1 December 2009, the European Union replaced the European Community and assumed all the rights and obligations of the European Community in respect of all

TABLE OF CONTENTS

Agreements for which the Director-General of the World Trade Organization is the depositary and to which the European Community is a signatory or a contracting party. We understand the reference in the Verbal Notes to the "European Community" to be a reference to the "European Communities". The European Union requested that the Panel replace "European Communities" with "European Union" in the title of the case, but the Panel decided not to make this change because China's request for consultations and for the establishment of a panel both occurred prior to 1 December 2009 and referred to the European Communities, as did the decision of the DSB establishing the Panel. However, all the submissions of the parties before the Panel came after that date and referred to the European Union, and the Panel made its findings with reference to the European Union. (Panel Report, paras. 6.4 and 6.5) In this Report, we too refer to the European Union.

CASES CITED IN THIS REPORT

Short title	Full case title and citation
Argentina – Ceramic Tiles	Panel Report, *Argentina – Definitive Anti-Dumping Measures on Imports of Ceramic Floor Tiles from Italy*, WT/DS189/R, adopted 5 November 2001, DSR 2001:XII, 6241
Argentina – Poultry Anti-Dumping Duties	Panel Report, *Argentina – Definitive Anti-Dumping Duties on Poultry from Brazil*, WT/DS241/R, adopted 19 May 2003, DSR 2003:V, 1727
Australia – Salmon	Appellate Body Report, *Australia – Measures Affecting Importation of Salmon*, WT/DS18/AB/R, adopted 6 November 1998, DSR 1998:VIII, 3327
Brazil – Desiccated Coconut	Appellate Body Report, *Brazil – Measures Affecting Desiccated Coconut*, WT/DS22/AB/R, adopted 20 March 1997, DSR 1997:I, 167
Brazil – Desiccated Coconut	Panel Report, *Brazil – Measures Affecting Desiccated Coconut*, WT/DS22/R, adopted 20 March 1997, as upheld by Appellate Body Report WT/DS22/AB/R, DSR 1997:I, 189

Short title	Full case title and citation
Brazil – Retreaded Tyres	Appellate Body Report, *Brazil – Measures Affecting Imports of Retreaded Tyres*, WT/DS332/AB/R, adopted 17 December 2007, DSR 2007:IV, 1527
Canada – Autos	Panel Report, *Canada – Certain Measures Affecting the Automotive Industry*, WT/DS139/R, WT/DS142/R, adopted 19 June 2000, as modified by Appellate Body Report WT/DS139/AB/R, WT/DS142/AB/R, DSR 2000:VII, 3043
Chile – Price Band System (Article 21.5 – Argentina)	Appellate Body Report, *Chile – Price Band System and Safeguard Measures Relating to Certain Agricultural Products – Recourse to Article 21.5 of the DSU by Argentina*, WT/DS207/AB/RW, adopted 22 May 2007, DSR 2007:II, 513
China – Auto Parts	Appellate Body Reports, *China – Measures Affecting Imports of Automobile Parts*, WT/DS339/AB/R, WT/DS340/AB/R, WT/DS342/AB/R, adopted 12 January 2009
China – Publications and Audiovisual Products	Appellate Body Report, *China – Measures Affecting Trading Rights and Distribution Services for Certain Publications and Audiovisual Entertainment Products*, WT/DS363/AB/R, adopted 19 January 2010
EC – Asbestos	Appellate Body Report, *European Communities – Measures Affecting Asbestos and Asbestos-Containing Products*, WT/DS135/AB/R, adopted 5 April 2001, DSR 2001:VII, 3243
EC – Bananas III	Appellate Body Report, *European Communities – Regime for the Importation, Sale and Distribution of Bananas*, WT/DS27/AB/R, adopted 25 September 1997, DSR 1997:II, 591
EC – Bananas III	Panel Reports, *European Communities – Regime for the Importation, Sale and Distribution of Bananas* ("*EC – Bananas III*"), WT/DS27/R/ECU (Ecuador) / WT/DS27/R/GTM, WT/DS27/R/HND (Guatemala and Honduras) / WT/DS27/R/MEX (Mexico) / WT/DS27/R/USA (US), adopted 25 September 1997, as modified by Appellate Body Report WT/DS27/AB/R, DSR 1997:II, 695 to DSR 1997:III, 1085

Short title	Full case title and citation
EC – Bananas III (Ecuador) (Article 22.6 – EC)	Decision by the Arbitrators, *European Communities – Regime for the Importation, Sale and Distribution of Bananas – Recourse to Arbitration by the European Communities under Article 22.6 of the DSU*, WT/DS27/ARB/ECU, 24 March 2000, DSR 2000:V, 2237
EC – Bed Linen	Panel Report, *European Communities – Anti-Dumping Duties on Imports of Cotton-Type Bed Linen from India*, WT/DS141/R, adopted 12 March 2001, as modified by Appellate Body Report WT/DS141/AB/R, DSR 2001:VI, 2077
EC – Chicken Cuts	Appellate Body Report, *European Communities – Customs Classification of Frozen Boneless Chicken Cuts*, WT/DS269/AB/R, WT/DS286/AB/R, adopted 27 September 2005, and Corr.1, DSR 2005:XIX, 9157
EC – Hormones	Appellate Body Report, *EC Measures Concerning Meat and Meat Products (Hormones)*, WT/DS26/AB/R, WT/DS48/AB/R, adopted 13 February 1998, DSR 1998:I, 135
EC – Poultry	Appellate Body Report, *European Communities – Measures Affecting the Importation of Certain Poultry Products*, WT/DS69/AB/R, adopted 23 July 1998, DSR 1998:V, 2031
EC – Salmon (Norway)	Panel Report, *European Communities – Anti-Dumping Measure on Farmed Salmon from Norway*, WT/DS337/R, adopted 15 January 2008, and Corr.1, DSR 2008:I, 3
EC – Sardines	Appellate Body Report, *European Communities – Trade Description of Sardines*, WT/DS231/AB/R, adopted 23 October 2002, DSR 2002:VIII, 3359
EC – Selected Customs Matters	Appellate Body Report, *European Communities – Selected Customs Matters*, WT/DS315/AB/R, adopted 11 December 2006, DSR 2006:IX, 3791
EC – Tube or Pipe Fittings	Appellate Body Report, *European Communities – Anti-Dumping Duties on Malleable Cast Iron Tube or Pipe Fittings from Brazil*, WT/DS219/AB/R, adopted 18 August 2003, DSR 2003:VI, 2613

Short title	Full case title and citation
EC – Tube or Pipe Fittings	Panel Report, *European Communities – Anti-Dumping Duties on Malleable Cast Iron Tube or Pipe Fittings from Brazil*, WT/DS219/R, adopted 18 August 2003, as modified by Appellate Body Report WT/DS219/AB/R, DSR 2003:VII, 2701
EC and certain member States – Large Civil Aircraft	Appellate Body Report, *European Communities and Certain Member States – Measures Affecting Trade in Large Civil Aircraft*, WT/DS316/AB/R, adopted 1 June 2011
Egypt – Steel Rebar	Panel Report, *Egypt – Definitive Anti-Dumping Measures on Steel Rebar from Turkey*, WT/DS211/R, adopted 1 October 2002, DSR 2002:VII, 2667
Guatemala – Cement I	Appellate Body Report, *Guatemala – Anti-Dumping Investigation Regarding Portland Cement from Mexico*, WT/DS60/AB/R, adopted 25 November 1998, DSR 1998:IX, 3767
Guatemala – Cement II	Panel Report, *Guatemala – Definitive Anti-Dumping Measures on Grey Portland Cement from Mexico*, WT/DS156/R, adopted 17 November 2000, DSR 2000:XI, 5295
India – Patents (US)	Appellate Body Report, *India – Patent Protection for Pharmaceutical and Agricultural Chemical Products*, WT/DS50/AB/R, adopted 16 January 1998, DSR 1998:I, 9
Japan – Agricultural Products II	Appellate Body Report, *Japan – Measures Affecting Agricultural Products*, WT/DS76/AB/R, adopted 19 March 1999, DSR 1999:I, 277
Japan – Apples	Appellate Body Report, *Japan – Measures Affecting the Importation of Apples*, WT/DS245/AB/R, adopted 10 December 2003, DSR 2003:IX, 4391
Japan – DRAMs (Korea)	Appellate Body Report, *Japan – Countervailing Duties on Dynamic Random Access Memories from Korea*, WT/DS336/AB/R and Corr.1, adopted 17 December 2007, DSR 2007:VII, 2703
Korea – Certain Paper	Panel Report, *Korea – Anti-Dumping Duties on Imports of Certain Paper from Indonesia*, WT/DS312/R, adopted 28 November 2005, DSR 2005:XXII, 10637
Korea – Certain Paper (Article 21.5 – Indonesia)	Panel Report, *Korea – Anti-Dumping Duties on Imports of Certain Paper from Indonesia – Recourse to Article 21.5 of the DSU by Indonesia*, WT/DS312/RW, adopted 22 October 2007, DSR 2007:VIII, 3369

Short title	Full case title and citation
Korea – Dairy	Appellate Body Report, *Korea – Definitive Safeguard Measure on Imports of Certain Dairy Products*, WT/DS98/AB/R, adopted 12 January 2000, DSR 2000:I, 3
Korea – Dairy	Panel Report, *Korea – Definitive Safeguard Measure on Imports of Certain Dairy Products*, WT/DS98/R and Corr.1, adopted 12 January 2000, as modified by Appellate Body Report WT/DS98/AB/R, DSR 2000:I, 49
Mexico – Anti-Dumping Measures on Rice	Appellate Body Report, *Mexico – Definitive Anti-Dumping Measures on Beef and Rice, Complaint with Respect to Rice*, WT/DS295/AB/R, adopted 20 December 2005, DSR 2005:XXII, 10853
Mexico – Anti-Dumping Measures on Rice	Panel Report, *Mexico – Definitive Anti-Dumping Measures on Beef and Rice, Complaint with Respect to Rice*, WT/DS295/R, adopted 20 December 2005, as modified by Appellate Body Report WT/DS295/AB/R, DSR 2005:XXIII, 11007
Mexico – Corn Syrup (Article 21.5 – US)	Appellate Body Report, *Mexico – Anti-Dumping Investigation of High Fructose Corn Syrup (HFCS) from the United States – Recourse to Article 21.5 of the DSU by the United States*, WT/DS132/AB/RW, adopted 21 November 2001, DSR 2001:XIII, 6675
Mexico – Olive Oil	Panel Report, *Mexico – Definitive Countervailing Measures on Olive Oil from the European Communities*, WT/DS341/R, adopted 21 October 2008, DSR 2008:IX, 3179
Mexico – Steel Pipes and Tubes	Panel Report, *Mexico – Anti-Dumping Duties on Steel Pipes and Tubes from Guatemala*, WT/DS331/R, adopted 24 July 2007, DSR 2007:IV, 1207
US – 1916 Act	Appellate Body Report, *United States – Anti-Dumping Act of 1916*, WT/DS136/AB/R, WT/DS162/AB/R, adopted 26 September 2000, DSR 2000:X, 4793
US – Anti-Dumping and Countervailing Duties (China)	Panel Report, *United States – Definitive Anti-Dumping and Countervailing Duties on Certain Products from China*, WT/DS379/R, adopted 25 March 2011, as modified by Appellate Body Report WT/DS379/AB/R
US – Carbon Steel	Appellate Body Report, *United States – Countervailing Duties on Certain Corrosion-Resistant Carbon Steel Flat Products from Germany*, WT/DS213/AB/R and Corr.1, adopted 19 December 2002, DSR 2002:IX, 3779

Short title	Full case title and citation
US – Continued Suspension	Appellate Body Report, *United States – Continued Suspension of Obligations in the EC – Hormones Dispute*, WT/DS320/AB/R, adopted 14 November 2008, DSR 2008:X, 3507
US – Continued Zeroing	Appellate Body Report, *United States – Continued Existence and Application of Zeroing Methodology*, WT/DS350/AB/R, adopted 19 February 2009
US – Corrosion - Resistant Steel Sunset Review	Appellate Body Report, *United States – Sunset Review of Anti-Dumping Duties on Corrosion-Resistant Carbon Steel Flat Products from Japan*, WT/DS244/AB/R, adopted 9 January 2004, DSR 2004:I, 3
US – Countervailing Measures on Certain EC Products	Appellate Body Report, *United States – Countervailing Measures Concerning Certain Products from the European Communities*, WT/DS212/AB/R, adopted 8 January 2003, DSR 2003:I, 5
US – FSC	Appellate Body Report, *United States – Tax Treatment for "Foreign Sales Corporations"*, WT/DS108/AB/R, adopted 20 March 2000, DSR 2000:III, 1619
US – Gasoline	Appellate Body Report, *United States – Standards for Reformulated and Conventional Gasoline*, WT/DS2/AB/R, adopted 20 May 1996, DSR 1996:I, 3
US – Hot-Rolled Steel	Appellate Body Report, *United States – Anti-Dumping Measures on Certain Hot-Rolled Steel Products from Japan*, WT/DS184/AB/R, adopted 23 August 2001, DSR 2001:X, 4697
US – Hot-Rolled Steel	Panel Report, *United States – Anti-Dumping Measures on Certain Hot-Rolled Steel Products from Japan*, WT/DS184/R, adopted 23 August 2001 modified by Appellate Body Report WT/DS184/AB/R, DSR 2001:X, 4769
US – Lamb	Appellate Body Report, *United States – Safeguard Measures on Imports of Fresh, Chilled or Frozen Lamb Meat from New Zealand and Australia*, WT/DS177/AB/R, WT/DS178/AB/R, adopted 16 May 2001, DSR 2001:IX, 4051
US – Lamb	Panel Report, *United States – Safeguard Measures on Imports of Fresh, Chilled or Frozen Lamb Meat from New Zealand and Australia*, WT/DS177/R, WT/DS178/R, adopted 16 May 2001, as modified by Appellate Body Report WT/DS177/AB/R, WT/DS178/AB/R, DSR 2001:IX, 4107

Short title	Full case title and citation
US – Oil Country Tubular Goods Sunset Reviews	Appellate Body Report, *United States – Sunset Reviews of Anti-Dumping Measures on Oil Country Tubular Goods from Argentina*, WT/DS268/AB/R, adopted 17 December 2004, DSR 2004:VII, 3257
US – Oil Country Tubular Goods Sunset Reviews (Article 21.5 – Argentina)	Panel Report, *United States – Sunset Reviews of Anti-Dumping Measures on Oil Country Tubular Goods from Argentina – Recourse to Article 21.5 of the DSU by Argentina*, WT/DS268/RW, adopted 11 May 2007, as modified by Appellate Body Report WT/DS268/AB/RW, DSR 2007:IX-X, 3609
US – Section 211 Appropriations Act	Appellate Body Report, *United States – Section 211 Omnibus Appropriations Act of 1998*, WT/DS176/AB/R, adopted 1 February 2002, DSR 2002:II, 589
US – Steel Safeguards	Appellate Body Report, *United States – Definitive Safeguard Measures on Imports of Certain Steel Products*, WT/DS248/AB/R, WT/DS249/AB/R, WT/DS251/AB/R, WT/DS252/AB/R, WT/DS253/AB/R, WT/DS254/AB/R, WT/DS258/AB/R, WT/DS259/AB/R, adopted 10 December 2003, DSR 2003:VII, 3117
US – Upland Cotton (Article 21.5 – Brazil)	Appellate Body Report, *United States – Subsidies on Upland Cotton – Recourse to Article 21.5 of the DSU by Brazil*, WT/DS267/AB/RW, adopted 20 June 2008, DSR 2008:III, 809
US – Wheat Gluten	Appellate Body Report, *United States – Definitive Safeguard Measures on Imports of Wheat Gluten from the European Communities*, WT/DS166/AB/R, adopted 19 January 2001, DSR 2001:II, 717
US – Zeroing (Japan) (Article 21.5 – Japan)	Appellate Body Report, *United States – Measures Relating to Zeroing and Sunset Reviews – Recourse to Article 21.5 of the DSU by Japan*, WT/DS322/AB/RW, adopted 31 August 2009

ABBREVIATIONS USED IN THIS REPORT

Abbreviation	Description
Anti-Dumping Agreement	*Agreement on Implementation of Article VI of the General Agreement on Tariffs and Trade 1994*

Abbreviation	Description
Basic AD Regulation	Council Regulation (EC) No. 1225/2009 of 30 November 2009 on protection against dumped imports from countries not members of the European Community, *Official Journal of the European Union*, L Series, No. 343 (22 December 2009) 51, and Corrigendum, *Official Journal of the European Union*, L Series, No. 7 (12 January 2010) 23 (Panel Exhibit CHN-3)
China's Accession Protocol	Protocol on the Accession of the People's Republic of China, WT/L/432
China's Accession Working Party Report	Report of the Working Party on the Accession of China, WT/ACC/CHN/49 and WT/ACC/CHN/49/Corr.1
Definitive Regulation	Council Regulation (EC) No. 91/2009 of 26 January 2009 imposing a definitive anti-dumping duty on imports of certain iron or steel fasteners originating in the People's Republic of China, *Official Journal of the European Union*, L Series, No. 29 (31 January 2009) 1 (Panel Exhibit CHN-4)
DSB	Dispute Settlement Body
DSU	*Understanding on Rules and Procedures Governing the Settlement of Disputes*
GATT 1994	*General Agreement on Tariffs and Trade 1994*
General Disclosure Document	European Commission, Anti-dumping proceeding concerning imports of certain iron or steel fasteners originating in the People's Republic of China, Proposal to impose definitive measures, 3 November 2008) (Panel Exhibit CHN-18)
Information Document	European Commission, Anti-dumping proceeding concerning imports of certain iron or steel fasteners originating in the People's Republic of China, Non-imposition of provisional anti-dumping measures, 4 August 2008 (Panel Exhibit CHN-17)
IT	Individual treatment
IT suppliers	Non-market economy suppliers that qualify for individual treatment
Kennedy Round Anti-Dumping Code	Kennedy Round *Agreement on Implementation of Article VI of the General Agreement on Tariffs and Trade*, BISD 15S/24, entered into force 1 July 1968
MET	Market economy treatment
MFN	Most favoured nation

Abbreviation	Description
NME	Non-market economy
Panel Report	Panel Report, *European Communities – Definitive Anti-Dumping Measures on Certain Iron or Steel Fasteners from China*, WT/DS397/R
PCN	Product Control Number
SCM Agreement	*Agreement on Subsidies and Countervailing Measures*
Vienna Convention	*Vienna Convention on the Law of Treaties*, done at Vienna, 23 May 1969, 1155 UNTS 331; 8 International Legal Materials 679
Working Procedures	*Working Procedures for Appellate Review*, WT/AB/WP/6, 16 August 2010
WTO	World Trade Organization
WTO Agreement	*Marrakesh Agreement Establishing the World Trade Organization*

I. INTRODUCTION

1. The European Union and China each appeals certain issues of law and legal interpretations developed in the Panel Report, *European Communities – Definitive Anti-Dumping Measures on Certain Iron or Steel Fasteners from China* (the "Panel Report").[2] The Panel was established on 23 October 2009 to consider a complaint by China concerning the consistency "as such" of Article 9(5) of Council Regulation (EC) No. 384/96 of 22 December 1995, as amended, on protection against dumped imports from countries not members of the European Community[3] with the *Agreement on Implementation of Article VI of the General Agreement on Tariffs and Trade 1994* (the "*Anti-Dumping Agreement*"), the *General Agreement on Tariffs and Trade 1994* (the "GATT 1994"), and the *Marrakesh Agreement Establishing the World Trade Organization* (the "*WTO Agreement*"), and the consistency of this measure, "as applied" in the fasteners investigation, with the *Anti-Dumping Agreement*; and the consistency of Council Regulation (EC) No. 91/2009 of 26 January 2009 imposing a definitive anti-dumping duty on imports of certain iron or steel fasteners originating in the People's Republic of China (the "Definitive Regulation")[4] with the *Anti-Dumping Agreement*. Council Regulation (EC) No. 384/96 was subsequently repealed and replaced by Council Regulation (EC) No. 1225/2009 of 30

[2] WT/DS397/R, 3 December 2010.

[3] *Official Journal of the European Communities*, L Series, No. 56 (6 March 1996) 2 (Panel Exhibit CHN-1).

[4] *Official Journal of the European Union*, L Series, No. 29 (31 January 2009) 1 (Panel Exhibit CHN-4).

November 2009, and China's submissions to the Panel addressed Council Regulation (EC) No. 1225/2009 (the "Basic AD Regulation").[5]

2. Before the Panel, China challenged the consistency of Article 9(5) of the Basic AD Regulation, "as such", with Articles 6.10, 9.2, 9.3, 9.4, and 18.4 of the *Anti-Dumping Agreement*, Articles I:1 and X:3(a) of the GATT 1994, and Article XVI:4 of the *WTO Agreement* because it requires exporters from non-market economies to satisfy certain criteria in order to receive individual dumping margins and individual duty rates. China also challenged Article 9(5) of the Basic AD Regulation, "as applied" in the fasteners investigation, under Articles 6.10, 9.2, and 9.4 of the *Anti-Dumping Agreement*. Additionally, China challenged various substantive and procedural aspects of the Definitive Regulation, imposing anti-dumping duties in the fasteners investigation, under Articles 2, 3, 4, 5, 6, and 12 of the *Anti-Dumping Agreement*. These included the Commission's determinations regarding standing, the definition of the domestic industry, the product under consideration, dumping and price undercutting, volume and impact of dumped imports, and causation. Procedurally, China's challenges dealt with the disclosure by the Commission of information relevant to the investigation, the treatment of confidential information, and the procedural aspects of individual treatment claims.

3. The Panel Report was circulated to Members of the World Trade Organization (the "WTO") on 3 December 2010. For the reasons set out in its Report, the Panel made the following findings.

The Panel found that the following claims were not within its terms of reference:

(a) the claim under Article 2.6 of the *Anti-Dumping Agreement* with respect to the definition of like product;

(b) the claim under Article 6.9 of the *Anti-Dumping Agreement* with respect to the alleged non-disclosure of aspects of the normal value determination; and

(c) the claim under Article 6.9 of the *Anti-Dumping Agreement* with respect to the procedural aspects of the domestic industry definition.

The Panel found that the European Union acted inconsistently with:

(a) Articles 6.10, 9.2, and 18.4 of the *Anti-Dumping Agreement*, Article I:1 of the GATT 1994, and Article XVI:4 of the *WTO Agreement* with respect to Article 9(5) of the Basic AD Regulation;

(b) Articles 6.10 and 9.2 of the *Anti-Dumping Agreement* with respect to the individual treatment determinations in the fasteners investigation;

[5] *Official Journal of the European Union*, L Series, No. 343 (22 December 2009) 51, and Corrigendum, *Official Journal of the European Union*, L Series, No. 7 (12 January 2010) 23 (Panel Exhibit CHN-3).

(c) Articles 3.1 and 3.2 of the *Anti-Dumping Agreement* with respect to the volume of dumped imports considered in the fasteners investigation;

(d) Articles 3.1 and 3.5 of the *Anti-Dumping Agreement* with respect to the causation analysis in the fasteners investigation;

(e) Articles 6.4 and 6.2 of the *Anti-Dumping Agreement* with respect to certain aspects of the normal value determination;

(f) Article 6.5.1 of the *Anti-Dumping Agreement* with respect to non-confidential versions of questionnaire responses of two European producers and Article 6.5 of the *Anti-Dumping Agreement* with respect to confidential treatment of information in the questionnaire response of the Indian producer;

(g) Article 6.5 of the *Anti-Dumping Agreement* with respect to the confidential treatment of the Eurostat data on total EU production of fasteners; and

(h) Article 6.5 of the *Anti-Dumping Agreement* by disclosing confidential information.

The Panel found that China had not established that the European Union had acted inconsistently with:

(a) Article 5.4 of the *Anti-Dumping Agreement* with respect to the standing determination in the fasteners investigation;

(b) Articles 4.1 and 3.1 of the *Anti-Dumping Agreement* with respect to the definition of domestic industry in the fasteners investigation;

(c) Articles 2.1 and 2.6 of the *Anti-Dumping Agreement* with respect to the product under consideration in the fasteners investigation;

(d) Article 2.4 of the *Anti-Dumping Agreement* with respect to the dumping determination in the fasteners investigation;

(e) Articles 3.1 and 3.2 of the *Anti-Dumping Agreement* with respect to the price undercutting determination in the fasteners investigation;

(f) Articles 3.1, 3.2, 3.4, and 3.5 of the *Anti-Dumping Agreement* with respect to the consideration of imports from non-sampled/unexamined producers and exporters as dumped in the fasteners investigation;

(g) Articles 3.1 and 3.4 of the *Anti-Dumping Agreement* with respect to the consideration of the consequent impact of dumped imports on the domestic industry;

(h) Articles 6.5, 6.4, and 6.2 of the *Anti-Dumping Agreement* in connection with the non-disclosure of the identity of the complainants and the supporters of the complaint;

(i) Articles 6.2 and 6.4 of the *Anti-Dumping Agreement* with respect to the confidential treatment of the Eurostat data on total EU production of fasteners;

(j) Articles 6.2 and 6.4 of the *Anti-Dumping Agreement* with respect to the procedural aspects of the domestic industry definition; and

(k) Article 6.1.1 of the *Anti-Dumping Agreement* with respect to the amount of time provided for responses to requests for information.

The Panel exercised judicial economy with regard to the following claims:

(a) Articles 9.3 and 9.4 of the *Anti-Dumping Agreement* and Article X:3(a) of the GATT 1994 with respect to Article 9(5) of the Basic AD Regulation;

(b) Article 9.4 of the *Anti-Dumping Agreement* with respect to the individual treatment determinations in the fasteners investigation;

(c) Articles 3.4 and 3.5 of the *Anti-Dumping Agreement* with respect to the volume of dumped imports considered in the fasteners investigation;

(d) Article 6.5.1 of the *Anti-Dumping Agreement* with respect to the questionnaire response of the Indian producer;

(e) Articles 6.2 and 6.4 of the *Anti-Dumping Agreement* with respect to the non-confidential versions of questionnaire responses of two European producers and the confidential treatment of information in the questionnaire response of the Indian producer; and

(f) Article 12.2.2 of the *Anti-Dumping Agreement* with respect to the procedural aspects of the individual treatment determinations.

4. On 25 March 2011, the European Union notified the Dispute Settlement Body (the "DSB") of its intention to appeal certain issues of law covered in the Panel Report and certain legal interpretations developed by the Panel, pursuant to Articles 16.4 and 17 of the *Understanding on Rules and Procedures Governing the Settlement of Disputes* (the "DSU"), and filed a Notice of Appeal[6] and an appellant's submission pursuant to Rules 20 and 21, respectively, of the *Working Procedures for Appellate Review* (the "*Working Procedures*").[7]

5. On 30 March 2011, China notified the DSB of its intention to appeal certain issues of law covered in the Panel Report and certain legal interpretations developed by the Panel, pursuant to Articles 16.4 and 17 of the DSU, and filed a Notice of Other Appeal[8] and an other appellant's submission pursuant to Rule 23(1) and (3), respectively, of the *Working Procedures*. On 12 April 2011, the

6 WT/DS397/7 (attached as Annex I to this Report).

7 WT/AB/WP/6, 16 August 2010.

8 WT/DS397/8 (attached as Annex II to this Report).

European Union and China each filed an appellee's submission.[9] On 15 April 2011, Brazil, Colombia, Japan, and the United States each filed a third participant's submission.[10] On the same day, Canada, Chile, India, Norway, the Separate Customs Territory of Taiwan, Penghu, Kinmen and Matsu, and Thailand each notified its intention to appear at the oral hearing as a third participant.[11] On 18 April 2011, Turkey notified its intention to appear at the oral hearing as a third participant.[12]

6. The oral hearing in this appeal was held on 4-6 May 2011. The participants and six of the third participants (Brazil, Colombia, India, Japan, Norway, and the United States) made oral statements.[13] The participants and third participants responded to questions posed by the Members of the Appellate Body Division hearing the appeal.

II. ARGUMENTS OF THE PARTICIPANTS AND THE THIRD PARTICIPANTS

A. Claims of Error by the European Union – Appellant

1. The Panel's Findings Regarding Article 9(5) of the Basic AD Regulation "As Such"

7. The European Union argues that the Panel erred in finding that Article 9(5) of the Basic AD Regulation is inconsistent with Articles 6.10, 9.2, and 18.4 of the *Anti-Dumping Agreement*, Article I:1 of the GATT 1994, and Article XVI:4 of the *WTO Agreement*[14], and asks the Appellate Body to reverse these findings by the Panel.[15]

(a) The Scope of Article 9(5) of the Basic AD Regulation

8. The European Union claims that the Panel erred in finding that Article 9(5) of the Basic AD Regulation concerns not only the imposition of anti-dumping duties but also the calculation of margins of dumping, and that the Panel erred in the application of Article 6.10 of the *Anti-Dumping Agreement* when finding that Article 9(5) of the Basic AD Regulation is, "as such", inconsistent with that provision. The European Union therefore contends that the Panel's finding of inconsistency with Article 6.10 was premised on an incorrect understanding of the scope of Article 9(5), since Article 6.10 addresses the determination of margins of dumping, while Article 9(5) is directed at the imposi-

---

9 Pursuant to Rules 22 and 23(4) of the *Working Procedures*.

10 Pursuant to Rule 24(1) of the *Working Procedures*.

11 Pursuant to Rule 24(2) of the *Working Procedures*.

12 Pursuant to Rule 24(4) of the *Working Procedures*.

13 Turkey made concluding remarks at the oral hearing.

14 European Union's appellant's submission, para. 14.

15 European Union's appellant's submission, para. 227.

tion of anti-dumping duties.[16] The European Union asks the Appellate Body to reverse these findings of the Panel.[17]

9. The European Union argues that, although the Panel considered that the meaning of Article 9(5) of the Basic AD Regulation was a "factual matter", this error can be reviewed by the Appellate Body because the examination by a panel of the municipal law of a WTO Member for purposes of determining whether the Member has complied with its WTO obligations is a legal characterization by a panel, which is subject to appellate review under Article 17.6 of the DSU.[18]

10. According to the European Union, an examination of Article 9(5) of the Basic AD Regulation on its face, based on its text and in the context of other articles of the Basic AD Regulation, shows that Article 9(5) deals exclusively with the imposition of anti-dumping duties.[19] The European Union contends that, in view of the "as such" nature of China's claim, any disagreement between the parties on the scope of the measure at issue should have been resolved by examining Article 9(5) on its face. Considering that the text of Article 9(5) makes it clear that, on its face, this provision relates to only the individual or country-wide imposition of anti-dumping duties, in the European Union's view, the Panel should have ended its examination of the scope of Article 9(5) at this stage. The European Union adds that, when Article 9(5) is read in the context of other provisions of the Basic AD Regulation, the same conclusion is reached regarding its meaning and content.[20]

11. The European Union claims that the Panel erred in concluding that nothing in the other articles of the Basic AD Regulation cited by the European Union "pertains to whether or not an individual margin will be calculated for any foreign producer or exporter", and asserts that other provisions of the Basic AD Regulation address directly or indirectly the separate threshold issue of the determination of individual dumping margins. The European Union makes reference to: Article 2(7) of the Basic AD Regulation, which determines whether suppliers should receive market economy treatment ("MET") and whether individual margins of dumping will be calculated for these suppliers; Article 11(4) of the Basic AD Regulation, which requires the calculation of individual margins of dumping in the context of new exporters' reviews; and Article 11(8) of the Basic AD Regulation, which requires that margins of dumping be established on an individual basis in the context of refund proceedings.[21] According to the European Union, the numerous references in the Basic AD Regulation to the determination of individual dumping margins make sense in view of the obligation set out in Article 9(4) to establish the ceiling for the amount of anti-dumping

---

16 European Union's appellant's submission, para. 88.

17 European Union's appellant's submission, para. 110.

18 European Union's appellant's submission, para. 89 (referring to Appellate Body Report, *US – Section 211 Appropriations Act*, para. 105; and Appellate Body Reports, *China – Auto Parts*, para. 225).

19 European Union's appellant's submission, para. 90.

20 European Union's appellant's submission, para. 95.

21 European Union's appellant's submission, para. 96.

duties by, *inter alia*, reference to the margin of dumping established. It is thus Article 9(4) that indicates that the EU authorities should calculate an individual dumping margin per supplier.[22]

12. The European Union further contends that the operation of Article 9(5) of the Basic AD Regulation in the context of anti-dumping investigations confirms that this provision addresses specifically the imposition of anti-dumping duties. The European Union explains that Article 9(5) serves to identify the relevant supplier in the context of imports from non-market economies ("NMEs") (that is, an independent supplier or the State and its related or controlled export entities) and that other relevant rules determine the proper duty rate for individual treatment ("IT") suppliers and non-IT suppliers. The Panel's finding that Article 9(5) determines whether an individual or country-wide dumping margin will be established for an exporter from an NME ignores the fact that the determination of the dumping margin for a supplier entitled to an individual dumping margin flows from the rule contained in Article 9(4) of the Basic AD Regulation, which China did not specify as the measure at issue in the present dispute.[23] Moreover, according to the European Union, an individual duty is not automatically based on an individual dumping margin, which serves as a ceiling for the amount of the anti-dumping duty.[24]

13. Finally, the European Union contends that, even if the determination of dumping and the imposition of duties are closely related issues, this does not mean that Article 9(5), which specifically addresses the imposition of anti-dumping duties, also incorporates by implication any other related issues that may derive as a consequence of its operation. The European Union emphasizes that such an approach should be rejected, particularly in the case of "as such" claims.[25]

(b) Article 6.10 of the *Anti-Dumping Agreement*

14. The European Union claims that the Panel erred in its interpretation and application of Article 6.10 of the *Anti-Dumping Agreement* and failed to comply with Article 11 of the DSU in finding that Article 9(5) of the Basic AD Regulation is inconsistent with Article 6.10 of the *Anti-Dumping Agreement* because it conditions the calculation of individual dumping margins for producers from NMEs on the fulfilment of the IT test.[26] The European Union requests the Appellate Body to reverse this finding by the Panel.[27]

15. The European Union contends that Article 6.10, first sentence, does not impose an unqualified obligation to determine individual dumping margins. The term "as a rule", which is inserted after the word "shall", indicates that the obli-

---

22 European Union's appellant's submission, para. 97.
23 European Union's appellant's submission, para. 104.
24 European Union's appellant's submission, para. 105.
25 European Union's appellant's submission, para. 107.
26 European Union's appellant's submission, para. 112.
27 European Union's appellant's submission, para. 157.

gation is only a general principle and not a strict obligation that is to be complied with in any and all circumstances.[28] Article 6.10 should not be read as being structured in the manner of a "rule/only exception"; rather, it expresses a preference for determining individual dumping margins and then refers to one affirmative situation (sampling) where such a preference "may" not be followed.[29] According to the European Union, there is no direct link between the general principle of the first sentence and the possibility of sampling in the second sentence of Article 6.10.

16. The European Union points out that earlier panels have interpreted Article 6.10 in a more flexible manner than this Panel, as not requiring the calculation of individual dumping margins for each known exporter or producer in all cases. The European Union refers to the panel in *Korea – Certain Paper*, which interpreted the term "exporter and producers" in Article 6.10 as permitting the combination of separate entities in a single supplier that is the "actual source of price discrimination".[30] The European Union also refers to the panel in *EC – Salmon (Norway)*, which found that the term "exporter and producers" in Article 6.10 means that an investigating authority may calculate dumping margins based on the producer's pricing behaviour, notwithstanding the existence of a known exporter for the product under investigation.[31]

17. According to the European Union, the fact that Article 6.10, first sentence, does not contain a strict rule, as the Panel found, is further supported by the existence of other situations where the preference does not need to be followed. In particular, the European Union refers to the following examples: (1) a non-cooperating exporter or producer for whom the dumping margin is calculated based on facts available, pursuant to Article 6.8 of the *Anti-Dumping Agreement*; (2) an exporter that exports the product of another supplier (mere "trader") and that is assigned the dumping margin of the actual supplier; (3) the situation where the actual producer of the product concerned cannot be identified; (4) the situation where an investigating authority has to calculate a single dumping margin, based on constructed normal value and export price, due to insufficient information; and (5) a known producer, related to an exporter or producer already subject to anti-dumping duties, that did not export the product during the period of investigation and that would not be entitled to an individual dumping margin in the investigation, nor in the context of a review pursuant to Article 9.5 of the *Anti-Dumping Agreement*.

18. The European Union observes that the Panel dismissed these examples on the grounds that they are directly based on other provisions of the *Anti-Dumping Agreement*, and that, "as such", they could not be considered even potentially as exceptions to the obligation to calculate individual dumping margins but rather

---

[28] European Union's appellant's submission, para. 114.

[29] European Union's appellant's submission, para. 117.

[30] European Union's appellant's submission, para. 120 (referring to Panel Report, *Korea – Certain Paper*, para. 7.161).

[31] European Union's appellant's submission, para. 121 (referring to Panel Report, *EC – Salmon (Norway)*, para. 7.178).

as specific rights and obligations otherwise provided for in the *Anti-Dumping Agreement*. The European Union contends that, in doing so, the Panel ignored basic principles of treaty interpretation, because, if other provisions of the *Anti-Dumping Agreement* (such as Article 6.8) directly and expressly permit departing from the "mandatory rule" contained in Article 6.10, first sentence, the only conclusion that the treaty interpreter can reach is that Article 6.10 cannot be interpreted in such a rigid manner.[32] The European Union submits that Article 9(5) of the Basic AD Regulation addresses a situation other than sampling where the preference expressed in Article 6.10 does not need to be followed. Therefore, Article 9(5) of the Basic AD Regulation is "as such" consistent with Article 6.10 of the *Anti-Dumping Agreement*.

19. The European Union claims that, even assuming that Article 6.10 is understood to contain a strict rule to requiring the determination of individual dumping margins for each known exporter or producer, the Panel erred in its application of Article 6.10 because it ignored the fact that Article 9(5) of the Basic AD Regulation aims at identifying the supplier that is the actual source of price discrimination in the context of imports from NMEs. In this respect, the European Union contends that the purpose of the IT test is to determine if the State and those entities that do not act independently from the State should be treated as a single supplier.[33]

20. The European Union relies on the findings of the panel in *Korea – Certain Paper*, which, in the European Union's view, stand for the proposition that, for the purpose of determining individual dumping margins, Article 6.10 permits investigating authorities to determine that two or more exporters and producers are part of the same entity.[34] The European Union adds that "[n]othing in the *Anti-Dumping Agreement* supports the proposition that the panel in *Korea – Certain Paper* explored the complete universe of relationships existing between separate entities to consider them as one single entity". According to the European Union, the *Anti-Dumping Agreement* contains provisions where, directly or indirectly, the relationship between two separate entities is relevant.[35]

21. The European Union argues that a determination of individual dumping margins for each legal entity, regardless of whether they are *de jure* or *de facto* related to each other, would be contrary to the object and purpose of Article 6.10 of the *Anti-Dumping Agreement*. Investigating authorities should be allowed to determine one dumping margin for related companies as a whole or for companies that, because of their close relationship, behave in the market as one single entity.[36]

22. The European Union points out that the purpose of imposing and collecting anti-dumping duties is to target the source of price discrimination and that a

---

32 European Union's appellant's submission, para. 122.
33 European Union's appellant's submission, para. 137.
34 European Union's appellant's submission, para. 139.
35 European Union's appellant's submission, para. 140.
36 European Union's appellant's submission, para. 141.

proper identification of the single exporter or producer in a case where several related companies exist allows for the imposition of anti-dumping duties on the actual source of price discrimination. In the view of the European Union, the identification of the actual source of price discrimination and the application of a single duty rate in the case of non-IT suppliers would avoid potential circumvention and additional dumping, which could occur if exports could be channelled by related companies through the supplier with the lowest duty rate.[37]

23. The European Union argues that the Article 9(5) criteria not only reflect elements that demonstrate direct or *de jure* control or interference by the State, but also reflect other elements that indirectly and *de facto* limit the capacity of the exporter to act free from State interference. Contrary to what the Panel found, the European Union contends that Article 9(5) does not merely relate to the role of the State in the way business is conducted in a given country, but it aims also at determining whether there is a close relationship between separate legal entities and the State in NMEs. Thus, the reasoning of the panel in *Korea – Certain Paper* is fully applicable to Article 9(5), considering that the objective of the IT criteria is to identify the actual source of price discrimination, that is, the single supplier of the product concerned, due to a close relationship.[38]

24. According to the European Union, whilst in the case of market economies, as established by the panel in *Korea – Certain Paper*, the close relationship between the separate legal entities has to be examined on a case-by-case basis, in NMEs, since the role of the State is different than in market economies, the presumption of State control is the general rule. Therefore, according to the European Union, the reasoning of the panel in *Korea – Certain Paper* fully applies in cases of imports from NMEs, starting with the presumption that all producers and exporters in an NME are, effectively, arms of the State. The criteria of the IT test are then applied to determine whether each individual producer or exporter can demonstrate that it acts independently from the State.[39]

25. The European Union further contends that the Panel acted inconsistently with Article 11 of the DSU, because it disregarded evidence submitted by the European Union concerning the nature of NMEs and China's status as an NME, as well as the fact that the Protocol on the Accession of the People's Republic of China (China's "Accession Protocol")[40] entitles the European Union to treat China as an NME until 2016. According to the European Union, this evidence, which was not contested by China, supports the presumption underlying Article 9(5) of the Basic AD Regulation that all producers and exporters in an NME constitute a single entity together with the State. However, in the European Union's view, the Panel ignored this evidence without providing reasoned and adequate explanations for its conclusion[41], and merely stated that it was not con-

---

[37] European Union's appellant's submission, para. 142.
[38] European Union's appellant's submission, para. 148.
[39] European Union's appellant's submission, para. 150.
[40] WT/L/432, 23 November 2001.
[41] European Union's appellant's submission, para. 154.

vinced by this argument and that the European Union had not pointed to any legal basis that would support it.

26. Finally, the European Union claims that the Panel erred in relying on the fact that the European Union applies a test such as the one in *Korea – Certain Paper* "in addition to" the IT test. The European Union remarks that its argument was not that the two tests are identical, but rather that the relationship between non-IT suppliers and the State "is similar to" the relationship that the panel in *Korea – Certain Paper* found between several legally distinct entities producing the product under investigation, for which the Korean authorities had calculated a single margin, treating them as a single producer. In this respect, the European Union argues, the application of both tests is irrelevant to the question of whether Article 9(5) of the Basic AD Regulation is consistent with Article 6.10 of the *Anti-Dumping Agreement*.[42]

(c) Article 9.2 of the *Anti-Dumping Agreement*

27. The European Union claims that the Panel erred in interpreting and applying Article 9.2 of the *Anti-Dumping Agreement* and violated Article 11 of the DSU when concluding that Article 9(5) of the Basic AD Regulation violates Article 9.2 of the *Anti-Dumping Agreement*, and requests the Appellate Body to reverse this finding by the Panel.[43]

28. The European Union claims that, like Article 6.10 of the *Anti-Dumping Agreement*, Article 9.2 does not contain a mandatory rule regarding the imposition of anti-dumping duties, but rather a principle or a preference. The European Union argues that Article 9.2 reflects a product-wide and country-wide approach in that it refers to the imposition of an anti-dumping duty on a "product", not a company.[44] The European Union contends that it is particularly significant that Article 9.2 refers to sources found to be dumped and causing *injury*, since injury is a country-wide, rather than a company-specific, concept.[45]

29. The European Union thus contends that, contrary to the Panel's interpretation, Article 9.2 does not impose an obligation to grant individual treatment to, or to impose individual anti-dumping duties on, exporters or producers. Article 9.2 merely contains an obligation to specify by name exporters or producers where practicable. This, according to the European Union, may serve to distinguish between exporters or producers included in the anti-dumping investigation and new exporters or producers that may request a review pursuant to Article 9.5 of the *Anti-Dumping Agreement*.[46]

30. The European Union contends that the Panel interprets Article 9.2 as providing for the same general rule (individual duties) and the same single exception (sampling) as contained in Article 6.10, which would make Article 9.2 re-

---

[42] European Union's appellant's submission, para. 155.
[43] European Union's appellant's submission, paras. 158 and 208.
[44] European Union's appellant's submission, para. 161.
[45] European Union's appellant's submission, para. 162.
[46] European Union's appellant's submission, para. 163.

dundant.[47] The European Union argues that the purpose of imposing anti-dumping duties (that is, to offset and to prevent dumping) also supports its interpretation that Article 9.2 does not require the imposition of individual anti-dumping duties on all known exporters and producers. In this respect, the European Union claims that, once dumping has been found to exist for the product concerned with respect to some investigated companies, a further examination of the pricing behaviour of other entities would not be required in order to impose anti-dumping duties in order to offset and prevent dumping.[48]

31. Assuming that Article 9.2 of the *Anti-Dumping Agreement* contained a strict rule to impose anti-dumping duties on an individual basis, the European Union submits that the Panel erred in finding that Article 9(5) of the Basic AD Regulation does not fall within the exception under Article 9.2, third sentence, which would only be available in cases where the authorities consider that, because of the large number of producers involved, it would be impracticable to name exporters or producers individually. The European Union is of the view that, like Article 6.10, Article 9.2 expressly permits the imposition of duties on a country-wide basis in cases other than the sampling scenario, in particular when it is "impracticable" to do so on an individual basis, consistently with the notion that these provisions should be interpreted in a flexible manner.[49]

32. The European Union points out that Article 9.4 of the *Anti-Dumping Agreement* addresses the specific situation of the imposition of anti-dumping duties when sampling is used, and contends that interpreting "impracticable" in Article 9.2 as referring only to sampling would make Article 9.4 redundant and unnecessary.[50]

33. The European Union argues that the Panel's interpretation of the term "impracticable" in Article 9.2 is both redundant and too rigid and that this term should be interpreted in a flexible manner.[51] According to the European Union, the notion of "impracticable" in Article 9.2 encompasses the notion of "ineffective". This situation is envisaged in Article 9(5) of the Basic AD Regulation, which provides for the imposition of country-wide duties, where anti-dumping duties cannot be imposed on an individual basis for "practical" reasons. The European Union explains that it would not be effective to impose individual anti-dumping duties on suppliers that are all related to the State, because this may lead to circumvention of the higher anti-dumping duties imposed on some individual exporters by channelling exports through those exporters for whom the lowest anti-dumping duties have been calculated.[52]

34. The European Union submits that its interpretation of the exception to the individual treatment of producers or exporters contemplated under Article 9.2 is also confirmed by the analysis of supplementary means of interpretation and, in

---

47 *Ibid.*
48 European Union's appellant's submission, para. 164.
49 European Union's appellant's submission, para. 168.
50 European Union's appellant's submission, para. 170.
51 European Union's appellant's submission, para. 174.
52 European Union's appellant's submission, para. 187.

particular, by the negotiating history and the circumstances at the conclusion of the Kennedy Round *Agreement on Implementation of Article VI of the General Agreement on Tariffs and Trade* (the "*Kennedy Round Anti-Dumping Code*").[53] According to the European Union, the negotiating history and the circumstances at the conclusion of Article 8(b) of the *Kennedy Round Anti-Dumping Code* show that negotiators were aware of the problems associated with imposing anti-dumping duties on imports from NMEs. They clarified that anti-dumping duties could be imposed on a country-wide basis in cases where it was "impracticable" to specify duties on an individual basis. The European Union notes that no limits were imposed on the notion of "impracticability", which included not only cases where suppliers could not be examined individually because they were too numerous or because they did not make themselves known or did not trade during the period examined, but also other situations, such as imports from NMEs. The notion of "impracticability" provided the necessary flexibility when imposing anti-dumping duties in order to remedy injurious dumping and, at the same time, preserved the rights of the other signatories through the obligation to provide refunds.[54]

35. The European Union further claims that the Panel erred in considering irrelevant the fact that Article 8 and Article 2(g) were introduced into the *Kennedy Round Anti-Dumping Code* together and for the first time. The European Union observes that Article 2(g), which incorporated the second *Ad* Note to Article VI:1 of the GATT 1994, specifically referred to a situation where "special difficulties ... in determining price comparability" existed and, thus, a situation where it was "impracticable" to use the normal methods for determining the existence of dumping.[55]

36. The European Union claims that the Panel erred in its application of Article 9.2 of the *Anti-Dumping Agreement*, which, in the European Union's view, does not exclude that the State could be considered as the actual source of price discrimination or as a single supplier for the purposes of imposing anti-dumping duties. The European Union argues that the terms "sources" and "supplier" in Article 9.2 may also include the State in cases where the State is an exporter or producer, because the use of these terms implies that anti-dumping measures aim at identifying the supplier that is the actual source of the price discrimination. This could be one exporter, one producer, or a group of related exporters and/or producers.[56]

37. The European Union argues that, in rejecting the notion that in NMEs the State can be presumed to be the source of price discrimination, the Panel acted inconsistently with its duties under Article 11 of the DSU, because it disregarded evidence presented by the European Union regarding NMEs in general and China's status as an NME, and failed to provide reasoned and adequate explana-

---

[53] BISD 15S/24, entered into force 1 July 1968.
[54] European Union's appellant's submission, para. 184.
[55] European Union's appellant's submission, para. 182.
[56] European Union's appellant's submission, para. 194.

tions for its findings. Although the Panel stated that it addressed this issue elsewhere in its findings, the European Union contends that no explanation was provided by the Panel as to why in NMEs the State cannot be presumed to be a producer and the actual source of price discrimination. To the extent that the Panel discussed this issue in its Report, the European Union argues that the Panel failed to provide a reasoned and adequate explanation for its finding and thus failed to make an objective analysis of the matter.[57]

38. The European Union claims that, in NMEs, because of State control over the means of production and State intervention in the economy, including international trade relations, all exports can be considered to emanate from the State, which can be considered as one single supplier whose dumping behaviour can be identified and addressed in accordance with the disciplines of the *Anti-Dumping Agreement*. The European Union further contends that it has shown that China is an NME and that, in accordance with paragraph 15(d) of China's Accession Protocol, the European Union is entitled to treat China as an NME in anti-dumping proceedings with all the consequences that this determination entails.[58]

39. The European Union argues that the Panel erred in finding that Article 9(5) of the Basic AD Regulation does not serve to identify the source of price discrimination, because it took a narrow view of the notion of "source of price discrimination" as being limited exclusively to the determination of export prices. In the view of the European Union, the source of price discrimination is both the determination of export prices and the determination of normal value, even though suppliers from NMEs may not actually control the determination of their normal value. In this respect, the European Union observes that, while anti-dumping disciplines address the phenomenon of international price discrimination, Article 2.1 of the *Anti-Dumping Agreement* does not require a conscious pricing decision with the intention of dumping by the entity concerned. Moreover, the European Union observes that the IT test criteria embodied in Article 9(5) are not limited to the determination of export prices, but aim at identifying whether the applicant company acts independently from the State in its export activities.[59]

40. In sum, the European Union claims that Article 9(5) serves to identify the relevant supplier in the context of imports from NMEs. The supplier will be the individual supplier if it can show that it meets the five criteria in the IT test. However, failure to meet these criteria will mean that the non-IT supplier is not the genuine exporter or producer, but an entity that does not act independently from the State and, thus, should be subject to the actual supplier, country-wide duty rate.[60]

---

[57] European Union's appellant's submission, para. 195.
[58] European Union's appellant's submission, para. 196.
[59] European Union's appellant's submission, para. 203.
[60] European Union's appellant's submission, para. 206.

(d) Article I:1 of the GATT 1994

41. The European Union claims that the Panel erred in the interpretation and application of Article I:1 of the GATT 1994 and acted inconsistently with Article 11 of the DSU, when it found that Article 9(5) of the Basic AD Regulation is inconsistent with the MFN obligation of Article I:1 of the GATT 1994. The European Union argues that it is entitled to grant formally different treatment to imports from market economies and from NMEs because such imports are different in nature. The European Union adds that the word "unconditionally" in Article I:1 does not preclude an advantage being subjected to conditions as long as this does not result in *de facto* discrimination.[61]

42. Moreover, the European Union claims that the alleged advantage granted to market economies was based on the nature of the suppliers involved, and not on the product itself. The European Union contends this was a "very important point that the Panel failed to acknowledge" since it means that discrimination between like products originating in different countries does not arise in this case.[62] The European Union further contends that, in assessing China's claim under Article I:1 of the GATT 1994, the Panel failed to fulfil its duties under Article 11 of the DSU, because it did not examine the evidence submitted by the European Union regarding China's status as an NME. The European Union asserts that it did demonstrate that market economies and NMEs, by definition, are in a different situation and that this evidence justifies the formally different treatment it conferred to imports from China.[63] This is so, the European Union argues, because China's status as an NME was not unilaterally determined by the European Union, but is based on paragraph 15(d) of China's Accession Protocol. According to the European Union, the Panel's failure to examine this evidence is contrary to its obligations under Article 11 of the DSU.[64]

43. The European Union also argues that the fact that under Article 9(5) of the Basic AD Regulation producers from NMEs may be able to demonstrate that they are independent from the State ensures that discrimination does not arise, because, if a supplier complies with the conditions of the IT test, it will be treated like a supplier of a market economy.[65] The European Union further contends that the fact that the Basic AD Regulation explicitly lists the NMEs whose producers will be subject to the IT test is irrelevant to the question of non-discrimination, because this list is based on evidence that the listed countries are in the same economic situation to be classified as NMEs and, thus, confers the same treatment to all countries in the same category.[66]

44. Finally, the European Union argues that, even if the Appellate Body were to consider that Article 9(5) of the Basic AD Regulation was inconsistent "as such" with Article I:1 of the GATT 1994, the different treatment of imports from

---

[61] European Union's appellant's submission, para. 212.
[62] European Union's appellant's submission, para. 213.
[63] European Union's appellant's submission, para. 214.
[64] European Union's appellant's submission, para. 215.
[65] European Union's appellant's submission, para. 217.
[66] European Union's appellant's submission, para. 218.

NMEs would be permitted by the provisions of the *Anti-Dumping Agreement*. The European Union remarks that the *lex specialis* principle and the *General Interpretative Note to Annex 1A of the WTO Agreement* make it clear that, when a provision of the *Anti-Dumping Agreement* conflicts with a provision of the GATT 1994, the former should prevail. In this respect, the European Union argues that a conflict between a provision of the GATT 1994 and a provision of the *Anti-Dumping Agreement* occurs not only in situations where a rule in the GATT 1994 prohibits what a rule in the *Anti-Dumping Agreement* requires; a conflict also exists when there is "incompatibility of contents". This scenario includes situations where an agreement prohibits what another permits. The European Union further notes that Article 9.2 of the *Anti-Dumping Agreement* already requires the imposition and collection of anti-dumping duties on a non-discriminatory basis.[67]

(e) Article XVI:4 of the *WTO Agreement* and Article 18.4 of the *Anti-Dumping Agreement*

45. As a consequence of the European Union's contention that the Panel wrongly found that Article 9(5) of the Basic AD Regulation is inconsistent "as such" with Articles 6.10 and 9.2 of the *Anti-Dumping Agreement*, the European Union also requests the Appellate Body to reverse the Panel's findings that the European Union acted inconsistently with Article XVI:4 of the *WTO Agreement* and Article 18.4 of the *Anti-Dumping Agreement* by failing to ensure the conformity of its laws, regulations, and administrative procedures with its obligations under the relevant agreements.

2. *The Panel's Findings Regarding Article 9(5) of the Basic AD Regulation "As Applied" in the Fasteners Investigation*

46. The European Union appeals the Panel's finding that Article 9(5) of the Basic AD Regulation, "as applied" in the fasteners investigation, is inconsistent with Articles 6.10 and 9.2 of the *Anti-Dumping Agreement*. The European Union argues that, since the Panel erred in finding that Article 9(5) of the Basic AD Regulation is inconsistent "as such" with the provisions of the *Anti-Dumping Agreement*, the Appellate Body should also reverse the Panel's "as applied" findings with respect to the determinations made in the fasteners investigation.[68]

47. The European Union argues that the Panel applied the "as such/as applied" distinction in a mechanical manner, and noted that there are measures where the result that is found to be WTO inconsistent "as such" may or may not take place in an "as applied" context, depending on the configuration of facts. The European Union contends that, in such cases, it cannot be found that the same measure "as applied" is WTO inconsistent since, in reality, the result does not take place.[69] The European Union points out that, while the Panel found Ar-

[67] European Union's appellant's submission, para. 222.
[68] European Union's appellant's submission, para. 228.
[69] European Union's appellant's submission, para. 230.

ticle 9(5) of the Basic AD Regulation to be "as such" inconsistent with the provisions of the *Anti-Dumping Agreement* and of the GATT 1994, in the fasteners investigation, each of the five cooperating sampled companies and each of the cooperating companies examined individually were granted individual treatment. Thus, according to the European Union, although the Panel found that Article 9(5) "as such" prevents the result that suppliers from NMEs are entitled to obtain from the obligations contained in the *Anti-Dumping Agreement* and the GATT 1994, in a case where all companies requesting individual treatment were granted such treatment, there is no basis for a finding of inconsistency "as applied". According to the European Union, for the Panel to say that there is a possibility that Article 9(5) affected participation by Chinese exporters in the fasteners investigation and/or the quality and quantity of information Chinese exporters provided to the Commission is pure speculation, and not based on evidence.[70]

48. The European Union argues that the Panel found that Article 9(5) of the Basic AD Regulation leads to a particular result in the absence of the required evidence to substantiate such a conclusion. According to the European Union, the Panel erred by concluding that, having found Article 9(5) of the Basic AD Regulation to be inconsistent "as such" with Articles 6.10 and 9.2 of the *Anti-Dumping Agreement*, "for the same reasons", its application in the fasteners investigation was also inconsistent with these two provisions. Therefore, even if the Appellate Body were to uphold the Panel's finding in respect of Article 9(5) "as such" and "as applied", the European Union requests the Appellate Body to modify the Panel's reasoning on this issue.[71]

3. *The Panel's Findings under Articles 6.4 and 6.2 of the* Anti-Dumping Agreement

49. The European Union requests the Appellate Body to reverse the Panel's finding that the European Union acted inconsistently with Articles 6.4 and 6.2 of the *Anti-Dumping Agreement* with respect to certain aspects of the normal value determination. In the European Union's view, the Panel erred in finding that Articles 6.4 and 6.2 required the Commission to disclose the factual determination of how it grouped product types for purposes of determining normal value. The European Union also maintains that the Panel made a purely consequential finding of violation of Article 6.2 that is incorrect given the flaws in the Panel's finding under Article 6.4. In addition, the European Union submits that the Panel disregarded certain important evidence on the record in its factual findings and thus violated Article 11 of the DSU.

---

[70] European Union's appellant's submission, para. 231.

[71] European Union's appellant's submission, para. 232.

(a) The "Information" Subject to the Obligations under Articles 6.4 and 6.2 of the *Anti-Dumping Agreement*

50. The European Union claims that the Panel erred when "it effectively found that Articles 6.4 and 6.2 required the EU investigating authorities to have disclosed the manner in which they decided to group product types for purposes of the normal value determination, prior to the disclosure of essential facts, and as part of their obligation under Article 6.4 to allow access to the file."[72] The European Union submits that such a factual determination by investigating authorities is not the kind of information that is covered by the obligation in Article 6.4 of the *Anti-Dumping Agreement*. Rather, the European Union contends that this is merely an essential factual determination that was disclosed at the end of the fasteners investigation in the final General Disclosure Document[73], in compliance with Article 6.9 of the *Anti-Dumping Agreement*. The European Union posits that a proper interpretation of the term "information" in Article 6.4, which takes into account the context of Article 6 as a whole, supports the proposition that factual determinations by investigating authorities are not subject to the obligation of Article 6.4.

51. The European Union contends that the term "information", read in the light of the sequence of rights and obligations set out in the various paragraphs of Articles 6.1 to 6.8 of the *Anti-Dumping Agreement*, refers to knowledge of facts as communicated by the interested parties or collected by the investigating authorities. Referring to the panels' findings in *Korea – Certain Paper*, *Korea – Certain Paper (Article 21.5 – Indonesia)*, and *US – Oil Country Tubular Goods Sunset Reviews (Article 21.5 – Argentina)*, the European Union contends that the term "information", as used in Article 6.4, concerns facts and "raw data", rather than "reasoning", factual determinations, or conclusions by the investigating authorities.[74] The European Union further submits that this view is confirmed by the Appellate Body's findings in *EC – Tube or Pipe Fittings*, which "assimilated" the term "information" in Article 6.4 with facts, evidence, or raw data that had not been disclosed to the interested parties.[75]

52. The European Union maintains that there is a logical sequence of events and corresponding rights and obligations that is reflected in the various paragraphs and subparagraphs of Article 6 of the *Anti-Dumping Agreement*. Specifically, the European Union submits that Articles 6.1 to 6.3 provide parties with the right to submit their own evidence in writing and to make their views known

---

[72] European Union's appellant's submission, para. 248.

[73] The General Disclosure Document (European Commission, Anti-dumping proceeding concerning imports of certain iron or steel fasteners originating in the People's Republic of China, Proposal to impose definitive measures, 3 November 2008) (Panel Exhibit CHN-18)) was the final disclosure document before the Commission issued the Definitive Regulation.

[74] European Union's appellant's submission, paras. 252 (quoting Panel Report, *Korea – Certain Paper (Article 21.5 – Indonesia)*, para. 6.82) and 253 (referring to Panel Report, *Korea – Certain Paper*, para. 7.199; and Panel Report, *US – Oil Country Tubular Goods Sunset Reviews (Article 21.5 – Argentina)*, para. 7.124).

[75] European Union's appellant's submission, para. 254 (referring to Appellate Body Report, *EC – Tube or Pipe Fittings*, paras. 138-141).

at an oral hearing. Articles 6.6 and 6.7, in turn, impose an obligation on investigating authorities to verify the information submitted by the parties, and Article 6.8 allows the use of "facts available" when any interested party does not provide necessary information. Thus, the European Union asserts, Article 6.4 is limited to addressing "the parties' right to know what *other interested parties have submitted* in terms of evidence and information".[76] Moreover, the European Union recalls that Article 6.9 requires that, before a final determination is made, the authorities inform all interested parties of "the essential facts under consideration which form the basis for the decision whether to apply definitive measures". In the European Union's view, the use of the phrase "essential facts" rather than the word "information" in Article 6.9 indicates that Articles 6.1 to 6.8 concern the information-gathering process, and Article 6.9 marks the end of the process and requires a disclosure of the authority's essential factual conclusions. The European Union further contends that the differences between the obligations under Article 6.4 and Article 6.9 are well established in WTO jurisprudence. For example, in *Guatemala – Cement II*, the panel found that Article 6.4 generally provides an "access to the file" right[77], whereas Article 6.9 provides for a disclosure of the basic factual findings in respect of the information received.

53. The European Union submits that the Panel failed to recognize the important differences between the various paragraphs of Article 6, and erroneously considered that Article 6.4 also applied in respect of the authorities' factual findings disclosed under Article 6.9 of the *Anti-Dumping Agreement*. This is because the Panel did not find that non-confidential evidence gathered by the Commission was not made available to the interested parties. Rather, the Panel's finding concerns the fact that the Commission in its General Disclosure Document stated that the normal value determination was based on a grouping of products as certain "product types", as opposed to Product Control Numbers ("PCNs")[78], which were reflected in the request for data in the questionnaires sent to the Chinese producers and exporters, but did not provide any information as to the relevant characteristics of those "product types". However, the European Union argues, the grouping of products is not raw data submitted by the parties or gathered by the Commission, but is "simply the determination by the European Commission of what constituted a proper way of grouping products per model or type, based on the information on product types which was in the public record".[79] The Panel thus erred in finding that the Commission was required by Article 6.4 to provide timely opportunities to the Chinese interested parties to see such "information".

---

76 European Union's appellant's submission, para. 260. (original emphasis)

77 European Union's appellant's submission, para. 268 (referring to Panel Report, *Guatemala – Cement II*, para. 8.230).

78 PCNs contain the following elements identified by the Commission: type of fasteners (by CN code); strength/hardness; coating; presence of chrome on coating; diameter; and length/thickness. (See Panel Report, para. 7.293)

79 European Union's appellant's submission, para. 274.

(b) Whether the "Information" Was Made Available to the Interested Parties in a "Timely" Manner within the Meaning of Article 6.4 of the *Anti-Dumping Agreement*

54. The European Union claims that the Panel failed to conduct an objective assessment of the facts when finding that the European Union acted inconsistently with Article 6.4 of the *Anti-Dumping Agreement* by not providing a timely opportunity for Chinese producers to see information regarding the product types on the basis of which normal value was established. Specifically, the European Union submits that the Panel disregarded certain critical evidence and thus failed to consider the evidence before it in its totality, as required by Article 11 of the DSU.

55. The European Union recalls that the Panel relied on the final General Disclosure Document, issued on 3 November 2008, to conclude that, for the first time during the investigation, the Chinese interested parties were informed that "the Commission based its normal value determination on 'product types', as opposed to PCNs", and that the General Disclosure Document did not "provide any information as to the relevant characteristics of those groups, or how they were determined".[80] However, the European Union argues, the Panel disregarded certain evidence on the record that contradicts this factual finding. Specifically, the Information Document[81], issued on 4 August 2008, contains the same paragraphs as those in the General Disclosure Document that the Panel referred to, with the exact same references to the use of "product types". The Information Document, signalling the use of "product types", was thus sent to all interested parties for comments three months before the issuance of the General Disclosure Document, yet no request to see the characteristics that formed the basis for the product types was received until 8 November 2008. Moreover, the Panel also ignored the fact that the Commission's decision to group product types according to the strength class and the distinction between standard and special fasteners was based on arguments and information submitted by the Chinese interested parties during the investigation. Indeed, the Chinese interested parties were able to make presentations on exactly those elements that were used by the Commission to group product types. Thus, in the European Union's view, it is clear that the interested parties had a timely opportunity to see information on the product types and to present their views.

56. The European Union further submits that, even assuming that the interested parties were only informed of the use of product types in the General Disclosure Document, the fact that the European Union ultimately disclosed the basis for the product types to the Chinese producers remains unchanged. On the basis of this disclosed information, a Chinese interested party submitted com-

---

[80] European Union's appellant's submission, para. 283 (quoting Panel Report, para. 7.485).

[81] European Commission, Anti-dumping proceeding concerning imports of certain iron or steel fasteners originating in the People's Republic of China, Non-imposition of provisional anti-dumping measures, 4 August 2008 (Panel Exhibit CHN-17).

ments in a letter dated 24 November 2008, in which it did not request an extension of time for making further presentations or submit any evidence relating to the need to make adjustments for differences affecting price comparability.[82] In the European Union's view, this letter, which the Panel ignored, demonstrates that a presentation was made on the basis of the "information" provided and therefore that the "information" was made available in a timely manner.

(c) The Panel's Finding under Article 6.2 of the *Anti-Dumping Agreement*

57. The European Union maintains that, because it has demonstrated that the Panel's finding under Article 6.4 was flawed, the Panel's "purely consequential" finding under Article 6.2 was also in error.[83] In addition, the European Union submits that Article 6.2 cannot be read to constitute a mere reiteration of the right under Article 6.4 to see the information.

58. The European Union contends that the Panel made a purely consequential finding of violation of Article 6.2 when it considered that the violation of Article 6.4 on access to information also constituted a violation of the general right of defence allegedly set forth in Article 6.2 of the *Anti-Dumping Agreement*. The European Union contends that the Panel made the error of reading the obligation in Article 6.4 into Article 6.2, thus erroneously collapsing both provisions, even though Article 6.2 sets forth an important but limited and specific obligation of its own. The European Union finds support for this view in the panel's finding in *Korea – Certain Paper* that Article 6.2 does not "address interested parties' right to see the information on the record".[84] The European Union further argues that the first sentence of Article 6.2, referring to the "full opportunity for the defence of [interested parties'] interests" cannot "be read as a catch-all due process provision", because doing so "would effectively render redundant *all* of the other provisions of Article 6 which impose specific obligations on investigating authorities".[85]

(d) Conclusion

59. In sum, the European Union asserts that a proper interpretation of the relevant provisions, as well as a proper assessment of the facts and evidence on the record, should have led the Panel to conclude that no violation of Article 6.4, and thus no consequential violation of Article 6.2, had been demonstrated. Therefore, the European Union requests the Appellate Body to reverse the Panel's finding that the European Union acted inconsistently with Articles 6.4

---

[82] Letter dated 24 November 2008 from Van Bael & Bellis to the European Commission on behalf of Kunshan Chenghe Standard Component Co. Ltd. (Panel Exhibit EU-12).

[83] European Union's appellant's submission, para. 275.

[84] European Union's appellant's submission, para. 276 (quoting Panel Report, *Korea – Certain Paper*, para. 7.306).

[85] European Union's appellant's submission, para. 277. (original emphasis)

and 6.2 of the *Anti-Dumping Agreement* concerning the product types used for purposes of normal value determination.

4. *The Panel's Findings under Articles 6.5 and 6.5.1 of the Anti-Dumping Agreement Regarding Non-Confidential Questionnaire Responses*

60. The European Union requests the Appellate Body to reverse the Panel's findings that the European Union acted inconsistently with Articles 6.5 and 6.5.1 of the *Anti-Dumping Agreement* with respect to confidentiality requests and non-confidential summaries of confidential information received in the fasteners investigation. Specifically, the European Union contends that the Panel erred in finding that the Commission acted inconsistently with Article 6.5.1 because it failed to require that domestic producers furnish appropriate statements of the reasons why information submitted in confidence was not susceptible of summary, and with Article 6.5 because it treated as confidential information received from the analogue country producer, Pooja Forge, without examining whether "good cause" supported this confidential treatment.

(a) Non-Confidential Summaries of Domestic Producers' Questionnaire Responses

61. The European Union claims that the Panel erred in its interpretation and application of the obligations contained in Article 6.5.1 of the *Anti-Dumping Agreement* when it found that the Commission failed to require domestic producers to provide "appropriate" statements of the reasons why summarization of confidential information was not possible. In the European Union's view, Article 6.5.1 imposes only a "best endeavours" obligation on investigating authorities to require parties to provide non-confidential summaries of information submitted in confidence, or, in the alternative, a statement of the reasons explaining why summarization is not possible.[86] The European Union contends that the Panel erred in finding that Article 6.5.1 further obliges investigating authorities to ensure that such summaries or statements of reasons are "appropriate".[87]

62. Under the interpretation of Article 6.5 of the *Anti-Dumping Agreement* proffered by the European Union, the only obligations imposed on investigating authorities are: (1) not to disclose confidential information without the specific permission of the submitting party; and (2) to require interested parties to provide non-confidential summaries of information submitted in confidence.[88] The European Union argues that Article 6.5 is therefore concerned "first and foremost" with assuring parties that information submitted in confidence will be treated as confidential and will not be disclosed without their permission.[89] Article 6.5.1, then, imposes a "best endeavours" obligation on authorities to require

---

[86] European Union's appellant's submission, para. 298.
[87] European Union's appellant's submission, para. 310.
[88] European Union's appellant's submission, para. 314.
[89] European Union's appellant's submission, para. 316.

that parties provide a non-confidential summary of information submitted in confidence so that other interested parties have a reasonable understanding of the substance of the confidential information.[90] In the European Union's view, it is also "permissible" for submitting parties not to summarize certain information, as long as they indicate that summarization is not possible, and provide a "statement of the reasons" as to why such summarization is not possible.[91] The European Union claims that, because Article 6.5 does not allow an authority to disregard information properly treated as confidential, regardless of whether or not a non-confidential summary or statement of reasons is provided, Article 6.5.1 cannot be read strictly to require that such summaries or statements be provided.[92] "Absent the necessary stick" that would allow an authority to penalize noncompliance, the European Union insists that Article 6.5.1 can only impose a "best efforts" obligation on authorities to "push interested parties to be as transparent as possible".[93] The European Union does not see that any "risk of abuse" would result from such an interpretation, as the Panel warned, as long as the request for confidential treatment is warranted.[94]

63. The European Union argues that prior WTO panels that interpreted Article 6.5.1 of the *Anti-Dumping Agreement* as imposing a duty on investigating authorities to require parties to submit a statement of reasons described the "outer boundaries of the obligation imposed by Article 6.5.1".[95] The panel's reasoning in *Mexico – Steel Pipes and Tubes* supports this argument, and stated that Articles 6.5 and 6.5.1 of the *Anti-Dumping Agreement* do not contain any obligation with regard to how an authority should comply with the requirements thereunder.[96] The European Union further alleges that the Panel misinterpreted the findings of the panel in *Mexico – Olive Oil* when it relied on that case for its conclusion that the *pro forma* "general statements" of the domestic producers were not sufficient to constitute an appropriate statement of reasons as to why summarization of confidential information was not possible.[97]

(b) Confidential Treatment of Information Obtained from Pooja Forge

64. The European Union contends that the Panel erred in making findings under Article 6.5 of the *Anti-Dumping Agreement* with regard to the confidential treatment of Pooja Forge's questionnaire responses, and that, substantively, the Panel also erred in its application of the chapeau of Article 6.5 to Pooja Forge. Specifically, the European Union argues that the claims relating to Pooja Forge's

[90] European Union's appellant's submission, para. 317.
[91] *Ibid.*
[92] European Union's appellant's submission, para. 320.
[93] European Union's appellant's submission, para. 321.
[94] European Union's appellant's submission, para. 322.
[95] European Union's appellant's submission, para. 327.
[96] European Union's appellant's submission, para. 328.
[97] European Union's appellant's submission, para. 329.

questionnaire response were not contained in China's panel request[98], and therefore not within the Panel's terms of reference, and that the Panel thus erred in making findings in this respect, contrary to Article 7.1 of the DSU. In the alternative, the European Union alleges that the manner in which China pursued its claim under Article 6.5, and the manner in which the Panel dealt with this claim, deprived the European Union of its due process rights. If the Appellate Body determines that the Panel did not err in considering this claim to be within its terms of reference and making findings on it, the European Union argues that the Panel nevertheless erred in its application of the chapeau of Article 6.5 because the requirement to show "good cause" in support of a request for confidential treatment applies only to "interested parties" and does not apply to analogue country producers.

(i) Terms of reference and due process

65. The European Union claims that the Panel did not have jurisdiction over China's claim under Article 6.5 relating to Pooja Forge's questionnaire responses, because this claim was not included in China's panel request as required under Article 6.2 of the DSU. The relevant portion of China's panel request did not mention the Indian producer, Pooja Forge, and "unambiguously states that China brings a claim only with regard to domestic producers".[99] The European Union acknowledges that it did not formally raise this challenge before the Panel, but states that the Panel had an obligation to examine its jurisdiction on its own motion, and that it failed to do so. In *Mexico – Corn Syrup (Article 21.5 – US)*, the Appellate Body explained that "panels cannot simply ignore issues which go to the root of their jurisdiction"[100], and in *Guatemala – Cement I*, it found that a panel must determine whether a party has "properly identified a relevant antidumping measure in its panel request" before it may find that a dispute is properly before it.[101] In making findings on this claim, then, the European Union argues, the Panel violated Article 7.1 of the DSU.[102]

66. Should the Appellate Body find that China's claims with respect to Pooja Forge's questionnaire response were within the Panel's terms of reference, the European Union argues that, in the alternative, the Panel violated its obligations under Article 11 of the DSU because the manner in which it dealt with this claim deprived the European Union of its rights to due process. Citing *US – Continued Zeroing*, the European Union argues that the Panel used its questions impermissibly to "make the case"[103] for China. Only in response to Panel Question 71 did

---

[98] European Union's appellant's submission, paras. 335-339.

[99] European Union's appellant's submission, para. 335.

[100] European Union's appellant's submission, para. 337 (quoting Appellate Body Report, *Mexico – Corn Syrup (Article 21.5 – US)*, para. 36).

[101] European Union's appellant's submission, para. 338 (quoting Appellate Body Report, *Guatemala – Cement I*, para. 88).

[102] European Union's appellant's submission, para. 339.

[103] European Union's appellant's submission, paras. 342 and 343 (quoting Appellate Body Report, *US – Continued Zeroing*, para. 343).

China begin to formulate its claims with respect to Pooja Forge's questionnaire response[104]; and only in response to Panel Question 103, after the second substantive meeting of the Panel with the parties, did China "finally clarif[y] that it actually made a claim under both Articles 6.5 and 6.5.1 with respect to Pooja Forge's questionnaire response".[105]

67. The European Union points out that the Panel itself admitted that the claim was unclear, and that this lack of clarity led it to pose questions to China in this regard.[106] Despite the Panel's suggestion to the contrary, the European Union claimed throughout this process that it was "not in a position to provide adequate responses due to the confusion" about China's claim.[107] For these reasons, the European Union requests the Appellate Body to reverse the Panel's finding that the European Union acted inconsistently with Article 6.5 of the *Anti-Dumping Agreement* with respect to confidential treatment of information in the questionnaire response of the Indian producer, Pooja Forge.

(ii) Application of Article 6.5 to analogue country producers

68. Substantively, the European Union argues that the Panel erred in its interpretation and application of Article 6.5 when it found that the Commission failed to require the Indian producer, Pooja Forge, to demonstrate that "good cause" existed for the confidential treatment of certain product type information in its questionnaire response. According to the European Union, Article 6.5 applies only to "parties to an investigation", which includes "interested parties" as defined in Article 6.11 of the *Anti-Dumping Agreement*.[108] The European Union contends that the Panel implicitly acknowledged this interpretation when it used the term "interested parties" in making its findings on this claim.[109] The definition of "interested parties" does not include producers from analogue third countries, and the European Union points out that it did not designate Pooja Forge an "interested party" in its regulation regarding the fasteners investigation, which it could have done under the last sentence of Article 6.11.[110] Therefore, because Pooja Forge could not be considered as an "interested party" in the fasteners investigation, the requirement in Article 6.5 to show "good cause" did not apply to it.[111]

69. The European Union emphasizes that this argument "is not pure textualism".[112] Rather, it is the interpretation that "makes the most sense in light of the

---

104 European Union's appellant's submission, para. 343.
105 European Union's appellant's submission, para. 344.
106 European Union's appellant's submission, para. 345 (quoting Panel Report, para. 7.522).
107 European Union's appellant's submission, para. 346.
108 European Union's appellant's submission, para. 349.
109 European Union's appellant's submission, para. 350.
110 European Union's appellant's submission, paras. 352 and 353 (quoting the Definitive Regulation, *supra*, footnote 4).
111 European Union's appellant's submission, para. 354.
112 European Union's appellant's submission, para. 356.

realities of investigations involving [NME] countries".[113] In NME investigations, authorities must rely on the willingness of third country producers to cooperate with the investigation, although they have no obligation to do so. The difficulty inherent in this situation is evidenced by the fact that the Commission found only two producers willing to cooperate in the fasteners investigation, of which only one, Pooja Forge, submitted information sufficiently detailed to serve as the basis for the establishment of normal value. The European Union argues that its investigating authorities have no coercive powers over analogue country producers, and therefore it would not be practicable to apply the requirements of Article 6.5 to these producers. According to the European Union, having reliable and verifiable third-party data is a benefit to the investigation, even if that data is provided on a confidential basis and without an assertion of "good cause".[114]

5. *The Panel's Findings under Articles 6.2 and 6.4 of the Anti-Dumping Agreement Regarding the Disclosure of the Identity of the Complainants*

70. The European Union requests the Appellate Body to reverse the Panel's determination that China's claim under Articles 6.4 and 6.2 of the *Anti-Dumping Agreement* regarding the identity of the complainants was within its terms of reference. Although the Panel found that the Commission had not violated these provisions by failing to disclose the identity of the complainants and the supporters of the complaint, the European Union nevertheless argues that the Panel should never have made findings on these claims because they were not included in China's panel request. In the European Union's view, Articles 6.4 and 6.2 contain multiple obligations, and it is therefore not sufficient simply to mention them without further elaboration.

71. Specifically, the European Union claims that China's panel request does not refer to the identity of the complainants within its claims under Articles 6.2 and 6.4, and the European Union stresses that, in this case, the mere listing of Articles 6.2 and 6.4 was not sufficient to present the problem clearly.[115] According to the European Union, the Panel mischaracterized the European Union's argument as claiming that China failed to provide "a brief summary of the legal basis for a claim under Articles 6,4 and 6.2". In the European Union's view, "[t]he issue was whether the way in which the panel request was made presented the problem clearly".[116] Specifically, the European Union challenges the Panel's interpretation that "the nature of the rights and obligations set forth in Articles 6.4 and 6.2 is such that a reference to these provisions, without further explanation, could suffice to put the responding Member on notice of the nature of the claim that the complainant might bring".[117] It argues that, while the Appellate

[113] *Ibid.*
[114] European Union appellant's submission, para. 357.
[115] European Union's appellant's submission, paras. 365 and 372.
[116] European Union appellant's submission, paras. 369 and 370.
[117] European Union's appellant's submission, paras. 378 and 379.

Body has found that in some instances it may be sufficient to list the provisions of WTO law under which a complaining party may later develop its arguments, the Appellate Body has also stated in *Korea – Dairy* that this would not be appropriate where the provisions listed contain not just one, distinct obligation, but multiple obligations.[118] According to the European Union, the fact that China made a claim under both Article 6.2 and Article 6.4 suggests that at least two obligations are necessarily involved, and that, furthermore, "these multiple obligations apply in multiple situations in the course of an anti-dumping investigation".[119]

B. Arguments of China – Appellee

1. The Panel's Findings Regarding Article 9(5) of the Basic AD Regulation "As Such"

72. China requests the Appellate Body to reject the European Union's appeal and to uphold the Panel's findings that Article 9(5) of the Basic AD Regulation is inconsistent with Articles 6.10, 9.2, and 18.4 of the *Anti-Dumping Agreement*, Article I:1 of the GATT 1994, and Article XVI:4 of the *WTO Agreement*.[120]

(a) The Scope of Article 9(5) of the Basic AD Regulation

73. China submits that the "meaning" or "scope" of Article 9(5) of the Basic AD Regulation is an issue of fact that the Appellate Body is not competent to review pursuant to Article 17.6 of the DSU. However, in the event that the Appellate Body were to consider itself competent to review this issue, China submits that the Panel correctly found that Article 9(5) concerns not only the imposition of anti-dumping duties but also the calculation of dumping margins.[121]

74. China submits that the issue of the "meaning" or "scope" of Article 9(5) of the Basic AD Regulation is an issue of fact that can only be reviewed in an appeal made on the basis of a claim under Article 11 of the DSU. Therefore, it rejects the European Union's argument that the scope of Article 9(5) of the Basic AD Regulation is a legal issue and hence subject to appellate review pursuant to Article 17.6 of the DSU. China contends that, since the "meaning" or "scope" of Article 9(5) was not clear on its face, the Panel's examination necessarily involved a factual assessment in relation to the operation of this provision in practice. As the Appellate Body stated in *China – Auto Parts*, "there may be instances in which a panel's assessment of municipal law will go beyond the text of an instrument on its face, in which case further examination may be required, and may involve factual elements".[122] In that dispute, the Appellate Body also

[118] European Union's appellant's submission, para. 381.
[119] European Union's appellant's submission, para. 382.
[120] China's appellee's submission, para. 364.
[121] China's appellee's submission, para. 67.
[122] China's appellee's submission, para. 73 (quoting Appellate Body Reports, *China – Auto Parts*, para. 225).

clarified that whenever a panel is required, in order to determine the meaning of a Member's municipal law, to "go beyond the text of an instrument on its face", the Appellate Body will not interfere lightly with the factual findings made by the panel in that respect.[123] China recalls that, in the case at issue, the "meaning" or "scope" of Article 9(5) was determined by the Panel not solely on the face of this provision, but also involved factual assessments regarding its operation in practice. Given that the "meaning" or "scope" of Article 9(5) of the Basic AD Regulation is an issue of fact and that the European Union failed to raise it under Article 11 of the DSU as a failure by the Panel to make an objective assessment of the facts, such a factual issue is not within the scope of the present appeal.

75. China contends that Article 9(5) of the Basic AD Regulation concerns not only the imposition of anti-dumping duties but also the determination of dumping margins. The fact that Article 9(5) does not contain the words "margins of dumping" is not sufficient, in China's view, automatically to conclude that Article 9(5) does not deal with dumping margins at all and relates only to the imposition of anti-dumping duties. In this regard, China agrees with the Panel's reasoning that it is necessary to look at the operation of Article 9(5) as a whole in order to clarify the meaning of that provision and, in particular, to determine whether it also concerns the calculation of dumping margins even if it does not expressly say so. The Panel correctly went beyond the mere text of Article 9(5) and also examined its context and operation, in accordance with the principles established by the Appellate Body in *US – Corrosion-Resistant Steel Sunset Review* and in *US – Carbon Steel*, in order to ascertain the meaning of that provision.[124]

76. China contests the European Union's assertion that the examination of the context provided by other articles of the Basic AD Regulation, such as Articles 2, 9(4), and 9(6), confirms that Article 9(5) relates only to the imposition of anti-dumping duties. However, China notes that none of these other provisions addresses the issue of whether the dumping margin for exporters or producers from NMEs is to be determined on an individual or country-wide basis. China disagrees with the European Union's contention that Article 9(5) of the Basic AD Regulation mirrors Article 9.2 of the *Anti-Dumping Agreement* concerning the imposition of duties and the obligation to determine individual margins of dumping for each known exporter or producer. Even assuming that this were correct, China points out that there is no provision in the Basic AD Regulation that mirrors Article 6.10 of the *Anti-Dumping Agreement* concerning dumping margin determinations. China submits that Article 9(4) of the Basic AD Regulation merely sets out the principle that the duty rate must not exceed the margin of dumping, but does not state how the dumping margin should be determined, or whether that margin has to be determined on an individual basis or on a country-wide basis for exporters from NMEs.[125] China thus contends that Article 9(5) is

[123] See China's appellee's submission, para. 74.

[124] China's appellee's submission, para. 82 (referring to Appellate Body Report, *US – Corrosion-Resistant Steel Sunset Review*, para. 168; and Appellate Body Report, *US – Carbon Steel*, para. 157).

[125] China's appellee's submission, para. 93.

the provision governing two separate, but very closely related, issues, namely, the determination of dumping margins and the imposition of anti-dumping duties. Therefore, meeting the five requirements for individual treatment listed under Article 9(5) not only determines whether the exporting producer is subject to an individual anti-dumping duty but also whether it qualifies for the determination of an individual dumping margin.

77. China notes that the operation of Article 9(5) of the Basic AD Regulation further confirms that this provision deals with both the determination of dumping margins as well as the imposition of duties. Contrary to what the European Union asserts, China contends that whether a Chinese exporter or producer is entitled to a determination of an individual dumping margin does not flow from Article 9(4), which establishes the requirement that the dumping margin be the ceiling of the anti-dumping duty, but rather flows from Article 9(5) of the Basic AD Regulation. Indeed, during the Panel proceedings, the European Union confirmed that the fact that an exporting producer is a "non-IT supplier", and therefore does not fulfil the Article 9(5) conditions, implies not only that it will receive a country-wide anti-dumping duty but also that no individual dumping margin will be determined for this exporting producer.[126] China recalls that, in order to impose an anti-dumping duty, the investigating authorities first have to determine a dumping margin, and thus considers it logical that an individual anti-dumping duty can only be imposed if the underlying dumping margin was also calculated on an individual basis.[127]

78. Thus, China submits that the examination of how Article 9(5) operates in practice clearly confirms the Panel's conclusion reached on the basis of an analysis of Article 9(5) in the context of the other provisions of the Basic AD Regulation, namely, that Article 9(5) deals not only with the imposition of anti-dumping duties but also with the determination of the dumping margins.[128]

(b) Article 6.10 of the *Anti-Dumping Agreement*

79. China submits that the Panel properly concluded that Article 9(5) of the Basic AD Regulation is inconsistent with Article 6.10 of the *Anti-Dumping Agreement* because it conditions the calculation of individual margins for producers from NMEs on the fulfilment of the IT test. China considers that the Panel did not err in finding that Article 6.10 of the *Anti-Dumping Agreement* contains a strict rule that an individual dumping margin be calculated for each known producer or exporter and that sampling is the only exception to that rule.[129]

80. China submits that the use of the word "shall" in the first sentence of Article 6.10 establishes the mandatory nature of this provision, and contends that if

[126] China's appellee's submission, para. 98 (referring to European Union's response to Panel Question 6(a)).
[127] China's appellee's submission, para. 106.
[128] China's appellee's submission, para. 107.
[129] China's appellee's submission, para. 111.

the drafters' intention indeed had been merely to express a preference, as the European Union contends, they would have used the word "should" instead of "shall". Likewise, they could have expressly mentioned that the derogation from the general rule was permitted in situations other than the one mentioned in the second sentence of Article 6.10. However, the drafters did not use any such words. In China's view, the expression "as a rule" is necessary to the extent that it creates a "link between the obligation contained in Article 6.10 first sentence which constitutes the rule and the exception to that rule included in the second sentence of that provision".[130] China asserts that the structure of Article 6.10 confirms the conclusion that the first sentence contains the main rule ("the authorities shall ... **determine**"), whereas the second sentence lays down the exception to that rule ("In cases where ... such a **determination** [is] impracticable").[131]

81. China points out that, even in cases where sampling is used, Article 6.10.2 requires investigating authorities to determine an individual margin for any exporter or producer not initially selected who submits the necessary information in time, except when this would be unduly burdensome to the authorities due to the large number of exporters or producers requesting individual examination. Therefore, Article 6.10.2 confirms the fundamental importance of the rule that margins of dumping be determined on an individual basis for each exporter or producer.[132] Indeed, reading Article 6.10, first sentence, as merely establishing a "preference", as the European Union submits, would mean that investigating authorities are merely invited to determine individual dumping margins. This conclusion would, in China's view, render the first sentence of Article 6.10 inutile.[133]

82. China recalls that a finding of the panel in *Mexico – Anti-Dumping Measures on Rice* confirmed that sampling is the only exception to the obligation contained in Article 6.10, first sentence. In that dispute, the panel stated that "[t]he exception to this rule is the case in which there are too many foreign producers or exporters so that an individual margin of dumping will only be calculated for a representative sample".[134] The use of the term "the" preceding the word "exception" indicates that the panel did not consider the second sentence of Article 6.10 to be merely an exception among various possible deviations from the rule. China characterizes the panel reports cited by the European Union, namely, *Korea – Certain Paper* and *EC – Salmon (Norway)*, as irrelevant to the point at issue, since neither panel in those disputes attempted to clarify whether the exception provided in Article 6.10, second sentence, is the only exception to the rule set out in the first sentence. China also considers that the European Union's reference to other provisions of the *Anti-Dumping Agreement* that would "pro-

---

130 China's appellee's submission, para. 114.

131 China's appellee's submission, para. 121. (original boldface)

132 China's appellee's submission, para. 125.

133 China's appellee's submission, para. 118.

134 China's appellee's submission, para. 126 (quoting Panel Report, *Mexico – Anti-Dumping Measures on Rice*, para. 7.137).

vide investigating authorities with certain flexibility in the application of the relevant rules"[135] does not support the European Union's position. On the contrary, Articles 2.4, 2.5, 5.8, 9.3.1, and 11.4 of the *Anti-Dumping Agreement*, by including the word "normally", rather support the view that, if the drafters had intended not to establish a strict obligation under the first sentence of Article 6.10, they would have used clearer wording to that effect, just like they did in the Articles referred to by the European Union.

83. China further asserts that none of the examples presented by the European Union convincingly shows that there are other hypothetical situations, apart from sampling, that may justify not calculating an individual margin for each known exporter or producer. Notably, in the case where an exporter or producer that initially agreed to cooperate decides to cease cooperating in the course of the investigation, the fact that the dumping margin for that exporter is based on best information available and, therefore, is *de facto* the same as the one determined for the other non-cooperating exporters does not render such dumping margin non-individual.[136] Similarly, in the case of an exporter who has not produced the product concerned during the period of investigation but merely "traded" this product, the fact that the investigating authorities may not calculate an individual dumping margin for this "trader" does not constitute an exception to Article 6.10, first sentence; rather, it is a possibility flowing directly from the general obligation in Article 6.10, first sentence, to determine an individual margin for "each known exporter **or** producer".[137] Lastly, in cases where a known producer did not export the product concerned during the period of investigation, China notes that no dumping margin—whether individual or collective—can be determined for a non-exporting producer, and once such a producer starts exporting it will receive, pursuant to Article 9.5 of the *Anti-Dumping Agreement*, an individual dumping margin unless that producer is related to existing producers or exporters.[138] China contends that the other two examples presented by the European Union are based on the European Union's unilateral practice and therefore are not relevant to the interpretation of Article 6.10, first sentence.[139]

84. China also rejects the European Union's alternative argument that Article 9(5) of the Basic AD Regulation is consistent with Article 6.10 of the *Anti-Dumping Agreement* because it "aims at identifying the relevant supplier in accordance with Article 6.10, first sentence".[140] Indeed, China contests the European Union's claim that "Article 9(5) of the Basic Regulation follows the same logic [as the *Korea – Certain Paper* test] and seeks to identify the relevant supplier in the specific context of imports from non-market economy countries",

---

[135] China's appellee's submission, para. 151 (quoting European Union's appellant's submission, para. 133).

[136] China's appellee's submission, para. 139.

[137] China's appellee's submission, para. 143. (original boldface)

[138] China's appellee's submission, para. 149.

[139] China's appellee's submission, paras. 146 and 147.

[140] China's appellee's submission, para. 165 (quoting European Union's appellant's submission, p. 47, heading (b)).

which is either a Chinese exporter acting independently from the State (IT supplier), or the State together with related export entities (non-IT suppliers) that are not acting independently from the State.[141] According to China, the European Union's anti-dumping practice confirms that the purpose of Article 9(5) is not to identify the "exporter" or "producer" within the meaning of Article 6.10, first sentence. Indeed, China notes that the IT test provided for in Article 9(5) of the Basic AD Regulation is only applied once the exporters or producers have been identified by the Commission. Therefore, the ultimate purpose of the IT test is not, as the European Union asserts, to identify the single supplier of the product under investigation. If the purpose of the IT test was indeed to identify the relevant supplier, such a test would not be carried out after the supplier has been identified by the Commission, but rather in order to identify such a supplier in the first place. China agrees with the Panel's finding that the fact that "the Commission first determine[s] which, if any, groups of companies should be considered as a single producer or exporter, and then applies the IT test to each 'single' producer or exporter it finds on the basis of that test ... clearly shows that the Commission itself distinguishes the test aimed at determining whether separate legal entities should be treated as a single exporter/producer for purposes of dumping determinations, from the IT test under Article 9(5) of the Basic AD Regulation".[142]

85. China further submits that, contrary to the *Korea – Certain Paper* test, Article 9(5) presumes that in NMEs all exporters or producers are related to the State and places the burden of proving the contrary on each exporter or producer, who are requested to provide evidence of complete fulfilment of the IT requirements under Article 9(5) in order to rebut this presumption. By contrast, under the *Korea – Certain Paper* test, it is for the investigating authorities to establish that there is a "sufficiently close structural and commercial relationship between individual producers to justify treating them as a single entity".[143] The Panel, therefore, correctly concluded that the "difference in the starting points of the two tests, and the different evidentiary burdens involved, ... show how different these two tests are".[144] China also notes that the Commission applies a test similar to the one in *Korea – Certain Paper* in all its anti-dumping investigations, irrespective of whether the importing country is a market economy or an NME; however, in cases where imports from NMEs are concerned, the Commission additionally applies the IT test.[145]

86. China recalls that the European Union justifies the reversal of the burden of proof under the IT test as compared to the *Korea – Certain Paper* test on the basis of the mere assertion that there is a presumption of State control in NMEs. For China, such a presumption lacks any legal basis. China notes that there are

[141] China's appellee's submission, para. 173 (referring to European Union's appellant's submission, para. 142).

[142] China's appellee's submission, para. 182 (quoting Panel Report, para. 7.97).

[143] China's appellee's submission, para. 186.

[144] China's appellee's submission, para. 187 (quoting Panel Report, para. 7.95).

[145] China's appellee's submission, para. 189.

also many State-owned or State-controlled companies in market economy countries, and fails to see why such companies receive an individual dumping margin whereas the same does not apply to the State-owned or State-controlled companies in NMEs. China also notes that the European Union refers to another presumption in order to justify the previous presumption of "State control", namely, that China is an NME and that the European Union is allowed to treat China as an NME by virtue of China's Accession Protocol. In this respect, China submits that China's Accession Protocol merely authorizes certain WTO Members to apply a temporary and limited derogation from certain rules of the *Anti-Dumping Agreement* concerning the determination of normal value, but in no case contains any general acknowledgement that China is an NME.[146] In any event, China points out that whether China is a market economy or an NME is irrelevant for the purposes of this case, because the first sentence of Article 6.10 of the *Anti-Dumping Agreement* does not distinguish between imports from market economies or NMEs in relation to the determination of dumping margins. China further notes that the Panel expressly and fully addressed this point. Accordingly, there is no basis for the European Union's additional claim that the Panel failed to act in accordance with its duty under Article 11 of the DSU to make an objective assessment of the facts.[147]

87. China further asserts that there are important differences between the test in *Korea – Certain Paper* and the Article 9(5) IT test because the nature of the relationship examined in these tests is fundamentally different: whereas the *Korea – Certain Paper* test examines the linkages between companies, the Article 9(5) IT test focuses on the relationship between companies and the State. For China, there is a fundamental difference between the examination of the structural and commercial relationship between different companies and the examination under Article 9(5), which relates to the political influence or interference the State exercises on the way business is conducted by the exporting producers concerned.[148] The panel in *Korea – Certain Paper* reached the conclusion that there was a close structural and commercial relationship among three companies on the basis of several factual findings, namely: (i) that the parent company had considerable controlling power; (ii) that there was commonality with respect to company management; (iii) that the companies harmonized their commercial activities to achieve common corporate objectives; and (iv) that the parent company acted practically as the sole channel for domestic sales. China contends that the IT test criteria in Article 9(5) relate to elements that are proper to the exercise of a governmental function in general, rather than to elements relevant to establishing State control, either *de jure* or *de facto*. Indeed, the IT test involves an assessment of whether exporters are free to repatriate capital and profits, whether export prices are freely determined, whether the majority of shares belong to private persons, whether exchange rate conversions are carried out at the market rate, and whether State interference is not such as to permit circumvention of

---

146 China's appellee's submission, para. 195.
147 China's appellee's submission, para. 197.
148 China's appellee's submission, para. 204.

anti-dumping measures when individual exporters are given different rates of duties. Therefore, in essence, the nature of the relationship examined by the IT test is not comparable to the one in *Korea – Certain Paper*. China further submits that, even assuming that the IT test criteria were seeking to identify circumstances of State control, those criteria are so strict that they disqualify Chinese exporters from individual treatment even in cases where there is no close relationship.[149]

88. Lastly, China notes that even assuming that the European Union seeks to identify a single exporter or producer by applying the IT test under Article 9(5), no individual dumping margin is ultimately calculated for the "State". Indeed, the principle that an "individual dumping margin" needs to be determined for each exporter or producer would require that an individual dumping margin be determined for the "State", that is, the group of companies found not to fulfil the IT conditions. According to China, the European Union does not determine such an individual dumping margin for the "State", but rather it determines a country-wide "residual" dumping margin that is, in most cases, based on "facts available" and applicable to all cooperating non-IT exporting producers as well as to all non-cooperating exporting producers.[150]

(c) Article 9.2 of the *Anti-Dumping Agreement*

89. China submits that the Panel correctly concluded that Article 9(5) of the Basic AD Regulation is inconsistent with Article 9.2 of the *Anti-Dumping Agreement*. Article 9.2 requires that anti-dumping duties be imposed on an individual basis and that a country-wide duty can only be imposed in the circumstances expressly referred to in Article 9.2, third sentence. Article 9.2, third sentence, however, does not authorize the automatic imposition of a country-wide duty in the case of imports from NMEs. Furthermore, the "State" cannot be regarded as a "supplier" or a "source" within the meaning of Article 9.2 of the *Anti-Dumping Agreement*.[151]

90. China submits that the fact that Article 9.2, first sentence, refers to the imposition of anti-dumping duties with respect to a "product" does not entail an authorization to impose country-wide duties. In China's view, there is no contradiction in acknowledging that the imposition of anti-dumping duties is made with respect to "products" as well as for each "producer" or "exporter" concerned. Indeed, the panel in *EC – Bed Linen* stated that "individual dumping margins are determined for each producer or exporter under investigation, and for each product under investigation".[152] China agrees with the Panel's interpretation of the word "sources" as necessarily referring to "producers" and/or "exporters" of the product under investigation. This reading finds support in Article 8 of the *Anti-Dumping Agreement*, which refers to "sources from which price

149 China's appellee's submission, para. 209.
150 China's appellee's submission, para. 211.
151 China's appellee's submission, para. 219.
152 China's appellee's submission, para. 224 (quoting Panel Report, *EC – Bed Linen*, para. 6.118).

undertakings have been accepted", when read in connection with Article 9.2, first sentence. By definition, only exporters—and not countries—may offer such price undertakings. China also finds support for that conclusion in the language of Article 9.2, itself referring to the "sources found to be dumped". Since dumping is determined on an individual basis, it follows that "sources found to be dumped" need to refer to exporters individually found to be dumping.[153] China characterizes the European Union's reference to the term "injury" in Article 9.2, first sentence, as entirely irrelevant for the purposes of determining whether Article 9.2 contains the obligation that anti-dumping duties must be imposed on an individual basis. Whereas the term "injury" is a country-wide rather than a company-specific concept, the panel in *EC – Salmon (Norway)* pointed out that "[t]he [*Anti-Dumping Agreement*] makes clear that a determination of dumping is individual" even though "a single injury determination is made in each investigation".[154]

91. China rejects the European Union's reading of the term "appropriate" in Article 9.2, first sentence, as referring to the "duty rate appropriate to the country concerned", and submits that the use of the word "appropriate" rather confirms the rule that anti-dumping duties must be imposed on an individual basis. The panel in *EC – Salmon (Norway)* defined the term "appropriate" as "'proper' or 'fitting' in the context of an anti-dumping investigation".[155] In this regard, China notes that the context of an anti-dumping investigation includes the determination of the dumping margin, which must, as a rule, be calculated on an individual basis, in accordance with Articles 2 and 6.10 of the *Anti-Dumping Agreement*. Therefore, an anti-dumping duty must be deemed to be "appropriate" for a particular exporting producer when it does not exceed the individual dumping margin determined for that exporting producer. China also notes that Article 9.2, first sentence, provides that an anti-dumping duty (singular) be collected in appropriate amounts (plural) on imports from all sources.[156]

92. With respect to the interpretation of Article 9.2, second sentence, of the *Anti-Dumping Agreement*, China submits that the Panel properly found that the obligation "to name" each "supplier" necessarily implies the obligation to impose anti-dumping duties on an individual basis. China also agrees with the Panel's interpretation of the term "suppliers", in the second and third sentences of Article 9.2, as referring to the individual foreign "producers" or "exporters" of the product subject to the anti-dumping investigation. In this respect, China rejects the European Union's argument that the second sentence of Article 9.2 merely imposes an obligation "to name", and that this "naming" obligation may serve to distinguish between exporters or producers who are subject to the anti-dumping duties on that product and those new exporters who may request a review under

---

[153] China's appellee's submission, para. 226.

[154] China's appellee's submission, para. 227 (quoting Panel Report, *EC – Salmon (Norway)*, para. 7.128).

[155] China's appellee's submission, para. 228 (quoting Panel Report, *EC – Salmon (Norway)*, para. 7.704).

[156] China's appellee's submission, para. 229.

Article 9.5 of the *Anti-Dumping Agreement*. China fails to see what utility an obligation to name each supplier would have if the general obligation set out in Article 9.2 was not to determine and impose the anti-dumping duties on an individual basis.[157]

93. China points out that Articles 6.10 and 9.4 of the *Anti-Dumping Agreement* are relevant context for the purposes of interpreting Article 9.2 and confirming that it contains an obligation to impose individual anti-dumping duties on each supplier. In China's view, the obligation to determine individual dumping margins contained in Article 6.10 would be rendered meaningless if no similar rule was contained in Article 9.2. In a similar vein, if, pursuant to the second sentence of Article 9.4, an individual anti-dumping duty must be imposed on those exporters or producers not included in the sample to the extent they provided the necessary information, it logically follows that an individual anti-dumping duty must necessarily be determined for those exporters/producers that are included in the sample (in case sampling is used), as well as all the exporters/producers that have provided the necessary information (if sampling is not used).[158] When Article 9.2 of the *Anti-Dumping Agreement* is read in its context it becomes clear that the investigating authorities have the general obligation to impose anti-dumping duties on an individual basis, and that the sole exception to that rule is the one identified in the third sentence of Article 9.2.

94. China contests the European Union's submission that the fact "that Article 9.2 does not require an individual imposition of anti-dumping duties on all known exporters or producers is also supported by the purpose of imposing anti-dumping duties", namely, to "offset *or* prevent dumping".[159] Article VI:2 of the GATT 1994 certainly provides that a Member may levy an anti-dumping duty on any product found to be dumped and not exceeding the dumping margin in respect of such a product "in order to offset or prevent dumping"; however, in China's view, this does not authorize Members to impose anti-dumping duties on the basis of whatever circumstances and pursuant to any methodology they wish to choose for the calculation of the margin of dumping.[160]

95. China agrees with the Panel's interpretation that the third sentence of Article 9.2 permits the imposition of country-wide duties when two conditions are met. First, there must be "several suppliers from the same country" and, second, it must be "impracticable to name all these suppliers". However, China rejects the European Union's interpretation of the term "impracticable" that leads the European Union to read Article 9.2 as permitting the imposition of anti-dumping duties on a country-wide basis in cases other than the sampling scenario. China considers that a proper interpretation of the word "impracticable" in accordance with Article 31 of the *Vienna Convention on the Law of Treaties*[161] (the "*Vienna*

[157] China's appellee's submission, para. 232.
[158] China's appellee's submission, para. 237.
[159] China's appellee's submission, para. 239 (quoting European Union's appellant's submission, para. 164 (original emphasis)).
[160] China's appellee's submission, para. 241.
[161] Done at Vienna, 23 May 1969, 1155 UNTS 331; 8 International Legal Materials 679.

Convention") does not lead to the conclusion, as the European Union submits, that the exception provided for in Article 9.2, third sentence, includes situations where the imposition of individual duties would be rendered "ineffective" (that is, by actually not offsetting or preventing dumping). The ordinary meaning of the word "impracticable" is "impossible in practice", but it does not encompass something that is "ineffective, not feasible or not suited for being used for a particular purpose".[162] China fails to see how something impossible "for practical reasons" would cover situations where the imposition of anti-dumping duties on an individual basis would be "ineffective" for the purpose of offsetting or preventing dumping.

96. China further notes that the word "impracticable" is used in other provisions of the *Anti-Dumping Agreement* and in other covered agreements. Article 6.10 of the *Anti-Dumping Agreement* expressly sets out that it is a "large number of producers or exporters" that makes individual dumping determinations "impracticable". It flows from the language of this provision that "impracticable" is something not feasible "for practical reasons". Similarly, Article 8.3 of the *Anti-Dumping Agreement* expressly establishes that an instance of impracticability is where "the number of actual or potential exporters is too great". China notes that, under the *Anti-Dumping Agreement*, the word "(im)practicable" is also used in Articles 6.1.1, 6.4, 6.13, 12.2.1, and paragraph 7 of Annex II thereto, and that in all these provisions this term refers to something which is (not) possible for practical reasons, and not to something which is (not) effective. Furthermore, the word "practicable" appears in Article 22.3 of the DSU. In this regard, the arbitrators in *EC – Bananas III (Ecuador) (Article 22.6 – EC)* emphasized the difference between the meaning of "practicable" and "effective" by stating that "the ordinary meaning of 'practicable' is 'available or useful in practice' … . In contrast, the term 'effective' connotes 'powerful in effect', 'making a strong impression', 'having an effect or result'".[163]

97. China also contests the European Union's argument that, since the purpose of imposing and collecting anti-dumping duties is to offset or prevent dumping, the imposition of duties on an individual basis becomes "impracticable" when such imposition renders the duties ineffective because they do not actually address the "source of price discrimination". China notes that the European Union fails to explain or define the vague concept of "source of price discrimination", and recalls that there is no rule in Article VI of the GATT 1994 or the *Anti-Dumping Agreement* that addresses it. China further submits that, even if the purpose of the *Anti-Dumping Agreement* is to offset or prevent dumping, nothing in the *Anti-Dumping Agreement* authorizes WTO Members to impose anti-dumping duties pursuant to any methodology they choose in clear deviation of the obligation set forth in Article 1 of the *Anti-Dumping Agreement*, which unambiguously provides that an anti-dumping measure shall only be applied

---

[162] China's appellee's submission, para. 249 (quoting European Union's appellant's submission, para. 172).

[163] China's appellee's submission, para. 264 (quoting Decision by the Arbitrators, *EC – Bananas III (Ecuador) (Article 22.6 – EC)*, paras. 70-72).

under the circumstances provided for in Article VI of the GATT 1994 and pursuant to investigations initiated and conducted in accordance with the provisions of the *Anti-Dumping Agreement*.[164] China also notes that, even assuming that the word "impracticable" would mean "ineffective", what is "impracticable" under Article 9.2, second sentence, is the action of "naming" the suppliers on an individual basis and not the action of "imposing" the duties on an individual basis.[165] Lastly, although in China's view there is no need to resort to supplementary means of interpretation within the meaning of Article 32 of the *Vienna Convention*, since the application of customary rules of interpretation enshrined in Article 31 do not leave its meaning ambiguous or obscure and do not lead to a result that is manifestly absurd or unreasonable, the *travaux préparatoires* confirm the understanding that "impracticable" only relates to the existence of "several suppliers from the same country" for the purposes of Article 9.2 of the *Anti-Dumping Agreement*.

98. In particular, China contends that an examination of the negotiating history of Article 8 of the *Kennedy Round Anti-Dumping Code* (now Article 9.2 of the *Anti-Dumping Agreement*) confirms that the drafters' aim was to clarify whether a Member would be authorized to impose anti-dumping duties only with respect to those particular exporters found to be dumped or, additionally, on all imports from the country of origin of the dumped imports.[166] China notes that no reference whatsoever to the specific issue of imports from NMEs can be found in the negotiating history of this provision. In addition, China submits that the fact that Article 2(g) of the *Kennedy Round Anti-Dumping Code* (which incorporates the second *Ad* Note to Article VI:1 of the GATT 1994) was also discussed, and eventually included in the *Anti-Dumping Code* during the Kennedy Round, does not demonstrate that the second *Ad* Note and Article 8 necessarily address the same issues.[167] On the contrary, in China's view, there is no link between the *Ad* Note and Article 9.2 of the *Anti-Dumping Agreement*.

99. China agrees with the Panel's interpretation of the terms "sources" and "suppliers" as referring to "the individual foreign producers or exporters of the product subject to the anti-dumping investigation".[168] With respect to the European Union's claim that the Chinese State can be deemed the actual "supplier", China submits that, even if the State could be regarded as a "supplier", it would nonetheless be necessary to prove that the State actually "exports" or "produces" the product concerned. In other words, the fact that the State may have some influence on the manner in which exporting producers conduct their business does not suffice to establish that the State itself is an "exporter" or a "producer". Regarding the European Union's assertion that the term "supplier" can also refer to the "actual source of price discrimination", China submits that there is no le-

[164] China's appellee's submission, para. 269.
[165] China's appellee's submission, para. 270.
[166] China's appellee's submission, paras. 274-285.
[167] China's appellee's submission, para. 286.
[168] China's appellee's submission, para. 292 (quoting Panel Report, para. 7.104).

gal basis, either in the wording of Article 9.2 or in the negotiating history of that provision, to support such a conclusion.[169]

100. China further submits that, even assuming that the words "source" or "supplier" could somehow include the concept of "actual source of price discrimination", the Panel correctly found that the State cannot be presumed to be the source of price discrimination. In China's view, the lack of any legal basis supporting such a presumption is sufficient to reject the European Union's claim and, therefore, the Panel did not fail to make an objective assessment of the matter as required by Article 11 of the DSU. Notably, the argument that the State in NMEs can be presumed to be the "source of price discrimination" flows from another presumption, namely, that China is indeed an NME, which China also contests. Indeed, China recalls that its Accession Protocol does not contain an understanding that China is an NME but merely contains the possibility, limited in time and only for specific WTO Members, to derogate from the general rules governing normal value determination. In China's view, the fact that many countries have expressly acknowledged that China is a market economy confirms this position.[170]

101. China contends that, even assuming that the terms "suppliers" or "sources" could be read as referring to the "source of price discrimination", the IT test contained in Article 9(5) of the Basic AD Regulation does not aim at identifying the "source of price discrimination". Indeed, if this were the case, there would be no reason for the European Union to apply different treatment to market economies and NMEs. China notes, instead, that, according to the European Union, the influence or interference by the State in NMEs makes the State the "source of price discrimination", whereas the same influence or interference by the State in market economies does not make the State the "source of price discrimination".[171]

(d) Article I:1 of the GATT 1994

102. China submits that the Panel properly found that Article 9(5) of the Basic AD Regulation is inconsistent with Article I:1 of the GATT 1994. China also submits that the Panel did not fail to comply with Article 11 of the DSU and that it did not err in finding that the *Anti-Dumping Agreement* does not allow for the different treatment of imports from NMEs provided for in Article 9(5) of the Basic AD Regulation.

103. China agrees with the Panel's conclusion that Article 9(5) of the Basic AD Regulation is inconsistent with the MFN obligation contained in Article I:1 of the GATT 1994. China contests the European Union's reading of the word "unconditionally" as permitting an advantage to be made available subject to conditions, as long as this does not result in *de facto* discrimination. Notably, in *Canada – Autos*, the panel clearly stated that once an advantage *per se* has been

---

[169] China's appellee's submission, para. 300.
[170] China's appellee's submission, para. 304.
[171] China's appellee's submission, para. 312.

granted to any product of a WTO Member, the obligation to accord it "unconditionally" to the like product of any other WTO Member means that "the extension of that advantage may not be made subject to conditions with respect to the situation or conduct of those countries".[172] In the light of this finding, subjecting the determination of individual dumping margins and imposition of individual duties (the advantage granted to all WTO Members that are considered market economies) to the fulfilment of the Article 9(5) IT test requirements (the condition imposed on China) is *de jure* inconsistent with the obligation set out in Article 1:1 of the GATT 1994. Only in the hypothetical situation in which the IT test was meant to apply to all countries—irrespective of their market economy or NME status—would it be necessary to prove that Article 9(5) results in *de facto* discrimination in order to find a violation of Article I:1 of the GATT 1994. China rejects the European Union's assertion that no discrimination arises under Article 9(5) of the Basic AD Regulation because imports from market economies are not "like" imports from NMEs. China also contends that whether or not imports from market economies and NMEs are different in nature is irrelevant for the purpose of the present dispute, precisely because the measure at issue is not origin-neutral on its face.[173]

104. China notes that the Panel addressed the European Union's argument that there is a difference in the nature of imports from NMEs, which justifies different treatment. In this respect, the Panel correctly concluded that the European Union merely asserted that imports from market economies and NMEs are different in nature, without providing sufficient factual evidence to support such a presumption. Notably, a panel's examination and weighing of the evidence submitted falls within the scope of the panel's discretion as the trier of the facts[174], and, in this case, the Panel did examine the evidence before it, but eventually concluded that it was insufficient to support the European Union's argument.

105. China further submits that the second *Ad* Note to Article VI:1 of the GATT 1994 does not reflect a recognition by Members that imports from market economies and NMEs are different in nature. In China's view, the *Ad* Note does not refer to NMEs but only to countries that have a complete or substantially complete monopoly of trade and where all domestic prices are fixed by the State, this not being China's case. Moreover, China recalls that the fact that exporters from NMEs may be able to show that they act independently from the State casts doubts on the alleged fundamental difference in nature between imports from market economies and NMEs. China also points out that nothing in its Accession Protocol can be read as an understanding that China is an NME. China argues that, pursuant to Section 15 of its Accession Protocol, WTO Members are only entitled to "use a methodology that is not based on a strict comparison with domestic prices or costs in China"[175] when determining normal value. By no means

---

172 China's appellee's submission, para. 323 (quoting Panel Report, *Canada – Autos*, para. 10.18).
173 China's appellee's submission, para. 328.
174 China's appellee's submission, para. 339 (quoting Appellate Body Report, *US – Wheat Gluten*, para. 151).
175 China's appellee's submission, para. 344.

does Section 15 of China's Accession Protocol authorize Members to derogate from the principles contained in the *Anti-Dumping Agreement* that dumping margins and anti-dumping duties must be determined and imposed on an individual basis. In any event, China submits that, even assuming that China's Accession Protocol would permit WTO Members to treat China as an NME, this would still fail to demonstrate that imports from NMEs are different in nature and thus that different treatment is justified.[176]

106. China requests the Appellate Body to uphold the Panel's finding that Article 9(5) of the Basic AD Regulation violates Article I:1 of the GATT 1994, even in the event it reverses the Panel's findings under Articles 6.10 and 9.2 of the *Anti-Dumping Agreement*. China rejects the European Union's argument that if Article 9(5) is found to be consistent with Articles 6.10 and 9.2 of the *Anti-Dumping Agreement* it must, by definition, also be consistent with Article I:1 of the GATT 1994 by virtue of the *lex specialis* principle contained in the *General Interpretative Note to Annex 1A of the WTO Agreement*. China recalls that the panel in *EC – Bananas III* established that a conflict only exists where obligations in different agreements cannot be complied with simultaneously.[177] Thus, it fails to see, in the present case, an actual conflict between the *Anti-Dumping Agreement* and Article I:1 of the GATT 1994. In China's view, even if the Appellate Body were to find that the *Anti-Dumping Agreement* is silent (hence does not expressly prohibit) on the question of whether investigating authorities may use special criteria when examining whether a country-wide or a company-specific duty must be imposed with respect to imports from NMEs only, it would still need to examine whether Article I:1 of the GATT 1994 prohibits treating WTO Members differently when deciding on the imposition of a country-wide or individual duty.[178]

(e) Article XVI:4 of the *WTO Agreement* and Article 18.4 of the *Anti-Dumping Agreement*

107. China requests the Appellate Body to uphold the Panel's finding that the European Union acted inconsistently with Article XVI:4 of the *WTO Agreement* and Article 18.4 of the *Anti-Dumping Agreement*. China submits that, for all the reasons above, the Appellate Body should also find that the European Union failed to "ensure the conformity of its laws, regulations and administrative procedures with its obligations as provided in the annexed Agreements", in accordance with Article XVI:4 of the *WTO Agreement*. Likewise, the European Union failed to "take the necessary steps, of a general or particular character, to ensure ... the conformity of its laws, regulations and administrative procedures with the

---

[176] China's appellee's submission, para. 345.

[177] China's appellee's submission, paras. 356 and 357 (referring to Panel Reports, *EC – Bananas III*, paras. 7.159 and 7.160).

[178] See China's appellee's submission, para. 359.

provisions of the [*Anti-Dumping Agreement*] ", in accordance with Article 18.4 of the *Anti-Dumping Agreement*.[179]

2. *The Panel's Findings Regarding Article 9(5) of the Basic AD Regulation, "As Applied" in the Fasteners Investigation*

108. China requests the Appellate Body to uphold the Panel's finding that the EU authorities violated Articles 6.10 and 9.2 of the *Anti-Dumping Agreement* with respect to the IT determinations in the fasteners investigation. China submits that a measure that is found to be "as such" inconsistent with WTO obligations will also necessarily be inconsistent "as applied". China notes that the European Union relies on the fact that all cooperating companies who requested individual treatment obtained it to contend that the application of Article 9(5) of the Basic AD Regulation did not actually lead to a denial of the rights contained in the relevant WTO rules, namely, individual treatment. China stresses that Article 9(5) not only prevents the result that suppliers from NMEs are entitled to obtain but also subjects them to an additional burden by requiring such exporters to request and demonstrate that they fulfil the conditions laid down in Article 9(5).[180] Therefore, the Panel correctly concluded that Article 9(5) of the Basic AD Regulation was inconsistent "as such" with Articles 6.10 and 9.2 of the *Anti-Dumping Agreement* and, for the same reasons, also inconsistent "as applied" in this investigation.[181]

3. *The Panel's Findings under Articles 6.4 and 6.2 of the Anti-Dumping Agreement*

109. China requests the Appellate Body to uphold the Panel's finding that the European Union acted inconsistently with Article 6.4 of the *Anti-Dumping Agreement* by not providing timely opportunities for the Chinese interested parties to see information regarding the product types on the basis of which normal value was established. In addition, China requests the Appellate Body to uphold the Panel's finding that the European Union acted inconsistently with Article 6.2 of the *Anti-Dumping Agreement* because the Chinese interested parties were not able to defend their interests. China requests the Appellate Body to dismiss in its entirety the European Union's appeal under these provisions.

(a) The "Information" Subject to the Obligations under Articles 6.4 and 6.2 of the *Anti-Dumping Agreement*

110. China submits that the product types used for the determination of normal value were correctly considered by the Panel as "information" within the meaning of Article 6.4 of the *Anti-Dumping Agreement*.

---

[179] China's appellee's submission, para. 363.
[180] China's appellee's submission, para. 369.
[181] China's appellee's submission, para. 370 (referring to Panel Report, para. 7.148).

111. With regard to the interpretation of Article 6.4, China maintains that the ordinary meaning of the term "information" indicates that it is a broad term covering any type of knowledge or facts and is not, as the European Union argues, limited to "facts and raw data rather than factual determinations and conclusions by the investigating authorities".[182] In China's view, this interpretation is confirmed by the other provisions of the *Anti-Dumping Agreement* in which the term is used, including Articles 2.4, 5.2, 8.6, and 11.2. This interpretation is also confirmed by the panel's finding in *Korea – Dairy* that the term "information" in Article 12.2 of the *Agreement on Safeguards* differs from "issues of fact and law" in that it is more general.[183]

112. China argues that none of the prior disputes relied upon by the European Union supports the interpretation that the term "information" is limited to "facts and raw data". The panel's finding in *Korea – Certain Paper (Article 21.5 – Indonesia)* merely confirms that the relevant information must be before the investigating authorities in the relevant anti-dumping proceeding and does not restrict the meaning of "information" to "raw data".[184] Moreover, the European Union's reliance on the panel's findings in *Korea – Certain Paper* is misplaced, because the panel's findings in that dispute actually support the view that the term "information" covers also the facts as processed by the investigating authority.[185] As for the panel's finding in *US – Oil Country Tubular Goods Sunset Reviews (Article 21.5 – Argentina)*, it merely indicates that Article 6.4 applies to "information" as opposed to the "reasoning", but does not suggest that the information is limited to raw data and facts.[186] China further argues that, in *EC – Tube or Pipe Fittings*, the Appellate Body did not assimilate the term "information" under Article 6.4 as "raw data", as the European Union argues[187], but merely noted the panel's factual finding that the authority's reasoning, as well as certain raw data, had not been disclosed to the interested parties.[188] In addition, the information found to be covered by Article 6.4 in that dispute contained data that had been treated, aggregated, and summarized by the investigating authority, as well as the authority's evaluation of these data. China adds that the "information" found to be subject to Article 6.4 in *EC – Tube or Pipe Fittings* is thus similar to the product types in the fasteners investigation, which are categories of products established on the basis of raw data provided by the Indian producer, Pooja Forge.

---

[182] China's appellee's submission, para. 380 (quoting European Union's appellant's submission, para. 253).

[183] China's appellee's submission, para. 379 (quoting Panel Report, *Korea – Dairy*, para. 7.125).

[184] China's appellee's submission, paras. 391 (quoting Panel Report, *Korea – Certain Paper (Article 21.5 – Indonesia)*, para. 6.82) and 392.

[185] See China's appellee's submission, para. 393 (referring to Panel Report, *Korea – Certain Paper*, para. 7.201).

[186] China's appellee's submission, para. 394 (quoting Panel Report, *US – Oil Country Tubular Goods Sunset Reviews (Article 21.5 – Argentina)*, para. 7.124).

[187] See European Union's appellant's submission, para. 254.

[188] China's appellee's submission, para. 395 (referring to Appellate Body Report, *EC – Tube or Pipe Fittings*, paras. 138-141).

113. China contends that the word "relevant" in Article 6.4 supports the interpretation that "information" under Article 6.4 is not limited to raw data and facts but any types of facts that the interested parties consider relevant to the presentation of the case. As for the context provided by the other paragraphs of Article 6, China argues that the European Union has erroneously tried to create an artificial division between the scope of the different obligations in Article 6, and appears to argue that there can be no overlap between such obligations. In China's view, there is a certain overlap between the different paragraphs of Article 6 and, in certain cases, one set of facts can give rise to a violation of several due process obligations. Specifically, the European Union's assertion that Articles 6.1 to 6.3 of the *Anti-Dumping Agreement* address only the right to submit a party's own evidence and arguments is incorrect in the light of the text of these provisions. This assertion also ignores the intertwined nature of a party's right to make submissions and its right to be informed of what the other interested parties submit.

114. In addition, China contends that the repeated reference to Article 6.5 in the other paragraphs of Article 6 illustrates the interrelated nature of the rights and obligations under Article 6, and undermines the artificial distinctions that the European Union has tried to draw among different paragraphs of Article 6. Furthermore, recalling its view that the term "information" in Article 6.4 has a broad connotation and may also include data that has been treated or organized by the investigating authority, China submits that the term "information" in Article 6.4 covers an even wider scope than "essential facts under consideration" in Article 6.9. Therefore, China argues, the distinction drawn by the European Union between "information" in Article 6.4 and "essential facts under consideration" in Article 6.9 is baseless. Finally, China submits that it would frustrate the object and purpose of the important obligations contained in Article 6 of the *Anti-Dumping Agreement* if the scope of the term "information" were to be interpreted restrictively, thereby depriving interested parties of their essential due process rights. In China's view, the sole limitations to the right granted in Article 6.4 are expressly laid down in the provision itself.

115. Turning to the facts of the fasteners investigation, China finds it "rather absurd" that the European Union seems to be arguing that the "product types" only need to be "disclosed by the investigating authorities as 'essential facts' under Article 6.9".[189] The European Union's argument would imply that, until the disclosure of the "essential facts" towards the end of the investigation, the interested parties would have no way of knowing the basis on which the products used for the normal value determination have been grouped into "product types". China argues that this would result in the interested parties not only being unable to comment on the appropriateness of the product categories but also, not knowing the physical characteristics of the product types, being unable to request adjustments pursuant to Article 2.4 of the *Anti-Dumping Agreement*. China adds that this would also be inconsistent with the requirement, in paragraph 151 of the Report of the Working Party on the Accession of China to the WTO (China's

[189] China's appellee's submission, para. 456.

"Accession Working Party Report")[190], that the process of investigation be transparent and that sufficient opportunity be given to Chinese producers and exporters to make comments.

(b) Whether the "Information" Was Made Available to the Interested Parties in a "Timely" Manner within the Meaning of Article 6.4 of the *Anti-Dumping Agreement*

116. China maintains that the European Union fails to demonstrate that the Panel acted inconsistently with Article 11 of the DSU in its assessment of the facts in relation to its finding that the European Union failed to make information available on a timely basis. China argues that the evidence referred to by the European Union was not deliberately disregarded by the Panel, and that, in any event, the conclusions the European Union draws from these pieces of evidence are incorrect and irrelevant.

117. China maintains that, during the Panel proceedings, the European Union did not refer to the Information Document in rebuttal of China's claim that the European Union acted inconsistently with Articles 6.2 and 6.4 of the *Anti-Dumping Agreement*. Rather, before the Panel, the European Union argued that the Information Document should not be taken into account because it was "an informal document that simply reflects a work in progress and has no legal status whatsoever in EU law or in the context of the *Anti-Dumping Agreement*."[191] Therefore, there is no basis for the European Union's assertion that the Panel disregarded the Information Document, when the European Union itself did not claim that this document constituted relevant evidence.

118. In any event, China considers that the Information Document should not lead to a conclusion different from that reached by the Panel. The parity of wording between the General Disclosure Document and the Information Document regarding "product types" does not, in China's view, detract from the Panel's conclusion on this issue for two main reasons. First, the relevant wording was a mere statement by the European Union that it had determined the normal value "per product type". However, in China's view, this did not change the impression by the Chinese producers since the mere reference to "product types" was made without clearly stating that these product types were different from the product types constructed on the basis of the full PCNs. Considering the consistent practice of the European Union in previous investigations to make the comparison on a PCN basis, this was not sufficient information to draw the necessary conclusions that there was a difference between the "product types" and the PCNs.

119. Second, China maintains that neither the Information Document nor the General Disclosure Document was specific enough to allow a Chinese producer

190 WT/ACC/CHN/49 and WT/ACC/CHN/49/Corr.1.

191 China's appellee's submission, para. 473 (quoting European Union's second written submission to the Panel, para. 120).

to know on which basis the comparison would be made. The General Disclosure Document did not provide any information as to the relevant characteristics of those product groups, or how they were determined, and the same applies to the Information Document. China argues that the "factual context supports an interpretation that the use of such ambiguous wording by the Commission was intentional"[192], as further illustrated by the very ambiguous reply of the Commission to the two Chinese exporters who had doubts regarding the comparison and requested clarification. To China, it was only when these exporters made a second request that the Commission clearly stated that the product types had not been constructed on the basis of the full PCNs, but were instead established on the basis of the strength class and the distinction between standard and special fasteners.

120. China further contends that, even assuming that the Chinese producers had been informed of the use of product types by either the Information Document or the General Disclosure Document, this would be irrelevant to the examination of whether the European Union complied with Article 6.4 of the *Anti-Dumping Agreement*. Article 6.4 requires an authority to provide "timely opportunities" to see the information requested by the interested parties. In the fasteners investigation, the Commission did not inform the Chinese interested parties about the basis of its normal value determination until one working day before the deadline to make comments, following two requests by the Chinese interested parties. Thus, the Panel's finding that the investigating authorities provided "timely opportunity" to see the information requested is properly supported by the relevant evidence on the record.

121. China submits that the contention put forward by the European Union regarding the ability of Chinese producers to make presentations on the basis of the "information" provided by the European Union was rightly dismissed by the Panel as irrelevant to its analysis under Article 6.4 of the *Anti-Dumping Agreement*. The comments by certain Chinese exporters referred to by the European Union were, according to China, made in a context that was completely unrelated to the determination of the product types that would be used for the comparison between normal value and export price. China submits that the Panel considered these "presentations" but rightly concluded that they were irrelevant to the assessment of China's claim under Article 6.4.

122. With respect to the letter of 24 November 2008[193], in which one of the Chinese interested parties who requested information concerning product types commented on this "information", China disagrees with the European Union that this piece of evidence indicated that a "timely opportunity" had been provided. China maintains that the content of the information given to the Chinese interested parties was not sufficient to enable a substantiated claim for additional adjustments. Specifically, the European Union did not provide the list of "product types" and their correlation with the PCNs, even though such information

[192] China's appellee's submission, para. 484.
[193] Panel Exhibit EU-12, *supra*, footnote 82.

had been requested. Furthermore, no precise information regarding the distinction between special and standard fasteners was provided by the Commission. China submits that the fact that the Chinese producer did not request an extension is irrelevant, because it was for the Commission to provide the information in a timely manner, and not for the interested parties to try to gain additional time. Thus, the Panel rightly decided not to rely on this letter in reaching its finding.

(c) The Panel's Finding under Article 6.2 of the *Anti-Dumping Agreement*

123. China submits that, although the European Union claims that the Panel's consequential finding under Article 6.2 is erroneous, it does not provide any additional arguments other than those it has provided in its arguments under Article 6.4 of the *Anti-Dumping Agreement*. Moreover, contrary to the European Union's assertion, the Panel did not read the obligation of Article 6.4 into Article 6.2, thus collapsing both provisions. Rather, even though there might be provisions more specific than Article 6.2 that govern a certain claim, it may be necessary for a panel to also address the claims under Article 6.2.

124. China further contends that the European Union's characterization of the Panel's finding under Article 6.2 as "purely consequential"[194] is erroneous. Rather, the Panel found a violation of Article 6.2 that was independent from Article 6.4, on the basis of the fact that the Chinese producers were denied a full opportunity for the defence of their interests because the Commission provided information concerning the product types used in the determination of the normal value only at a very late stage of the proceedings. Thus, according to China, the Panel found a twofold violation of Article 6.2: (i) the consequential violation resulting from Article 6.4; and (ii) a separate violation resulting from the Commission's failure adequately to provide information that would have allowed the Chinese producers to defend their interests in the investigation.

(d) Conclusion

125. On the basis of the above arguments, China requests the Appellate Body to uphold the Panel's findings that the European Union acted inconsistently with Articles 6.2 and 6.4 of the *Anti-Dumping Agreement* with respect to aspects of the normal value determination, and in particular the information on "product types", their characteristics, and their relationship with the PCNs.

---

[194] China's appellee's submission, para. 505 (quoting European Union's appellant's submission, paras. 236, 244, 247, and 275).

4. *The Panel's Findings under Articles 6.5 and 6.5.1 of the Anti-Dumping Agreement Regarding Non-Confidential Questionnaire Responses*

126. China requests the Appellate Body to uphold the Panel's findings that the European Union acted inconsistently with Articles 6.5 and 6.5.1 of the *Anti-Dumping Agreement* with respect to the non-confidential questionnaire responses of domestic producers, and the confidential treatment of Pooja Forge's questionnaire responses. Specifically, China agrees with the Panel that Article 6.5.1 requires investigating authorities to ensure that parties provide "appropriate" non-confidential summaries of information submitted in confidence, or, in exceptional circumstances, "appropriate" statements of reasons explaining why summarization is not possible. China further maintains that the Panel rightly determined that it could make findings on China's claims regarding the questionnaire responses of Pooja Forge. On the substance of this claim, China asserts that Article 6.5 applies to analogue country producers because they can be considered "parties to an investigation", or, in the alternative, because the European Union created a new class of "interested parties" when it employed an alternative method of determining normal value using analogue country producers.

(a) Non-Confidential Summaries of Domestic Producers' Questionnaire Responses

127. China agrees with the Panel that Article 6.5.1 of the *Anti-Dumping Agreement* requires an investigating authority to ensure that, where information provided in confidence is not susceptible to non-confidential summary, an "appropriate" statement of reasons explaining why summarization is not possible is required. According to China, Article 6.5.1 entails a two-part obligation. First, Article 6.5.1 obliges an investigating authority to require non-confidential summaries of confidential information, or, where applicable, statements of the reasons why summarization is not possible. Second, an investigating authority must require that these summaries or statements be "appropriate" to satisfy Article 6.5.1.[195] In China's view, interpreting this provision in a way that would allow less than "appropriate" compliance with its terms would render the obligation useless and would violate a corollary to the general rule of interpretation that an interpreter should not adopt a reading that reduces the provisions of treaty "to redundancy or inutility".[196]

128. China reminds the Appellate Body that, as several panel reports have already recognized, the *Anti-Dumping Agreement* is aimed at WTO Members, not private parties[197], and it is for the investigating authority of a Member, therefore, to determine whether a party has substantiated its claim that summarization of confidential information is not possible.[198] China disagrees with the European

[195] China's appellee's submission, para. 523.
[196] China's appellee's submission, paras. 523 and 524.
[197] China's appellee's submission, para. 525.
[198] China's appellee's submission, para. 527.

Union that authorities are not given a "stick"[199] with which to enforce such an obligation, and suggests that both Article 6.5.2[200] and Article 6.8[201] allow authorities to disregard information that is not submitted in compliance with Article 6.5 as a whole. Furthermore, China contends that the European Union's obligations under Article 6.5.1 are not affected by the fact that Chinese exporters did not affirmatively request improved summaries[202], or by the fact that exporters were able to make presentations on the issues to which the confidential information related without having received improved summaries.[203]

129. Contrary to the European Union's interpretation, China argues that Article 6.5 is only one aspect of the overall transparency requirement contained in both Articles 6.5 and 6.5.1, and that Article 6.5.1 "narrowly circumscribes" the right to confidential treatment.[204] Therefore, notwithstanding the protection of confidentiality, interested parties must be given access to non-confidential summaries of confidential information in order to allow them the exercise of their basic procedural rights. Only in the exceptional circumstance that summarization is not possible can one derogate from the obligation to provide a non-confidential summary. In China's view, if these conditions are not met, confidential treatment must be denied or the information must be disregarded.[205] Read within the overall framework of Article 6, then, confidential treatment is rather an exception to the main objective to ensure that interested parties have a full opportunity for the defence of their interests.[206]

130. China further submits that the language of Article 6.5.1—that authorities "shall require" non-confidential summaries, and that these summaries "shall be" sufficiently detailed—does not suggest only a "best endeavours" obligation. Rather, Article 6.5.1 contains "an obligation to achieve the required result, irrespective of the nature of the endeavours undertaken by the investigating authorities".[207] But even if Article 6.5.1 did contain a "best endeavours" obligation, China argues that the European Union still failed to comply with it. The panel in *Egypt – Steel Rebar* analyzed what is meant by a party's "best endeavours", and found that the term "connotes efforts going beyond those that would be considered 'reasonable' in the circumstances" and implies a "high level of effort".[208] While the Commission may have requested that domestic producers submit non-confidential summaries, it did not do so with respect to the provision of statements of reasons explaining why summarization was not possible in the case that

[199] China's appellee's submission, para. 530 (quoting European Union's appellant's submission, para. 321).
[200] China's appellee's submission, para. 531.
[201] China's appellee's submission, para. 532.
[202] China's appellee's submission, para. 534.
[203] China's appellee's submission, para. 535.
[204] China's appellee's submission, paras. 537 and 538.
[205] China's appellee's submission, para. 538.
[206] China's appellee's submission, paras. 540 and 541.
[207] China's appellee's submission, para. 549.
[208] China's appellee's submission, para. 551 (quoting Panel Report, *Egypt – Steel Rebar*, para. 7.244).

no summary was provided.[209] China urges the Appellate Body to accept the findings of the panel in *Mexico – Olive Oil*, which held that an investigating authority should examine a party's reasons for not summarizing confidential information to determine whether they constitute exceptional circumstances.[210] It also disputes the European Union's reading of that case as factually distinguishable from the fasteners investigation.[211]

(b) Confidential Treatment of Information Obtained from Pooja Forge

(i) Terms of reference and due process

131. In response to the European Union's terms of reference challenge, China requests the Appellate Body to uphold the Panel's findings that China's claims regarding Pooja Forge's questionnaire responses were properly before it. The European Union did not raise this claim before the Panel, and China contends that the European Union therefore waived its right to have this objection heard before the Appellate Body.[212] China cites the Appellate Body Report in *Mexico – Corn Syrup (Article 21.5 – US)* for the proposition that a Member who "fails to raise objections in a timely manner, notwithstanding one or more opportunities to do so", may be deemed to have waived its rights to have a panel consider such objections.[213]

132. Even if the Appellate Body finds that the European Union did not waive its right to raise this objection on appeal, China argues that its claim under Article 6.5 regarding Pooja Forge's questionnaire responses was within the panel's terms of reference. In China's view, its panel request satisfied the requirements of Article 6.2 of the DSU because the legal basis of the claim was clear. China observes that the Appellate Body has drawn a distinction between "claims" and "arguments"[214], and maintains that Article 6.2 therefore does not require it to explain "*why* and *how* the measure at issue violates the provisions" listed in the panel request.[215] By including certain of its arguments in its panel request, China asserts that it merely foreshadowed arguments that it would later develop in its submissions before the Panel, and that this cannot be interpreted as narrowing the scope of its claim.[216] Furthermore, China explains, the reference in its panel request to "domestic producers" only related to its claims under Article 6.5.1, and not to its claims under Article 6.5, which the Panel found to have been violated with regard to the questionnaire responses submitted by Pooja Forge on a

[209] China's appellee's submission, para. 552.

[210] China's appellee's submission, para. 557 (quoting Panel Report, *Mexico – Olive Oil*, para. 7.92).

[211] China's appellee's submission, para. 558.

[212] China's appellee's submission, para. 570.

[213] China's appellee's submission, para. 574 (quoting Appellate Body Report, *Mexico – Corn Syrup (Article 21.5 – US)*, para. 50).

[214] China's appellee's submission, para. 578 (quoting Appellate Body Report, *Korea – Dairy*, para. 139; and Appellate Body Report, *EC – Bananas III*, para. 141).

[215] China's appellee's submission, para. 577.

[216] China's appellee's submission, para. 584.

confidential basis.[217] Finally, China notes that the sufficiency of a panel request under Article 6.2 of the DSU entails a two-stage test, articulated by the panel in *EC – Bed Linen* as follows: "first, examination of the text of the request for establishment itself, in light of the nature of the legal provisions in question; second, an assessment of whether the respondent has been prejudiced by the formulation of claims in the request for establishment, given the actual course of the panel proceedings."[218] China claims that the European Union's failure to even raise this claim before the Panel confirms that its ability to defend its interests was not prejudiced.

133. Regarding the European Union's alternative claim, China points out that the Panel examined the issue of due process and sufficiently addressed the European Union's concerns when it dealt with this claim. Having determined that China had not offered arguments or evidence relating to any category of information besides "product types", the Panel limited China's claims with regard to Pooja Forge to the confidential information relating to this category only.[219] In any event, China submits that the Panel did not make the case for China, and highlights several submissions made by China to the Panel, which it argues were sufficient for the Panel to have reached the finding it ultimately made. These submissions were not limited to responses to the Panel's questions, moreover, but also consisted of the submission of the non-confidential version of Pooja Forge's questionnaire responses itself, as well as arguments China made in its second written submission to the Panel.[220] Finally, in China's view, the European Union was not deprived of an "adequate opportunity" to respond to China's claims. Rather, the European Union chose not to respond because it felt the claim "should be dismissed without entering into the substance".[221]

(ii) Application of Article 6.5 to analogue country producers

134. China disagrees with the European Union's claim that Article 6.5 of the *Anti-Dumping Agreement* did not apply to Pooja Forge because it was not an "interested party". China argues that Article 6.5 applies expressly to "parties to an investigation", which is a broader concept than "interested parties" as defined in Article 6.11, and would include analogue third country producers participating in the investigation. This interpretation is supported by the subsequent use of more general terms, such as "a person supplying the information" and "the supplier of the information".[222] China claims that the consistent use of a term other than "interested parties" leads to the conclusion that a different meaning is intended, and that therefore Pooja Forge did not need to come within the definition

---

[217] *Ibid.*
[218] China's appellee's submission, para. 585 (quoting Panel Report, *EC – Bed Linen*, para. 6.26).
[219] China's appellee's submission, para. 588.
[220] China's appellee's submission, paras. 591 and 592.
[221] China's appellee's submission, para. 593.
[222] China's appellee's submission, para. 602.

of "interested parties" to be considered a "party to the investigation".[223] China observes that Pooja Forge submitted an extensive amount of data, that this data was used by the Commission as the basis for calculating normal value, and that the Commission even visited Pooja Forge in order to verify such data.[224] Therefore, in China's view, Pooja Forge "took part in" the fasteners investigation, and should be considered a "party to the investigation".[225]

135. In response to the European Union's argument that it does not make sense, in the light of the realities of NME anti-dumping investigations, to apply the requirements of Article 6.5 to analogue country producers, China asserts that the opposite is true. In China's view, investigating authorities enjoy a high margin of discretion in determining normal value in the context of investigations involving NME countries, and, therefore, it is even more important that the process be as transparent as possible, and that sufficient opportunity be given to Chinese producers to view and make comments on information relating to normal value.[226]

136. Even if the Appellate Body determines that Article 6.5 applies only to "interested parties", as defined by Article 6.11, China suggests that Pooja Forge should be considered an "interested party" in the fasteners investigation. The Appellate Body in *Japan – DRAMs (Korea)* found that "interested parties" should also include those entities whose participation is relevant "for carrying out an objective investigation and for obtaining information or evidence relevant to the investigation at hand"[227], and China contends that an analogue producer falls directly within the Appellate Body's description. China further argues that the European Union itself designated Pooja Forge as an "interested party", for purposes of Article 6.5, by including in documents intended solely for analogue country producers instructions on submitting confidential information in compliance with Article 6 of the *Anti-Dumping Agreement.*[228]

5. *The Panel's Findings under Articles 6.2 and 6.4 of the Anti-Dumping Agreement Regarding the Disclosure of the Identity of the Complainants*

137. China counters the European Union's terms of reference challenge regarding the disclosure of the identity of the complainants under Articles 6.4 and 6.2 of the *Anti-Dumping Agreement* by pointing out that the European Union fails to distinguish between "claims" and "arguments", and thereby identifies the wrong standard for determining whether a panel request summarizes the legal basis of

---

[223] China's appellee's submission, para. 599.
[224] China's appellee's submission, para. 603.
[225] *Ibid.*
[226] China's appellee's submission, para. 606 (quoting China's Accession Working Party Report, para. 151).
[227] China's appellee's submission, para. 608 (quoting Appellate Body Report, *Japan – DRAMs (Korea)*, para. 242).
[228] China's appellee's submission, paras. 609-611.

the complaint in a way that is "sufficient to present the problem clearly".[229] China urges the Appellate Body to follow the standard developed in previous Appellate Body reports, which, in its view, requires that "the identification of the legal basis of the claim must shed light on the nature of the obligation at issue so that the respondent is able to defend itself".[230]

138. China argues that it "precisely" identified its claim when it stated in its panel request that the measure at issue violated Articles 6.4 and 6.2 of the *Anti-Dumping Agreement* "because the [European Union] failed to ensure throughout the investigation to Chinese producers/exporters the full opportunity for the defense of their interests and failed to provide timely opportunities for them to see all information that is relevant to the presentation of their cases".[231] According to China, this was sufficient to identify its "claims", and China had no obligation to include "arguments" explaining how the European Union had violated its obligations. Moreover, the fact that China did include several arguments in its panel request should not be interpreted as limiting the scope of its claims to those arguments only.[232] Furthermore, China disagrees with the European Union that its panel request was not specific enough to "present the problem clearly", because Articles 6.4 and 6.2 together contain multiple obligations. With regard to Article 6.2, China emphasizes that it included only the first sentence of this provision in its claim, and did not intend to invoke the entire Article.[233] China contends that, while there may be multiple ways in which these provisions can be violated, the same is true for all provisions of the *Anti-Dumping Agreement*, and does not imply that each contains multiple obligations.[234]

139. Finally, China contends that the Appellate Body's examination of the sufficiency of a panel request must take into account whether or not a respondent's ability to defend itself "was prejudiced, given the actual course of the proceedings".[235] In China's view, "irrespective" of whether China's panel request complied with Article 6.2 of the DSU, the European Union cannot succeed in a terms of reference challenge unless it successfully demonstrates such prejudice.[236] Given the unambiguous statement of China's claims in its first written submission to the Panel, and in its subsequent clarifications in response to the Panel's questions, China insists that the European Union cannot show that its ability to defend itself was prejudiced in this case.[237]

---

[229] China's appellee's submission, paras. 626-628.

[230] China's appellee's submission, para. 633 (referring to Appellate Body Report, *EC – Bananas III*, para. 141; Appellate Body Report, *US – Carbon Steel*, para. 130; and Appellate Body Report, *Korea – Dairy*, paras. 124 and 127)..

[231] China's appellee's submission, para. 634.

[232] China's appellee's submission, paras. 635-638 (quoting Appellate Body Report, *EC – Selected Customs Matters*, para. 153).

[233] China's appellee's submission, para. 645.

[234] China's appellee's submission, para. 648.

[235] China's appellee's submission, para. 632 (quoting Appellate Body Report, *Korea – Dairy*, para. 127).

[236] China's appellee's submission, para. 653.

[237] China's appellee's submission, paras. 654-658.

C. *Claims of Error by China – Other Appellant*

1. *The Panel's Findings under Articles 4.1 and 3.1 of the Anti-Dumping Agreement*

140. China requests the Appellate Body to reverse the Panel's finding that the European Union did not act inconsistently with Articles 4.1 and 3.1 of the *Anti-Dumping Agreement* with respect to the definition of the domestic industry in the fasteners investigation. First, China alleges that the Panel erred in finding that the European Union did not act inconsistently with Articles 4.1 and 3.1 of the *Anti-Dumping Agreement* by excluding from the definition of the domestic industry producers who did not support the complaint against injurious dumping and producers that made themselves known more than 15 days after the publication of the Notice of Initiation of the investigation. In addition, China asserts that the Panel erred in rejecting China's claim that the domestic industry in the fasteners investigation, comprising producers accounting for 27 per cent of total estimated EU production of fasteners, did not include producers whose collective output "constitutes a major proportion of the total domestic production" within the meaning of Article 4.1 of the *Anti-Dumping Agreement*. Finally, China claims that the Panel erred in finding that the European Union did not act inconsistently with Articles 4.1 and 3.1 of the *Anti-Dumping Agreement* by making an injury determination on the basis of a sample of producers that was not representative of the domestic industry.

(a) Exclusion of Certain Producers

141. China claims that the Panel failed to conduct an objective assessment of the facts, as required by Article 11 of the DSU and Article 17.6 of the *Anti-Dumping Agreement*, in finding that the European Union did not exclude producers that did not support the complaint from the definition of domestic industry. China further argues that the Panel erred in its interpretation of Article 4.1 of the *Anti-Dumping Agreement*, and acted inconsistently with Article 11 of the DSU, in finding that the European Union did not violate Article 4.1 of the *Anti-Dumping Agreement* by excluding from the definition of domestic industry the producers that did not come forward within 15 days of the initiation of the anti-dumping investigation. China also submits that the Panel erred in its interpretation of Article 3.1 of the *Anti-Dumping Agreement* by rejecting China's claim under that provision simply because it had rejected China's claim under Article 4.1 of that Agreement.

(i) Exclusion of producers who did not support the complaint

142. China recalls the Appellate Body's finding in respect of Article 11 of the DSU that "the question whether a panel has made an 'objective assessment' of

the facts is a *legal* one, that may be the subject of an appeal."[238] Moreover, the Appellate Body has found that, in carrying out its mandate under Article 11 of the DSU, "a panel has the duty to examine and consider **all** the evidence before it, not just the evidence submitted by one or the other party, and to evaluate the relevance and probative [force] of each piece thereof."[239] The Appellate Body has also emphasized that panels cannot make affirmative findings that lack a basis in the evidence contained in the panel record.[240]

143. Turning to the facts of this case, China submits that it claimed before the Panel that the European Union erroneously excluded from the definition of the domestic industry all producers who did not support the complaint regarding the alleged injurious dumping caused by imports of fasteners from China. The Panel, however, failed to conduct an objective assessment of the facts, and erroneously found that the Commission did not exclude producers unsupportive of the complaint from the definition of the domestic industry. China alleges that, in reaching its finding, the Panel relied solely on the European Union's factual assertion that at least one producer who did not affirmatively state support for the complaint at the pre-initiation stage was included in the definition of the domestic industry. According to China, this assertion of the European Union was not substantiated by evidence, even though evidence in this regard "was clearly accessible to the [European Union] as investigating authorities".[241] For example, the European Union could have provided the list of the complainants and supporters who had come forward before the initiation. Yet, in response to the concern raised by China concerning the reliability of this statement, the Panel stated that it "ha[d] no reason to doubt the European Union's assertion of fact in this regard".[242] Therefore, China submits, "by treating as an established fact a mere assertion made by the [European Union] without supporting evidence, the Panel committed an egregious error and therefore failed to make an objective assessment of the facts as required by Article 11 of the DSU".[243]

144. China further maintains that the Panel "disregarded the explanation put forward by China"[244], as well as other relevant evidence, which showed that the Commission knew whether the producer who had allegedly remained silent before initiation of the investigation in fact supported the complaint. China submits that, as indicated by the European Union's response to a question posed by the Panel, the Commission enquired into the position of all known producers regard-

---

[238] China's other appellant's submission, para. 46 (quoting Appellate Body Report, *US – Wheat Gluten,* para. 151 (original emphasis); and referring to Appellate Body Report, *EC – Hormones*, para. 132).

[239] China's other appellant's submission, para. 50 (quoting Appellate Body Report, *Korea – Dairy*, para. 137). (boldface added by China)

[240] China's other appellant's submission, para. 50 (referring to Appellate Body Report, *US – Carbon Steel*, para. 142, in turn referring to Appellate Body Report, *US – Wheat Gluten*, paras. 161 and 162).

[241] China's other appellant's submission, para. 65.

[242] China's other appellant's submission, para. 63 (quoting Panel Report, footnote 473 to para. 7.214).

[243] China's other appellant's submission, para. 66.

[244] China's other appellant's submission, para. 69.

ing the complaint and, consequently, must have been aware of the position of the producer who had allegedly remained silent prior to initiation but was included in the domestic industry definition subsequent to initiation.[245] Moreover, the Information Document, which was issued by the Commission several months before concluding the investigation, made it clear that the Commission enquired into, and knew, the position of all known producers regarding the complaint. In "ignoring"[246] such evidence, the Panel failed to make an objective assessment, as required by Article 11 of the DSU, when it found that the fact asserted by the European Union, that a producer who had remained silent in the pre-initiation stage was included in the definition of the domestic industry, necessarily demonstrated that the Commission did not exclude producers unsupportive of the complaint.

145. China asserts, furthermore, that the Panel acted inconsistently with Article 11 of the DSU because it "ignored" the following three pieces of evidence submitted by China demonstrating that the European Union excluded from the domestic industry definition all producers unsupportive of the complaint.[247] Specifically, recital 114 of the Definitive Regulation defines the domestic industry as 45 EC producers who "supported the complaint and fully cooperated in the investigation". The Panel acknowledged that the wording of the Definitive Regulation meant that "only producers expressing support for the complaint were included in the domestic industry".[248] However, the Panel "disregarded the unambiguous wording" of the Definitive Regulation in its assessment of facts[249], and failed to explain why it did not consider this evidence relevant to its finding.

146. In addition, China maintains that, before the Panel, it referred to the Information Document issued by the Commission half a year before the publication of the Definitive Regulation, in which the Commission explained its preliminary determinations in the fasteners investigation. China argues that the Information Document shows that the domestic industry was initially defined as comprising only the 86 producers who supported the complaint and fully cooperated in the investigation. However, the Panel decided not to rely on the Information Document, finding that it was "a working document reflecting progress in the investigation to that point, with no legal status in EU law", and thus did not constitute "part of the measure" at issue before the Panel.[250] According to China, the Panel erroneously disregarded this evidence, because the Information Document is part of the record of the investigation and a relevant piece of evidence. Finally, China contends that it submitted to the Panel a letter sent by the Commission in response to two Chinese producers' requests for clarification

245 China's other appellant's submission, para. 82 (referring to European Union's responses to Panel Questions 88 and 89).
246 China's other appellant's submission, para. 82.
247 China's other appellant's submission, para. 85.
248 China's other appellant's submission, para. 89 (quoting Panel Report, para. 7.214).
249 China's other appellant's submission, para. 89.
250 China's other appellant's submission, para. 92 (quoting Panel Report, para. 7.214).

regarding certain aspects of the General Disclosure Document.[251] In the letter, the Commission stated that the volume of production of the Community industry indicated in the General Disclosure Document corresponded to "the Community producers that supported the complaint and fully cooperated in the investigation".[252] In China's view, this evidence demonstrates that only producers supporting the complaint were included in the domestic industry definition. The Panel, however, did not refer to this letter and thus "totally ignored" the evidence in its analysis.[253]

147. On this basis, China requests the Appellate Body to reverse the Panel's finding that the European Union did not exclude producers who did not support the complaint from the definition of the domestic industry. China further requests the Appellate Body to complete the analysis and find that the European Union excluded from the definition of the domestic industry the producers who did not support the complaint and that, in so doing, the European Union acted inconsistently with Article 4.1 of the *Anti-Dumping Agreement*. China argues that, apart from the two exceptions provided in Article 4.1, no other categories of producers may be excluded by the investigating authorities from the definition of the domestic industry. China finds support for its position in the text of Article 4.1, as well as in the finding of the panel in *EC – Salmon (Norway)* that, under Article 4.1, it is not permissible to exclude from the domestic industry definition certain categories of producers of the like product other than those set out in paragraphs (i) and (ii) of that provision.[254]

(ii) Exclusion of producers who did not come forward within 15 days of the initiation of the investigation

148. China claims that the Panel erred in the legal interpretation, and acted inconsistently with Article 11 of the DSU, in finding that the European Union did not act inconsistently with Article 4.1 of the *Anti-Dumping Agreement* by excluding from the domestic industry definition all producers who did not come forward within 15 days of the initiation of the investigation.

149. According to China, the Panel erred in the interpretation of Article 4.1 when finding that "nothing in Article 4.1 ... would preclude investigating authorities from establishing deadlines for companies to come forward in order to

[251] Letter from the European Commission dated 18 November 2008 to Van Bael & Bellis in response to letter from Van Bael & Bellis dated 12 November 2008, submitted to the Panel as Panel Exhibit CHN-39. The General Disclosure Document, *supra*, footnote 73, was the final disclosure document before the Commission issued the Definitive Regulation.

[252] China's other appellant's submission, para. 97 (quoting Panel Exhibit CHN-39, *supra*, footnote 251, p. 1). (underlining by China omitted)

[253] China's other appellant's submission, para. 99.

[254] Under Article 4.1(i), domestic producers that are related to the exporters or importers or are themselves importers of the allegedly dumped product may be excluded. Article 4.1(ii) further provides that domestic industry may be limited to include only those producers within a particular geographic region, if certain criteria are met.

be considered for inclusion in the domestic industry".[255] In China's view, Article 4.1 prohibits the exclusion of any categories of producers, except for those provided under paragraphs (i) and (ii), and the prohibition applies to producers defined as a category on the basis of the time period within which they must come forward. China submits that the imposition of a deadline for domestic producers to come forward may be permissible by reasons of the necessity for the investigating authorities to conclude the investigations within the time-limit prescribed in Article 5.10 of the *Anti-Dumping Agreement*. The deadline, however, must be balanced with the fundamental due process rights enjoyed by interested parties. Therefore, any deadline granted by the investigating authorities to domestic producers to come forward must be "reasonable" and "sufficient".[256] China further submits that a deadline would not be permissible if the investigating authorities continue to consider the inclusion of producers who come forward after the deadline, but ultimately decide not to include such producers, because this would constitute a deliberate exclusion process inconsistent with Article 4.1 of the *Anti-Dumping Agreement*.

150. China maintains that the Panel failed to conduct an objective assessment of the facts, as required by Article 11 of the DSU, when finding that the European Union "did not act to exclude" producers who did not make themselves known within 15 days of the initiation of the investigation.[257] China submits that both the Definitive Regulation and the Information Document indicate that the domestic industry consists of EC producers who expressed a wish to be included in the sample within the 15-day deadline. Moreover, as the Panel also noted, there seemed to have been "a process of considering additional producers for inclusion in the domestic industry", although none of the producers so considered were, in the end, included in the domestic industry.[258] In China's view, this shows that the Commission envisaged including producers other than those who had come forward within the 15-day period but decided not to do so. In the light of the above evidence, China argues, the Panel should have concluded that the Commission acted to exclude producers who had not come forward within the 15-day deadline.

151. Furthermore, China asserts that the Panel failed to conduct an objective assessment of the facts, as required by Article 11 of the DSU, in finding that China had not established that the 15-day period granted by the Commission was insufficient or unreasonable. China contends that it substantiated, before the Panel, the insufficiency and unreasonableness of the 15-day deadline with the following arguments and evidence. First, the 15-day deadline is "very short and makes it much more likely that complainants and companies supporting the investigation", rather than producers opposing the investigation, will come forward within the prescribed period.[259] China submits that this argument is sup-

---

[255] China's other appellant's submission, para. 123 (quoting Panel Report, para. 7.219).
[256] China's other appellant's submission, para. 125.
[257] China's other appellant's submission, para. 117 (quoting Panel Report, para. 7.215).
[258] China's other appellant's submission, para. 120 (quoting Panel Report, para. 7.215).
[259] China's other appellant's submission, para. 135.

ported by the evidence, which shows that the 46 producers that made up the domestic industry all supported the complaint and all came forward within the 15-day deadline. In addition, as shown by the Information Document, "a large number of" producers who opposed the complaint or did not express an opinion were not included in the domestic industry definition.[260] Furthermore, by requiring producers to come forward within 15 days and express a willingness to be included in the sample within that deadline, the European Union adopted an approach that was "fundamentally non-objective", because producers opposing the investigation were less likely to be willing to be part of the sample.[261] Finally, China asserts that the 15-day deadline to respond to the sampling form is not the same as the period in which an interested party was requested to make itself known under the Notice of Initiation, which was a 40-day period. China contends, therefore, that it properly substantiated its argument before the Panel that the 15-day deadline was unreasonable and therefore inconsistent with Article 4.1 of the *Anti-Dumping Agreement*.

152. On this basis, China requests the Appellate Body to reverse the Panel's finding that the Commission "did not act to exclude"[262] producers who did not make themselves known within 15 days of the initiation of the investigation, and that "the mere fact that the domestic industry as ultimately defined does not include any particular proportion of producers … who did not come forward within the 15-day period, does not demonstrate that the European Union acted inconsistently with Article 4.1 of the [*Anti-Dumping Agreement*] in defining the domestic industry."[263] China further requests the Appellate Body to conclude that the 15-day period granted to domestic producers to come forward was not reasonable or sufficient and that the European Union acted inconsistently with Article 4.1 by setting such a deadline.

(iii) Inconsistency with Article 3.1 of the *Anti-Dumping Agreement*

153. China alleges that the Panel erred in its interpretation of Article 3.1 of the *Anti-Dumping Agreement* in dismissing China's claim under that provision because it found that the European Union did not act inconsistently with Article 4.1 of the *Anti-Dumping Agreement* with respect to the definition of the domestic industry. According to China, the separate claims made by China on two different legal bases under Article 4.1 and Article 3.1 required the Panel to examine whether the exclusion from the domestic industry of the producers who did not support the complaint and the producers who did not come forward within the 15-day deadline was inconsistent with the requirements under each of those provisions.

---

[260] China's other appellant's submission, para. 136.
[261] China's other appellant's submission, para. 137.
[262] Panel Report, para. 7.215. See also China's other appellant's submission, para. 141.
[263] Panel Report, para. 7.219. See also China's other appellant's submission, para. 141.

154. China contends that Article 3.1 of the *Anti-Dumping Agreement* requires the injury determination to be based on "positive evidence" and to involve an "objective examination" of, *inter alia*, the impact of dumped imports on domestic producers. Thus, by excluding the producers who did not support the complaint from the definition of the domestic industry, the European Union's action was "fundamentally biased and non-objective", because it "favour[ed] the interests of a group of interested parties, namely the complainants".[264] Moreover, the exclusion of the producers who did not make themselves known within the 15-day deadline was also "bias[ed]" and "non-objective"[265], because the European Union included only those producers who came forward within that deadline and expressed a willingness to be part of the sample. In China's view, the domestic industry must first be defined from which a sample may be selected. By including in the domestic industry definition only those producers willing to be part of the sample, the European Union's approach confused two different steps in the process of selecting a sample. Because producers not willing to be included in the sample "probably [did] not support the investigation"[266], this approach made it more likely that only those companies supporting the complaint would be included in the domestic industry definition and, hence, made it more likely to find injury. Therefore, China asserts, by including in the domestic industry only those producers who came forward within the 15-day deadline and expressed their willingness to be part of the sample, the European Union acted inconsistently with Article 3.1 of the *Anti-Dumping Agreement* by failing to make an objective examination of the impact of the dumped imports on the domestic industry.

155. On this basis, China requests the Appellate Body to reverse the Panel's finding that "China [made] no other allegations in support of its claim of violation of Article 3.1"[267] of the *Anti-Dumping Agreement* and its claim must therefore be rejected, and to conclude that the European Union acted inconsistently with that provision with respect to the definition of the domestic industry.

(b) "A Major Proportion" of the Total Domestic Production

156. China submits that the Panel erred in rejecting China's claim that the domestic industry as defined by the European Union did not include domestic producers whose collective output of the like product constitutes a "major proportion" of the total domestic production. According to China, the Panel erroneously concluded that the fact that the Commission relied on a presumption that 25 per cent of total domestic production constituted "a major proportion" within the meaning of Article 4.1 of the *Anti-Dumping Agreement* was, in itself, insufficient to demonstrate that the definition of the domestic industry in this dispute is inconsistent with Article 4.1. Moreover, the Panel erroneously concluded that

---

264 China's other appellant's submission, para. 155.
265 China's other appellant's submission, para. 156.
266 China's other appellant's submission, para. 162.
267 Panel Report, para. 7.221. See also China's other appellant's submission, para. 171.

the non-quantitative factors raised by China were not relevant to the examination of whether the domestic industry defined by the Commission met the requirement of "a major proportion" under Article 4.1.

(i) The interpretation of the term "a major proportion"

157. China submits that the interpretation of the term "a major proportion" on the basis of its ordinary meaning and in the light of the context leads to only one permissible interpretation, which is different from the one followed by the Panel. Quoting the relevant dictionary definitions, China argues that "a major proportion" means a "share" of the whole that is "unusually important, serious or significant".[268] Therefore, the domestic producers whose production makes up a major proportion must be representative of the whole. As support, China recalls the Appellate Body's finding in *US – Lamb* that the words "as a whole" and "a major proportion" in Article 4.1(c) of the *Agreement on Safeguards* address "the representative nature of producers making up the domestic industry"[269], as well as the panel's finding in that dispute that the words relate to the "representativeness of the data pertaining to the condition of the domestic industry".[270] China submits that, although the Panel found that the word "major" means "important, serious, or significant", the Panel failed to take into account the "representative" requirement under the phase "a major proportion".[271]

158. According to China, the reference to "the domestic producers as a whole", which constitutes the immediate context of the phrase "a major proportion", indicates that "[t]he reason for permitting the domestic industry to be defined as those producers constituting only a 'major proportion' is to address the practical impossibility for investigating authorities in some cases to obtain the requested information from all the producers of the like product."[272] China recalls that paragraphs (i) and (ii) of Article 4.1 expressly authorize the exclusion from the definition of the domestic industry of two categories of producers. In China's view, it would be superfluous to set out precise conditions for the application of the two exclusions if investigating authorities could in any event exclude from the definition of the domestic industry any other producers they wish as long as the remaining producers still constitute a major proportion. Moreover, given the requirement under Article 3.1 that an injury determination "be based on positive evidence and involve an objective examination", China argues that "a major proportion" must be sufficiently representative of the domestic production

[268] China's other appellant's submission, paras. 185 (quoting *The New Shorter Oxford English Dictionary*, 4th edn, L. Brown (ed.) (Clarendon Press, 1993), Vol. 2, p. 2381) and 188 (quoting *ibid.*, Vol. 1, p. 1670).

[269] China's other appellant's submission, para. 185 (quoting Appellate Body Report, *US – Lamb*, para. 91).

[270] China's other appellant's submission, para. 186 (quoting Panel Report, *US – Lamb*, para. 7.73). (underlining by China omitted)

[271] China's other appellant's submission, para. 190.

[272] China's other appellant's submission, para. 195.

"as a whole" to ensure that the examination carried out with respect to the industry, as defined, is "objective" within the meaning of Article 3.1 of the *Anti-Dumping Agreement.*

159. Therefore, China submits, whether the requirement of "a major proportion" is met must be assessed in the light of the specific circumstances of a case, including "the practical feasibility for the investigating authorities to include more producers than those actually included, the number of producers and the exclusion of certain categories of producers from the scope of the domestic industry".[273]

(ii) Whether the domestic industry defined in the fasteners investigation meets the requirement on "a major proportion"

160. China maintains that, as indicated in the Definitive Regulation in the fasteners investigation, the EU producers whose output represented 27 per cent of the total domestic production constituted "the Community industry within the meaning of Articles 4(1) and 5(4) of the [Basic AD Regulation]."[274] Articles 4(1) and 5(4) of the Basic AD Regulation are largely similar to Articles 4.1 and 5.4 of the *Anti-Dumping Agreement*, except that Article 4(1) of the Basic AD Regulation defines "a major proportion" as being equal to 25 per cent of the total domestic production, namely, the minimum benchmark for meeting the standing requirement contained in Article 5(4). Thus, it is "not disputed" that the Commission concluded in the fasteners investigation "that the domestic producers making up the domestic industry constituted a 'major proportion' solely because they represented more than 25% of the total domestic production".[275]

161. China contends that Article 5.4 of the *Anti-Dumping Agreement* merely lays down a standard for determining whether the standing requirement is met and an investigation may be initiated. Article 4.1, in contrast, defines the "domestic industry" and is therefore a very different exercise than that of measuring the degree of support for a complaint within the meaning of Article 5.4. Therefore, in China's view, it is "legally incorrect" to establish an automatic link between the requirement on "a major proportion" and the 25 per cent minimum benchmark for meeting the standing requirement.[276] Moreover, China submits that whether the requirement on "a major proportion" is met may not be determined in the abstract, on the basis of a quantitative benchmark, but depends on the facts of the case. In China's view, by relying on this rule when defining the domestic industry, without assessing the specific circumstances in this case, the Commission acted inconsistently with Article 4.1 of the *Anti-Dumping Agreement.*[277] Thus, the Panel "made a fundamental legal error in finding that 'the as-

[273] China's other appellant's submission, para. 201.
[274] China's other appellant's submission, para. 211 (quoting Definitive Regulation, *supra*, footnote 4, recital 114).
[275] China's other appellant's submission, para. 216.
[276] China's other appellant's submission, para. 237.
[277] See China's other appellant's submission, paras. 223-228 and 240.

sertion that the Commission relied on a presumption is not alone sufficient to demonstrate, *prima facie*, that the definition of domestic industry in this case is inconsistent with Article 4.1 of the [*Anti-Dumping Agreement*].'"[278]

162. China further maintains that the Panel erred in failing to consider certain non-quantitative factors that China argued were relevant to the examination of whether the requirement of "a major proportion" was met in the fasteners investigation. Specifically, China argues that, by excluding from the domestic industry definition the producers who opposed the complaint or remained silent, the "domestic industry" as defined by the Commission was not representative of the whole industry and, thus, not "a major proportion" of the production of that industry.[279] Furthermore, the Panel erred in finding that the possibility or feasibility for the investigating authority to include more producers in the domestic industry definition, and the reasons why it did not do so, was irrelevant to an examination of whether the requirement on "a major proportion" was met. As shown by the relevant evidence, the Commission had identified at the outset of the investigation "at least 114 producers representing 45% of the total domestic production".[280] However, the Commission ultimately excluded more than half of these producers from the domestic industry definition, even though it would have been possible for it to include more producers. Finally, China asserts that the number of producers constituting the domestic industry is relevant to a determination of whether a certain percentage in terms of the volume of production constitutes a major proportion. Yet, the Panel failed to take into account the fact that, although there were more than 300 producers of fasteners in the European Union, the domestic industry definition only included 45 producers. In China's view, "[t]his is a very limited proportion which cannot be considered a 'major proportion'".[281]

163. On this basis, China requests the Appellate Body to reverse the Panel's finding that, "[e]ven assuming non-quantitative factors are relevant to the definition of a domestic industry under Article 4.1, we do not consider that the factors China raises in this regard are relevant in this case, or in general."[282] China further requests the Appellate Body to conclude that, in the light of these non-quantitative factors, the domestic producers constituting the domestic industry in the fasteners investigation did not represent a "major proportion" of the domestic industry.

(c) The Representativeness of the Sample of Domestic Producers in the Injury Determination

164. China submits that the Panel erred in rejecting China's claim that the European Union acted inconsistently with Article 3.1 of the *Anti-Dumping*

---

278 China's other appellant's submission, para. 227 (quoting Panel Report, para. 7.225).
279 See China's other appellant's submission, paras. 245-249.
280 China's other appellant's submission, para. 254.
281 China's other appellant's submission, para. 258.
282 Panel Report, para. 7.230. See also China's other appellant's submission, para. 259.

Agreement in the selection of a sample of the domestic producers for purposes of the injury determination. China alleges that the Panel made the following two specific errors.

165. First, China asserts that the Panel wrongly rejected China's contention that, because "only a statistically valid sample will be sufficiently representative for purposes of an injury determination"[283], the sample of producers selected by the Commission on the basis of the largest volume of production that could reasonably be investigated was not representative of the domestic industry. According to China, despite the absence of a specific provision in the *Anti-Dumping Agreement* addressing the issue of sampling of the domestic industry for purposes of assessing injury, "the investigating authorities are bound by the obligation laid down in Article 3.1 of the [*Anti-Dumping Agreement*] that the injury determination involve[s] an objective examination and be based on positive evidence."[284] China asserts that, in the context of the dumping determination, pursuant to Article 6.10 of the *Anti-Dumping Agreement*, limiting a sample to the largest percentage of the volume of the exports that can reasonably be investigated may be justified in the light of the "possibility for subsequent refunds if an individual producer is not actual[ly] dumping".[285] Because "there is no similar system which would take into account the absence of injury with respect to certain domestic producers", it is "fundamental" that a sample in the injury context be sufficiently representative of the domestic industry as a whole.[286] Therefore, in China's view, a sample cannot merely be based on the largest volume that can reasonably be investigated, but should take into account other criteria, such as, the use of a statistically valid sample.

166. Second, China alleges that the Panel erred in concluding that China had not demonstrated "that the EU investigating authority could have carried out the entire injury examination for the domestic industry it had defined, or at least included more producers in the sample".[287] China submits that, as it demonstrated before the Panel, the Commission examined certain injury factors with respect to the entire domestic industry as defined, that is, the 45 domestic producers. Thus, contrary to the Panel's finding, the Commission could have also analyzed the other injury factors for the entire domestic industry as defined, rather than with respect to only the sampled producers.

167. On this basis, China requests the Appellate Body to reverse the Panel's finding that the European Union did not act inconsistently with Article 3.1 of the *Anti-Dumping Agreement* in the selection of a sample of the domestic industry, and to conclude that the European Union, by selecting the sample for the injury determination solely on the basis of the volume of production, and by including in the sample only six producers representing 17.5 per cent of total domestic

---

[283] China's other appellant's submission, para. 265 (quoting Panel Report, para. 7.239).

[284] China's other appellant's submission, para. 270.

[285] China's other appellant's submission, para. 272 (quoting Panel Report, *EC – Salmon (Norway)*, footnote 309 to para. 7.132).

[286] China's other appellant's submission, para. 272.

[287] China's other appellant's submission, para. 276 (quoting Panel Report, para. 7.240).

production, acted inconsistently with Article 3.1 of the *Anti-Dumping Agreement*.[288]

2. *The Panel's Findings under Article 2.4 of the Anti-Dumping Agreement*

168. China requests the Appellate Body to reverse the Panel's finding that the European Union did not act inconsistently with Article 2.4 of the *Anti-Dumping Agreement* with respect to the comparison of the export price and normal value in the dumping determination. China claims that the Panel also acted inconsistently with Article 11 of the DSU by not addressing China's argument that the Commission failed to indicate to the interested parties what information was necessary to ensure a fair comparison. China further submits that the Panel erred in its interpretation and application of Article 2.4, and acted inconsistently with Article 11 of the DSU, in rejecting China's claim that the Commission failed to make adjustments for the differences in physical characteristics identified in the PCNs. Finally, China maintains that the Panel erred in the interpretation and application of Article 2.4 of the *Anti-Dumping Agreement* in rejecting China's claim that the Commission failed to make adjustments for quality differences.

(a) The Panel's Treatment of China's Argument

169. China recalls that, at the outset of the fasteners investigation, the Chinese producers were requested to provide product information on the basis of the PCNs identified by the Commission, and "it was clear"[289] that the PCNs would be used for the purposes of ensuring a fair comparison between the export price and the normal value. Although the Commission later decided not to use the PCNs for purposes of price comparison, and instead relied on certain "product types", it did not inform the Chinese producers of this change until one working day before the deadline for submitting comments on the General Disclosure Document. Before the Panel, China claimed that, under the last sentence of Article 2.4 of the *Anti-Dumping Agreement*, the Commission was required to inform the Chinese producers of the fact that the comparison was not made on the basis of the PCNs and to provide them with a sufficient opportunity to comment. However, the Panel did not address this argument, noting that this was "the main argument China raise[d] in connection with its claim under Articles 6.2, 6.4, 6.5 and 6.9 of the [*Anti-Dumping Agreement*]"[290], and did not explain why it was not necessary to examine the argument in the context of China's claim under Article 2.4 of the *Anti-Dumping Agreement*. China maintains that the Panel thus failed to address a substantial argument by China that was central in the assessment of whether the European Union acted inconsistently with Article 2.4 of the *Anti-Dumping Agreement*. The Panel's failure to address this argument "deprive[d]

[288] See China's other appellant's submission, paras. 275 and 278; and Panel Report, para. 7.241.

[289] China's other appellant's submission, para. 297.

[290] China's other appellant's submission, para. 314 (quoting Panel Report, para. 6.98).

China of a complete resolution of the matter at issue" and "would ... constitute a false exercise of judicial economy".[291]

170. China therefore requests the Appellate Body to find that the Panel acted inconsistently with Article 11 of the DSU by failing to address China's argument under the last sentence of Article 2.4 of the *Anti-Dumping Agreement*. In the event the Appellate Body considers that the Panel "implicitly rejected China's argument"[292], China requests the Appellate Body to find that the Panel erred in its interpretation and application[293] of Article 2.4 of the *Anti-Dumping Agreement*.

171. China further requests the Appellate Body to complete the analysis and find that the Commission's failure to inform the interested parties of the change in the basis for price comparison constitutes a violation of Article 2.4 of the *Anti-Dumping Agreement*. China submits that the relevant factual findings of the Panel in its examination of China's claim under Articles 6.2 and 6.4 of the *Anti-Dumping Agreement* provide the factual basis for completing the analysis. Specifically, the Panel found that the "Chinese producers were informed very late in the proceedings of the product types that formed the basis of the comparisons underlying the Commission's dumping determinations" and that, despite their request, the Chinese producers "were not given a timely opportunity to see the relevant information by the Commission".[294] Moreover, the Panel correctly found that, without the information concerning the basis on which the comparison will actually be made, "it would be difficult if not impossible, for foreign producers to request adjustments that they consider necessary in order to ensure a fair comparison."[295] China therefore submits that the Commission was under an obligation to inform the interested parties of the basis on which the comparison between the export price and the normal value was made, and to provide sufficient time for the interested parties to comment or request adjustments. Because the Commission failed to do so, China requests the Appellate Body to find that the European Union failed to "indicate to the parties in question what information is necessary to ensure a fair comparison" and imposed "an unreasonable burden of proof on those parties"[296], and thus acted inconsistently with Article 2.4 of the *Anti-Dumping Agreement*.

---

[291] China's other appellant's submission, para. 312.

[292] China's other appellant's submission, para. 315.

[293] Although China's other appellant's submission alleges that the Panel erred in its interpretation (see para. 296), China clarified at the oral hearing that its claim also covers the Panel's application of Article 2.4 to the facts of the case.

[294] China's other appellant's submission, para. 325 (quoting Panel Report, para. 7.492).

[295] China's other appellant's submission, para. 326 (quoting Panel Report, para. 7.491).

[296] China's other appellant's submission, para. 332.

(b) Physical Differences

(i) The Panel's interpretation and application of Article 2.4

172. China submits that the Panel erred in its interpretation and application[297] of Article 2.4 of the *Anti-Dumping Agreement* in rejecting China's argument that the European Union acted inconsistently with Article 2.4 of the *Anti-Dumping Agreement* by failing to evaluate, and make adjustments for, physical characteristics identified in the PCNs.

173. China submits that, under Article 2.4 of the *Anti-Dumping Agreement*, the requirement to make due allowance for physical differences means that the investigating authority must at least evaluate identified differences with a view to determining whether or not an adjustment is required. China alleges that this is confirmed by relevant findings of the panels in *Argentina – Ceramic Tiles* and *EC – Tube or Pipe Fittings*.[298] In the light of the fact that the Commission initially identified the physical characteristics reflected in the PCNs as "necessary to make a 'fair comparison'" but later decided to base the comparison on product types instead[299], China contends that Article 2.4 imposes a "twofold obligation"[300] on the Commission. Specifically, the Commission was required to: (i) first evaluate all differences in physical characteristics that had been identified in the PCNs to determine whether they affected price comparability; and (ii) conclude, on the basis of such an evaluation, that adjustments were indeed required so as to ensure a fair comparison.[301] Yet, the Commission failed to do either.

174. China maintains that, in rejecting China's argument that the Commission acted inconsistently with Article 2.4, the Panel erroneously found that there was no evidence on the record demonstrating that the PCN elements necessarily affected price comparability. In China's view, the Panel failed to distinguish between the two-step analysis that the Commission was required to conduct, because its finding only concerned the second step described above. Indeed, the relevant findings of the Panel make it clear that the physical characteristics in the PCNs constitute differences that had been identified by the investigating authorities. Specifically, the Panel found that the fact that the Commission sought information on the basis of PCNs "suggest[ed] ... that these elements might affect price comparability".[302] China further contends that, because the interested parties were under the impression that the price comparison was being made on the basis of the PCNs, they made no requests for adjustments during the investiga-

[297] Although China's other appellant's submission alleges that the Panel erred in its interpretation (see paras. 296, 344, and 367), China clarified at the oral hearing that its claim also covers the Panel's application of Article 2.4 to the facts of the case.

[298] See China's other appellant's submission, paras. 353 and 354 (quoting Panel Report, *Argentina – Ceramic Tiles*, para. 6.113; and Panel Report, *EC – Tube or Pipe Fittings*, para. 7.157).

[299] China's other appellant's submission, para. 337.

[300] China's other appellant's submission, para. 346.

[301] See China's other appellant's submission, para. 346.

[302] China's other appellant's submission, para. 359 (quoting Panel Report, para. 7.301). (underlining by China omitted)

tion concerning the physical characteristics reflected in the PCNs. Nonetheless, as China submitted before the Panel, the interested parties stressed throughout the investigation the importance of using the PCNs for purposes of ensuring a fair comparison. However, the Panel failed to "come to the logical conclusion" that, because the physical characteristics "*might* affect price comparability", they had been identified as differences that the Commission was required to evaluate.[303]

175. China also takes issue with the Panel's finding that, although information organized on the basis of the PCNs may well facilitate the comparison process, "the obligation to make a fair comparison under Article 2.4 does not vary depending on the form in which information is requested or received."[304] In China's view, because the Commission had identified certain physical characteristics as possibly affecting price comparability, it was required to evaluate those characteristics to determine whether adjustments were necessary to ensure a fair comparison.

176. On this basis, China requests the Appellate Body to reverse the Panel's finding that "the argument that the Commission should have considered whether the elements excluded from the comparison nonetheless required adjustments does not amount to a *prima facie* case of violation of Article 2.4"[305], and find that the European Union's failure to evaluate the differences identified through the PCNs constitutes a violation of Article 2.4 of the *Anti-Dumping Agreement*.

(ii) The Panel's failure to make an objective assessment of the facts

177. China submits that the Panel failed to make an objective assessment of the facts in finding that China pointed to no evidence that was before the investigating authority in support of its claim that the PCN characteristics indicated differences affecting price comparability. As a preliminary matter, China recalls that the Commission, by failing to inform the interested parties of the basis for the price comparison, made it impossible for the Chinese producers to request adjustments and provide the necessary evidence.

178. Moreover, China contends that it demonstrated to the Panel that there was evidence before the Commission showing that the PCN characteristics were differences affecting price comparability and warranting adjustments. Specifically, the fact that certain physical characteristics were reflected in the PCNs shows that such characteristics affect price comparability, because reliance on PCNs had been identified by the investigating authorities at the beginning of the investigation as being necessary to ensure a fair comparison. In addition, several of the PCN characteristics were used by the Commission for purposes of the price undercutting analysis between the Chinese and European fasteners producers in the injury determination, including the type of coating applied and the use of

---

303 China's other appellant's submission, para. 361. (original emphasis)

304 China's other appellant's submission, para. 365 (quoting Panel Report, para. 7.303).

305 China's other appellant's submission, para. 368 (quoting Panel Report, para. 7.306).

expensive chrome on coating. China also alleges that it referred the Panel to the following three pieces of additional evidence to demonstrate that the PCN characteristics necessarily affected price comparability: (i) a statement by the EU producers, in the context of a discussion on the comparability between EU and Chinese fasteners, regarding the fact that raw materials represent 40 to 55 per cent of the costs and may be lower for products with a little diameter; (ii) a statement by the Chinese Chamber of Commerce, in the same context, that it was necessary to add to the differences reflected in the PCNs a distinction between standard and special fasteners; and (iii) a presentation on behalf of a Chinese interested party that the PCN characteristics are not sufficiently detailed to differentiate interims of the quality of fasteners. China therefore asserts that, by ignoring the above evidence, the Panel failed to make an objective assessment of the facts, as required by Article 11 of the DSU.

179. China further maintains that Article 17.6(i) of the *Anti-Dumping Agreement* requires the Panel to determine whether the Commission's establishment of the facts was proper and whether its evaluation of those facts was unbiased and objective. Because the Commission "ignored the evidence before it that demonstrated that the PCN characteristics could affect price comparability", "it is clear" that the Commission's establishment of the facts was not proper and its evaluation of those facts was not unbiased and objective.[306] Thus, the Panel, by finding that it would be inappropriate for it to consider whether the PCN characteristics reflect differences affecting price comparability, "ignored the duty imposed upon it by Article 17.6 (i)" of the *Anti-Dumping Agreement*.[307]

180. On this basis, China requests the Appellate Body to reverse the above Panel findings. China further requests the Appellate Body to complete the analysis and find that the European Union acted inconsistently with Article 2.4 of the *Anti-Dumping Agreement* by not making the necessary adjustments for the differences in physical characteristics identified in the PCNs. This is because an objective and unbiased investigating authority should have concluded, on the basis of all the elements before the Commission, that the PCN characteristics described in this case indicate differences affecting price comparability and that, accordingly, these had to be accounted for by means of adjustments.

(c) Quality Differences

181. China asserts that the Panel erred in the interpretation and application of Article 2.4 of the *Anti-Dumping Agreement* in rejecting China's claim that the European Union acted inconsistently with that provision by not making the necessary adjustments for quality differences affecting price comparability.

182. China recalls that, under Article 2.4, investigating authorities must at least evaluate identified differences in physical characteristics with a view to determining whether or not an adjustment is necessary to ensure a fair comparison of the export price and the normal value. In this case, "[i]t is not disputed that at

306 China's other appellant's submission, para. 387.
307 China's other appellant's submission, para. 386.

least one of the Chinese exporters" sent a letter requesting adjustments for differences in quality between Indian and Chinese fasteners.[308] Moreover, the Commission "acknowledge[d] the existence of quality differences" in the Definitive Regulation by stating that "[a]ny perceived differences in quality, which may subsist from a user's point of view, can be dealt with through an adjustment for physical differences".[309] The Commission also stated in a letter to some Chinese exporters that adjustments were made for the cost of quality control that "reflects the general difference in quality level".[310] This, in China's view, also shows that quality differences had been identified and that the Commission should have evaluated such differences. China therefore contends that the Panel erred in not concluding that the Commission acted inconsistently with Article 2.4 of the *Anti-Dumping Agreement* by not evaluating the identified quality differences.

183. China further submits that, in finding that the Commission did not act inconsistently with Article 2.4 of the *Anti-Dumping Agreement*, the Panel "ignore[d] the fact" that the Commission acknowledged the existence of quality differences. According to China, there is a duty on the investigating authority to request the necessary information if it feels that a claimed adjustment is not sufficiently substantiated. Therefore, "at the very least, the Commission should have sought additional information on this issue."[311] China thus maintains that the Panel erred in law by failing to conclude that the failure of the Commission to indicate further information that would be necessary to ensure a fair comparison and the failure to make appropriate adjustments was inconsistent with Article 2.4 of the *Anti-Dumping Agreement*.

3. *The Panel's Findings under Articles 6.5, 6.2, and 6.4 of the Anti-Dumping Agreement Regarding the Disclosure of the Identity of the Complainants*

184. China requests the Appellate Body to reverse the Panel's findings that the European Union did not act inconsistently with Articles 6.5, 6.4, and 6.2 of the *Anti-Dumping Agreement* when it failed to disclose to Chinese producers the identity of the complainants and the supporters of the complaint. China argues that the complainants' allegation of "potential commercial retaliation" was not sufficient to satisfy the requirement to show "good cause" under Article 6.5, and that the Panel violated Article 11 of the DSU in its evaluation of this claim. Assuming the Appellate Body finds that the identity of the complainants and the supporters of the complaint were not properly treated as confidential information, China requests the Appellate Body to complete the analysis to find that the

[308] China's other appellant's submission, para. 410.

[309] China's other appellant's submission, para. 411 (quoting Definitive Regulation, *supra*, footnote 4, recital 52).

[310] China's other appellant's submission, para. 413 (quoting Letter dated 21 November 2008 from the European Commission to Van Bael & Bellis replying to Van Bael & Bellis' letter dated 17 November 2008 (Panel Exhibit CHN-31), point 5).

[311] China's other appellant's submission, para. 420.

European Union therefore also violated Articles 6.4 and 6.2 of the *Anti-Dumping Agreement* when it failed to disclose this information to Chinese exporters upon request.

(a) The Complainants' "Good Cause" Showing

185. China claims that the Panel erred in finding that the Commission had established that "good cause" existed for the confidential treatment of the identity of the complainants and the supporters of the complaint under Article 6.5 of the *Anti-Dumping Agreement*. China observes that the requirement to show "good cause" is, in the words of the panel in *Mexico – Steel Pipes and Tubes*, of "critical importance" to preventing parties from abusing the privileges of confidential treatment, and in "preserving the balance between the interests of confidentiality and the ability of another interested party to defend its rights throughout an anti-dumping investigation".[312] In China's view, while every request for confidentiality requires an evidentiary showing of "good cause", in the case of information that is not "by nature" confidential, such as the identity of the complainants, "a higher threshold needs to be met".[313]

186. China argues that the Panel erred in its interpretation of the "good cause" requirement, because, in its view, Article 6.5 does not apply to commercial retaliation that is merely hypothetical in nature. China contends that, in the complaint, domestic producers requested confidential treatment of their identity because of a "potential retaliation" that "could" happen, but did not allege or show that any "significantly adverse effect" "'would' happen if confidential treatment [was] not granted". In China's view, Article 6.5 refers to situations that "*would have* a significantly adverse effect" upon the parties supplying the information, and that the complainants' use of the word "could" suggests that "the likelihood of the detrimental effect to occur is rather remote".[314]

187. According to China, the complainants failed to provide any evidence to support the assertion in the complaint that a threat of potential commercial retaliation existed. The Panel itself acknowledged that the "*only evidence* before the Commission was the complaint" and that "[t]he Commission relied on this statement, although there is no indication that the complainants submitted evidence to support their concern in this regard."[315] In China's view, the reasoning included in the complaint, that retaliation could come from the complainants' customers who also bought the subject products from China, was a "mere statement" and clearly does not amount to an evidentiary showing. China contends that an interpretation of Article 6.5 that does not require an evidentiary showing to support "good cause" "is contrary to both the text and *ratio legis* of Article

---

312 China's other appellant's submission, para. 447 (quoting Panel Report, *Mexico – Steel Pipes and Tubes*, para. 7.380).
313 China's other appellant's submission, para. 449.
314 China's other appellant's submission, paras. 450-453.
315 China's other appellant's submission, para. 458 (quoting Panel Report, para. 7.453).

6.5" and "seriously undermines the delicate balance sought in that provision to protect the interests of all interested parties".[316]

188. China further argues that the evidentiary burden of proof under Article 6.5 rests with the party requesting confidential treatment, and that the Panel violated Article 11 of the DSU when it impermissibly shifted this burden on China. The Panel found that China did not "contest the factual assertion" contained in the complaint, and had not "proffered any evidence, or even argued, that this assertion was unfounded, unreasonable, or untrue".[317] It similarly found that evidence of "potential commercial retaliation" is not likely to be obtainable, and that therefore, the allegation of the complainants would be sufficient "unless there is some reason to believe that the fear of retaliation is unreasonable, unfounded, or untrue – and China has proffered none".[318] In China's view, it was up to the complainants in the investigation to present "compelling evidence" to support their allegation, and it was not China's responsibility to present evidence before a WTO panel that no "good cause" existed.[319] Moreover, even if China had an obligation to offer evidence against the complainants' allegation of potential commercial retaliation, it was prevented from doing so because it was never given access to those complainants' identity.[320]

189. Before the Panel, China claimed that the Commission's disclosure of the sampled producers' identity in the context of the injury determination demonstrated that good cause could not have existed for the Commission's earlier confidential treatment of those producers' identity as complainants and supporters of the complaint. By disclosing the names of the sampled producers, China submits, the Commission thereby also revealed the names of several complainants and/or supporters of the complaint. The fact that the domestic producers did not request that their identity be kept confidential in this context as well, demonstrates, in China's view, that no "good cause" existed to treat their identity as confidential earlier in the proceedings.[321] On appeal, China claims that the Panel erred in rejecting this argument because the Panel record contains clear evidence showing that the entire domestic industry as defined by the Commission, and therefore also the domestic producers sampled for purposes of the injury determination, consisted only of complainants and supporters of the complaint.[322]

190. China also claims that the Panel erred in finding that the identification of companies as sampled producers would not cause the same concerns for those companies as their identification as complainants and supporters, and that in the fasteners investigation it was not the case that the sampled producers were necessarily complainants or supporters of the complaint. China argues that the former argument is "unfounded" because the Panel did not explain why sampled

[316] China's other appellant's submission, para. 463.
[317] China's other appellant's submission, para. 464 (quoting Panel Report, para. 7.452).
[318] China's other appellant's submission, para. 464 (quoting Panel Report, para. 7.453).
[319] China's other appellant's submission, paras. 464 and 467.
[320] China's other appellant's submission, para. 468.
[321] China's other appellant's submission, para. 471.
[322] China's other appellant's submission, paras. 473 and 474.

producers would not have the same concerns as complainants and supporters. As to the latter, China submits that this conclusion was erroneous, because it was based on the European Union's "mere assertion" that "at least one company included in the sample was not, in fact, either a complainant or supporter of the complaint".[323]

(b) Disclosure under Articles 6.4 and 6.2 of the *Anti-Dumping Agreement*

191. Assuming that the Appellate Body reverses the Panel's finding that the European Union properly treated the identity of the complainants as confidential information under Article 6.5 of the *Anti-Dumping Agreement*, China requests that the Appellate Body also reverse the Panel's consequential findings under Articles 6.4 and 6.2 of the *Agreement*, and find instead that the Commission's failure to disclose the identity of the complainants was inconsistent with both provisions.[324] To this end, China argues that the identity of the complainants and the supporters of the complaint should have been disclosed in compliance with Article 6.4 because this information was "used" by the Commission in their standing determination, and was therefore "'relevant' to the presentation of [the Chinese producers'] cases" in this regard.[325] China also argues that the identity of the complainants should have been disclosed under Article 6.2 of the *Anti-Dumping Agreement* in order to provide the producers with a "full opportunity for the defence of their interests".[326] According to China, Article 6.2 is "so broad" that a violation of Article 6.4 "necessarily entails a violation of Article 6.2".[327] Even independently of a violation of Article 6.4, however, China submits that the Commission violated Article 6.2 because, as a result of the Commission's failure to disclose the names of these companies, the Chinese producers were not given an opportunity properly to examine and present arguments regarding the Commission's standing determination.[328]

4. *The Panel's Findings that the MET/IT Claim Form Was Not a "Questionnaire" for Purposes of Article 6.1.1 of the Anti-Dumping Agreement*

192. China requests the Appellant Body to reverse the Panel's finding that the Commission did not act inconsistently with its obligations under Article 6.1.1 of the *Anti-Dumping Agreement* when it allowed Chinese producers only 15 days from the publication of the Notice of Initiation of the investigation to submit a claim form requesting market economy and/or individual treatment ("the MET/IT Claim Form"). Specifically, China argues that the Panel erred in

[323] China's other appellant's submission, para. 477 (quoting Panel Report, footnote 940 to para. 7.454).
[324] China's other appellant's submission, para. 482.
[325] China's other appellant's submission, paras. 483 and 484.
[326] China's other appellant's submission, para. 487.
[327] *Ibid.*
[328] China's other appellant's submission, para. 488.

finding that the 30-day time-limit required for the submission of "questionnaires" in Article 6.1.1 applies only to "the initial comprehensive questionnaire" issued in an investigation.[329] In the alternative, China contends that the Panel erred in finding that the MET/IT Claim Form was not the initial, comprehensive questionnaire sent to foreign exporters in an NME investigation.

193. China submits that the Panel erred in interpreting the term "questionnaires" as referring only to "the initial comprehensive questionnaire issued in an anti-dumping investigation to each of the interested parties by an investigating authority at or following the initiation of an investigation, which questionnaire seeks information as to all relevant issues pertaining to the main questions that will need to be decided (dumping, injury and causation)".[330] Instead, China urges the Appellate Body to find that the term "questionnaires" includes all information requests made through a series of questions that are su30bstantial enough to warrant verification, as long as extending a full 30-day deadline would not prevent the investigating authorities from complying with the overall timeframe set out in Article 5.10 of the *Anti-Dumping Agreement* for the completion of an investigation.[331]

194. China observes that the ordinary meaning of the term "questionnaire" is quite broad and would on its face cover every document used by an investigating authority to seek information in the form of "a formulated series of questions".[332] China also emphasizes the fact that Article 6.1.1 uses the plural form of this term, which suggests that the provision would not only apply to multiple questionnaires, but that each foreign producer may receive more than one questionnaire requiring a 30-day deadline throughout the course of the investigation.[333] China argues that Articles 6.1 and 6.2 of the *Anti-Dumping Agreement* provide the appropriate context for the interpretation of Article 6.1.1, and notes that the Appellate Body has found that these provisions "set out the fundamental due process rights" in anti-dumping investigations and provide for "liberal opportunities for respondents to defend their interests".[334] China claims that the reference to a "questionnaire" in paragraphs 6 and 7 of Annex I to the *Anti-Dumping Agreement* (Procedures for On-the-Spot Investigations pursuant to Paragraph 7 of Article 6) shows that the term refers to information requests that are "so substantial" that they require verification by the investigating authority—a characterization that would cover the MET/IT Claim Form.[335] Finally, China argues that the purpose of the time-limit set out in Article 6.1.1, that investigating authorities retain the ability to "control and expedite the investigating process", does not imply that the term "questionnaires" can refer to only one document.[336]

---

329 China's other appellant's submission, para. 501 (quoting Panel Report, para. 7.574).
330 *Ibid.*
331 China's other appellant's submission, para. 538.
332 China's other appellant's submission, para. 509.
333 China's other appellant's submission, para. 510.
334 China's other appellant's submission, para. 513 (quoting Appellate Body Report, *US – Oil Country Tubular Goods Sunset Reviews*, para. 241).
335 China's other appellant's submission, para. 526.
336 China's other appellant's submission, para. 533.

China claims that the Commission's ability to complete the fasteners investigation in a timely manner would not have been frustrated by allowing the Chinese producers a full 30 days to submit the MET/IT Claim Form.[337]

195. Even if the Appellate Body determines that the Panel was correct in its interpretation of the term "questionnaires" in Article 6.1.1, China argues that the Panel violated Article 11 of the DSU and Article 17.6(i) of the *Anti-Dumping Agreement* when it failed to find that, for the foreign exporters of an NME country, the MET/IT Claim Form is the initial, comprehensive questionnaire. China submits that the MET/IT Claim Form includes many of the same issues covered in other initial questionnaires, and that the Panel's own admission that not all initial questionnaires will cover the same material, suggests that the MET/IT Claim Form need not have covered all the issues involved in the investigation to be considered the "initial questionnaire".

D. Arguments of the European Union – Appellee

1. The Panel's Findings under Articles 4.1 and 3.1 of the Anti-Dumping Agreement

196. The European Union requests the Appellate Body to reject China's appeal against the Panel's finding that the European Union did not act inconsistently with Articles 4.1 and 3.1 of the *Anti-Dumping Agreement* with respect to the definition of the domestic industry in the fasteners investigation. The European Union maintains that, as the Panel properly found, the European Union did not exclude from the definition of the domestic industry those producers who did not support the complaint. Nor did the European Union act inconsistently with Articles 4.1 and 3.1 of the *Anti-Dumping Agreement* by not including in the domestic industry definition those producers who made themselves known more than 15 days after the publication of the Notice of Initiation of the investigation. The European Union further submits that the Panel correctly rejected China's assertion that the domestic industry defined by the Commission, consisting of those producers whose output accounted for 27 per cent of total domestic production, did not meet the requirement of "a major proportion" under Article 4.1 of the *Anti-Dumping Agreement*. Finally, with respect to China's claim regarding the representativeness of the sample for purposes of the injury determination, the European Union contends that the claim was not properly before the Panel and therefore outside the scope of appellate review. In any event, the European Union asserts that China's arguments in support of this claim are without merit.

(a) Exclusion of Certain Producers

197. The European Union submits that China fails to demonstrate that the Panel acted inconsistently with Article 11 of the DSU and Article 17.6(i) of the *Anti-Dumping Agreement* in finding that the European Union did not exclude producers who did not support the complaint from the definition of domestic

[337] China's other appellant's submission, para. 536.

industry. Moreover, China has not demonstrated that the Panel erred in its interpretation of Article 4.1 of the *Anti-Dumping Agreement*, or acted inconsistently with Article 11 of the DSU, in rejecting China's allegation that the exclusion of the producers who did not come forward within the 15-day deadline was inconsistent with Article 4.1 of the *Anti-Dumping Agreement*. In addition, China fails to demonstrate that the Panel erred in law when it rejected China's "consequential"[338] claim under Article 3.1 of the *Anti-Dumping Agreement*.

(i) Exclusion of producers who did not support the complaint

198. The European Union maintains that "[i]t is well established" that a panel, as the trier of facts, enjoys a substantial margin of discretion. The discretion is not boundless, and there could be a failure to make an objective assessment of the facts in the event of "deliberate disregard" and refusal to consider the evidence, or in case of the "wilful distortion" or "misrepresentation" of the evidence.[339] In the European Union's view, the relevant jurisprudence under Article 11 of the DSU suggests that a violation of that provision is not "simply an error of judgment in the appreciation of evidence but rather 'an egregious error that calls into question the good faith of a panel'".[340]

199. Turning to the facts of the case, the European Union submits that the Panel properly took into consideration, as part of the totality of evidence before it, the "information provided by the [European Union] that at least one producer that had remained silent prior to initiation and thus had not 'supported the complaint' was included in the definition of the domestic industry".[341] The Panel "was right to assume good faith on the part of the [European Union]"[342], and there was no reason to doubt the veracity of the information in the light of the relevant evidence on the record. Specifically, the European Union provided the name of the producer in question, rather than giving "a vague reference to an unidentified mysterious producer that could not be verified".[343] Moreover, contrary to China's assertion that the European Union should have provided the list of complainants and supporters in order to prove the information it provided, the European Union indicated to the Panel its willingness to provide the list, but also highlighted the fact that the list had been treated as confidential. The Panel did not request to see the list, and it is not within the Appellate Body's mandate to examine now evidence in respect of which factual findings have been made by the Panel.

200. Moreover, the European Union contends, the information it provided to the Panel concerning the producer who had not supported the complaint was

338 European Union's appellee's submission, para. 107.

339 European Union's appellee's submission, para. 50 (quoting Appellate Body Report, *EC – Hormones*, para. 133). (underlining by the European Union omitted)

340 *Ibid.*

341 European Union's appellee's submission, para. 53.

342 European Union's appellee's submission, para. 61.

343 European Union's appellee's submission, para. 57.

"mainly to *confirm* the [other] information already provided by the [European Union] that no producer was excluded for reason of the fact that it did not support the complaint".[344] Specifically, the European Union maintains that it submitted evidence in the form of the sampling forms sent upon the initiation of the investigation to all known producers for purposes of defining the domestic industry, which did not include a question concerning support for the complaint. Moreover, recitals 23 to 25 of the Definitive Regulation also confirm that all those producers who responded to the sampling forms within the 15-day deadline and indicated their willingness to cooperate were included in the domestic industry definition, regardless of whether they supported the complaint. Thus, the European Union contends, China erroneously suggests that the European Union made a "mere assertion"[345] when it provided the name of the producer who had not supported the complaint. On the contrary, this evidence was supported and confirmed by other evidence on the record. The Panel therefore did not act inconsistently with Article 11 of the DSU because it took into account all of the above evidence in its assessment of the facts.

201. The European Union further submits that there is no basis for China's allegation that the Commission knew whether the sampled producer who had not supported the complaint at the time of initiation actually supported the investigation when it came forward after initiation. In the European Union's view, China "speculates" about what the Commission could have known regarding the producer's position in respect of the complaint, "when it has been established as a matter of fact that this was a producer that (i) was silent before initiation and (ii) subsequently ... return[ed] a sampling form in which no question was asked about support for the complaint".[346] Therefore, the Panel properly found that, "[w]hile China continues to assert that the Commission inquired as to the position of EU producers with respect to the complaint, the only evidence before the Panel, the sampling forms, does not support that assertion."[347] The European Union asserts that the "evidence" provided by China in this regard was based on "certain unfortunate statements in the Information Document and in [the Definitive Regulation]".[348] Such statements, according to the European Union, were due to certain "confusion"[349] between the issue of the standing requirement and the definition of the domestic industry, which was caused by the Commission's inquiry, after the initiation of the investigation, concerning the Chinese interested parties' allegation that the standing requirement had not been met. Although China disagrees with the weight given by the Panel to the alleged "evidence", a panel's examination and weighing of the evidence submitted falls within the scope of the panel's discretion as the trier of the facts.

---

344 European Union's appellee's submission, para. 58. (original emphasis)

345 European Union's appellee's submission, para. 59 (quoting China's other appellant's submission, para. 66).

346 European Union's appellee's submission, para. 63.

347 European Union's appellee's submission, para. 64 (quoting Panel Report, para. 6.75).

348 European Union's appellee's submission, footnote 47 to para. 65.

349 *Ibid.*

202. Finally, the European Union maintains that, in alleging that the Panel "disregarded"[350] three pieces of evidence and thus acted inconsistently with Article 11 of the DSU, China's claim merely concerns the Panel's appreciation of the evidence within the boundary of its discretion as the trier of facts. Specifically, the Panel rightly relied on recitals 23 to 25 of the Definitive Regulation, which show that support for the complaint was not a condition for being included in the domestic industry definition, despite the reference to "producers supporting the complaint" in the definition of the domestic industry under the Definitive Regulation. "Similarly", the European Union argues, "the Panel put the confused statements in the informal Information Document in context by pointing to the fact that this was a mere working document with no legal status in the [European Union]."[351] Finally, the European Union asserts that the Panel did not err in not expressly addressing the letter referred to by China, because a panel "is not required to discuss, in its report, each and every piece of evidence".[352] In any event, China misinterprets the letter it sought to rely on, which does not state that support for the complaint was a condition for inclusion in the domestic industry definition.

203. On this basis, the European Union submits that China's allegation that the Panel committed egregious error in not giving the same weight to the evidence as did China, and acted inconsistently with Article 11 of the DSU, must fail.

(ii) Exclusion of producers who did not come forward within 15 days of the initiation of the investigation

204. The European Union asserts that China fails to establish that the Panel erred in the legal interpretation, and acted inconsistently with Article 11 of the DSU, in finding that the European Union did not act inconsistently with Article 4.1 of the *Anti-Dumping Agreement* by excluding from the domestic industry definition all producers who did not come forward within 15 days following the initiation of the investigation.

205. The European Union contends that China accepts that it is "permissible"[353] to impose a deadline for domestic producers to come forward, which undermines its assertion that Article 4.1 prohibits the exclusion of any categories of producers except for those provided under paragraphs (i) and (ii). Moreover, there is no basis for China's argument that the imposition of a deadline for producers to come forward is "inadmissible if the investigating authorities ... consider the inclusion of producers that did not come forward within the deadline

[350] European Union's appellee's submission, para. 68 (quoting China's other appellant's submission, para. 85).
[351] European Union's appellee's submission, para. 72.
[352] European Union's appelles's submission, para. 73 (quoting Appellate Body Report, *Brazil – Retreaded Tyres*, para. 202).
[353] European Union's appellee's submission, para. 78 (quoting China's other appellant's submission, para. 125).

and finally decide not to include them".[354] Indeed, China does not explain why it accepts that deadlines may be used, but then objects to the fact that such deadlines are actually applied by the authorities. The European Union submits that investigating authorities are entitled, under Article 6.14 of the *Anti-Dumping Agreement*, to maintain control over the investigations and to impose deadlines in order to be able to proceed expeditiously with the investigation. Moreover, the authorities are required to impose such deadlines in order to comply with their obligation under Article 5.10 of the *Anti-Dumping Agreement* to conclude the investigation within 12 to 18 months. The European Union further submits that, in the fasteners investigation, the 15-day deadline excluded producers irrespective of their support for the complaint and was a reasonable and objective way of defining the domestic industry.

206. The European Union maintains that there is no basis for China's allegation that the Panel acted inconsistently with Article 11 of the DSU in finding that the European Union did not deliberately exclude producers that came forward after the 15-day deadline. The Information Document, to which China refers in support of its claim, merely reflects, "in a somewhat confused manner"[355], the fact that the Commission accommodated the Chinese interested parties' allegation, that the standing requirement had not been met, by contacting additional domestic producers concerning their production volume and their position regarding the complaint. Moreover, the Panel examined the relevant evidence and found that "the fact that the Commission considered including [the additional producers in] the domestic industry supports our view that it did not simply exclude producers who did not come forward within the 15-day period."[356] In the European Union's view, China's allegation that the Panel acted inconsistently with Article 11 of the DSU in reaching this finding is "based on a wilful misreading of the Panel Report", because the Panel simply "reached the factual conclusion that the authorities applied the deadline they had set for domestic producers but that in so doing the authorities had not been deaf to requests from exporters to contact more producers".[357]

207. The European Union argues that China's assertion that the Panel acted inconsistently with Article 11 of the DSU in finding that China had not demonstrated the unreasonableness of the 15-day deadline is also without merit. As the Panel correctly found, China submitted no evidence regarding the alleged unreasonable or insufficient nature of the 15-day deadline. China's mere "speculation" that a deadline as short as 15 days makes it more likely that only complainants and supporters would come forward does not amount to such evidence.[358] Moreover, contrary to China's argument, linking the possibility of being included in the domestic industry to a producer's willingness to be included in the sample is

---

[354] European Union's appellee's submission, para. 81 (quoting China's other appellant's submission, para. 126).
[355] European Union's appellee's submission, para. 89.
[356] European Union's appellee's submission, para. 90 (quoting Panel Report, para. 7.215).
[357] European Union's appellee's submission, para. 91.
[358] European Union's appellee's submission, para. 96.

unrelated to the question of whether the 15-day deadline is reasonable. This is because the information requested in the sampling form, concerning the products produced and the volume of production, was easy to provide, and the indication of willingness to be included in the sample only required the ticking of the appropriate box on the form. Finally, the European Union contends that China's assertion that the 15-day deadline to respond to the sampling form is not the same as the period in which an interested party was requested to make itself known under the Notice of Initiation is "simply incorrect". This is so because the Notice of Initiation clearly provides for a 15-day period for being included in the domestic industry, and a 40-day period for interested parties to make themselves known "unless otherwise specified".[359]

208. On this basis, the European Union requests the Appellate Body to reject China's above claims and arguments, as well as China's request for completion of the analysis.

(iii) Inconsistency with Article 3.1 of the *Anti-Dumping Agreement*

209. The European Union maintains that the Panel correctly determined that China failed to make a *prima facie* case under Article 3.1 of the *Anti-Dumping Agreement* because its arguments under that provision were dependent on its arguments under Article 4.1 of the *Anti-Dumping Agreement*. In support of its appeal under Article 3.1, China simply repeats its arguments concerning the alleged exclusion of the producers who did not support the complaint, and the alleged unreasonableness of the 15-day deadline. These are the same arguments China had raised under Article 4.1 of the *Anti-Dumping Agreement*, which the Panel properly rejected. Thus, given the Panel's findings under Article 4.1, and given the fact that China's arguments under Article 3.1 were identical to those under Article 4.1, the Panel did not err in rejecting China's claim under Article 3.1. The European Union adds that China's appeal does not identify any error of law in the Panel's finding under Article 3.1, but merely describes the alleged errors committed by the Commission in its definition of the domestic industry. Thus, the European Union contends that, because China "never developed an independent argument under Article 3.1 of the *Anti-Dumping Agreement*"[360], the Appellate Body must also reject China's appeal under that provision.

210. The European Union further submits that China's argument that the manner in which the Commission defined the domestic industry was biased must also be rejected. China's assertion that "[c]ompanies opposing the investigation are much less likely to be willing to be part of the sample than companies supporting the investigation"[361] is "purely speculative".[362] Even if it were true, this

[359] European Union's appellee's submission, para. 101. (boldface by the European Union omitted)
[360] European Union's appellee's submission, para. 108.
[361] European Union's appellee's submission, para. 113 (quoting China's second written submission to the Panel, para. 548).
[362] European Union's appellee's submission, para. 113.

does not mean that an authority cannot use cooperation as a criterion for defining the domestic industry. In the absence of subpoena powers, the Commission was entitled to continue its investigation on the basis of facts made available by the cooperating producers, as long as their output represented a major proportion of the total domestic production. Finally, the European Union submits that Article 3.1 of the *Anti-Dumping Agreement* only requires that the authorities conduct an objective examination of positive evidence in respect of the domestic industry as defined under Article 4.1. Article 3.1 thus concerns only the manner in which data from those producers included in the domestic industry definition is examined, an issue not raised in China's appeal under that provision.

211. On this basis, the European Union requests the Appellate Body to reject China's appeal under Article 3.1 of the *Anti-Dumping Agreement*.

(b) "A Major Proportion" of the Total Domestic Production

212. As a preliminary matter, the European Union submits that it wishes to express its concern about what it views as a change in China's position with regard to the interpretation of the term "a major proportion" under Article 4.1 of the *Anti-Dumping Agreement*. Before the Panel, China agreed with the interpretation of the panel in *Argentina – Poultry Anti-Dumping Duties* that "major" means "important, serious or significant", with which the European Union also agreed. Although China's original position had been that "a major proportion" must be as close as possible to 100 per cent, it "clearly abandoned its original position" by acknowledging that "major" in abstract terms could even be a percentage lower than 25 per cent.[363] Thus, noting the agreement between the parties on the interpretation of the term "a major proportion", the Panel focused its examination on whether China met its burden of proving that, in this dispute, 27 per cent of the total domestic production was not a major proportion. Thus, in the European Union's view, because the Panel "relied on" the agreement between the parties regarding the legal interpretation in developing its reasoning, it is "simply not credible, nor appropriate" for China to assert on appeal that the interpretation put forward by the Panel is not permissible.[364]

213. The European Union further submits that, as the Panel correctly found, despite the alleged presumption relied on by the Commission in defining the domestic industry, China failed to establish that the output of the domestic industry as defined by the Commission, representing 27 per cent of total domestic production, did not constitute "a major proportion" within the meaning of Article 4.1 of the *Anti-Dumping Agreement*. Finally, China's allegation that the Panel erred in rejecting certain non-quantitative factors is also unfounded. These non-quantitative factors include the alleged exclusion of certain producers, the practical possibility to obtain information from all producers, and the number of producers.

---

363 European Union's appellee's submission, para. 138.

364 European Union's appellee's submission, para. 141.

(i) The interpretation of the term "a major proportion"

214. The European Union submits that, because the text of Article 4.1 of the *Anti-Dumping Agreement* refers to "a major proportion" and does not use terms such as "the majority", this provision does not require that the domestic industry consist of producers representing more than 50 per cent of the domestic production. This interpretation is supported by the panel's finding in *Argentina – Poultry Anti-Dumping Duties*[365], and China does not argue otherwise. The European Union further maintains that, on the basis of its ordinary meaning, the term "a major proportion" means an "important, serious or significant" proportion of total domestic output. Although the dictionary definition relied on by China defines the word "major" as "*unusually* important, serious or significant"[366], the European Union submits that the qualifying term "unusually" is not particularly meaningful.

215. The European Union agrees with China's argument that, in order to represent a "proportion", the production of domestic producers concerned must constitute a "part" or "share" of the whole. However, the European Union asserts that China "makes an unsubstantiated leap of logic when it states that '[*i*]*n other words*, they must be representative of the whole'".[367] There is nothing inherently "representative" in the term "proportion", because the term simply refers to a ratio. Moreover, because Article 4.1 refers to the "collective output", the term "a major proportion" is to be examined in relation to the quantity of production. The European Union further contends that the Appellate Body's finding in *US – Lamb*, to which China refers in support of its position, addresses the meaning of "producers as a whole", and not "a major proportion", and therefore does not lend support to China's position.[368]

216. The European Union submits that, without any basis, China asserts that "[t]he reason for permitting the domestic industry to be defined as those producers constituting only a 'major proportion' is to address the practical impossibility for investigating authorities in some cases to obtain the requested information from all the producers of the like product."[369] The European Union maintains that Article 4.1 merely refers to two alternative options for defining the domestic industry, and the word "or" indicates that there is no hierarchy or preference between these two options. Moreover, contrary to China's assertions, paragraphs (i) and (ii) of Article 4.1 do not limit the discretion of the investigating authority, but merely allow the investigating authority to limit the total number of eligible

[365] European Union's appellee's submission, para. 147 (referring to Panel Report, *Argentina – Poultry Anti-Dumping Duties*, paras. 7.341 and 7.342).

[366] European Union's appellee's submission, para. 142 (referring to China's other appellant's submission, paras. 10, 188 and 189). (emphasis added by the European Union)

[367] European Union's appellee's submission, para. 151 (referring to China's other appellant's submission, para. 185). (emphasis added by the European Union)

[368] European Union's appellee's submission, para. 153 (quoting Appellate Body Report, *US – Lamb*, para. 91).

[369] European Union's appellee's submission, para. 155 (quoting China's other appellant's submission, para. 195).

producers. The European Union emphasizes that its interpretation would not, as China suggests, lead to arbitrary exclusion of categories of producers. Rather, if the authority acts in an objective and unbiased manner in defining the domestic industry by, for example, including only those producers willing to cooperate, the definition of the domestic industry will be consistent with Article 4.1, even if it consists of producers whose output represents less than 100 per cent of the total domestic production. Finally, the European Union disagrees with China's argument that Article 3.1 of the *Anti-Dumping Agreement* provides contextual support for the proposition that the term "a major proportion" requires that the domestic industry so defined must be representative of the domestic producers as a whole. Rather, Article 3.1 imposes obligations in respect of injury determination, and does not impose any obligations in respect of the definition of the domestic industry.

(ii) Whether the domestic industry defined in the fasteners investigation meets the requirement on "a major proportion"

217. The European Union submits that it is for China, as the complaining party, to make a *prima facie* case that the European Union failed properly to define the domestic industry in the fasteners investigation because the collective output representing 27 per cent of total domestic production did not constitute "a major proportion" within the meaning of Article 4.1 of the *Anti-Dumping Agreement*. Before the Panel, although China argued that the Commission wrongly relied on a presumption that producers accounting for 25 per cent of total domestic production constituted a major proportion of domestic production, China also accepted that, depending on the circumstances, even a percentage of less than 25 per cent could be sufficient. Thus, the Panel correctly required China to provide evidence demonstrating that, in this dispute, 27 per cent was not an important, serious, or significant part of total domestic production.

218. In the European Union's view, China effectively alleges that authorities are under an independent obligation to explain the basis for their conclusion that a certain percentage of production is "major" in the circumstances of the case. However, Article 4.1 does not impose such an obligation. This is confirmed by the panel's finding in *Argentina – Poultry Anti-Dumping Duties* that authorities are not under an obligation to elucidate how they found that a percentage lower than 50 per cent could be considered "a major proportion".[370] The European Union maintains that, before the Panel, China did not deny that the domestic industry as defined included large and small companies, as well as producers of different types of fasteners. Moreover, during the fasteners investigation, the Chinese exporters did not question the representativeness of the domestic industry definition, and the Commission was therefore under no obligation to address such concerns. In this regard, China's argument on appeal that the Commission

[370] European Union's appellee's submission, para. 178 (referring to Panel Report, *Argentina – Poultry Anti-Dumping Duties*, para. 7.343).

relies on a rule that automatically equates "a major proportion" with 25 per cent of total domestic production "is in error and entirely irrelevant".[371] This is because China did not challenge the relevant provision of the European Union's Basic AD Regulation concerning such a "rule". Thus, these provisions are not before the Appellate Body and, in any event, there is no evidence on the record demonstrating that the Basic AD Regulation sets forth a mandatory rule preventing the Commission from concluding, in the specific circumstances of a case, that 25 per cent does not amount to a major proportion.

219. The European Union nonetheless maintains that the Basic AD Regulation reflects its position that Article 5.4 of the *Anti-Dumping Agreement* provides important contextual guidance concerning the meaning of the term "a major proportion" in Article 4.1 of that Agreement. Specifically, Article 5.4 provides that a request for initiation of an anti-dumping investigation must be made "by or on behalf of the domestic industry", and that this will be the case when it is established that domestic producers supporting the application represent at least 25 per cent of total domestic production. Therefore, it is "permissible to consider that producers that represent 25 [per cent] or more of domestic production can *legitimately* represent a major proportion of total production and that, as explained before, this was the case in the fasteners investigation."[372]

220. With regard to China's claim that the Panel failed to consider certain non-quantitative factors, the European Union asserts that China merely repeats the arguments in support of its view that the term "a major proportion" requires the domestic industry so defined be representative of the domestic producers as a whole. The European Union agrees that authorities cannot deliberately exclude a category of producers. However, if the exclusion only results from the application of a reasonable deadline, or the consequence of the fact that the industry is fragmented, it is not inconsistent with Article 4.1 of the *Anti-Dumping Agreement*. Furthermore, contrary to China's assertion, the number of producers is not a relevant element in the definition of the domestic industry, because Article 4.1 concerns the volume of production.

221. On this basis, the European Union submits that the Panel properly found that China failed to demonstrate, *prima facie*, that the definition of domestic industry in this case is inconsistent with Article 4.1 of the *Anti-Dumping Agreement*, and requests the Appellate Body to reject China's appeal.

(c) The Representativeness of the Sample of Domestic Producers in the Injury Determination

222. The European Union alleges, as a preliminary matter, that China's appeal concerns the Panel's rejection of a claim that was not within the Panel's terms of reference. In its request for the establishment of a panel[373], China alleged that the European Union acted inconsistently with Articles 4.1 and 3.1 of the *Anti-*

[371] European Union's appellee's submission, para. 186.
[372] European Union's appellee's submission, para. 187. (original emphasis)
[373] WT/DS397/3, 13 October 2009.

Dumping Agreement because the Commission conducted the injury determination on the basis of a sample of producers accounting for only 17.5 per cent of the total European Union production of the like product in 2006. However, in its second written submission before the Panel, China raised the "entirely new claim" that the European Union acted inconsistently with Article 3.1 of the *Anti-Dumping Agreement* by using a sample on the basis of the largest volume that can be reasonably investigated, thereby failing to use a sampling technique that guaranteed that the sample was sufficiently representative of the domestic industry.[374] The European Union argues that this new claim is in no way related to China's claim under Article 3.1 of the *Anti-Dumping Agreement* listed in its panel request, and is therefore not properly before the Appellate Body.

223. The European Union submits that China's claim under Article 3.1 of the *Anti-Dumping Agreement* is in any event without merit. Article 3.1 does not prescribe any methodology for sampling in the injury determination. Although Article 6.10 of the *Anti-Dumping Agreement*, concerning sampling in the dumping determination, is not directly applicable in the context of injury determinations, the fact that the Commission followed one of the two sampling methodologies provided in that provision indicates that its method was not unreasonable or biased. Moreover, as the Panel correctly found, China failed to present any factors other than volume that should have been taken into account. The European Union further maintains that there is no basis for China's claim that the Commission could have included more domestic producers in the sample. The Panel properly found that the mere fact that certain macro-economic factors were examined on the basis of data from all 45 producers making up the domestic industry does not demonstrate that the Commission could have examined all micro-economic factors on the same basis. This finding falls within the Panel's discretion as the trier of facts, and China makes no claim under Article 11 of the DSU in this regard.

224. On this basis, the European Union requests the Appellate Body to reject China's appeal of the Panel's finding that the sample selected by the Commission was not inconsistent with Article 3.1 of the *Anti-Dumping Agreement*.

2. *The Panel's Findings under Article 2.4 of the Anti-Dumping Agreement*

225. The European Union requests the Appellate Body to reject China's appeal of the Panel's finding that the European Union did not act inconsistently with Article 2.4 of the *Anti-Dumping Agreement* in respect of the comparison of the export price and normal value in the dumping determination. According to the European Union, each of China's three claims on appeal is without merit and should be rejected.

---

[374] European Union' appellee's submission, para. 214.

(a) The Panel's Treatment of China's Argument

226. The European Union submits that China's allegation of a violation of Article 11 of the DSU by the Panel for its alleged failure to address China's argument on the EU authorities' lack of communication on the information required to ensure a fair comparison is baseless.

227. The European Union maintains that the "factual premise for China's claim is in error"[375], because China did not make a claim, nor a substantial argument, before the Panel concerning the Commission's alleged failure to inform interested parties of the fact that PCNs were not used in price comparison. Rather, China raised this issue before the Panel in its second written submission merely in rebuttal of the European Union's argument that no interested parties had requested adjustments, and in support of its claim that adjustments should have been made. The Panel therefore did not "ignore[] a substantial argument put forward by China"[376], because the Panel was not requested to opine on such an argument. The European Union further submits that China's references to the Appellate Body's findings on "false exercise of judicial economy" are "completely besides the point", given that those findings deal with the decision of a panel not to address certain "claims" before it, not "arguments".[377] Moreover, because panels have the discretion to address only those arguments they deem necessary to resolve a particular claim, "the fact that a particular argument relating to that claim is not specifically addressed in the 'Findings' section of a panel report will not, in and of itself, lead to the conclusion that that panel has failed to make the 'objective assessment of the matter before it' required by Article 11 of the *DSU*".[378] Thus, the European Union submits that China fails to demonstrate that the Panel acted inconsistently with Article 11 of the DSU by not addressing China's argument.

228. The European Union further contends that China fails to substantiate its alternative claim that, should the Appellate Body consider that the Panel implicitly rejected China's argument, the Appellate Body should find that the Panel erred in its interpretation of Article 2.4 of the *Anti-Dumping Agreement*. In the European Union's view, given that the Panel did not make a finding in this respect, and did not exceed the boundaries of its discretionary authority in not addressing China's argument, there is no basis for the Appellate Body to review this alleged error in law in respect of a non-existent finding.

---

375 European Union's appellee's submission, para. 249.

376 European Union's appellee's submission, para. 252 (quoting China's other appellant's submission, para. 306).

377 European Union's appellee's submission, para. 255.

378 European Union's appellee's submission, para. 255 (quoting Appellate Body Report, *EC – Poultry*, para. 135).

(b) Physical Differences

(i) The Panel's interpretation and application of Article 2.4

229. The European Union maintains that China's allegation of the Panel's error in the interpretation and application of Article 2.4 of the *Anti-Dumping Agreement*, concerning the Commission's obligation to evaluate all PCN characteristics and to make necessary adjustments, is equally without merit. According to the European Union, the Panel's legal interpretation of Article 2.4 of the *Anti-Dumping Agreement* "is in line with the interpretation" advocated by China that an authority must evaluate identified differences potentially affecting price comparability.[379] This is confirmed by the Panel's finding that, under Article 2.4, the authorities "must take steps to achieve clarity as to the adjustment claimed and then determine **whether and to what extent that adjustment is merited**".[380]

230. The European Union submits that China's appeal does not concern an issue of law, but rather concerns China's disagreement with the Panel's factual finding regarding the role and relevance of the PCN characteristics, and fails to "convincingly" challenge this finding under Article 11 of the DSU.[381] The European Union recalls China's argument before the Panel that, because the PCN characteristics had been identified by the authorities themselves as affecting price comparability, the Commission had an obligation at least to evaluate whether these differences indeed affected price comparability or not, and should subsequently have concluded that adjustments were indeed required. Thus, China's argument is premised on the assumption that the Commission had identified PCN characteristics as affecting price comparability. The Panel, however, disagreed with the "factual premise" of China's assertion[382], finding, instead, that the fact that the Commission used the PCNs as a tool for information gathering did not imply that the Commission identified each of the PCN characteristics as necessarily affecting price comparability. The Panel further found that China pointed to no evidence that was before the investigating authority in support of its assertion that the Commission considered all PCN characteristics as necessarily affecting price comparability. In the European Union's view, these are factual findings unrelated to whether or not there exists a distinction, as alleged by China, between the evaluation of identified differences and the making of adjustments for differences affecting price comparability.

231. The European Union further maintains that, in any event, pursuant to a proper interpretation of Article 2.4 of the *Anti-Dumping Agreement*, the European Union complied with its obligations under that provision. First, Article 2.4 requires an investigating authority to request information that may be necessary

---

[379] European Union's appellee's submission, para. 272.

[380] European Union's appellee's submission, para. 271 (quoting Panel Report, para. 7.298, in turn quoting Panel Report, *EC – Tube or Pipe Fittings*, para. 7.158 (boldface added by the Panel)).

[381] European Union's appellee's submission, para. 263.

[382] European Union's appellee's submission, para. 267.

for ensuring a fair comparison and to determine whether any adjustments are warranted. The European Union requested all interested parties to organize product information on the basis of the PCNs "merely [as] a tool"[383] to help matching export sales to domestic sales in the analogue country. Second, under Article 2.4, it is the obligation of the producers from the country under investigation to substantiate their claim for adjustment. The European Union recalls that the interested parties emphasized, throughout the fasteners investigation, the importance of the distinction between standard and special fasteners, and the Commission took into account this distinction in the product types used for purposes of price comparison. Third, under Article 2.4, an investigating authority is only required to adjust for differences that are demonstrated to affect price comparability, and not for any other differences. Consistent with this obligation, the Commission determined that only one of the PCN characteristics, that is, strength, was demonstrated to affect price comparability. In this respect, the European Union argues that China makes an inaccurate factual statement that "interested parties have stressed throughout the investigation that it was of fundamental importance that the comparison be made on the PCN basis".[384] Therefore, the Commission complied with all of the obligations under Article 2.4 of the *Anti-Dumping Agreement* and conducted a fair comparison between normal value and export price by making a comparison between fasteners on the basis of their strength class and whether they were special or standard fasteners.

232. On this basis, the European Union requests the Appellate Body to reject China's appeal against the Panel's finding that the Commission did not act inconsistently with Article 2.4 of the *Anti-Dumping Agreement* in not making adjustments for alleged differences indicated through the PCN characteristics.

(ii) The Panel's failure to make an objective assessment of the facts

233. The European Union submits that, before addressing China's specific claims, it may be useful to recall the role of the PCNs in the fasteners investigation. According to the European Union, the PCNs are an information-gathering tool, consisting of "a very preliminary listing" of potentially relevant product features that may or may not affect price comparability.[385] Whether the PCNs will ultimately be used depends on numerous factors, including the arguments of the parties, and the practical limitations of the information available. In the fasteners investigation, the European Union argues, the failure of the Indian producer to provide the information in the detailed manner required by the PCNs implied that a different approach based on product types became preferable. Furthermore, the evidence on the record indicates that strength class and the distinction between standard and special fasteners, on the basis of which the Commis-

---

383 European Union's appellee's submission, para. 277.

384 European Union's appellee's submission, para. 287 (quoting China's other appellant's submission, para. 360).

385 European Union's appellee's submission, para. 292.

sion determined the product types, were two main characteristics referred to by the interested parties in the course of the investigation, including the Chinese interested parties. The European Union further submits that the Chinese interested parties did not raise any other characteristics affecting price comparability during the investigation, even after they were informed that the price comparison was done on the basis of product types rather than PCNs. China's argument, that the interested parties did not request adjustments because they assumed that any differences affecting price comparability would be taken into account by the PCN characteristics, is contradicted by the fact that the Chinese interested parties presented arguments during the investigation regarding the importance of strength class even though strength class was one of the PCN characteristics.

234. Turning to China's allegation that the Panel acted inconsistently with Article 11 of the DSU, the European Union maintains that China has not pointed to any evidence that was disregarded by the Panel. First, China repeats its erroneous assertion that the fact that certain physical characteristics were reflected in the PCNs provides evidence that such characteristics affect price comparability. Yet, as the Panel correctly found, the use of the PCNs as an information-gathering tool did not mean that the characteristics indicated therein necessarily affect price comparability. Second, although China submitted to the Panel that the Commission should have made adjustments for PCN characteristics such as the type of coating and the use of chrome, it did not made such claims before the Commission. The European Union emphasizes that the Panel's duty was to review whether the Commission's determination was reasonable in the light of the evidence before the Commission, rather than assertions made during the Panel proceedings. Third, with regard to the three pieces of evidence that China alleges it submitted to the Panel, the first two were statements by the EU industry made in the context of discussions concerning the comparability between EU and Chinese fasteners, and thus did not concern the issue of price comparability between Indian and Chinese fasteners. As for the third piece of evidence, it concerns a presentation on behalf of a Chinese interested party stressing the need to differentiate fasteners based on standard market and niche products, which also does not address the alleged importance of the PCN characteristics. Thus, China fails to demonstrate that the Panel wilfully disregarded, distorted, or refused to consider the evidence submitted by China. Rather, the Panel examined all evidence in its totality, including China's acknowledgement that no interested parties raised any factors affecting price comparability other than those taken into account by the Commission, and reached its conclusion on that basis. The Panel did not violate Article 11 of the DSU simply because it did not discuss every piece of evidence or every argument made by China.

235. The European Union contends that China neither substantiates, nor provides any evidence for, its allegation that the Panel acted inconsistently with Article 17.6(i) of the *Anti-Dumping Agreement*. As the Panel found, China had pointed to no evidence that was before the investigating authorities in support of its assertion that all PCN characteristics constituted differences affecting price comparability. Because the task of the Panel was to review the reasonableness of

the Commission's determination, the Panel rightly considered that it should not engage in a review of such evidence to determine whether it would have reached a different conclusion. Therefore, China's appeal in this respect, as well as its request for completion of the analysis, must be rejected.

(c) Quality Differences

236. The European Union maintains that, although China alleges that the Panel erred in its legal interpretation, China's appeal does not point to any legal errors by the Panel in the interpretation of Article 2.4 of the *Anti-Dumping Agreement*. Rather, the interpretation advanced by China is in line with the Panel's finding that an authority must examine whether and to what extent adjustments must be made. The European Union further submits that it agrees that characteristics that have been acknowledged to affect price comparability, or for which the requisite evidence has been provided, must be evaluated in order to determine whether and to what extent adjustments may need to be made.

237. In this dispute, however, there was no evidence of any difference in quality that affected price comparability between Chinese and Indian fasteners. Specifically, with respect to the letter from one Chinese producer requesting adjustments for quality differences, the Panel correctly found that the letter was not supported by any evidence. Moreover, China's assertion that the Commission failed to evaluate, and make adjustments for, quality differences is based on a misreading of the Definitive Regulation. As the Panel rightly found, the recital in the Definitive Regulation to which China referred concerns fasteners produced in China and in the European Union, and does not even mention fasteners produced in India. Moreover, the letter from the Commission to some Chinese exporters does not refer to any quality differences, but indicates that the only difference for which an adjustment was made consisted of the fact that the Indian producer regularly checked the quality before shipping, whereas the Chinese producers generally did not do so.

238. Therefore, the European Union argues, China's claim under Article 2.4 of the *Anti-Dumping Agreement* is based on the erroneous factual premise that the Commission acknowledged that certain quality differences existed. Given that the Panel correctly found that there was no evidence showing that the Commission made such an acknowledgement, the European Union requests the Appellate Body to reject China's appeal that the Panel erred in finding that the Commission did not act inconsistently with Article 2.4 of the *Anti-Dumping Agreement* by not evaluating, and making adjustments for, quality differences.

3. The Panel's Findings under Article 6.5, 6.2, and 6.4 of the Anti-Dumping Agreement Regarding the Disclosure of the Identity of the Complainants

239. The European Union requests the Appellate Body to uphold the Panel's findings under Article 6.5 of the *Anti-Dumping Agreement* with respect to the disclosure of the identity of the complainants and the supporters of the com-

plaint. As a preliminarily matter, the European Union raises two jurisdictional concerns. First, the European Union points out that the claim under Article 11 of the DSU brought by China in its other appellant's submission was not included in its Notice of Other Appeal, and is therefore not properly before the Appellate Body.[386] Second, in the European Union's view, China's argument regarding the disclosure of the identity of the sampled producers seems to challenge the Panel's weighing of the evidence, and should more properly have been raised under Article 11 of the DSU. As Article 11 was not mentioned in China's Notice of Other Appeal in this context, this claim too should be dismissed by the Appellate Body as outside the scope of appellate review.[387] Substantively, the European Union argues that the Panel correctly found that the European Union acted consistently with Article 6.5 when it treated the complainants' identity as confidential in order to prevent commercial retaliation by some of their customers. As a consequence of upholding the Panel's finding in this regard, the European Union also requests the Appellate Body to uphold the Panel's consequential finding that the European Union acted consistently with Articles 6.4 and 6.2 of the *Anti-Dumping Agreement*.

(a) The Complainants' "Good Cause" Showing

240. The European Union observes, at the outset, that China does not challenge the Panel's findings that the Commission's standing determination was consistent with its obligations under the *Anti-Dumping Agreement*, and China thereby "confirms" that the identity of these companies was a "non-issue from the point of view of the interested parties' rights of defence".[388] In response to China's specific claims, the European Union disagrees with China's suggestion that a higher threshold must be reached in order to show "good cause" in the case of information that is not "by nature" confidential. Rather, the European Union concurs with the Panel's determination that the relevant issue was "whether the justification based on potential commercial retaliation provided by the complainants in the fasteners investigation could amount to 'good cause' in the sense of Article 6.5".[389]

241. Regarding China's claim that the complainants were required to demonstrate the commercial retaliation "would", as opposed to "could", happen, the European Union contends that "China's distinction is artificial".[390] The use of the term "would" in Article 6.5 appears as part of some examples of information that is confidential by nature, and does not imply that in all cases the submitting party must show that harm will unavoidably result. In the European Union's view, China's proposition does not appear to cover a "risk" that some harm might occur, and ignores the purpose of Article 6.5, which is "precisely to make sure that a feared adverse effect ... remains hypothetical and does not actually material-

[386] European Union's appellee's submission, para. 362.
[387] European Union's appellee's submission, para. 363.
[388] European Union's appellee's submission, para. 365.
[389] European Union's appellee's submission, para. 369.
[390] European Union's appellee's submission, para. 371.

ise".[391] In the European Union's view, China's interpretation would alter the balance under Article 6.5, not in favour of parties requesting confidential treatment of their information, but decidedly against them, and would "discourage the initiation of investigations and cooperation overall".[392]

242. The European Union counters China's claim that the Panel relied on a "mere assertion" to justify "good cause" by arguing that the Panel did examine "the evidence in light of the specific justification provided as 'good cause'", and took into consideration the "particular standard of review" the Panel had in reviewing decisions of an investigating authority.[393] The European Union asserts that commercial retaliation can be carried out in sophisticated and subtle ways, and therefore a party's ability to supply proof that such retaliation might occur is very difficult.[394] Given this difficulty, the Panel logically looked next for any evidence to show "that the fear of retaliation was unreasonable, unfounded or untrue".[395] The Panel did not violate Article 11 of the DSU in expecting that China should provide evidence in this respect because, the European Union argues, the normal rules of dispute settlement proceedings in fact require the complainant—in this case China—to make a *prima facie* case of inconsistency.[396] In any event, the European Union claims that the Panel did not find that "no evidence" existed to support the complainants' assertion that their customers also purchased the subject product from Chinese producers. Rather, this assertion itself was "essential" to the Panel's findings and "served to substantiate" the complainants' concerns about commercial retaliation.[397] Further, the European Union explains that the fact that more evidence of potential commercial retaliation was not disclosed does not imply that such evidence was not before the Commission, particularly with regard to the nature and operation of the fasteners market itself.[398]

243. The European Union considers that China's claim regarding the disclosure of the identity of the sampled domestic producers essentially challenges the Panel's weighing of the evidence and, as an Article 11 claim has not been raised, therefore falls outside of the scope of this appeal.[399] China's claim relies on its own allegation that the evidence before the Panel unequivocally demonstrated that all sampled producers were also supporters of the complaint, and that the disclosure of the sampled producers' identity effectively disclosed the identity of the supporters of the complaint as well. The European Union contends, however, that China's presentation of the evidence is incomplete, and that the same document extensively cited by China also states that the data and figures presented "correspond to ***two different sets of companies***", referring to the sets of compa-

---

391 *Ibid.*.
392 European Union's appellee's submission, para. 372.
393 European Union's appellee's submission, para. 375.
394 European Union's appellee's submission, para. 376.
395 European Union's appellee's submission, para. 378 (quoting Panel Report, para. 7.453).
396 European Union's appellee's submission, para. 378.
397 European Union's appellee's submission, para. 379.
398 European Union's appellee's submission, para. 380 and footnote 338 thereto.
399 European Union's appellee's submission, para. 363.

nies who either supported the complaint or cooperated with the investigation.[400] China's claim that the Panel relied solely on the European Union's assertion that "at least one company included in the sample was not, in fact, either a complainant or supporter of the complaint" is, in the European Union's view, not only "unfounded", but also "blatantly outside the Appellate Body's jurisdiction".[401] Finally, the European Union emphasizes the fact that it is specifically the identification of a company as an initiator of an investigation that would create a hazard "analogous to the risk of a whistleblower".[402]

(b) Disclosure under Articles 6.4 and 6.2 of the *Anti-Dumping Agreement*

244. The European Union raises no substantive arguments in response to China's request that the Appellate Body complete the analysis to find that, because the identity of the complainants was not properly treated as confidential, the Commission's failure to disclose the company names was also inconsistent with Article 6.4 and 6.2 of the *Anti-Dumping Agreement*. If the Appellate Body determines that these claims were within the Panel's jurisdiction, the European Union requests that the Panel's findings that the European Union did not act inconsistently with Articles 6.4 and 6.2 be upheld. Because China's claims under Articles 6.4 and 6.2 are "entirely dependent" on its claim under Article 6.5, the European Union maintains that the Panel did not err in finding that the identity of the complainants was confidential information under Article 6.5, and therefore cannot have erred in finding that the European Union did not violate Articles 6.4 and 6.2.

4. *The Panel's Findings that the MET/IT Claim Form Was Not a "Questionnaire" for Purposes of Article 6.1.1 of the Anti-Dumping Agreement*

245. As a preliminary matter, the European Union argues that China can only succeed on its claims under Article 6.1.1 of the *Anti-Dumping Agreement* if the Appellate Body reverses the Panel's interpretation of the term "questionnaires", because China's alternative claim under Article 11 of the DSU was not mentioned in its Notice of Other Appeal and is therefore not properly before the Appellate Body. The European Union requests, however, that the Appellate Body uphold the Panel's findings under Article 6.1.1, because its interpretation of the term "questionnaires" is also supported by two previous panel reports[403], and because the alternative interpretation suggested by China would render the meaning of the term "questionnaires" "arbitrary and dependent on a case-by-case

[400] European Union's appellee's submission, para. 384 (quoting European Union's oral statement at the second Panel meeting, paras. 100 and 101). (boldface added by the European Union on appeal)
[401] European Union's appellee's submission, para. 387.
[402] European Union's appellee's submission, para. 385.
[403] European Union's appellee's submission, paras. 410-415 (quoting Panel Report, *Egypt – Steel Rebar*, paras. 7.276 and 7.277; and Panel Report, *US – Anti-Dumping and Countervailing Duties (China)*, paras. 15.23-15.37).

analysis".[404] In fact, the European Union states that it adopts the panel's reasoning in *US – Anti-Dumping and Countervailing Duties (China)*, which dealt with the parallel provision in the *Agreement on Subsidies and Countervailing Measures* (the "*SCM Agreement*"), as its own.[405]

246. The European Union further argues that the dictionary definition of the word "questionnaire" does not amount to its "ordinary meaning" for purposes of interpretation, because this can only be discerned with reference to its context and in the light of its object and purpose. As the panel in *US – Anti-Dumping and Countervailing Duties (China)* found, the broad language in the chapeau of Article 6.1 confirms the fact that not every request for information will fall under "the specific 30-day 'ample opportunity' rule" set out in Article 6.1.1.[406] The European Union contends that this contextual interpretation of the term "questionnaires" as applying only to the initial, comprehensive questionnaire is further supported by the consistent use of the singular form of the term in footnote 15 of Article 6.1.1, and in Annex I to the *Anti-Dumping Agreement*.[407] The European Union further argues that the question of whether or not an information request is "so substantial" that it warrants verification, or whether allowing 30 days for its return will interfere with the authority's timely completion of the investigation, are both issues that will require a case-by-case determination depending on the circumstances in a particular investigation, and should not form part of the definition of the term "questionnaires".[408]

247. Should the Appellate Body find that China's alternative claims are properly raised on appeal, the European Union asserts that the Panel rightly found that the MET/IT Claim Form did not constitute a "questionnaire" under the Panel's interpretation. Although some of the information contained in the MET/IT Claim Form may overlap with information requested in more comprehensive questionnaires, the European Union argues that the MET/IT Claim Form serves an entirely different purpose from such questionnaires, and is much narrower in scope.[409] Were the Appellate Body to agree with China's suggested application of Article 6.1.1, it would have to find that every information request that "plays a role" in the investigation would fall under the term "questionnaire" and require 30 days for completion[410], a result the European Union urges the Appellate Body to reject.

[404] European Union's appellee's submission, para. 418.
[405] European Union's appellee's submission, para. 416.
[406] European Union's appellee's submission, para. 420.
[407] European Union's appellee's submission, para. 420.
[408] European Union's appellee's submission, paras. 421-423.
[409] European Union's appellee's submission, para. 429.
[410] European Union's appellee's submission, para. 431.

E. *Arguments of the Third Participants*

1. *Brazil*

248. Brazil disagrees with the Panel's finding that there is solely one exception to the obligation in Article 6.10 of the *Anti-Dumping Agreement* to determine individual dumping margins to each known exporter or producer of the product under investigation. Brazil contends that there are various plausible interpretations of the second sentence of Article 6.10 of the *Anti-Dumping Agreement.* In cases where multiple interpretations of a treaty provision are "possible", the Appellate Body has clearly stated that customary rules of interpretation require interpreters to avoid assuming that the most burdensome obligation was the one intended by the drafters of the treaty.[411] In Brazil's view, it seems "reasonable" to interpret the second sentence of Article 6.10 as one specific, but not the sole, exception to the first sentence of Article 6.10. Indeed, the use of "as a rule" in the first sentence of Article 6.10 reveals the general nature of the obligation, merely expressing preference for the use of a specific methodology. This conclusion is further confirmed by the French and the Spanish versions, which begin, respectively, with the expressions "*en règle générale*" and "*por regla general*". In contrast, there are no limiting or restrictive expressions, such as "unless" or "only in cases where", in the second sentence of Article 6.10 of the *Anti-Dumping Agreement.*[412]

249. Brazil contends that one of the situations in which the general rule of individual dumping margin calculation contained in the first sentence of Article 6.10 of the *Anti-Dumping Agreement* is not applicable is where prices and costs are not established according to market economy rules. This conclusion is supported in Article 2.7 of the *Anti-Dumping Agreement,* which refers to the second *Ad* Note to Article VI:1 of the GATT 1994, and, in the particular case of China, reinforced by paragraph 15(a)(ii) of China's Accession Protocol. Pursuant to these provisions, investigating authorities may use, when determining the dumping margin, a different methodology for price comparability than the one resulting from Articles 2 and 6.10 of the *Anti-Dumping Agreement.* Brazil notes that, in *Korea – Certain Paper*, the panel recognized that there may be situations in which treating separate legal entities as a single exporter for determining dumping margins is a proper, WTO-consistent methodology.[413] Although this precedent refers to an investigation concerning companies that operated under market economy conditions, it is Brazil's contention that in the case of NMEs the motives for "single exporter" treatment are all the more justified.[414] The Panel itself recognized that it is possible to consider all companies operating under NME conditions as one single exporter together with the State, but such a statement

411 Brazil's third participant's submission, para. 12 (referring to Appellate Body Report, *EC – Hormones*, para. 165).
412 Brazil's third participant's submission, para. 9.
413 Brazil's third participant's submission, para. 26 (referring to Panel Report, *Korea – Certain Paper*, para. 7.161).
414 Brazil's third participant's submission, para. 28.

seems to be in contradiction with the Panel's final conclusion that sampling is the only exception to the obligation to determine individual dumping margins.[415]

250. Regarding the presumption established by Article 9(5) of the Basic AD Regulation with respect to the relationship between investigated companies and the State in NMEs, Brazil considers that the Panel erred in finding that such a presumption has no legal basis. In Brazil's view, investigating authorities are permitted under WTO law to place on Chinese exporters or producers the burden of proving that their industry is subject to market economy conditions in its functioning, which includes showing that they operate independently from the State. The expressions "can/cannot clearly show" in Article 15(a)(i) and (ii) are the key textual element indicating that the treatment accorded to Chinese exporters or producers is dependent upon their capacity to show that market economy conditions prevail in their industry. Brazil further contends that, since NME conditions constitute a factor that Members have recognized to affect price comparability, information on price comparability falls into the scope of Article 2.4 of the *Anti-Dumping Agreement*. Therefore, placing the burden of proof regarding the existence of market economy conditions on the Chinese exporters or producers is permitted under Article 2.4 of the *Anti-Dumping Agreement*, as long as this burden is reasonable.[416]

251. With respect to Article 9.2 of the *Anti-Dumping Agreement*, Brazil rejects the Panel's conclusion that, given the similarities between Article 9.2 and Article 6.10 of the *Anti-Dumping Agreement*, the obligation to name the suppliers corresponds to the obligation to calculate individual dumping margins.[417] Brazil submits that the *Anti-Dumping Agreement* addresses, in distinct provisions, the determination of dumping margins and the imposition of anti-dumping duties, and considers that the Panel's parallelism between these core provisions is far-fetched. The textual differences between Article 9.2 and Article 6.10 are a clear indication that Members intended them to have different scopes. In addition, both in *US – Gasoline* and *EC – Hormones*, the Appellate Body affirmed that a treaty interpreter must not ignore the choice of different words in the text of treaty provisions.[418] In referring to the naming of the concerned suppliers, Article 9.2 of the *Anti-Dumping Agreement* does not establish any other obligation than the *naming* itself, thus there is no need for the investigating authorities to impose different duties on each of them. In Brazil's view, the investigating authorities may rightfully impose the same anti-dumping duty to all known exporters or producers as long as it is equal to, or less than, the smallest dumping margin established to these exporters/producers.[419]

[415] Brazil's third participant's submission, para. 30.
[416] Brazil's third participant's submission, para. 40.
[417] Brazil's third participant's submission, para. 45.
[418] Brazil's third participant's submission, paras. 49 and 50 (referring to Appellate Body Report, *US – Gasoline*, p. 17, DSR 1996:I, 3, at 16; and Appellate Body Report, *EC – Hormones*, para. 164).
[419] Brazil's third participant's submission, para. 56.

2. *Colombia*

252. With respect to the interpretation of Article 6.10 of the *Anti-Dumping Agreement*, Colombia disagrees with the Panel's finding that the rule in this provision does not admit more exceptions than only sampling. Colombia considers that a single dumping margin can also be determined if, after having assessed the evidence available, the investigating authorities conclude that the producers and exporters in an NME are deemed a single entity with the State. Colombia considers, however, that there is no direct legal basis within the WTO legal framework for a general presumption that all producers and exporters in an NME are a single entity with the State for the purposes of the determination of a dumping margin and the imposition of anti-dumping duties. Therefore, the assessment of a link between the producers/exporters and the State is a matter of evidence and should be done on a case-by-case basis. Colombia reads Article 9(5) of the Basic AD Regulation as setting out the evidentiary threshold to establish a link between producers/exporters and the State in NMEs for the purposes of the dumping margin determination. In Colombia's view, as long as this threshold provides the elements to collect the evidence necessary to demonstrate that such a link does not exist, it is consistent with Article 6.10 of the *Anti-Dumping Agreement*. Colombia further submits that the Appellate Body can take into account China's Accession Protocol and the Accession Working Party Report as guidance in relation to the Members' concerns regarding anti-dumping investigations concerning products from China.[420]

253. Colombia disagrees with the Panel's interpretation of Article 9.2 of the *Anti-Dumping Agreement* and rejects the Panel's conclusion that Article 9.2 does not permit the imposition of a single country-wide anti-dumping duty in an investigation involving an NME. In Colombia's view, rejecting the European Union's interpretation of the term "appropriate" in Article 9.2, as referring to the duty rate appropriate to the country concerned, could lead to a situation where, even if the "appropriate" amount of anti-dumping duty to be collected is a country-wide one, such country-wide anti-dumping duty cannot be imposed. This would limit the possibility for Members to collect the appropriate amount of anti-dumping duties in a given case.[421] Colombia reiterates its understanding that, since there is no legal basis for a general evidentiary presumption that producers and exporters act as a single entity under the control of the State in NMEs, an investigating authority needs a factual basis to support a conclusion that a single, country-wide anti-dumping duty must be imposed. Article 9(5) of the Basic AD Regulation sets out the evidentiary threshold that the European Union applies to determine what type of relationship exists between exporters and producers and the State in NMEs, and, as long as such threshold provides evidence of a link, this can be considered as a factual basis for the imposition of a single, country-wide anti-dumping duty.[422]

---

[420] Colombia's third participant's submission, para. 13.
[421] Colombia's third participant's submission, para. 23.
[422] Colombia's third participant's submission, para. 28.

254. Colombia agrees with the Panel's finding that the determination of how to group products by product type was the kind of "information" covered by the requirements of Article 6.4 of the *Anti-Dumping Agreement*. In *EC – Tube or Pipe Fittings*, the panel defined the kind of information that Article 6.4 requires authorities to disclose as "information that would not initially be in the possession of an interested party and would therefore be unknown or unfamiliar to an interested party if it were not disclosed to that party in the course of an investigation".[423] Taking this definition into consideration, Colombia submits that the qualification of how to group the products in the investigation falls within the scope of information covered by Article 6.4 of the *Anti-Dumping Agreement*, and highlights the fact that product grouping defines how the producers and exporters under investigation will substantiate their defence.[424]

3. *Japan*

255. Japan agrees with the Panel's finding that the first sentence of Article 6.10 establishes an obligation to determine an individual dumping margin for each individual exporter or producer concerned, with only one exception, namely, the possibility of sampling specified in the second sentence of Article 6.10. In Japan's view, Article 6.10 is purely procedural in nature, in the sense that it imposes a procedural obligation to determine individual margins of dumping for each known exporter or producer, and it is not concerned with substantive issues regarding the determination of individual dumping margins.[425] Therefore, provisions covering substantive issues, such as Articles 2 and 6.8 of the *Anti-Dumping Agreement*, cannot be deemed exceptions to the rule set out in Article 6.10. In addition, the manner in which an investigating authority may define "exporter" or "producer" within the meaning of the first sentence of Article 6.10 has nothing to do with the relationship between the first and the second sentences of the Article 6.10 of the *Anti-Dumping Agreement*.[426]

256. Japan further submits that the Panel's reading of *Korea – Certain Paper* may be too narrow, especially in its application in the context of NMEs. In Japan's view, the principles derived from that precedent—that is, that distinct legal entities may be treated as a single exporter or producer if they "are in a relationship close enough to support that treatment"[427]—equally apply to the relationship between the State and private legal entities. In that sense, Japan has doubts as to whether the operation of Article 9(5) of the Basic AD Regulation is indeed "fundamentally different" from the test in *Korea – Certain Paper* as the Panel concluded. Japan also queries whether the question of who carries the burden of proving whether distinct entities are in a close enough relationship to be consid-

---

[423] Colombia's third participant's submission, para. 30 (quoting Panel Report, *EC – Tube or Pipe Fittings*, para. 7.208).
[424] Colombia's third participant's submission, para. 32.
[425] Japan's third participant's submission, para. 8.
[426] Japan's third participant's submission, para. 9.
[427] Japan's third participant's submission, para. 14 (quoting Panel Report, *Korea – Certain Paper*, para. 7.161).

ered a single exporter or producer is relevant for the interpretation of Article 6.10 of the *Anti-Dumping Agreement*, insofar as this provision makes no reference to the burden of proof. In any event, Japan considers that Article 15(a) and (d) of China's Accession Protocol, which places the burden of proof on the producers under investigation or on China itself, appears to provide relevant context in that respect.[428]

257. Japan supports the Panel's finding that "sources" and, by implication, "suppliers" in Article 9.2 of the *Anti-Dumping Agreement* can be interpreted as referring to the State where it is demonstrated that the State is the actual producer or exporter of the product in question.[429] Likewise, Japan supports the European Union's argument that the State can be the source of price discrimination. However, Japan queries whether the Panel provided a sufficient basis to conclude that Article 9.2 of the *Anti-Dumping Agreement* prohibits Members to presume that the State in an NME is the source of price discrimination. In Japan's view, it is at least questionable whether Members would not, in any event, be allowed to presume that the Chinese State is the source of price discrimination on the basis of Article 15(a) and (d) of China's Accession Protocol, read together with paragraph 151 of China's Accession Working Party Report. Japan maintains, however, that any presumption in that regard must be rebuttable.[430]

258. Japan disagrees with the Panel's finding that the term "impracticable" in Article 9.2 of the *Anti-Dumping Agreement* must be interpreted as in Article 6.10, namely, in reference to a large number of producers or exporters. In Japan's view, the impracticability of naming all the suppliers, as provided for in the third sentence of Article 9.2, relates to the collection of the appropriate amount of anti-dumping duties, as provided for in the first sentence of Article 9.2. A high risk of circumvention may be one reason for it to be impracticable to name each individual producer or exporter for which an anti-dumping margin was calculated.[431] Given the context, the scope of the third sentence of Article 9.2 could well be given a broader interpretation than the situation described in the second sentence of Article 6.10, namely, the sampling exception. Japan notes that there is no reference in the text of either Article 9.2 or Article 6.10 indicating that the exceptions contained respectively in the third and second sentences of each provision must be read together; and it adds that whereas Article 6.10 explicitly qualifies the "impracticability" as referring to only one specific situation ("where the number of exporters, producers, importers or types of products involved is so large"), Article 9.2 provides no such explicit, nor even implicit, limitation.[432]

---

428 Japan's third participant's submission, para. 18.

429 Japan's third participant's submission, para. 20 (referring to Panel Report, footnote 278 to para. 7.103).

430 Japan's third participant's submission, para. 24.

431 Japan's third participant's submission, para. 33.

432 Japan's third participant's submission, para. 36.

4. *United States*

259. The United States argues that the Panel erred in its interpretation that Article 6.10 of the *Anti-Dumping Agreement* prohibits investigating authorities from requiring NME exporters or producers to show their independence from the State before providing them with an individual margin of dumping. In the United States' view, the Panel's interpretation of Article 6.10 as prescribing a single rule for how investigating authorities must weigh evidence in all cases does not accord with the recognition elsewhere in the WTO Agreements that NMEs may present additional factual complexities in an anti-dumping investigation.[433] The United States maintains that the interpretative second *Ad* Note to Article VI:1 of the GATT 1994 recognizes that price comparisons with domestic prices may not be possible in an NME where State interference is pervasive, and allows Members to apply an alternative price comparison methodology by basing the normal value on data from an analogue country. Moreover, China's Accession Protocol recognizes the pervasive government interference in the Chinese economy, allowing Members to establish different evidentiary requirements for firms operating in China. Specifically, the Protocol recognizes that, absent a demonstration to the contrary by Chinese producers, government interference will prevent market principles from functioning in the relevant industry producing the product under consideration.[434]

260. The United States further submits that the Panel erred in its interpretation that Article 6.10 of the *Anti-Dumping Agreement* prohibits an investigating authority from using criteria, such as those established in Article 9(5) of the Basic AD Regulation, to determine whether a firm is sufficiently separate from the State to determine an individual margin of dumping for that entity. According to the United States, the *Anti-Dumping Agreement* neither defines "exporter" nor "producer", nor sets out criteria for the investigating authority to examine before concluding that a particular firm or group of firms constitute an "exporter" or "producer".[435] Therefore, the determination of whether a firm constitutes the relevant exporter or producer, including the selection of criteria to employ in making this determination, would appear to fall within the discretion of the investigating authority. The United States contends that, in a NME such as China, State interference could exert influence over firms and prices, thus making the State analogous to a parent company that makes business decisions for the individual firms. Furthermore, there is substantial evidence that such State interference exists in the Chinese economy, such as concerns expressed by Members in this regard during China's accession negotiations.[436] Therefore, contrary to the Panel's finding, it is logical for the European Union's investigating authority to confirm that a Chinese company functions as an exporter or producer separate from the State before assigning an individual dumping margin to that company.

---

[433] United States' third participant's submission, p. 12.

[434] United States' third participant's submission, para. 13.

[435] United States' third participant's submission, para. 16.

[436] United States' third participant's submission, para. 19 (referring to China's Accession Working Party Report, paras. 50, 51, and 150).

The United States disagrees with China's argument that requiring companies from NMEs to demonstrate that they qualify for individual dumping margins results in the application of a rigid and burdensome rule to Chinese firms. Rather, such a requirement provides investigating authorities with the necessary flexibility to respond to changes in these NMEs.[437]

261. The United States maintains that the Panel erred in its application of Article I:1 of the GATT 1994 in finding that Article 9(5) of the Basic AD Regulation is inconsistent with that provision. In the United States' view, Chinese products pose "methodological challenges to investigating authorities" in determining costs and prices in connection with those products due to pervasive State interference.[438] Thus, Article 9(5) of the Basic AD Regulation is designed to address a particular condition associated with the nature of China's economy. Moreover, several WTO rules, including the second *Ad* Note to Article VI:1 of the GATT 1994 and China's Accession Protocol, explicitly recognize that, in the context of anti-dumping and countervailing duty proceedings, products from one Member may be treated differently from those of another Member. The United States further contends that the Panel misinterpreted Article 9 of the *Anti-Dumping Agreement* when finding that Article 9(5) of the Basic AD Regulation is inconsistent with Article 9.2 of the *Anti-Dumping Agreement* because Article 9.2 requires an authority to "name the supplier or suppliers of the product concerned" when imposing a duty. According to the United States, the imposition of anti-dumping duties is always with respect to products, not individual exporters or producers.[439] Thus, the concept of imposing duties on exporters or producers, on which the Panel relied in reaching its finding, has no basis in the *Anti-Dumping Agreement*. Moreover, the obligation to "name the supplier" under Article 9.2 does not require an authority to calculate individual margins of dumping for each exporter or producer.

262. The United States submits that, although it does not take a position on the particular facts at issue in this dispute, it agrees with China that a definition of the domestic industry that is narrowly limited to those parties who actively support or otherwise wish to participate in the investigation does not permit an "objective examination" of whether the domestic industry is experiencing material injury, within the meaning of Article 3.1 of the *Anti-Dumping Agreement*.[440] This is because those producers most likely to participate are those who supported the complaint who had the "least healthy economic performance". The United States also agrees with China that the Panel's analysis under Article 3.1 was flawed insofar as it did not account for the European Union's failure to make active efforts to collect data on all known EU fastener producers. In this respect, the United States disagrees with the Panel's suggestion that the European Union's exclusion of most known EU fastener producers from its definition of the domestic industry may be justified by the fragmented nature of this industry.

---

[437] United States' third participant's submission, para. 21.
[438] United States' third participant's submission, para. 23.
[439] United States' third participant's submission, para. 26.
[440] United States' third participant's submission, para. 41.

263. The United States disagrees with the Panel's finding that the European Union is allowed to use a process that favours complainants and supporters to be included in the domestic industry definition "so long as the producers that are included account for a sufficient quantity of domestic production to be considered a 'major proportion'".[441] In the United States' view, such an interpretation renders meaningless the two exceptions covered under subparagraphs (i) and (ii), which expressly allow investigating authorities to depart from the inclusive standard defined in Article 4.1. Finally, the United States disagrees with the European Union's argument that the "major proportion" referenced by Article 4.1 should be interpreted to mean producers accounting for at least 25 per cent of total domestic production in the light of the 25 per cent benchmark under Article 5.4 of the *Anti-Dumping Agreement* for determining the sufficiency of standing. In the United States' view, the 25 per cent standing requirement under Article 5.4 should not be read as setting a benchmark for the "major proportion" requirement under Article 4.1 for defining the relevant domestic industry, given that the 25 per cent standing requirement itself must be judged against a broader domestic industry defined under Article 4.1 as "domestic producers as a whole" or "those of them whose collective output ... constitutes a major proportion of the total domestic production".[442]

264. The United States submits that the Panel correctly interpreted Article 6.1.1 of the *Anti-Dumping Agreement* in finding that the 30-day response period prescribed in that provision applies only to the original anti-dumping questionnaire. The United States recalls that, in *Egypt – Steel Rebar*, the panel explained that the term "questionnaire" refers to one particular request for information made by the investigating authority.[443] Moreover, the panel in *US – Anti-Dumping and Countervailing Duties (China)* similarly found that the term "questionnaires" in Article 12.1.1 of the *SCM Agreement* refers to the initial comprehensive questionnaire issued by an investigating authority covering the issues on which the investigating authority will have to make determinations in relation to subsidization of the investigated product, injury, and causation.[444] The United States further submits that paragraphs 6 and 7 of Annex I to the *Anti-Dumping Agreement* refer to "the questionnaire" in the singular. In the United States' view, given the breadth of information requested in the initial anti-dumping questionnaire, it is logical that the *Anti-Dumping Agreement* seeks to provide a minimum time period for respondent firms to collect the necessary data. However, the opportunity to claim MET or IT is merely a precursor to the issuance of the actual anti-dumping questionnaire, and hence not subject to the obligations in Article 6.1.1 of the *Anti-Dumping Agreement.*[445]

[441] United States' third participant's submission, para. 46 (quoting Panel Report, para. 7.230).

[442] United States' third participant's submission, para. 47.

[443] United States' third participant's submission, para. 32 (referring to Panel Report, *Egypt – Steel Rebar*, para. 7.7276).

[444] United States' third participant's submission, para. 33 (referring to Panel Report, *US – Anti-Dumping and Countervailing Duties (China)*, para. 15.37).

[445] United States' third participant's submission, para. 35.

III. ISSUES RAISED IN THIS APPEAL

265. The following issues are raised in the appeal by the European Union:

(a) whether the Panel erred in finding that Article 9(5) of the Basic AD Regulation is inconsistent "as such" with Articles 6.10 and 9.2 of the *Anti-Dumping Agreement* and with Article I:1 of the GATT 1994, and in particular:

(i) whether the Panel erred in finding that Article 9(5) of the Basic AD Regulation concerns not only the imposition of anti-dumping duties, but also the calculation of margins of dumping;

(ii) whether the Panel erred in its interpretation of Article 6.10 of the *Anti-Dumping Agreement* and in finding that Article 9(5) of the Basic AD Regulation is inconsistent with Article 6.10 of the *Anti-Dumping Agreement*, because it conditions the determination of individual dumping margins for exporters or producers from NMEs on the fulfilment of the IT test;

(iii) whether the Panel erred in its interpretation of Article 9.2 of the *Anti-Dumping Agreement* and in finding that Article 9(5) of the Basic AD Regulation is inconsistent with Article 9.2 of the *Anti-Dumping Agreement*, because it conditions the imposition of individual duties on exporters or producers from NMEs on the fulfilment of the IT test;

(iv) whether the Panel erred in finding that Article 9(5) of the Basic AD Regulation violates the MFN obligation in Article I:1 of the GATT 1994; and

(v) whether, in making the findings that Article 9(5) of the Basic AD Regulation is inconsistent "as such" with Articles 6.10 and 9.2 of the *Anti-Dumping Agreement* and with Article I:1 of the GATT 1994, the Panel acted inconsistently with its obligations under Article 11 of the DSU;

(b) whether the Panel erred in finding that the European Union acted inconsistently with Article XVI:4 of the *WTO Agreement* and Article 18.4 of the *Anti-Dumping Agreement* by failing to ensure the conformity of its laws, regulations, and administrative procedures with its obligations under the relevant agreements;

(c) whether the Panel erred in finding that Article 9(5) of the Basic AD Regulation is inconsistent with Articles 6.10 and 9.2 of the *Anti-Dumping Agreement* "as applied" in the fasteners investigation;

(d) whether the Panel erred in the interpretation and application of Article 6.4 of the *Anti-Dumping Agreement*, and acted inconsistently with Article 11 of the DSU, in finding that the European Union acted inconsistently with Article 6.4 of the *Anti-Dumping Agreement* by failing to provide a timely opportunity for the Chinese exporters to see the product types used by the Commission for purposes of comparing the export price and the normal value in the dumping determination;

(e) whether the Panel erred in finding that, by failing to provide a timely opportunity for the Chinese exporters to see the product types, the European Union also acted inconsistently with Article 6.2 of the *Anti-Dumping Agreement* by failing to ensure all interested parties had a full opportunity for the defence of their interests;

(f) whether the Panel erred in its interpretation and application of Articles 6.5 and 6.5.1 of the *Anti-Dumping Agreement* with regard to the European Union's treatment of confidential information, and in particular:

    (i) whether the Panel erred in finding that the European Union failed to ensure that the two domestic producers, Agrati and Fontana Luigi, provided appropriate statements of the reasons why information provided in confidence was not susceptible of summary;

    (ii) whether the claim that the European Union failed to establish that "good cause" existed to support the confidential treatment of information submitted by the analogue country producer participating in the investigation, Pooja Forge, was within the Panel's terms of reference under Article 6.2 of the DSU; and if so

    (iii) whether Panel erred in finding that the European Union failed to establish that "good cause" existed to support the confidential treatment of information submitted by Pooja Forge;

    (iv) whether, in addressing China's claim that no "good cause" supported the confidential treatment of information submitted by Pooja Forge, the Panel acted inconsistently with its obligations under Article 11 of the DSU, and deprived the European Union of its right to due process; and

(g) whether the Panel erred in finding that China's claims before the Panel under Articles 6.2 and 6.4 of the *Anti-Dumping Agreement* regarding the disclosure of the identity of the complainants and the supporters of the complaint were within the Panel's terms of reference under Article 6.2 of the DSU.

266. The following issues are raised in the other appeal by China:

(a) whether the Panel erred in rejecting China's claim that the domestic industry in the fasteners investigation did not include producers whose collective output "constitutes a major proportion of the total domestic production" within the meaning of Article 4.1 of the *Anti-Dumping Agreement*, and in particular:

    (i) whether the Commission erroneously relied on a presumption that 25 per cent of the total domestic production constituted "a major proportion", and therefore failed to define the domestic industry in the fasteners investigation consistently with Article 4.1; and

    (ii) whether other specific circumstances of the fasteners investigation were relevant to the examination of the domestic industry definition in the fasteners investigation under Article 4.1 of the *Anti-Dumping Agreement*;

(b) whether the Panel erred in rejecting China's claim that the European Union acted inconsistently with Article 3.1 of the *Anti-Dumping Agreement* by making an injury determination on the basis of a sample of producers that was not representative of the domestic industry;

(c) whether the Panel erred in finding that the European Union did not act inconsistently with Articles 4.1 and 3.1 of the *Anti-Dumping Agreement* by excluding certain producers from the definition of the domestic industry, and in particular:

    (i) whether the Panel acted inconsistently with its obligations under Article 11 of the DSU and Article 17.6 of the *Anti-Dumping Agreement* in finding that the European Union did not exclude from the definition of the domestic industry those producers who did not support the complaint;

    (ii) whether the Panel erred in the interpretation and application of Article 4.1 of the *Anti-Dumping Agreement*, and acted inconsistently with Article 11 of the DSU, in finding that the European Union did not act inconsistently with Article 4.1 of the *Anti-Dumping Agreement* by excluding from the definition of the domestic industry producers who did not make themselves known within 15 days of the publication of the Notice of Initiation; and

    (iii) whether the Panel erred in the interpretation and application of Article 3.1 of the *Anti-Dumping Agreement* in rejecting China's claim that the European Union acted inconsistently with that provision by excluding certain producers;

(d) whether the Panel erred in finding that the Commission did not act inconsistently with Article 2.4 of the *Anti-Dumping Agreement* in the dumping determination in the fasteners investigation, and in particular:

(i) whether the Panel acted inconsistently with Article 11 of the DSU, and erred in its interpretation and application of Article 2.4 of the *Anti-Dumping Agreement*, in not addressing China's argument that the Commission failed to inform the interested parties of the "product types" it used to compare the export price and normal value;

(ii) whether the Panel erred in the interpretation of Article 2.4 of the *Anti-Dumping Agreement*, and acted inconsistently with Article 11 of the DSU, when finding that the Commission did not have to make adjustments for the physical differences reflected in the Product Control Number (the "PCN"); and

(iii) whether the Panel erred in the interpretation and application of Article 2.4 of the *Anti-Dumping Agreement* in finding that the European Union did not have to make adjustments for alleged quality differences;

(e) whether the Panel erred in its interpretation and application of Articles 6.5 and 6.5.1 of the *Anti-Dumping Agreement* with regard to the European Union's treatment of confidential information, and in particular:

(i) whether the Panel erred in finding that the European Union did not act inconsistently with its obligations under Article 6.5 when the Commission granted the request to treat the identity of the complainants and the supporters of the complaint as confidential; and

(ii) whether the Panel acted inconsistently with Article 11 of the DSU in its evaluation of the above claim when it impermissibly shifted the burden to China to show that the "good cause" alleged for the confidential treatment of the complainants' identity was unfounded;

(f) if the Appellate Body finds that the Panel erred in finding that "good cause" existed to support the confidential treatment of the identity of the complainants and supporters of the complaint, whether the European Union also violated Articles 6.2 and 6.4 of the *Anti-Dumping Agreement* when it failed to disclose the identity of the complainants and the supporters of the complaint to the Chinese producers;

(g) whether the Panel erred in its interpretation and application of Article 6.1.1 of the *Anti-Dumping Agreement*, and in particular of the term "questionnaire", when it found that the European Union did not act inconsistently with this provision by allowing Chinese exporters less than 30 days to submit the Market Economy Treatment and/or Individual Treatment Claim Form; and

(h) whether the Panel acted inconsistently with Article 11 of the DSU and Article 17.6 of the *Anti-Dumping Agreement* when it concluded that the Market Economy Treatment and/or Individual Treatment Claim Form did not fall under the definition of "questionnaires" as interpreted by the Panel.

IV. THE PANEL'S FINDINGS REGARDING ARTICLE 9(5) OF THE BASIC AD REGULATION "AS SUCH"

A. *Introduction*

267. Before the Panel, China claimed that Article 9(5) of Council Regulation (EC) No. 1225/2009 of 30 November 2009 (the "Basic AD Regulation")[446] is inconsistent "as such" with Articles 6.10, 9.2, 9.3, and 9.4 of the *Anti-Dumping Agreement* as well as Articles I:1 and X:3(a) of the GATT 1994. China also claimed that, as a consequence of the fact that Article 9(5) of the Basic AD Regulation is inconsistent with the provisions of the *Anti-Dumping Agreement* and of the GATT 1994, this measure is also inconsistent with Article XVI:4 of the *WTO Agreement* and Article 18.4 of the *Anti-Dumping Agreement*.

268. The Panel found that Article 9(5) of the Basic AD Regulation is inconsistent with Articles 6.10 and 9.2 of the *Anti-Dumping Agreement* because it requires that a country-wide dumping margin be determined and a country-wide duty be imposed with respect to producers or exporters from non-market economies ("NMEs") unless such producers or exporters show, on the basis of the criteria set out in that provision, that they are independent of their State.[447] The Panel also found that Article 9(5) of the Basic AD Regulation violates the most favoured nation ("MFN") obligation of Article I:1 of the GATT 1994 because its application will, in certain situations, result in imports of the same product from different WTO Members being treated differently in anti-dumping investigations conducted by the European Union.[448]

269. As a consequence of its findings that Article 9(5) of the Basic AD Regulation is inconsistent with Articles 6.10 and 9.2 of the *Anti-Dumping Agreement*, the Panel also found that the European Union acted inconsistently with Article XVI:4 of the *WTO Agreement* and Article 18.4 of the *Anti-Dumping Agreement* by failing to ensure the conformity of its laws, regulations, and administrative procedures with its obligations under the relevant agreements.[449]

---

[446] *Official Journal of the European Union*, L Series, No. 343 (22 December 2009) 51, and Corrigendum, *Official Journal of the European Union*, L Series, No. 7 (12 January 2010) 23 (Panel Exhibit CHN-3).

[447] Panel Report, paras. 7.98 and 7.112.

[448] Panel Report, para. 7.124.

[449] Panel Report, para. 7.137. Having found that Article 9(5) is inconsistent "as such" with Articles 6.10 and 9.2 of the *Anti-Dumping Agreement* and with Article I:1 of the GATT 1994, the Panel exercised judicial economy in respect of China's claims under Articles 9.3 and 9.4 of the *Anti-Dumping Agreement* and Article X:3(a) of the GATT 1994. (*Ibid.*, paras. 7.116, 7.118, and 7.133)

270. The European Union appeals these findings and requests the Appellate Body to: (i) reverse the Panel's finding that Article 9(5) of the Basic AD Regulation concerns not only the imposition of anti-dumping duties, but also the calculation of margins of dumping, and find instead that Article 9(5) of the Basic AD Regulation, on its face, deals with only the individual or country-wide imposition of anti-dumping duties in respect of imports from NMEs; (ii) reverse the Panel's finding that Article 9(5) of the Basic AD Regulation is inconsistent with Article 6.10 of the *Anti-Dumping Agreement*, since that finding was premised on the Panel's incorrect understanding of the scope of Article 9(5) of the Basic AD Regulation; (iii) reverse the Panel's finding that Article 9(5) of the Basic AD Regulation is inconsistent with Article 6.10 of the *Anti-Dumping Agreement* because it conditions the determination of individual dumping margins for producers or exporters from NMEs on the fulfilment of the individual treatment ("IT") test; (iv) reverse the Panel's finding that Article 9(5) of the Basic AD Regulation is inconsistent with Article 9.2 of the *Anti-Dumping Agreement* because it conditions the imposition of individual duties on producers or exporters from NMEs on the fulfilment of the IT test; (v) reverse the Panel's finding that Article 9(5) of the Basic AD Regulation violates the MFN obligation under Article I:1 of the GATT 1994; and (vi) reverse the Panel's consequential findings that the European Union acted inconsistently with Article XVI:4 of the *WTO Agreement* and Article 18.4 of the *Anti-Dumping Agreement* by failing to ensure the conformity of its laws, regulations, and administrative procedures with its obligations under the relevant agreements.

271. Before turning to the specific issues on appeal, we consider it useful to outline the measure at issue in this dispute, that is, the Basic AD Regulation and, in particular, Article 9(5).

B. *The Measure at Issue*

272. Article 9(5) of the Basic AD Regulation provides that "[a]n anti-dumping duty shall be imposed in the appropriate amounts in each case, on a non-discriminatory basis on imports of a product from all sources found to be dumped and causing injury, except for imports from those sources from which undertakings under the terms of this Regulation have been accepted." It further establishes that the regulation imposing the anti-dumping duty shall specify the duty "for each supplier or, if that is impracticable, and in general where Article 2(7)(a) applies, the supplying country concerned". Article 2(7)(a) provides that, in the case of imports from NMEs, normal value shall not be determined based on prices paid or payable in the ordinary course of trade by independent customers in the exporting country, but based on an alternative methodology, such as the price or constructed value in a market economy third country.

273. To provide the relevant context for Article 9(5), we note that Article 2 of the Basic AD Regulation addresses the determination of dumping, including the determination of normal value. The rules set out in Article 2(1) to (6) closely mirror the provisions of Article 2.2 of the *Anti-Dumping Agreement*, and con-

cern the determination of normal value in respect of imports from market economies. Article 2(7) of the Basic AD Regulation contains specific rules on the determination of normal value in anti-dumping investigations involving NMEs. It groups NMEs into two categories—(i) NMEs that are not WTO Members and (ii) NMEs that are WTO Members (and Kazakhstan)—and establishes different rules for determining normal value for these categories.

274. Article 2(7)(a) applies to NMEs that are not Members of the WTO, including Albania, Armenia, Azerbaijan, Belarus, Georgia, North Korea, Kyrgyzstan, Moldova, Mongolia, Tajikistan, Turkmenistan, and Uzbekistan.[450] It provides that, for these countries, normal value is determined on the basis of the price or constructed value in a market economy third country, or the price from such a third country to other countries, including the European Union, or, where this is not possible, on any other reasonable basis, including the price actually paid or payable in the European Union for the like product duly adjusted if necessary to include a reasonable profit margin. Article 2(7)(b), which applies to "imports from the People's Republic of China, Vietnam and Kazakhstan and any [NME] country which is a member of the WTO at the date of the initiation of the investigation"[451] provides that if it is shown, on the basis of properly substantiated claims by one or more producers subject to the investigation and in accordance with the criteria and procedures set out in Article 2(7)(c), that "market economy conditions prevail" for them, normal value is determined for those producers in accordance with the rules in Article 2(1) to (6) applicable to market economies. Article 2(7)(b) further provides that, when this is not the case, normal value will be determined on the basis of Article 2(7)(a), that is, on the basis of the price or constructed value in a market economy third country, or the price actually paid or payable in the European Union for the like product. Article 2(7)(c) sets out the criteria that a foreign producer has to fulfil in order to demonstrate that it operates under market economy conditions, and thus that "market economy conditions prevail". These criteria are generally referred to as the market economy treatment test ("MET test").[452] The determination of export

---

[450] See corrigendum to Basic AD Regulation, *supra*, footnote 5.

[451] *Ibid.*

[452] Specifically, Article 2(7)(c) sets out the following criteria for the MET test. To demonstrate that they operate under market economy conditions, producers must show that:

- decisions of firms regarding prices, costs and inputs, including for instance raw materials, cost of technology and labour, output, sales and investment, are made in response to market signals reflecting supply and demand, and without significant State interference in this regard, and costs of major inputs substantially reflect market values;
- firms have one clear set of basic accounting records which are independently audited in line with international accounting standards and are applied for all purposes;

prices to which the normal value is compared in order to calculate the margin of dumping is dealt with in Article 2(8) and (9). Article 2(8) provides that the export price shall be the price actually paid or payable for the product when sold for export from the exporting country to the European Union. Article 2(9) sets out alternative methods for the determination of export prices under certain specified circumstances that are not relevant in this dispute.

275. Article 9(5) of the Basic AD Regulation sets out the modalities for the imposition of anti-dumping duties. Article 9(5) requires that, in principle, a duty be specified for each "supplier" of a product found to be dumped. It then provides for two exceptions to this principle: (i) where it is "impracticable" to specify the duty for each supplier; and (ii) where Article 2(7)(a) of the Basic AD Regulation applies—that is, where normal value for NME suppliers is determined on the basis of market economy third country prices or one of the other methods set forth in that provision. In these situations, the regulation imposing the duty shall specify a single duty rate for the supplying country concerned, a so-called country-wide duty, which will apply to all suppliers and imports from that country.

276. Article 9(5), however, exempts from the country-wide duty rate those NME suppliers that qualify for individual treatment ("IT suppliers"). An exporter from an NME may qualify for individual treatment and be granted an individual duty if it meets all of the following conditions:

(a) in the case of wholly or partly foreign owned firms or joint ventures, exporters are free to repatriate capital and profits;

(b) export prices and quantities, and conditions and terms of sale are freely determined;

(c) the majority of the shares belong to private persons; state officials appearing on the board of directors or holding key management positions shall either be in minority or it must be demonstrated that the company is nonetheless sufficiently independent from State interference;

(d) exchange rate conversions are carried out at the market rate; and

(e) State interference is not such as to permit circumvention of measures if individual exporters are given different rates of duty.

– the production costs and financial situation of firms are not subject to significant distortions carried over from the former non-market economy system, in particular in relation to depreciation of assets, other write-offs, barter trade and payment via compensation of debts;
– the firms concerned are subject to bankruptcy and property laws which guarantee legal certainty and stability for the operation of firms; and
– exchange rate conversions are carried out at the market rate.

277. These criteria are generally referred to as the "IT test". If an exporter demonstrates that it meets these conditions and is thus entitled to individual treatment, the EU authorities will specify an individual duty rate for that exporter. Such an individual rate is determined by comparing the normal value from the market economy third country with the exporters' actual export prices. Exporters that fail to satisfy the IT test will be subject to the country-wide duty rate.

278. Thus, when an exporter from a WTO Member that the European Union treats as an NME is subject to an anti-dumping investigation, the following possibilities with respect to the determination of normal value and the imposition of an anti-dumping duty apply. If the NME exporter or producer satisfies the MET test according to the criteria set out in Article 2(7)(c), then, according to Article 2(7)(b), its normal value will be determined on the same basis as for exporters from market economies, that is, prices paid or payable, in the ordinary course of trade, by independent customers in the exporting country. Moreover, according to Article 9(5), an individual duty rate will be specified for that supplier.

279. If the NME exporter fails to meet the MET test, then its normal value will be determined on the basis of an alternative method (usually on the basis of prices in a market economy third country). Whether an individual or a country-wide duty rate will be specified for that supplier will depend on whether the exporter requests and obtains individual treatment, pursuant to Article 9(5). Thus, if the NME exporter that has not fulfilled the MET test makes such a request and demonstrates that it meets the criteria in Article 9(5) of the Basic AD Regulation—that is, the IT test—an individual duty rate will be specified for the NME exporter on the basis of a comparison of the alternative third country normal value with its own export prices.[453]

280. An NME exporter that does not meet the IT test will be subject to a country-wide duty rate. The determination of the export price used to calculate that country-wide duty rate will depend on the level of cooperation on the part of the non-IT exporters altogether. If the level of cooperation is high—that is, if the cooperating non-IT exporters account for almost 100 per cent of all exports—the export price will be based on a weighted average of the actual price of all export transactions effected by these exporters. If, however, the level of cooperation is low—that is, if the cooperating non-IT exporters account for significantly less than 100 per cent of all exports—the Commission will resort to facts available to complete the missing information. Recourse to facts available will depend on the degree of non-cooperation and may include statistical import data.[454]

281. In sum, Article 2(7) of the Basic AD Regulation determines whether a supplier from an NME will receive market economy treatment, that is, whether

[453] For an NME exporter or producer who meets the MET test, an individual duty will be specified on the basis of a comparison between that exporter's *domestic* normal value and its export price; by contrast, for an NME exporter or producer who meets the IT test, an individual duty will be calculated on the basis of a comparison between that exporter's export price and a *market economy third country* normal value.

[454] Panel Report, para. 7.50.

the normal value for its imports will be determined on the basis of its domestic prices or costs or on the basis of an alternative methodology. Article 9(5) of the Basic AD Regulation determines whether a supplier from an NME will receive an individual or a country-wide anti-dumping duty. According to Article 9(5), NME suppliers that have fulfilled the MET test under Article 2(7) will automatically receive individual duties; NME suppliers that have not fulfilled the MET test under Article 2(7) will receive country-wide duties, but will receive individual duties if they fulfil the IT test set out in Article 9(5).

282. In this dispute, China does not challenge the European Union's alternative methodology to determine normal value for imports from NMEs on the basis of a market economy third country, nor does it challenge the criteria to grant market economy treatment to WTO NME suppliers set forth in Article 2(7). China directs its challenge to the rules regarding the specification of individual and country-wide duties for NME suppliers, including the IT test, which are contained in Article 9(5) of the Basic AD Regulation.

C. Section 15 of China's Accession Protocol

283. Before addressing the appeal by the European Union of the Panel's findings under Articles 6.10 and 9.2 of the *Anti-Dumping Agreement*, we address the claim by the European Union that the Protocol on the Accession of the People's Republic of China (China's "Accession Protocol")[455], and in particular Section 15, allows the European Union to treat China as an NME for the purpose of applying anti-dumping rules and, in particular, Article 9(5) of the Basic AD Regulation.

284. The European Union argues that China's Accession Protocol contains an understanding that China is not yet a market economy and that, while it does not speak directly to the issue of whether Chinese suppliers must receive individual treatment with respect to the calculation of dumping margins and the imposition of anti-dumping duties, it "does not narrow the universe of situations where the *Anti-Dumping Agreement* permits a flexible application of the rules".[456] The European Union highlights that the reference in paragraph 15(a)(i) and (ii) of China's Accession Protocol to "the manufacture, production and sale of that product" suggests that the term "market economy conditions" also "encompasses the situation where State intervention in the economy including international trade is so substantial that operators cannot act independently from the State in their export activities".[457] China responds that Section 15 of its Accession Protocol does not contain "an official recognition by China" that it is an NME, but only "a temporary and limited derogation from the rules in the [*Anti-Dumping Agreement*]" on the determination of the normal value in anti-dumping investigations initiated with respect to imports from China.[458]

---

455 WT/L/432, 23 November 2001.

456 European Union's appellant's submission, para. 49.

457 European Union's appellant's submission, para. 46.

458 China's appellee's submission, para. 49.

285. We begin by observing that Section 15 of China's Accession Protocol contains a similar acknowledgment of the difficulties in determining price comparability as the one contained in the second *Ad* Note to Article VI:1 of the GATT 1994, in respect of imports from China.[459] The second *Ad* Note to Article VI:1 recognizes that, in the cases of imports from countries where the State has a complete or substantially complete monopoly of trade and where all domestic prices are fixed by the State, importing Members may determine that a comparison with domestic prices in such a country may not be appropriate due to special difficulties in determining price comparability. This provision allows investigating authorities to disregard domestic prices and costs of such an NME in the determination of normal value and to resort to prices and costs in a market economy third country. Article 2.7 of the *Anti-Dumping Agreement* states that Article 2 is without prejudice to the second *Ad* Note to Article VI:1 of the GATT 1994, and thus incorporates the second *Ad* Note to Article VI:1 into the *Anti-Dumping Agreement*.[460]

---

[459] Section 15 of China's Accession Protocol, entitled "Price Comparability in Determining Subsidies and Dumping", reads in relevant part:

> Article VI of the GATT 1994, the Agreement on Implementation of Article VI of the General Agreement on Tariffs and Trade 1994 ("*Anti-Dumping Agreement*") and the SCM Agreement shall apply in proceedings involving imports of Chinese origin into a WTO Member consistent with the following:
>
> (a) In determining price comparability under Article VI of the GATT 1994 and the *Anti-Dumping Agreement*, the importing WTO Member shall use either Chinese prices or costs for the industry under investigation or a methodology that is not based on a strict comparison with domestic prices or costs in China based on the following rules:
>
> (i) If the producers under investigation can clearly show that market economy conditions prevail in the industry producing the like product with regard to the manufacture, production and sale of that product, the importing WTO Member shall use Chinese prices or costs for the industry under investigation in determining price comparability;
>
> (ii) The importing WTO Member may use a methodology that is not based on a strict comparison with domestic prices or costs in China if the producers under investigation cannot clearly show that market economy conditions prevail in the industry producing the like product with regard to manufacture, production and sale of that product.
>
> ...
>
> (d) Once China has established, under the national law of the importing WTO Member, that it is a market economy, the provisions of subparagraph (a) shall be terminated provided that the importing Member's national law contains market economy criteria as of the date of accession. In any event, the provisions of subparagraph (a)(ii) shall expire 15 years after the date of accession. In addition, should China establish, pursuant to the national law of the importing WTO Member, that market economy conditions prevail in a particular industry or sector, the non-market economy provisions of subparagraph (a) shall no longer apply to that industry or sector.

[460] The second *Ad* Note to Article VI:1 of the GATT 1994 reads as follows:

> It is recognized that, in the case of imports from a country which has a complete or substantially complete monopoly of its trade and where all domestic prices are fixed

286. According to paragraph 15(a) of China's Accession Protocol, it is incumbent upon Chinese producers to "clearly show" that market economy conditions prevail in the industry producing the like product in order for Chinese prices or costs to be used when determining price comparability. If Chinese producers are not able to "clearly show" that market economy conditions prevail in the industry in question, the importing WTO Member may use an alternative methodology that is not based on a strict comparison with domestic prices or costs in China, such as using surrogate third country or constructed normal value.

287. We note that paragraph 15(a) of China's Accession Protocol places the burden on the Chinese producers clearly to show that market economy conditions prevail in the industry producing the like product with respect to its manufacture, production, and sale. If such a showing is made, the importing Member shall use Chinese prices and costs in determining price comparability. Like the second *Ad* Note to Article VI:1 of the GATT 1994, paragraph 15(a) of China's Accession Protocol permits importing Members to derogate from a strict comparison with domestic prices or costs in China, that is, in respect of the determination of the normal value. This is indicated by the text of paragraph 15(a), which, in respect of the determination of price comparability, refers to "*Chinese* prices or costs" or "a methodology that is not based on a strict comparison with *domestic* prices or costs in China".[461]

288. We do not consider that the references in paragraph 15(a)(i) and (ii) to producers having to show that "market economy conditions prevail ... with regard to the manufacture, production and *sale*"[462] of a product means that paragraph 15(a) permits any derogations also with respect to the determination of

---

> by the State, special difficulties may exist in determining price comparability for the purposes of paragraph 1, and in such cases importing Members may find it necessary to take into account the possibility that a strict comparison with domestic prices in such a country may not always be appropriate.

We observe that the second *Ad* Note to Article VI:1 refers to a "country which has a complete or substantially complete monopoly of its trade" and "where all domestic prices are fixed by the State". This appears to describe a certain type of NME, where the State monopolizes trade and sets all domestic prices. The second *Ad* Note to Article VI:1 would thus not on its face be applicable to lesser forms of NMEs that do not fulfil both conditions, that is, the complete or substantially complete monopoly of trade and the fixing of all prices by the State.

Furthermore, the reference in the second *Ad* Note to Article VI:1 to a strict "comparison with domestic prices" not always being "appropriate" provides flexibility only in respect of the determination of normal value. The recognition of special difficulties in determining price comparability in the second *Ad* Note to Article VI:1 does not mean that importing Members may depart from the provisions regarding the determination of export prices and the calculation of dumping margins and anti-dumping duties set forth in the *Anti-Dumping Agreement* and in the GATT 1994. While the second *Ad* Note to Article VI:1 refers to difficulties in determining price comparability in general, the text of this provision clarifies that these difficulties relate exclusively to the normal value side of the comparison. This is indicated by the operative part in the third sentence of this provision, which only allows importing Members to depart from a "strict comparison with *domestic* prices".

The second *Ad* Note to Article VI:1 was added to the GATT 1947 following the 1954-1955 Review Session. (L/334, adopted 3 March 1955, p. 2, para. 6, and Annex I, Section I.B, p. 10; BISD 3S/222, at 223, para. 6)

[461] Emphasis added.

[462] Emphasis added.

export prices. We reach this conclusion because, when producers are not able to show that market economy conditions prevail (including with regard to the *sale* of the product), paragraph 15(a) makes it clear that all an importing WTO Member is allowed to do as a consequence is to "use a methodology that is not based on a strict comparison with *domestic prices or costs in China*".[463]

289. Paragraph 15(d) of China's Accession Protocol establishes that the provisions of paragraph 15(a) expire 15 years after the date of China's accession (that is, 11 December 2016). It also provides that other WTO Members shall grant before that date the early termination of paragraph 15(a) with respect to China's entire economy or specific sectors or industries if China demonstrates under the law of the importing WTO Member "that it is a market economy" or that "market economy conditions prevail in a particular industry or sector". Since paragraph 15(d) provides for rules on the termination of paragraph 15(a), its scope of application cannot be wider than that of paragraph 15(a). Both paragraphs concern exclusively the determination of normal value. In other words, paragraph 15(a) contains special rules for the determination of normal value in anti-dumping investigations involving China. Paragraph 15(d) in turn establishes that these special rules will expire in 2016 and sets out certain conditions that may lead to the early termination of these special rules before 2016.

290. In our view, therefore, Section 15 of China's Accession Protocol does not authorize WTO Members to treat China differently from other Members except for the determination of price comparability in respect of domestic prices and costs in China, which relates to the determination of normal value. We consider that, while Section 15 of China's Accession Protocol establishes special rules regarding the domestic price aspect of price comparability, it does not contain an open-ended exception that allows WTO Members to treat China differently for other purposes under the *Anti-Dumping Agreement* and the GATT 1994, such as the determination of export prices or individual versus country-wide margins and duties.[464]

291. Finally, we note that China's claim before the Panel concerned the determination of individual and country-wide dumping margins and duties, not the possibility of resorting to alternative methodologies in the calculation of normal value in anti-dumping investigations involving China.

---

[463] Emphasis added.

[464] Paragraph 150 of China's Accession Working Party Report states that several WTO Members noted that China was continuing the process of transition towards a full market economy and also refers to possible special difficulties in determining price comparability and to the possibility that a strict comparison with domestic costs and prices in China might not always be appropriate. It states:

> Several members of the Working Party noted that China was continuing the process of transition towards a full market economy. Those members noted that under those circumstances, in the case of imports of Chinese origin into a WTO Member, special difficulties could exist in determining cost and price comparability in the context of anti-dumping investigations and countervailing duty investigations. Those members stated that in such cases, the importing WTO Member might find it necessary to take into account the possibility that a strict comparison with domestic costs and prices in China might not always be appropriate.

D. *The Scope of Article 9(5) of the Basic AD Regulation*

292. We now turn to the European Union's appeal of the Panel's findings concerning the scope of Article 9(5) of the Basic AD Regulation. The Panel found that "Article 9(5) of the Basic AD Regulation concerns not only the imposition of anti-dumping duties but also the calculation of margins of dumping".[465] The Panel reasoned that, as a general matter, "there is a close and necessary link between the calculation of a margin of dumping and the imposition of an anti-dumping duty"[466] and that "normally, an investigating authority would calculate the margin of dumping and impose the consequent anti-dumping duty on the same basis", whether this is producer specific or country-wide.[467] Specifically, the Panel found that, "in operation, the result of the IT test in Article 9(5) of the Basic AD Regulation determines the nature of the margin calculation the EU authorities will undertake, either individual or country-wide".[468]

293. The European Union claims that Article 9(5) of the Basic AD Regulation, examined on its face and based on its text and in the context of other Articles of the Basic AD Regulation, shows that it "deals exclusively with the imposition of anti-dumping duties"[469] and does not address the calculation of dumping margins or whether such dumping margins should be calculated on an individual or a country-wide basis. According to the European Union, the determination of the dumping margin for a supplier entitled to an individual dumping margin flows from the rule contained in Article 9(4) rather than 9(5) of the Basic AD Regulation, which China did not specify as the measure at issue in the present dispute.

294. China contends that the Panel's finding on the "meaning" and "scope" of Article 9(5) of the Basic AD Regulation is an issue of fact that the Appellate Body is not competent to review pursuant to Article 17.6 of the DSU. China submits that the meaning and scope of Article 9(5) is not clear "on its face", and its determination involves the Panel's findings on relevant factual elements with which the Appellate Body will not lightly interfere. China contends that, because the European Union has failed to raise a claim under Article 11 of the DSU in this respect, the Panel's finding regarding the meaning and scope of Article 9(5) of the Basic AD Regulation is not subject to our review in this case. In the alternative, assuming that we were to consider ourselves competent to review this issue, China submits that the Panel correctly found that Article 9(5) of the Basic AD Regulation concerns not only the imposition of anti-dumping duties but also the calculation of dumping margins.[470]

---

465 Panel Report, para. 7.77.

466 Panel Report, para. 7.72.

467 Panel Report, para. 7.74.

468 The Panel found that it is undisputed that, where according to Article 9(5) country-wide duties are imposed on NME producers that fail the IT test, the European Commission calculates only a country-wide dumping margin for such producers (and not individual margins), while in respect of producers that pass the IT test, an individual margin is calculated and an individual duty is imposed. (Panel Report, para. 7.77)

469 European Union's appellant's submission, para. 90.

470 China's appellee's submission, para. 67.

295. We begin by addressing China's preliminary objection that the Panel's finding concerning the meaning and scope of Article 9(5) of the Basic AD Regulation is a matter of fact that is not subject to appellate review pursuant to Article 17.6 of the DSU. We disagree with China and the Panel.[471] On several occasions, the Appellate Body has clarified that municipal law may serve both as evidence of facts and evidence of a Member's compliance or non-compliance with its international obligations.[472] In particular, in *US – Section 211 Appropriations Act*, the Appellate Body stated that, when a panel examines the municipal law of a WTO Member for the purpose of determining whether that Member has complied with its WTO obligations, that examination is a legal characterization by a panel and is therefore subject to appellate review under Article 17.6 of the DSU.[473]

296. In *China – Auto Parts*, the Appellate Body stated that it could review the panel's findings regarding the meaning of municipal law to the extent that the panel conducted its examination of municipal law for purposes of determining whether the Member had complied with its WTO obligations. The Appellate Body recognized that there will be instances in which a panel's assessment of municipal law will go beyond the text of the instrument on its face, in which case further examination may be required, and may involve factual elements. The Appellate Body explained that it would not lightly interfere with a panel's assessment of municipal law that went beyond the text of an instrument on its face and involved such factual elements.[474] The Appellate Body clarified that the examination of a municipal legal instrument will focus on its text, but may also include the context of the provision and the "overall structure and logic"[475] of the municipal law.[476] In this dispute, the Panel did not review factual elements concerning the application of Article 9(5), such as pronouncements by EU domestic courts or opinions of legal experts or recognized scholars[477], but assessed Article 9(5) of the Basic AD Regulation, based on the text of the provision, its context, and its operation.[478]

---

471 At the outset of its analysis of the scope of Article 9(5) of the Basic AD Regulation, the Panel stated that it fell upon it "to clarify the scope/operation of Article 9(5) of the Basic AD Regulation as a factual matter before engaging in a substantive analysis of China's claims". (Panel Report, para. 7.68)

472 Appellate Body Report, *India – Patents (US)*, paras. 65 and 66; Appellate Body Report, *US – Hot-Rolled Steel*, para. 200; Appellate Body Report, *China – Publications and Audiovisual Products*, paras. 177 and 178; Appellate Body Report, *US – Corrosion-Resistant Steel Sunset Review*, para. 168; Appellate Body Report, *US – Carbon Steel*, paras. 156 and 157.

473 Appellate Body Report, *US – Section 211 Appropriations Act*, para. 105.

474 Appellate Body Reports, *China – Auto Parts*, para. 225.

475 Appellate Body Reports, *China – Auto Parts*, para. 238.

476 Appellate Body Reports, *China – Auto Parts*, paras. 225-245; Appellate Body Report, *China – Publications and Audiovisual Products*, para. 177.

477 Appellate Body Report, *US – Carbon Steel*, para. 157.

478 The Panel stated that:

> … the meaning of national law of a WTO Member is a *matter of fact* for panels to establish. We note that the European Union has not provided any evidence of the meaning of Article 9(5) of the Basic AD Regulation, such as, for instance, an interpretation from the EU courts having relevant jurisdiction. Thus, we consider that it

297. Therefore, we conclude that the Panel's assessment of the meaning and scope of Article 9(5) of the Basic AD Regulation, which is based on the text of the provision, its context within the structure of the other relevant provisions of the Regulation, and its operation is not a "factual matter" and is not excluded from appellate review. Rather, the Panel examined Article 9(5) for the purpose of determining its consistency with a number of provisions of the *Anti-Dumping Agreement* and the GATT 1994, which, as a matter of legal characterization, is subject to appellate review according to Article 17.6 of the DSU.

298. Having clarified that the Panel's findings concerning the meaning and scope of Article 9(5) of the Basic AD Regulation are subject to appellate review, we now turn to the European Union's appeal that the Panel erred in finding that Article 9(5) of the Basic AD Regulation concerns not only the imposition of anti-dumping duties but also the calculation of margins of dumping.

299. The European Union contends that, even if the determination of dumping and the imposition of duties are closely related issues, this does not mean that "any consequence of the Article 9(5) determination, such as the nature of the dumping margin calculation, was part of the measure at issue".[479] The European Union contends that provisions of the Basic AD Regulation other than Article 9(5) speak directly or indirectly to the separate issue of the determination of dumping margins and whether those determinations are individual or country-wide. In particular, the European Union refers to: (i) Article 2(7), as the basis on which a supplier meeting the MET test would be assigned an individual margin of dumping; (ii) Article 9(4), which establishes the ceiling for the amount of anti-dumping duties by reference to the margin of dumping to be established; (iii) Article 9(6), which addresses the calculation of dumping margins and the imposition of anti-dumping duties in the context of sampling; (iv) Article 11(4), which provides for the calculation of individual margins of dumping for new exporters in reviews; and (v) Article 11(8), which requires that the dumping margin be established on an individual basis in refund proceedings. According to the European Union, these provisions address the separate issue of the individual determination of dumping margins.[480]

300. Like the Panel, we note that the text of Article 9(5) of the Basic AD Regulation does not explicitly mention dumping margins. However, we observe that Article 9(5) requires that an anti-dumping duty "be imposed in the appropriate amounts in each case" and that such duty be specified for each supplier or in certain circumstances for the supplying country concerned. We agree with the Panel that there is "a close and necessary link" between the calculation of a dumping margin and the imposition of an anti-dumping duty.[481] In particular, we consider that the determination of a dumping margin is a prerequisite for the

---

falls upon us to clarify the scope/operation of Article 9(5) of the Basic AD Regulation *as a factual matter* before engaging in a substantive analysis of China's claims.

(Panel Report, para. 7.68 (emphasis added; footnotes omitted))

[479] European Union's appellant's submission, para. 108.

[480] European Union's appellant's submission, para. 96.

[481] Panel Report, para. 7.72.

imposition of an anti-dumping duty and that, therefore, a duty cannot be imposed unless a margin has been calculated, in part because the margin sets the ceiling on the amount of anti-dumping duty that may be imposed. Moreover, the requirement in Article 9(5) that the amount of the duty be "appropriate" also presupposes that an individual duty be based on an individual margin, and a country-wide duty be based on a country-wide margin. It thus follows that, if individual duties are imposed, individual margins are calculated; if country-wide duties are imposed, country-wide margins are calculated.[482]

301. We are not persuaded that any of the other provisions of the Basic AD Regulation cited by the European Union addresses the question of whether individual or country-wide dumping margins should be calculated. Article 2 of the Basic AD Regulation, like Article 2 of the *Anti-Dumping Agreement*, is entitled "Determination of Dumping", and contains rules concerning the determination of normal value and export price, the comparison between normal value and export price, and methodologies to determine the existence of margins of dumping. Article 2 of the Basic AD Regulation, however, like Article 2 of the *Anti-Dumping Agreement*, does not contain a rule that requires that dumping margins be determined for each individual exporter or producer. More specifically, Article 2(7) of the Basic AD Regulation does not establish that individual margins of dumping will be calculated for NME suppliers if they fulfil the MET test. Article 2(7) only provides that, in the case of imports from NMEs, the normal value shall be determined on the basis of an alternative methodology and not based on domestic prices or costs, unless exporters from NMEs are able to show that market economy conditions prevail by demonstrating that they fulfil the criteria of the MET test. Article 2(7), however, is silent about the calculation of individual margins and duties. It is Article 9(5) of the Basic AD Regulation that establishes that individual duties will be specified for NME suppliers that have fulfilled the MET test; it also stipulates that, for NME suppliers that did not fulfil the MET test, an individual duty will be specified only if they fulfil the IT test.

302. Furthermore, Article 9(4) of the Basic AD Regulation, which appears to implement Article 9.3 of the *Anti-Dumping Agreement*, does not address the issue of the type of dumping margins that should be calculated for NME suppliers. Article 9(4) of the Basic AD Regulation concerns another issue, that is, the ceiling amount of anti-dumping duties, which must not exceed the dumping margin. This ceiling applies regardless of whether dumping margins have been calculated for each individual supplier or for all suppliers from a given country. Indeed, Article 9(4) does not mention at all individual margins or duties, as it is concerned with the maximum ceiling applicable to duties, regardless of whether these duties are imposed on an individual or a country-wide basis.

303. We observe that Article 9(6) of the Basic AD Regulation, which appears to implement Article 9.4 of the *Anti-Dumping Agreement*, addresses the specific situation of the dumping margins and anti-dumping duties that are determined and imposed on non-sampled producers, where the European Commission re-

---

[482] See Panel Report, para. 7.74.

sorts to sampling. It requires that the anti-dumping duty applied to exporters or producers not included in the sample, who have made themselves known and provided sufficient information within three weeks of initiation of the investigation, should not exceed the weighted average margin of dumping established for the parties in the sample. Article 9(6) thus provides that the margin of sampled exporters be averaged; this determination of a weighted average is consequential to the calculation of individual margins for those sampled exporters, which Article 9(6) does not regulate.

304. Article 11(4) of the Basic AD Regulation, which appears to implement Article 9.5 of the *Anti-Dumping Agreement*, requires that a review be carried out for the purpose of determining individual margins for new exporters. Article 11(4) does not exclude the application of Article 9(5) to new exporters from NMEs. In other words, an exporter from an NME that applies for a new exporter review under Article 11(4) would nevertheless have to fulfil the conditions of Article 9(5) if it wants to obtain individual dumping margins and duties. Moreover, Article 11(4) does not speak to the calculation of individual margins for exporters or producers who are not "new exporters or producers". Finally, Article 11(8) of the Basic AD Regulation allows an importer to request refunds, and requires that for this purpose the dumping margin for the relevant exporter be established on an individual basis.

305. All of these provisions of the Basic AD Regulation presuppose the prior determination of dumping margins under a different rule; moreover, none of these provisions addresses the specific question of whether individual or country-wide margins should be determined for exporters or producers. We, therefore, agree with the Panel that none of these other provisions of the Basic AD Regulation cited by the European Union implements the requirement contained in Article 6.10 of the *Anti-Dumping Agreement* that, as a rule, individual margins of dumping have to be determined for each exporter or producer.[483]

306. By contrast, Article 9(5) of the Basic AD Regulation, which establishes the circumstances under which anti-dumping duties must be specified on an individual or a country-wide basis, by necessary implication, also requires that dumping margins be determined on such a basis. The fact that other provisions of the Basic AD Regulation cited by the European Union presuppose the determination of a dumping margin supports the view that it is Article 9(5) that regulates the circumstances under which dumping margins should be determined on an individual basis. To suggest that no provision in the Basic AD Regulation implements the requirement of Article 6.10 of the *Anti-Dumping Agreement* that, as a rule, individual dumping margins be determined for each exporter or producer, would result in a lacuna that is not consistent with the structure and operation of the Basic AD Regulation and with the other rules in the Regulation, which presuppose the existence of such a rule.

[483] Panel Report, para. 7.75.

307. We also consider that the calculation of country-wide margins for non-IT suppliers cannot be described as "any consequence"[484] or as merely a potential consequence of the Article 9(5) determination, as it is directly and necessarily associated with the rule in Article 9(5) that requires the specification of country-wide duties for non-IT suppliers. In other words, it seems to us that the calculation of dumping margins and of the amount of duties are closely linked, in that the method used to determine dumping margins is reflected in the imposition of duties. As a consequence, individual duties presuppose individual margins and country-wide duties presuppose country-wide margins. Therefore, we do not consider that, as the European Union argues[485], by addressing the country-wide dumping margin calculation that results from the operation of Article 9(5), the Panel incorrectly expanded the scope of the measure at issue.

308. In the light of the above, we consider that the Panel did not err in finding that Article 9(5) of the Basic AD Regulation not only concerns the imposition of anti-dumping duties but also the calculation of dumping margins, and that it could be challenged "as such" under Article 6.10 of the *Anti-Dumping Agreement*, which addresses the calculation of margins of dumping for each exporter or producer.[486]

E. Articles 6.10 and 9.2 of the Anti-Dumping Agreement

309. Having concluded that Article 9(5) of the Basic AD Regulation regulates not only the imposition and collection of anti-dumping duties but also the determination of dumping margins, and whether these are determined on an individual or a country-wide basis, we now turn to the Panel's interpretation and application of Articles 6.10 and 9.2 of the *Anti-Dumping Agreement*.

310. The Panel ultimately found that Article 9(5) of the Basic AD Regulation is inconsistent with Articles 6.10 and 9.2 of the *Anti-Dumping Agreement* because it requires the determination of country-wide dumping margins for and the imposition of country-wide anti-dumping duties on exporters or producers from NMEs, unless such producers or exporters show, on the basis of the criteria set out in that provision, that they are independent from the State (IT test).[487] We address below first the Panel's interpretation of Articles 6.10 and 9.2 and then its application of these provisions.

1. Interpretation of Articles 6.10 and 9.2 of the Anti-Dumping Agreement

(a) Article 6.10 of the *Anti-Dumping Agreement*

311. In its analysis of the consistency of Article 9(5) of the Basic AD Regulation with Article 6.10 of the *Anti-Dumping Agreement*, the Panel observed that

---

[484] European Union's appellant's submission, para. 108.
[485] See European Union's appellant's submission, para. 108.
[486] Panel Report, para. 7.77.
[487] Panel Report, paras. 7.98 and 7.112.

"the first sentence of Article 6.10 provides that the investigating authorities must, 'as a rule', calculate an individual dumping margin for each known exporter or producer of the product under investigation"[488] and that "[t]he wording of Article 6.10, particularly the fact that the exception is stated immediately after the rule, seems to suggest that sampling is the sole exception to the rule of individual margins".[489]

312. The European Union claims that Article 6.10 should not be read as establishing a rule subject to a single exception and that it does not impose an unqualified obligation, but rather states a preference for determining individual dumping margins. The European Union maintains that the term "as a rule", which is inserted after the word "shall", "indicate[s] that the obligation is only a general principle and not a strict obligation that is to be complied with in any and all circumstances".[490] The European Union observes that Article 6.10 refers to one affirmative situation (sampling) where such a preference "may" not be followed, and argues that "sampling" is not the only situation in which a Member is not required to determine individual dumping margins.[491] According to the European Union, that Article 6.10, first sentence, does not contain a strict rule, as the Panel found, but a preference, is borne out by the existence of other situations where the preference does not need to be followed.

313. China responds that the use of the word "shall" in the first sentence of Article 6.10 establishes the mandatory nature of this provision, and that "sampling" is the only exception to this rule. In China's view, the expression "as a rule" is necessary to the extent that it creates a "link between the obligation contained in Article 6.10 first sentence which constitutes the rule and the exception to that rule included in the second sentence of that provision".[492] According to China, if the drafters' intention was to allow more exceptions than "sampling", they would have expressly mentioned that the derogation from the general rule was permitted in situations other than the one mentioned in the second sentence of Article 6.10.[493]

314. We observe that two main interpretative questions are raised in respect of the Panel's findings under Article 6.10. First, whether the first sentence of Article 6.10, through the use of the terms "shall" and "as a rule", expresses a mandatory rule or a mere preference to determine individual margins of dumping. Second, whether "sampling", as permitted by the second sentence, is the only exception to the rule formulated in the first sentence.

---

488 Panel Report, para. 7.88.

489 Panel Report, para. 7.90. Investigating authorities may resort to sampling when the number of exporters, producers, importers or types of products is so large as to make individual dumping margin determinations impracticable. In such cases, the authorities may limit their examination either: (i) to a reasonable number of interested parties or products by using samples, which are statistically valid; or (ii) to the largest percentage of the volume of exports from the country in question that can reasonably be investigated.

490 European Union's appellant's submission, para. 114.

491 European Union's appellant's submission, para. 117.

492 China's appellee's submission, para. 114.

493 China's appellee's submission. para. 123.

315. Article 6.10 of the *Anti-Dumping Agreement* reads:

> The authorities shall, as a rule, determine an individual margin of dumping for each known exporter or producer concerned of the product under investigation. In cases where the number of exporters, producers, importers or types of products involved is so large as to make such a determination impracticable, the authorities may limit their examination either to a reasonable number of interested parties or products by using samples which are statistically valid on the basis of information available to the authorities at the time of the selection, or to the largest percentage of the volume of the exports from the country in question which can reasonably be investigated.[494]

316. We note that the auxiliary verb "shall" is commonly used in legal texts to express a mandatory rule. In the phrase "[t]he authorities *shall, as a rule,* determine an individual margin of dumping for each known exporter or producer"[495], "shall" is followed by the term "as a rule". The definition of the latter term includes "usually" and "more often than not".[496] The combination of the terms "shall" and "as a rule" does not connote a mere preference. Had the drafters of Article 6.10 wanted to avoid formulating an obligation to determine individual dumping margins, they would have used terms such as "it is desirable" or "in principle" instead of "shall".

317. Although the term "shall" renders the rule in the first sentence of Article 6.10 mandatory, this obligation is qualified by the term "as a rule", and this qualification must have a meaning. In our view, the term "as a rule" in the first sentence indicates that this obligation is not absolute, and foreshadows the possibility of exceptions. Absent the insertion of "as a rule" in the first sentence of Article 6.10, the obligation to determine individual margins would be difficult to reconcile with other provisions of the *Anti-Dumping Agreement* that permit derogations from the rule to determine individual dumping margins. However, while the term "as a rule" should be read as modifying the obligation to determine individual margins, it does not render it a mere preference. Otherwise, the use of "shall" in the first sentence would be deprived of its ordinary meaning.

---

[494] Article 6.10.2 reads:

> In cases where the authorities have limited their examination, as provided for in this paragraph, they shall nevertheless determine an individual margin of dumping for any exporter or producer not initially selected who submits the necessary information in time for that information to be considered during the course of the investigation, except where the number of exporters or producers is so large that individual examinations would be unduly burdensome to the authorities and prevent the timely completion of the investigation. Voluntary responses shall not be discouraged.

[495] Emphasis added.

[496] *Shorter Oxford English Dictionary*, 6th edn, A. Stevenson (ed.) (Oxford University Press, 2007), Vol. 1, p. 126.

318. The second sentence of Article 6.10 allows investigating authorities to depart from the obligation to determine individual dumping margins in cases where the number of exporters, producers, importers, or types of products is so large as to make such determinations impracticable. In such cases, the authorities may limit their examination either: (i) to a reasonable number of interested parties or products by using samples, which are statistically valid; or (ii) to the largest percentage of the volume of exports from the country in question that can reasonably be investigated. This limited examination is generally referred to as "sampling", even where a statistically valid sample is not used but the second alternative for limiting the examination is used.[497] Sampling is the only exception to the determination of individual dumping margins that is expressly provided for in Article 6.10.

319. According to Article 6.10.2, even if the authorities have limited their examination based on sampling, they are nevertheless required to determine an individual margin of dumping for any exporter or producer not initially selected for individual examination if that exporter submits the necessary information in time during the investigation. We observe, however, that Article 6.10.2 also permits investigating authorities not to determine individual dumping margins for exporters or producers who are not initially selected for sampling, even if they submit the necessary information on time, if the number of producers is so large that individual examinations of each of them would be unduly burdensome and prevent the timely completion of the investigation. Again, a derogation from the rule that an individual margin be determined is explicitly provided for in Article 6.10.2. We find relevant context to the interpretation of Article 6.10 also in Article 9.5 of the *Anti-Dumping Agreement.* Article 9.5 requires investigating authorities to determine individual dumping margins for exporters or producers who have not exported the product during the period of investigation. However, when new exporters cannot show that they are not related to any of the exporters or producers that are subject to the anti-dumping duties, such an individual determination is not required. Thus, an exception permitting derogation from the rule requiring the determination of individual margins for new exporters is again expressly provided for in Article 9.5.

320. By inserting the term "shall, as a rule", the drafters of Article 6.10 were careful not to express an obligation that would conflict with other provisions in the *Anti-Dumping Agreement* permitting derogation from the rule to determine individual margins of dumping apart from the sampling exception, and would oblige investigating authorities to determine individual margins of dumping in all cases. However, in our view, such exceptions must be provided for in the covered agreements, so as to avoid the circumvention of the obligation to determine individual margins of dumping in Article 6.10. The term "as a rule" in the first sentence not only anticipates the exception that follows in the second sentence of Article 6.10, but also other provisions in the *Anti-Dumping Agreement* that allow Members to depart from the requirement to determine individual mar-

[497] Panel Report, para. 7.85.

gins of dumping. At the same time, we do not consider that the flexibility provided by the term "as a rule" goes as far as providing Members with an open-ended possibility to create exceptions, which would erode the obligatory character of Article 6.10. It would be incompatible with the existence of such an obligation if Members were free to depart from it by unilaterally determining what qualifies as an applicable exception. The general rule, that is, the obligation to determine individual margins of dumping for each known exporter or producer, applies, unless derogation from it is provided for in the covered agreements.

321. In support of its position that sampling is not the only exception to the determination of individual dumping margins and that other exceptions not specified in the *Anti-Dumping Agreement* are allowed, the European Union cites several examples of other situations where the rule to determine individual dumping margins of Article 6.10 need not be observed.

322. The first example cited by the European Union concerns a non-cooperating exporter or producer for whom the dumping margin is calculated based on facts available. We observe, however, that Article 6.8 of the *Anti-Dumping Agreement* allows an investigating authority to rely on "facts available" if an exporter or producer does not cooperate, and that the margin applied to the non-cooperating exporter or producer would still be an individual one even if it is calculated based on facts available rather than on information provided by the exporter or producer.

323. The second example put forward by the European Union, namely, a "mere trader" that exports the product of another producer and that is assigned the dumping margin of the actual producer, is clearly based on the first sentence of Article 6.10, which refers to "exporters or producers". The reference to "exporters *or* producers"[498] allows investigating authorities not to determine a separate margin of dumping for the producer and the exporter of the same product, but a single one for both. This, however, does not constitute an exception to the requirement to determine individual margins, but rather constitutes an application of this very rule.

324. The third example cited by the European Union refers to cases where an authority is unable to identify the actual producer of the product concerned. This situation is compatible with the correct interpretation of the first sentence of Article 6.10, which requires that individual dumping margins be determined merely for each "known" exporter or producer. When an investigating authority is not able to identify an exporter or producer, it cannot be considered as "known" within the meaning of Article 6.10, and thus the authority cannot be expected to calculate an individual margin for that exporter or producer.

325. The fourth example provided by the European Union concerns those situations where an authority decides to construct normal value and export prices for all producers or exporters on the basis of the same information because it is unable to verify all the necessary information. We observe that the possibility of

---

[498] Emphasis added.

resorting to constructed normal value and export price is explicitly provided for in Article 2 of the *Anti-Dumping Agreement* and, as such, it cannot be characterized as a non-specified exception to Article 6.10. In any event, the fact that an authority may have to construct normal value and/or export price for one or more exporters or producers does not necessarily imply a departure from the rule in Article 6.10. Dumping margins based on constructed normal value and export price based on the same information for many suppliers are not the same as a country-wide margin.

326. Finally, in its fifth example, the European Union refers to the situation of a known producer that does not export the product during the period of investigation and that will not be entitled to an individual dumping margin because it is related to existing exporters or producers. As noted above[499], this situation is expressly provided for in Article 9.5 of the *Anti-Dumping Agreement*, which establishes that new exporters or producers will be entitled to individual duties in a review only if they can show that they are not related to any of the exporters or producers subject to the original investigation.

327. We thus consider that the examples cited by the European Union involve situations that either do not constitute departures from the individual margins rule or are provided for in Article 6.10 itself or in other provisions of the *Anti-Dumping Agreement*. Indeed, the term "as a rule" in the first sentence of Article 6.10 anticipates the possibility of departures from the general rule, but as explained above, any such exceptions must be provided for in the covered agreements. In this respect, we consider that the examples cited by the European Union are consistent with the binding nature of the rule set forth in the first sentence of Article 6.10 and, therefore, do not support the European Union's claim that Article 6.10 states a mere preference.

328. Having said that, we do not find any provision in the covered agreements that would allow importing Members to depart from the obligation to determine individual dumping margins only in respect of imports from NMEs. We have explained above[500] that Section 15 of China's Accession Protocol permits derogation in respect of the domestic price or normal value aspect of price comparability, but does not address the export price aspect of price comparability. It, therefore, has no entailment in respect of the obligation in Article 6.10 of the *Anti-Dumping Agreement* to determine individual dumping margins. In our view, therefore, Section 15 of China's Accession Protocol does not provide a legal basis for flexibility in respect of export prices and for justifying an exception to the requirement to determine individual dumping margins in Article 6.10 of the *Anti-Dumping Agreement*.

329. In the light of the above, we interpret Article 6.10 of the *Anti-Dumping Agreement* as expressing an obligation, rather than a preference, for authorities to determine individual margins of dumping. This obligation is qualified and is subject not only to the exception specified for sampling in the second sentence

---

[499] See *supra*, para. 319.
[500] See *supra*, section IV.C of this Report.

of Article 6.10, but also to other exceptions to the rule to determine individual dumping margins that are provided for in the covered agreements.

(b) Article 9.2 of the *Anti-Dumping Agreement*

330. In its analysis of the consistency of Article 9(5) of the Basic AD Regulation with Article 9.2 of the *Anti-Dumping Agreement*, the Panel noted important similarities between Article 9.2 and Article 6.10 of the *Anti-Dumping Agreement*. Although Article 6.10 concerns dumping margin calculations and Article 9.2 concerns duty imposition, these two provisions relate to "the same general obligation" to "provide individual treatment" to exporters and producers in the context of anti-dumping proceedings.[501] The Panel interpreted Article 9.2 of the *Anti-Dumping Agreement* as requiring investigating authorities to name the individual suppliers, that is, the exporters or producers, on whom anti-dumping duties are imposed, except when the number of exporters or producers is so large that it would be impracticable to do so, in which case the authorities would be allowed to name the supplying country. Accordingly, the Panel concluded that Article 9.2 "does not ... allow the imposition of a single country-wide anti-dumping duty in an investigation involving [an NME]".[502]

331. There are a number of interpretative questions that arise under Article 9.2. The first question is whether the first and second sentences of Article 9.2 require investigating authorities to specify anti-dumping duties for individual suppliers or merely to specify the names of the suppliers of the product concerned. The second question concerns the scope of the exception to this rule contained in the third sentence of Article 9.2 that permits the authorities to name the supplying country concerned when it is "impracticable" to name all individual suppliers. Specifically, the question is whether this exception is limited to the sampling scenario or whether it also covers situations where it would not be "effective" to impose individual duties in respect of NMEs, as the European Union suggests.

332. Article 9.2 of the *Anti-Dumping Agreement* provides:

> When an anti-dumping duty is imposed in respect of any product, such anti-dumping duty shall be collected in the appropriate amounts in each case, on a non-discriminatory basis on imports of such product from all sources found to be dumped and causing injury, except as to imports from those sources from which price undertakings under the terms of this Agreement have been accepted. The authorities shall name the supplier or suppliers of the product concerned. If, however, several suppliers from the same country are involved, and it is impracticable to name all these suppliers, the authorities may name the sup-

[501] Panel Report, para. 7.108.
[502] Panel Report, para. 7.112.

> plying country concerned. If several suppliers from more than one country are involved, the authorities may name either all the suppliers involved, or, if this is impracticable, all the supplying countries involved.

333. The European Union claims on appeal that, like Article 6.10 of the *Anti-Dumping Agreement*, Article 9.2 does not contain a mandatory rule regarding the imposition of individual anti-dumping duties, but merely a principle or a preference. The European Union argues that Article 9.2 of the *Anti-Dumping Agreement* reflects a product-wide and country-wide approach in that it refers to the imposition of an anti-dumping duty on a "product", not a company.[503]

334. China responds that "the wording of Article 9.2 read in its context" (including Article 6.10) "confirms that Article 9.2 contains the obligation for investigating authorities to impose anti-dumping duties on an individual basis and that the only exception to that rule is the one identified in Article 9.2, third sentence".[504] China submits that there is no contradiction in acknowledging that the imposition of anti-dumping duties is made with respect to "products" as well as for each "producer" or "exporter" concerned. In China's view, the fact that Article 9.2, first sentence, refers to the imposition of anti-dumping duties with respect to a "product" does not entail an authorization to impose country-wide duties.[505]

335. We observe that the fact that anti-dumping duties are imposed on products is not inconsistent with the requirement that dumping margins and anti-dumping duties be specified for each individual supplier. The *Anti-Dumping Agreement* contains rules that focus on products as well as importers, exporters, and producers. Article 9.2 itself refers to both products and suppliers. We do not consider, therefore, that a focus on products in certain provisions of the *Anti-Dumping Agreement* is inconsistent with the requirement that anti-dumping duties be specified by supplier in the appropriate amounts in each case.

336. Article 9.2 states that anti-dumping duties "*shall* be collected in the appropriate amounts in each case" and that "authorities *shall* name the supplier or suppliers of the product concerned".[506] It is thus clear from the wording of this provision, which uses the auxiliary verb "shall", that the collection in appropriate amounts of anti-dumping duties and the naming of the supplier are of a mandatory nature. The mandatory nature of the first and second sentences of Article 9.2 can be contrasted with the preference expressed in the second sentence of Article 9.1 for duties lesser than the margin of dumping, if lesser duties are adequate to remove the injury to the domestic industry. To express such a preference, Article 9.1 uses the expression "it is desirable".

---

503 European Union's appellant's submission, paras. 160 and 161.
504 China's appellee's submission, para. 238.
505 China's appellee's submission, para. 225.
506 Emphasis added.

337. The European Union claims that Article 9.2 does not impose an obligation to grant individual treatment to exporters or producers, but merely contains an obligation to "specify by name" exporters or producers.[507] According to the European Union, the term "appropriate" in the first sentence of Article 9.2 may be interpreted as referring to "the duty rate appropriate to the country concerned", and the "source" found to be dumped and causing injury within the meaning of Article 9.2 "could be the relevant country".[508] China rejects the European Union's reading of the term "appropriate" in Article 9.2, first sentence, as referring to the "duty rate appropriate to the country concerned", and submits that the use of the word "appropriate" rather "confirms" the rule that "anti-dumping duties must be imposed on an individual basis".[509]

338. We note that Article 9.2 of the *Anti-Dumping Agreement* requires that anti-dumping duties be collected on a non-discriminatory basis from "all sources" found to be dumped and causing injury, except from "those sources" from which price undertakings have been accepted. We agree with the Panel that the term "sources", which appears twice in the first sentence of Article 9.2, has the same meaning and refers to individual exporters or producers and not to the country as a whole.[510] This is indicated by the fact that price undertakings mentioned in the first sentence of Article 9.2 are accepted, according to Article 8 of the *Anti-Dumping Agreement*, from individual exporters and not from countries. Therefore, the requirement under Article 9.2 that anti-dumping duties be collected in appropriate amounts in each case and from all sources relates to the individual exporters or producers subject to the investigation.[511]

339. We have concluded above that Article 6.10 of the *Anti-Dumping Agreement* contains an obligation to determine individual dumping margins for each exporter or producer, except when sampling is used or if a derogation is otherwise provided for in the covered agreements. We observe that, where an individual margin of dumping has been determined, it flows from the obligation contained in the first sentence of Article 9.2 that the *appropriate* amount of anti-dumping duty that can be imposed also has to be an individual one. We do not see how an importing Member could comply with the obligation in the first sentence of Article 9.2 to collect duties in the *appropriate* amounts in each case if, having determined individual dumping margins, it lists suppliers by name, but imposes country-wide duties. In other words, unless sampling is used, the *appropriate* amount of an anti-dumping duty in each case is one that is specified by supplier, as further clarified and confirmed by the obligation to name suppliers in the second sentence of Article 9.2.[512]

---

[507] European Union's appellant's submission, para. 163.

[508] European Union's appellant's submission, para. 161.

[509] China's appellee's submission, para. 228.

[510] Panel Report, para. 7.103.

[511] We address below the situation where an authority can demonstrate that "exporters or producers" constitute a single entity with the State.

[512] The requirement in Article 9.2 to specify duties by individual suppliers is also consistent with the obligation in that provision not to discriminate in the collection of duties on imports from all sources

340. The second sentence of Article 9.2 contains a requirement that authorities name the supplier or suppliers of the product concerned. It is not clear from the terms of the second sentence alone what the purpose of naming suppliers would be, considering that the term "name" can be defined simply as "mention or specify by name".[513] However, in our view, the content of the obligation "to name" is clarified by the requirements in the first sentence that anti-dumping duties be collected in the appropriate amounts on a non-discriminatory basis from all sources.

341. An interpretation of Article 9.2, second sentence, as requiring the specification of anti-dumping duties by individual suppliers is also confirmed by the context provided by Article 9 of the *Anti-Dumping Agreement* as a whole. Article 9 of the *Anti-Dumping Agreement* sets forth specific rules concerning the imposition of anti-dumping duties. Paragraph 1 states that it is desirable that the duty be less than the margin if a lesser duty would be adequate to remove injury; paragraph 2 requires that duties be imposed in the appropriate amounts and that authorities name suppliers, unless to do so would be impracticable; paragraph 3 states that the amount of the duty should not exceed the dumping margin; paragraph 4 sets forth rules for the application of anti-dumping duties to imports from exporters or producers not included in the sample; and paragraph 5 provides for reviews to determine individual margins for new exporters or producers. All the paragraphs of Article 9 set forth rules concerning the imposition of anti-dumping duties, as reflected in the title of this provision, "Imposition and Collection of Anti-Dumping Duties". All the paragraphs of Article 9, read together, thus suggest that the obligation to name individual suppliers in the second sentence of paragraph 2 is closely related to the imposition of individual anti-dumping duties and that the requirement to name suppliers that are subject to imposition and collection of anti-dumping duties should be interpreted as a requirement to specify duties for each supplier.[514]

342. Having concluded that the first and second sentences of Article 9.2 contain obligations to specify individual anti-dumping duties and to name suppliers, we now turn to the third sentence of Article 9.2. It provides for an exception, which allows importing Members to specify duties for the supplying country concerned, where specification of individual suppliers is "impracticable".

found to be dumped and causing injury. In this case, if an individual dumping margin has been determined for each exporter or producer consistently with Article 6.10, the principle of non-discrimination requires that each exporter or producer obtains an anti-dumping duty that corresponds to its individual dumping margin.

[513] *Shorter Oxford English Dictionary*, 6th edn, A. Stevenson (ed.) (Oxford University Press, 2007), Vol. 2, p. 1887.

[514] We also note that Article 9(5) of the Basic AD Regulation, which according to the European Union "bring[s] into the EU's legal order" and "mirrors the language of Article 9.2 of the *Anti-Dumping Agreement*" (European Union's appellant's submission, para. 95), appears to interpret the first two sentences of Article 9.2 as containing a requirement to specify anti-dumping duties by individual suppliers. Article 9(5) of the Basic AD Regulation states in relevant part that "[t]he Regulation imposing the duty *shall specify the duty for each supplier* or, if that is impracticable, and in general where Article 2(7)(a) applies, the supplying country concerned". (emphasis added)

343. The European Union claims that the Panel erred in finding that Article 9(5) of the Basic AD Regulation does not fall within the exception under Article 9.2, third sentence, of the *Anti-Dumping Agreement*. It argues that, like Article 6.10, Article 9.2 expressly permits the imposition of duties on a country-wide basis in cases other than "sampling", in particular when it is "impracticable" to impose duties and name suppliers on an individual basis, consistently with the notion that these provisions "should ... be interpreted in a flexible manner".[515] China submits that the Panel correctly concluded that Article 9.2 requires that anti-dumping duties be imposed on an individual basis and that a country-wide duty can only be imposed in the circumstances described in Article 9.2, third sentence. In China's view, however, the third sentence does not authorize generally the imposition of a country-wide duty in the case of imports from NMEs.

344. We observe that there is significant parallelism between Article 6.10 and Article 9.2 of the *Anti-Dumping Agreement*. Article 6.10 requires the determination of individual margins of dumping, which corresponds to the obligation to impose anti-dumping duties on an individual basis in Article 9.2. We further note that the fact that the same term "impracticable" is used in both Article 6.10 and Article 9.2 to describe when the exception applies provides an indication that both exceptions refer to the situation where an authority determines dumping margins based on sampling.

345. The interpretative question before us, however, does not concern the precise scope of the exception in the third sentence of Article 9.2, and whether it exactly overlaps with the exception for sampling in Article 6.10 or it has a broader scope. Rather, the issue is whether this exception may be interpreted as permitting the situation envisaged in Article 9(5) of the Basic AD Regulation, that is, the imposition of a country-wide duty on suppliers from NMEs that do not fulfil the IT test under Article 9(5). In particular, we need to ascertain whether it can be considered "impracticable" to impose individual anti-dumping duties on suppliers from NMEs that do not meet the IT test.

346. The European Union contends that the exception in the third sentence of Article 9.2 covers situations such as those envisaged in Article 9(5) of the Basic AD Regulation, which provides for the imposition of country-wide duties where anti-dumping duties cannot be imposed on an individual basis for "practical" reasons.[516] The European Union explains that it would not be "effective" to impose individual anti-dumping duties on suppliers that are all related to the State, because this may lead to the circumvention of the higher anti-dumping duties imposed on some individual exporters by channelling exports through related exporters with the lowest anti-dumping duties.[517]

---

515 European Union's appellant's submission, para. 168.
516 European Union's appellant's submission, para. 172.
517 European Union's appellant's submission, para. 186.

347. We observe that the dictionary definition of the word "impracticable" is "[n]ot practicable; unable to be carried out or done; impossible in practice".[518] The dictionary definition of the word "ineffective" is "[n]ot producing any, or the desired effect; ineffectual, inoperative, inefficient".[519] It is evident from the dictionary definitions that "impracticable" and "ineffective" describe different qualities or characteristics of an action. Thus, the notion of "ineffective" is not included in the notion of "impracticable". In particular, we observe that the notion of "ineffective" is concerned with bringing about or producing an effect or result, which is absent from the notion of "impracticable", which describes the action itself.

348. The reasons adduced by the European Union to justify the imposition of a country-wide duty on non-IT suppliers from NMEs focus on effectiveness rather than on practicability. In other words, if the State in an NME were able to circumvent individual anti-dumping duties imposed on suppliers by channelling exports through the exporter with the lowest duty rate, this may mean that individual anti-dumping duties are "ineffective" to counter dumping, not that their imposition is "impracticable". In our view, Article 9.2, third sentence, allows Members to name the supplying country concerned only when it is impracticable to name individual suppliers; it does not permit naming the supplying country when the imposition of individual duties is ineffective because it may result in circumvention of the anti-dumping duties.

349. We further note that the very content and structure of Article 9(5) of the Basic AD Regulation reveals that the IT test and "impracticability" in Article 9.2 refer to different situations. We recall that Article 9(5) of the Basic AD Regulation states in relevant part:

> An anti-dumping duty shall be imposed in the appropriate amounts in each case, on a non-discriminatory basis on imports of a product from all sources found to be dumped and causing injury, except for imports from those sources from which undertakings under the terms of this Regulation have been accepted. The Regulation imposing the duty shall specify the duty for each supplier or, if that is impracticable, *and* in general where Article 2(7)(a) applies, the supplying country concerned. (emphasis added)

350. Thus, Article 9(5) itself distinguishes situations where the imposition of individual duties would be "impracticable" from situations where Article 2(7)(a) applies, that is, where exporters from NMEs will receive a country-wide duty unless they meet the IT test. The use of the conjunction "and" in Article 9(5)

---

[518] *Shorter Oxford English Dictionary*, 6th edn, A. Stevenson (ed.) (Oxford University Press, 2007), Vol. 1, p. 1332.

[519] *Shorter Oxford English Dictionary*, 6th edn, A. Stevenson (ed.) (Oxford University Press, 2007), Vol. 1, p. 1363.

suggests that these are two separate situations justifying departure from the individual duty rule and that the imposition of country-wide duties on NME suppliers does not fall within the "impracticability" exception, because it is reflected as a separate exception.

351. In the light of the above, we do not consider that the exception in the third sentence of Article 9.2 of the *Anti-Dumping Agreement*, which permits naming the supplying country where naming individual suppliers is "impracticable", authorizes the European Union to impose country-wide duties on suppliers from NMEs that do not meet the IT test in Article 9(5) of the Basic AD Regulation.

352. The European Union further submits that its interpretation of the exception to the individual treatment of suppliers in the third sentence of Article 9.2, as permitting the imposition of country-wide duties on suppliers from NMEs who do not qualify for individual treatment under Article 9(5), is also confirmed by the analysis of supplementary means of interpretation. In particular, the European Union refers to the negotiating history and the circumstances of the conclusion of the *Kennedy Round Anti-Dumping Code*.[520]

353. We have concluded above, based on the text of the provision read in its context, that Article 9.2 of the *Anti-Dumping Agreement* requires the imposition of anti-dumping duties on an individual basis and that the exception in the third sentence of Article 9.2 does not justify the imposition of country-wide duties on non-IT suppliers from NMEs. We, therefore, consider that we do not need to have recourse to supplementary means of interpretation under Article 32 of the *Vienna Convention*, such as the preparatory work of the treaty and the circumstances of its conclusion, in order to confirm or determine the meaning resulting from the application of Article 31.

354. We thus conclude that Article 9.2 of the *Anti-Dumping Agreement* requires investigating authorities to specify an individual duty for each supplier, except where this is impracticable, when several suppliers are involved. We reach this conclusion by reading the first sentence of Article 9.2 in conjunction with the second sentence of Article 9.2. The first sentence requires investigating authorities to collect anti-dumping duties in the appropriate amounts in each case and on a non-discriminatory basis on imports from all sources—that is, suppliers—while the second sentence requires investigating authorities to name the supplier or suppliers of the product concerned. We also consider that the exception in the third sentence of Article 9.2 does not allow the imposition of a single country-wide anti-dumping duty in investigations involving NMEs where the imposition of individual duties is alleged to be "ineffective", but is not "impracticable".

---

520 European Union's appellant's submission, para. 175.

2. *Application of Articles 6.10 and 9.2 of the Anti-Dumping Agreement*

355. The European Union claims that, even assuming that the Panel correctly interpreted Articles 6.10 and 9.2 of the *Anti-Dumping Agreement*, it erred in the application of Articles 6.10 and 9.2 and, in doing so, also acted inconsistently with Article 11 of the DSU. The European Union argues that the Panel ignored its contention that the function of the IT test in Article 9(5) of the Basic AD Regulation is to identify the actual source of price discrimination in the context of imports from NMEs, and thus determine if the State and those entities that do not act independently from the State in NMEs should be treated as a single supplier for the purposes of Articles 6.10 and 9.2.[521] The European Union relies on the findings of the panel in *Korea – Certain Paper*, which, in its view, stand for the proposition that, for the purpose of determining individual dumping margins, Article 6.10 permits investigating authorities to determine that two or more exporters and producers are part of the same entity.[522]

356. The Panel found that, unlike the test in *Korea – Certain Paper*, the IT test does not serve the purpose of establishing whether the State and the exporters or producers are in fact a single entity, nor does it identify the actual source of price discrimination.[523] Moreover, the Panel found that the IT test, unlike the test in *Korea – Certain Paper*, is based on a presumption that in NMEs the State and the exporters constitute a single legal entity and that such a presumption has no legal foundation in the covered agreements.

357. In the next sections, we first address the questions of whether the presumption in Article 9(5) of the Basic AD Regulation that in NMEs all exporters and producers are related to the State is consistent with the provisions of the *Anti-Dumping Agreement* and whether the Panel acted inconsistently with Article 11 of the DSU because it disregarded evidence submitted by the European Union relating to such a presumption. We then address the question of whether an importing Member may determine that the exporters and producers from an NME constitute a single legal entity together with the State for the purposes of applying Articles 6.10 and 9.2 of the *Anti-Dumping Agreement*; more specifically, we will explore whether the operation of the IT test results in the identification of such a single entity.

(a) Whether the European Union Is Entitled to Presume that in NMEs the State and the Exporters Constitute a Single Entity

358. The panel in *Korea – Certain Paper* found that Article 6.10 could be interpreted as allowing the treatment of legally separate entities as a single supplier in "circumstances where the structural and commercial relationship between the

---

[521] European Union's appellant's submission, para. 191.

[522] European Union's appellant's submission, para. 139 (referring to Panel Report, *Korea – Certain Paper*, paras. 7.163-7.168).

[523] Panel Report, paras. 7.94 and 7.106.

companies in question is sufficiently close to be considered as a single exporter or producer".[524] The panel then went on to find that the majority shares of the three companies in question were owned by the same parent company, which had thus considerable controlling power over the operations of the three companies concerned; that there were important commonalities of management between the three companies where most of the directors of each company were present on the board of directors of the other companies; and that the three companies had the ability to shift production amongst themselves, to harmonize commercial activity and basic common corporate objectives, and to make their domestic sales through the same company. Accordingly, the panel concluded that these companies were in a structural and commercial relationship that justified treating them as a single exporter or producer for purposes of Article 6.10 of the *Anti-Dumping Agreement*.[525]

359. We recall that under the IT test in Article 9(5) of the Basic AD Regulation an exporter from an NME that did not qualify for market economy treatment under Article 2(7)(c) is not entitled to an individual anti-dumping duty unless it can demonstrate that:

> (a) in the case of wholly or partly foreign owned firms or joint ventures, exporters are free to repatriate capital and profits;
>
> (b) export prices and quantities, and conditions and terms of sale are freely determined;
>
> (c) the majority of the shares belong to private persons; state officials appearing on the board of directors or holding key management positions shall either be in minority or it must be demonstrated that the company is nonetheless sufficiently independent from State interference;
>
> (d) exchange rate conversions are carried out at the market rate; and
>
> (e) State interference is not such as to permit circumvention of measures if individual exporters are given different rates of duty."

360. The Panel considered that there is a fundamental difference between the IT test and the test applied by the panel in *Korea – Certain Paper*. In its view, the latter test requires investigating authorities to demonstrate the existence of a close structural and commercial relationship between a number of producers such that they constitute a single supplier for which a single dumping margin may be calculated and a single anti-dumping duty may be applied. By contrast, under the IT test, the European Union presumes that in NMEs all exporters and producers are related to the State (and subject to a country-wide dumping margin and anti-dumping duty) unless a producer demonstrates that it has no such relationship with the State and thus qualifies for individual treatment. According to

---

[524] Panel Report, *Korea – Certain Paper*, para. 7.162.
[525] Panel Report, *Korea – Certain Paper*, para. 7.168.

the Panel, applying such a presumption to NME producers "would seriously undermine the logic of Article 6.10", which requires that individual margins be calculated for each known exporter or producer.[526]

361. The European Union submits that in the case of market economies, as found by the panel in *Korea – Certain Paper*, the close relationship between separate legal entities has to be established by the investigating authority on a case-by-case basis; by contrast, in NMEs "the presumption of State control is the general rule".[527] The European Union also contends that the Panel acted inconsistently with Article 11 of the DSU, because it disregarded evidence submitted by the European Union concerning the nature of NMEs and China's status as an NME, as well as the fact that China's Accession Protocol entitles the European Union to treat China as an NME until 2016. This evidence, which, according to the European Union, was not contested by China, supports the presumption underlying Article 9(5) of the Basic AD Regulation that all producers and exporters in an NME constitute a single entity together with the State.

362. China responds that the presumption advocated by the European Union that in NMEs the State and exporters constitute a single entity has no legal basis in the covered agreements and China's Accession Protocol in particular. China further argues that its Accession Protocol does not reflect a general understanding or recognition that China is an NME. Paragraph 15(a) merely authorizes WTO Members to apply until 2016 a temporary and limited derogation from certain rules in the *Anti-Dumping Agreement* concerning normal value. Pursuant to paragraph 15(d), these Members may discontinue the application of paragraph 15(a) prior to that date with respect to certain industries or the entire economy.[528] In any event, China points out that whether China is a market economy or an NME is irrelevant for the purposes of this case, because there is no basis under Articles 6.10 and 9.2 of the *Anti-Dumping Agreement* to distinguish between imports from market economies and imports from NMEs in relation to the determination of individual dumping margins and anti-dumping duties.

363. We recall that Article 9(5) of the Basic AD Regulation establishes a presumption that producers or exporters that operate in NMEs are not entitled to individual treatment; in order to qualify for such treatment, NME exporters bear the burden to demonstrate that they satisfy the criteria of the IT test. We observe that under Articles 6.10 and 9.2 of the *Anti-Dumping Agreement* it is the investigating authority that is called upon to make an objective affirmative determination, on the basis of the evidence that has been submitted or that it has gathered in the investigation, as to who is the known exporter or producer of the product concerned. It is, therefore, the investigating authority that will determine whether one or more exporters have a relationship with the State such that they can be considered as a single entity and receive a single dumping margin and a single anti-dumping duty. In other words, where certain exporters or producers

526 Panel Report, para. 7.96.
527 European Union's appellant's submission, para. 150.
528 China's appellee's submission, para. 195.

are separate legal entities, that evidence will be taken into account in treating them as separate exporters or producers for purposes of Articles 6.10 and 9.2 of the *Anti-Dumping Agreement*. An investigating authority, however, may also need to consider other evidence that demonstrates that legally distinct exporters or producers are in a sufficiently close relationship to constitute a single entity and should thus receive a single dumping margin and anti-dumping duty. By contrast, under Article 9(5) of the Basic AD Regulation, country-wide dumping margins and country-wide anti-dumping duties are established for exporters from NME WTO Members unless such exporters request individual treatment and demonstrate that they satisfy all criteria of the IT test. Failure to meet only one of those criteria leads to denial of individual treatment.

364. We consider that placing the burden on NME exporters to rebut a presumption that they are related to the State and to demonstrate that they are entitled to individual treatment runs counter to Article 6.10, which "as a rule" requires that individual dumping margins be determined for *each known exporter or producer*, and is inconsistent with Article 9.2 that requires that individual duties be specified by *supplier*. Even accepting in principle that there may be circumstances where exporters and producers from NMEs may be considered as a single entity for purposes of Articles 6.10 and 9.2, such singularity cannot be presumed; it has to be determined by the investigating authorities on the basis of facts and evidence submitted or gathered in the investigation.

365. We are also of the view that no other provision in the *Anti-Dumping Agreement* or in other covered agreements provides a legal basis for the European Union's presumption in Article 9(5) of its Basic AD Regulation that results in exporters and producers from NMEs having to demonstrate that they are unrelated to the State in order to qualify for individual treatment. In particular, we do not consider that there is a legal basis in the provisions of China's Accession Protocol for a presumption that country-wide dumping margins be calculated and country-wide duties be imposed on all Chinese exporters of a product under investigation. We have explained above that Section 15 of China's Accession Protocol is silent as to the individual and country-wide determination of dumping margins and imposition of anti-dumping duties. Section 15 only permits derogations in respect of the use of domestic prices and costs—that is, normal value—but not in respect of export prices in the calculation of margins and the consequential imposition of duties.

366. It is true that paragraph 15(a) of China's Accession Protocol places the burden on Chinese exporters to "clearly show" that market economy conditions prevail in order for the importing WTO Members to be obliged to use Chinese domestic prices and costs in determining price comparability. However, this rule concerns only the normal value aspect of price comparability, and does not permit derogation from the disciplines of the *Anti-Dumping Agreement* regarding export price. Paragraph 15(a) of China's Accession Protocol does not provide a legal basis for a presumption that an exporter's individual export prices cannot be used and that, as a consequence, country-wide export prices should be used and hence country-wide margins should be determined and country-wide duties

should be imposed. Neither can paragraph 15(d) be interpreted as authorizing WTO Members to treat China as an NME for matters other than the determination of normal value. As explained above, paragraph 15(d) does not pronounce generally on China's status as a market economy or NME. Rather, it permits an importing WTO Member to specify when the special rules regarding normal value contained in paragraph 15(a) no longer apply—that is, either in 2016 or earlier—if China establishes that it is a market economy or that market economy conditions exist in specific industries. In the light of the above, we conclude that there is no legal basis in the covered agreements for the general presumption that in an NME the State and all exporters are sufficiently related to constitute a single entity, for which a single export price and hence a single duty can be determined.

367. In our view, whether the European Union's presumption under Article 9(5) of its Basic AD Regulation that in NMEs the State and all exporters constitute a single entity is consistent with Articles 6.10 and 9.2 of the *Anti-Dumping Agreement* is a legal question, not a factual one that depends on the economic structure of a particular WTO Member. Rather, the economic structure of a WTO Member may be used as evidence before an investigating authority to determine whether the State and a number of exporters or producers subject to an investigation are sufficiently related to constitute a single entity such that a single margin should be calculated and a single duty be imposed on them. It cannot, however, be used to imply a legal presumption that has not been written into the covered agreements.

368. The European Union submitted to the Panel evidence that it claimed supported the presumption in Article 9(5) of the Basic AD Regulation that the State and the exporters are to be treated as a single entity. In particular, the European Union provided a definition of an NME. It referred to situations where the "State control over the means of production and State intervention in the economy, including international trade, imply that all the means of production and natural resources belong to one entity, the State" and where "[a]ll imports from non-market economy countries are therefore considered to emanate from a single supplier, the State" so that "[t]he State in this sense can be considered as one supplier".[529] The European Union also pointed to paragraph 15(d) of China's Accession Protocol which, it argues, allows it to treat China as an NME until 2016 and provided other evidence concerning China's intervention in its economy and international trade.[530]

369. We have explained above why we conclude that Section 15 of China's Accession Protocol does not provide a legal basis for the European Union's presumption in Article 9(5) of the Basic AD Regulation. We are also of the view that the evidence submitted by the European Union concerning NMEs in general

---

[529] European Union's appellant's submission, para. 152 (quoting European Union's first written submission to the Panel, para. 61).

[530] European Union's appellant's submission, para. 51. These include publications providing definitions of NMEs and describing mechanisms relating to how the Chinese Government intervenes in the economy and international trade.

and China in particular is not relevant to the *legal* question of whether the European Union is permitted to presume under Article 9(5) of the Basic AD Regulation that the State and the exporters are a single exporter for purposes of Articles 6.10 and 9.2 of the *Anti-Dumping Agreement*. The review of this evidence reveals that it is possible that in specific circumstances an investigating authority may reach the conclusion that the State and certain exporters are so closely related that they constitute a single entity. However, the evidence submitted by the European Union cannot establish that the economic structure in China justifies a general presumption that the State and all the exporters in all industries that might be subject to an anti-dumping investigation constitute a single legal entity, where no legal basis for such a presumption is provided for in the covered agreements. Consequently, whether the Panel considered this evidence is of no relevance to the question of whether a legal presumption exists or whether the Panel made an objective assessment of the matter pursuant to Article 11 of the DSU.

370. We have concluded above that a presumption that the State and all exporters or producers in all industries in NMEs are sufficiently related to constitute a single entity lacks a legal basis in the covered agreements. As such, the European Union's presumption is inconsistent with Articles 6.10 and 9.2 of the *Anti-Dumping Agreement*, which requires individual treatment for each exporter or producer. Moreover, the evidence the European Union submitted to the Panel regarding the operation of NMEs in general and China in particular was not relevant to the legal question of whether a presumption is permitted. Therefore, irrespective of the evidence presented by the European Union, the Panel did not err in finding that the European Union had not shown a legal basis for its presumption. Thus, we also find that the Panel did not fail to comply with its duties under Article 11 of the DSU in its assessment of the evidence submitted by the European Union in support of its presumption.

(b) Whether in NMEs the State and the Exporters Can Be Considered as a Single Entity

371. The Panel understood the panel in *Korea – Certain Paper* to have found that Article 6.10 of the *Anti-Dumping Agreement* does not preclude investigating authorities from treating multiple legally distinct entities as a single exporter or producer for purposes of an anti-dumping investigation where the structural and commercial relationship between the companies in question is sufficiently close for them to be considered as a single exporter or producer.[531] The Panel also stated that it is possible in principle for an investigating authority to determine that "one or more nominally distinct producer(s) or exporter(s) is/are, in fact, sufficiently related to the State to justify concluding that they are a single producer or exporter".[532]

531 Panel Report, para. 7.92.
532 Panel Report, para. 7.94.

372. The Panel distinguished the situation before the panel in *Korea – Certain Paper* from Article 9(5) of the Basic AD Regulation on the ground that the criteria of the IT test in Article 9(5) do not concern the structural and commercial relationship between distinct legal entities, but are concerned with the role of the State in the way business is conducted in a given country. The Panel noted that, under the European Union's approach, the State would be considered as a "parent company" for potentially thousands of distinct legal entities producing and exporting a product under investigation. The Panel considered that this was not a plausible application of the reasoning of the panel in *Korea – Certain Paper*.[533]

373. The Panel also found that the IT test does not aim at ascertaining whether the State is the "source of price discrimination" as the European Union claims. According to the Panel, even if an exporter from an NME is able to determine its export prices—which would suggest that it is not the State that is the source of the price discrimination—it would fail the IT test unless it meets all of the other criteria.[534]

374. In our view, the panel in *Korea – Certain Paper* did not develop an interpretation that expanded the meaning of the term "each known exporter or producer", nor did it read new exceptions into Article 6.10 of the *Anti-Dumping Agreement*. Rather, that panel considered that there may be situations where several closely related suppliers may be deemed a single supplier for the purposes of Article 6.10 and referred to a "structural and commercial relationship".[535] In the present dispute, the Panel did not exclude the possibility that in a given investigation the authorities might determine that one or more legally distinct exporter(s) or producer(s) is/are, in fact, sufficiently related to the State to justify a conclusion that they are a single exporter or producer. In such a situation, the Panel noted, the authorities could well treat the exporter(s) or producer(s) and the State as a single exporter and calculate a single dumping margin for, and assign a single duty to, that single exporter.[536]

375. Articles 6.10 and 9.2 of the *Anti-Dumping Agreement* require respectively that individual dumping margins be determined for *each exporter or producer* and that individual anti-dumping duties be imposed on individual *suppliers*. These requirements for individual treatment are respected, the European Union contends, as long as a single country-wide margin and duty is determined for the single State entity.

376. In our view, Articles 6.10 and 9.2 of the *Anti-Dumping Agreement* do not preclude an investigating authority from determining a single dumping margin and a single anti-dumping duty for a number of exporters if it establishes that they constitute a single exporter for purposes of Articles 6.10 and 9.2 of the *Anti-Dumping Agreement*. Whether determining a single dumping margin and a

---

[533] Panel Report, para. 7.93.

[534] Panel Report, para. 7.106.

[535] That panel report was not appealed and the issue of whether several suppliers can be considered as a single supplier that is assigned an individual margin and duty, if they are in a sufficiently close commercial and structural relationship, has not been addressed by any other panel.

[536] Panel Report, para. 7.94.

single anti-dumping duty for a number of exporters is inconsistent with Articles 6.10 and 9.2 will depend on the existence of a number of situations, which would signal that, albeit legally distinct, two or more exporters are in such a relationship that they should be treated as a single entity. These situations may include: (i) the existence of corporate and structural links between the exporters, such as common control, shareholding and management; (ii) the existence of corporate and structural links between the State and the exporters, such as common control, shareholding and management; and (iii) control or material influence by the State in respect of pricing and output. We note that the *Anti-Dumping Agreement* addresses pricing behaviour by exporters; if the State instructs or materially influences the behaviour of several exporters in respect of prices and output, they could be effectively regarded as one exporter for purposes of the *Anti-Dumping Agreement* and a single margin and duty could be assigned to that single exporter. In our view, however, this is not the function of the IT test.

377. The IT test contained in Article 9(5) of the Basic AD Regulation has a different function than the determination of whether several distinct exporters constitute a single exporter because of structural and commercial integration or due to control or material influence by the State. The function of the IT test is to determine whether exporters or producers are sufficiently distinct from the State to overcome the presumption of singularity, such that they should be entitled to individual treatment pursuant to Article 9(5). Such a test cannot be used to determine whether distinct exporters are sufficiently integrated with each other or with the State to constitute a single exporter. Nonetheless, given that the purpose of the IT test is to demonstrate the independence of exporters from State interference, we do not exclude that some of its elements would be relevant to the question of integration, while others would not.

378. Only one of the five criteria of the IT test, for example, directly relates to the structural relationship of the company with the State: the requirement that the majority of the shares belong to private persons and that State officials holding management positions be in the minority. Another criterion relates to the State interference with prices and output. All the other criteria, however, appear to be related to State interference with exporters or State intervention in the economy in general and are likely to lead to the denial of individual treatment with respect to exporters that have little or no structural or commercial relationship with the State and whose pricing and output decisions are not interfered with by the State. This is because the criteria of the IT test apply on a cumulative basis and that failure to comply with only one of them will result in the denial of individual treatment under Article 9(5).

379. Moreover, by focusing on State interference with exporters and State intervention in the economy in general, the IT test captures broader market distortions in the economy and different kinds of interferences by the State than that of the control or material influence by the State over the exporters in respect of pricing and output of a particular like product. As a consequence, the cumulative criteria of the IT test are likely to result in the denial of individual treatment

where the relationship between individual exporters and the State is not such as to justify treating the State and one or several exporters as a single entity for the purposes of Articles 6.10 and 9.2 of the *Anti-Dumping Agreement*.

380. Therefore, even if, as the European Union argues, the purpose of the IT test was to identify the actual source of price discrimination, we cannot see why the failure to comply with one of the criteria of the IT test provides conclusive evidence that the price discrimination by individual suppliers can be attributed to the State, when some of the criteria do not touch on the question of whether an exporter is free to determine its own prices. We thus consider that the IT test is not capable of establishing whether, similar to the situation in *Korea – Certain Paper*, the State and one or more exporters can be deemed a single entity for purposes of Articles 6.10 and 9.2 of the *Anti-Dumping Agreement*. Nevertheless, the test developed by the panel in *Korea – Certain Paper* may not capture all situations where the State effectively controls or materially influences and coordinates several exporters such that they can be considered a single entity. The panel in *Korea – Certain Paper* addressed the question of when two or more legally distinct private companies can be deemed a "single exporter" under Article 6.10 of the *Anti-Dumping Agreement* due to their commercial and structural relationship. The situation analyzed by the panel in *Korea – Certain Paper* presents some relevance to the determination of whether the State and several exporters constitute a single entity. However, the criteria used for determining whether a single entity exists from a corporate perspective, while certainly relevant, will not necessarily capture all situations where the State controls or materially influences several exporters such that they could be considered as a single entity for purposes of Articles 6.10 and 9.2 of the *Anti-Dumping Agreement* and be assigned a single dumping margin and anti-dumping duty.

381. Criteria relating to corporate structure may in certain circumstances be relevant to the determination of whether the State and certain exporters constitute a single entity. In other circumstances, however, an investigating authority might have to take into account factors and positive evidence other than those establishing a corporate or commercial relationship in assessing whether the State and a number of exporters are a single entity and that, therefore, the State is the source of price discrimination. These, for instance, may include evidence of State control or instruction of, or material influence on, the behaviour of certain exporters in respect of pricing and output. These criteria could show that, even in the absence of formal structural links between the State and specific exporters, the State in fact determines and materially influences prices and output.

382. In the light of the above, we are of the view that in principle there may be situations where nominally distinct exporters may be considered as a single entity for the purpose of determining individual dumping margins and anti-dumping duties under Articles 6.10 and 9.2 of the *Anti-Dumping Agreement*, due to State's control or material influence in and coordination of these exporters' pricing and output. We reiterate, however, that the IT test in Article 9(5) of the Basic AD Regulation is not directed at such an inquiry.

383. We further note that, even where it could be determined that particular exporters that are related constitute a single supplier, Articles 6.10 and 9.2 of the *Anti-Dumping Agreement* would nonetheless require the determination of an individual dumping margin for the single entity, which should be based on the average export prices of each individual exporter, and the imposition of a corresponding single anti-dumping duty. Instead, the European Union does not determine such a single dumping margin for the State and non-IT suppliers, but rather calculates a country-wide dumping margin and duty. If cooperating non-IT exporters account for significantly less than 100 per cent of all exports, this duty will be based on facts available for the missing information.[537] Such a country-wide dumping margin and duty is applicable to all cooperating non-IT exporters as well as to all non-cooperating exporters.[538]

384. In our view, only a dumping margin that is based on a weighted average of the export prices of each individual exporter that forms part of the single entity would be consistent with the obligation in Article 6.10 to determine an individual dumping margin for the single entity that is composed of several legally distinct exporters. We also do not consider that a country-wide duty imposed on a group of exporters could be considered as being "collected in the appropriate amounts in each case" within the meaning of Article 9.2 of the *Anti-Dumping Agreement*, to the extent it is determined for the group of fully cooperating non-IT exporters on the basis of facts available because cooperating exporters account for significantly less than 100 per cent of all exports.

3. *Conclusions under Articles 6.10 and 9.2 of the Anti-Dumping Agreement*

385. In the light of all of the above, we therefore *uphold*, albeit for different reasons, the Panel's findings, in paragraphs 7.98 and 7.112 of the Panel Report, that Article 9(5) of the Basic AD Regulation is inconsistent "as such" with Articles 6.10 and 9.2 of the *Anti-Dumping* Agreement, because it conditions the determination of individual dumping margins for and the imposition of individual anti-dumping duties on NME exporters or producers to the fulfilment of the IT test. We also find that the Panel did not act inconsistently with Article 11 of the DSU in finding that Article 9(5) of the Basic AD Regulation is inconsistent "as such" with Articles 6.10 and 9.2 of the *Anti-Dumping Agreement*.

F. *Article I:1 of the GATT 1994*

386. The Panel considered that Article 9(5) of the Basic AD Regulation constitutes a rule or formality, maintained by the European Union in connection with importation. According to the Panel, Article 9(5) results in imports of the same

---

[537] If the level of co-operation is high, that is, if the cooperating non-IT exporters account for close to 100 per cent of all exports, the export price will be based on a weighted average of the actual price of all export transactions effected by these exporters.

[538] Panel Report, para. 7.50.

product from different WTO Members being treated differently in anti-dumping investigations. The Panel reasoned that imports from NMEs may be treated differently from imports of like products from market economy countries only to the extent that a relevant provision of the covered agreements allows for such differential treatment.[539] The Panel found that the European Union had not demonstrated that any provision of the *Anti-Dumping Agreement*, or any other provision of the WTO covered agreements, allows for the specific different treatment of imports from NMEs that is provided for in Article 9(5) of the Basic AD Regulation. Moreover, the Panel considered that the European Union had not established a sufficient factual basis to conclude that there was a relevant difference in the nature of the imports concerned from NMEs as compared to those from other WTO Members, and stated that this argument by the European Union was merely an assumption.[540]

387. Regarding Article I:1 of the GATT 1994, the Panel therefore concluded:

> [I]t is clear that the application of Article 9(5) will, in certain situations, result in imports of the same product from different WTO Members being treated differently in anti-dumping investigations conducted by the European Union. Thus, we consider that Article 9(5) violates the MFN obligation of Article I:1 of the GATT 1994.[541]

388. The European Union claims that the Panel erred in the interpretation and the application of Article I:1 of the GATT 1994, and acted inconsistently with Article 11 of the DSU, when it found that Article 9(5) of the Basic AD Regulation is inconsistent with the MFN obligation of Article I:1 of the GATT 1994. The European Union contends that the alleged advantage granted to market economies was based on the nature of the suppliers involved, and not on the product itself, and that this means that discrimination between like products originating in different countries does not arise in this case.[542] The European Union argues that it is entitled to grant different treatment to imports from market economies and from NMEs because such imports are different in nature. The European Union adds that the word "unconditionally" in Article I:1 does not preclude an advantage being subjected to conditions as long as this does not result in *de facto* discrimination.[543]

389. China responds that the Panel properly found that Article 9(5) of the Basic AD Regulation is inconsistent with Article I:1 of the GATT 1994, because the different treatment that the European Union provides in its anti-dumping investigations to imports from NME and non-NME WTO Members "cannot be

---

[539] The Panel mentioned the second *Ad* Note to Article VI:1 of the GATT 1994 and Section 15 of China's Accession Protocol as examples of relevant provisions allowing for differential treatment in respect of the determination of normal value. (Panel Report, footnote 306 to para. 7.125)

[540] Panel Report, paras. 7.124 and 7.125.

[541] Panel Report, para. 7.124.

[542] European Union's appellant's submission, para. 213.

[543] European Union's appellant's submission, para. 212.

justified on the ground that the origin of the product somehow reflects a difference in nature".[544] China also submits that the Panel did not fail to comply with Article 11 of the DSU and that it did not err in finding that the *Anti-Dumping Agreement* does not allow for the different treatment of imports from NMEs provided for in Article 9(5) of the Basic AD Regulation.

390. Article I:1 of the GATT 1994 requires that:

> [w]ith respect to customs duties and charges of any kind imposed on or in connection with importation or exportation or imposed on the international transfer of payments for imports or exports, and with respect to the method of levying such duties and charges, and with respect to all rules and formalities in connection with importation and exportation, and with respect to all matters referred to in paragraphs 2 and 4 of Article III, any advantage, favour, privilege or immunity granted by any Member to any product originating in or destined for any other country shall be accorded immediately and unconditionally to the like product originating in or destined for the territories of all other Members.

391. Article VI:2 of the GATT 1994 states that:

> [i]n order to offset or prevent dumping, a Member may levy on any dumped product an anti-dumping duty not greater in amount than the margin of dumping in respect of such product. For the purposes of this Article, the margin of dumping is the price difference determined in accordance with the provisions of paragraph 1.

392. We observe that Article VI of the GATT 1994 permits the imposition of anti-dumping duties, which may otherwise be inconsistent with other provisions of the GATT 1994, such as Article I:1.[545] Therefore, in our view, a preliminary question to be addressed before determining whether an anti-dumping duty has been imposed inconsistently with Article I:1 of the GATT 1994 is whether the anti-dumping duty had been imposed consistently with Article VI of the GATT 1994.

---

[544] China's appellee's submission, para. 330.

[545] This relationship is also reflected in Article II:2(b) of the GATT 1994, which states that:

> Nothing in this Article shall prevent any Member from imposing at any time on the importation of any product:
>
> ...
>
> (b) any anti-dumping or countervailing duty applied consistently with the provisions of Article VI.

393. In *Brazil – Desiccated Coconut*, the Appellate Body upheld the panel's finding that the applicability of Article VI of the GATT 1994 to a countervailing duty investigation also determined the applicability of Articles I and II of the GATT 1994. The panel had found that Article VI of the GATT 1994 did not apply to a countervailing duty measure that was the result of an investigation initiated prior to 1 January 1995. Moreover, the panel had found that, if Article VI of GATT 1994 does not constitute applicable law, claims under Articles I and II, which derive from claims of inconsistency with Article VI of the GATT 1994, cannot succeed.[546]

394. Article 9(5) of the Basic AD Regulation regulates the conditions under which an anti-dumping duty is to be imposed by the European Union. In its panel request, however, China did not raise a claim under Article VI of the GATT 1994 in respect of Article 9(5) of the Basic AD Regulation. Thus, it was not argued before the Panel and it is not disputed before us whether Article 9(5) of the Basic AD Regulation is applied consistently with the provisions of Article VI of the GATT 1994. This has significant implications for the question of whether Article 9(5) of the Basic AD Regulation is inconsistent with Article I:1 of the GATT 1994.

395. The Panel, however, found that Article 9(5) of the Basic AD Regulation is inconsistent with Article I:1 of the GATT 1994, without addressing the preliminary question that arises in this case of whether Article 9(5) of the Basic AD Regulation was consistent with Article VI of the GATT 1994. The Panel did not engage with the implications of the absence of a claim under Article VI of the GATT 1994 for a claim under Article I:1 of the GATT 1994. Nor did the Panel consider the relationship between Article VI of the GATT 1994 and the provisions of the *Anti-Dumping Agreement*, which according to Article 1 of the *Anti-Dumping Agreement* "govern the application of Article VI of the GATT 1994".[547] We thus consider that the Panel's finding under Article I:1 of the GATT 1994 lacks an essential step in the sequence of its legal analysis, that is, the determination of whether and under what circumstances an anti-dumping measure that is inconsistent with the *Anti-Dumping Agreement* may be reviewed under Article I:1 of the GATT 1994 in the absence of a review under Article VI of the GATT 1994.

396. As we explained above, China did not claim before the Panel that Article 9(5) of the Basic AD Regulation is inconsistent with Article VI of the GATT 1994, nor did the parties present arguments in this dispute in respect of the rela-

---

[546] Appellate Body Report, *Brazil – Desiccated Coconut*, p. 21, DSR 1997:I, 167, at 185; Panel Report, *Brazil – Desiccated Coconut*, paras. 280 and 281.

[547] Article 1 of the *Anti-Dumping Agreement* states that "[t]he following provisions govern the *application* of Article VI of the GATT 1994 insofar as action is taken under anti-dumping legislation or regulations." (emphasis added) We further note that Article 18.1 of the *Anti-Dumping Agreement* states that no specific action against dumping "can be taken except in accordance with the provisions of GATT 1994, as interpreted by this Agreement". The Panel did not analyze the implications of the terms "application" in Article 1 and "as interpreted" in Article 18 of the *Anti-Dumping Agreement* with respect to the relationship between the obligations in the *Anti-Dumping Agreement* and Articles VI and I of the GATT 1994.

tionship between the provisions of the *Anti-Dumping Agreement* and those of Articles VI and I of the GATT 1994. Thus, we do not consider it appropriate to explore further ourselves the implications of the absence of a claim under Article VI of the GATT 1994 for a claim under Article I:1 of the GATT 1994.

397. In addition, we have already upheld the Panel's findings that Article 9(5) of the Basic AD Regulation is inconsistent "as such" with Articles 6.10 and 9.2 of the *Anti-Dumping Agreement* and we consider that a ruling under Article I:1 of the GATT 1994 is unnecessary for purposes of resolving this dispute.

398. Therefore, for the reasons given above, we decline to rule on the Panel's finding that Article 9(5) of the Basic AD Regulation is inconsistent with Article I:1 of the GATT 1994 and declare this finding moot and of no legal effect. We see no need to address the claim by the European Union that the Panel acted inconsistently with Article 11 of the DSU, because we have declared the Panel's finding that Article 9(5) of the Basic AD Regulation is inconsistent with Article I:1 of the GATT 1994 moot and of no legal effect.

G. Article XVI:4 of the WTO Agreement and Article 18.4 of the Anti-Dumping Agreement

399. Article XVI:4 of the *WTO Agreement* requires WTO Members to ensure that their laws, regulations, and administrative provisions are consistent with the provisions of the covered agreements. Article 18.4 of the *Anti-Dumping Agreement* requires each Member to take all necessary steps to ensure the conformity of its laws, regulations, and administrative procedures with the provisions of the *Anti-Dumping Agreement*. Having concluded that Article 9(5) of the Basic AD Regulation is inconsistent with Articles 6.10 and 9.2 of the *Anti-Dumping Agreement* "as such", the Panel also found that:

> … the European Union has acted inconsistently with Article XVI:4 of the WTO Agreement and Article 18.4 of the [*Anti-Dumping Agreement*] by failing to ensure the conformity of its laws, regulations and administrative procedures with its obligations under the relevant Agreements.[548]

400. As a consequence of the European Union's contention that the Panel wrongly found that Article 9(5) of the Basic AD Regulation is inconsistent "as such" with Articles 6.10 and 9.2 of the *Anti-Dumping Agreement*, the European Union also requests the Appellate Body to reverse the Panel's findings that the European Union acted inconsistently with Article XVI:4 of the *WTO Agreement* and Article 18.4 of the *Anti-Dumping Agreement* by failing to ensure the conformity of its laws, regulations, and administrative procedures with its obligations under the relevant agreements.

---

[548] Panel Report, para. 7.137.

401. We have upheld the Panel's findings that Article 9(5) of the Basic AD Regulation is inconsistent with Articles 6.10 and 9.2 of the *Anti-Dumping Agreement* "as such". As a consequence, we also *uphold* the Panel's finding, in paragraph 7.137 of the Panel Report, that the European Union has acted inconsistently with Article XVI:4 of the *WTO Agreement* and Article 18.4 of the *Anti-Dumping Agreement* by failing to ensure the conformity of its laws, regulations, and administrative procedures with its obligations under the relevant Agreements.

V. THE PANEL'S FINDINGS REGARDING ARTICLE 9(5) OF THE BASIC AD REGULATION "AS APPLIED" IN THE FASTENERS INVESTIGATION

402. The Panel considered that the fact that all the requests for individual treatment were granted to all Chinese producers or exporters that requested such treatment in the underlying investigation did not preclude it from considering whether the application of Article 9(5) of the Basic AD Regulation in the fasteners investigation was inconsistent with the *Anti-Dumping Agreement*. The Panel further noted that the very existence of Article 9(5) of the Basic AD Regulation as part of the legal framework that applies to anti-dumping investigations conducted by the European Union may have discouraged other Chinese producers from coming forward and cooperating and from requesting individual treatment in the investigation at issue.[549]

403. Thus, having found that Article 9(5) of the Basic AD Regulation is inconsistent with Articles 6.10 and 9.2 of the *Anti-Dumping Agreement* "as such", the Panel considered that it was "difficult to see how its application in this investigation could be considered consistent with the obligations of the European Union under the [*Anti-Dumping Agreement*]" and found that "for the same reasons, its application in the fasteners investigation was also inconsistent with these two provisions".[550]

404. The European Union argues that, since the Panel erred in finding that Article 9(5) of the Basic AD Regulation is inconsistent "as such" with the provisions of the *Anti-Dumping Agreement*, the Appellate Body should also reverse the Panel's "as applied" findings with respect to the determinations made in the fasteners investigation.[551] Moreover, the European Union claims that the Panel found that Article 9(5) "as such" prevents the result that suppliers from NMEs are entitled to obtain from the European Union's compliance with the obligations contained in the *Anti-Dumping Agreement* and the GATT 1994. However, in a case where all companies requesting individual treatment were granted such treatment, there is no basis for a finding of inconsistency "as applied" because the result obtained by these companies was the same as it would have been had

549 Panel Report, footnote 334 to para. 7.148.
550 Panel Report, para. 7.148.
551 European Union's appellant's submission, para. 228.

the European Union complied with its obligation. According to the European Union, for the Panel to say that there is a possibility that Article 9(5) affected participation by Chinese exporters in the fasteners investigation and/or the quality and quantity of information Chinese exporters provided to the Commission is pure "speculation", and "not based on evidence".[552]

405. China submits that a measure that is found to be "as such" inconsistent with WTO obligations will also necessarily be inconsistent "as applied". China argues that Article 9(5) of the Basic AD Regulation not only prevents the result that suppliers from NMEs are entitled to obtain but also subjects them to an additional burden by requiring such exporters to request and demonstrate that they fulfil the conditions laid down in Article 9(5).[553]

406. We observe that in the fasteners investigation the European Union applied Article 9(5) of the Basic AD Regulation. Those Chinese suppliers that were not granted market economy treatment under Article 2(7) of the Basic AD Regulation and requested individual treatment pursuant to Article 9(5) obtained it, once they had demonstrated that they fulfilled each and every requirement of the IT test. If Article 9(5) would not condition the granting of individual treatment on the fulfilment of the IT test, all exporters from NMEs that are WTO Members would be entitled to individual treatment, based on Articles 6.10 and 9.2 of the *Anti-Dumping Agreement*, regardless of whether they qualify for market economy treatment under Article 2(7) or not. Article 9(5) of the Basic AD Regulation subjects the right of NME exporters to individual treatment to a number of conditions, which are not provided for under Articles 6.10 and 9.2 of the *Anti-Dumping Agreement* as a prerequisite for obtaining individual treatment. The fact that in this investigation all suppliers who requested individual treatment under Article 9(5) met the burden of demonstrating that they fulfil all the conditions set out in Article 9(5) does not, in our view, render this specific application of Article 9(5) consistent with the *Anti-Dumping Agreement*.

407. We also disagree with the argument of the European Union that there are two categories of measures that can be found "as such" inconsistent: measures whose application will always produce an inconsistent result and "measures where the result which is found WTO inconsistent may or may not take place in an 'as applied' context depending on the configuration of facts".[554] In our view, any instance of application of a measure that is "as such" inconsistent with a covered agreement will produce an inconsistent result even in a situation where suppliers succeed in demonstrating the conditions of the IT test and qualify ultimately for individual treatment. In other words, granting individual treatment without conditioning it on the fulfilment of the IT test would be consistent "as applied", while granting or denying individual treatment subject to the fulfilment of the IT test and the administrative burden it imposes remain inconsistent "as applied".

552 European Union's appellant's submission, para. 231.
553 China's appellee's submission, para. 369.
554 European Union's appellant's submission, para. 230.

408. Granting individual treatment subject to the fulfilment of the IT test would produce a result that may be less inconsistent than a complete denial of individual treatment, but it would nevertheless fall short of the requirements in Articles 6.10 and 9.2 of the *Anti-Dumping Agreement*. We see a difference between the granting of individual treatment without additional obstacles pursuant to Articles 6.10 and 9.2 and the granting of individual treatment subject to a showing that the conditions of the IT test have been fulfilled. The existence of the IT test itself, even where exporters succeed in demonstrating that they meet its conditions, places an additional burden on those exporters who apply for individual treatment, and it has a potential impact on those exporters who may be discouraged by the administrative burden from cooperating with the investigating authority and from requesting individual treatment. The very existence of the IT test adversely affected Chinese exporters who were concerned by the fasteners investigation. These exporters bore the burden of demonstrating that they were entitled to individual treatment, whereas under the *Anti-Dumping Agreement* no such demonstration is required, and for this reason alone it is possible that some exporters did not apply for individual treatment.

409. In the light of the above, having upheld the Panel's findings that Article 9(5) of the Basic AD Regulation is inconsistent "as such" with Articles 6.10 and 9.2 of the *Anti-Dumping Agreement*, we also *uphold* the Panel's finding, in paragraph 7.148 of the Panel Report, that Article 9(5) of the Basic AD Regulation is inconsistent with Articles 6.10 and 9.2 of the *Anti-Dumping Agreement* "as applied" in the fasteners investigation.

VI. CHINA'S OTHER APPEAL OF THE PANEL'S FINDINGS UNDER ARTICLES 4.1 AND 3.1 OF THE *ANTI-DUMPING AGREEMENT*

A. Introduction

410. We turn now to address China's other appeal of the Panel's findings that the European Union did not act inconsistently with Articles 4.1 and 3.1 of the *Anti-Dumping Agreement* with respect to the definition of the domestic industry in the fasteners investigation. We begin our analysis with the interpretation of these provisions, in particular the term "a major proportion" in Article 4.1 of the *Anti-Dumping Agreement*. We then examine China's allegation that the Panel erred in rejecting China's claim that the domestic industry defined in the fasteners investigation did not include producers whose collective output "constitutes a major proportion of the total domestic production" within the meaning of Article 4.1 of the *Anti-Dumping Agreement*. Next, we address China's claims that the Panel erred in finding that: (i) the European Union did not act inconsistently with Article 3.1 of the *Anti-Dumping Agreement* by making an injury determination on the basis of a sample of producers that were not representative of the domestic industry; and (ii) the European Union did not act inconsistently with

Articles 4.1 and 3.1 of the *Anti-Dumping Agreement* by excluding certain producers from the definition of the domestic industry.

B. *Interpretation of Articles 4.1 and 3.1 of the Anti-Dumping Agreement*

411. Article 4.1 of the *Anti-Dumping Agreement* provides that the term "domestic industry" must be defined as referring to the "domestic producers *as a whole* of the like product" or "those of them whose collective output of the products constitutes *a major proportion* of the total domestic production", except in two specific circumstances that are not relevant in this dispute.[555] Article 4.1 thus juxtaposes two methods for defining the term "domestic industry". By using the term "a major proportion", the second method focuses on the question of *how much* production must be represented by those producers making up the domestic industry when the domestic industry is defined as less than the domestic producers as a whole. In answering this question, Article 4.1 does not stipulate a specific proportion for evaluating whether a certain percentage constitutes "a major proportion".[556]

412. The absence of a specific proportion does not mean, however, that any percentage, no matter how low, could automatically qualify as "a major proportion". Rather, the context in which the term "a major proportion" is situated indicates that "a major proportion" should be properly understood as a relatively high proportion of the total domestic production. Specifically, when read in the light of the phrase "the domestic producers as a whole", the term "those of them" in the second method for defining the domestic industry clearly refers to those producers among "domestic producers as a whole". Thus, the collective output of "those" producers must be determined in relation to the production of the domestic producers as a whole. Moreover, the term "a major proportion" is immediately followed by the words "of the total domestic production". "A major proportion", therefore, should be understood as a proportion defined by reference to the total production of domestic producers as a whole. "A major proportion" of such *total* production will standardly serve as a substantial reflection of the total domestic production. Indeed, the lower the proportion, the more sensitive an investigating authority will have to be to ensure that the proportion used substantially reflects the total production of the producers as a whole.

413. In our view, the above interpretation is confirmed by the purpose of defining the domestic industry under the *Anti-Dumping Agreement*. As footnote 9

---

555 Emphasis added. Under Article 4.1(i), domestic producers that are related to the exporters or importers or are themselves importers of the allegedly dumped product may be excluded. Article 4.1(ii) further provides that the domestic industry may be limited to include only those producers within a particular geographic region, if certain criteria are met.

556 One panel has found that "Article 4.1 of the [*Anti-Dumping*] *Agreement* does not require Members to define the 'domestic industry' in terms of domestic producers representing the majority, or 50+ per cent, of total domestic production". (Panel Report, *Argentina – Poultry Anti-Dumping Duties*, para. 7.341)

to Article 3 of the *Anti-Dumping Agreement* indicates[557], the domestic industry forms the basis on which an investigating authority makes the determination of whether the dumped imports cause or threaten to cause material injury to the domestic producers. In this respect, Article 3.1 requires that an injury determination be based on "positive evidence". Pursuant to Article 3.4, such "positive evidence" includes relevant economic factors and indices collected from the domestic industry, which have a bearing on the state of the industry. Naturally, the "positive evidence" to be used in an injury determination requires wide-ranging information concerning the relevant economic factors in order to ensure the accuracy of an investigation concerning the state of the industry and the injury it has suffered. Thus, "a major proportion of the total domestic production" should be determined so as to ensure that the domestic industry defined on this basis is capable of providing ample data that ensure an accurate injury analysis.

414. Moreover, Article 3.1 requires that a determination of injury "involve an objective examination" of, *inter alia*, the impact of the dumped imports on domestic producers. The Appellate Body has found that an "objective examination" in accordance with Article 3.1 "requires that the domestic industry, and the effects of dumped imports, be investigated in an unbiased manner, without favouring the interests of any interested party, or group of interested parties, in the investigation".[558] In other words, to ensure the accuracy of an injury determination, an investigating authority must not act so as to give rise to a material risk of distortion in defining the domestic industry, for example, by excluding a whole category of producers of the like product. The risk of introducing distortion will not arise when no producers are excluded and the domestic industry is defined as "the domestic producers as a whole". Where a domestic industry is defined as those producers whose collective output constitutes a major proportion of the total domestic production, it follows that the higher the proportion, the more producers will be included, and the less likely the injury determination conducted on this basis would be distorted. Therefore, the above interpretation is also consistent with the requirement under Article 3.1 that an injury determination be based on an objective examination of the impact of the dumped imports on domestic producers.

415. We recognize that obtaining information regarding domestic producers may be difficult, particularly in special market situations, such as a fragmented industry with numerous producers. In such special cases, the use of "a major proportion" within the meaning of Article 4.1 provides an investigating authority with some flexibility to define the domestic industry in the light of what is reasonable and practically possible. The practical constraint on an authority's ability to obtain information regarding the domestic producers may also mean that, in

---

[557] Footnote 9 states that:

> Under this Agreement the term "injury" shall, unless otherwise specified, be taken to mean material injury to a domestic industry, threat of material injury to a domestic industry or material retardation of the establishment of such an industry and shall be interpreted in accordance with the provisions of [Article 3].

[558] Appellate Body Report, *US – Hot-Rolled Steel*, para. 193.

such special cases, what constitutes "a major proportion of the total domestic production" may be lower than what is ordinarily permissible in a less fragmented market.

416. Nonetheless, while the proportion of total production that qualifies as "a major proportion" in such a special market situation may be lower than in a normal case, this does not change the purpose of defining the domestic industry, that is, to provide the basis for the injury determination. As in a normal case, the domestic industry defined in such a special case also must ensure that the subsequent injury analysis is based on positive evidence and involves an objective examination pursuant to Article 3.1 of the *Anti-Dumping Agreement*. An injury determination regarding a fragmented industry must therefore cover a large enough proportion of total domestic production to ensure that a proper injury determination can be made pursuant to Article 3.1. Thus, even if what constitutes "a major proportion" may be lower in the light of the practical constraints on obtaining information in a special market situation, an investigating authority bears the obligation to ensure that the way in which it defines the domestic industry does not introduce a material risk of skewing the economic data and, consequently, distorting its analysis of the state of the industry.

417. Finally, we turn to examine the interpretation advanced by the European Union that Article 5.4 of the *Anti-Dumping Agreement* provides important contextual guidance concerning the interpretation of the term "a major proportion" in Article 4.1 of that Agreement. Article 5.4, which contains the standing requirement for the initiation of an investigation, provides certain numerical benchmarks for evaluating whether a complaint to initiate an anti-dumping investigation has sufficient support by domestic producers. Specifically, Article 5.4 states that an investigation "shall not be initiated" unless the application "has been made *by or on behalf of the domestic industry*".[559] It then provides that "[t]he application shall be considered to have been made 'by or on behalf of the domestic industry' if it is supported by those domestic producers whose collective output constitutes more than 50 per cent of the total production of the like product produced by that portion of the domestic industry expressing either support or opposition to the application." Furthermore, "no investigation shall be initiated when domestic producers expressly supporting the application account for less than 25 per cent of total production of the like product produced by the domestic industry."

418. According to the European Union, it is "permissible to consider that producers that represent 25% or more of domestic production can *legitimately* represent a major proportion of total production".[560] In our view, however, there is no textual basis for such a proposition. Articles 4.1 and 5.4 concern two different aspects of an anti-dumping investigation. Article 4.1 defines the whole universe of the domestic industry relevant to the injury determination in an anti-dumping investigation. By contrast, Article 5.4 concerns the question of whether an appli-

559 Emphasis added.

560 European Union's appellee's submission, para. 187. (original emphasis)

cation is made "by or on behalf of the domestic industry", and requires a minimum benchmark defined as expressions of support from those producers representing at least 25 per cent of the "total production ... by the *domestic industry*".[561] Therefore, the 25 per cent benchmark under Article 5.4 does not address the question of how the entire universe of the domestic industry *itself* should be defined. The European Union's recourse to the negotiating history regarding Articles 4.1 and 5.4 of the *Anti-Dumping Agreement* is also unavailing. Although the European Union asserts that the "discussions on major proportion and standing went hand in hand" during the negotiations, this does not change the fact that no agreement was reached in setting a specific proportion for determining what, in abstract, constitutes "a major proportion".[562]

419. In sum, a proper interpretation of the term "a major proportion" under Article 4.1 requires that the domestic industry defined on this basis encompass producers whose collective output represents a relatively high proportion that substantially reflects the total domestic production. This ensures that the injury determination is based on wide-ranging information regarding domestic producers and is not distorted or skewed. In the special case of a fragmented industry with numerous producers, the practical constraints on an authority's ability to obtain information may mean that what constitutes "a major proportion" may be lower than what is ordinarily permissible in a less fragmented industry. However, even in such cases, the authority bears the same obligation to ensure that the process of defining the domestic industry does not give rise to a material risk of distortion. A complainant alleging an inconsistency under the second method for defining the domestic industry bears the burden to prove its claim and to demonstrate that the domestic industry definition does not meet the standard of "a major proportion". Nonetheless, a domestic industry defined on the basis of a proportion that is low, or defined through a process that involves active exclusion of certain domestic producers, is likely to be more susceptible to a finding of inconsistency under Article 4.1 of the *Anti-Dumping Agreement*.

C. *Whether 27 Per Cent of Total Domestic Production in the Fasteners Investigation Constitutes "a major proportion" within the Meaning of Article 4.1 of the Anti-Dumping Agreement*

420. China appeals the Panel's finding that China did not establish that the domestic industry defined in the fasteners investigation did not include domestic producers whose collective output constituted a "major proportion" of the total domestic production. According to China, the Panel erroneously concluded that the fact that the Commission relied on a presumption that 25 per cent of total domestic production constituted "a major proportion" within the meaning of Article 4.1 of the *Anti-Dumping Agreement* was insufficient to demonstrate that the definition of the domestic industry in this dispute was inconsistent with Article 4.1. Moreover, China alleges that the Panel erroneously concluded that certain

---

561 Emphasis added.

562 European Union's appellee's submission, para. 184.

specific circumstances in the fasteners investigation, such as the possibility of including more producers in the domestic industry definition than were included by the Commission[563], were not relevant to the examination of whether the domestic industry defined by the Commission met the requirement of "a major proportion" under Article 4.1.

421. We recall that, with regard to the definition of the domestic industry in the fasteners investigation, recital 114 of the Definitive Regulation provided that:

> [t]he production of the Community producers that supported the complaint and fully cooperated in the investigation represents 27,0% of the production of the product concerned in the Community. It is *therefore* considered that these companies constitute the Community industry *within the meaning of Articles 4(1) and 5(4) of the basic Regulation.*[564] (emphasis added)

422. As the European Union acknowledges[565], in relation to the total domestic production, 27 per cent is at the lower end of the spectrum. Indeed, a figure as low as 27 per cent can hardly be considered a substantial reflection of the total. Nonetheless, the European Union alleges that the fasteners industry is "known to be" a fragmented industry with many producers[566], and China does not dispute this. The practical constraints on obtaining information from domestic producers in such a market may mean that what normally would not qualify as "a major proportion" may in these circumstances suffice, provided that the process of defining the domestic industry does not introduce material risks of distortion. Nonetheless, as further discussed below, the Commission failed to ensure that the domestic industry definition would not introduce a material risk of distortion to the injury analysis by relying on a minimum benchmark irrelevant to the issue of what constitutes "a major proportion", and by excluding certain known producers on the basis of a self-selection process among the producers.

423. The evidence on the record shows that, in the fasteners investigation, the Commission applied a minimum benchmark of 25 per cent in defining the domestic industry. As the European Union explains, Articles 4(1) and 5(4) of the Basic AD Regulation[567], which "link[] the 'major proportion' requirement to the

---

563 See China's other appellant's submission, paras. 250-254. Other specific circumstances alleged by China include: (i) whether the producers included in the domestic industry definition were representative of the entire EU industry; and (ii) the fact that the number of producers included in the domestic industry definition (45) was much smaller than the total number of known EU producers (318). (See *ibid.*, paras. 247-249 and 255-258)

564 Definitive Regulation, *supra*, footnote 4, recital 114.

565 European Union's responses to questioning at the oral hearing.

566 European Union's appellee's submission, para. 191. See also European Union's second written submission to the Panel, para. 122.

567 Specifically, Article 4(1) of the Basic AD Regulation states that "the term 'Community industry' shall be interpreted as referring to the Community producers as a whole of the like products or to

objective benchmark of Article 5.4 of the *Anti-Dumping Agreement* as a legitimate presumption"[568], reflect its position that producers that represent 25 per cent or more of domestic production represent a major proportion of total production. We recall that recital 114 of the Definitive Regulation provides that the producers whose output represents 27 per cent of the total domestic production constitutes the domestic industry "within the meaning of Articles 4(1) and 5(4)" of the Basic AD Regulation. This indicates that the Commission considered that producers representing 27 per cent of the total domestic production were sufficient to constitute the domestic industry simply because they fulfilled the 25 per cent test set out in Articles 4(1) and 5(4) of the Basic AD Regulation. The European Union confirms this understanding in stating that it is "permissible to consider that producers that represent 25% or more of domestic production can *legitimately* represent a major proportion of total production and ... this was the case in the fasteners investigation."[569]

424. We note that China has not challenged Articles 4(1) and 5(4) of the Basic AD Regulation, as such, and that the meaning and scope of these provisions were not examined by the Panel. These provisions are therefore not before us. Nonetheless, China challenges the application of these provisions in the fasteners investigation, arguing that the Commission was not permitted to apply a minimum benchmark, but was required to examine the specific circumstances to determine whether the standard of "a major proportion" was met.[570]

425. The Definitive Regulation indicates, and the European Union confirms, that the Commission applied the 25 per cent test under Articles 4(1) and 5(4) of the Basic AD Regulation in the fasteners investigation and concluded that the producers representing 27 per cent of the total domestic production constituted the domestic industry. However, as explained above, we disagree with the European Union's position that 25 per cent of total domestic production can be presumed to meet the requirement of "a major proportion" under Article 4.1 of the *Anti-Dumping Agreement*. In our view, the 25 per cent benchmark in Article 5.4 of the *Anti-Dumping Agreement* concerns the issue of standing and does not address the question of what constitutes "a major proportion" in Article 4.1. Thus, the Commission determined that a proportion as small as 27 per cent met the standard of "a major proportion" simply because it exceeded a benchmark that was irrelevant to the issue of the definition of the domestic industry. As a result of the application of a benchmark wholly unrelated to the proper interpretation of the term "a major proportion", the domestic industry defined in the fasteners

---

those of them whose collective output of the products constitutes a major proportion, *as defined in Article 5(4)*, of the total Community production of those products". (Basic AD Regulation, *supra*, footnote 5, Article 4(1) (emphasis added)) Article 5(4) of the Basic AD Regulation, in turn, transcribes the standing requirement provided in Article 5.4 of the *Anti-Dumping Agreement*, including the minimum benchmark of "25% of total production of the like product produced by the Community industry". (*Ibid.*, Article 5(4))

[568] European Union's appellee's submission, para. 186.

[569] European Union's appellee's submission, para. 187. (original emphasis) See also European Union's response to Panel Question 32, para. 98.

[570] See China's other appellant's submission, paras. 223-243.

investigation covered a low proportion of domestic production, which significantly restricted the data coverage for conducting an accurate and undistorted injury determination.

426. Moreover, as noted above, recital 114 of the Definitive Regulation defines the domestic industry as including "the Community producers that supported the complaint and fully cooperated in the investigation". We note that the issue of whether the domestic industry, as defined, included only those "producers that supported the complaint" is disputed between the parties, and we will address that issue in the next subsection. It is not disputed, however, that the Commission limited the definition of the domestic industry to those producers who "fully cooperated in the investigation". In this respect, the Definitive Regulation provides that:

> … in view of the large number of producers, sampling of the domestic industry was proposed. ... In order to enable the Commission to decide whether sampling would be necessary, and if so to select a sample, Community producers were requested to make themselves known within 15 days from the date of the initiation of the investigation and to provide basic information on their production and sales, and the names and activities of all their related companies involved in the production and/or selling of the product concerned … *46 Community producers that produced the product concerned in the Community during the investigation period and expressed a wish to be included in the sample within the aforesaid period were considered as cooperating companies and were taken into account in the selection of the sample* ... These Community producers represented over 30% of the estimated production in the Community in 2006. *These producers are considered to constitute the Community industry as mentioned in recital 114.*[571] (emphasis added)

427. In our view, by defining the domestic industry on the basis of willingness to be included in the sample, the Commission's approach imposed a self-selection process among the domestic producers that introduced a material risk of distortion. First, we fail to see the reason why a producer's willingness to be included in the *sample* should affect its eligibility to be included in the *domestic industry*, which is a universe of producers that is by definition wider than the sample. As China argues on appeal, the Commission's approach "confuses

[571] Panel Report, para. 7.212 (quoting Definitive Regulation, *supra*, footnote 4, recitals 23-25). As noted above, one producer among the 46 cooperating producers was later found not to be cooperating and was dropped from the definition of the domestic industry, reducing the proportion of the total domestic production represented by the domestic industry to 27 per cent.

two different steps", because the domestic industry should be defined first, before a sample may be selected from the producers included in the domestic industry.[572]

428. We note that the Panel expressed "sympathy for the European Union's view that producers who do not support the complaint are not likely to cooperate, and thus cannot effectively be considered as part of the domestic industry unless they specifically come forward and agree to participate in the investigation."[573] However, the evidence on the record shows more producers "specifically [came] forward"[574] than were ultimately included in the domestic industry definition. As the European Union explained before the Panel, the Commission contacted 318 known producers requesting certain basic information, and 70 companies responded by providing the requested information within the 15-day deadline, including information on their production and sales.[575] Thus, as China submits, the Commission identified, and obtained information from, more producers than those it ultimately included in the domestic industry definition.[576]

429. According to the European Union's explanation, the Commission excluded 25 of these 70 producers from the domestic industry definition for various reasons, one of which was the producers' expressed unwillingness to be part of the sample.[577] However, as noted above, the sample of domestic producers is a smaller universe than the domestic industry, and the unwillingness to be part of the sample should not affect whether a producer should be part of the domestic industry. This is confirmed by the relevant facts in the fasteners investigation.

---

[572] China's other appellant's submission, para. 163.

[573] Panel Report, para. 7.215. Although we also recognize the potential difficulty in obtaining information from non-cooperating companies, we note that the Commission was not entirely without any ability to solicit information. Article 6(3) of the Basic AD Regulation, for instance, provides that "[t]he Commission may request Member States to supply information, and Member States shall take whatever steps are necessary in order to give effect to such requests." Article 6(4) further provides that "[t]he Commission may request Member States to carry out all necessary checks and inspections, particularly amongst importers, traders and Community producers, and to carry out investigations in third countries, provided that the firms concerned give their consent and that the government of the country in question has been officially notified and raises no objection."

[574] Panel Report, para. 7.215.

[575] Upon the Panel's request, the European Union provided the list of the 70 EU producers, including the names of the related companies involved in the production and/or selling of the product concerned. (See List of "Sampling Form for Community Producers" for inspection by interested parties (Panel Exhibit EU-19))

[576] China alleges on appeal that 114 producers, whose output represented 45 per cent of total domestic production, came forward and provided relevant information. China also alleges that the Commission could have included these 114 producers in the domestic industry definition. (See China's other appellant's submission, paras. 253 and 254) This is a factual issue disputed between the parties and on which we make no finding. Section VI.E of this Report contains our detailed analysis of the participants' dispute on appeal concerning certain factual issues before the Panel.

[577] The European Union explained before the Panel that the Commission disregarded 25 of the 70 producers who responded because they: (i) did not produce the product concerned; (ii) did not wish to be included in the sample; or (iii) refused to provide, or did not send, an open version of their reply. (See European Union's response to Panel Question 31, para. 93) We found no evidence on the record regarding how many of these producers were excluded for the sole reason that they were unwilling to be included in the sample.

Specifically, the Commission selected six producers as part of the sample, obtained relevant information from them, and verified the information on their premises.[578] The Commission then used the information obtained from the sampled producers for its analysis of the "microeconomic" injury factors, but conducted its analysis of the "macroeconomic" injury factors on the basis of information obtained from all of the 45 producers included in the domestic industry definition.[579] Thus, by including only those willing to be part of the *sample* in the domestic industry definition, the Commission's approach shrank the universe of producers whose data could have been used for part of the injury determination. Even though, due to the fragmented nature of the fasteners industry, the practical constraints on obtaining information may justify the inclusion of a smaller proportion of domestic production in the domestic industry definition, the Commission's approach in excluding those who provided relevant information but were unwilling to be part of the sample was unrelated to, and cannot be justified by, such practical constraints.

430. In sum, in the fasteners investigation, the collective output of those producers included in the domestic industry definition, which accounted for 27 per cent of the total domestic production, represented a low proportion in relation to the total. The fragmented nature of the fasteners industry, however, might have permitted such a low proportion due to the impracticality of obtaining more information, provided that the process with which the Commission defined the industry did not give rise to a material risk of distortion. Yet, we note that the Commission applied a minimum benchmark of 25 per cent in defining what constituted "a major proportion of total domestic production", even though this benchmark does not address the standard of "a major proportion" or the practicality of achieving a higher proportion. Moreover, by limiting the domestic industry definition to those producers willing to be part of the sample, the Commission excluded producers that provided relevant information. In so doing, the Commission reduced the data coverage that could have served as a basis for its injury analysis and introduced a material risk of distorting the injury determination. Therefore, we consider that the Panel erred in finding that "the European Union did not act inconsistently with Article 4.1 of the [*Anti-Dumping Agreement*] in defining a domestic industry comprising producers accounting for 27 per cent of total estimated EU production of fasteners."[580]

D. *The Consistency of the Sample with Article 3.1 of the Anti-Dumping Agreement*

431. China alleges that the Panel erred in rejecting its claim that the European Union violated Article 3.1 of the *Anti-Dumping Agreement* because the Com-

---

578 See Definitive Regulation, *supra*, footnote 4, recitals 27, 28, 36, and 37.

579 The "microeconomic" factors were stocks, profitability and cash flow, investment, return on investments, ability to raise capital, and wages. The "macroeconomic" factors were production, production capacity, capacity utilisation, sales, market share, average prices, employment, and productivity. (See Panel Report, para. 7.385)

580 Panel Report, para. 7.230.

mission made an injury determination with respect to a sample of producers that was not representative.[581] China argued before the Panel that, even assuming that the domestic industry was correctly defined, the sample selected by the Commission for purposes of the injury determination was inconsistent with Article 3.1 of the *Anti-Dumping Agreement* because it was not representative of the domestic industry. According to China, the sample was selected on the sole basis of production volume of the like product rather than on the basis of a statistically valid sample.[582] China also argued that the Commission could have carried out the examination of all injury factors with respect to the entire domestic industry it had defined, or at least with respect to more producers than those included in the sample.[583]

432. The Panel rejected these arguments. The Panel found that, "in the absence of any arguments concerning relevant factors either ignored or dismissed by the investigating authority, and given that the sample selected does appear to include producers whose production is representative of that of the industry defined in the investigation, ... China has not demonstrated that the sample selected is not representative of the domestic industry solely because it was selected on the basis of volume of production."[584] Moreover, the Panel stated that it "cannot accept the contention that only a statistically valid sample will be sufficiently representative for purposes of an injury determination".[585] The Panel also found that the fact that the Commission examined certain injury factors with respect to the entire domestic industry did not, as China contended, demonstrate that the Commission could have carried out its examination of all injury factors with respect to the entire domestic industry it had defined, or could have at least included more producers in the sample. On appeal, China claims that the Panel erred in its interpretation and application of Article 3.1 of the *Anti-Dumping Agreement* in reaching these findings.[586]

433. As a preliminary matter, we note the European Union's assertion that China's appeal concerns a claim that was not included in China's panel request and therefore is not properly before the Appellate Body.[587] According to the European Union, China's claim that the European Union violated Article 3.1 of the *Anti-Dumping Agreement* by failing to use a sampling technique that guarantees that the sample is sufficiently representative of the domestic industry was "suddenly" raised at the second substantive meeting before the Panel and constitutes a new claim not included in the request for consultations or for Panel establishment.[588]

---

581 China's other appellant's submission, paras. 267 and 278.

582 See Panel Report, para. 7.237.

583 See Panel Report, para. 7.240.

584 Panel Report, para. 7.238.

585 Panel Report, para. 7.239.

586 See China's other appellant's submission, para. 267.

587 European Union's appellee's submission, para. 213.

588 European Union's appellee's submission, para. 214. The European Union raised the same objection before the Panel. (See Panel Report, footnote 509 to para. 7.237)

434. In its panel request, China claimed that the European Union violated Article 3.1 of the *Anti-Dumping Agreement* by conducting the injury determination on the basis of a sample of producers accounting for only 17.5 per cent of the total domestic production.[589] China's claim in its panel request thus alerted the European Union to the fact that China considered that the sample was deficient for conducting a proper injury analysis, at least in terms of the volume of production. Thus, like the Panel, we consider that China merely developed a new argument in support of its claim under Article 3.1 of the *Anti-Dumping Agreement* when alleging that the selected sample was also not representative of the domestic industry. Therefore, we agree with the Panel's finding that China's argument did not constitute an entirely new claim, as alleged by the European Union, but was rather a newly developed argument in support of China's claim that the European Union "failed to make a determination of injury with respect to the relevant domestic industry, in part because the sample included producers accounting for only 17.5 per cent of domestic production".[590]

435. Turning to the substance of China's claims, we note that the *Anti-Dumping Agreement* is silent on the issue of whether sampling may be used for purposes of the injury determination. The Agreement thus does not prevent an authority from using samples to determine injury, and China does not contest this view.[591] In the fasteners investigation, the Commission selected a sample comprising six producers, whose output accounted for approximately 65 per cent of the production of the 45 domestic producers defined by the Commission as the domestic industry. The Commission chose these producers on the basis of their production volumes, "so as to achieve the largest representative volume of production of the like product produced in the Community which could reasonably be investigated within the time available".[592] China submits that a sample that is selected merely on the basis of the "largest volume that can reasonably be investigated" is not appropriate to satisfy the requirement under Article 3.1 of the *Anti-Dumping Agreement* that an injury determination involve an objective examination of the effects of the dumped imports, because such a sample is not representative of the domestic industry.[593] Rather, China argues, other methods, such as a statistically valid sample, should be used.

436. We note that, because the *Anti-Dumping Agreement* does not specify whether sampling is allowed for purposes of an injury determination, it also does not contain guidance on how sampling should be conducted. Thus, we see no basis for China's argument that a sample selected on the basis of the largest volume that can reasonably be investigated, rather than a statistically valid sample, necessarily means that an injury determination conducted on this basis is inconsistent with Article 3.1 of the *Anti-Dumping Agreement*. Although we do not disagree with the view that a sample must be properly representative of the do-

[589] WT/DS397/3, para. (ii)(k)(iv).
[590] Panel Report, footnote 509 to para. 7.237.
[591] See Panel Report, para. 7.239.
[592] Panel Report, para. 7.216 (quoting Definitive Regulation, *supra*, footnote 4, recital 27).
[593] China's other appellant's submission, para. 271.

mestic industry defined by the investigating authority, we disagree with China's contention that the only way to ensure representativeness is through a statistically valid sample. In our view, as long as the domestic industry is defined consistently with the *Anti-Dumping Agreement*, and that the sample selected is representative of the domestic industry, an investigating authority has discretion in deciding the method with which it selects a sample. A statistically valid sample is a proper way to ensure the representativeness of the sample. Yet, the *Anti-Dumping Agreement* imposes no obligation on an investigating authority always to resort to statistically valid samples.

437. China further argues that, as it demonstrated to the Panel, the Commission conducted its analysis of the "macroeconomic" injury factors on the basis of the information from all of the 45 producers included in the domestic industry definition. China therefore asserts that, if the Commission was in a position to analyze the macroeconomic injury factors for the domestic industry as defined, it could also have analyzed the "microeconomic" injury factors for the domestic industry as defined rather than only for the sampled domestic producers. However, as the Panel correctly found, China has not provided any arguments or evidence to substantiate its assertion.[594]

438. On this basis, we decline to uphold China's claims that the Panel erred in rejecting the contention that only a statistically valid sample would be sufficiently representative of the domestic industry, and in finding that China had not demonstrated that the Commission could have carried out its entire injury examination for the domestic industry it had defined, or could have at least included more producers in the sample. We note that China's above claims concern the issue of whether the sample *itself* selected in the investigation was consistent with Article 3.1 of the *Anti-Dumping Agreement*. In declining to uphold China's claim, therefore, our finding is limited to the issue of whether the *sample* was inconsistent with Article 3.1 of the *Anti-Dumping Agreement*, and does not address the issue of whether *the domestic industry defined by the Commission* in the fasteners investigation was consistent with this provision.

E. Exclusion of Certain Producers

1. The Exclusion of Producers Who Did Not Support the Complaint

439. China claims that, in finding that the European Union did not act inconsistently with Article 4.1 of the *Anti-Dumping Agreement*, the Panel failed to conduct an objective assessment of the facts, as required by Article 11 of the DSU and Article 17.6[595] of the *Anti-Dumping Agreement*, in finding that the

---

[594] Moreover, we note that China has not appealed the Panel's finding that the European Union did not act inconsistently with Articles 3.1 and 3.4 of the *Anti-Dumping Agreement* by basing its examination of "microeconomic" injury factors on the sampled producers. (See Panel Report, para. 7.395)

[595] China did not provide any arguments specifically regarding Article 17.6 of the *Anti-Dumping Agreement* in support of its claim under Article 4.1 of that Agreement. Moreover, we recall that the Appellate Body has found that "it is inconceivable that Article 17.6(i) should require anything other

European Union did not exclude from the definition of domestic industry those producers who did not support the complaint lodged against imports of fasteners from China. Specifically, China claims that the Panel: (i) "disregarded"[596] certain evidence submitted by China, that is, the Information Document[597] issued by the Commission during the investigation, and a letter sent by the Commission; (ii) accepted an "unsubstantiated"[598] factual assertion by the European Union that at least one producer included in the domestic industry definition did not support the investigation; and (iii) drew an incorrect inference from that factual assertion.

440. Article 11 of the DSU states, in relevant part, that:

> ... a panel should make an objective assessment of the matter before it, including an objective assessment of the facts of the case and the applicability of and conformity with the relevant covered agreements, and make such other findings as will assist the DSB in making the recommendations or in giving the rulings provided for in the covered agreements.

441. Pursuant to Article 11 of the DSU, a panel, as a trier of facts, must base its findings on a sufficient evidentiary basis on the record[599], may not apply a double standard of proof[600], and its treatment of the evidence must not "lack even-handedness".[601] Moreover, the duty to make an objective assessment of the facts of the case "requires a panel to consider evidence before it in its totality, which includes consideration of submitted evidence in relation to other evidence"[602], and a panel should not disregard evidence that is relevant to the case of one of the parties.[603] The Appellate Body has also clarified, however, that a panel is "entitled, in the exercise of its discretion, to determine that certain elements of evidence should be accorded more weight than other elements".[604] In doing so, a panel "is not required to discuss, in its report, each and every piece of evidence."[605] Moreover, "in view of the distinction between the respective roles

than that panels make an *objective* 'assessment of the facts of the matter'." (Appellate Body Report, *US – Hot Rolled Steel*, para. 55 (original emphasis)) In the light of these findings, and the absence of arguments by China concerning Article 17.6 of the *Anti-Dumping Agreement*, we do not separately address, in our analysis, China's claim under this provision.

596 China's other appellant's submission, p. 47, heading (F).

597 European Commission, Anti-dumping proceeding concerning imports of certain iron or steel fasteners originating in the People's Republic of China, Non-imposition of provisional anti-dumping measures, 4 August 2008 (Panel Exhibit CHN-17).

598 China's other appellant's submission, p. 38, heading (D).

599 See Appellate Body Report, *US – Continued Zeroing*, para. 338.

600 See Appellate Body Report, *Korea – Dairy*, para. 137.

601 Appellate Body Report, *US – Upland Cotton (Article 21.5 – Brazil)*, para. 292.

602 Appellate Body Report, *US – Continued Zeroing*, para. 331.

603 Appellate Body Reports, *US/Canada – Continued Suspension*, paras. 553 and 615.

604 Appellate Body Report, *EC – Asbestos*, para. 161.

605 Appellate Body Report, *Brazil – Retreaded Tyres*, para. 202.

of the Appellate Body and panels", the Appellate Body will not "interfere lightly" with the panel's fact-finding authority[606], and "cannot base a finding of inconsistency under Article 11 simply on the conclusion that [it] might have reached a different factual finding from the one the panel reached".[607]

442. Thus, not every error allegedly committed by a panel amounts to a violation of Article 11 of the DSU. It is incumbent on a participant raising a claim under Article 11 on appeal to explain *why* the alleged error *meets* the standard of review under that provision. An attempt to make every error of a panel a violation of Article 11 of the DSU is an approach that is inconsistent with the scope of this provision. In particular, when alleging that a panel ignored a piece of evidence, the mere fact that a panel did not explicitly refer to that evidence in its reasoning is insufficient to support a claim of violation under Article 11. Rather, a participant must explain why such evidence is so material to its case that the panel's failure explicitly to address and rely upon the evidence has a bearing on the objectivity of the panel's factual assessment. It is also unacceptable for a participant effectively to recast its arguments before the panel under the guise of an Article 11 claim. Instead, a participant must identify specific errors regarding the objectivity of the panel's assessment. Finally, a claim that a panel failed to comply with its duties under Article 11 of the DSU must stand by itself and should not be made merely as a subsidiary argument or claim in support of a claim that the panel failed to apply correctly a provision of the covered agreements.[608] With these considerations in mind, we turn to review China's appeal against the Panel's finding regarding the alleged exclusion of certain producers from the definition of the domestic industry.

443. The Panel noted the European Union's explanation that, at the time of initiation, the Commission sent sampling forms to 318 EU producers of fasteners, requesting them to provide certain information within 15 days, and to indicate whether they would be willing to be included in the sample.[609] The Panel also noted that the sampling forms do not contain any questions concerning whether the producers supported or opposed the application.[610] On the basis of the sampling forms received, the Commission defined the domestic industry in the fasteners investigation as including 45 EU producers, representing 27 per cent of the total EU production, all of whom responded to the request for information within the 15-day deadline and indicated that they would be willing to be part of the sample.[611] According to recital 114 of the Definitive Regulation, these

[606] See Appellate Body Report, *US – Wheat Gluten*, para. 151; Appellate Body Report, *EC – Sardines*, para. 299; and Appellate Body Report, *US – Carbon Steel*, para. 142.

[607] Appellate Body Report, *US – Wheat Gluten*, para. 151.

[608] See Appellate Body Report, *US – Steel Safeguards*, para. 498; and Appellate Body Report, *Chile – Price Band System (Article 21.5 – Argentina)*, para. 238.

[609] Panel Report, para. 7.213 (referring to European Union's response to Panel Question 88, para. 17).

[610] Panel Report, para. 7.213 (referring to Non-confidential Sampling Form of Agrati (Panel Exhibit EU-30) and Non-confidential Sampling Form of Fontana Luigi (Panel Exhibit EU-31)).

[611] Panel Report, paras. 7.212 (referring to Definitive Regulation, *supra*, footnote 4, recitals 22-25) and 7.216.

EU producers "supported the complaint and fully cooperated in the investigation".[612] The European Union explained that, despite the stipulation in recital 114, the issue of support was in fact only relevant to the determination of whether the complaint for the initiation of the fasteners investigation had met the *standing* requirement. The sampling forms sent for purposes of defining the domestic industry did not concern the issue of standing. Rather, they concerned the issue of cooperation, that is, whether a producer would be willing to be part of the sample.[613]

444. In the Panel's view, "by using the term 'producers that supported the complaint'", the Definitive Regulation "suggest[ed]" that only producers expressing support for the complaint were included in the domestic industry.[614] Notwithstanding recital 114 of the Definitive Regulation, the Panel did not immediately reach a finding that producers not supporting the complaint were excluded. Rather, the Panel went on to review several other pieces of evidence as well as the parties' relevant arguments. The Panel noted China's contention that the Commission was aware of the positions of the EU producers with regard to the investigation and defined the domestic industry on the basis of the producers' support for the investigation. According to China, the Information Document, sent to the parties at the time the Commission decided not to issue a provisional measure[615], indicates that, of the 114 domestic producers who came forward with relevant information, 86, representing 36 per cent of estimated EU production, supported the complaint, while 25, accounting for 9 per cent of EU production, opposed the complaint, and three did not express an opinion.[616]

445. The Panel did not rely on the Information Document, but accepted the European Union's contention that the Information Document was "a working document reflecting progress in the investigation to that point, with no legal status in EU law, which was made available to the parties despite there being no obligation to do so, and is not the measure before us".[617] Therefore, the Panel "[did] not consider the representations in the Information Document as constituting part of the measure which [it] must evaluate."[618] Moreover, the Panel noted the European Union's explanations that:

> ... based on arguments made by Chinese exporters, it continued to consider the question of standing after the initiation, that this continued examination confused the question of the definition of the domestic industry, and that *the "unfortunate standard for-*

---

[612] Panel Report, para. 7.212 (quoting Definitive Regulation, *supra*, footnote 4, recital 114).

[613] See European Union's response to Panel Question 31, para. 97; and European Union's response to Panel Question 89, para. 18.

[614] Panel Report, para. 7.214 (referring to European Union's response to Panel Question 30, para. 88).

[615] Definitive Regulation, *supra*, footnote 4, recital 5; Information Document , *supra*, footnote 81.

[616] Information Document, *supra*, footnote 81, pp. 5-6.

[617] Panel Report, para. 7.214 (referring to European Union's response to Panel Question 30, para. 88).

[618] Panel Report, para. 7.214.

> *mulation" in the Definitive Regulation (referring to the use of the term "producers that supported the complaint" with respect to the domestic industry),* did not affect the definition of the domestic industry, with respect to which no distinction was made between producers who supported the complaint and those that did not.[619] (emphasis added; footnotes omitted)

446. The European Union further explained before the Panel that revisiting the issue of standing was a "mistake" because it caused "confusion"[620], as demonstrated by certain inaccuracies in the Information Document. Specifically, the European Union submitted that 70 companies (rather than 114 companies indicated in the Information Document) came forward after initiation and provided the information requested in the Notice of Initiation within the 15-day deadline.[621] Only 46 of these 70 producers were considered as cooperating and were included in the domestic industry definition, as confirmed by recital 25 of the Definitive Regulation.[622] In making this determination, the issue of support was not considered by the Commission. However, as a result of the parallel processes on the determination of the domestic industry definition and on the determination of standing, all of the companies that submitted information, before and after the 15-day deadline, were "wrongly grouped together in the 114 companies that the Information [D]ocument refers to".[623]

447. On appeal, China alleges that the Panel violated Article 11 of the DSU because it "disregarded and ignored evidence submitted by China", including the Information Document, even though such evidence demonstrated that the Commission excluded from the domestic industry all producers who did not support the complaint.[624] China submits that, although the Information Document did not constitute part of the measure at issue, it was nonetheless a piece of evidence and "plainly relevant" for purposes of examining the issue of the definition of the domestic industry.[625]

448. We have sympathy for China's argument that whether the Information Document could be taken into account as a piece of relevant evidence should not

---

[619] Panel Report, para. 7.214 (referring to European Union's response to Panel Question 89, para. 18; and the European Union's response to Panel Question 34, para. 105).

[620] Panel Report, footnote 357 to para. 7.170 (quoting European Union's response to Panel Question 31).

[621] Upon the Panel's request, the European Union provided the list of the 70 EU producers, including the names of the related companies involved in the production and/or selling of the product concerned. (See List of "Sampling Form for Community Producers" for inspection by interested parties (Panel Exhibit EU-19))

[622] European Union's response to Panel Question 31, paras. 92-94. As noted above, one producer among the 46 cooperating producers was later found not to be cooperating and was dropped from the definition of the domestic industry. (See *supra*, footnote 571)

[623] European Union's response to Panel Question 31, para. 97.

[624] China's other appellant's submission, p. 47, heading (F).

[625] China's other appellant's submission, para. 93.

depend on its legal status under EU law. Although this document is not part of the measure at issue as a document issued by the Commission during the investigation, it could nonetheless shed light on aspects of the investigation. At the same time, we note that the Panel did pose certain questions to the European Union concerning the Information Document[626], and therefore did not simply disregard or ignore the evidence submitted by China. Moreover, the European Union's explanation regarding the "confused" and "parallel" processes between the determination of the domestic industry definition and the determination of standing cast doubt on the reliability of the representations regarding the domestic industry contained in the Information Document. We do not, therefore, consider that the Panel exceeded its margin of discretion under Article 11 of the DSU in deciding to attribute less weight than China did to the Information Document in reaching its finding.

449. China claims that the Panel also disregarded a letter sent by the Commission to two Chinese exporters in response to their request for clarification regarding certain production figures contained in the Definitive Regulation.[627] Specifically, the letter explains that the figure on production volume by the domestic industry in recital 128 of the Definitive Regulation corresponds to "the Community producers that supported the complaint and fully cooperated in the investigation". China asserts that, even though this letter "unambiguously demonstrates" that only producers supporting the complaint were included in the domestic industry[628], the Panel "totally ignored and disregarded"[629] this evidence.

450. The reference in the letter to "the Community producers that supported the complaint and fully cooperated in the investigation" repeats the same phrase contained in recital 114 of the Definitive Regulation. As discussed above, the European Union explained to the Panel that this "unfortunate standard formulation" remained in the Definitive Regulation as a result of the confusion between the issue of standing and the domestic industry definition.[630] Moreover, as the trier of facts, "[a] panel enjoys discretion in assessing whether a given piece of evidence is relevant for its reasoning, and is not required to discuss, in its report, each and every piece of evidence".[631] Given that the information in the letter essentially replicates the information in the Definitive Regulation, and in the light of the European Union's explanation regarding the background of such evi-

[626] For example, the Panel asked the European Union to clarify whether the number of producers who came forward within the 15-day deadline was 114, as indicated by the Information Document, and whether the number of producers expressing willingness to be included in the sample was 86, as indicated by the Information Document, or 46, as indicated in the Definitive Regulation. (See Panel Question 31)

[627] Letter from the European Commission dated 18 November 2008 to Van Bael & Bellis in response to letter from Van Bael & Bellis dated 12 November 2008 (Panel Exhibit CHN-39).

[628] China's other appellant's submission, para. 98.

[629] China's other appellant's submission, para. 99.

[630] Panel Report, para. 7.214 (quoting European Union's response to Panel Question 89, para. 18).

[631] Appellate Body Report, *Brazil – Retreaded Tyres*, para. 202.

dence, we do not consider that the Panel erred in not explicitly mentioning or relying on this letter in reaching its finding.

451. Finally, China alleges that the Panel erroneously accepted as a fact the unsubstantiated statement of the European Union that at least one producer who did not support the complaint was included in the domestic industry and in the sample. According to China, in asserting this fact, the European Union was required to present relevant evidence by, for example, providing the list of complainants and supporters who had come forward before the initiation.[632] Since the European Union did not do so, China claims that the Panel failed to make an objective assessment of the facts as required by Article 11 of the DSU by merely accepting the European Union's factual assertion.

452. The European Union made the above statement in response to the Panel's question regarding whether support for the investigation was used as a criterion in determining the definition of the domestic industry. The European Union maintained that support was not used as a criterion, and named a producer included in the sample who "had not supported the complaint", because it "was not a complainant, nor a supporter of the complaint" and "had remained silent at the pre-initiation phase".[633] The Panel, on the basis of this explanation by the European Union, found that "the fact that at least one producer who did not affirmatively state support for the complaint was included in the domestic industry" "demonstrated" that the Commission did not exclude producers not supporting the complaint from the domestic industry.[634] We note that, before the initiation of the investigation, the Commission sent forms to all producers listed in the complaint brought by certain EU producers against imports of fasteners from China, so as to verify whether they supported or opposed the complaint (the "standing forms").[635] On appeal, the European Union clarifies that the producer it referred to before the Panel had not returned the standing form, and that the Commission was simply not aware of whether that producer supported, opposed, or was neutral to, the investigation on fasteners from China. Thus, in our view, there is evidence that the Commission had no knowledge of this particular producer's position regarding the complaint.

453. Moreover, we note that, subsequent to the initiation of the investigation, this producer was sent a sampling form and returned the form within the 15-day deadline. It is noteworthy that the sampling forms sent upon initiation did not contain any questions relating to support for or opposition to the complaint, and that the sampling forms were sent to *all* EU fasteners producers known to the Commission when the investigation was initiated. This evidence lends support to the European Union's contention that the only relevant criterion for inclusion in the domestic industry definition was that a producer must return the completed

---

632 China's other appellant's submission, para. 65.

633 European Union's response to Panel Question 89, para. 19.

634 Panel Report, para. 7.215.

635 See Extract from the Non-Confidential File: To Be Integrated in the File for Inspection by Interested Parties: Note for the File dated 8 November 2007 and attached documents (Panel Exhibit EU-6).

form within 15 days and indicate that it would be willing to be included in the sample. In the light of the above analysis, there is no basis to interfere with the Panel's assessment of the facts.

454. In sum, the Panel had before it several pieces of evidence relating to the issue of whether the Commission excluded producers who did not support the complaint from the definition of the domestic industry. There was evidence that supported China's position that only those producers who supported the complaint were included in the domestic industry definition. Such evidence included recital 114 of the Definitive Regulation and a letter sent by the Commission to the Chinese interested parties. There was also evidence that indicated that support was not a condition for inclusion in the domestic industry definition. Such evidence included recitals 22 to 25 of the Definitive Regulation, which explain, *inter alia*, the process of defining the domestic industry and the fact that sampling forms were sent to all known producers at the beginning of the investigation for purposes of defining the domestic industry. As the Panel found, no question was asked in the sampling form regarding support for or opposition to the investigation. In addition, the Panel accepted, with reason, the European Union's factual representation that one producer who did not affirmatively express a position regarding the complaint was nonetheless sent the sampling form and included in the domestic industry definition. The Panel examined and engaged with the above evidence, and ultimately came to the conclusion that China had not demonstrated that the Commission excluded producers who did not support the complaint from the domestic industry it defined. Our review of the Panel's reasoning does not indicate that the Panel exceeded its margin of discretion in its weighing of various pieces of evidence and in drawing its conclusions on this basis. Although the Panel attributed different weight to certain evidence than did China, this is insufficient to demonstrate that the Panel's assessment of the facts was not objective. Moreover, even if we might have reached a different conclusion had we been asked to review such evidence *de novo*, we are mindful that we "cannot base a finding of inconsistency under Article 11 simply on the conclusion that we might have reached a different factual finding from the one the panel reached".[636] We therefore decline to uphold China's appeal in this regard.

2. *The Exclusion of Producers Who Did Not Respond within 15 Days*

455. China claims that the Panel erred in the interpretation of Article 4.1 of the *Anti-Dumping Agreement* when finding that "nothing in Article 4.1 ... would preclude investigating authorities from establishing deadlines for companies to come forward in order to be considered for inclusion in the domestic industry".[637] Moreover, China asserts that the Panel failed to conduct an objective assessment of the facts, as required by Article 11 of the DSU, when finding that the Commission "did not act to exclude" producers that did not make themselves

---

636 Appellate Body Report, *US – Wheat Gluten*, para. 151.

637 China's other appellant's submission, para. 123 (quoting Panel Report, para. 7.219).

known within 15 days following the initiation of the investigation[638], and that the 15-day deadline was not insufficient or unreasonable.

456. In the finding challenged by China, the Panel stated that:

> ... while it seems clear that producers who did not make themselves known within the 15-day period established at initiation were not included in the domestic industry, we find that the investigating authority did not act to exclude such producers. *There seems to have been a process of considering additional producers* for inclusion in the domestic industry, based on arguments made by the exporters.[639] (emphasis added)

457. Relevant evidence before the Panel nonetheless indicates that the Commission excluded producers who did not make themselves known within the 15-day deadline from the definition of the domestic industry. Before the Panel, the European Union submitted that, upon initiation of the fasteners investigation, the Commission invited all known producers to come forward and indicate willingness to participate within 15 days, and did not include producers who made themselves known after the 15-day deadline.[640] As noted above, the European Union also explained before the Panel that the Commission revisited the issue of standing after initiation in response to comments by the Chinese interested parties. Thus, subsequent to the 15-day deadline, the Commission collected information concerning additional producers, including data on their production volumes and their views on the complaint.[641] This process, according to the European Union, was confused with the issue of the domestic industry definition in the Information Document. This confusion was clarified under the Definitive Regulation, which makes it clear that "the domestic producers that ... constitute[d] the domestic industry [were] those that ma[d]e themselves known within 15 days following initiation, provide[d] the requested information and express[ed] their willingness to participate in the investigation".[642] The European Union repeated these explanations several times during the Panel proceedings.[643] On appeal, the European Union similarly states that, after receiving information

---

638 China's other appellant's submission, para. 117 (quoting Panel Report, para. 7.215).

639 Panel Report, para. 7.215.

640 See European Union's first written submission to the Panel, para. 302.

641 See European Union's response to Panel Question 31, para. 97.

642 European Union's response to Panel Question 31, para. 97.

643 For example, in response to questions posed by China after the first Panel meeting, the European Union stated that "[i]t is clear that this determination was based on those producers that came forward within the 15-day deadline and indicated their willingness to cooperate (see recital 24 of Council Regulation No 91/2009)". (European Union's response to China's Question 4 after the first Panel meeting, para. 10) In response to the Panel's question following the second Panel meeting, the European Union maintained that "[a]ll known producers were contacted regardless of whether they supported or opposed the complaint and all were invited to come forward. Those that did so within the deadline, and that indicated a willingness to cooperate with the authorities were considered as part of the domestic industry." (European Union's response to Panel Question 89, para. 18)

provided by the additional producers contacted after the 15-day deadline, the Commission "decided to simply stick to the objective and reasonable deadline of 15 days it had set at the time of initiation in a transparent and predictable manner".[644]

458. Thus, the evidence on the record, including the Definitive Regulation and the European Union's explanations, shows that the Commission excluded producers who did not make themselves known within the 15-day deadline from the definition of domestic industry. The Panel, in reaching its finding that the Commission "did not act to exclude" such producers, stated that "[t]here *seems to* have been a process of considering additional producers for inclusion in the domestic industry, based on arguments made by the exporters".[645] On the basis of the European Union's explanations, this "process of considering additional producers" was conducted for purposes of re-examining the issue of standing, and was not done in order to define the domestic industry.

459. Nonetheless, even though the Panel mistakenly concluded that the Commission did not exclude producers not responding within the 15-day deadline, this did not affect the Panel's final conclusion. The Panel found that "none of the producers [considered after the deadline] were in the end included in the domestic industry".[646] Moreover, the Panel found it "reasonable for investigating authorities to impose deadlines for domestic producers to make themselves known and then define the domestic industry on the basis of those that come forward within that deadline".[647] The Panel also found that there was "no basis for concluding that the 15-day period was necessarily insufficient" for purposes of defining the domestic industry.[648] The Panel therefore found that the European Union did not act inconsistently with Article 4.1 of the *Anti-Dumping Agreement*, even if it did not include producers not responding within 15 days.

460. In our view, in applying Article 4.1 to the facts of the case, the Panel correctly found that it was reasonable for the Commission to set a deadline by which producers were required to make themselves known. Given the multiple steps that must be carried out in an anti-dumping investigation and the time constraint on an investigation, an investigating authority must be allowed to set various deadlines to ensure an orderly conduct of the investigation. Indeed, as Article 5.10 of the *Anti-Dumping Agreement* provides, "[i]nvestigations shall, except in special circumstances, be concluded within one year, and in no case more than 18 months, after their initiation." Moreover, Article 6.14 states that the rules of procedures set out in Article 6 of the *Anti-Dumping Agreement* "are not intended to prevent the authorities of a Member from proceeding *expeditiously*".[649] In this regard, the Appellate Body has found that:

---

644 European Union's appellee's submission, para. 92.
645 Panel Report, para. 7.215. (emphasis added)
646 Panel Report, para. 7.215.
647 Panel Report, para. 7.219.
648 *Ibid.*
649 Emphasis added.

> [i]nvestigating authorities must be able to control the conduct of their investigation and to carry out the multiple steps in an investigation required to reach a final determination. Indeed, in the absence of time-limits, authorities would effectively cede control of investigations to the interested parties, and could find themselves unable to complete their investigations within the timelimits mandated under the *Anti-Dumping Agreement.*[650]

We therefore disagree with China's assertion that the Panel erred in the interpretation of Article 4.1 when finding that "nothing in Article 4.1 ... would preclude investigating authorities from establishing deadlines for companies to come forward in order to be considered for inclusion in the domestic industry".[651]

461. China further submits that, even if the imposition of a deadline for domestic producers to come forward may be permissible for reasons of necessity, any deadline granted by the investigating authorities to domestic producers to come forward must be "reasonable" and "sufficient".[652] In this respect, China submits that the Panel acted inconsistently with Article 11 of the DSU by "ignor[ing] the 'evidence'" submitted by China in order to demonstrate that the 15-day deadline was insufficient and unreasonable.[653] First, China maintains that, as it argued before the Panel, the 15-day deadline was "very short and makes it much more likely that complainants and [supporters of] the investigation", rather than producers opposing the investigation, will come forward within the deadline.[654] China submits that, in support of this argument, it referred the Panel to the Information Document, which shows that, among the 114 producers who made themselves known up to the date the Information Document was published, 25 producers representing 9 per cent of EU production opposed the complaint. Yet, China argues, because of the 15-day deadline, these 25 producers were not included in the domestic industry.[655]

462. We note that China again sought to rely on the Information Document in support of this claim. As discussed above, in the light of the European Union's explanation as to the inaccuracies contained in the Information Document, we do not consider that the Panel failed to conduct an objective assessment of the facts in not relying on the Information Document for its decision. Moreover, even assuming that the representations in the Information Document could be relied upon, we fail to see how these representations demonstrate that the imposition of a 15-day deadline influenced whether the producers opposing the complaint

---

[650] Appellate Body Report, *US – Hot-Rolled Steel*, para. 73 (quoting Panel Report, *US – Hot-Rolled Steel*, para. 7.54).

[651] Panel Report, para. 7.219.

[652] China's other appellant's submission, para. 125.

[653] China's other appellant's submission, para. 130.

[654] China's other appellant's submission, para. 135.

[655] China's other appellant's submission, para. 136; China's first written submission to the Panel, para. 244.

would respond to the request for information. Indeed, the Information Document states that, among the 114 producers who "came forward and provided the requested information *within the deadline*"[656], 25 were opposed to the complaint. It does not state that all of these 25 producers came forward after the 15-day deadline, and therefore does not support China's assertion that, *because of the deadline*, those who opposed the complaint were excluded from the definition of the domestic industry.

463. China further argues that, by requiring producers to come forward within 15 days and express willingness to be included in the sample within that deadline, the Commission adopted an approach that was "fundamentally non-objective", because producers opposing the investigation were less likely to be willing to be part of the sample.[657] China, however, has not substantiated this assertion. In any event, China's argument does not concern the reasonableness of the 15-day deadline *per se*. Rather, it concerns the question of whether the definition of the domestic industry was consistent with the *Anti-Dumping Agreement* when it was determined on the basis of producers' willingness to cooperate by being included in the sample.

464. In sum, we do not consider that the Panel erred in its interpretation or application of Article 4.1 of the *Anti-Dumping Agreement*, or acted inconsistently with Article 11 of the DSU, when finding that "the mere fact that the domestic industry as ultimately defined does not include any particular proportion of producers expressing different views with respect to the complaint, or producers who did not come forward within the 15-day period, does not demonstrate that the European Union acted inconsistently with Article 4.1 of the [*Anti-Dumping Agreement*] in defining the domestic industry."[658] We therefore decline to uphold China's appeal in this respect.

3. *The Exclusion of Producers under Article 3.1 of the Anti-Dumping Agreement*

465. China claims that the Panel erred in its interpretation of Article 3.1 of the *Anti-Dumping Agreement* by dismissing China's claim under that provision that the Commission erroneously excluded from the domestic industry definition those producers who did not support the complaint and did not come forward within the 15-day deadline simply because it had rejected China's same claim under Article 4.1 of the *Anti-Dumping Agreement*.

466. Before the Panel, China argued that, "by defining the domestic industry as including only those producers that supported the complaint and excluding

---

[656] Information Document, *supra*, footnote 81, p. 5. (emphasis added) We recall the European Union's assertion that these 114 producers actually include those who came forward after the 15-day deadline. (See *supra*, para. 446) However, China has not expressed its disagreement with these factual assertions, and instead seeks to rely on certain representations made in the Information Document.

[657] China's other appellant's submission, para. 137.

[658] Panel Report, para. 7.219.

those who did not, the [European Union] conducted a biased analysis favouring the interests of the complainants", and that "[s]uch an analysis is not 'objective' as required by Article 3.1 of the [*Anti-Dumping Agreement*]".[659] China also argued that, by setting the 15-day period granted to domestic producers for indicating their willingness to be included in the sample, the Commission "acted in a non-objective manner in that only producers supporting the investigation were included in the domestic industry".[660] China then repeated the arguments it had made under Article 4.1 as to why the 15-day period was insufficient and unreasonable for purposes of defining the domestic industry.[661] The Panel rejected China's claim, finding, instead, that:

> China asserts that it is only possible to undertake an objective examination pursuant to Article 3.1 if the result of the examination is not predetermined by the way the domestic industry is defined. We do not disagree. However, we have rejected China's position with respect to this aspect of its claim challenging the domestic industry definition in this case. China makes no other allegations in support of its claim of violation of Article 3.1, and we therefore dismiss that aspect of China's claim.[662] (footnote omitted)

467. In our analyses in the preceding two subsections, we have declined to uphold China's appeal of the Panel's findings that the European Union did not act inconsistently with Article 4.1 of the *Anti-Dumping Agreement* by excluding producers from the domestic industry definition who did not support the complaint and who did not respond to the sampling forms within 15 days. Given that, with regard to these aspects of the fasteners investigation, China has not provided arguments under Article 3.1 that differ from those under Article 4.1, we also decline to uphold China's appeal of the Panel's finding that the European Union did not act inconsistently with Article 3.1 of the *Anti-Dumping Agreement* by excluding these producers from the domestic industry.

F. Conclusion

468. In sum, with regard to China's other appeal of the Panel's findings under Articles 4.1 and 3.1 of the *Anti-Dumping Agreement*, we have reached the following findings. We find that the Panel erred in finding that "the European Union did not act inconsistently with Article 4.1 of the [*Anti-Dumping Agreement*] in defining a domestic industry comprising producers accounting for 27 per cent of total estimated EU production of fasteners" on the basis that the collective output of these producers represented "a major proportion" of the total

[659] China's first written submission to the Panel, para. 244.
[660] China's second written submission to the Panel, para. 577.
[661] See China's second written submission to the Panel, paras. 578-580.
[662] Panel Report, para. 7.221.

domestic production.[663] However, we find that the Panel did not err in finding that China failed to establish that the European Union acted inconsistently with Article 3.1 of the *Anti-Dumping Agreement* by making an injury determination on the basis of a sample of producers that was allegedly not representative. We also do not consider that the Panel erred in its interpretation or application of Articles 4.1 and 3.1 of the *Anti-Dumping Agreement*, or acted inconsistently with Article 11 of the DSU, when finding that "the mere fact that the domestic industry as ultimately defined does not include any particular proportion of producers expressing different views with respect to the complaint, or producers who did not come forward within the 15-day period, does not demonstrate that the European Union acted inconsistently with Article 4.1 of the [*Anti-Dumping Agreement*] in defining the domestic industry"[664] or acted inconsistently with Article 3.1 of that Agreement.

VII. APPEAL OF THE PANEL'S FINDINGS REGARDING ASPECTS OF THE DUMPING DETERMINATION IN THE FASTENERS INVESTIGATION UNDER ARTICLES 6.4, 6.2, AND 2.4 OF THE *ANTI-DUMPING AGREEMENT*

A. *Introduction*

469. We turn now to address the European Union's and China's appeals of the Panel's findings regarding certain aspects of the Commission's dumping determination in the fasteners investigation. Specifically, the European Union appeals the Panel's finding that it acted inconsistently with Articles 6.4 and 6.2 of the *Anti-Dumping Agreement* by not providing a timely opportunity for Chinese interested parties to see the product types used by the Commission for purposes of comparing export price and normal value in the dumping determination. China appeals the Panel's finding that the European Union did not act inconsistently with Article 2.4 of the *Anti-Dumping Agreement* by failing to make a "fair comparison" between the export price and the normal value in the dumping determination. We begin our analysis with a description of the relevant factual background underlying both the European Union's and China's claims. We then discuss the relevant interpretation of the provisions of the *Anti-Dumping Agreement* under which the European Union's and China's claims are raised. Next, we address the specific claims and arguments raised on appeal.

B. *The Relevant Factual Background*

470. The Panel found that, in the questionnaires sent to the producer in India, Pooja Forge[665], and to the Chinese producers, the Commission requested that

---

[663] Panel Report, para. 7.230.

[664] Panel Report, para. 7.219.

[665] We recall that, due to the European Union's designation of China as an NME, and the fact that MET was not granted to the Chinese producers in the fasteners investigation, the Commission established the normal value on the basis of the prices of fasteners sold in the analogue country, India. The

information on the investigated products be reported on the basis of categories defined by Product Control Numbers ("PCNs").[666] The Panel noted that the following six elements made up the PCNs identified by the Commission: type of fasteners (by CN code); strength/hardness; coating; presence of chrome on coating; diameter; and length/thickness. All but two of these elements, in turn, are further divided into sub-categories, each of which is assigned a code in the form of a number or a letter. The elements contained in the PCNs thus represent 38 narrowly defined specifications of fasteners. The questionnaire provided, as an example, a product having the following characteristics: "self-tapping screw, case hardening, not coated, diameter 4,2 millimeters, length 13 millimeters". On the basis of the corresponding numbers and letters assigned to each of the characteristics, this product would have a PCN of 2XNR042013.[667]

471. The questionnaire sent to Pooja Forge also requested that information be provided on the basis of the same PCNs. However, Pooja Forge did not provide information categorized on the basis of the PCNs as requested. Because the normal value in the fasteners investigation was established on the basis of the information provided by Pooja Forge, the Commission could not base its comparison between the normal value and export price on full PCNs.[668] Therefore, it resorted to the use of "product types" defined by two factors, strength class and the distinction between standard and special fasteners, in the price comparisons for the dumping determination.[669]

472. The Panel found that the Chinese producers were informed very late in the proceedings of the product types that formed the basis of the comparisons underlying the Commission's dumping determinations. Specifically, the General Disclosure Document, issued towards the end of the investigation on 3 November 2008, indicated that the Commission based its normal value determination on product types, but did not specify the number of, or relevant characteristics of, the product types or how they were determined.[670]

473. On 8 November 2008, two Chinese producers sought clarification from the Commission regarding the product types used, and specifically asked for a linkage between the PCNs on which the Chinese producers based their questionnaire submissions and the product types eventually used by the Commission.

Commission identified two Indian companies that produced the fasteners that were the subject of the investigation, and one of them, Pooja Forge, cooperated with the investigation. (See Definitive Regulation, *supra*, footnote 4, recitals 38 and 92)

666 See Panel Report, para. 7.292 (referring to European Commission, Anti-Dumping Questionnaire for Chinese Exporters/Producers (Panel Exhibit CHN-51), pp. 11-13).

667 See Panel Exhibit CHN-51, *supra*, footnote 666, pp. 11-13.

668 See Panel Report, para. 7.293 (referring to European Union's response to Panel Question 43(b)).

669 See Panel Report, para. 7.293 (referring to Definitive Regulation, *supra*, footnote 4, recital 102; and Panel Exhibit CHN-31, *supra*, footnote 310, p. 2).

670 See Panel Report, para. 7.485. In addition, under the heading "Comparison", the General Disclosure Document stated that the price comparison between the fasteners from China and those sold by Pooja Forge on the Indian market was "made by distinguishing between standard and special fastener types". (General Disclosure Document, *supra*, footnote 73, para. 93) The same statement is also contained in recital 102 of the Definitive Regulation.

According to the Panel, this letter "clearly convey[ed] these two Chinese producers' request to see information regarding the product types that established the basis of the Commission's normal value determination and the relationship between these product types and the PCNs pertaining to the Chinese producers' products".[671] The Commission replied on 13 November 2008, stating that, "beside[s] product characteristics as specified in the PCN, a distinction was introduced between standard and special products since this was found to have a significant impact on prices".[672] It went on to say that, for these two Chinese producers, "their entire export volume was considered as being standard products".[673] The Panel found that this response did "not explain how the product types were established in the determination of normal value, or the relevant characteristics of those product types".[674]

474. On 17 November 2008, the Chinese producers again sought clarification. They noted that the non-confidential version of Pooja Forge's questionnaire response contained no indication that Pooja Forge reported sales on the basis of PCNs. Thus, the Chinese producers asked:

> In abstract terms, was normal value established on a PCN basis, or were more general types of [the Indian producer's] fasteners matched with groups of PCNs from our clients? In that context, it would still be very useful for us if we could have a listing simply of which type of fastener or which PCNs of [the Indian producer] were matched with the PCNs of our clients.[675]

The Panel described this letter as "clearly repeat[ing] these Chinese producers' request to see information on the basis of which product types for the Indian producer were established".[676]

475. The Commission replied in a letter dated 21 November 2008 that the comparison "was not made on the basis of the full PCN, but on part [*sic*] of the characteristics of the product, namely the strength class as well as the abovementioned distinction between special and standard products".[677] The Panel found that this was the first time the Commission clearly informed the Chinese producers that it did not make its findings based on PCNs, but on the characteristics of strength class and the distinction between standard and special fasteners. The

[671] Panel Report, para. 7.486.

[672] Panel Report, para. 7.487 (quoting Email Message dated 13 November 2008 from the European Commission to Van Bael & Bellis (Panel Exhibit CHN-29), p. 1).

[673] Panel Report, para. 7.487 (quoting Panel Exhibit CHN-29, *supra*, footnote 672, p. 1).

[674] Panel Report, para. 7.487.

[675] Panel Report, para. 7.488 (quoting Letter dated 17 November 2008 from Van Bael & Bellis to the European Commission concerning the Definitive Disclosure Document: Request for Information II on behalf of Kunshan Chenghe Standard Component Co. Ltd and Ningbo Jinding Fastening Piece Co. Ltd. (Panel Exhibit CHN-30), p. 2). (emphasis omitted)

[676] Panel Report, para. 7.488.

[677] Panel Report, para. 7.489 (quoting Panel Exhibit CHN-31, *supra*, footnote 310, p. 2).

letter came one working day before the deadline to make comments on the General Disclosure Document.[678]

476. The Panel record indicates that, on 24 November 2008, two days after the deadline for comments, one Chinese producer sent another letter to the Commission, expressing the view that it was not possible for it to comment on the Commission's dumping determination without knowing what types or groups of products of Pooja Forge were actually matched with the Chinese products.[679]

477. Thus, the Panel's factual findings, as well as the Panel record, indicate the following timeline relating to the relevant events that occurred in the context of the Commission's dumping determination:

Timeline of Relevant Events

9 November 2007	Notice of Initiation
3 November 2008	General Disclosure Document
8 November 2008	First request for clarification
13 November 2008	Commission response
17 November 2008	Second request for clarification
21 November 2008	Commission response clarifying product types
22 November 2008	Deadline for comments on General Disclosure Document
24 November 2008	Comments by the Chinese producer

C. *The Relevant Interpretation of Articles 6.4 and 2.4 of the Anti-Dumping Agreement*

478. Article 6.4 of the *Anti-Dumping Agreement* provides:

> The authorities shall whenever practicable provide timely opportunities for all interested parties to see all information that is relevant to the presentation of their cases, that is not confidential as defined in paragraph 5, and that is used by the authorities in an anti-dumping investigation, and to prepare presentations on the basis of this information.

479. The Appellate Body has found that Article 6.4 refers to "provid[ing] timely opportunities for all interested parties to see all information that is rele-

---

678 Panel Report, para. 7.489.

679 Letter dated 24 November 2008 from Van Bael & Bellis on behalf of Kunshan Chenghe Standard Component Co. Ltd. to the European Commission, Comments on the Definitive Disclosure Document (Panel Exhibit CHN-59), p. 4.

vant to the presentation of *their* cases", and that the possessive pronoun "their" "clearly refers to the earlier reference in that sentence to 'interested parties'".[680] Therefore, it is the interested parties, rather than the authority, who determine whether the information is in fact "relevant" for the purposes of Article 6.4.[681] Moreover, according to the Appellate Body, whether the information was "used" by the authority does not depend on whether the authority specifically relied on that information. Rather, it depends on whether the information is related to "a required step in the anti-dumping investigation".[682] Thus, Article 6.4 concerns information relating to "issues which the investigating authority is required to consider under the [*Anti-Dumping Agreement*], or which it does, in fact, consider, in the exercise of its discretion, during the course of an anti-dumping investigation."[683]

480. The interested parties' right under Article 6.4, therefore, is to see *all* non-confidential information relevant to the presentation of their cases and used by the investigating authority. Article 6.4 thus applies to a broad range of information that is used by an investigating authority for purposes of carrying out a required step in an anti-dumping investigation. We note the European Union's view that the term "information" in Article 6.4 "concerns facts and raw data rather than factual determinations and conclusions by the investigating authorities".[684] In our view, there is no textual basis in Article 6.4 for limiting information "relevant to the presentation of [parties'] cases" and "used by the authorities" to facts or raw data unprocessed by the authorities. Indeed, the broad range of information subject to the obligation under Article 6.4 may take various forms, including data submitted by the interested parties, and information that has been processed, organized, or summarized by the authority. We do not see why only facts and raw data would be relevant to the parties' presentation of their cases. A proper interpretation of Article 6.4 does not mean, however, that an investigating authority's reasoning or internal deliberation in reaching its final determination is also subject to the obligation under Article 6.4. Article 6.4 concerns the information that is used by an authority, rather than an authority's detailed analysis of the information, or the determination it reaches based on such information.

481. The European Union also argues that the context of Article 6.4, as provided by the other paragraphs of Article 6, confirms that the obligation under Article 6.4 only concerns facts and raw data submitted by interested parties. The European Union submits that Articles 6.1 to 6.3 provide parties the right to submit their *own* information, and Articles 6.6 and 6.7 impose an obligation on investigating authorities to verify the information submitted by the parties. Article 6.8, in turn, allows the use of "facts available" when an interested party does not provide necessary information.[685] Thus, the European Union asserts, Article 6.4

680 Appellate Body Report, *EC – Tube or Pipe Fittings*, para. 145. (original emphasis)
681 See Appellate Body Report, *EC – Tube or Pipe Fittings*, para. 145.
682 Appellate Body Report, *EC – Tube or Pipe Fittings*, para. 147.
683 Panel Report, *EC – Salmon (Norway)*, para. 7.769. (footnotes omitted)
684 European Union's appellant's submission, para. 253.
685 European Union's appellant's submission, paras. 258, 259, 262, and 263.

is limited to addressing "the parties' right to know what *other interested parties have submitted* in terms of evidence and information".[686] In our view, however, the European Union's recourse to the other paragraphs under Article 6 is unavailing. The only qualification on the term "information" under Article 6.4 is that it is "relevant to the presentation of their cases", "not confidential as defined in paragraph 5", and "used by the authorities in an anti-dumping investigation". Article 6.2 further confirms that access to all such information is important because, without such information, the interested parties may not have "a full opportunity for the defence of their interests". Moreover, where the term "information" is to be specifically qualified, the relevant paragraphs under Article 6 clearly provide so. For example, Article 6.3 refers to "oral information", Article 6.5 applies to information that is "by nature confidential", and Article 6.6 concerns information "supplied by interested parties". Without such qualifications, we see no textual basis in Article 6.4, or contextual basis under Article 6, for limiting the term "information" in Article 6.4 to only that provided by other interested parties.

482. The European Union further argues that, pursuant to Article 6.9, the authorities must inform all interested parties of "the essential facts under consideration which form the basis for the decision" before a final determination is made. In the European Union's view, the use of the phrase "essential facts" rather than the word "information" in Article 6.9 indicates that Articles 6.1 to 6.8 concern the information-gathering process. The European Union also argues that Article 6.9 marks the end of the process and requires a disclosure of the authority's essential factual conclusions[687], and that the "product types" used to compare export price and normal value fall into the category of essential facts.[688] The European Union further contends that the differences between the obligations under Articles 6.4 and 6.9 are "well established in WTO jurisprudence". For example, the European Union argues that in *Guatemala – Cement II* the panel found that Article 6.4 generally provided an "access to the file"[689] right, whereas Article 6.9 required more and could not be satisfied "simply by offering to provide interested parties with copies of all information in the file".[690]

483. The differences alleged by the European Union between Article 6.9 and the other paragraphs of Article 6 do not, in our view, restrict the meaning of the word "information" in Article 6.4 to the narrow scope the European Union attributes to it. As discussed above, Article 6.4 refers broadly to "*all* information that is relevant to the presentation of [the interested parties'] cases". Such information may come in different forms, including not only "facts or raw data" submitted by the other parties, but also information that an investigating authority organizes, processes, or summarizes at each stage of an anti-dumping investiga-

686 European Union's appellant's submission, para. 260. (original emphasis)

687 European Union's appellant's submission, paras. 264 and 265.

688 European Union's responses to questioning at the oral hearing.

689 European Union's appellant's submission, para. 261 (quoting Panel Report, *Guatemala – Cement II*, para. 8.133).

690 Panel Report, *Guatemala – Cement II*, para. 8.230.

tion. Although Article 6.9 refers to "the essential facts under consideration which form the basis" for the authority's final determination, we do not consider that what the terms "information" and "essential facts" refer to must be mutually exclusive. Depending on the specific circumstances of a case, the "information" relevant to the presentation of an interested party's case can be a broader concept than the essential facts relied on by the authority, or it may overlap with such "essential facts". The "essential facts" under Article 6.9, which form the basis for a final determination, are those that are material for the authority's decision, whereas "information" that is relevant to the presentation of a party's case, and used by the authority, is not necessarily what the authority relies on in reaching its final determination. Moreover, information within the meaning of Article 6.4 has to be provided to interested parties in a timely fashion throughout the investigation. It is not sufficient to provide such information only "before a final determination is made" within the meaning of Article 6.9. In sum, we consider that the European Union's reliance on the context of Article 6.4 is unavailing to its position.

484. The European Union refers to the panel's finding in *Korea – Certain Paper* to point out that what had to be disclosed upon request in that dispute were the actual figures for cost of manufacture, expenses or profits used in the calculation of the constructed normal value.[691] The European Union further submits that the Appellate Body's finding in *EC – Tube or Pipe Fittings*, that the European Communities was required to disclose a document containing a summary of the "raw data"[692] on some of the injury factors under Article 3.4 of the *Anti-Dumping Agreement*, also supports its understanding of the term "information" in Article 6.4. However, the fact that the findings in prior disputes under Article 6.4 may have concerned such "raw data" only shows that that was the "information" at issue in those disputes. The particular "information" found to be subject to Article 6.4 in specific disputes, however, does not limit the scope of the term in Article 6.4 in all disputes arising under that provision. Moreover, with regard to the Appellate Body's finding in *EC – Tube or Pipe Fittings*, to the extent that the European Union uses the term "raw data"[693] to mean information submitted by the parties and not processed by the investigating authority, we note that this view is contradicted by the facts at issue in that dispute. Rather, the "information" relevant to the Appellate Body's finding under Article 6.4 in that case consisted of data that had been aggregated and summarized by the Commission as well as the Commission's evaluation of this data. More specifically, the "information" contained worksheets prepared by the European investigating authority

[691] European Union's appellant's submission, para. 253 (referring to Panel Report, *Korea – Certain Paper*, para. 7.199).
[692] European Union's appellant's submission, para. 254 (referring to Appellate Body Report, *EC – Tube or Pipe Fittings*, paras. 138-141).
[693] European Union's appellant's submission, para. 254.

regarding the injury factors listed in Article 3.4 on the basis of evidence submitted by the interested parties.[694]

485. In sum, under Article 6.4 of the *Anti-Dumping Agreement*, what information is considered "relevant to the presentation of [the interested parties'] cases" and "used by the authorities" would depend on the specific "step" of the anti-dumping investigation and the particular issue before the investigating authority. We recall that, in this dispute, China claims that the Commission failed to provide timely opportunities for the Chinese producers to see certain information relevant to the comparison between the export price and normal value for purposes of the dumping determination in the fasteners investigation. We therefore focus our analysis on the type of "information" covered under Article 6.4 and when it has to be disclosed, in the context of the comparison between the export price and normal value within the meaning of Article 2.4 of the *Anti-Dumping Agreement*.

486. Article 2.4 of the *Anti-Dumping Agreement* provides, in relevant part:

> A fair comparison shall be made between the export price and the normal value. This comparison shall be made at the same level of trade, normally at the ex-factory level, and in respect of sales made at as nearly as possible the same time. Due allowance shall be made in each case, on its merits, for differences which affect price comparability, including differences in conditions and terms of sale, taxation, levels of trade, quantities, physical characteristics, and any other differences which are also demonstrated to affect price comparability. ... The authorities shall indicate to the parties in question what information is necessary to ensure a fair comparison and shall not impose an unreasonable burden of proof on those parties. (footnote omitted)

487. As the Appellate Body has explained:

> [U]nder Article 2.4, the obligation to ensure a "fair comparison" lies on the *investigating authorities*, and not the exporters. It is those authorities which, as part of their investigation, are charged with comparing normal value and export price and determining whether there is dumping of imports.[695] (original emphasis)

488. However, this does not mean that the interested parties do not have a role to play in the process of ensuring a fair comparison. Rather, panels in previous

---

[694] Panel Report, *EC – Tube or Pipe Fittings*, para. 7.307 and footnote 256 thereto. See also China's appellee's submission, para. 397.

[695] Appellate Body Report, *US – Hot-Rolled Steel*, para. 178.

disputes have found that exporters bear the burden of substantiating, "as constructively as possible"[696], their requests for adjustments reflecting the "due allowance" within the meaning of Article 2.4. If it is not demonstrated to the authorities that there is a difference affecting price comparability, there is no obligation to make an adjustment.[697] Moreover, the fair comparison obligation does not mean that the authorities must accept each request for an adjustment. The authorities "must take steps to achieve clarity as to the adjustment claimed and then determine whether and to what extent that adjustment is merited".[698]

489. The process of making a fair comparison must also be understood in the light of the last sentence of Article 2.4, which requires an investigating authority to "indicate to the parties in question what information is necessary to ensure a fair comparison and shall not impose an unreasonable burden of proof on those parties". The last sentence of Article 2.4 thus adds a procedural requirement to the general obligation of investigating authorities to ensure a fair comparison. The sentence imposes an obligation on the investigating authority to tell the parties what information the authority will need in order to ensure a fair comparison. Thus, whereas the exporters may be required to "substantiate their assertions concerning adjustments"[699], the last sentence of Article 2.4 requires the investigating authorities to "indicate to the parties" what information these requests should contain, so that the interested parties will be in a position to make a request for adjustments. This process has been described as a "dialogue"[700] between the authority and the interested parties.

490. In our view, as a starting point for the dialogue between the investigating authority and the interested parties to ensure a fair comparison, the authority must, at a minimum, inform the parties of the product groups with regard to which it will conduct the price comparisons. For example, the authority may choose to make comparisons of transaction prices for a number of groups of goods within the like product that share common characteristics, thus minimizing the need for adjustments, or it may choose to make adjustments for each difference affecting price comparability to either the normal value or the export price of each transaction to be compared.[701] Without knowing which particular method the authority will use to categorize the products for purposes of price comparison, it would not be possible for the interested parties to know what information will be necessary for purposes of ensuring a fair comparison, and to request adjustments accordingly. Thus, as the Panel correctly found in its analysis of China's claim under Article 6.4 of the *Anti-Dumping Agreement*:

> Ensuring that the comparison of normal value and export price is based on comparable goods is, as

[696] Panel Report, *EC – Tube or Pipe Fittings*, para. 7.158.
[697] Panel Report, *Korea – Certain Paper*, para. 7.147.
[698] Panel Report, *EC – Tube or Pipe Fittings*, para. 7.158.
[699] *Ibid.*
[700] Panel Report, *Egypt – Steel Rebar*, para. 7.352.
[701] See Panel Report, para. 7.297.

> provided for in Article 2.4, an obligation on investigating authorities. Foreign producers have a role in that process, by requesting due allowance for differences demonstrated to affect price comparability. In order to fulfil their role, and thus ensure that their interest in a fair comparison is protected, however, it is necessary that they know the basis on which the investigating authority undertakes to make the comparison of normal value and export price, and in sufficient time to allow the exporters to make and substantiate requests for due allowance.[702]

491. Furthermore, in an anti-dumping investigation of imports from NMEs, where the normal value is not established on the basis of the foreign producers' domestic sales, but is established on the basis of the domestic sales in an analogue country, the investigating authority's obligation to inform the interested parties of the basis of the price comparison is even more pertinent for ensuring a fair comparison. This is because foreign producers are unlikely to have knowledge of the specific products and pricing practices of the producer in an analogue country. Unless the foreign producers under investigation are informed of the specific products with regard to which the normal value is determined, they will not be in a position to request adjustments they deem necessary.

492. With the above interpretation in mind, we turn to review the European Union's and China's claims and arguments raised on appeal.

D. The European Union's Appeal of the Panel's Findings under Articles 6.4 and 6.2 of the Anti-Dumping Agreement

493. The European Union appeals the Panel's finding that the European Union acted inconsistently with Articles 6.4 and 6.2 of the *Anti-Dumping Agreement* when the Commission failed to disclose information regarding the product types to Chinese producers until one working day before the deadline for submitting comments. Specifically, the Panel found that, by failing to disclose information regarding the product types, "the European Union failed to provide a timely opportunity for the Chinese [interested parties] to see information"[703] pertaining to the basis on which the Commission made the comparison of normal value and export price, in violation of Article 6.4 of the *Anti-Dumping Agreement.* Because the Commission failed to disclose the product types on a timely basis, the Panel also found that it had denied the Chinese interested parties a "full opportunity for the defence of their interests", in violation of Article 6.2 of the *Anti-Dumping Agreement.*[704]

---

702 Panel Report, para. 7.491.
703 Panel Report, para. 7.492.
704 Panel Report, para. 7.495.

494. The European Union's appeal under Article 6.4 is based on the following two grounds. First, the European Union maintains that the grouping of products into product types was a "factual determination" made by the Commission and was not "information" as that term is used in Article 6.4 of the *Anti-Dumping Agreement*.[705] Second, the European Union argues that the Panel violated Article 11 of the DSU in making its determination under Article 6.4 because it refused to consider certain evidence regarding the "timeliness" of the Commission's disclosure, and therefore did not consider the evidence in its totality.[706]

495. With respect to the first ground of appeal, as discussed above, we disagree with the European Union's view that the term "information" in Article 6.4 only "concerns facts and raw data rather than factual determinations and conclusions by the investigating authorities".[707] Rather, Article 6.4 applies to a broad range of information that is relevant to the presentation of the interested parties' cases and is used by an investigating authority for purposes of carrying out a required step in an anti-dumping investigation. Such information includes evidence submitted by the interested parties, as well as data processed, organized, or summarized by the authority. An authority's reasoning or internal deliberation in reaching a determination, however, does not constitute "information" subject to the obligation under Article 6.4.

496. In this dispute, the product types used by the Commission concerned "a required step"[708] in an anti-dumping investigation, namely, the comparison between export price and normal value for purposes of the dumping determination. The product types used by the Commission for purposes of the dumping determination were particularly relevant to the interested parties' cases, given the factual background of this case. We recall that the questionnaire sent to the Chinese producers and the Indian producer requested that products be identified on the basis of PCNs, thus leaving at least two Chinese exporters[709] with the impression that such PCNs would be used for purposes of the comparison between export price and normal value. As the Panel noted, "it appears from the structure of the questionnaires that [requests for adjustments to ensure a fair comparison] will not be necessary because of the categorization of the product according to PCN groups".[710] Indeed, by using the PCNs as the organizing principle when gathering product information from the interested parties, the Commission's approach created a reasonable expectation that price comparisons would be conducted on a very particular basis. Moreover, in the light of the very precise nature of the physical characteristics listed under the PCNs, it was also reasonable to assume that few adjustments would be necessary, as prices of narrowly defined products

---

705 European Union's appellant's submission, para. 248.

706 European Union's appellant's submission, para. 279.

707 European Union's appellant's submission, para. 253.

708 Appellate Body Report, *EC – Tube or Pipe Fittings*, para. 147.

709 These two producers later requested the Commission to clarify the meaning of "product types" used in the dumping determination.

710 Panel Report, para. 7.491.

by the Chinese producers would have been compared to prices of equally narrowly defined products in the analogue country, India.

497. Nonetheless, although the Chinese producers provided information on the basis of PCNs, the Indian producer, Pooja Forge, did not provide information on that basis. Consequently, the Commission decided to use a different method of product grouping to conduct the comparison, namely, what it called "product types", which it defined on the basis of two factors: strength class and the distinction between standard and special fasteners. The product types used by the Commission were thus a critical piece of information relating to a required step in the investigation, and these product types were in turn established on the basis of the product information provided by the Indian producer. They were not simply the Commission's reasoning in reaching its final determination.

498. Moreover, we recall that the PCNs include six elements further divided into 38 specifications, which could have resulted in hundreds of different combinations. Yet, the PCN characteristics and the product types overlap only with regard to one element, namely, the strength class. Thus, the differences between the PCNs and the product types used by the Commission could have prompted the Chinese producers to request that adjustments be made for any differences that might have affected price comparability between the Chinese and Indian fasteners, within the meaning of Article 2.4 of the *Anti-Dumping Agreement.* Indeed, without knowing what constituted "product types", "it would be difficult if not impossible, for foreign producers to request adjustments that they consider necessary in order to ensure a fair comparison."[711] Thus, the information concerning the product types, including their characteristics and how they were determined, constituted "information" within the meaning of Article 6.4 of the *Anti-Dumping Agreement*, because they were used in the dumping determination made by the Commission[712], and were indispensible to the parties' presentation of their cases concerning the dumping determination.

499. Turning to the European Union's claim that the Panel violated Article 11 of the DSU, we recall that, as discussed above in section VI.E, not every error allegedly committed by a panel amounts to a violation of Article 11 of the DSU. Rather, a participant claiming that a panel ignored certain evidence, and hence acted inconsistently with Article 11, must explain why the evidence is so material to its case that the panel's failure to address such evidence has a bearing on the objectivity of the panel's factual assessment.

500. In this regard, we note the European Union's assertion that "[o]ne *might* wrongly conclude from the Panel's findings" that the Chinese producers requesting to see the product types were unable to make any presentations due to time constraints.[713] According to the European Union, one Chinese producer "did submit comments" on the requested information in a letter dated

[711] *Ibid.*
[712] See Panel Report, *EC – Salmon (Norway)*, para. 7.769.
[713] European Union's appellant's submission, para. 291. (emphasis added)

24 November 2008[714] and, in that letter, it did not request an extension of the time for making presentations.[715] The European Union argues that this letter shows that "timing was *not* the problem for the interested parties", but the letter was not mentioned by the Panel in its reasoning.[716] In our view, the assertion that the Panel's findings "might" give a certain impression does not explain why the Panel's alleged "disregard" of a piece of evidence calls into question the objectivity of the Panel's factual assessment. On its face, such a claim simply does not rise to the level of egregiousness that a violation of Article 11 of the DSU requires.[717]

501. The European Union further submits that the Panel disregarded the Information Document, which "signall[ed] the use of 'product types'" three months prior to the issuance of the General Disclosure Document.[718] Thus, in the European Union's view, any "problem with the timing of the disclosure" regarding product types "was in large part due to the fact that the Chinese interested parties never requested to see the basis for the product type groupings until very late in the proceedings."[719]

502. Although the European Union's argument suggests that the Information Document was an important piece of evidence supporting its position, a review of the relevant evidence indicates the contrary. The Information Document, like the General Disclosure Document, stated that the Commission based its normal value determination on product types, but did not specify the relevant characteristics of the product types or how they were determined.[720] Moreover, as the Panel properly found, the correspondence between the Commission and the two Chinese producers requesting clarification regarding the product types showed that "until the receipt of the General Disclosure Document, the Chinese producers were under the impression that the Commission would make its dumping determinations on the basis of PCNs, as requested in the questionnaires sent to the Chinese and the Indian producers".[721] It should also be recalled that the "information" sought by the Chinese producers was a clarification of what constituted "product types" as referenced in the General Disclosure Document. Thus, the fact that the Information Document referred to the concept of product types does not alter the Panel's ultimate finding that the Commission did not disclose the requested clarification until one working day before the deadline for com-

[714] European Union's appellant's submission, para. 291. (emphasis omitted)
[715] European Union's appellant's submission, para. 292.
[716] European Union's appellant's submission, para. 294. (original emphasis)
[717] In any event, we note that, in the letter referred to by the European Union, the Chinese producer expressed the view that it was not possible to comment on the Commission's dumping determination without knowing what types or groups of products of Pooja Forge were actually matched with the Chinese products. The letter thus shows that the Chinese producers still considered the information provided by the Commission insufficient for them to comment properly on the dumping determination. This letter, therefore, does not lend support to the European Union's position, and the Panel acted properly in not relying on this evidence for reaching its finding.
[718] European Union's appellant's submission, para. 284.
[719] European Union's appellant's submission, para. 286.
[720] Information Document, *supra*, footnote 81, p. 12.
[721] Panel Report, para. 7.490.

ments. We therefore do not agree with the European Union's assertion that the Panel erroneously ignored the evidence contained in the Information Document in reaching its finding.

503. The European Union also claims that, because some Chinese producers submitted information describing certain characteristics that, they believed, distinguished different types of fasteners, and because the product types used for purposes of the dumping determination reflected the same characteristics, the Chinese producers "clearly were able to make presentations based on this 'information'".[722] Specifically, the European Union refers to a submission made on 22 February 2008 by Jiaxing Association of Fastener Import & Export Companies ("Jiaxing Association") describing the difference between fasteners produced by Chinese producers and those produced by EU producers. Jiaxing Association argued that the Chinese companies mostly produced standard fasteners in lower strength classes, while EU producers mostly produced non-standard fasteners in higher strength classes[723], and that fasteners by Chinese and EU producers were not competitive with each other. The European Union asserts that "the Panel's conclusion that Chinese producers were not given a timely opportunity to 'see information relevant to the presentation of their cases' is flawed as the alleged 'information' was no other than what the Chinese interested parties had been presenting as being the main characteristics for distinguishing between product types throughout the investigation."[724]

504. However, the evidence that the European Union claimed the Panel "disregarded" was not apposite to the issue examined by the Panel under Article 6.4 of the *Anti-Dumping Agreement*. As discussed, what information may be considered "relevant for the presentation" of the interested parties' cases under Article 6.4 depends on the particular stage of the anti-dumping investigation and the specific issue before the investigating authority. China's claim and the Panel's finding under Article 6.4 concern the information on product types that the Commission used for purposes of price comparisons between fasteners produced by the Indian producer (rather than EU producers) and by the Chinese producers in its dumping determination. Thus, the information contained in Jiaxing Association's submission, which was made in a context unrelated to the issue of price comparisons between the Indian and Chinese fasteners, cannot be considered as information that the two Chinese producers requested as relevant to the presentation of their cases regarding the dumping determination. Therefore, we do not consider that the Panel erred in not relying on the evidence concerning Jiaxing Association's submission in making its finding under Article 6.4.

505. In sum, we consider that the product types used by the Commission for purposes of comparing the export price and normal value in the fasteners investigation constituted "information relevant to the presentation" of the Chinese

722 European Union's appellant's submission, para. 288.

723 Jiaxing Association of Fasteners Import & Export Companies, Submission of 22 February 2008 (Panel Exhibit EU-13), p. 4. The two Chinese producers requesting clarification regarding product types were not part of this association.

724 European Union's appellant's submission, para. 288 (referring to Panel Report, para. 7.492).

parties' case. This is because, without such information, "it would be difficult if not impossible, for foreign producers to request adjustments that they consider necessary in order to ensure a fair comparison."[725] We further consider that the Panel correctly found that the European Union violated Article 6.4 of the *Anti-Dumping Agreement* "by not providing a timely opportunity for Chinese producers to see information regarding the product types on the basis of which normal value was established".[726] We therefore decline to accept the European Union's appeal of these findings.

506. With regard to the Panel's finding under Article 6.2 of the *Anti-Dumping Agreement*, the European Union maintains that, because it has demonstrated that the Panel's finding under Article 6.4 was flawed, the Panel's "purely consequential" finding under Article 6.2 was also in error.[727] In the light of our finding that the Panel did not err in reaching its finding under Article 6.4, we also disagree with the European Union's assertion that the Panel's finding under Article 6.2 was in error.

507. The European Union further submits that the first sentence of Article 6.2, which provides that all interested parties "shall have a full opportunity for the defence of their interests", cannot "be read as a catch-all due process provision" because doing so "would effectively render redundant *all* of the other provisions of Article 6 which impose specific obligations on investigating authorities".[728] We recall that, in the fasteners investigation, the Chinese producers could not make relevant requests for adjustment in order to ensure a fair comparison within the meaning of Article 2.4 of the *Anti-Dumping Agreement*, because they were not informed, in a timely manner, of the basis on which the export price and normal value was compared. Consequently, they did not have a full opportunity to defend their interests in relation to the Commission's dumping determination. Thus, contrary to the European Union's assertion, the Panel did not simply treat Article 6.2 as a "catch-all due process provision". Rather, the Panel's finding is consistent with the Appellate Body's interpretation, in *EC – Tube or Pipe Fittings*, that the "presentations" referred to in Article 6.4 "logically are the principal mechanisms through which an exporter subject to an anti-dumping investigation can defend its interests" within the meaning of Article 6.2.[729] On this basis, we consider that the Panel properly found that "the Chinese exporters could not defend their interests in this investigation because the Commission only provided information concerning the product types used in the determination of the normal value at a very late stage of the proceedings" and that, therefore, "the European Union acted inconsistently with Article 6.2" of the *Anti-Dumping Agreement*.[730]

---

[725] Panel Report, para. 7.491.
[726] Panel Report, para. 7.494.
[727] European Union's appellant's submission, para. 275.
[728] European Union's appellant's submission, para. 277. (original emphasis)
[729] Appellate Body Report, *EC – Tube or Pipe Fittings*, para. 149.
[730] Panel Report, para. 7.495.

E. China's Other Appeal of the Panel's Findings under Article 2.4 of the Anti-Dumping Agreement

508. China alleges that the Panel erred in finding that the European Union did not fail to conduct a fair comparison between the export price and normal value within the meaning of Article 2.4 of the *Anti-Dumping Agreement*. Specifically, China asserts that the Panel erred in not addressing a "substantial argument"[731] that China raised on the basis of the last sentence of Article 2.4, which requires that the authorities indicate to the parties what information is necessary to ensure a fair comparison. China also contends that the Panel's failure to address its arguments is inconsistent with a correct interpretation and application of Article 2.4.[732] China therefore requests the Appellate Body to complete the analysis by applying Article 2.4 to the facts, and to find that the Commission's failure to indicate to the Chinese producers the information necessary to ensure a fair comparison constituted a violation of Article 2.4 of the *Anti-Dumping Agreement*.[733] Furthermore, China alleges that the Panel erred in its interpretation of Article 2.4 of the *Anti-Dumping Agreement*, and acted inconsistently with Article 11 of the DSU, when finding that the Commission did not have to make adjustments for the physical differences reflected in the PCN characteristics. Finally, China maintains that the Panel erred in its interpretation and application of Article 2.4 of the *Anti-Dumping Agreement* when finding that the Commission did not have to make adjustments for quality differences.[734] We turn now to address each of these claims.

509. China alleges that, contrary to its duty under Article 11 of the DSU, the Panel failed to address "one of China's main arguments concerning its claim of violation of Article 2.4" of the *Anti-Dumping Agreement*, that is, the argument with regard to the Commission's failure to inform the interested parties of the "product types" on the basis of which the comparison was made between the normal value and export price.[735] We note that, in its first written submission to the Panel, China maintained that the Commission failed to disclose "the list of product types on the basis of which normal value had been determined and how these product types had been compared with the PCNs of the Chinese exporting producers"[736], although China did not specifically refer to the last sentence of Article 2.4. In its second written submission, China, for the first time before the Panel, referenced the last sentence of Article 2.4 and argued that, because the Commission failed to indicate to the parties in question what information was

---

731 China's other appellant's submission, para. 306.

732 Although China's other appellant's submission alleges that the Panel erred in its interpretation (see para. 296), China clarified at the oral hearing that its claim also covers the Panel's application of Article 2.4 to the facts of the case.

733 See China's other appellant's submission, paras. 315-334.

734 Although China's other appellant's submission alleges that the Panel erred in its interpretation (see paras. 296 and 367), China clarified at the oral hearing that its claim also covers the Panel's application of Article 2.4 to the facts of the case.

735 China's other appellant's submission, para. 311.

736 China's first written submission to the Panel, para. 372.

necessary to ensure a fair comparison, the European Union violated Article 2.4.[737]

510. The Panel did not address this argument in its findings under Article 2.4 of the *Anti-Dumping Agreement*. Regarding China's request during the interim review stage that the Panel address this argument, the Panel responded:

> With respect to China's concern that the Panel failed to address its argument that, by failing to inform the Chinese producers of its decision not to base the dumping determinations on full PCNs, the European Union violated Article 2.4 of the [*Anti-Dumping Agreement*], we recall that this is the main argument China raises in connection with its claim under Articles 6.2, 6.4, 6.5 and 6.9 of the [*Anti-Dumping Agreement*], which is addressed in the Report at paragraphs 7.477-7.483.[738]

511. The above review of China's arguments before the Panel indicates that China did not raise a separate claim under the last sentence of Article 2.4, but referred to that sentence in support of its claim that the Commission acted inconsistently with the obligation to conduct a fair comparison under Article 2.4 of the *Anti-Dumping Agreement*. On appeal, China has also characterized its allegation under the last sentence of Article 2.4 as an "argument put forward by China".[739] Thus, we disagree with China's view that the Panel's failure to address this argument constitutes "a false exercise of judicial economy"[740], because the issue of judicial economy is only relevant to the manner in which a panel deals with a party's *claims*. Moreover, as the Appellate Body has found, a panel has the discretion "to address only those arguments it deems necessary to resolve a particular claim" and "the fact that a particular argument relating to that claim is not specifically addressed in the 'Findings' section of a panel report will not, in and of itself, lead to the conclusion that that panel has failed to make the 'objective assessment of the matter before it' required by Article 11 of the DSU".[741]

512. Although the Panel's failure to address China's argument does not rise to the level of a violation of Article 11 of the DSU, we nonetheless consider that, in the light of its findings under Article 6.4 of the *Anti-Dumping Agreement*, the Panel should have considered China's argument under the last sentence of Article 2.4 of the *Anti-Dumping Agreement* in reaching its finding. As discussed above, Article 2.4 obliges investigating authorities to indicate to the parties what information is necessary to ensure a fair comparison and requires an investigating authority, at a minimum, to inform the parties of the products or product groups used for purposes of the price comparison. This will then allow the par-

---

[737] China's second written submission to the Panel, paras. 778-787 and 796.
[738] Panel Report, para. 6.98.
[739] China's other appellant's submission, para. 306.
[740] China's other appellant's submission, para. 312.
[741] Appellate Body Report, *EC – Poultry*, para. 135. (emphasis omitted)

ties to decide whether a request for adjustment regarding any differences affecting price comparability should be made.

513. We recall that, in the fasteners investigation, the structure of the questionnaire sent to the Chinese producers suggested that requests for adjustments would not be necessary because of the categorization of the product under investigation according to PCN groups. However, the Commission decided to use a different method of product grouping to conduct the comparison, namely, the "product types" defined on the basis of strength class and the distinction between standard and special fasteners. As noted above, significant differences existed between PCNs and the "product types" defined by the Commission. Had the Chinese producers known that these product types were used instead of PCNs, such differences could have prompted the Chinese producers to request adjustments within the meaning of Article 2.4. In this respect, the Panel correctly found, in its analysis under Article 6.4, that, without knowing what "product types" were used by the Commission, "it would be difficult if not impossible, for foreign producers to request adjustments that they consider necessary in order to ensure a fair comparison."[742] Thus, the facts of the case indicate that, because the Commission did not clearly indicate the product types used for purposes of price comparisons until very late in the proceedings, the European Union acted inconsistently with its obligations under Article 2.4 by depriving the Chinese producers of the ability to request adjustments for differences that could have affected price comparability.

514. The Panel found, however, that the European Union acted consistently with Article 2.4 of the *Anti-Dumping Agreement*. In so finding, the Panel analyzed China's claim under Article 2.4 in isolation from its analysis under Article 6.4 of that Agreement. Specifically, in disagreeing with China's argument that the Commission should have made adjustments for differences reflected in the PCN codes, the Panel stated that, "in the course of the investigation at issue, none of the Chinese producers argued that there were factors which affected price comparability within the meaning of Article 2.4 other than those used by the Commission to categorize the product for comparison purposes, that is, strength class (which was an element of the PCNs) and the distinction between standard and special fasteners (which was not an element of the PCNs)".[743] The Panel further stated that, "[g]iven the absence of such a request [for adjustments for differences affecting price comparability] from the Chinese exporters, and any showing that there was a factor which affected price comparability which should have been apparent to the Commission", China's claim was unfounded and must be rejected.[744]

515. Yet, as the Panel found in the context of Article 6.4, "[i]n a case such as this one, where it appears from the structure of the questionnaires that such requests will not be necessary because of the categorization of the product accord-

742 Panel Report, para. 7.491.
743 Panel Report, para. 7.306.
744 *Ibid.*

ing to PCN groups, *we consider that it is not unreasonable for exporters to not request specific adjustments which are already reflected in those PCN groups*."[745] The Panel further found that "Chinese producers were informed very late in the proceedings of the product types that formed the basis for the comparisons underlying the Commission's dumping determinations."[746] Thus, because of the Commission's failure to provide a timely opportunity to see the information concerning the basis of the price comparisons, the Chinese producers were precluded from requesting any adjustments for purposes of ensuring a fair comparison. The "absence"[747] of a request from the Chinese producers for adjustments on the basis of the PCN characteristics, therefore, should not have prevented a finding of inconsistency under Article 2.4. On the contrary, it further demonstrates that, due to the Commission's failure to indicate what information was necessary for a fair comparison, the Chinese producers were unable to exercise their rights under Article 2.4 to ensure that the Commission conducted a fair comparison of the export price and the normal value. Thus, in failing to consider the last sentence of Article 2.4 in the light of the relevant facts of the case and its finding under Article 6.4, the Panel erred in its application of Article 2.4 of the *Anti-Dumping Agreement*.

516. China further maintains that the Panel erred in the interpretation of Article 2.4 of the *Anti-Dumping Agreement* by failing to distinguish between two obligations encompassed under that provision: first, the obligation for an investigating authority to evaluate identified differences that might affect price comparability; second, the obligation of the authority to make adjustments if it finds that the differences indeed affected price comparability. In this dispute, China argues, because the Commission requested information on the basis of PCNs at the beginning of the investigation, the physical characteristics indicated in the PCNs were identified by the Commission.[748] Thus, even in the absence of a request, the Commission should have evaluated whether any of the identified differences could have had an impact on the prices compared.

517. The Panel, quoting the panel's finding in *EC – Tube or Pipe Fittings*, found that the investigating authorities "must take steps to achieve clarity as to the adjustment claimed and whether and to what extent that adjustment is merited".[749] Logically, as a step "to achieve clarity as to the adjustment claimed", authorities must first evaluate the differences identified to assess whether they affect price comparability. Therefore, we do not consider that the Panel's interpretation of Article 2.4 differs from China's view that an investigating authority must evaluate identified differences and then make adjustments.[750] We are less convinced, however, by China's assertion that the authority must evaluate any identified differences, regardless of whether a request for adjustment has been

[745] Panel Report, para. 7.491. (emphasis added)
[746] Panel Report, para. 7.492.
[747] Panel Report, para. 7.306.
[748] China's other appellant's submission, para. 360.
[749] Panel Report, para. 7.298 (quoting Panel Report, *EC – Tube or Pipe Fittings*, para. 7.158).
[750] See also European Union's appellee's submission, para. 272.

made. It is likely that, in an anti-dumping investigation, the differences between the products sold in the foreign producer's domestic and export markets would be numerous. Differences between the products, however, would not always affect price comparability and require adjustments by the authorities. China's assertion may place an undue burden on an investigating authority to assess each difference in order to determine whether adjustment is needed in every case, even without a request by the interested party.

518. China further argues that the Panel failed to conduct an objective assessment of the facts, as required by Article 11 of the DSU, in finding that China did not provide evidence in support of its claim that the PCN characteristics necessarily affected price comparability.[751] In addition, according to China, the Panel acted inconsistently with Article 17.6(i) of the *Anti-Dumping Agreement* when it found that, because the Commission did not conclude that the PCN characteristics indicated differences affecting price comparability, it was inappropriate for the Panel to consider this issue itself.[752] China requests the Appellate Body to complete the analysis and find that "an unbiased and objective investigating authority in this situation could only have concluded that such adjustments had to be made."[753]

519. We emphasize that our finding above, that the Panel failed properly to apply Article 2.4 of the *Anti-Dumping Agreement*, does not suggest that the PCN characteristics *necessarily* reflect differences that affect price comparability. Neither does it suggest that the Commission, had it examined the characteristics, would have made adjustments. Rather, the authorities "must take steps to achieve clarity as to the adjustment claimed and then determine whether and to what extent that adjustment is merited".[754] Thus, it is the investigating authority's duty to review the requested adjustments in order to determine whether any physical differences identified before it are differences that affect price comparability within the meaning of Article 2.4.

520. In this dispute, because the Chinese producers were not able to claim adjustments, the Commission did not examine the issue of whether any of the PCN characteristics, when compared to the product types used to establish the normal value, were differences that affect price comparability. The numerous PCN characteristics were thus not compared with the product types chosen by the Commission and discussed for purposes of price comparison. In this context, it was therefore reasonable for the Panel to state that, "while it may be plausible that the PCN characteristics described in this case indicate differences affecting price comparability"[755], there is no evidence on the Panel record that would support this conclusion. Moreover, it was the Commission's duty to review any requested

---

751 See China's other appellant's submission, para. 383.

752 See China's other appellant's submission, para. 386. See also Panel Report, para. 7.302.

753 China's other appellant's submission, para. 400.

754 Panel Report, *EC – Tube or Pipe Fittings*, para. 7.158.

755 Panel Report, para. 7.302. The Panel recalled that the PCN characteristics were: type of fasteners (by CN code); strength/hardness; coating; presence of chrome on coating; diameter; and length/thickness. (*Ibid.*, footnote 617 to para. 7.302)

adjustments to determine whether the request would be warranted. As the Panel rightly found, absent any discussion during the investigation at issue, it was not appropriate, nor feasible, for the Panel to assume the role of an investigating authority and analyze the differences between each of the narrowly defined PCN characteristics and the product types used by the Commission.[756] Similarly, it is not within our mandate to review whether the various PCN characteristics reflect physical differences that would have affected price comparability in the fasteners investigation, in the absence of any factual findings in this regard by the Commission or by the Panel. Therefore, we decline to accept China's claim that the Panel acted inconsistently with Article 11 of the DSU, or Article 17.6(i) of the *Anti-Dumping Agreement*, and, consequently, we also decline China's request for completion of the analysis.

521. Finally, China alleges that the Panel erred in its interpretation and application of Article 2.4 of the *Anti-Dumping Agreement* in disagreeing with China's argument that the European Union violated that provision because the Commission failed to evaluate, and make adjustments for, quality differences[757] between Indian and Chinese fasteners, even though China demonstrated to the Panel that one Chinese producer requested such an adjustment.[758] According to China, the Commission was under a duty at least to evaluate the claimed differences in quality between the Indian and Chinese products. Moreover, because "the quality differences affected price comparability, the Commission was required to make the necessary adjustments".[759]

522. In reaching the finding challenged by China, the Panel noted China's assertion that, at recital 52 of the Definitive Regulation, the Commission "acknowledged" that there were quality differences between Indian and Chinese fasteners.[760] Recital 52 states, in relevant part:

> The submission from the PRC authorities mentioned in recital 48 enclosed an analysis report detailing alleged quality differences between fasteners of a given standard (DIN 933 is used as an example) manufactured in the Community and the PRC. ... Any perceived differences in quality, which may subsist from a user's point of view, can be dealt with through an adjustment for physical differences (see recital 103) but do not mean that the two products are not comparable.

523. In reviewing recital 52, the Panel found that China's argument was based on a misreading of that recital. Specifically, the Panel found that "recital 52 relates to the issue of like product, not dumping determinations", and that "it refers

---

[756] See Panel Report, para. 7.302.
[757] We recall that quality is not one of the characteristics identified in the PCNs.
[758] China's other appellant's submission, paras. 405 and 406.
[759] China's other appellant's submission, para. 408.
[760] Panel Report, para. 7.307.

to an analysis of differences between fasteners produced in China, and fasteners produced in the European Union", which China alleged in support of its argument that Chinese and EU fasteners are not comparable, and therefore should not be considered "like".[761] Furthermore, the Panel noted that "China's argument seem[ed] to rest on the premise that the Commission stated in recital 52 that any perceived quality differences *would* be dealt with through adjustments, and that therefore such adjustments should have been made."[762] The Panel observed, however, "that recital 52 says that any perceived differences in quality *can* be dealt with through adjustments", and "it is clear that this recital does not even address any differences between Indian and Chinese fasteners."[763] On the basis of its review, therefore, the Panel concluded:

> Thus, despite the reference to recital 103 [in recital 52], where the Commission explains the adjustment made for differences in the cost of quality control between Indian and Chinese producers, we do not see what relevance recital 52 has to the issue raised by China, that the Commission should have made an adjustment for quality differences between Chinese and Indian fasteners.[764]

524. On appeal, although China claims that the Panel erred in its interpretation and application of Article 2.4 of the *Anti-Dumping Agreement* in finding that the Commission was not required to make adjustments for quality differences, it does not provide any specific argument that addresses such an error in legal interpretation. Rather, China's appeal hinges on its disagreement with the Panel concerning the meaning and scope of the above recital in the Definitive Regulation. In our view, the Panel's finding, that recital 52 of the Definitive Regulation did not support the view that the Commission acknowledged quality differences between Indian and Chinese fasteners, was based on a reasoned analysis of the text of the measure at issue. As the Panel correctly found, recital 52 "does not even address any differences between Indian and Chinese fasteners".[765] Moreover, China has not identified any specific differences in quality that had been identified during the fasteners investigation. We therefore see no basis for China's argument that Recital 52 of the Definitive Regulation demonstrates that these quality differences were "identified".[766]

525. China further argues that it submitted to the Panel a letter sent by the Commission in reply to questions by certain Chinese exporters, in which the Commission stated that "[p]hysical differences are addressed by ... adjustment

---

[761] Panel Report, para. 7.308.

[762] Panel Report, para. 7.309 (referring to China's response to Panel Question 94). (original underlining)

[763] Panel Report, para. 7.309. (original underlining)

[764] Panel Report, para. 7.309.

[765] *Ibid.*

[766] China's other appellant's submission, para. 412.

for the cost of quality control which reflects the general difference in quality level."[767] China maintains that this letter demonstrated that the Commission was aware of a "general difference in quality level".[768]

526. The Panel dismissed the relevance of the letter, finding that "nothing in this letter indicates that any evidence was proffered to the Commission to demonstrate that this alleged difference in quality affected price comparability", and that the letter did not clearly show that the Commission acknowledged that there were quality differences affecting price comparability.[769] In our view, the Panel's finding is properly premised on the content of the letter. The letter clearly shows that it concerns adjustments for "cost of quality control" rather than any differences in quality of the fasteners by Chinese and Indian producers. Moreover, on appeal, China did not raise any claims under Article 11 of the DSU alleging that the Panel's above review of a piece of evidence submitted by China was inconsistent with its obligation to conduct an objective assessment of the facts. Thus, it is not for us to second-guess the Panel's conclusion on the basis of its assessment of this evidence. We consider, therefore, that China's claim is not properly substantiated and should therefore be dismissed. Consequently, China's allegation that the Commission should have made adjustments for such "acknowledged" differences in quality also cannot stand.[770]

F. Conclusion

527. In sum, with respect to the Panel's findings on certain aspects of the dumping determination, we *find* that the Panel correctly found that the European Union violated Article 6.4 of the *Anti-Dumping Agreement* "by not providing a timely opportunity for Chinese producers to see information regarding the product types on the basis of which normal value was established".[771] The Panel also correctly found that, in view of the Commission's failure to disclose the information on the product types on a timely basis, the European Union denied the Chinese producers a "full opportunity for the defence of their interests", in violation of Article 6.2 of the *Anti-Dumping Agreement*.[772] We further find that, in failing to take into account the last sentence of Article 2.4 in the light of the relevant facts of the case and its finding under Article 6.4 of the *Anti-Dumping Agreement*, the Panel erred in its application of Article 2.4 of that Agreement. We *find*, instead, that, in not disclosing the information on the product types on a timely basis, the European Union acted inconsistently with Article 2.4 of the *Anti-Dumping Agreement* by failing to indicate to the parties in question what information was necessary to ensure a fair comparison.

---

[767] China's other appellant's submission, para. 413 (quoting Panel Exhibit CHN-31, *supra*, footnote 310, point 5).

[768] China's other appellant's submission, para. 414.

[769] Panel Report, para. 7.311.

[770] China's other appellant's submission, para. 418.

[771] Panel Report, para. 7.494.

[772] Panel Report, para. 7.495.

528. However, we do not find that the Panel erred in its interpretation of Article 2.4 of the *Anti-Dumping Agreement* by failing to distinguish between an investigating authority's obligation to evaluate identified differences that might affect price comparability, and to make adjustments if it finds that the differences indeed affected price comparability. Neither do we find that the Panel acted inconsistently with Article 11 of the DSU or Article 17.6 of the *Anti-Dumping Agreement* in finding that the Commission was not required to make adjustments for the physical differences between the characteristics reflected in the PCNs and the product types. Finally, we *find* that the Panel did not err in the interpretation and application of Article 2.4 of the *Anti-Dumping Agreement* in rejecting China's argument that the Commission acted inconsistently with that provision by failing to evaluate, and to make adjustments for, quality differences.

VIII. CONFIDENTIAL TREATMENT AND THE DISCLOSURE OF INFORMATION UNDER ARTICLES 6.5 AND 6.5.1 AND ARTICLES 6.2 AND 6.4 OF THE *ANTI-DUMPING AGREEMENT*

A. Introduction

529. We will now turn to the participants' various appeals regarding the Commission's treatment of confidential information under Articles 6.5 and 6.5.1 of the *Anti-Dumping Agreement*, and the disclosure of information under Articles 6.2 and 6.4 of the *Anti-Dumping Agreement*.

530. According to Article 6.5 of the *Anti-Dumping Agreement*, information that is "by nature" confidential or that is "provided on a confidential basis" shall, upon "good cause" shown, be treated as such by the investigating authorities. Article 6.5.1 of the *Anti-Dumping Agreement* requires that parties submitting confidential information also furnish a non-confidential summary thereof, in sufficient detail to permit a reasonable understanding of the substance of the information submitted in confidence. In exceptional circumstances, parties may indicate that confidential information is not susceptible of summary, and a statement of the reasons why summarization is not possible must be provided.

531. The participants raise on appeal several issues under Articles 6.5 and 6.5.1. We will address first the European Union's appeal of the Panel's finding that the European Union acted inconsistently with Article 6.5.1 because two domestic producers[773] provided insufficient statements of the reasons why they could not provide non-confidential summaries of information submitted in confidence. The European Union claims on appeal that Article 6.5.1 does not require investigating authorities to ensure that producers provide "appropriate" statements of the reasons why summarization is not possible, because, in the European Union's view, this provision imposes only a "best endeavours" obligation on investigating authorities.

[773] EU producers A. Agrati S.p.A. and Fontana Luigi S.p.A.

532. Next, we will address the European Union's second claim under Article 6.5 regarding the confidential treatment of the "product type" information submitted by the analogue country producer, whose data the Commission used for the determination of normal value *in lieu* of Chinese domestic prices. We begin by addressing the European Union's preliminary objection that this claim was not within the Panel's terms of reference, and that the Panel's consideration and ruling on this claim deprived the European Union of its due process rights. Then, we will address the issue raised by the European Union as to whether the requirement in Article 6.5 to show "good cause" for confidential treatment applies to an analogue country producer not designated as an "interested party" under Article 6.11 of the *Anti-Dumping Agreement*.

533. We will then turn to the claims raised by China in its Notice of Other Appeal regarding the Panel's finding that "potential commercial retaliation" justified the confidential treatment of the identity of the complainants and supporters of the complaint. China claims that the complainants did not make a sufficient "good cause" showing for treating the identity of the complainants and supporters as confidential, and that the Panel erred in both its application of the burden of proof and in its rejection of China's argument that the Commission's disclosure of the complainants' identity in another context undermined the "good cause" alleged.

534. Finally, we will address the European Union's appeal under Article 6.2 of the DSU that the Panel erred in finding that China's claims under Articles 6.2 and 6.4 of the *Anti-Dumping Agreement* challenging the non-disclosure of the identity of the complainants and supporters were within the Panel's terms of reference, despite the lack of an explicit reference in the panel request to China's claim regarding the non-disclosure of the identity of the complainants and supporters.[774] Since in China's view no "good cause" was shown under Article 6.5 to treat the identity of the complainants and the supporters of the complaint as confidential, China claimed that the non-disclosure of their identity to the Chinese exporters and producers was inconsistent with the transparency and due process requirements of Articles 6.2 and 6.4. The European Union contends on appeal that China's claims under Articles 6.2 and 6.4 with respect to the non-disclosure of the identity of the complainants were not within the Panel's terms of reference because they were not included in the panel request.

B. *Confidential Treatment of Information under Articles 6.5 and 6.5.1 of the Anti-Dumping Agreement*

535. We begin with an interpretation of Articles 6.5 and 6.5.1 of the *Anti-Dumping Agreement*. Articles 6.5 and 6.5.1 set out specific rules governing

[774] We recall that Article 6.2 of the *Anti-Dumping Agreement* provides that interested parties be given a full opportunity to defend their interests throughout an investigation. Article 6.4 in turn requires that the authorities provide timely opportunities for interested parties to see all non-confidential information relevant to the presentation of their cases. (See *supra*, paras. 478 and 507)

an investigating authority's acceptance and treatment of confidential information. The provisions read as follows:

> 6.5 Any information which is by nature confidential (for example, because its disclosure would be of significant competitive advantage to a competitor or because its disclosure would have a significantly adverse effect upon a person supplying the information or upon a person from whom that person acquired the information), or which is provided on a confidential basis by parties to an investigation shall, upon good cause shown, be treated as such by the authorities. Such information shall not be disclosed without specific permission of the party submitting it.
>
> 6.5.1 The authorities shall require interested parties providing confidential information to furnish non-confidential summaries thereof. These summaries shall be in sufficient detail to permit a reasonable understanding of the substance of the information submitted in confidence. In exceptional circumstances, such parties may indicate that such information is not susceptible of summary. In such exceptional circumstances, a statement of the reasons why summarization is not possible must be provided.

536. Under Article 6.5, authorities must treat information submitted by parties to an investigation as confidential if it is "by nature" confidential, or if it is "provided on a confidential basis" and "upon good cause shown". The confidentiality of information that is "by nature" confidential will often be readily apparent. Article 6.5 provides illustrative examples of information that falls into the category of "by nature" confidential, including information that is sensitive "because its disclosure would be of significant competitive advantage to a competitor or because its disclosure would have a significantly adverse effect upon a person supplying the information or upon a person from whom that person acquired the information". One type of such information is commercially sensitive information not typically disclosed in the normal course of business, and which would likely be regularly treated as confidential in anti-dumping investigations.[775] The question of whether information is "by nature" confidential depends on the *content* of the information. Information that is "provided on a confidential basis" is not necessarily confidential by reason of its content, but rather, confidentiality arises from the circumstances in which it is provided to the authorities. These two categories may, in practice, overlap.

537. The requirement to show "good cause" for confidential treatment applies to both information that is "by nature" confidential and that which is provided to

---

[775] This could be the case, for example, for certain profit or cost data or proprietary customer information.

the authority "on a confidential basis".[776] The "good cause" alleged must constitute a reason sufficient to justify the withholding of information from both the public and from the other parties interested in the investigation, who would otherwise have a right to view this information under Article 6 of the *Anti-Dumping Agreement*. Put another way, "good cause" must demonstrate the risk of a potential consequence, the avoidance of which is important enough to warrant the non-disclosure of the information. "Good cause" must be assessed and determined objectively by the investigating authority, and cannot be determined merely based on the subjective concerns of the submitting party.

538. We find that the examples provided in Article 6.5 in the context of information that is "by nature" confidential are helpful in interpreting "good cause" generally, because they illustrate the type of harm that might result from the disclosure of sensitive information, and the protectable interests involved. Article 6.5 states that the disclosure of such information "would be of significant competitive advantage to a competitor" or "would have a significantly adverse effect upon a person supplying the information or upon a person from whom that person acquired the information". These examples suggest that a "good cause" which could justify the non-disclosure of confidential information might include an advantage being bestowed on a competitor, or the experience of an adverse effect on the submitting party or the party from which it was acquired. These examples are only illustrative, however, and we consider that a wide range of other reasons could constitute "good cause" justifying the treatment of information as confidential under Article 6.5.

539. In practice, a party seeking confidential treatment for information must make its "good cause" showing to the investigating authority upon submission of the information. The authority must objectively assess the "good cause" alleged for confidential treatment, and scrutinize the party's showing in order to determine whether the submitting party has sufficiently substantiated its request. In making its assessment, the investigating authority must seek to balance the submitting party's interest in protecting its confidential information[777] with the prejudicial effect that the non-disclosure of the information may have on the transparency and due process interests of other parties involved in the investigation to present their cases and defend their interests. The type of evidence and the extent of substantiation an authority must require will depend on the nature of the information at issue and the particular "good cause" alleged. The obligation remains with the investigating authority to examine objectively the justification given for the need for confidential treatment. If information is treated as confidential by an authority without such a "good cause" showing having been made, the authority would be acting inconsistently with its obligations under Article 6.5 to grant such treatment only "upon good cause shown".

---

[776] See Panel Report, para. 7.451; Panel Report, *Korea – Certain Paper*, para. 7.335; and Panel Report, *Guatemala – Cement II*, para. 8.219.

[777] Where necessary, the authority must also consider the submitting party's relationship with the source of the confidential information.

540. In examining the scope of Article 6.5, we note that it extends the need to request confidential treatment to information submitted by "parties to an investigation" rather than those in the specifically defined group of "interested parties". As such, Article 6.5 does not limit the protection afforded to sensitive information to the "interested parties" expressly listed under Article 6.11 of the *Anti-Dumping Agreement.*[778] In our view, the term "parties to an investigation" refers to any person who takes part or is implicated in the investigation.[779] Moreover, Article 6.11 does not contain an exhaustive list of "interested parties", but states that "'interested parties' shall *include*" the persons or groups listed in that Article. In our view, the persons expressly listed in Article 6.11 are those who are in every case considered to be "interested parties", but are not the only persons who may be considered "interested parties" in a particular investigation. We do not believe that an investigating authority is relieved of its obligations under Article 6.5 merely because a participant in the investigation does not appear on the list of "interested parties" in Article 6.11.[780] Rather, once "good cause" is shown, confidential treatment of sensitive information must be afforded to any party who takes part or is implicated in the investigation or in the provision of information to an authority. Pursuant to Article 6.5 such parties include persons supplying information, persons from whom confidential information is acquired, and parties to an investigation.

541. Whenever information is treated as confidential, transparency and due process concerns will necessarily arise because such treatment entails the with-

[778] Article 6.11 of the *Anti-Dumping Agreement* reads:

For the purposes of this Agreement, "interested parties" shall include:

(i) an exporter or foreign producer or the importer of a product subject to investigation, or a trade or business association a majority of the members of which are producers, exporters or importers of such product;

(ii) the government of the exporting Member; and

(iii) a producer of the like product in the importing Member or a trade and business association a majority of the members of which produce the like product in the territory of the importing Member.

This list shall not preclude Members from allowing domestic or foreign parties other than those mentioned above to be included as interested parties.

[779] The panel in *Argentina – Poultry Anti-Dumping Duties* analyzed a similar term in Article 6.1.2 of the *Anti-Dumping Agreement*, that is, "other interested parties participating in the investigation", and developed a similar interpretation of this term. (Panel Report, *Argentina – Poultry Anti-Dumping Duties*, para. 7.153)

[780] We note, in this respect, the European Union's argument that the "good cause" requirement for confidential treatment of information in Article 6.5 does not apply to analogue country producers like Pooja Forge, because they do not fall within the definition of "interested parties" under Article 6.11 of the *Anti-Dumping Agreement*. (European Union's appellant's submission, paras. 349-354) In the fasteners investigation, the Commission did not determine normal value on the basis of the information from Chinese producers and exporters, and decided to seek information from analogue country producers. The Indian company Pooja Forge participated in the investigation at the request of the Commission, and provided substantial amounts of information that was used as the basis for determining normal value. In our view, the decision by the Commission to determine normal value based on information from an analogue country producer, and the participation of Pooja Forge in the investigation, require that Pooja Forge be afforded the protection of sensitive information upon "good cause" shown and the obligations of both Articles 6.5 and 6.5.1 apply.

holding of information from other parties to an investigation. Due process requires that interested parties have a right to see the evidence submitted or gathered in an investigation, and have an adequate opportunity for the defence of their interests.[781] As the Appellate Body has stated, "that opportunity must be meaningful in terms of a party's ability to defend itself".[782]

542. Articles 6.5 and 6.5.1 accommodate the concerns of confidentiality, transparency, and due process by protecting information that is by nature confidential or is submitted on a confidential basis and upon "good cause" shown, but establishing an alternative method for communicating its content so as to satisfy the right of other parties to the investigation to obtain a reasonable understanding of the substance of the confidential information, and to defend their interests. As the Panel found, "Article 6.5.1 serves to balance the goal of ensuring that the availability of confidential treatment does not undermine the transparency of the investigative process".[783] In respect of information treated as confidential under Article 6.5, Article 6.5.1 obliges the investigating authority to require that a non-confidential summary of the information be furnished, and to ensure that the summary contains "sufficient detail to permit a reasonable understanding of the substance of the information submitted in confidence".[784] The sufficiency of the summary provided will therefore depend on the confidential information at issue, but it must permit a reasonable understanding of the substance of the information withheld in order to allow the other parties to the investigation an opportunity to respond and defend their interests.

543. Article 6.5.1 contemplates that in "exceptional circumstances" confidential information may not be "susceptible of summary". In such exceptional circumstances, a party may indicate that it is not able to furnish a non-confidential summary of the information submitted in confidence, but it is nevertheless required to provide a "statement of the reasons why summarization is not possible". Article 6.5.1 relieves a party of its duty to provide a non-confidential summary of information submitted in confidence only if doing so "is not possible". It is not enough for a party simply to claim that providing a summary would be burdensome or costly. Summarization of information will not be possible where no alternative method of presenting that information can be developed that would not, either necessarily disclose the sensitive information, or necessarily

---

[781] Appellate Body Report, *Australia – Salmon*, para. 272.

[782] Appellate Body Report, *US – Gambling*, para. 270.

[783] Panel Report, para. 7.515.

[784] The panel in *Mexico – Steel Pipes and Tubes* made a similar finding:

> We consider that the conditions set out in Article 6.5, chapeau, and 6.5.1 are of critical importance in preserving the balance between the interests of confidentiality and the ability of another interested party to defend its rights throughout an anti-dumping investigation. For precisely this reason, we consider it paramount for an investigating authority to ensure that the conditions in these provisions are fulfilled. We consider it equally important for a WTO Panel called upon to review an investigating authority's treatment of confidential information strictly to enforce these conditions, while remaining cognizant of the applicable standard of review.

(Panel Report, *Mexico – Steel Pipes and Tubes*, para. 7.380)

fail to provide a sufficient level of detail to permit a reasonable understanding of the substance of the information submitted in confidence.

544. Where information is kept confidential upon "good cause" shown, and it is not possible to provide a non-confidential summary of the information that permits a reasonable understanding of its substance, the balance struck under Articles 6.5 and 6.5.1 is altered, and the due process rights of other parties to the investigation are not fully respected. Therefore, when it is not possible to furnish a non-confidential summary, Article 6.5.1 requires a party to identify the exceptional circumstances and provide a statement explaining the reasons why summarization is not possible. For its part, the investigating authority must scrutinize such statements to determine whether they establish exceptional circumstances[785], and whether the reasons given appropriately explain why, under the circumstances, no summary that permits a reasonable understanding of the information's substance is possible.[786] As the Panel found, "in the absence of scrutiny of non-confidential summaries or stated reasons why summarization is not possible by the investigating authority, the potential for abuse under Article 6.5.1 would be unchecked unless and until the matter were reviewed by a panel."[787] This "would obviously defeat the goal of maintaining transparency during the course of the investigation itself that is one of the purposes of Article 6.5".[788] In sum, Article 6.5.1 imposes an obligation on the investigating authorities to ensure that sufficiently detailed non-confidential summaries are submitted to permit a reasonable understanding of the substance of the confidential information; and, in exceptional circumstances, to ensure that parties provide a statement appropriately explaining the reasons why particular pieces of confidential information are not susceptible of summary.

C. Domestic Producers' Statements of the Reasons Why Summarization of Confidential Information Was Not Possible

545. We turn next to the European Union's appeal of the Panel's finding that the Commission failed to ensure that two domestic producers complied with the requirements of Article 6.5.1 of the *Anti-Dumping Agreement*, and thus the European Union acted inconsistently with that provision.[789] In the fasteners in-

---

785 The panel in *Mexico – Olive Oil* came to a similar conclusion in its interpretation of the parallel provisions of the *SCM Agreement*, finding that:

> ... the investigating authority should examine the reasons given for not summarizing the confidential information and determine whether, indeed, these reasons constitute "exceptional" circumstances.

(Panel Report, *Mexico – Olive Oil*, para. 7.92)

786 We note that various methods of summarization are used by parties and investigating authorities in anti-dumping investigations, such as indexing data, providing trends analysis, and aggregating data from multiple producers. Where a certain method might be expected to be used for the specific type of information in question, it would be incumbent on the submitting party to explain, *inter alia*, why present circumstances prevent it from employing that method.

787 Panel Report, para. 7.515.

788 *Ibid.*

789 Panel Report, paras. 7.516 and 7.517.

vestigation, two domestic producers, A. Agrati S.p.A ("Agrati") and Fontana Luigi S.p.A. ("Fontana Luigi"), submitted a substantial amount of information to the Commission on a confidential basis. As required by Article 6.5.1, each producer provided, in addition to the non-confidential version of its questionnaire response, summaries for most of the information submitted in confidence. For certain categories of information, however, no non-confidential summaries were provided, and only limited statements were provided relating to the lack of such summaries.

546. The Panel found that the statements provided by the two producers were not sufficient to comply with the requirement under Article 6.5.1 that, in the exceptional circumstance in which confidential information is not susceptible of summary, parties provide a statement of the reasons why summarization is not possible. The Panel found that the statements submitted by these producers did not "relate to any of the specific information for which no non-confidential summary [was] provided, or to anything having to do with [the producer] itself, the party supplying it".[790] Specifically, the Panel found that Agrati's statement simply asserted that the confidential information could not be summarized. The Panel further noted that, in certain cases, Agrati's assertion that it could not summarize the information was undermined by the fact that other domestic producers were able to produce summaries of the same types of information.[791] In the case of Fontana Luigi, the Panel found that the producer did not even assert that the information was not susceptible of summary, but only stated that the various questionnaire responses were "by nature confidential".[792] The Panel further found that there was no evidence "that would even suggest that the Commission ever considered whether [the producers'] stated reason for the lack of a non-confidential summary of such information ... was more than *pro forma*", and concluded that the European Union thereby violated its obligations under Article 6.5.1 to ensure that an appropriate statement of reasons was provided.[793]

547. On appeal, the European Union contends that Articles 6.5 and 6.5.1 impose only two requirements on investigating authorities, that is, to treat information as confidential, upon good cause shown, and to require parties to provide non-confidential summaries of information submitted in confidence. The second, third, and fourth sentences of Article 6.5.1 impose only a "best endeavours" obligation on the investigating authority to ensure that non-confidential summaries provided include "sufficient detail to permit a reasonable understanding" of the underlying information, or to require that a statement of reasons be provided where summarization is not possible.[794] There is no basis, in the European Union's view, for the Panel's finding that investigating authorities must ensure that parties provide "appropriate" non-confidential summaries or "appropriate" state-

---

790 *Ibid.*
791 Panel Report, para. 7.516.
792 Panel Report, para. 7.517.
793 Panel Report, paras. 7.516 and 7.517. (original emphasis)
794 European Union's appellant's submission, para. 317.

ments of the reasons why summarization is not possible.[795] According to the European Union, had the drafters intended Article 6.5.1 to impose a strict obligation on investigating authorities in these respects, the provision would have given authorities the power to penalize non-compliance, for example, by disregarding confidential information when no non-confidential summary, or no statement of reasons explaining why summarization is not possible, is provided.[796]

548. In response, China submits that, as the Panel found, Article 6.5.1 entails a two-part obligation. First, Article 6.5.1 obliges an investigating authority to require non-confidential summaries of confidential information, or, where applicable, statements of the reasons why summarization is not possible. Second, an investigating authority must further require that these summaries or statements be "appropriate" to satisfy the requirements of Article 6.5.1.[797] In China's view, interpreting this provision in a way that would allow less than "appropriate" summaries and statements would render the obligation "useless", and would violate the interpretative principle that an interpreter should not adopt a reading that reduces the provisions of a treaty "to redundancy or inutility".[798]

549. As we have found above, contrary to the European Union's contention, Article 6.5.1 imposes an obligation on investigating authorities to ensure that parties to an investigation provide non-confidential summaries in sufficient detail to permit a reasonable understanding of the substance of the information submitted in confidence; and, in the exceptional circumstances in which summarization of confidential information is not possible, that statements be provided appropriately explaining the reasons why this is so.[799] The European Union is correct that the *Anti-Dumping Agreement* does not provide for specific sanctions to penalize parties if they fail to provide a sufficient non-confidential summary or a statement of the reasons why summarization is not possible. The *Anti-Dumping Agreement* places a number of obligations on investigating authorities to make a fair and objective assessment of particular issues in every investigation and to balance the rights and obligations of the interested parties subject to that investigation, with limited power to impose sanctions on a non-complying party. However, this does not derogate from the obligatory nature of the requirements. It does not mean, as the European Union argues, that an investigating authority must merely make best efforts to ensure that such summaries or statements of reasons are provided. The obligation rests on the Members to comply with the requirements of Article 6.5.1, and it is left to each Member to determine how they will do so.

550. In this instance, the Panel found that the non-confidential version of the questionnaire response submitted by Agrati contained non-confidential summaries of information submitted in confidence relating to some injury factors, but

795 European Union's appellant's submission, paras. 298 and 321.
796 European Union's appellant's submission, para. 319.
797 China's appellee's submission, para. 523.
798 China's appellee's submission, paras. 524 and 527.
799 See *supra*, paras. 542-544.

not others.[800] For those where a non-confidential summary was not provided, the following statement was included: "[t]he information cannot be summarized without disclosing confidential information which can cause a damage to our company. The information has been provided as limited."[801]

551. In respect of the second domestic producer, Fontana Luigi, while the initial questionnaire response contained "almost no non-confidential summarized information regarding injury factors", a follow-up response based on a specific request by the Commission contained non-confidential summaries for the majority of the information submitted in confidence.[802] However, no summaries were provided for information regarding distribution systems and price settings. The reason given as to why a summary could not be provided was simply that "[the] information is by nature confidential because its disclosure would be of significant competitive advantage to a Competitor."[803]

552. As we have found above, where a party claims that it cannot provide a non-confidential summary of information submitted in confidence, Article 6.5.1 requires an investigating authority to ensure that, in the exceptional circumstances in which confidential information is not susceptible of summary, a submitting party provide instead a statement appropriately explaining the reasons why summarization of that particular information is not possible. As we have also found, summarization of confidential information will not be possible where no alternative method of presenting the information can be developed that would not, either necessarily disclose the sensitive information, or necessarily fail to provide a sufficient level of detail to permit a reasonable understanding of the substance of the information submitted in confidence.

553. Neither of the statements provided by Agrati or Fontana Luigi indicated why the information for which no non-confidential summary was provided presented an "exceptional circumstance" to justify the lack of a summary, nor did either statement provide reasons explaining why summarization of a particular category of information was not possible. With respect to Agrati, its statement asserting for each category that "[t]he information cannot be summarized without disclosing confidential information" speaks to a justification for providing confidential treatment in the first place. It does not address the issue of why

[800] Agrati included a non-confidential summary for employment, sales and re-sales of the subject product, inventories, production, capacity and capacity utilization. No summary was provided for factors such as return on investment, investments, profitability, cash flows, cost of production, suppliers of direct (raw) materials, volume of raw materials used in production, extraordinary items with respect to costs, list of all sales to unrelated domestic customers, and allocation of different cost elements among different types of products. (See Panel Report, para. 7.516)

[801] Panel Report, para. 7.516.

[802] These non-confidential summaries relate to information concerning volume of production, production capacity, capacity utilization, total purchases in volume and value, stocks in volume of finished goods, sales and re-sales in value and volume both to related and unrelated companies, captive use, cost of production, consumption of raw material, profitability for the product in question and total company profitability, cash flows, investments, returns on net assets, and employment and labour costs both for the product concerned and for the company. (See Panel Report, para. 7.517 (referring to Annexes to Fontana Luigi's Non-confidential Questionnaire Response (Panel Exhibit EU-28))

[803] Panel Report, para. 7.517.

summarization of the information is not possible, or why the particular information presents exceptional circumstances that would justify a failure to provide a non-confidential summary. Nor can the single statement repeated by Agrati be read as adequate justification for treating a number of different pieces of information as equally unsusceptible to summarization. Furthermore, Agrati's assertion that it could not summarize information was undermined by the fact that Fontana Luigi was able to produce summaries of the same types of information.[804] We agree with the Panel that Agrati's statement did not "relate to any of the specific information for which no non-confidential summary [was] provided or to anything having to do with Agrati itself".[805] Therefore, we consider that the Commission failed to ensure that Agrati provided an appropriate statement of why summarization of certain portions of its questionnaire response was not possible.

554. With respect to Fontana Luigi, we note that its statement that the non-summarized information is "by nature confidential because its disclosure would be of significant competitive advantage to a Competitor" also addresses the reasons for seeking confidential treatment in the first place rather than demonstrating that summarization of the information is not possible. Indeed, Fontana Luigi did not even assert that the confidential information could not be summarized, much less make the case that the information at issue qualified as an "exceptional circumstance" under Article 6.5.1. In the complete absence of any statement of reasons why summarization of the confidential information was not possible, we agree with the Panel that the European Union, in accepting these statements as sufficient, did not meet its obligations under Article 6.5.1.

555. Moreover, the Panel record does not indicate that the Commission examined these statements to evaluate their consistency with Article 6.5.1.[806] In its appellant submission, the European Union states that it had requested improved non-confidential summaries from the domestic producers, and that, because interested parties did not complain further about the non-confidential file, "the authorities considered that there was no need to insist further".[807] The European Union further states that "no further investigation was conducted in respect of the few pieces of information for which no summary was provided and for which a statement of reasons was offered."[808] Article 6.5.1 of the *Anti-Dumping Agreement* requires an investigating authority to scrutinize the reasons given by the party to determine whether they establish exceptional circumstances, and whether the reasons given appropriately explain why summarization is not possible. We do not consider that the European Union did so in this case.

[804] Panel Report, para. 7.516.

[805] *Ibid.*

[806] For both producers, the Panel stated that "[t]here is nothing in the Definitive Regulation, or any other evidence that has been proffered, that would even suggest that the Commission ever considered whether [the parties'] stated reason for the lack of a non-confidential summary ... was more than *pro forma*." (Panel Report, paras. 7.516 and 7.517)

[807] European Union's appellant's submission, para. 332.

[808] *Ibid.*

556. For these reasons, we *uphold* the Panel's findings, in paragraphs 7.516 and 7.517 of the Panel Report, that the European Union acted inconsistently with its obligations under Article 6.5.1 of the *Anti-Dumping Agreement* when it failed to ensure that the domestic producers Agrati and Fontana Luigi provide appropriate statements as to why summarization of confidential information was not possible.

D. *Confidential Treatment of Information Submitted by the Analogue Country Producer, Pooja Forge*

557. We turn next to the European Union's appeal of the Panel's finding that the European Union acted inconsistently with its obligations under Article 6.5 of the *Anti-Dumping Agreement* "with respect to the treatment of the confidential information in Pooja Forge's questionnaire response".[809]

558. In the fasteners investigation, the Commission applied Article 2(7) of its Basic AD Regulation to China and therefore did not determine normal value on the basis of the information from Chinese producers and exporters. Rather, the Commission sought information from analogue country fastener producers and ultimately found one company in India, Pooja Forge, that was willing to respond to requests for information from the Commission. Pooja Forge provided substantial amounts of information that was used as the basis for determining normal value. When it returned its questionnaire, Pooja Forge submitted a non-confidential version of its response, in which it designated large portions as confidential, or left them blank.[810] China contended that this information should not have been granted confidential treatment by the Commission. The Panel determined that "China [had] not put forward any evidence or arguments with respect to the confidential treatment of any other category of information than that concerning product types", and limited its analysis to that category.[811] The Panel went on to find that Pooja Forge did not assert or show any "good cause" for treating such "product type" information as confidential, nor did it provide a non-confidential summary or a statement of why summarization of the confidential information was not possible.[812] On this basis, the Panel concluded that the European Union acted inconsistently with its obligations under Article 6.5 of the *Anti-Dumping Agreement* because it treated "product type" information as confi-

---

[809] Panel Report, para. 7.525.

[810] The Panel found that the non-confidential response contained information on company turnover, production, capacity and capacity utilization, but did not include information on sales to independent customers, costs or profits. (Panel Report, para. 7.518)

[811] The Panel noted in this respect that, in its second written submission to the Panel, China claimed that the non-confidential summary of Pooja Forge's questionnaire response "does not contain *any information*, and in particular information on the 'product types' on the basis of which the information has been provided by this producer", and the Panel decided to limit its analysis to the confidential treatment of "product types". (Panel Report, para. 7.524 and footnote 1041 thereto (quoting China's second written submission to the Panel, para. 1110 (original emphasis)) We recall that the term "product types", as used in the fasteners investigation, refers to the product categories upon which the Commission based its comparison between normal value and export price.

[812] Panel Report, para. 7.525.

dential without requiring Pooja Forge to show "good cause" for such treatment.[813]

559. The European Union appeals the Panel's findings regarding the confidential treatment of Pooja Forge's questionnaire response on procedural and substantive grounds. First, the European Union contends that China's claim regarding the Commission's confidential treatment of information submitted by Pooja Forge was not within the Panel's terms of reference[814], or, in the alternative, that the manner in which China and the Panel dealt with this claim over the course of the proceedings deprived the European Union of its rights to due process, and that the Panel made the case for the complainant.[815] Second, the European Union claims that the Panel erred in finding that the requirement to show "good cause" for confidential treatment of information in Article 6.5 applies also to analogue third country producers. In the European Union's view, the requirements of Article 6.5 apply only to "interested parties", as that term is defined in Article 6.11 of the *Anti-Dumping Agreement*, and a third country producer like Pooja Forge is not an "interested party" under that provision.[816] The European Union further argues that this interpretation makes sense in the context of an investigation involving an analogue country producer, because it would be too difficult to recruit companies willing to participate in such an investigation if they had to comply with the requirements of Articles 6.5 and 6.5.1.[817]

560. China contends that its claim under Article 6.5 challenging the Commission's confidential treatment of information submitted by Pooja Forge was within the Panel's terms of reference. China argues that the Appellate Body should in any case reject the European Union's appeal, because the European Union did not raise this issue "promptly" before the Panel, and thereby waived its rights to have such an objection considered on appeal.[818] China further contends that Article 6.2 of the DSU requires a party to list its *claims* in the panel request, but does not require a party to include its *arguments* explaining how the identified measure violates the responding party's obligations under a provision.[819] On the substance of the European Union's claim, China points out that, by its own terms, Article 6.5 applies to "parties to an investigation", and not to "interested parties", and that the former term is a more inclusive concept that would also cover an analogue country producer.[820] China argues that, due to the broad discretion investigating authorities have in determining an alternative normal value for NME countries, it is particularly important that the transparency requirements contained in Article 6.5 are strictly enforced.[821] Finally, China argues that, even if Article 6.5 applies only to "interested parties" within the meaning of Ar-

813 Panel Report, para. 7.525.
814 European Union's appellant's submission, paras. 335 and 336.
815 European Union's appellant's submission, paras. 343 and 344.
816 European Union's appellant's submission, paras. 349-353.
817 European Union's appellant's submission, para. 356.
818 China's appellee's submission, paras. 572-575.
819 China's appellee's submission, para. 578.
820 China's appellee's submission, paras. 599-603.
821 China's appellee's submission, para. 606.

ticle 6.11, it should nevertheless apply to Pooja Forge, because the Commission designated the company an "interested party" by virtue of Pooja Forge's involvement in the investigation.[822]

561. Regarding the Panel's terms of reference, the European Union acknowledges that it did not raise its challenge in this respect before the Panel.[823] The Appellate Body has found that parties are required to raise procedural objections "promptly"[824], but also that matters going to the jurisdiction of a panel are "fundamental" and can therefore be raised at any stage in a proceeding, including on appeal.[825] If a claim is not within a panel's terms of reference, the panel does not have the jurisdiction to hear the claim. Moreover, a party's failure to raise a timely jurisdictional objection cannot operate to cure such a jurisdictional defect. We therefore find that the European Union's failure to raise its terms of reference claim promptly before the Panel does not bar it from bringing this challenge on appeal.

562. Article 6.2 of the DSU lays out the key requirements for a panel request and, by implication, the establishment of a panel's terms of reference under Article 7.1 of the DSU. The complaining party must identify the specific measure at issue and provide a brief summary of the legal basis of the complaint, sufficient to present the problem clearly. The Appellate Body has found that the panel request "assists in determining the scope of the dispute" in respect of each measure, and "consequently, establishes and delimits the jurisdiction of the panel".[826] The panel request also serves the important due process objective of notifying the respondent of the nature of the case it must defend.[827] As the Appellate Body stated in *EC and certain member States – Large Civil Aircraft*, "[t]his due process objective is not constitutive of, but rather flows from, the proper establishment of a panel's jurisdiction".[828] The panel request must therefore be examined "as it existed at the time of filing" in order to determine whether a particular claim falls within the panel's terms of reference.[829] For its part, a panel must "scrutinize carefully the panel request, read as a whole, and on the basis of the language used"[830], in order to determine whether it is "sufficiently precise"[831] to

822 China's appellee's submission, paras. 608-611.

823 European Union's appellant's submission, para. 337.

824 Appellate Body Report, *US – Carbon Steel*, para. 123; Appellate Body Report, *Mexico – Corn Syrup (Article 21.5 – US)*, para. 50; Appellate Body Report, *US – FSC*, para. 166; Appellate Body Report, *US – 1916 Act*, para. 54.

825 Appellate Body Report, *EC and certain member States – Large Civil Aircraft*, para. 791; Appellate Body Report, *US – Carbon Steel*, para. 123; Appellate Body Report, *Mexico – Corn Syrup (Article 21.5 – US)*, para. 36; Appellate Body Report, *US – 1916 Act*, para. 54.

826 Appellate Body Report, *EC and certain member States – Large Civil Aircraft*, para. 640.

827 See Appellate Body Report, *US – Carbon Steel*, para. 126 (referring to Appellate Body Report, *Brazil – Desiccated Coconut*, p. 22, DSR 1997:I, 167, at 186). Appellate Body Report, *EC – Chicken Cuts*, para. 155; and Appellate Body Report, *US – Zeroing (Japan) (Article 21.5 – Japan)*, para. 108.

828 Appellate Body Report, *EC and certain member States – Large Civil Aircraft*, para. 640.

829 Appellate Body Report, *EC and certain member States – Large Civil Aircraft*, para. 642.

830 Appellate Body Report, *US – Carbon Steel*, para. 127; Appellate Body Report, *US – Oil Country Tubular Goods Sunset Reviews*, paras. 164 and 169; Appellate Body Report, *US – Continued Zeroing*, para. 161; Appellate Body Report, *US – Zeroing (Japan) (Article 21.5 – Japan)*, para. 108.

comply with Article 6.2 of the DSU. A party's later submissions may be referenced where the meanings of the terms used in the panel request are not clear on their face, but the content of these subsequent submissions "cannot have the effect of curing the failings of a deficient panel request".[832]

563. Turning to the European Union's appeal, we note that China stated in its panel request that the European Union had violated:

> ... Articles 6.2, 6.4, 6.5 and 6.5.1 of the [*Anti-Dumping Agreement*] because the EC failed to ensure that domestic producers provided non-confidential summaries of confidential information they submitted or because the EC wrongly treated information as being confidential, thereby preventing Chinese producers to have the full opportunity for the defence of their interests.[833]

We read China's panel request as containing the claims that: (i) the European Union failed to ensure that domestic producers provided non-confidential summaries of information submitted as confidential; or (ii) the European Union wrongly treated information as being confidential, and thereby prevented Chinese producers from having a full opportunity to defend their interests.

564. The claim subject to the European Union's terms of reference challenge is whether the European Union wrongly treated information submitted by Pooja Forge in its questionnaire response regarding "product types" as confidential. Because Pooja Forge is not a domestic producer, this claim cannot fall under the first phrase in the panel request. However, the language of the second phrase, "the [European Union] wrongly treated information as being confidential", is broad enough to capture China's claim regarding the confidential treatment of information submitted by Pooja Forge. A claim that "the [European Union] wrongly treated information as confidential" implies that the European Union did so in circumstances where "good cause" was not shown, and so falls within the scope of Article 6.5 of the *Anti-Dumping Agreement*. The fact that the first phrase refers to "domestic producers" does not, in our view, limit or reduce the scope of the second phrase. We therefore *find* that China's claim under Article 6.5 of the *Anti-Dumping Agreement* regarding the Commission's confidential treatment of information submitted by Pooja Forge was within the Panel's terms of reference.

565. As we have found that this claim was properly before the Panel, we turn to the substantive arguments and claims raised by the European Union on appeal. The European Union submits that, through the manner in which the Panel

---

[831] Appellate Body Report, *EC – Bananas III*, para. 142; Appellate Body Report, *US – Zeroing (Japan) (Article 21.5 – Japan)*, para. 108.

[832] Appellate Body Report, *EC and certain member States – Large Civil Aircraft*, para. 642; Appellate Body Report, *EC – Bananas III*, para. 143; Appellate Body Report, *US – Carbon Steel*, para. 127.

[833] WT/DS397/3, p. 5.

dealt with its claim under Article 6.5, the Panel deprived it of its due process rights and thus acted inconsistently with Article 11 of the DSU. The European Union further claims that the Panel violated Article 11 of the DSU also because it impermissibly "made the case" for China through its questioning during the proceedings related to this claim.[834] Specifically, the European Union argues that, but for the Panel's questioning, China would not have articulated its argument, or established a *prima facie* case, that "good cause" had not been shown to justify the Commission's treatment of information submitted by Pooja Forge as confidential.

566. We note at the outset that the burden rests on the complainant to substantiate its claims with legal arguments and evidence in its written and oral submissions to the panel. While the DSU, and Article 11 in particular, require a panel to make an objective assessment of the matters that are before it, the panel must turn its attention to and direct its questions at claims and arguments that the parties have articulated. Where a complainant has failed to set forth arguments in its submissions before a panel sufficient to substantiate its claims, a panel may not use its interrogative powers to make good the absence of relevant substantiating arguments and evidence.[835] We should not be understood to suggest, however, that, where arguments have been affirmatively *raised* by the parties, the panel should not fully scrutinize such evidence and argumentation. Where there is an *absence* of argumentation, however, a panel cannot intervene to raise arguments on a party's behalf and make the case for the complainant.

567. We recall that, in reviewing the European Union's argument that China failed to substantiate its claim under Article 6.5, the Panel stated that "the way in which China had pursued this claim in this dispute is far from ideal", and that it was "particularly troubled by the fact that the claim was not developed at all in China's first written submission".[836] The Panel explained that China's "fail[ure] to put forward a fuller explanation of and argument in support of its claim ... left the European Union in a difficult position in attempting to respond to a claim that was unclear".[837] The Panel determined, however, that China ultimately provided, "in its second written submission and its answer to [Panel] question 71, a sufficiently clear argument in support of its claim to allow the European Union an adequate opportunity to respond".[838]

568. We too are troubled by the way in which China pursued its claim under Article 6.5 regarding the confidential treatment of "product type" information submitted by Pooja Forge. As the Panel found, China did not articulate a "good cause" claim or argument under Article 6.5 in its first written submission. The arguments China did make in its first submission were limited to the deficiency of the non-confidential version of Pooja Forge's questionnaire response,

---

834 European Union's appellant's submission, paras. 340-347.

835 See also Appellate Body Report, *US – Continued Zeroing*, para. 343; Appellate Body Report, *Japan – Agricultural Products II*, para. 129.

836 Panel Report, para. 7.522.

837 *Ibid.*

838 *Ibid.*

which is a claim under Article 6.5.1, and not related to the issue of whether "good cause" for confidential treatment was shown under Article 6.5.

569. The Panel record indicates that, at the first meeting of the parties, the claims regarding Pooja Forge were not addressed by either party in its oral statement. After the first meeting of the parties, referring to China's first written submission, the Panel asked China the following:

> Question 71: The Panel notes that in the heading of its claim regarding alleged deficiencies in questionnaire responses, China also refers to questionnaire responses by the producer in the analogue third country. The body of China's argumentation in this regard, however, does not make reference to this issue. Please elaborate.

China submitted its response to this question on the same day that it filed its second written submission. China's answer to Panel Question 71 stated, in part:

> In China's view, a lot of (if not all) **information was considered as confidential although no "good cause" was shown**. In this respect, China *inter alia* refers to the fact that not even the categorizations ("product types") used for the provision of the data were disclosed. This information is obviously not confidential and China therefore fails to see any "good cause" for the confidential treatment of this information. Indeed, no "good cause" can be shown for treating the product types applied for the data to be provided, as confidential. By granting confidential treatment to these data, the EU violated Article 6.5 of the [*Anti-Dumping Agreement*].[839] (original boldface)

570. Although China mentioned, for the first time, the issue of "good cause" in its above response, it did not provide any further arguments or evidence in this respect. In its second written submission, China stated that it had not dropped its claim under Article 6.5 "as far as it relates to the deficient character of the questionnaire response of the producer in the analogue country".[840] China then stated that the non-confidential version of Pooja Forge's questionnaire response "does not contain *any information*, and in particular information on the "product types" on the basis of which the information has been provided by this producer which is obviously not confidential".[841] These arguments, however, addressed the issue of whether the non-confidential summary provided by Pooja Forge met the requirement of Article 6.5.1. They were not relevant to the issue of whether

839 China's responses to Panel Question 71, p. 113.

840 China's second written submission to the Panel, para. 1110.

841 China's second written submission to the Panel, para. 1110. (original emphasis)

"good cause" was shown under Article 6.5 for treating the information submitted by Pooja Forge in its questionnaire response as confidential.[842]

571. The Panel record further indicates that, at the second meeting of the parties, China merely repeated the same argument it had put forward in its second written submission, that Pooja Forge's non-confidential questionnaire response was inadequate.[843] China did not raise the issue of the lack of a "good cause" showing in its oral statement at that meeting. Following the second meeting of the parties, the Panel asked China to clarify whether it "expect[ed] a finding" regarding the issue of "good cause" under Article 6.5, or a finding regarding the consistency of the non-confidential summary of Pooja Forge's questionnaire response with Article 6.5.1.[844]

572. In response, China stated that it sought, first, a finding under Article 6.5, and second, if the Panel concluded that the information was properly treated as confidential, a finding under Article 6.5.1 that the European Union failed to require Pooja Forge to furnish a "non-confidential summary" of such information "in sufficient detail to permit a reasonable understanding of the substance of the information submitted in confidence".[845] However, in support of these claims, China again merely reiterated its argument that Pooja Forge's questionnaire response "[did] not contain any information at all and, in particular, concerning the 'product types'".

573. Thus, as the Panel record clearly shows, the only time that China used the term "good cause" was in its response to Panel Question 71, and there it was used in a cursory manner that only asserted a claim, without providing substantiating arguments or evidence. Throughout the Panel proceedings, China focused on the lack of information regarding "product types" in the non-confidential version of the questionnaire response, rather than the lack of a "good cause" showing for confidential treatment in the first place.

---

[842] Although addressed to China, the European Union submitted its own comments in response to Panel Question 71, stating that, to the extent that China maintains its claims with regard to Pooja Forge, "the Panel should simply rule that China has failed to make a *prima facie* case", because it "failed to provide any evidence in accordance and within the deadlines set out in paragraph 16 of the Panel's working procedures". (European Union's response to Panel Question 71 after the first Panel meeting, para. 170)

[843] In response, the European Union stated that the Panel's *Working Procedures* prevented it from allowing China to articulate its arguments so late in the proceedings, and asserted that "the Panel should not go any further because China had its opportunity to try to make its case but it failed to even try". (Panel Report, para. 7.520)

[844] Panel Question 103, which reads in full:

> With respect to the claim regarding the non-confidential versions of the questionnaire responses of the two EU producers and that of the Indian producer, the Panel notes that, in its written submissions, China refers to Article 6.5 only but in its response to Question [71] from the Panel it refers to Article 6.5.1. China's panel request refers both to Article 6.5 and 6.5.1. Please explain whether China expects a finding under the chapeau of Article 6.5 or under Article 6.5.1 from the Panel with respect to this claim.

[845] China's response to Panel Question 103 after the second Panel meeting, p. 24.

574. Rule 4 of the Panel's Working Procedures requires that, "[b]efore the first substantive meeting of the panel with the parties, the parties to the dispute shall transmit to the panel written submissions in which they present the facts of the case and their arguments." As described above, the Panel record shows that China asserted its claim under Article 6.5 regarding the lack of a "good cause" showing for the confidential treatment of Pooja Forge's questionnaire response only in response to questions from the Panel, and articulated this claim only after the parties had provided the Panel with written submissions and had attended a substantive meeting. We do not find that assertions made so late in the proceedings, and only in response to questioning by the Panel, can comply with either Rule 4 of the Panel's Working Procedures, or the requirements of due process of law. The late assertion of a claim under Article 6.5 with respect to the lack of a "good cause" showing for confidential treatment of Pooja Forge's "product type" information, and the absence of proper argumentation and of the provision of relevant evidence in support of this assertion, demonstrates that the European Union was not called upon to respond to China's claim under Article 6.5.

575. In the light of the above, we *find* that China failed to substantiate its claim under Article 6.5 of the *Anti-Dumping Agreement* that the confidential treatment of the "product type" information submitted by Pooja Forge in its questionnaire response was improper. Therefore, we *reverse* the Panel's finding, in paragraph 7.525 of the Panel Report, that the European Union acted inconsistently with its obligations under Article 6.5 of the *Anti-Dumping Agreement* "with respect to the treatment of confidential information submitted by Pooja Forge". Having reversed the Panel's finding on this basis, we see no need to make a separate finding under Article 11 of the DSU that the Panel, as argued by the European Union, deprived it of its due process rights and impermissibly made the case for China.[846]

E. Confidential Treatment of the Identity of the Complainants

576. We now turn to China's other appeal of the Panel's findings under Article 6.5 of the *Anti-Dumping Agreement* that the European Union did not err in treating the identity of the complainants and supporters of the complaint as confidential. In the fasteners investigation, the complainants and supporters of the complaint requested the Commission to grant such treatment in order "to avoid a potential retaliation which could be carried out by some of their Customers who also buy products directly from P.R. China".[847] The complainants alleged that, if these customers knew which European producers had requested or supported the initiation of this investigation, they might discontinue purchasing fasteners from those producers. The Commission accepted this request and granted confidential treatment.

577. The Panel found that, although the complainants' "good cause" showing was limited to the allegation contained in the complaint, this was not a "fatal lack

846 European Union's appellant's submission, paras. 340-347.

847 Panel Report, para. 7.448.

of evidence" under Article 6.5.[848] In the Panel's view, the reason for the confidential treatment provided in the complaint, that the retaliation could be carried out by customers who also bought products from Chinese producers, "substantiated their assertion to a certain degree by explaining the circumstances which they thought showed that commercial retaliation could happen".[849] The Panel stated that "unless there is some reason to believe that the fear of retaliation is unreasonable, unfounded, or untrue—and China has proffered none—we consider that the allegation of the complainants in this case is a sufficient basis for the Commission's conclusion."[850] The Panel therefore concluded that the European Union had not acted inconsistently with Article 6.5 when it treated the complainants' identity as confidential based on their allegation of potential commercial retaliation.[851]

578. On appeal, China argues that the Panel erred in finding that the "potential commercial retaliation" alleged by the complainants satisfied the "good cause" requirement of Article 6.5. China claims that the commercial retaliation asserted by the complainants was not sufficient to constitute "good cause", because it was "merely hypothetical".[852] China further submits that the complainants failed to provide any evidence to support the assertion of potential commercial retaliation contained in the complaint.[853] Moreover, China claims that the Panel erred in the interpretation of Article 6.5, and acted inconsistently with Article 11 of the DSU, when it shifted the burden to China to show that the complainants' assertion of potential commercial retaliation was "unfounded, unreasonable, or untrue".[854] China contends that it demonstrated that this assertion was unfounded when it argued that the same producers' identity were in fact disclosed as sampled producers in the context of the Commission's injury determination.[855] Finally, should the Appellate Body find that no "good cause" existed to treat the identity of the complainants and supporters as confidential under Article 6.5, China asks the Appellate Body to complete the analysis under Articles 6.2 and 6.4 of the *Anti-Dumping Agreement* and find that the European Union's failure to disclose the identity of the complainants and supporters was also inconsistent with these provisions.[856]

579. In response, the European Union argues that China's claim ignores the fact that the purpose of protecting confidential information under Article 6.5 is to ensure that any adverse consequences resulting from the disclosure of sensitive information remain hypothetical.[857] According to the European Union, the Panel did not rely on a "mere assertion", but evaluated the evidence in the light

848 Panel Report, para. 7.453.
849 *Ibid.*
850 *Ibid.*
851 Panel Report, para. 7.455.
852 China's other appellant's submission, paras. 450-453.
853 China's other appellant's submission, paras. 458 and 459.
854 China's other appellant's submission, paras. 464-467 (referring to Panel Report, para. 7.453).
855 China's other appellant's submission, paras. 471-477.
856 China's other appellant's submission, paras. 482-488.
857 European Union's appellee's submission, para. 371.

of the specific justification given.[858] In addition, the European Union points out that the claim China raises under Article 11 of the DSU was not included in its Notice of Other Appeal, and that it is therefore not properly before the Appellate Body.[859] In any event, the European Union asserts that the Panel did not err in shifting the burden of proof to China, because, having brought the claim before the Panel, it was up to China to make out a *prima facie* case of inconsistency.[860] Regarding the disclosure of the identity of the sampled producers later in the investigation, the European Union contends that China's claim relates to the Panel's weighing of the evidence, and therefore should have been brought under Article 11 of the DSU, which China did not do.[861] On the substance of the argument, the European Union counters that not all of the sampled producers were supporters of the complaint, and that the sampled producers that merely cooperated in the investigation did not face the same risks in having their identity disclosed as the complainants.[862]

580. As a preliminary matter, we address the European Union's challenge that China's claim under Article 11 of the DSU in relation to the Panel's finding that "good cause" had been shown for the confidential treatment by the Commission of the complainants' identity is not properly before us because that claim was not mentioned in China's Notice of Other Appeal. China contends that the language of its Notice of Other Appeal was sufficient to notify the European Union of the nature of China's claim despite the absence of an explicit listing of Article 11 of the DSU in this respect. China further observes that, under the new *Working Procedures* that entered into force on 15 September 2010, the Notice of Other Appeal and the other appellant's submission are filed on the same day. Therefore, any doubt about whether a claim was raised in China's Notice of Other Appeal would have been easily dispelled by its other appellant's submission.[863]

581. We are not convinced by China's arguments. Rules 20(2)(d)(ii) and 23(2)(c)(ii)(B) of the *Working Procedures* require a participant to include in its Notice of Appeal or Notice of Other Appeal "a list of the legal provision(s) of the covered agreements that the panel is alleged to have erred in interpreting or applying". The Appellate Body has recognized the due process function that a Notice of Appeal fulfils, emphasizing:

> ... the important balance that must be maintained between the right of Members to exercise the right of appeal meaningfully and effectively, and the right of appellees to receive notice through the Notice of

---

858 European Union's appellee's submission, para. 375 (referring to China's other appellant's submission, para. 462).
859 European Union's appellee's submission, para. 362.
860 European Union's appellee's submission, para. 378.
861 European Union's appellee's submission, para. 363.
862 European Union's appellee's submission, para. 385.
863 China's responses to questioning at the oral hearing.

> Appeal of the findings under appeal, so that they may exercise their right of defence effectively.[864]

582. If an appellee is not notified of the claims raised by the appellant or other appellant in the Notice of Appeal or Other Appeal, those claims are not properly within the scope of the appeal, and the Appellate Body will not make findings thereon.[865] China failed to list Article 11 of the DSU in its Notice of Other Appeal with regard to the confidential treatment of the identity of the complainants and supporters of the complaint, and we therefore find that this claim under Article 11 is not properly before us. Thus, absent a claim under Article 11 of the DSU, we are not called upon to evaluate whether the Panel made an objective assessment of the facts or to examine the Panel's weighing of the evidence before it.

583. We recall that, in addition to its claim under Article 11, which we find to be outside the scope of our review, China also raises the following four arguments as to why the Panel erred in finding that confidential treatment of the identity of the complainants and supporters of the complaint was not inconsistent with Article 6.5 of the *Anti-Dumping Agreement*. First, China alleges that the Panel relied upon the hypothetical character of commercial retaliation that "could" happen, rather than that "would" happen.[866] Second, China argues that the Panel relied on a mere assertion contained in the complaint, and did not require any evidence in support of this assertion.[867] Third, China maintains that the Panel shifted the burden to China to show that the assertion contained in the complaint was "unfounded, unreasonable, or untrue".[868] Fourth, China asserts that the Panel erroneously rejected China's argument that the later disclosure of the complainants' and supporters' identity as sampled producers undermined the allegation that "good cause" existed for the non-disclosure of the identity of the same producers as complainants.[869]

584. On this basis, we do not understand China to argue that "commercial retaliation" may not constitute a "good cause" justification for confidential treatment. In this respect, we agree with the Panel that "nothing in Article 6.5 ... would exclude potential commercial retaliation from constituting good cause for the confidential treatment of any information, including the identity of complainants", and China does not challenge this finding.[870]

585. Rather, we understand China to argue that the Commission erred in concluding that a showing of "good cause" was made by the complainants and that the Panel erred in upholding the Commission's conclusion. We have set out

---

[864] Appellate Body Report, *US – Countervailing Measures on Certain EC Products*, para. 62.

[865] See Appellate Body Report, *US – Countervailing Measures on Certain EC Products*, para. 72; Appellate Body Reports, *EC – Bananas III (Article 21.5 – Ecuador II)/EC – Bananas III (Article 21.5 – US)*, para. 285; and Appellate Body Report, *Japan – Apples*, paras. 124-128.

[866] China's other appellant's submission, para. 454.

[867] China's other appellant's submission, para. 455.

[868] China's other appellant's submission, para. 464 (referring to Panel Report, para. 7.453).

[869] China's other appellant's submission, para. 471.

[870] Panel Report, para. 7.452.

above that the standard of "good cause" requires that a balance be struck between the proprietary interests of those seeking protection of information and the transparency and due process that should be accorded to parties that require access to information to defend their interests. On the basis of this test, it is for the investigating authority to strike that balance and to make an objective determination of whether "good cause" has been shown. Based on this test, a panel may review such a determination on the basis of relevant facts and legal arguments. Thus, China's appeal requires us to examine whether the Panel, in reviewing the Commission's determination, made an error in its legal interpretation of Article 6.5 or incorrectly applied Article 6.5 to the ascertained facts on record in this case. With this in mind, we turn to review China's four arguments set out above.

586. First, China contends that a party requesting confidential treatment must demonstrate that potential commercial retaliation "would" happen if the information was disclosed, and it is insufficient merely to show that such retaliation "could" happen. The question before us, therefore, is whether the Panel made an error in the interpretation and application of Article 6.5 because a request to treat information as confidential requires a demonstration that disclosure "would" give rise to the potential for retaliation, and not simply that it "could" do so.

587. As we have found above, "good cause" can be shown when the party requesting confidential treatment demonstrates the risk of a potential adverse consequence. The purpose of granting confidential treatment in this situation is "precisely to make sure that the feared adverse effect, in this case 'potential commercial retaliation', remains hypothetical, and does not actually materialize".[871] We consider that China's argument that the complainants had to demonstrate that potential commercial retaliation "would" happen—rather than "could" happen—mistakes the nature of the inquiry. Rather, China's claim relates to the gravity and likelihood of the risk of the occurrence of potential commercial retaliation that a complainant alleges, which is a question of degree. We do not consider that the degree of risk of commercial retaliation is an issue of law. The degree of risk does not define what constitutes "good cause" within the meaning of Article 6.5. Nor do we consider the degree of risk to be an application of the "good cause" standard to ascertained facts. Rather, it is a matter relevant to the extent and nature of the evidence required by an investigating authority to support a showing of "good cause". In reviewing the authority's determination of "good cause", the Panel's assessment of the likelihood that commercial retaliation will occur goes to the Panel's weighing of the evidence. Thus, we consider that China's challenge is directed at the Panel's assessment of whether the kind and extent of evidence before the Commission was sufficient for the Commission to have reached the conclusion that a showing of "potential commercial retaliation" as "good cause" had been made.

588. Absent a claim that the Panel failed to conduct an objective assessment of the facts, this is not a matter to be reviewed by us on appeal. The level of risk and, more particularly, the likelihood or probability that such risk may come

---

[871] Panel Report, para. 7.453.

about are matters of degree and must be assessed on the facts, and the Panel conducted such an assessment in reaching its finding. No claim under Article 11 of the DSU has been properly raised on appeal, and therefore the question before us is whether the Panel made an error of legal interpretation or application. No such error, however, has been demonstrated. Consequently, this factual determination by the Panel warrants no interference by us.

589. Second, with regard to China's claim that the Panel relied on a mere assertion in reaching its finding, we recall that the Panel noted that the complainants alleged in the complaint that confidential treatment of the complainants' and supporters' identity was necessary because retaliation "could be carried out by some of their Customers who also buy products directly from P.R. China".[872] According to the Panel, "'potential commercial retaliation' is not a sufficiently concrete phenomenon that evidence of its existence is likely to be obtainable".[873] The Panel considered that the Commission could rely on the factual circumstance of having customers in common with Chinese suppliers who might be negatively affected by the complainants' actions as evidence of a risk of commercial retaliation. The Panel went on to state that, "unless there is some reason to believe that the fear of retaliation is unreasonable, unfounded or untrue—and China has proffered none—we consider that the allegation of the complainants in this case is a sufficient basis for the Commission's conclusion".[874] The Panel concluded that "China [did] not contest the factual assertion that some of the customers of the complainants and the supporters of the application also bought the subject product from Chinese producers."[875] The Panel found that, "by stating that their customers were also themselves importers of the subject product from China, the complainants substantiated their assertion to a certain degree by explaining the circumstances which they thought showed that commercial retaliation could happen."[876]

590. We do not believe that the Panel, in making these findings, misinterpreted Article 6.5 of the *Anti-Dumping Agreement* or misapplied the correct interpretation of that provision to the ascertained facts before it. Rather, the Panel found that the assertion contained in the complaint demonstrated "good cause" for treating the complainants' identity confidential, because potential commercial retaliation could occur due to the uncontested fact that the complainants had customers in common with Chinese suppliers. Moreover, we do not think that China's argument is directed at whether the Panel erred in its interpretation of Article 6.5 or application of that provision to the facts of the case. Rather, China's argument that the Panel relied on this "mere assertion"[877] in reaching its finding concerns the Panel's weighing of the evidence before it. Yet, as stated

872 Panel Report, para. 7.448 (quoting European Industrial Fasteners Institute (EIFI), Complaint against Imports of Carbon Steel Fasteners from China, 24 September 2007 (Panel Exhibit CHN-15)).
873 Panel Report, para. 7.453.
874 *Ibid.*
875 Panel Report, para. 7.452.
876 Panel Report, para, 7.453.
877 China's other appellant's submission, para. 455.

above, we are not called upon to assess whether the Panel exceeded its authority as the trier of facts in reviewing the Commission's decision to keep the identity of the complainants and supporters confidential, because no claim under Article 11 of the DSU has properly been raised in this respect.

591. Third, China argues that the Panel shifted the burden to China to show that the assertion contained in the complaint was "unfounded, unreasonable, or untrue".[878] We recall that, before the Panel, China claimed that the European Union had acted inconsistently with Article 6.5 by accepting the assertion of "potential commercial retaliation" in the complainants' request as a sufficient showing of "good cause" for the confidential treatment of their identity. In raising this claim before the Panel, it was for China to make out a *prima facie* case that no "good cause" had been demonstrated by the complainants, and that the Commission's decision to grant the complainants' request to treat their identity as confidential was inconsistent with Article 6.5. The Panel did not err, therefore, in asking China to present legal and factual arguments to substantiate its claim that "good cause" was not shown, or, as the Panel put it, China had to show that the complainants' assertion of potential commercial retaliation was "unreasonable, unfounded, or untrue".[879] We thus do not find that the Panel shifted the burden of proof to China by requesting it to do so. As described above, the Panel reviewed the Commission's determination, and explained why it considered that the complainants' assertion of "potential commercial retaliation" provided a sufficient showing of "good cause" for confidential treatment of the complainants' identity. In our view, the thrust of China's challenge regarding these findings is again directed mainly at the Panel's weighing of the evidence. As no claim under Article 11 of the DSU has been properly raised in this regard, we decline to examine further these findings of the Panel.

592. Finally, we recall that the Panel rejected China's argument that the disclosure of the identity of the complainants and supporters as sampled producers undermined the allegation that "good cause" existed for the non-disclosure of the identity of the same producers or supporters. China's argument on appeal relies on its challenge of the Panel's finding under Article 4.1 of the *Anti-Dumping Agreement* that the domestic industry from which the sampled producers were drawn were *not all* complainants or supporters of the complaint, because the view of at least one of the sampled producers regarding support or opposition to the complaint was unknown to the Commission.[880] We have found above that the Panel did not err in finding that at least one producer who did not affirmatively state support for the complaint was included in the domestic industry and selected for the sample.[881] Therefore, China's contention that all producers included in the sample were complainants or supporters of the complaint has not been established before the Panel, nor did the Panel make a factual finding to that effect. Hence, we also do not agree that the disclosure of the identity of the

[878] China's other appellant's submission, para. 464 (referring to Panel Report, para. 7.453).
[879] Panel Report, para. 7.453.
[880] See *supra*, para. 451.
[881] See *supra*, para. 452.

sampled producers demonstrates, as China contends, that no "good cause" was shown for keeping the identity of the complainants and supporters confidential. Moreover, we find again that China's challenge concerns the Panel's factual findings and its weighing of the evidence. We recall that China did not properly raise a claim under Article 11 of the DSU with respect to the Panel's disposition of its argument that the later disclosure of the complainants' identity as sampled producers undermined the allegation that "good cause" existed for the non-disclosure of their identity as complainants. Moreover, China has not pointed to any specific error in the Panel's legal interpretation or application of Article 6.5 to the facts of the case. We therefore decline to address further China's argument in this regard.

593. Based on the foregoing, we *uphold* the Panel's finding, in paragraph 7.455 of the Panel Report, that the European Union did not act inconsistently with its obligations under Article 6.5 of the *Anti-Dumping Agreement* when the Commission granted the request to treat the identity of the complainants and supporters as confidential.[882]

F. *Whether China's Claim under Articles 6.2 and 6.4 of the Anti-Dumping Agreement Regarding the Non-Disclosure of the Identity of the Complainants Was within the Panel's Terms of Reference*

594. The European Union appeals the Panel's finding that China's claims under Articles 6.2 and 6.4 of the *Anti-Dumping Agreement* with respect to the non-disclosure of the identity of the complainants and supporters were within the Panel's terms of reference.[883] The European Union raises this procedural challenge in its Notice of Appeal independently of China's substantive claims in its Notice of Other Appeal that the confidential treatment of the identity of the complainants and supporters is inconsistent with Article 6.5. The European Union appeals the Panel's terms of reference finding notwithstanding the fact that the Panel subsequently found that the confidential treatment of the complainants' identity was not inconsistent with Article 6.5 and that, as a consequence, the European Union had not acted inconsistently with Article 6.2 or 6.4.[884]

595. As we have discussed above, Article 6.2 of the DSU requires a complaining party to identify in its panel request the specific measure at issue and provide

---

[882] China requests us to complete the analysis under Articles 6.2 and 6.4 of the *Anti-Dumping Agreement* regarding the alleged failure to disclose the identity of the complainants only if we reverse the Panel's finding under Article 6.5 that a "good cause" showing of "potential commercial retaliation" had been made. Having upheld this finding of the Panel under Article 6.5, we consider China's request for completion of the analysis under Articles 6.2 and 6.4 moot.

[883] European Union's appellant's submission, para. 361 (referring to Panel Report, para. 7.458).

[884] The Panel reached this finding because information that is properly treated as confidential under Article 6.5 is not subject to the requirement in Article 6.4 to provide timely opportunities for all interested parties to see all information that is relevant to the presentation of their cases. Moreover, the Panel found that the requirement in Article 6.2 that interested parties have a full opportunity for the defence of their interests throughout the anti-dumping investigation is also conditional upon the need to preserve confidentiality.

a brief summary of the legal basis of the complaint, sufficient to "*present the problem clearly*".[885] If a party fails in its panel request to "present the problem clearly", the claim in question is outside the panel's jurisdiction, and cannot be heard.

596. China's panel request states that the Definitive Regulation was inconsistent with:

> ... Articles 6.2 and 6.4 of the [*Anti-Dumping Agreement*] and paragraph 151(c)(e) of the *Working Party Report on the Accession of China* because the EC failed to ensure throughout the investigation to Chinese producers/exporters the full opportunity for the defence of their interests and failed to provide timely opportunities for them to see all information that is relevant to the presentation of their cases, including, but not limited to the composition of the domestic industry, data concerning normal value determination, information on the adjustments for differences affecting price comparability, Eurostat data on the basis of which are based the total EC production and EC consumption figures.[886]

China's panel request contains four claims under Articles 6.2 and 6.4 of the *Anti-Dumping Agreement* relating to: (i) the composition of the domestic industry; (ii) data concerning normal value determination; (iii) information on the adjustments for differences affecting price comparability; and (iv) Eurostat data on which total EU production and consumption figures are based.

597. We find that China's claim regarding the disclosure of the identity of the complainants and supporters does not fall within the scope of any of the four above descriptions. The Panel did not find otherwise, but considered that China's panel request should not be read as being limited to the specific descriptions contained in the request because they are preceded by the phrase "including, but not limited to".[887] The Appellate Body has previously found, however, that this phrase cannot operate to include any and all other claims not specifically in-

---

[885] Emphasis added. As we have also stated above, the panel request "establishes and delimits the jurisdiction of the panel" and also serves the important due process objective of notifying the respondent of the nature of the case it must defend. (Appellate Body Report, *EC and certain member States – Large Civil Aircraft*, para. 640. See Appellate Body Report, *US – Carbon Steel*, para. 126 (referring to Appellate Body Report, *Brazil – Desiccated Coconut*, p. 22, DSR 1997:I, 167, at 186; also Appellate Body Report, *EC – Chicken Cuts*, para. 155; and Appellate Body Report, *US – Zeroing (Japan) (Article 21.5 – Japan)*, para. 108)) This request must be examined as it existed at the time of submission and, if deficiencies exist, they cannot be cured through the examination of the party's subsequent submissions. (Appellate Body Report, *EC and certain member States – Large Civil Aircraft*, para. 642; Appellate Body Report, *EC – Bananas III*, para. 143; Appellate Body Report, *US – Carbon Steel*, para. 127)

[886] China's panel request (Panel Report, Annex G, p. G-9).

[887] Panel Report, para. 7.458.

cluded in the request.[888] Rather, each claim must be presented in a manner that "presents the problem clearly" within the meaning of Article 6.2 of the DSU. China emphasizes the distinction between "claims" and "arguments", and asserts that the above descriptions represent "arguments" that need not be included in a panel request at all pursuant to Article 6.2. This, however, does not mean that the mere listing of Articles 6.2 and 6.4 of the *Anti-Dumping Agreement*, without more, succeeded in "present[ing] the problem clearly" in respect of the alleged failure to disclose the identity of the complainants and the supporters of the complaint.

598. Therefore, we disagree with the Panel that the "nature" of the obligations in Articles 6.2 and 6.4 of the *Anti-Dumping Agreement* is such that a complaining party need only list these Articles in order to satisfy the requirements in Article 6.2 of the DSU to "provide a brief summary of the legal basis of the complaint sufficient to present the problem clearly", and to notify the respondent and third parties of the nature of the case raised. We are of the view that the obligations contained in Articles 6.2 and 6.4 of the *Anti-Dumping Agreement* are relatively broad in scope and apply on a continuous basis throughout an investigation. The variety of claims contained in the panel request itself attests to this fact. It may be possible in some circumstances to refer to the initial written submissions of the parties to clarify the meaning of the terms used in a panel request. In this case, however, we do not believe that China's claim under Articles 6.2 and 6.4 challenging the non-disclosure of the complainants' and supporters' identity can be read into the terms actually used in the panel request by recourse to clarification found in China's submissions.

599. We therefore *reverse* the Panel's finding, in paragraph 7.458 of the Panel Report, that China's claims under Articles 6.2 and 6.4 of the *Anti-Dumping Agreement* regarding the non-disclosure of the identity of the complainants and the supporters of the complaint were within the Panel's terms of reference. As a consequence, we declare moot the Panel's subsequent finding, in paragraph 7.459 of the Panel Report, that the European Union did not act inconsistently with Articles 6.2 and 6.4 of the *Anti-Dumping Agreement* by not disclosing the identity of the complainants and the supporters of the complaint.

IX. TIME-LIMIT FOR SUBMISSION OF THE MET/IT CLAIM FORM

600. We turn now to address China's appeal of the Panel's finding that the "Market Economy Treatment and/or Individual Treatment Claim Form" (the "MET/IT Claim Form") in the fasteners investigation was not subject to the 30-day period for reply provided in Article 6.1.1 of the *Anti-Dumping Agreement*. To provide the relevant background, we recall that, when an anti-dumping investigation involves an NME, the European Union applies an alternative method for calculating normal value, pursuant to Article 2(7) of the Basic AD Regulation,

888 Appellate Body Report, *India – Patents (US)*, para. 90.

using data from a market economy third country or using a constructed value and also calculates a country-wide anti-dumping duty for all exporters pursuant to Article 9(5) of the Basic AD Regulation.[889] However, if they satisfy certain criteria, NME exporters can individually establish that they operate under market conditions (under the "MET test"), or, in the alternative, that their export prices are free from State intervention (under the "IT test").[890] If an exporter satisfies the MET test, both normal value and export price will be calculated based on its own domestic sales data, and it will receive an individual dumping margin and individual duty, thereby receiving the same treatment as market economy exporters.[891] If an exporter does not fulfil the MET test, but satisfies the IT test, its dumping margin will be calculated based on a comparison of an alternative normal value calculation and that particular exporter's export price, such that it will receive an individual dumping margin and duty rather than a country-wide duty.[892] For purposes of determining what kind of treatment NME exporters will receive during the investigation, the Commission distributes to each exporter a single form entitled "Market Economy Treatment and/or Individual Treatment Claim Form" (the MET/IT Claim Form). The Commission distributed these forms in the fasteners investigation, and gave Chinese producers 15 days from the date of publication of the Notice of Initiation of the investigation to complete them.[893]

601. China argued before the Panel that the European Union acted inconsistently with Article 6.1.1 of the *Anti-Dumping Agreement* because the Commission failed to allow the Chinese exporters and producers at least 30 days to complete the MET/IT Claim Forms, counted one week from the date on which they were sent out by the investigating authority. The Panel rejected China's claim. It found that the 30-day period stipulated in Article 6.1.1 applies only to "questionnaires", which it defined as "the initial comprehensive questionnaire issued in an anti-dumping investigation to each of the interested parties by an investigating authority at or following the initiation of an investigation, which ... seeks information as to all relevant issues pertaining to the main questions that will need to be decided (dumping, injury and causation)".[894] The Panel examined the MET/IT Claim Form and concluded that the form was not a "questionnaire" within the meaning of Article 6.1.1, and that the European Union was not obliged to give producers at least 30 days for its submission.[895]

602. On appeal, China claims that the Panel erred in its interpretation of the term "questionnaires" in Article 6.1.1 of the *Anti-Dumping Agreement*, as well as in its application of this interpretation to the MET/IT Claim Form. China argues

889 Panel Report, para. 7.47.
890 See *supra*, section IV.B of this Report for a detailed description of the MET and IT tests contained in the Basic AD Regulation.
891 Panel Report, para. 7.47.
892 Panel Report, paras. 7.48 and 7.49.
893 Panel Report, para. 7.567.
894 Panel Report, para. 7.574.
895 Panel Report, para. 7.577.

that the proper interpretation of the term "questionnaires" covers all "information requests ... which are so substantial that they deserve verifications being carried out and [which] do not prevent the investigating authorities from complying with the time-frames set out in the [*Anti-Dumping Agreement*]".[896] In the alternative, if the Appellate Body upholds the Panel's interpretation of the term "questionnaires", China argues that the Panel acted inconsistently with Article 11 of the DSU and Article 17.6 of the *Anti-Dumping Agreement* when it found that the MET/IT Claim Form did not fall within its definition of that term.[897]

603. The European Union requests the Appellate Body to uphold the Panel's interpretation of Article 6.1.1 of the *Anti-Dumping Agreement* and argues that China's interpretation "would make the meaning of the term 'questionnaires' arbitrary and dependent on a case-by-case analysis".[898] The European Union also argues that the Panel's determination that the MET/IT Claim Form was not a "questionnaire" for purposes of Article 6.1.1 was correct, because the MET/IT Claim Form is narrow in scope and serves a different purpose from "the initial comprehensive questionnaire" distributed in an anti-dumping investigation.[899] The European Union further submits that China's claims under Article 11 of the DSU and Article 17.6 of the *Anti-Dumping Agreement* are not properly before the Appellate Body because they are not included in China's Notice of Other Appeal.[900]

604. As a preliminary matter, we agree that China's Notice of Other Appeal does not explicitly mention claims under Article 11 of the DSU and Article 17.6 of the *Anti-Dumping Agreement*[901] in connection with its claim that the Panel erred in its application of Article 6.1.1 of the *Anti-Dumping Agreement*. In its Notice of Other Appeal, China "seeks review of the Panel's conclusions and findings concerning China's claim that the European Union violated Article 6.1.1 of the [*Anti-Dumping Agreement*]". China asserts that "the Panel erred in its interpretation of the term 'questionnaire' in Article 6.1.1", and that "even assuming that the Panel did not err in its interpretation of the term 'questionnaire' ... the Panel erroneously concluded that the MET/IT claim form was not a 'questionnaire' according to this definition". China also requests the Appellate Body "to reverse the Panel's findings and to conclude that the 'MET/IT claim form' is a questionnaire within the meaning of Article 6.1.1 of the [*Anti-Dumping Agreement*] and to complete the analysis by finding that the [European Union] violated Article 6.1.1 of the [*Anti-Dumping Agreement*]".

---

[896] China's other appellant's submission, para. 538.
[897] China's other appellant's submission, para. 544.
[898] European Union's appellee's submission, para. 418.
[899] European Union's appellee's submission, para. 429.
[900] European Union's appellee's submission, para. 405.
[901] We note that the European Union has not raised this challenge in its appellee's submission, but we recall that matters going to the jurisdiction of a panel are fundamental and can therefore be raised at any stage in a proceeding. (See Appellate Body Report, *EC and certain Member States – Large Civil Aircraft*, para. 791; and Appellate Body Report, *US – Carbon Steel*, para. 123)

605. Accordingly, it is clear from the face of the Notice of Other Appeal that this ground of China's other appeal was raised only under Article 6.1.1 of the *Anti-Dumping Agreement*. As discussed above[902], under Rules 20(2)(d)(ii) and 23(2)(c)(ii) of the *Working Procedures*, only claims under those provisions of the covered agreements specifically listed in a Notice of Appeal or Other Appeal are properly raised on appeal. Therefore, as China's claims under Article 11 of the DSU and Article 17.6 of the *Anti-Dumping Agreement* regarding the MET/IT Claim Form were not included in its Notice of Other Appeal, we decline to make findings upon them. We proceed next to address the remaining issues raised in China's other appeal under Article 6.1.1 of the *Anti-Dumping Agreement*.

606. Articles 6.1 and 6.1.1 of the *Anti-Dumping Agreement* read as follows:

> 6.1 All interested parties in an anti-dumping investigation shall be given notice of the information which the authorities require and ample opportunity to present in writing all evidence which they consider relevant in respect of the investigation in question.
>
> 6.1.1 Exporters or foreign producers receiving questionnaires used in an anti-dumping investigation shall be given at least 30 days for reply.[*] Due consideration should be given to any request for an extension of the 30-day period and, upon cause shown, such an extension should be granted whenever practicable.
>
> [* original footnote 15] As a general rule, the time-limit for exporters shall be counted from the date of receipt of the questionnaire, which for this purpose shall be deemed to have been received one week from the date on which it was sent to the respondent or transmitted to the appropriate diplomatic representative of the exporting Member or, in the case of a separate customs territory Member of the WTO, an official representative of the exporting territory.

607. The Panel began its interpretation of the term "questionnaires" in Article 6.1.1 by referring to a dictionary definition, namely "a formulated series of questions by which information is sought from a selected group".[903] The Panel determined that this definition "[did] not suffice to answer the question before [it]", because applying such a definition "could make it impossible for the authorities to obtain necessary information while still respecting the time limits on investigation set forth in Article 5.10 of the [*Anti-Dumping Agreement*]".[904]

---

[902] See *supra*, paras. 581 and 582.

[903] Panel Report, para. 7.571 (quoting *The New Shorter Oxford English Dictionary*, 4th edn, L. Brown (ed.) (Clarendon Press, 1993), Vol. 2, p. 2447).

[904] Panel Report, para. 7.571.

608. The Panel went on to analyze the context of the term "questionnaires" in Article 6.1.1 provided by other provisions of the *Anti-Dumping Agreement* that contain the term, including Annex I on Procedures for On-the-Spot Investigations Pursuant to Paragraph 7 of Article 6.[905] Annex I states, in paragraphs 6 and 7 respectively, that "[v]isits to explain the questionnaire should only be made at the request of an exporting firm" and that such visits "should be carried out after the response to the questionnaire has been received". The Panel found that these references suggest that "'the questionnaire' is a substantial enough information request to warrant a visit to verify the information", "that it is sent early in the investigation", and that a verification visit is "a significant event" not likely to be repeated with respect to multiple "questionnaires".[906] In addition to Annex I, the Panel also emphasized the use of the singular form of the term in footnote 15 of Article 6.1.1, which states that "the time-limit for *exporters* shall be counted from the date of receipt of *the* questionnaire".[907] The Panel opined that, if the drafters had intended the obligation in Article 6.1.1 to apply to more than one questionnaire, they might have used a plural or indefinite formulation in the footnote, such as, "'any' or 'a' 'questionnaire'".[908] Instead, in the Panel's view, the language of the footnote suggests that a single questionnaire is sent to each recipient. The Panel found that the term "questionnaires" in the first sentence of Article 6.1.1 refers to:

> ... one kind of document in an investigation. Turning to the question of what that document might be, we note that the considerations of context ... suggest that it refers to the initial comprehensive questionnaire issued in an anti-dumping investigation to each of the interested parties by an investigating authority at or following the initiation of an investigation, which questionnaire seeks information as to all relevant issues pertaining to the main questions that will need to be decided (dumping, injury and causation).[*]
>
> [* original footnote 1123] We recognize that there may be differences in the initial comprehensive questionnaires sent to the different interested parties, reflecting their different activities and interests in the investigation. Moreover, depending on how a Member organizes the conduct of anti-dumping investigations, there may be separate and distinct initial questionnaires concerning the issues of dumping and injury and causation. These circumstances do not affect our fundamental conclusion, that the ini-

905 Panel Report, para. 7.572 (quoting Panel Report, *Egypt – Steel Rebar*, para. 7.276).
906 Panel Report, footnote 1122 to para. 7.574.
907 Panel Report, para. 7.573. (emphasis added by the Panel)
908 Panel Report, para. 7.573.

> tial comprehensive document, or set of documents, covering all of these issues are encompassed by the term "questionnaires" in Article 6.1.1.[909]

609. The question before us is whether the Panel erred in defining the term "questionnaires" in Article 6.1.1 in this manner. The interpretation of Article 6.1.1 requires that the provision be read in its proper context, in particular Article 6.1, which it follows. Article 6.1 states that "[a]ll interested parties in an anti-dumping investigation shall be given notice of the information which the authorities require and ample opportunity to present in writing all evidence which they consider relevant in respect of the investigation in question." Article 6.1 thus requires an investigating authority to give interested parties: (i) notice of the information the authority requires; and (ii) "ample opportunity" to present their evidence in writing. Where a specific request for information is made by an investigating authority, what constitutes "ample opportunity" to respond will depend upon the specific nature and scope of the request.[910] Along with Article 6.2 of the *Anti-Dumping Agreement*, the Appellate Body has found that the language in Article 6.1 provides for the "fundamental due process rights" of interested parties in an anti-dumping investigation.[911] Together, these provisions "suggest there should be liberal opportunities for respondents to defend their interests".[912]

610. Read in this context, Article 6.1.1 is concerned with the circumstance in which "[e]xporters or foreign producers" are asked to complete "questionnaires", and requires the investigating authority to allow these responding parties at least 30 days from the date of receipt to submit responses. Domestic producers can control the timing of the submission of a request for initiation of an anti-dumping investigation because it is their complaint that triggers the authority's investigative process. The complaining producers therefore have an opportunity to gather much of the evidence necessary to support their complaint in advance. The responding parties, on the other hand, typically receive no notice until the initiation of the investigation. Article 6.1.1 protects exporters and foreign producers by requiring investigating authorities to provide them with at least 30 days to reply to "questionnaires", and by allowing that extensions should be granted whenever practicable, upon cause shown. This indicates to us that the specific due process interest of exporters and foreign producers to be afforded an ample opportunity to respond has been expressly provided for.[913]

---

909 Panel Report, para. 7.574.

910 See Panel Report, *US – Anti-Dumping and Countervailing Duties (China)*, para. 15.23, where that panel made a similar finding.

911 Appellate Body Report, *US – Oil Country Tubular Goods Sunset Reviews*, para. 241.

912 *Ibid.*

913 Footnote 15 of Article 6.1.1 ensures that foreign exporters receive a full 30 days for completion and submission of the questionnaires, by specifying that this period "shall be counted from the date of receipt of the questionnaire, which for this purpose shall be deemed to have been received one week from the date on which it was sent".

611. The proper interpretation of Article 6.1.1 must also take into considerations the interests of investigating authorities in controlling their investigative process and bringing investigations to a close within a stipulated period of time. Article 5.10 of the *Anti-Dumping Agreement* requires that investigations be completed within 12 months or, in special circumstances, no more than 18 months. In this vein, Article 6.14 of the *Anti-Dumping Agreement* states that none of the procedures set out under Article 6 is intended "to prevent the authorities of a Member from proceeding expeditiously" in reaching their determinations. The balance between a party's "ample opportunity" and the investigating authority's interest in controlling the investigative process was articulated by the Appellate Body in *Mexico – Anti-Dumping Measures on Rice*, where it found that:

> ... the due process rights in Article 6 of the *Anti-Dumping Agreement*—which include the right to 30 days for reply to a questionnaire—"cannot extend indefinitely" but, instead, are limited by the investigating authority's need "to 'control the conduct' of its inquiry and to 'carry out the multiple steps' required to reach a timely completion" of the proceeding. As such, the time-limits for completing an investigation serve to circumscribe the obligation in Article 6.1.1 to provide all interested parties 30 days to reply to a questionnaire.[914] (emphasis omitted; footnotes omitted)

612. Therefore, while Article 6.1.1 captures a specific due process concern as indicated above, the "questionnaires" referred to in that Article do not refer to every request for information made by an investigating authority to exporters or foreign producers. Rather, the "questionnaires" must be substantial requests, distributed early in the investigation, when a 30-day timeframe for the response would not lead to a delay in the completion of the investigation. They afford the investigating authority an early opportunity to solicit relevant information from exporters and foreign producers on key aspects of the investigation that is to be conducted by the authority.

613. Based on these considerations, we conclude that the meaning and scope of the term "questionnaires" in Article 6.1.1 of the *Anti-Dumping Agreement*, and its application to specific kinds of documents, must reflect a balance between the due process requirement to provide parties with an "ample opportunity" to submit all information they consider responsive to a questionnaire request in an anti-dumping investigation, and the overall timeframe imposed on the investigation under Article 5.10, along with the need for authorities to proceed expeditiously as contemplated in Article 6.14. We therefore find that the "questionnaires" referred to in Article 6.1.1 are a particular type of

---

[914] Appellate Body Report, *Mexico – Anti-Dumping Measures on Rice*, para. 282. See also Appellate Body Report, *US – Oil Country Tubular Goods Sunset Reviews*, paras. 241 and 242; and Appellate Body Report, *US – Hot-Rolled Steel*, para. 73.

document containing substantial requests for information, distributed early in an investigation, and through which the investigating authority solicits a substantial amount of information relating to the key aspects of the investigation that is to be conducted by the authority (that is, dumping, injury, and causation). While in many investigations one "questionnaire" may be employed to solicit such information on these aspects of the investigation, we consider that, depending on how different Members organize the conduct of the investigation process, a party may receive several substantial requests soliciting such comprehensive information that are "questionnaires" within the meaning of Article 6.1.1.

614. Having defined the kind of information requests that qualify as "questionnaires", we now turn to examine the MET/IT Claim Form at issue in this case. The European Commission distributes MET/IT Claim Forms to exporters and foreign producers in countries specified as NMEs under Article 2(7) of its Basic AD Regulation. The form is 14 pages long and contains questions regarding corporate identity and other corporate information, primary materials and other cost components for the product concerned, industrial property rights, labour rights and working conditions, production facilities and production, sales prices, financial statements, and accounting principles and practice. The purpose of the MET/IT Claim Form is to determine whether a particular exporter or producer from an NME country should be treated as a market economy exporter or producer, despite the exporting country's designation as an NME; or, if a particular exporter cannot satisfy this MET test, whether that exporter should nonetheless be granted "individual treatment" in the determination of margins and duties because it is sufficiently independent from the State to satisfy the IT test.[915] The Panel found that questions contained in the MET/IT Claim Form "are not relevant in all investigations, and are not directly related to the determinations of dumping, injury and causation".[916] Rather, the information solicited is necessary for the determination of whether an exporter or foreign producer operates under market economy conditions, or whether its export activities are independent from State intervention.[917]

615. We recall that Article 6.1 of the *Anti-Dumping Agreement* requires investigating authorities to give all interested parties "ample opportunity" to submit evidence that they consider relevant to the investigation, and that this obligation applies also to information requests that cannot be considered "questionnaires". In our view, the determinations made regarding MET and IT treatment are important for NME exporters and foreign producers.[918] The MET/IT Claim Form was the first request for information received by the Chinese exporters in the fasteners investigation, and their responses were subject to verification.[919] While much of the information requested would seem to be readily accessible to the

---

915 European Commission, Market Economy Treatment and/or Individual Treatment Claim Form (MET/IT Claim Form) (Panel Exhibit CHN-72).

916 Panel Report, para. 7.577.

917 Panel Report, para. 7.576.

918 Panel Report, para. 7.577. See *supra*, paras. 600 and 614.

919 Panel Report, para. 7.577.

responding party, the form requests certain production and sales data for "the product concerned" that may need to be collected and reported in a form that is not regularly kept by the company, and could therefore involve a certain amount of time and effort for completion.[920] Given the consequences of MET/IT status for exporters and foreign producers, and the amount of information solicited in the MET/IT Claim Form, we consider that, under the requirements of Article 6.1, a deadline of 15 days from the date of publication of the Notice of Initiation was too short and did not provide parties with "ample opportunity" to submit all evidence in support of their requests for MET or IT treatment. However, China has not invoked Article 6.1 in this case. Rather, China has limited its claim to the specific time period required for the submission of "questionnaires" under Article 6.1.1, and it is under this provision that we are called upon to make findings.

616. In determining whether an information request is a "questionnaire" under Article 6.1.1, as we have defined this term above, an investigating authority must ascertain whether it is a substantial request seeking to elicit from exporters and foreign producers comprehensive information regarding the key aspects of the anti-dumping determination, that is, dumping, injury, and causation. While the length and complexity of the request are not irrelevant, the determination of whether a particular request for information constitutes a "questionnaire" depends on the content and purpose of the request for information.

617. In order to make determinations on the key aspects of dumping, injury, and causation, pursuant to Articles 2 and 3 of the *Anti-Dumping Agreement*, investigating authorities need to collect, among other things, information on exporters' products, domestic and export sales, production and production capacity, cost of production, and factors relevant to adjustments to carry out a fair comparison. The typical anti-dumping questionnaire used by the Commission for exporters therefore solicits information relating to all of these factors. More specifically, the questionnaire solicits information regarding specifications of export and domestic products, comparison of export and domestic products, turnover, total quantity and value of sales, production and capacity statistics, stocks, employment, investments, export sales to related and unrelated customers in the European Union, domestic sales to related and unrelated customers, accounting system and policies, production process and cost of production, allowances on export sales, and allowances on domestic sales.[921]

618. By contrast, the MET/IT Claim Form is employed by the Commission for a different specifically defined purpose: to select those exporters or producers that operate under market economy conditions or that are sufficiently independ-

---

[920] For example, the MET/IT Claim Form requests Chinese exporters to submit monthly production figures for the product concerned, or, if foreign owned, total volume of production during the investigation period, a list of average unit costs of primary materials, and an explanation of how these materials are procured, including a list of suppliers. (See Panel Exhibit CHN-72)

[921] For purposes of this discussion, we refer to the anti-dumping questionnaire sent to exporters and producers of farmed salmon from Norway, which was provided to the Panel by China as Exhibit CHN-63.

ent from the State to justify different treatment from non-qualifying NME exporters or producers. In determining whether an exporter or foreign producer operates under market conditions under the MET test, the Commission examines factors including: (i) the "decisions of firms regarding prices, costs and inputs"; (ii) their accounting standards; (iii) the extent to which production costs are "subject to significant distortions"; (iv) the applicability of "bankruptcy and property laws which guarantee legal certainty and stability"; and (v) whether "exchange rate conversions are carried out at the market rate".[922] In order to establish whether an exporter or foreign producer is sufficiently independent from the State under the IT test, the Commission will determine whether: (i) it is "free to repatriate capital and profits"; (ii) "export prices and quantities, and conditions and terms of sale are freely determined"; (iii) "the majority of the shares belong to private persons"; (iv) "exchange rate conversions are carried out at the market rate"; and (v) "State interference [would] permit circumvention of measures if individual exporters are given different rates of duty".[923]

619. China argues that much of the information solicited in the MET/IT Claim Form is *also* relevant to the determinations of dumping, injury, and causation, and that it is therefore similar enough to the European Union's typical anti-dumping questionnaire discussed above to constitute a "questionnaire" for purposes of Article 6.1.1. However, a comparison of these two information requests shows that a typical anti-dumping questionnaire solicits different information and for a different purpose than the MET/IT Claim Form. The latter form solicits information regarding factors such as what bankruptcy or property laws are applicable, whether companies are free to repatriate capital and profits, or whether the majority of the shares belong to private parties that may be of relevance for determining whether exporters operate independently from the State; however, such information is not relevant for the purpose of determining dumping, injury, or causation.

620. Even where the MET/IT Claim Form and the typical "questionnaire" solicit similar information, that information is used for a different purpose. For example, in making its dumping determination, the Commission examines in detail and on a product-by-product basis, factors such as product specifications, sales, and prices in order to make its comparison between export price and normal value. In order to do so, the Commission collects data from exporters to determine *actual* export quantities and prices, production costs, and capacity.[924]

---

922 Basic AD Regulation, *supra*, footnote 5, Article 2(7)(c).

923 Basic AD Regulation, *supra*, footnote 5, Article 9(5).

924 For example, the typical questionnaire sent by the Commission to exporters in an anti-dumping investigation requests submission of, *inter alia*, total production and purchases of the product concerned, capacity and capacity utilization including how these factors are calculated, the country of origin and specific sources of purchases of the product, descriptions of production lines and major components, and descriptions of the manufacturing process and production facilities used for each product, including the raw materials used, relationship to the supplier, other products manufactured in the same facilities, other companies involved in the manufacturing process, and the number of days the product concerned is on average held in inventory before sale. All product information must be submitted on the basis of PCNs, which the exporter must create "for each unique combination of

621. By contrast, the MET/IT Claim Form requests production information for the different and specific purpose of determining whether "the production costs and financial situation of firms" are "subject to significant distortions", and whether the "decisions" of NME exporters and producers regarding prices, costs, and inputs are "made in response to market signals reflecting supply and demand, and without significant State interference", such that its production costs "substantially reflect market values".[925] If the MET test is not satisfied, the Commission analyzes the production data submitted to determine, under the IT test, whether export prices and quantities "are freely determined"[926] for the purpose of assessing whether the exporter operates independently from the State. The MET/IT Claim Form requests much less detailed information than the typical anti-dumping questionnaire; it requests that exporters submit monthly production figures for the product concerned, or, if foreign owned, total volume of production during the investigation period, a list of average unit costs of primary materials, and an explanation of how these materials are procured, including a list of suppliers.[927] The MET/IT Claim Form does not request this data to be submitted based on narrowly defined PCNs or other product categories, but only requests that it be submitted for the "product concerned". This information could not serve as the basis for the Commission's determination of actual export prices, as required for a dumping determination.

622. In sum, the categories of information solicited by the MET/IT Claim Form relate to the factors used under the MET and IT tests for the purpose of determining whether an exporter operates under market conditions or, if not, whether it operates independently from the State. The factors examined by the Commission, such as restrictions on repatriation of capital and profits, composition of board members and shareholders, and exchange rate conversions[928], are not relevant to the Commission's dumping, injury, and causation determinations. Nor is information solicited in the MET/IT Claim Form regarding restrictions on the import of raw materials used, required business authorizations, and information regarding relevant barter or counter trade[929] relevant to the determinations of dumping, injury, and causation. We conclude that the content of the information requested under the MET/IT Claim Form is qualitatively different from the content of the information requested in a typical anti-dumping questionnaire.[930]

623. Therefore, based on the content of the MET/IT Claim Form and the purpose for which it is used, we find that the MET/IT Claim Form is not an infor-

product characteristics" using a table provided by the Commission. (See Panel Exhibit CHN-63, *supra*, footnote 921)

925 Basic AD Regulation, *supra*, footnote 5, Article 2(7)(c).

926 Basic AD Regulation, *supra*, footnote 5, Article 9(5)(b).

927 MET/IT Claim Form, *supra*, footnote 915, pp. 8 and 10.

928 Basic AD Regulation, *supra*, footnote 5, Article 9(5).

929 MET/IT Claim Form, *supra*, footnote 914, pp. 8, 10, 13, and 14.

930 We find that China's further arguments regarding the length and substantial nature of the request, as well as its importance to Chinese exporters and producers, are similarly unavailing. As we have found above, these factors should be taken into consideration when determining whether a party was given "ample opportunity" to present evidence under Article 6.1.

mation request soliciting from the Chinese exporters and producers a substantial amount of information upon which the Commission would base its determinations regarding the key aspects of an anti-dumping investigation.[931] We therefore *uphold* the Panel's finding, in paragraph 7.579 of the Panel Report, that the MET/IT Claim Form is not a "questionnaire" within the meaning of Article 6.1.1 of the *Anti-Dumping Agreement* and, that, therefore, the European Union did not act inconsistently with its obligations under Article 6.1.1 when it did not provide Chinese exporters with 30 days to submit their responses.

X. FINDINGS AND CONCLUSION

624. For the reasons set out in this Report, the Appellate Body:

(a) with respect to Article 9(5) of the Basic AD Regulation[932]:

(i) *upholds* the Panel's finding, in paragraph 7.77 of the Panel Report, that Article 9(5) of the Basic AD Regulation concerns not only the imposition of anti-dumping duties, but also the calculation of dumping margins, and that it could be challenged "as such" under Article 6.10 of the *Anti-Dumping Agreement*, which addresses the calculation of margins of dumping for each exporter or producer;

(ii) *upholds*, albeit for different reasons, the Panel's finding, in paragraph 7.98 of the Panel Report, that Article 9(5) of the Basic AD Regulation is inconsistent "as such" with Article 6.10 of the *Anti-Dumping Agreement*, because it conditions the determination of individual dumping margins for exporters or producers from NMEs on the fulfilment of the IT test;

(iii) *upholds*, albeit for different reasons, the Panel's finding, in paragraph 7.112 of the Panel Report, that Article 9(5) of the Basic AD Regulation is inconsistent "as such" with Article 9.2 of the *Anti-Dumping Agreement*, because it conditions the imposition of individual duties on exporters or producers from NMEs on the fulfilment of the IT test;

(iv) *finds* that, in making the findings that Article 9(5) of the Basic AD Regulation is inconsistent "as such" with Articles 6.10 and 9.2 of the *Anti-Dumping Agreement*, the Panel did not act inconsistently with Article 11 of the DSU;

(v) *declares moot and of no legal effect* the Panel's finding, in paragraph 7.127 of the Panel Report[933], that Article 9(5) of

[931] Panel Report, para. 7.577.
[932] See also Panel Report, para. 8.2(a).
[933] *Ibid.*

the Basic AD Regulation is inconsistent with the MFN obligation in Article I:1 of the GATT 1994;

(vi) *upholds* the Panel's finding, in paragraph 7.137 of the Panel Report[934], that the European Union has acted inconsistently with Article XVI:4 of the *WTO Agreement* and Article 18.4 of the *Anti-Dumping Agreement* by failing to ensure the conformity of its laws, regulations, and administrative procedures with its obligations under the relevant agreements;

(vii) *upholds* the Panel's finding, in paragraph 7.148 of the Panel Report[935], that Article 9(5) of the Basic AD Regulation is inconsistent with Articles 6.10 and 9.2 of the *Anti-Dumping Agreement* "as applied" in the fasteners investigation;

(b) with respect to the Panel's findings under Articles 4.1 and 3.1 of the *Anti-Dumping Agreement*[936]:

(i) *finds* that the Panel erred in finding, in paragraph 7.230 of the Panel Report, that "the European Union did not act inconsistently with Article 4.1 of the [*Anti-Dumping Agreement*] in defining a domestic industry comprising producers accounting for 27 per cent of total estimated EU production of fasteners" on the basis that the collective output of these producers represented "a major proportion" of the total domestic production;

(ii) *finds* that the Panel did not err in finding, in paragraph 7.241 of the Panel Report, that China failed to establish that the European Union acted inconsistently with Article 3.1 of the *Anti-Dumping Agreement* in the selection of a sample of the domestic industry for purposes of making an injury determination; and

(iii) *finds* that the Panel did not err in its interpretation or application of Articles 4.1 and 3.1 of the *Anti-Dumping Agreement*, or acted inconsistently with Article 11 of the DSU and Article 17.6 of the *Anti-Dumping Agreement*, when finding, in paragraph 7.219 of the Panel Report, that "the mere fact that the domestic industry as ultimately defined does not include any particular proportion of producers expressing different views with respect to the complaint, or producers who did not come forward within the 15 day period, does not demonstrate that the European Union acted inconsistently with Article 4.1 of the [*Anti-Dumping*

---

[934] *Ibid.*

[935] See also Panel Report, para. 8.2(b).

[936] *Ibid.*

Agreement] in defining the domestic industry" or acted inconsistently with Article 3.1 of that Agreement;

(c) with respect to the Panel's findings regarding certain aspects of the dumping determination in the fasteners investigation:

(i) *finds* that the Panel did not err in finding, in paragraph 7.494 of the Panel Report[937], that the European Union violated Article 6.4 of the *Anti-Dumping Agreement* "by not providing a timely opportunity for Chinese producers to see information regarding the product types on the basis of which normal value was established";

(ii) *finds* that the Panel did not err in finding, in paragraph 7.495 of the Panel Report[938], that "the Chinese exporters could not defend their interests in this investigation because the Commission only provided information concerning the product types used in the determination of the normal value at a very late stage of the proceedings" and that, therefore, "the European Union acted inconsistently with Article 6.2" of the *Anti-Dumping Agreement*;

(iii) *finds* that the Panel did not act inconsistently with Article 11 of the DSU in not addressing China's argument that the European Union failed to inform the interested parties of the "product types" it used to compare the export price and normal value;

(iv) *finds* that the Panel erred in its application of Article 2.4 of the *Anti-Dumping Agreement* by failing to take into account the last sentence of Article 2.4 in the light of the relevant facts of the case and of its finding under Article 6.4 of the *Anti-Dumping Agreement*; and *finds*, instead, that, in not disclosing the information on the product types on a timely basis, the European Union acted inconsistently with Article 2.4 of the *Anti-Dumping Agreement* by failing to indicate to the parties in question what information was necessary to ensure a fair comparison;

(v) *finds* that the Panel did not err in its interpretation of Article 2.4 of the *Anti-Dumping Agreement* when finding, in paragraph 7.306 of the Panel Report, that the European Union did not act inconsistently with Article 2.4 of that Agreement by not making adjustments for every element of the PCN;

(vi) *finds* that the Panel did not act inconsistently with Article 11 of the DSU, when finding, in paragraph 7.302 of the

[937] See also Panel Report, para. 8.2(e).

[938] *Ibid.*

Panel Report, that there is no inherent reason to conclude that every element of the PCN necessarily reflects a difference that affects price comparability; and

(vii) *finds* that the Panel did not err in its interpretation and application of Article 2.4 of the *Anti-Dumping Agreement* in finding, in paragraph 7.311 of the Panel Report, that the European Union did not have to make adjustments for alleged quality differences;

(d) with respect to Articles 6.5 and 6.5.1 of the *Anti-Dumping Agreement*:

(i) *upholds* the Panel's findings, in paragraphs 7.516 and 7.517 of the Panel Report[939], that the European Union failed to ensure that the domestic producers, Agrati and Fontana Luigi, provide appropriate statements of the reasons why information provided in confidence was not susceptible of summary;

(ii) *finds* that China's claim under Article 6.5 that the European Union failed to establish that "good cause" existed to support the confidential treatment of information submitted by the analogue country producer participating in the investigation, Pooja Forge, was within the Panel's terms of reference; but *finds* that China failed to substantiate this claim; and therefore

(iii) *reverses* the Panel's finding, in paragraph 7.525 of the Panel Report[940], that the European Union acted inconsistently with its obligations under Article 6.5 with respect to the treatment of confidential information submitted by Pooja Forge; and

(iv) *upholds* the Panel's finding, in paragraph 7.455 of the Panel Report[941], that the European Union did not act inconsistently with its obligations under Article 6.5 when the Commission granted the request to treat the identity of the complainants and the supporters of the complaint as confidential; and

(v) *finds* that China's claim under Article 11 of the DSU regarding the confidential treatment of the identity of the complainants and the supporters of the complaint is not within the scope of this appeal because it was not included in China's Notice of Other Appeal;

---

939 See also Panel Report, para. 8.2(f).

940 *Ibid.*

941 See also Panel Report, para. 8.3(h).

(e) *reverses* the Panel's finding, in paragraph 7.458 of the Panel Report, that China's claims under Articles 6.2 and 6.4 of the *Anti-Dumping Agreement* regarding the non-disclosure of the identity of the complainants were within its terms of reference under Article 6.2 of the DSU; and therefore, declares *moot* the Panel's finding, in paragraph 7.459 of the Panel Report[942], that the European Union did not act inconsistently with Articles 6.2 and 6.4 of the *Anti-Dumping Agreement* by not disclosing the identity of the complainants and the supporters of the complaint; and

(f) with respect to Article 6.1.1 of the *Anti-Dumping Agreement*:

(i) *upholds* the Panel's finding, in paragraph 7.579 of the Panel Report[943], that the "'Market Economy Treatment and/or Individual Treatment claim form' is not a 'questionnaire' within the meaning of Article 6.1.1"; and that, therefore, the European Union did not act inconsistently with its obligations under Article 6.1.1 of the *Anti-Dumping Agreement* when it did not provide the Chinese exporters with 30 days to submit their responses; and

(ii) *finds* that China's claims under Article 11 of the DSU and Article 17.6 of the *Anti-Dumping Agreement* regarding the Market Economy Treatment and/or Individual Treatment Claim Form are not within the scope of this appeal because these claims were not included in China's Notice of Other Appeal.

625. The Appellate Body *recommends* that the DSB request the European Union to bring its measures, found in this Report and in the Panel Report as modified by this Report, to be inconsistent with the *Anti-Dumping Agreement* and the *WTO Agreement*, into conformity with its obligations under those Agreements.

---

942 *Ibid.*

943 See also Panel Report, para. 8.3(k).

ANNEX I

WORLD TRADE ORGANIZATION

WT/DS397/7
29 March 2011
(11-1542)

Original: English

EUROPEAN COMMUNITIES[1] – DEFINITIVE ANTI-DUMPING MEASURES ON CERTAIN IRON OR STEEL FASTENERS FROM CHINA

Notification of an Appeal by the European Union under Article 16.4 and Article 17 of the Understanding on Rules and Procedures Governing the Settlement of Disputes (DSU), and under Rule 20(1) of the Working Procedures for Appellate Review

The following notification, dated 25 March 2011, from the Delegation of the European Union, is being circulated to Members.

Pursuant to Article 16.4 and Article 17.1 of the *DSU* the European Union hereby notifies to the Dispute Settlement Body its decision to appeal to the Appellate Body certain issues of law covered in the Panel Report and certain legal interpretations developed by the Panel in the dispute *European Communities – Definitive Anti-Dumping Measures on Certain Iron or Steel Fasteners from China* (WT/DS397). Pursuant to Rule 20(1) of the *Working Procedures for Ap-*

[1] On 1 December 2009, the Treaty of Lisbon amending the Treaty on European Union and the Treaty establishing the European Community (done at Lisbon, 13 December 2007) entered into force. On 29 November 2009, the WTO received a Verbal Note (WT/L/779) from the Council of the European Union and the Commission of the European Communities stating that, by virtue of the Treaty of Lisbon, as of 1 December 2009, the "European Union" replaces and succeeds the "European Community". On 13 July 2010, the World Trade Organization received a Verbal Note (WT/Let/679) from the Council of the European Union confirming that, with effect from 1 December 2009, the European Union replaced the European Community and assumed all the rights and obligations of the European Community in respect of all Agreements for which the Director-General of the World Trade Organization is the depositary and to which the European Community is a signatory or a contracting party.

pellate Review, the European Union simultaneously files this Notice of Appeal with the Appellate Body Secretariat.

For the reasons to be further elaborated in its submissions to the Appellate Body, the European Union appeals, and requests the Appellate Body to reverse and/or modify the findings, conclusions and recommendations of the Panel, with respect to the following errors of law and legal interpretations contained in the Panel Report.

I. COUNCIL REGULATION NO. 1225/2009 ("THE BASIC AD REGULATION")

The Panel erred in its interpretation and application of Articles 6.10, 9.2 and 18.4 of the *Anti-Dumping Agreement*, Article I:1 of the *GATT 1994* and Article XVI:4 of the *WTO Agreement* and failed to make an objective assessment pursuant to Article 11 of the *DSU* when it concluded that Article 9(5) of the Basic AD Regulation is, as such, inconsistent with those provisions.[2] In particular:

(a) the Panel erred in the application of Article 6.10 of the *Anti-Dumping Agreement* when finding that Article 9(5) of the Basic AD Regulation concerns not only the imposition of anti-dumping duties but also the calculation of margins of dumping.[3] Based on its incorrect understanding of the scope of Article 9(5) of the Basic AD Regulation, the Panel wrongly concluded that Article 9(5) of the Basic AD Regulation, as such, is inconsistent with Article 6.10 of the *Anti-Dumping Agreement*[4];

(b) the Panel erred in the interpretation and application of Article 6.10 of the *Anti-Dumping Agreement* and also violated Article 11 of the *DSU* when finding that Article 9(5) of the Basic AD Regulation is, as such, inconsistent with Article 6.10 of the *Anti-Dumping Agreement* in that it conditions the calculation of individual margins for producers from non-market economy countries on the fulfilment of the Individual Treatment (IT) test[5];

(c) the Panel erred in the interpretation and application of Article 9.2 of the *Anti-Dumping Agreement* and also violated Article 11 of the *DSU* when finding that Article 9(5) of the Basic AD Regulation is, as such, inconsistent with the obligation laid down in Article 9.2 of the *Anti-Dumping Agreement*, which does not allow the imposition of a single country-wide anti-dumping duty in an investigation involving a non-market economy country[6];

---

2 Panel Report, para. 8(2)(a).
3 Panel Report, para. 7.77.
4 Panel Report, para. 7.98.
5 Panel Report, paras. 7.96 and 7.98.
6 Panel Report, para. 7.112 and footnote 278.

(d) the Panel erred in the interpretation and application of Article I:1 of the *GATT 1994* and also violated Article 11 of the *DSU* when finding that Article 9(5) of the Basic AD Regulation violates the MFN obligation of Article I:1 of the *GATT 1994*.[7] Moreover, the Panel erred when concluding that the *Anti-Dumping Agreement* does not allow for the different treatment of imports from non-market economy countries provided for in Article 9(5) of the Basic AD Regulation[8]; and

(e) the Panel erred when finding that the EU acted inconsistently with Article XVI:4 of the *WTO Agreement* and Article 18.4 of the *Anti-Dumping Agreement* by failing to ensure the conformity of its laws, regulations and administrative procedures with its obligations under the relevant agreements.[9]

II. COUNCIL REGULATION NO. 91/2009 (FASTENERS INVESTIGATION)

The Panel erred in the interpretation and application of Articles 6.2, 6.4, 6.5, 6.5.1, 6.10 and 9.2 of the *Anti-Dumping Agreement* and also violated Articles 6.2, 7.1 and 11 of the *DSU* when it concluded that the EU acted inconsistently with those provisions of the *Anti-Dumping Agreement* in the fasteners investigation.[10] In particular:

(a) the Panel erred in its interpretation and application of Articles 6.10 and 9.2 of the *Anti-Dumping Agreement* when finding that, having found that Article 9(5) of the Basic AD Regulation is, as such, inconsistent with those provisions, its application in the fasteners investigation was, for the same reasons, inconsistent with these two provisions[11];

(b) the Panel erred in the interpretation and application of Articles 6.2 and 6.4 of the *Anti-Dumping Agreement* and violated Article 11 of the *DSU* when finding that the EU violated these provisions by not providing a timely opportunity for Chinese producers to see information regarding the product types on the basis of which normal value was established, information relevant to the presentation of their case[12];

(c) the Panel erred in the interpretation and application of Article 6.5.1 of the *Anti-Dumping Agreement* when finding that the European investigating authorities had violated that provision in that

7 Panel Report, paras. 7.124, 7.126 and 7.127.

8 Panel Report, para. 7.125 and footnote 307.

9 Panel Report, para. 7.137.

10 Panel Report, paras. 8(2)(b), 8(2)(e) and 8(2)(f).

11 Panel Report, para. 7.148.

12 Panel Report, paras. 7.494 and 7.495.

they failed to ensure Agrati's and Fontana Luigi's compliance with the requirements of Article 6.5.1[13];

(d) the Panel acted inconsistently with Articles 6.2, 7.1 and 11 of the *DSU* when addressing in substance China's claim under Article 6.5 of the *Anti-Dumping Agreement* in connection with Pooja Forge[14];

(e) the Panel erred in the interpretation and application of Article 6.5 of the *Anti-Dumping Agreement* when it considered that, absent a showing of "good cause", the European investigating authorities were not entitled to grant confidential treatment to information submitted by Pooja Forge, the analogue country producer[15]; and

(f) the Panel acted inconsistently with Article 6.2 of the *DSU* when considering that the issue of "the identity of the complainants and supporters" was properly identified in China's Panel Request under its claims referring to Article 6.2 and 6.4 of the *Anti-Dumping Agreement*.[16]

---

13 Panel Report, paras. 7.516 and 7.517.

14 Panel Report, paras. 7.518-7.526.

15 Panel Report, para. 7.525.

16 Panel Report, para. 7.458.

ANNEX II

WORLD TRADE ORGANIZATION

WT/DS397/8
5 April 2011

(11-1682)

Original: English

EUROPEAN COMMUNITIES[1] – DEFINITIVE ANTI-DUMPING MEASURES ON CERTAIN IRON OR STEEL FASTENERS FROM CHINA

Notification of an Other Appeal by China under Article 16.4 and Article 17 of the Understanding on Rules and Procedures Governing the Settlement of Disputes (DSU), and under Rule 23(1) of the Working Procedures for Appellate Review

The following notification, dated 30 March 2011, from the Delegation of the People's Republic of China, is being circulated to Members.

Pursuant to Article 16.4 and Article 17 of the DSU, the People's Republic of China hereby notifies to the Dispute Settlement Body its decision to appeal to the Appellate Body certain issues of law covered in the Report of the Panel and certain legal interpretations developed by the Panel in its Report in the dispute *European Communities – Definitive Anti-Dumping Measures on Certain Iron or Steel Fasteners from China* (WT/DS397/R). Pursuant to Rule 23(1) of the *Work-*

---

[1] On 1 December 2009, the *Treaty of Lisbon amending the Treaty on European Union and the Treaty establishing the European Community* (done at Lisbon, 13 December 2007) entered into force. On 29 November 2009, the World Trade Organization received a Verbal Note (WT/L/779) from the Council of the European Union and the Commission of the European Communities stating that, by virtue of the *Treaty of Lisbon*, as of 1 December 2009, the "European Union" replaces and succeeds the "European Community". On 13 July 2010, the World Trade Organization received a second Verbal Note (WT/Let/679) from the Council of the European Union confirming that, with effect from 1 December 2009, the European Union replaced the European Community and assumed all the rights and obligations of the European Community in respect of all Agreements for which the Director-General of the World Trade Organization is the depositary and to which the European Community is a signatory or a contracting party.

ing Procedures for Appellate Review, China simultaneously files this Notice of Other Appeal with the Appellate Body Secretariat.

China seeks review by the Appellate Body of the following aspects of the Report of the Panel:

1. China seeks review of the Panel's conclusions and findings concerning China's claim that the European Union violated Articles 4.1 and 3.1 of the AD Agreement with respect to the definition of domestic industry in the fasteners investigation by excluding from the definition of the domestic industry the producers that made themselves known after the 15-day deadline following the publication of the Notice of Initiation and the producers that did not support the complaint (paragraphs 7.209 – 7.221 and paragraph 8.3(b) of the Panel Report). China has identified, *inter alia*, the following errors in the issues of law and legal interpretations developed by the Panel:

- The Panel failed to make an objective assessment of the facts in violation of, *inter alia*, Article 11 of the DSU and Article 17.6 of the AD Agreement in connection with China's claim that the EU violated Articles 4.1 and 3.1 of the AD Agreement by excluding from the definition of the domestic industry producers that did not support the complaint, since:
    - the Panel erroneously accepted as a "fact" the unsubstantiated statement of the EU that "at least one producer which was not a complainant, and had remained silent prior to initiation, was not only included in the domestic industry, but was selected for the sample"[2];
    - the Panel erroneously concluded that the fact that "at least one producer which was not a complainant, and had remained silent prior to initiation, was not only included in the domestic industry, but was selected for the sample" demonstrated that "the EU investigating authority, in this case, did [not], in fact, exclude producers that did not support the complaint from the domestic industry"[3] and erroneously ignored the explanation put forward by China pointing out that such conclusion cannot be and was not correct;
    - the Panel disregarded and ignored the evidence submitted by China which demonstrated that the EU excluded from the domestic industry all producers that did not support the complaint.

China requests the Appellate Body to reverse the Panel's findings and to complete the analysis by finding that it has been demonstrated that the EU excluded from the definition of the domestic industry the producers that did not

---

2 Panel Report, para. 7.214.
3 Panel Report, para. 7.215.

support the complaint. China further requests the Appellate Body to complete the analysis by finding that the exclusion from the definition of the domestic industry of the producers that did not support the complaint is inconsistent with Article 4.1 of the AD Agreement.

- The Panel erred in its interpretation of Article 4.1 of the AD Agreement when examining China's claim that the exclusion from the domestic industry of producers that did not come forward within 15 days as of the date of publication of the Notice of Initiation was inconsistent with Article 4.1 and failed to make an objective assessment of the facts in violation of Article 11 of the DSU in connection with that claim:
    - the Panel failed to make an objective assessment of the facts as required by Article 11 of the DSU when it concluded that the "EU did not act to exclude"[4] producers that did not make themselves known within 15 days as of the date of initiation of the investigation;
    - the Panel erred in its interpretation of Article 4.1 of the AD Agreement when concluding that there is nothing in Article 4.1 which would preclude investigating authorities from establishing deadlines for companies to come forward in order to be considered for inclusion in the domestic industry;
    - the Panel failed to make an objective assessment of the facts as required by Article 11 of the DSU when concluding that China has not demonstrated that "the 15 days allowed by the Commission was insufficient".[5]

China requests the Appellate Body to reverse the Panel's findings and to complete the analysis by finding that, on the basis of the facts before the Panel, it has been demonstrated that the EU acted to exclude from the definition of the domestic industry the producers which did come forward within 15 days as of the date of publication of the Notice of Initiation and that, therefore, the EU acted in violation of Article 4.1 of the AD Agreement. China furthermore requests the Appellate Body to conclude that it has been demonstrated that the 15-day period granted to the domestic producers to come forward was not "reasonable" or "sufficient" and that therefore the EU acted in violation of Article 4.1 of the AD Agreement.

- The Panel erred in dismissing China's claim that the EU violated Article 3.1 of the AD Agreement by excluding from the domestic industry the producers which did not come forward within 15 days

[4] *Ibid.*

[5] Panel Report, para. 7.219.

as of the date of the Notice of Initiation and the producers which did not support the complaint.

China requests the Appellate Body to reverse the Panel's findings and to conclude that the EU violated Article 3.1 since it failed to make an injury determination which is based on an "objective examination" as required by Article 3.1 of the AD Agreement.

2. China seeks review of the Panel's conclusions and findings concerning China's claim that the European Union violated Articles 4.1 and 3.1 of the AD Agreement with respect to the definition of domestic industry in the fasteners investigation because the domestic industry as defined by the EU did not include domestic producers whose collective output of the like product constitutes a major proportion of the total domestic production (paragraphs 7.222 – 7.230 and para. 8.3(b) of the Panel Report). China has identified, *inter alia*, the following errors in the issues of laws and of legal interpretations developed by the Panel:

- The Panel failed to make a correct interpretation of the terms "major proportion" which is based on the ordinary meaning of these terms and in light of their context, pursuant to the principles of treaty interpretation of the Vienna Convention on the Law of Treaties, and, as a result, made the following erroneous findings and conclusions:

  (i) the Panel erroneously concluded that the fact that the Commission relied on a presumption is not alone sufficient to demonstrate, *prima facie*, that the definition of the domestic industry in this case is inconsistent with Article 4.1 of the AD Agreement;

  (ii) the Panel erroneously concluded that the non-quantitative factors raised by China are not relevant in this case or in general.

China requests the Appellate Body to reverse the Panel's findings and to conclude that, by considering that producers accounting for 25% of total domestic production necessarily constitute a major proportion, the EU violated Article 4.1 of the AD Agreement and that the "non-quantitative factors" identified by China are relevant for the purposes of determining whether the major proportion requirement is satisfied and had to be considered by the Commission in the fasteners investigation. China further requests the Appellate Body to conclude that, in light of these non-quantitative factors, the domestic producers constituting the domestic industry in the fasteners investigation did not represent a "major proportion" of the domestic industry.

3. China seeks review of the Panel's conclusions and findings concerning China's claim that the European Union violated Articles 3.1 and 4.1 of the AD Agreement since it made an injury determination with respect to a sample of producers that was not representative (paragraphs 7.234 to 7.241 and 8.3(b) of the Panel Report). China identified, *inter alia*, the following errors in the issues of law and of legal interpretations developed by the Panel:

- The Panel erroneously concluded that "it cannot accept the contention that only a statistically valid sample will be sufficiently representative for purposes of an injury determination";
- the Panel erroneously concluded that China has not demonstrated that the EU investigating authority could have carried out its injury examination for the domestic industry it had defined, or at least include more producers in the sample.

China requests the Appellate Body to reverse the Panel's findings and to conclude that the EU violated Article 3.1 of the AD Agreement.

4. China seeks review of the Panel's conclusions and findings concerning China's claim that the European Union violated Article 2.4 of the AD Agreement with respect to the dumping determination in the fasteners investigation (paragraphs 7.291 – 7.311 and para. 8.3(d) of the Panel Report). China has identified, *inter alia*, the following errors in the issues of laws and legal interpretations developed by the Panel:

- The Panel failed to make an objective assessment of the matter as required by Article 11 of the DSU by failing to address China's argument that the EU violated Article 2.4 since the Commission failed to indicate to the interested parties what information was necessary to ensure a fair comparison and made it impossible for them to claim adjustments for differences affecting price comparability and, to the extent the Panel would have implicitly concluded that such a failure was not inconsistent with Article 2.4 of the AD Agreement, the Panel failed to make a correct interpretation of Article 2.4 of the AD Agreement;
- the Panel erred in its interpretation of Article 2.4 of the AD Agreement when it rejected China's argument that the EU violated Article 2.4 by failing to evaluate whether the characteristics identified in the PCNs affected price comparability and whether adjustments for these differences in physical characteristics were warranted;
- the Panel did not make an objective assessment of the facts as required by Article 11 of the DSU and Article 17.6 of the AD Agreement when it concluded that China has pointed to no evidence supporting the conclusion that the PCN characteristics indicated differences affecting price comparability and when claiming that "it would be inappropriate for us, under the standard of review to consider it ourselves";
- the Panel erred in its interpretation of Article 2.4 of the AD Agreement when it rejected China's claim that the EU violated Article 2.4 of the AD Agreement by failing to make the necessary adjustments for quality differences.

China requests the Appellate Body to reverse the Panel's findings and to conclude that, on the basis of the facts before the Panel, it has been demonstrated that the EU violated Article 2.4 of the AD Agreement with respect to each of the identified issue mentioned above.

5. China seeks review of the Panel's conclusions and findings concerning China's claim that the EU violated Articles 6.5, 6.4 and 6.2 of the AD Agreement in connection with the non-disclosure of the identity of the complainants and of the supporters of the complaint (paragraphs 7.445 – 7.459 and para. 8.3(h) of the Panel Report). China has identified, *inter alia*, the following errors in the issues of laws and legal interpretations developed by the Panel in its findings concerning China's claim under Article 6.5 of the AD Agreement:

- The Panel erred in its interpretation of the "good cause" requirement when ignoring the difference between a hypothetical potential retaliation which "could" happen and a retaliation which "would" happen;
- the Panel erred in law in considering that the "good cause" requirement was satisfied without supporting evidence provided by the parties requesting confidential treatment;
- the Panel erred in rejecting China's argument that no good cause was established since the seven EU producers that made up the sample for purposes of the Commission's injury determination were also complainants and supporters and that they did not ask the Commission to treat their identity as confidential information.

China requests the Appellate Body to reverse the Panel's findings and to conclude that the EU violated Article 6.5 of the AD Agreement through the non-disclosure of the identity of the complainants and of the supporters of the complaint. China also requests the Appellate Body to reverse the Panel's findings concerning China's claim under Articles 6.4 and 6.2 of the AD Agreement and to complete the analysis by finding that the EU's failure to disclose the identity of the complainants and of the supporters of the complaint is also inconsistent with Articles 6.4 and 6.2 of the AD Agreement.

6. China seeks review of the Panel's conclusions and findings concerning China's claim that the EU violated Article 6.1.1 of the AD Agreement by limiting the time period for the submission of MET/IT claim form to 15 days as of the date of publication of the Notice of Initiation (paragraphs 7.566 – 7.579 and 8.3(k) of the Panel Report). China has identified, *inter alia*, the following errors in the issues of law and legal interpretations developed by the Panel:

- The Panel erred in its interpretation of the term "questionnaire" in Article 6.1.1 of the AD Agreement by adopting an interpretation which is not consistent with the ordinary meaning of that word in light of its context and the object and purpose as required by the principles of treaty interpretation included in the Vienna Convention on the Law of Treaties;

- even assuming that the Panel did not err in its interpretation of the term "questionnaire" in that it would refer to "the initial comprehensive questionnaire issued in an anti-dumping investigation to each of the interested parties by an investigating authority at or following the initiation of an investigation, which seeks information as to all relevant issues pertaining to the main questions that will need to be decided (dumping, injury and causation)", the Panel erroneously concluded that that the MET/IT claim form was not a "questionnaire" according to this definition.

China requests the Appellate Body to reverse the Panel's findings and to conclude that the "MET/IT claim form" is a questionnaire within the meaning of Article 6.1.1 of the AD Agreement and to complete the analysis by finding that the EU violated Article 6.1.1 of the AD Agreement.

Cumulative List of Published Disputes

www.ingramcontent.com/pod-product-compliance
Ingram Content Group UK Ltd.
Pitfield, Milton Keynes, MK11 3LW, UK
UKHW041453071026
15587UKWH00010B/1004
* 9 7 8 1 1 0 7 0 3 3 7 3 3 *